Principles of Operations Research for Management

Irwin Series in Quantitative Analysis for Business

Consulting Editor   ROBERT B. FETTER   *Yale University*

Principles of Operations Research for Management

FRANK S. BUDNICK

Department of Management Science
University of Rhode Island

RICHARD MOJENA

Department of Management Science
University of Rhode Island

THOMAS E. VOLLMANN

Department of Operations and Systems Management
Indiana University

1977

Richard D. Irwin, Inc. Homewood, Illinois 60430

ISBN 0-256-01796-4
Library of Congress Catalog Card No. 76–49311
Printed in the United States of America

To our parents

Preface

THIS TEXTBOOK is primarily intended for use in a one-semester course in management science, operations research, or quantitative methods in schools of management or business administration. Specifically, it is designed for the increasingly required course in OR/MS at the junior-senior and MBA levels. The textbook is also suitable for OR/MS courses which are designed for majors in economics, public administration, and health administration. Additionally, it may be appropriate as a primary or supplementary source in a two-semester course for undergraduate majors in OR/MS.

Objectives and Orientation

Our primary objective can be stated succinctly: *to make believers out of potential users of quantitative techniques.* To accomplish this we present a *comprehensive* and (we hope) lucid survey of OR/MS techniques in a *decision-making* context.

An important aspect of this decision orientation is reflected in the design of Chapter 1. An eight-step *decision paradigm,* which includes the scientific method, is developed in depth. This chapter is obviously an important one and we are committed to making it more meaningful than the typical introductory chapter of books in this area. Succeeding chapters integrate and reinforce this paradigm.

The emphasis on managerial decision making dictates a strong *applications orientation;* however, this does not imply a superficial or "cookbook" treatment of the models and their solutions, for we are convinced that a reasonable amount of theoretical foundations is required to avoid

ix

misapplications and incorrect decision implications. In effect, we have attempted to suppress mathematical rigor without sacrificing *conceptual rigor*. For the most part, proofs and other mathematical developments that are of interest to the quantitatively inclined either have been relegated to appendices or have been identified as advanced (**) sections and exercises that can be omitted without loss of continuity.

Topical Coverage

The extensive topical coverage within this book may appear to belie our claim that it has been primarily designed for a one-semester course for nonspecialists of OR/MS. One of our primary objectives is to treat important topics that traditionally have been perceived as advanced at a level that is intuitively appealing and comprehensible to the nonspecialist. These topics include integer, goal, nonlinear, and heuristic programming, system dynamics, queuing optimization models, stochastic inventory models, sequential decision processes, and others.

To avoid the impression that OR/MS is a narrow field that is restricted by highly simplified assumptions about the real world, we have included many sections which *overview* the essence of specialized or otherwise mathematically advanced topics, e.g., "Advanced Linear Programming" (section 10.3), "Inventory Control Systems" (section 11.6), "Other Stochastic Processes" (section 15.6), and "Other Decision Structures" (section 17.7).

To lend perspective to many of the models, a number of chapters include *assessments* of what has been presented. For example, see section 8.5 (integer programming), section 9.6 (dynamic programming), section 10.5 (nonlinear programming), section 12.8 (queuing theory), section 14.6 (PERT/CPM), section 15.7 (stochastic processes), and section 17.8 (decision analysis).

Finally, the extensive coverage of topics allows the instructor to *tailor* the course to his/her philosophy and to the particular level of the students. For example, a mathematical programming emphasis would stress Chapters 2–10, whereas a stochastic models emphasis would stress Chapters 11–17; a course for undergraduate nonmajors of OR/MS would cover fewer topics than the equivalent course for MBA students, and a two-semester course for undergraduate majors would cover most of the topics, including many of the advanced sections.

As much as possible, we have attempted to facilitate this type of "weaving" through the book by identifying advanced sections with double asterisks (**) and by the conscious ordering of sections. For example, the instructor can choose to cover the formulation of transportation and integer programming models, without having to treat algorithms, simply by assigning the first two sections of Chapter 7 and the first three sections of Chapter 8.

At the University of Rhode Island, we have successfully (in our own "biased" opinion) used the manuscript with undergraduate and graduate business students and with undergraduate majors in management science. Based on this experience, we provide specific suggestions for structuring the course in the *Instructor's Manual*.

Examples and Exercises

Since the book is intended for users rather than designers of quantitative techniques, there is a strong emphasis on realistic scenarios through examples and exercises. Exercises are found both within the chapter (*follow-up exercises*) and at the end of the chapter (*additional exercises*). Follow-up exercises serve to reinforce, integrate, and extend immediately preceding material, whereas the chapter-end exercises offer an opportunity for review and new scenarios. The importance we place on these is evidenced by the following statistics: The textbook has a total of 808 exercises, many with multiple parts; the mean number of exercises per chapter, excluding the first and last chapters and the appendices, is 47.

The portfolio of applications includes those in the *traditional functional areas of business* (e.g., finance, marketing, accounting, management, production); those that can be classified as *classic OR* (e.g., traveling salesman, paper trim, knapsack, caterer, reliability, replacement); and those that include the *public sector* (e.g., urban systems, environmental protection, health care delivery, emergency response systems). We have particularly made an effort to provide meaningful applications in the public sector, in keeping with the realization of recent years that the management process transcends private enterprise.

In our years of teaching and class testing of the manuscript, we have found that diversity and richness of applications is appealing to students, better highlights the benefits of quantitative modeling, and reveals important similarities across decision making environments. A convenient reference for locating page numbers for the applications in the book is provided following the preface.

Prerequisites

The only prerequisites assumed for the text are understandings of basic algebra and basic statistics. Additional quantitative prerequisites are either reviewed in appendices or developed as necessary. For example, appendices are included on determinants, systems of simultaneous equations, and fundamentals of matrix algebra; basic concepts in probability and statistics are reviewed in a chapter-length appendix; and calculus, where required, is developed in an intuitive and expedient manner within an applications context. It should be noted, however, that chapters are written in such a manner that calculus is not required for their coverage (excepting Chapters 2 and 3 and some advanced materials elsewhere).

Acknowledgments

We wish to express our deep appreciation to many who have contributed to this project, both explicitly and implicitly: to Rudolph P. Lamone, University of Maryland, for philosophical direction and detailed reviews of the manuscript; to Albert J. Simone, University of Cincinnati, for philosophical direction and several scenarios of applications; to Richard R. Weeks, University of Rhode Island, for consistent administrative support over the course of this arduous project; to Robert B. Fetter, Yale

University, and Claude McMillan, Jr., University of Colorado, for helpful reviews of the manuscript; to Linda Hemphill, for her patience in typing through several drafts of the manuscript and in preparing the hundreds of copies for class testing; to Mary Jane DeFazio, for numerous corrections and "grunt" work on the *Instructor's Manual;* to Sue Rubinsky for her "clutch" typing in the end; to our students who suffered through "ditto" copies for class testing, yet managed to provide invaluable corrections and suggestions for subsequent revisions; to our immediate families, who remained cheerfully supportive in spite of our frequent absences; and to the administrative staffs of Indiana University and, in particular, the University of Rhode Island, for unflagging administrative support over the three-year course of this project.

March 1977   FRANK S. BUDNICK
                                                       RICHARD MOJENA
                                                       THOMAS E. VOLLMANN

PAGE REFERENCES FOR APPLICATIONS

PRIVATE SECTOR

Accounting-Finance

capital budgeting, 116, 291, 322, 688
capital expansion, 134, 306, 307
credit control, 613
financial management, 121, 426, 530
portfolio management, 92, 137, 376, 385, 649
stock market, 530, 594, 647
timing sale of asset, 59

Management

agricultural management, 92, 134, 347, 566
forest management, 386, 686
maintenance, 465, 614
personnel, 135, 385, 462
pollution control, 82, 466
port facility management, 527
project management, 535, 574, 636
purchasing, 136, 307
scheduling, 310
ski resort management, 576
solid waste management, 123, 179, 189
typing pool, 465
workforce planning, 339

Marketing

advertising, 53, 68, 88
brand switching, 589, 606
media mix, 91, 118, 269, 352, 355, 357, 638
new product introduction, 658
physical distribution, 114, 230, 639
pricing, 37, 63, 74, 91, 386, 641
product development, 81, 572
reservation system, 466
sales allocation, 62, 271, 640
warehouse location, 289

Production

assembly, 574
assembly line balancing, 632
assignment of facilities to locations (plant layout), 626
blending, 105, 123, 136
inventory control, 403, 409, 414, 424, 507, 618, 685
job shop scheduling, 635
pipeline construction, 689
plant distribution, 271
product mix, 109, 361, 384
production-inventory control, 234, 326
production-vendor, 135
solar energy design, 350, 529
trim loss (cutting stock), 138

Classic OR

cargo loading, 139, 276, 346, 366, 385
caterer, 231
diet, 139, 311
knapsack, 291
queues, 443, 445, 447, 449, 451, 453, 455, 457, 462, 466, 467
reliability, 333
replacement, 56, 59, 64, 348
set covering, 284, 308
shortest route, 315, 336, 349
traveling salesman, 285

PUBLIC SECTOR

blood banking, 414
budget allocation, 309
campaign tour, 285
car pooling, 387
charity, 63
committee assignment, 233
contract awards, 136, 268
court scheduling, 267, 306
desegregation, 641
disaster airlift, 305
emergency response, 34, 64, 95, 272, 647

environmental protection, 687
fire station allocation, 93, 284, 345
forest management, 686
funds allocation, 346
gasoline panic, 464
highway patrol, 654
highway management, 577
hospital administration, 137, 443, 593, 615, 707, 721
job retraining, 308
nuclear power plant, 664

Contents

Special Issues in Problem Formulation. Selected References. Additional Exercises.

Quantitative Decision Making:
A Perspective

THE KEY FEATURE of this chapter is a paradigm (pattern or framework) for decision making; we see eight somewhat distinct steps to problem identification and solution, and find this eight-step paradigm to be a useful way to consider critical aspects of the problem-solving environment. We also believe that the paradigm permits us as authors to make a better selection and structure of quantitative materials, and gives you as a reader an important framework for integrating quantitative decision making.

1.1 OBJECTIVES

Someone wisely said that if you do not care where you are going any road will take you there. We do care where we are going, and identify with the advertising slogan: "Getting there can be half the fun." We feel deeply obligated to explicitly state our objectives, chart our collective course toward achieving those objectives, and thereafter measure up to a critical appraisal of how well we have succeeded.

Credo

We believe that quantitative techniques can be integrated usefully into any nontrivial decision process. Quantitative approaches to decision making typically involve the construction and manipulation of mathematical models of the decision environment. It is our contention that the incorporation of quantitative analysis as *one input* to the decision process can be of considerable aid in making better decisions.

Having stated our belief in quantitative approaches, we now identify what well may be a shocking fact: Real-world applications of quantitative models can only be described as disappointing. Many of the models you will study in this book have existed for two decades; yet their use, although established in large organizations and on the increase in general, does not measure up to early expectations. It is critical for you to understand the reasons for both past successes and failures, and a major objective of this book is devoted to providing that understanding.

We offer three reasons for the failure of quantitative analysis to realize its potential. First, many quantitative model-building attempts have not given proper attention to the users or consumers. The persons who ultimately make the decisions have to understand the models, believe in their results, and feel that the objectives or criteria expressed in the models are harmonious with their own objectives. Second, the primary academic orientation toward quantitative techniques has been with the development of new theory rather than with the effective application of existing theory. Recent developments indicate a redress of this imbalance, a trend which we strongly endorse. Finally, fault does not lie entirely with the quantitative specialist. Resistance to change when confronted with a new technology and a lack of proper quantitative foundations are two closely related deficiencies in many decision makers. Increased emphasis on behavioral science, integration of quantitative materials, and accessibility of computer power in college curricula constitute basic fundamentals for improved quantitative decision making.

We view this book as appropriate for future users of quantitative model building. Not surprisingly, we make a commitment to applications because we want the book to be as useful as possible. It is our hope that you can leave your course with a quantitative point of view, a belief in the superiority of quantitative methods for solving many kinds of problems, a knowledge of how to construct certain kinds of models, an awareness of pitfalls awaiting the unwary, an understanding of how to correctly use specialists in certain model-building areas, and most importantly of all, a deep appreciation of the decision-making process and the role of quantitative techniques in that process.

Orientation

Our orientation, as reflected by the title of the book, is toward the use of **operations research (OR)** as an approach to managerial decision making. The field of operations research, or **management science (MS),** is concerned with the development and application of quantitative techniques to the solution of problems faced by managers of public and private organizations. More specifically, theory and methodology (tools) in mathematics, probability, statistics, and computing are adapted and applied to the identification, formulation, solution, validation, implementation, and control of administrative or decision-making problems.[1]

Our commitment to applications should not be interpreted as an avoid-

---

[1] In schools of business administration or management, MS and OR are essentially synonymous. Where OR is housed in, say, schools of engineering, the emphasis tends to be on mathematical proofs and, of course, on nonbusiness applications.

ance of rigorous material. Although rigor will not be developed for rigor's sake alone, we maintain that a certain degree of quantitative sophistication is necessary to clearly understand basic techniques and their assumptions, limitations, extensions, and reasons for failure. Our interest is in good applications, and good must be distinguished from bad on a technical as well as on an applied basis.

An applications orientation results in the presentation of many techniques by example. We have attempted to make the examples realistic, rich, and varied. Because there are many ways of looking at the same problem, several examples will be revisited in subsequent chapters. Since management is a general process, the examples will be based upon public as well as private sectors, on large firms as well as on small firms. Furthermore, we will try to show how problem structure in one decision-making situation is very similar to problem structure in other kinds of decision-making situations.

A Decision-Making Paradigm

The balance of this chapter is devoted to a process of applying quantitative models for decision making that we believe is essential to successful real-world applications. This process is organized in an eight-step paradigm, or framework for decision making, which incorporates **scientific methodology** (steps II–VI). We want to make it clear that this paradigm is not to be regarded as a rigid set of steps that one enters at one end and proceeds through on a direct course to the other end. On the contrary, a great deal of cycling back and forth through the steps in any particular problem should be expected. The ideas included in the eight-step paradigm will be utilized and reemphasized in subsequent chapters. We will not, however, subject you to the drill of squeezing each problem through all eight steps of the following paradigm.

    I.   Recognition of a Need. (The perception that some action needs to be taken, or perhaps taken better.)

    II.   Problem Formulation. (Translation of the perceived need into an explicit statement of both the need and the criteria by which problem solution is to be judged.)

    III.   Model Construction. (Construction of a mathematical replica or representation of the problem.)

    IV.   Data Collection. (The specific inputs to the model which reflect actual problem conditions.)

    V.   Model Solution. (Manipulation of the input data to produce results.)

    VI.   Model Validation and Sensitivity Analysis. (Testing model results to ensure validity and the implications of errors in estimating input data.)

    VII.   Interpretation of Results and Implications. (Broad reexamination of problem criteria in light of model results.)

    VIII.   Decision Making, Implementation, and Control. (Behavioral and technical change requirements in both short-run and long-run conditions.)

1.2 STEP ONE—NEED RECOGNITION

Recognition of a need involves a perception on the part of some decision maker that some action needs to be taken, or perhaps taken better. Implied in this perception are objectives or criteria on the part of the decision maker, the need to identify measures which reflect these objectives or criteria, and the proper relationship between the decision maker and individuals with expert knowledge in model building.

Criteria or Objectives

In any decision-making environment, goals, objectives, or criteria are used to assess the status quo. When the assessment is negative, the decision-making process has been started. Some people like to think of goals as being more broad in orientation than objectives, which in turn are less specific than criteria. We will not make this distinction, since one person's criterion might be another person's goal; we will generally use the term criterion as somewhat all-encompassing and at the same time will often use the management science term "objective function." All of these terms have the same purpose in decision making: *criteria dictate, direct, or drive the decision-making process*.

Criteria are possessed by individuals as well as by organizational entities, such as departments, companies, hospitals, or city governments. For example, a manager in an industrial firm has personal aspirations, and the company has profit, growth, and other objectives; a medical doctor has personal as well as professional objectives such as income and experience while the hospital has objectives such as care, reputation, fiduciary responsibility, cost minimization, and so forth; the town mayor might be interested in political patronage and getting reelected in addition to being a good representative of the people, and the town has objectives of providing community services, minimizing the tax burden, or providing a healthy environment in which to bring up children.

One of the critical problems in decision making stems from the fact that there are many criteria involved in any decision; in fact, it is probably fair to say that there are *too* many. The decision maker has many objectives, and those objectives have to be balanced with criteria of other individuals and organizational subunits. What we have, then, is a set or system of criteria which operates throughout the decision-making process. Need might be recognized in terms of only one criterion or the perception may take place in terms of several criteria. Recent research efforts in management science include the development of models which address **multiple criteria,** as illustrated in Chapter 10.

One of the primary problems in decision making within a multicriteria environment is what we will refer to as **goal congruence.** That is, criteria sets or systems need to be established so that they are consistent: Achievement of the company manager's goals should not be inconsistent with company criteria; the doctor's goals must not be realized at the expense of the goals of the patient or hospital; and the town mayor's objectives should not be at the expense of the constituents. In step seven of our decision-making paradigm, we will see that, laudible as goal congruency may be, it will never be achieved perfectly. Suboptimization within organizational units is a fact of life.

Surrogates

All high-level (ultimate or universal) criteria tend to be vague. The manager of a company might want "fulfillment from life." How does the company know when it is maximizing profits? What is professional status for a doctor? How do we maximize community services?

In any decision-making environment, ultimate criteria will always be nebulous and it is necessary to establish **surrogates,** or stand-ins, by which we can judge particular actions. A surrogate for a person's standard of living (ultimate criterion) might be personal income or annual percentage growth in personal income. The performance (ultimate criterion) of a company is often measured in terms of surrogate criteria such as profit as a percentage of sales, return on stockholder's equity, market share, or percentage growth in sales. Hospitals are continually evaluated by accrediting agencies as well as by boards of directors in terms of such measures as the number of patient-days spent in the hospital per death, percentage occupancy in the maternity section, and so forth. Even successful politicians are concerned with the margin by which they have won. Professional plant location specialists evaluate towns in terms of such measures as tax rate, assessed evaluation, student-faculty ratios in schools, and so forth.

The purpose of a surrogate criterion is to reduce a nebulous, though terribly important objective, into some less nebulous objective, hopefully one that can be measured. For example, although we cannot really assess patient care, we could take a measure of how many hospital beds are in use each day.

Surrogate criteria are always necessary, but they are simultaneously dangerous. They are necessary because, for example, it is obviously ludicrous to tell the town garbage collector to "maximize community service." On the other hand, the garbage collector's performance could be evaluated in terms of the number of complaints received, the weekly truck mileage, or the number of town residents per employee (perhaps compared to other towns). The danger in using these surrogates is that they are not "the ultimate criteria." It is always possible to improve performance in terms of a surrogate while performance in terms of ultimate criteria is degraded. For example, running garbage trucks less frequently decreases mileage, and transferring all terminally ill patients to nursing homes reduces hospital death rates. (By the way, this is a common practice!)

The User-Designer Concept

Recognition of a need implies someone, or perhaps some group, has a need, or at least is in the organizational position where the need occurs. In this book we will call these people **users. Designers,** on the other hand, are not primarily associated with the problem criteria. They are individuals who have specialized kinds of knowledge or skills. In this book, we will be concerned primarily with the interaction between designers, who are experts in operations research, and managerial users, who have decisions to make. The **user-designer concept** refers to a style of problem investigation which more thoroughly involves the user in the analysis; the result is an accelerated evolution in problem formulation, model building, and problem solution, as well as a sharply increased likelihood of implemented results.

The user-designer concept attempts to overcome a communications gap. The gap is potentially dangerous when one considers problem analysis in an evolutionary context. The following is not unusual:

> A designer first identifies as well as is practicable the problem delineated by the user. The designer then selects or develops a model or models, collects appropriate data, manipulates the model, makes inferences, and thereafter proposes a solution to the problem. If the solution seems appropriate to the user, it meets the original statement of needs; however, once the solution has been accepted and a decision has been made, very often new problems and criteria, perhaps more basic and fundamental, are perceived by the user, necessitating further model building, problem solutions, and decisions. But this next decision is not the last. The user's perception of the needs or problems continues to change, improve, or sharpen in an evolutionary manner.

It should be emphasized that evolution in the user's needs (demanding new model-building efforts and appropriate decisions) does not mean that the user did a "poor job" in the initial recognition of the problem or in defining the criteria dictating the problem. Many important problems or potential opportunities can be identified only after models have been formulated or decisions have been made for different problems. Evolution is inevitable, should be expected, and should be sought.

When one considers problem solving–decision making in an evolutionary context, an interesting question arises as to where one should start. It is the authors' opinion that many failures of quantitative models have been due to a tendency to formulate models or investigate problems that users are not ready for. Taking the evolutionary approach, however, means that we should not be concerned so much with where we start as with where we finish. The moral to the story seems to be: "Start with whatever problem is perceived by the user, but create a model-building environment which is upward-compatible." It is interesting to speculate that upward-compatibility increasingly will be facilitated as future managers (today's students) formally incorporate quantitative methods as part of their repertoire for decision making.

The rather abstract ideas presented above will now be reinforced with two brief examples.

Example 1.1 Metropolitan Boston Transit Authority—MBTA

An increasing number of complaints, unfavorable newspaper editorials, and statements by politicians about the subway service in Boston caused the governing board of the MBTA to question present operations. The board asked the subway operations manager to identify ways to improve service.

What are the criteria for a problem like this? Who has the criteria? Clearly, there are criteria for the taxpayers of Massachusetts who subsidize metropolitan mass transportation. There are also subway-user criteria, as well as criteria possessed by individuals and organizational entities concerned with transportation issues (subways, buses, trains, expressways, toll bridges, and so on). Other criteria that well may be important include those possessed by politicians, newspapers, lobbying groups, or other power sources that can exert pressure on subway operations.

The use of surrogates is obviously needed in this problem. Examples might include net profit or loss from operations, number of passengers, passenger-miles traveled, passenger waiting times, passenger travel times, ticket price per ride, breakdown frequency, equipment utilization, number of robberies in subway stations, wages of personnel, percentage of minority persons employed, automobile gasoline consumption, expressway traffic counts, and bonded debt levels.

Some of these surrogates conflict with others; for example, reducing the price per ride might reduce the net profit from operations. Others are more consistent, such as reducing both breakdown frequencies and passenger waiting. Moreover, potential conflicts exist: All trains could spend more time undergoing preventive maintenance, which would leave fewer trains in service. Finally, as noted in the discussion of surrogates, improvement in terms of these stand-ins may work to the detriment of the ultimate goals. For example, subway commuters might want to reach work in less time (passenger travel time minimization becomes the surrogate); the act of closing every other subway station will reduce travel time but might increase the time between leaving the house and arriving at the job.

To illustrate how the user-designer interaction *might* occur for this MBTA example, assume that the user is the operations manager, that equipment utilization and net return from operations are the major surrogate criteria, and that the problem has evolved to the stage of making a decision about reduced fares during nonpeak hours in order to stimulate subway travel.

In Chapter 2, you will see one model for dealing with this problem. In using the model it will be necessary to ascertain whether the model is valid and whether correct decision implications can be drawn from it. Of much more fundamental importance, however, is the question of whether this model can be used at all: Is it compatible with the MBTA operations manager's style of thinking? Can the manager understand the model, both in its present formulation and in its logical extensions? Are the initial decision implications consonant with the operations manager's perceived decision alternatives? How robust is the model? That is, to what extent can the model permit open-ended evolution in problem delineation?

Example 1.2   Gotham City Hospital—GCH

In recent years the complexities of administering the operations of hospitals have fostered an increasing number of OR applications for improving operations.[2] For example, the arrival and departure of patients have

---

[2] See David H. Stimson and Ruth H. Stimson, *Operations Research in Hospitals: Diagnosis and Prognosis* (Chicago: Hospital Research and Educational Trust, 1972).

been treated in the context of queuing models; the management of medical supplies has relied on inventory models; and the scheduling of beds and nonemergency surgery have benefited from mathematical programming.

GCH is a medium-sized hospital which is experiencing "growing pains." In recent weeks a large number of complaints have suggested that the waiting times of patients in the emergency room have been too long.

Follow-up Exercise

1. What is a reasonable set of ultimate goals for GCH? List surrogate criteria that might reflect these goals. Illustrate the user-designer concept with yourself in the role of "expert" consultant on some system or procedure that could be used to reduce the long waiting times. Make any assumptions you need to but explicitly state them. Particularly note conflicting surrogate criteria and how these conflicts can be resolved.

1.3 STEP TWO—PROBLEM FORMULATION

Once a need is clearly recognized, including some understanding of appropriate surrogate criteria, the decision-making process logically requires a formal problem statement to delineate the boundaries of the investigation. It is analogous to working with an architect on the design of a house; at some point the architect understands your needs well enough to formulate a specific plan. And, as with the architect's formulation, revisions may be made in the problem statement as the investigation is carried out.

The most critical concept in problem formulation is the process of explicitly and unambiguously stating the essentials of a problem: relevant variables and parameters, constraints or restrictions, and surrogate criteria or objective functions. The explicit statement of the problem represents our "blueprint" which guides us as we "build" our problem solution. Without the blueprint, the chances of achieving a match between problem solution and basic criteria are sharply reduced.

Variables, Parameters, and Constraints

The basic building blocks for a quantitative problem statement are variables, parameters, and constraints. Variables are measurable factors which bear on the problem of interest. Generally a distinction is made between **controllable variables** and **uncontrollable variables.** The former are those under the direct control of the decision maker and are often termed **decision variables.** Conversely, uncontrollable variables affect the criteria for decision making but are *exogenous* or not subject to direct manipulation by the decision maker. For example, a controllable variable in an inventory problem is the level at which to restock inventory, and an uncontrollable variable might be the demand for the item being inventoried.

Parameters are measurable conditions inherent in the structure of the problem. In mathematical terms, they are typically identified as **constants.** The cost of stocking (carrying) a unit of a product over some period of time and the cost of ordering or the start-up cost of producing a batch of items are examples of parameters for an inventory problem.

Constraints represent restrictions which are placed on the controllable and uncontrollable variables. In actual practice, very few problems can be considered as unconstrained. For the inventory example, constraints might be placed on the amount of capital invested in inventory or on the amount of space allocated to inventory.

The Objective Function

Ideally, the criteria for a given problem can be redefined structurally as a single measurable surrogate criterion, or **objective function,** the value

FIGURE 1–1
Criteria and Tradeoffs for a Queuing Problem

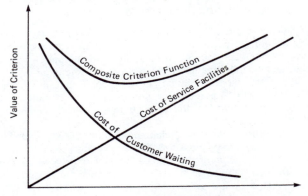

(a) Number of Service Facilities

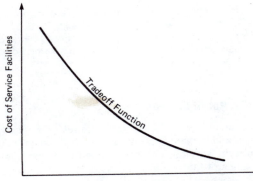

(b) Cost of Customer Waiting

of which is influenced by the controllable and uncontrollable variables, parameters, and constraints.

✳   In *multiple criteria* problems, either it is not feasible or it is not desirable to redefine criteria into a single measurable criterion. For example, a decision as to the number of servers to include in a queuing system might be based on criteria such as average number of customers in line, average waiting time per customer, or utilization of the service facility. In this case, a composite criterion function (Figure 1–1a) or a tradeoff function (Figure 1–1b) between surrogate criteria may resolve conflicts. If appropriate costs can be assigned to customer waiting, then the composite criterion function in Figure 1–1a becomes a total cost function. (Do you agree with the indicated conflict in Figure 1–1a?) Other approaches which are more direct have been applied to multiple criteria problems. In Chapter 10 we present one of these procedures in detail.

Example 1.3   Quantitative Butchers, Inc.—QBI

QBI specializes in blending meatloaf mixtures. The original recipe called for 50 percent beef, 20 percent pork, and 30 percent veal by weight. Over time, however, it has been found that these proportions can be varied somewhat without significantly changing the taste of the meatloaf.

After some taste experimentation, it was found that the ground beef could range from 40 to 60 percent, the pork from 20 to 30 percent, the veal from 10 to 40 percent, and that the pork content must be no more than 150 percent of the veal content.

The ultimate criteria for QBI include long-term growth, community relationships, and reputation. The surrogate criteria critical to their meatloaf mix problem are to maintain quality by keeping within the mixture percentage constraints and to make the mix at the lowest cost per pound. The sales price is not affected by the exact composition of the mix.

The decision variables for this problem are the proportions of each meat in the mixture. Uncontrollable variables include the available supply of meats and their wholesale prices. Parameters include various costs; the taste percentages are parameters as well as constraints.

In Chapter 4 the management science model called linear programming will be applied to this problem. You will see how beef, pork, and veal can be traded-off for each other, how changes in prices for the ingredients affect the optimal mixture, and how other kinds of interesting questions can be examined; for instance, what if the problem is formulated in terms of protein content as well as taste, and soybeans are allowed as an additional ingredient?

Example 1.4   Police Patrol Sectors

A city has a fixed number of police officers, patrol cars, paddywagons, motorcycles, scooters, and horses. The officers can walk beats, ride in cars, direct traffic, and so forth, and they can be assigned to different days of the week and different times of the day and night.

Follow-up Exercise

2. Suppose you were a consultant with a management consulting group and you were to advise the city described above how to use its police officers effectively. What are some ultimate criteria? (Keep in mind the various societal perspectives.) What are surrogates that can be used to measure these criteria? Define some controllable and uncontrollable variables, parameters, and constraints which may be relevant. List some tradeoffs in the surrogate criteria. Can you think of tradeoffs in the controllable variables?

1.4 STEP THREE—MODEL CONSTRUCTION

Once an explicit formulation of the problem has been achieved, the next step is to construct a replica or representation of the problem, that is, a mathematical model.

Mathematical Models

A **mathematical model** explicitly states the mathematical structure which relates the inputs (controllable and uncontrollable variables, constraints, and parameters) to the outputs (values for the criterion as expressed through the objective function).[3] Models are used in place of the real system for many reasons—economy and range of experimentation being two important ones. Good models capture the essence of reality and are robust; that is, they have the ability to remain appropriate as evolution in problem delineation occurs.

The following illustrates a mathematical model (as developed in Example 2.3).

Minimize

$$\overline{T} = \tfrac{1}{3}\,(x/v_x + y/v_y) \tag{1.1}$$

subject to

$$x \cdot y = A \tag{1.2}$$

where the controllable variables x and y represent the dimensions of a rectangular police patrol sector; v_x and v_y denote the uncontrollable variables average travel velocities for a patrol vehicle in the x directions and y directions, respectively; $\overline{T}$ is the criterion, average response time of a patrol vehicle; and Equation (1.2) represents an area constraint for the sector (the parameter A represents area). Equation (1.1) is typically

---

[3] Mathematical models represent a subset of **symbolic models,** the latter including both mathematical and logical structures. **Iconic models** (for example, sculpture, globe of the earth, wind tunnel airfoil) and **analogue models** (for example, graphs, maps) are not of significant interest to OR.

termed the objective function. The constant $\frac{1}{3}$ represents a parameter which results from the development of the model. (Can you relate this model to Example 1.4?)

The Model-Building Process

The use of quantitative representations of reality is the key feature which differentiates quantitative decision making from decision making in general. Model building is essentially a process of deciding what features or aspects of a complex real-world problem are to be represented for analysis. In this process, all eight steps of the paradigm play a role.

We noted in the introduction to the eight-step paradigm that it should not be regarded as a rigid set of steps which is entered at one end and completed mechanistically. Figure 1–2 shows this graphically. On the left side of the figure, the real world has been depicted as a large system or set. Within that set is a smaller system of interest such as the MBTA. Based upon the recognition of a need, the clockwise flow leads to a model of the real system, back to implemented changes in the real system, back to problem formulation, and so forth.

The Role of Criteria

Figure 1–2 depicts a criteria hub or center to the decision-making process. Earlier in this chapter the notion of a set of criteria which drives, directs, or dictates the decision-making process was presented. Similarly, criteria drive, direct, or dictate the model-building process. Put very simply, models are built for particular purposes.

The above paragraph may seem repetitious or intuitively obvious, but it is worth emphasizing that in this process an abstract statement and actual practice can be dramatically separated. Experience indicates that the greatest deficiency in model-building efforts may be the lack of a clearly delineated set of criteria. It can virtually be *guaranteed* that you will fall into this trap during your quantitative analysis course, as well as in other endeavors. Indeed, one of the most important lessons for you to learn from this course is how to fall into the trap less frequently and how to recognize the condition sooner when it occurs.

Suppose, for example, that you are asked to construct a diagrammatic or flowchart model of a bank teller's operation. To make the task even simpler, suppose that only checks are cashed by the bank teller. How would you construct such a model? What features or aspects of the teller's job would you include? How would you relate the model features? Does the teller always count out the paper money before the silver? Is it necessary to include the counting of silver separately from that of paper money? Is it necessary to include the process of counting money separately from the process of account verification?

The only way one can adequately answer such questions is to consult the criteria system. That is, *why* is this model being built and what questions are to be examined with the model? If one were interested in knowing how to improve the teller's efficiency or speed, a reasonable approach might be to break the task into very small detail, such as studying the

FIGURE 1–2

The Decision-Making Process

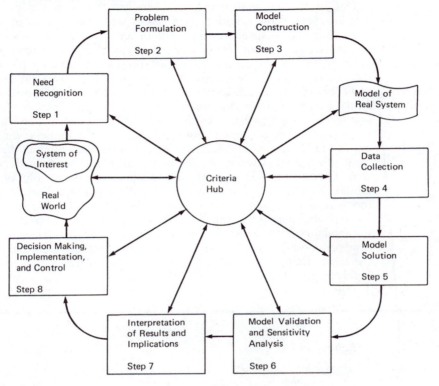

individual hand motions involved in counting silver and paper money. If, however, one were willing to accept the present job methods, but were concerned with how many teller stations to have open at various times during the day, then selection of model entities (and the concomitant data collection process) would be quite different.

Level of Aggregation

The criteria system not only dictates the appropriate entities to be represented in a model, but also the *way* they are to be represented. The necessary degree of detail, or what is often called the appropriate **level of aggregation,** can be determined only by falling back on the criteria system. As stated above, the major reason for using a model is economy; a model is an abstract that contains the essence of the real—but only the essence—for a particular set of criteria. It therefore follows that the essence implies a necessary level of detail, and the necessary level will vary for different problems.

In several places, the notion of recycling in the analytical process has been discussed. Recycling suggests evolution in the model-building process. As that evolution occurs, the appropriate level of aggregation often changes.

One of the authors once had a very interesting experience with the level-of-aggregation question. The issue was the subject of classroom discussion and assigned reading, but in an abstract way. At the end of one class day, students were asked to prepare an initial design proposal for a digital simulation model of beef production. During the next class session, two students were asked to put their design on the blackboard, and other students added relevant features. As the session progressed, the model became more and more detailed and complicated (that is, it had a *low* level of aggregation). Typical additions included provision for meat products that were canned, institutional uses, TV dinners, the corn-hog cycle, the inventory of beef held on the hoof at slaughter houses, and meat substitutes. After about two hours, all blackboards in the classroom were covered, and it was difficult to make any sense out of the total model. Finally, the students suggested that perhaps they were getting too complex in their approach. A lively discussion ensued in which it became abundantly clear that no objectives had been explicitly stated for the model-building exercise. The objectives were thereafter stated to show how commodity markets with feedback can be modeled through industrial dynamics simulations (Chapter 13). At that point, a relatively simple, highly aggregated model was constructed.

Follow-up Exercise

3. Gotham City Hospital (GCH) is contemplating the expansion of its emergency room facilities. GCH estimates that during the busiest two-hour period of the day, one to six patients will arrive every five minutes. Patients require between 10 and 60 minutes for treatment; it can be assumed that arrivals and departures take place only at five-minute intervals (for example, a patient will stay for 20 or 25 minutes but not 23 minutes). A crap-shooting friend observed that the number of patients arriving in a five-minute period can be "simulated" by the throw of a die, and that treatment time can be "simulated" by two dice with the value of the dice multiplied by five. List controllable and uncontrollable variables, parameters, constraints, and surrogate criteria which seem relevant. In what way does this problem relate to Figure 1–1? Formulate the problem at a high level of aggregation; then formulate the problem at a more disaggregated level. Can you formulate and operationalize a model to help GCH? What data would you need?

1.5 STEP FOUR—DATA COLLECTION

Once a model has been formulated, it is usually necessary to collect data for the modeling process. It is worth noting again that the role of criteria is all-important; we must have data oriented toward the decision to be made. Although it is conceptually correct to think of criteria dictating problem formulation, which in turn dictates model selection, which in turn dictates data collection, the flow can be reversed; that is, existing data may help in model selection. It might be desirable to have one set of data, but if another set is readily available, it *may* be possible (but not ideal) to select a model which could utilize the data and still achieve valid results.

Systems of Measurement and Scales

The collection of data implies a system of measurement. For example, if an aerospace engineer is considering the lift characteristics of various airfoil configurations, a unit of measurement is needed for lift (Would you believe pounds?); a study of refinery capacity requires a unit of measurement for flows through various processing units, say, cubic feet per minute or barrels per day; and an OR model for production scheduling needs cost data in units of dollars per item and technological data in units of labor hours per item.

The unit of measurement in turn implies one of the following scales of measurement: nominal, ordinal, interval, or ratio. A **nominal scale** is simply a scale with mutually exclusive categories, for example, colors and makes of automobiles. An **ordinal scale** consists of mutually exclusive categories which have rank order; that is, the magnitudes of numbers have relative but not absolute meaning. For example, suppose that some commodity is graded excellent, good, or fair. The numbers three, two, and one can be associated with these grades, but one would not want to conclude that the absolute difference between excellent and good is the same as that between good and fair or that excellent is three times as desirable as fair.

An **interval scale** has the additional property that equal differences between numbers represent equal differences in the attribute which those numbers measure. Interval scales set the origin or zero point arbitrarily, such as $0°C$ or noon and midnight for clocks. For example, suppose the dollar is chosen as the unit of measurement for disposable income. For an economic study, the difference between $1,000 and $5,000 is the same as the difference $5,000 and $9,000; however, if these same figures are used to measure the attribute of economic well-being, then $5,000 may represent more well-being than $1,000 and less well-being than $9,000 but the differences in well-being are not necessarily equal.

Finally, a **ratio scale,** in addition to the properties of the interval scale, has the properties that the numbers are proportional to the attribute they represent and the zero point is meaningful. For example, suppose a Volkswagen is priced at $4,000 and a Porsche at $16,000. If the attribute is costliness, then the Porsche is four times as costly as the Volkswagen; if the attribute is quality, then based on this unit of measurement, we cannot conclude that the Porsche is four times better than the Volkswagen.

The upshot of the preceding discussion is that very close attention must be paid to the relationship between the global criterion (attribute), the unit of measurement (scale) for the surrogate criterion, and the form of the mathematical or statistical analysis. This latter item is of special im-

portance because the simple mathematical operation of summation requires the assumption of at least the interval scale. (Can you explain
why?)

Estimation and Forecasting

Typically, problem formulation and model selection require the analyst
to estimate and forecast parameters and values for uncontrollable
variables. Both of these procedures can be accomplished either statistically
or subjectively.

Statistical estimation requires the ability to access data which are available in objective form (**hard data**) either through sampling from primary
and secondary documents or through sample surveys. In either case,
these procedures require sound sample designs in order to (1) avoid biases
and misinterpretations and (2) obtain probabilistic estimates of the
variability of the sample statistics.

In applications which are time-dependent, parameters and uncontrollable variables must be estimated using **statistical forecasting models.**
For example, the demands for blood types in a blood-bank inventory
model exhibit both seasonal and trend patterns which can be estimated by
exponential smoothing models or **regression models.** Appendix A, at the
end of the book, presents statistical estimation and forecasting in greater
detail.

In many cases, statistical estimation and forecasting may be impossible,
too costly, or unwarranted—so we turn to **subjective estimation.** For
example, historical demand or cost data for the introduction of a totally
new product are unavailable, and market testing may be too costly. It is
possible, however, to generate so-called **soft data** by polling individuals
with expertise. In some cases, the estimates can be as accurate as (or
more accurate than) statistical procedures, and in other cases, decisions
may be fairly insensitive to variations in the estimates.

The term soft data can also include the measurement of attributes which
are inherently difficult to quantify, for example, preferences (as in
Example 1.5, which follows), opinions, "quality," and so forth. If these
aspects are important to the problem being analyzed, their lack of "hard-
ness" should not discourage their use in a quantitative model. The use of
sensitivity analysis (as described in Section 1.7) and careful attention to
scaling can go a long way toward compensating for their lack of explicit-
ness.

When misapplied, statistical estimation and forecasting give the illusion
of accuracy by providing precision (Think about it!); if the data you
use are "dirty" and biased (*G*arbage *I*n), then your model results may be
quite unuseable (*G*arbage *O*ut). As you might expect, GIGO presents a
formidable real-world problem to the OR analyst which can be devastating
if ignored.

Management Information Systems

The desires to include soft data and to use open-ended sensitivity
analyses imply evolution in problem delineation as well as continual im-

perfection in the statement of criteria. The ability to explore alternative solutions will be partially based upon the robustness of the underlying data. Computerized **management information systems (MIS)** can permit robust data collection by allowing more data to be held in a basic disaggregated format. Combining or accumulating can be done for particular problems at hand without destroying the original identity of the basic data. Disaggregated data can be assembled or combined in many different forms depending upon user-oriented inquiries, assumptions, or hypotheses. It follows that augmenting such a computerized data bank with a bank of computerized models provides an opportunity for *man-machine interaction* leading to rapid evolution in problem delineation—model formulation—problem solution. MIS also has important implications for control (Section 1.9 and Chapter 18.).

Example 1.5 Committee Assignments

Fifty members of a college faculty are to be assigned to eight standing committees according to their preferences. Two numbering schemes for assessing committee preferences are being considered.

(1) Each faculty member ranks the committees in order of preference from one to eight.
(2) Each faculty member assigns a weight on a scale of zero to one indicating dispreference for each committee; a weight of zero means highest preference.

Follow-up Exercises

4. What is the attribute being measured here? What type of scale is (1)? Is (2) more nearly an interval scale than (1)? Why isn't (2) a true interval scale? If the criterion is to minimize overall faculty dispreference, then which scale would you recommend? Why? Are these "hard" or "soft" data? (We will return to this problem in Example 7.3.)

5. For the police patrol sector problem, indicate units of measurement and scale considerations for the surrogate criteria, variables, and parameters either given in Equations (1.1) and (1.2) or identified in Exercise 2. Identify and discuss the issues involved in estimating or forecasting these values. What source(s) would you use for data collection? Can you think of other considerations which might require special attention?

6. Consider the same issues for GCH (Example 1.2 and Exercise 3).

1.6 STEP FIVE—MODEL SOLUTION

Model solution is obviously an important aspect of operations research; indeed, the major part of this book is devoted to a careful development of solution procedures. In many ways, however, it is the most straightforward aspect of the decision-making process. Furthermore, great skill in this area does not by itself insure superior decisions.

Solution Procedures

In a general sense, the solution of a model consists of finding those values for the controllable variables which result in outcomes that are judged superior in terms of criteria. Because there is great variety in the solution procedures for models in operations research, we have adopted the concept of taxonomic structure from the biological sciences in an attempt to categorize quantitative techniques and to provide you with a "road map" to the materials covered in the text. Figure 1–3 presents our

FIGURE 1–3

Taxonomy of OR Models

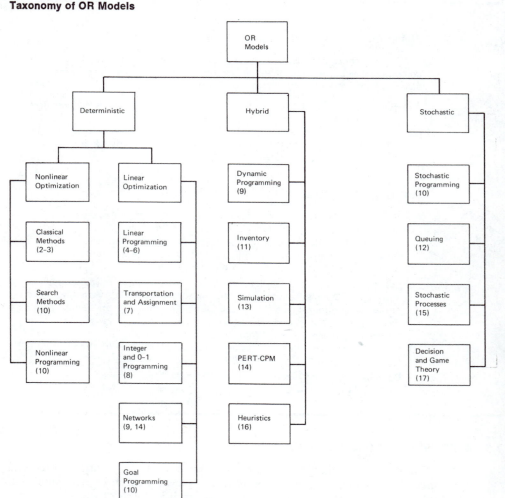

taxonomy of OR models. For ease of reference, the chapters which treat these models are parenthetically inserted in the blocks.

Taxonomy of OR Models

Models are dichotomized as either **deterministic** (nonprobabilistic) or **stochastic** (probabilistic). Some models, however, are treated more appropriately as **hybrids** of these two categories. Deterministic models, as opposed to stochastic models, assume that values for all uncontrollable variables and parameters are known with certainty and are fixed. As we all know, however, the real world is probabilistic. So why bother with deterministic models? First, mathematical modeling is more tractable under deterministic assumptions than under probabilistic assumptions (as you will come to realize). In other words, certain complex processes can be feasibly modeled and solved deterministically but not probabilistically. Second, some real-world systems are stable enough to be modeled effectively by deterministic approaches. Finally, a feature of all deterministic modeling allows the introduction of uncertainties: sensitivity analysis (step six of the paradigm).

Most of the deterministic models can be characterized as those which optimize (maximize or minimize) some objective function (surrogate criterion expressed in terms of variables and parameters) usually subject to a set of constraints; that is,

optimize

$$z = f(\mathbf{X}, \mathbf{Y})$$

subject to   (1.3)

$$\mathbf{G(X, Y)} \left(\begin{matrix} \leq \\ = \\ \geq \end{matrix} \right) \mathbf{B}$$

where z is the criterion of interest expressed as a function of $\mathbf{X}$, the set of controllable variables, and $\mathbf{Y}$, the set of uncontrollable variables; $\mathbf{G(X, Y)}$ is the set of constraints expressed as functions of the controllable and uncontrollable variables; and $\mathbf{B}$ represents the set of right-hand–side constants associated with the set of constraints. Note that the constraint set can consist of inequality as well as equality relationships. Procedures for solving models of the type given by Equation (1.3) are collectively called **mathematical programming.**

The distinction between **linear** and **nonlinear optimization models** is based on the nature of the objective function and/or constraints; for example, **linear programming** models are characterized by a linear objective function and linear constraints. **Transportation** and **assignment models** can be viewed as special cases of linear programming, whereby certain efficiencies can be realized in the solution procedures. When the decision variables in linear optimization models are restricted to either integer or 0–1 values, so-called **integer** and **0–1 programming models** are appropriate. **Network models** represent these types of problems in terms of flow diagrams. **Goal programming models** optimize a multiple criteria objective function which is linear subject to a set of linear constraints.

For each of these linear models, the solution procedure is based on a specific iterative algorithm. An **iterative algorithm** is a solution procedure which starts with some solution (complete or partial) and then proceeds to better or more complete solutions by a set of rules. The procedure is repeatedly applied until no further improvement in the objective function is achieved or until some stopping condition is met.

Nonlinear optimization models are classified more by the method of solution than by the structure of the model: **Classical methods** apply differential calculus, **search methods** use gradient and hill-climbing techniques, and **nonlinear programming methods** apply special **algorithms** (solution procedures) to exploit certain mathematical structures in the functional relationships.

Stochastic programming algorithms treat the parameters of optimization models as random variables from specified sampling distributions. Thus, they represent an area of mathematical programming which relaxes some of the deterministic assumptions.

Queuing models (as do inventory and competitive models) occupy a special category in that they have been developed specifically for a given area of application. Queuing models essentially attempt to predict the operating characteristics (for example, average length of queue, utilization of service facilities, and so forth) of queuing systems. In some cases, these models can be formulated in terms of a surrogate cost criterion and solved by an optimization procedure.

Models of **stochastic processes** attempt to characterize the behavior of certain probabilistic processes by systems of mathematical equations. Attention is usually focused on the ability to predict the behavior of the system (including surrogate criteria) rather than on the need to optimize some objective function. For example, these models have predicted market shares of specific products, have been applied to equipment replacement and reliability problems, and have characterized certain equipment failure and queuing phenomena.

Decision theory represents a formalized approach to decision making under uncertainty which incorporates and integrates concepts from utility theory, probability distribution theory, and Bayesian probability theory. **Game theory** is a related approach to characterizing the behavior of decision making under conflict or competition.

Dynamic programming is an approach to optimization which is uniquely suited to many deterministic and probabilistic problems; several models include deterministic and probabilistic representations: **PERT-CPM** is an approach to planning, scheduling, and controlling complex projects which can be characterized as networks; **heuristic models** apply "rules-of-thumb" to problems which otherwise cannot be solved feasibly, efficiently, or optimally; **inventory models,** both deterministic and stochastic, specify inventory policies which minimize expected cost.

Simulation is an important form of deterministic and stochastic modeling which represents the behavior of complex systems by computerized mathematical or logical models. By properly representing the uncertainties, relationships, and interactions of individual components in a system, it is possible to reproduce that system artificially. As opposed to the physical simulation of systems (for example, space flight simulators, wind tunnel models, planetariums, and so forth) OR simulation models represent the system with mathematical approaches especially suited to manipulation by digital computers. Simulation is particularly valuable for the investigation of problems too complex to be analyzed by other OR procedures.

In concluding this section, we might note that Figure 1–3 omits "cross-fertilization." For example, certain inventory models, decision theory models, and stochastic processes can be characterized as probabilistic dynamic programming models; game theory models can be formulated in terms of linear programming; queuing models can be treated as stochastic processes; and simulations of inventory and queuing systems are common.

1.7 STEP SIX—MODEL VALIDATION AND SENSITIVITY ANALYSIS

Once a solution to the model is generated, there is a critical need for postsolution analysis. This analysis should focus upon the validity of the model as well as the validity of the solution.

Model Validation

Model validation is concerned with whether the model accurately represents the problem environment. Although we treat it as step six in our paradigm, you should not be misled to believe that validation necessarily follows solution. Validation is a continuous procedure which begins in the model construction phase and ends only when the environmental conditions from which the original problem was identified no longer exist.

The validation process needs to be both objective and subjective. Although in this text we will emphasize objective validation tests, in the last analysis the decision maker has to believe in the model. A good deal of this belief is a natural by-product of the user-designer concept; the inclusion of inputs and opinions from independent, unbiased sources also fosters belief.

Perhaps the greatest pitfall concerns models which contain structural limitations which do not accurately represent the way in which variables are actually related to one another. For example, many models assume that production output is linearly proportionate to the level of production input. This may not be a valid assumption when the effects of economies of scale are significant. Once again this illustrates the very important need for users to intimately understand the structural assumptions which are made in the statement or derivation of the model.

The model validation process can also indicate certain variables that were included are either not significant or their influence runs counter to the anticipated effect. For instance, in Forrester's *Urban Dynamics* models, decision variables such as expenditures on low-cost housing and job retraining produce results that are either insignificant or counterintuitive. In contrast, models often exclude variables which are significant in the problem. The exclusion of the industrial sector in a pollution model would be a gross logical error.

The problem of determining whether variables and models are significant is one which often can be resolved by the use of statistical tools such as correlation and regression analyses and the analysis of variance and covariance. For example, an analysis of variance can be used to test for significant differences in mean criterion values between the models and reality for various levels of the variables.

Solution Validation

Once a solution has been found, decision makers should be concerned with (a) whether the solution is better than other alternatives and (b) the degree of stability in the results.

The most common benchmark for evaluating a solution is the level of performance of the existing system. The comparison can be based on historical levels of performance, using actual data gathered in the past, or on projected performance. Obviously, a favorable comparison is essential if the solution is to be considered further. Moreover, any increase in the cost of implementing the new solution should be more than offset by projected benefits.

Decision makers also need to be concerned about the stability of the results from the model. Stability, in this instance, refers to the sensitivity of the recommended decisions and the projected measures of system performance to changes in model parameters. In most models, the degree of accuracy of the parameters depends upon the appropriateness of the data available and the validity of the procedures used in analyzing the data. **Sensitivity analysis** is concerned with determining the amount by which these parameter estimates can be in error before the generated decision alternative will no longer be superior to others.

1.8 STEP SEVEN—INTERPRETATION OF RESULTS AND IMPLICATIONS

This step is concerned with a critical examination of user objectives or criteria and the evaluation of those criteria in light of model results. For example, are the tradeoffs and criteria valid for the ranges implied in the solution? That is, do the explicit surrogate criteria still hold, or are there other objectives that must be considered? What are the implications of the decision indicated by the solution for other systems not included in the model? An important part of this step is an understanding of the term "optimum."

Satisficing

The word "optimum" has a particular meaning in management science. If a solution is said to be the optimum, that means that the solution is the best and it can be mathematically *proven* to be the best. The optimal solution, however, is always relative to a carefully stated criteria set, and the criteria will almost always be surrogate criteria.

We have noted several times that real-world problems tend to have many nebulous criteria. It is extremely difficult, if not impossible, to find a solution that is truly optimal (within the tight definition given above). An alternative to achieving "optimal" solutions is to achieve "satisfactory" solutions; "satisficing" becomes the goal instead of "optimizing," and the decision maker accepts decisions that are satisfactory or "good" instead of "best." To arrive at a decision which results in satisfactory levels of all criteria, the decision maker must be concerned with the tradeoffs between them. (Remember the tradeoff concept as presented in Figure 1–1?)

An obvious problem with satisficing is the determination of what represents a good or satisfactory solution. It is much easier to specify the absolute best than to settle for something less—particularly when the decision maker does not *know* how far away from optimal a given solution lies.

Suboptimization

The concept of "suboptimization" refers to the penalty one pays for less than perfect overall system design or global decision making. It *always* exists, and occurs for many reasons, including noncongruency of criteria, poor choices of surrogate criteria, omitted criteria, and poor tradeoffs of the criteria. The analytical process almost assures suboptimization since usually a small subset of the entire system is chosen for analysis.

To illustrate the concept of suboptimization, consider a firm structured along functional lines. Marketing would like to maximize customer service by never being out of products (implying high inventories). Finance would like to minimize the cost of inventory holding and replenishment. Clearly, these surrogate criteria are in conflict, and the global criteria for the firm such as profits and long-term growth may be suboptimized.

It is almost impossible to accurately assess the degree of suboptimization at the highest system level. Who knows how much more profit a company might have been able to make with better decisions? And, even if it were possible to determine the ultimate profit potential, profit is only one surrogate. One possible way to cope with this dilemma is to make comparisons of companies within an industry, metropolitan hospitals of similar size, mass transit systems for different cities, and so forth. Useful as these comparisons may be, the goals or objectives derived from them are "suboptimal" rather than "optimal."

Although the management science models in this text will always address less than the "total system," the results of the analysis often will force better total-system thinking. If an optimum-producing model indicates one decision, and the decision makers choose another, there are natural tendencies to ask why. The resultant analysis should lead to an improvement in suboptimization.

1.9 STEP EIGHT—DECISION MAKING, IMPLEMENTATION, AND CONTROL

After determining the validity of a solution and verifying its consistency with global criteria, one might think that the decision is automatic. In one sense, this is true, but in another sense it is not. The modeling process of operations research may properly be viewed as providing an input or set of inputs to a decision maker. Other inputs can be equally as important, including those of a purely qualitative or subjective nature. In fact most OR results are treated as initial plans which can be modified by intangible considerations.

Decision Rule Formulation

For some kinds of problems, decision makers jump from step one, recognition of a need, to step eight, decision making. This seems particularly appropriate for actions such as driving a car or putting one's hand on a hot stove. In both cases, formal analysis is not needed; automatic or programmed behavior prevails.

Decision rule formulation is essentially a process of building programmed decision responses. When a problem with the same basic structure comes up again and again, it is often advisable to invest analytic effort in understanding the structure of the problem rather than expending all of the effort on solving the problem. The result is a rule or set of rules for automatically dealing with future problems as they arrive.

In many ways, decision rule formulation is at the heart of the management process. It involves analysis of problem situations—and the development of policies and procedures to cover those problems. A good example of this process may be seen in inventory control procedures. Thirty years ago, inventory problems were attacked with incomplete policy and an army of clerks. Today, most inventory problems can be handled by standard computerized approaches which incorporate statistical forecasting with a set of programmed decision rules. Employees who used to spend a great deal of their time placing orders, such as buyers in department stores, now spend their time on much more constructive and interesting work, such as analysis of the product line.

Implementation

The decision maker not only has to identify good decision alternatives but also has to select alternatives that are capable of being implemented. This implies an assessment of the organizational climate for change and the decision maker's abilities to move the organization.

The behavioral aspects of change are exceedingly important to the successful implementation of management science results. This is particularly so when the systems approach is being used since the widening scope of analysis is even more likely to touch increasing numbers of individuals and organizational subunits.

To a great extent, the user-designer concept enhances the likelihood of successful implementation of management science results because decision makers who are in the best position to implement are (hopefully) active participants in the analytical process. In the last chapter we will provide a more detailed treatment of caveats regarding resistance to change.

Control

The final concept that we want to identify as part of the decision-making process is control or monitoring of the system following implementation of the solution. Control processes are necessary to assure that the implemented solution in fact results in the predicted changes in system performance. Beyond initial implementation, controls are necessary for maintenance of the solution. Organizations are set within dynamic environments, and changes within the environment can have significant implications regarding the continuing validity of models and their solutions. Feedback-control mechanisms will be treated in Chapter 18.

1.10 IMPACT OF OPERATIONS RESEARCH/MANAGEMENT SCIENCE

The impact of OR/MS in its less than three decades of existence as a formal field of study has been nothing short of remarkable. Although we

TABLE 1–1

OR/MS Applications

Public Sector	Private Sector
Urban–Social	Service
City planning	Portfolio management
Courtroom congestion and scheduling	Insurance and risk management
Income maintenance and family assistance	Location of retail facilities
	Fleet scheduling
Air-water pollution control	Actuarial science
Solid waste disposal	Professional sports drafts
Educational planning and schoolbus scheduling	Feedlot optimization
	Auditing strategies
Manpower planning	Advertising media mix
Air and highway traffic patterns	Airplane scheduling
Mass transit systems	Telephone switching
Regional and world development	Transportation scheduling
Public utilities regulation	Utilization of banking facilities
Population planning	
Natural resources planning and allocation	Industrial
Municipal zoning	Food and chemical blending
Emergency response systems	Production scheduling
Law enforcement	Optimal inventory policies
Political campaign strategies*	Distribution of products
	Working capital management
	Capital budgeting
Health	Advertising strategies and market shares
Health indices construction	
Evaluating health care delivery systems	Product safety testing
Blood inventory policies	Assignment of facilities
Hospital admissions	Planning, scheduling, and controlling complex projects
Diagnostics	
Disease control	New product introduction
Dietary planning	Plant layouts
Hospital utilization and scheduling	Quality control
	Replacement and servicing policies
Aerospace–Military	Queuing analysis of facilities
Inventory, distribution, maintenance of equipment	
Reliability of space vehicles	
Satellite queuing	
Missile defense and allocation	
Search and rescue efforts	

* Don't blame us for Watergate!

have already indicated reasons for various shortcomings in the field (Section 1.1) and we offer a critique in the final chapter, the fact remains that the quantitative analysis of managerial, economic, and social problems has proliferated, has become entrenched, and is maturing. To wit: Numerous graduate programs of study offer OR/MS degrees; many corporations, consulting companies, and universities put on nationally based seminars on specific modeling procedures; OR/MS departments are well-established in relatively large corporations and governmental agencies; management consulting groups provide OR/MS services to small and medium-sized organizations; and several personnel placement companies specialize in searching for and placing individuals with OR/MS expertise.

To give you an idea of the areas and scope of OR/MS applications, we have compiled a partial list of real-world applications in Table 1–1. Subsequent chapters will provide greater detail in relating specific applications to specific models.

2

Classical Deterministic
Models I

A PRESUMPTION throughout this text is that the criteria upon which decisions are made are quantifiable and can be represented by mathematical functions. The mathematical relationships used to represent these criteria are often referred to as objective functions, as defined in Chapter 1.

The next two chapters will focus upon a group of problem structures which can be represented mathematically by so-called **classical deterministic models,** as opposed to probabilistic models. When problems can be represented accurately by such models, we will show that solutions can be generated rather easily through the use of the calculus. The present chapter treats **single-variable optimization** problems, and the next chapter presents more advanced topics such as *n*-variable optimization and optimization with constraints. In subsequent chapters, calculus-based solutions will be demonstrated for continuous dynamic programming models (Example 9.7), inventory models (Chapter 11), and queuing optimization models (Section 12.7).

Since the solution techniques particularly involve differential calculus, it is assumed that most readers are familiar with elementary rules for finding derivatives. If you are not familiar with the concepts and techniques of differential calculus, you must carefully study Sections 2.3 and 2.4. We strongly believe that these fundamentals can be mastered if (*a*) you have a rudimentary knowledge of algebra and (*b*) you make a commitment. Calculus is not as esoteric as you might believe. Try it, you might even like it. Besides, it has snob appeal. If you are familiar with calculus, a reading of Sections 2.3 and 2.4 should serve to clear the "cobwebs."

It is important to note that our efforts in not only this chapter but also most of the remaining chapters are primarily aimed at developing your expertise for a particular subset of the eight-step paradigm of Chapter 1: problem formulation, model building, and model solution, including sensitivity analysis and interpretation of results.

2.1 MATHEMATICAL REPRESENTATION OF FUNCTIONS

Before discussing the mathematical representation of objective functions, a discussion of functional notation is appropriate.

Functional Notation

A **function** is a mathematical relationship for which the value of a particular variable is determined from the values of one or more other variables. For example, the relationship

$$y = f(x) \tag{2.1}$$

implies some association between the variables x and y. Specifically, Equation (2.1) indicates that the variable y is a function of, or depends upon, the variable x. In this context, y is called the **dependent (criterion) variable** and x the **independent (predictor) variable.** Equation (2.1) is read "y is a function of x" where the expression $f(x)$ can be verbalized as "f of x." $f(x)$ is the value of the algebraic function f at x.

Example 2.1

Starting salaries for drivers of trucks for the Humorous Ice Cream Company are based upon an incentive system. Salaries are dependent upon the sales generated by each driver. This salary-sales relationship might be expressed symbolically as

$$y = f(x)$$

or

$$\text{Salary} = f(\text{dollar sales})$$

where "salary" is the criterion variable and "dollar sales" is the independent variable. The precise relationship between the two variables might be expressed as

$$y = 50 + 0.25x$$

where $y =$ weekly salary in dollars and $x =$ weekly sales in dollars.

You should notice that in this example $f(x)$ involves a constant term (50). The occurrence of constant terms is common in mathematical functions. In this situation drivers are paid a base weekly salary of $50 and receive a commission of 0.25 on every dollar of sales. For example, if a driver were to generate $250 in sales during a given week, the salary of $112.50 can be determined easily by substituting 250 for x in the above linear function.

In many instances, the criterion variable depends upon more than one variable. Consequently, a more general functional representation of the association between some criterion variable, *y*, and a set of *n* independent variables is

$$y = f(x_1, x_2, x_3, \ldots, x_n). \tag{2.2}$$

Representation through Continuous Mathematical Functions

A not insignificant number of models in economics and management utilize discrete or integer variables. Units of a product, number of employees, and dollars and cents are all examples of variables characterized by discrete values. In most cases, functions which are based on variables which are continuous—time, length, volume—can be treated more readily than discrete functions. Indeed, differential calculus rests on the premise that the function being treated is continuous. Fortunately, discrete functional relationships often can be approximated quite well by continuous mathematical functions, as the subsequent example illustrates.

Example 2.2

A certain company is interested in studying how sales revenue for a district responds to different levels of assigned sales personnel per district. Figure 2–1 reflects empirical data gathered within a representative sales

FIGURE 2–1

Empirical Data for Example 2.2

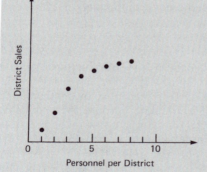

district where the number of personnel assigned ranged from one to eight. Each data point reflects the number of personnel in the district and the associated level of sales for the district. The data seem to indicate a diminishing returns effect beyond three people. Note that the function is discrete since both sales and personnel, assuming the latter cannot be split among districts, are discrete variables. As Figure 2–2 indicates, however,

FIGURE 2–2

Continuous Function for Example 2.2

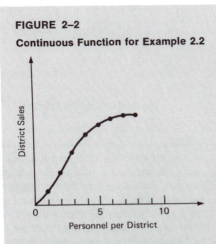

a continuous function can be approximated by fitting a smooth curve to the plotted data. Although the curve extrapolates between integer values of the variable, the important feature is that it provides a fairly accurate portrayal of the relationship between district sales and number of personnel assigned per sales district.

You will find in this chapter that where criterion relationships or objective functions can be represented by continuous mathematical functions, the laws of differential calculus provide a convenient search procedure for identifying conditions of optimality.

The Concept of Optimality

Returning to a statement made in the introduction to this chapter, we presumed that the criteria upon which decisions are made are often quantifiable and capable of being represented by mathematical functions called objective functions. The ultimate purpose for making a decision is to try to influence the objective function in a favorable direction. Optimization is the state of either minimization or maximization of the chosen measure of effectiveness. For example, the objective in a hospital emergency room might be to minimize the average waiting time between arrival at the hospital and attendance by medical personnel. In Example 2.2, the company might be interested in determining the number of personnel it should assign to a particular district in order to maximize district profits.

In a situation where the criterion variable depends upon one independent variable, the relationship graphed in Figure 2–3 could represent such an objective function. This continuous objective function is rather strange looking, but it is useful in demonstrating some concepts of optimality. Assume that the independent variable, x, can have values ranging between $x = 0$ and $x = x_m$.

Given that variable x represents the independent variable, a function is said to reach a **relative** or **local maximum** at a point $x = x_a$ if $f(x_a)$ is greater than the value of $f(x)$ for any adjacent value of x. Similarly, a function is said to reach a **relative** or **local minimum** at a point $x = x_b$ if $f(x_b)$ is less than the value of $f(x)$ for any adjacent value of x. For example, in Figure 2–3 relative maxima occur at points a and c on the curve. If you select an adjacent point on either side of $x = x_a$, then the value of the criterion variable is less than $f(x_a)$. The same argument applies to adjacent points surrounding $x = x_c$. Following the definition of a relative minimum, one would conclude that relative minima occur at points b and

FIGURE 2–3

Minima and Maxima

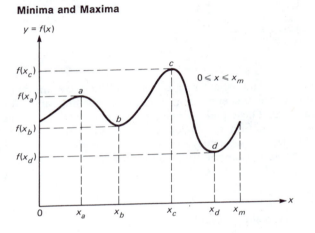

d on the curve. For values of the independent variable adjacent to either $x = x_b$ or $x = x_d$, the value of the criterion variable is greater than $f(x_b)$ or $f(x_d)$, respectively.

A function is said to have an **absolute** or **global maximum** at a point $x = x_c$ if $f(x_c)$ is greater than $f(x)$ for any other allowable value of x. The global maximum in Figure 2–3 occurs at point c where $x = x_c$. That is, $f(x_c)$ is larger than that for any other value of x within the region $0 \leq x \leq x_m$. Similarly, a function is said to have an **absolute** or **global minimum** at point $x = x_d$ if $f(x_d)$ is less than $f(x)$ for any other allowable value of x. In Figure 2–3, the global minimum occurs at $x = x_d$. $f(x_d)$ is less than $f(x)$ for any other value of x, where $0 \leq x \leq x_m$. It should be noted that a local maximum or minimum can also be a global maximum or minimum.

End points on a function can be significant in identifying optimal values for a criterion variable. Consider Figure 2–4 as an example. In this situation, the allowable values of x range from $x = x_a$ to $x = x_d$. A quick glance at this figure indicates that the global maximum for the criterion variable occurs not at $f(x_b)$, the local maximum, but when $x = x_d$; the

FIGURE 2–4

Global Minimum and Maximum End Points

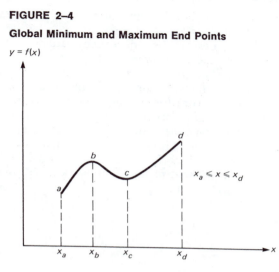

global minimum occurs when $x = x_a$, not at the local minimum $f(x_c)$. Notice that these are the end points on the allowable range for the independent variable. These end points are not candidates for local optima, however, for examination of adjacent points on both sides of the end point is impossible. Consequently, in examining for global optimum points, one should evaluate the function not only at the local maxima and minima but also at the end values of the allowable range for the independent variable.

Manipulation of Decision Variables

The ideal circumstances within a decision-making situation are that the criterion variable is totally controllable by the decision maker. Although it is rare that the decision maker has such powers (monopolistic conditions might approximate this situation), most decision makers are capable of partially controlling the relative achievement of their objectives. They do so by making decisions concerning the variables over which they have control. Such **endogenous** or **decision variables** might include the level of manpower resources to hire, the amount of money to allocate to advertising, the number of and timing of daily runs of a mass transit system, the hours of operation of a bank, the number of sections of a required college mathematics course to offer during a semester, and so forth. Note that decision variables are represented as independent variables (usually x's) in mathematical functions.

Realistically, there may be practical, competitive, or legal restrictions on the values that independent variables can assume. For example, budget considerations could set restrictions on the number of persons who may be hired or upon the allowable amounts of money which can be expended for advertising. It is within these limits of control that the

FIGURE 2–5

Manipulation for Achieving Optimization

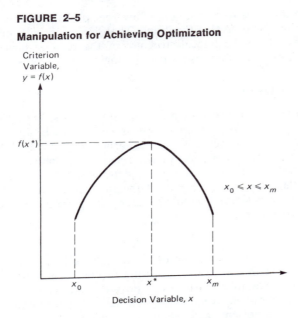

Decision Variable, x

decision maker hopes to influence the value of the objective function in the most favorable direction.

If the objective function looks like that in Figure 2–5, and if the goal is to maximize the value of the criterion variable, then the decision maker would like to manipulate the value of x as close to x^* as possible. In many cases, the way in which the criterion variable and the decision variable are interrelated may be unknown. Only through a trial-and-error procedure might the decision maker realize the best value to assign to the decision variable. But trial-and-error decisions by managers might lead to either a short life for the business or a shorter career for the decision maker. The greater the degree of understanding about the relationship which exists between the relevant variables, the greater the likelihood that a systematic and efficient search procedure can be identified.

2.2 WHERE DO THE RELATIONSHIPS COME FROM?

This book necessarily presents in detail many of the solution techniques for quantitative models of decision processes. In doing so, however, we do not want you to lose sight of the importance of and the pitfalls associated with the *formulation* of quantitative models. One of the traditional areas of neglect in discussing classical optimization theory is the whole question of the source of a model. As a systems analyst or management scientist, chances are slim that a decision maker will come to you and lay a quadratic profit equation on your desk to be solved. And yet, many calculus texts would lead the student to believe that the extent of one's interest should simply be to solve *predetermined* systems of equations.

This section attempts to create greater awareness of the source of these criterion equations or objective functions. The discussion will focus upon those situations where the logical structure of the relationships between variables is *well-defined* and those where the logical structure is *ill-defined*.

Logical Structure Well-Defined

There are a variety of problem situations in which the logical structure of the way in which variables interrelate is well-defined. This generally means that a systematic observation of the variables of interest leads to an exact mathematical representation of the relationship between variables. A classic example of this situation is the determination of total revenue for a firm. If the firm sells each unit at the same price, p, total revenue from selling q units is simply found by multiplying price per unit times the number of units sold, or

$$TR = p \cdot q.$$

This model is, under the assumption of a constant selling price, a logical and deterministic representation of the total revenue function.

The following example illustrates a decision situation in which the interrelationships between variables are well-defined either by their obvious structure or by assumptions made about the structure.

Example 2.3   Police Patrol Sectors[1]

In recent years, management scientists have focused greater attention upon urban service systems. One area of special interest has been that of improving the effectiveness of emergency-response systems. Emergency-response systems are exemplified by police response, ambulance response, and fire department response to calls for service. This example relates to how cities might go about the process of deciding upon optimal dimensions of patrol sectors for any emergency-response unit. In order to avoid confusion, we will cast the example within the framework of police patrol sector design, but the analysis can be extended to include any of the other response systems.

Suppose that a rectangular patrol sector is to be designed for a police patrol car so as to minimize the average travel time to incidents. The assumptions will be made that a patrol car responds only to the calls in its patrol sector and that a call for assistance is equally likely to originate from any point in the patrol sector. In addition, it will be assumed that at the instant a call occurs, the patrol car is equally likely to be at any point within the patrol sector. Statistically, it is being assumed that the positions of the patrol car and the calls for service are independent variables and that their values are uniformly distributed over the patrol sector.

Figure 2–6 illustrates some of the other aspects of the problem. The fig-

[1] The motivation for this example came from the work of Richard C. Larson, *Urban Police Patrol Analysis* (Cambridge, Mass.: The M.I.T. Press, 1972).

FIGURE 2–6

Rectangular Patrol Sector

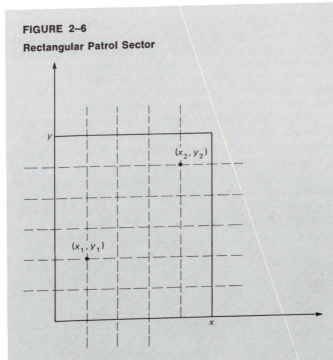

ure portrays a system of city blocks. The patrol sector in this application will be assumed rectangular with dimensions x by y (the decision variables). In addition, the directions of travel are parallel to the boundaries of the patrol area. This means that travel distances are computed on a "right-angle" basis. If a call is received at the location (x_2, y_2) and the patrol unit is currently located at (x_1, y_1), the patrol unit must follow the existing pattern of streets, combining an easterly movement with one in a northerly direction.

Travel speeds within a city can vary according to direction of travel, time of day, and section of the city. This model will assume that *effective* speeds can be determined. Effective travel speeds in the x and y directions, respectively, are defined by v_x and v_y. For the incident-patrol locations in Figure 2–6, the distances traveled in the x and y directions would be computed as:

$$d_x = |x_2 - x_1|$$

and

$$d_y = |y_2 - y_1|.$$

Total travel time is

$$T = t_x + t_y$$

where t_x = travel time in the x direction, and t_y = travel time in the y direction; or, since travel time is the distance traveled divided by the travel speed,

$$T = d_x/v_x + d_y/v_y.$$

The overall objective for the police administrator in this example is to determine the dimensions of the rectangular patrol sector which would minimize the criterion variable "average travel time "($\overline{T}$) for responding to calls for service. (If it is assumed that there is no delay between receiving a call and dispatching a car, then the objective translates into one of minimizing average *response* time to a call for assistance.)

It can be shown that the *average* distance traveled in the x and y directions for uniformly distributed incidence and patrol car locations are, respectively,

$$\overline{d}_x = x/3 \text{ and } \overline{d}_y = y/3$$

where x and y are the dimensions of the sector. If locations were recorded and the travel distances were noted in both the x and y directions for a large number of crimes, the *average* travel distances in the x and y directions would statistically tend toward the d_x and d_y values as indicated above. Consequently, the objective function in this problem becomes

$$\overline{T} = \frac{1}{3}\frac{x}{v_x} + \frac{1}{3}\frac{y}{v_y}$$
$$= \frac{1}{3}\left(\frac{x}{v_x} + \frac{y}{v_y}\right)$$

where $\overline{T}$ is the average travel time.

As this problem is formulated, the mathematical solution is trivial. Average travel time equals 0 when $x = y = 0$. It is apparent that the information is insufficient to determine a realistic solution to the problem. One condition which police planners often attempt to create is equal workloads for patrol cars. A way of approximating this condition is to assume that the number of calls received is proportional to the area of the sector patrolled. Thus, another condition in the above model is that the area of each sector must be predetermined. If the area of each sector is denoted as A, then it can be stated that $A = x \cdot y$.

The final statement of the problem is to minimize

$$\overline{T} = \frac{1}{3}\left(\frac{x}{v_x} + \frac{y}{v_y}\right) \qquad (2.3)$$

such that

$$x \cdot y = A. \qquad (2.4)$$

Logical Structure Ill-Defined

There are many situations in which the logical interrelationships existing between variables are not known exactly. Consequently it is more difficult to mathematically formulate an objective function. In such cases, it is necessary to collect relevant data through sampling in order to determine whether any regular pattern of behavior is apparent. If a pattern does seem to exist, then a curve-fitting procedure may be employed to quantitatively model the relationship. The means of fitting the curve might range from simply "eyeballing" to more rigorous procedures such as regression analysis (as discussed in Appendix A at the end of the book).

The following example illustrates a situation in which the logical structure is not defined sufficiently to simply write down the relevant system of equations.

Example 2.4   Single Product Pricing Problem

The Metropolitan Boston Transit Authority (MBTA) is attempting to smooth its demand for subway services. The subway system operates at capacity during the early morning and late afternoon rush hours, while it operates far below capacity during the late morning and early afternoon hours. The MBTA wants to stimulate greater demand during off-peak hours and to encourage riders who do not need to travel during peak hours to travel at other times. Housewives (or househusbands) shopping in the city during the day are examples of this category of riders.

The MBTA has been experimenting with off-peak fares in order to determine the effects upon demand. Currently, a program entitled "dime-time" allows passengers to travel for $0.10 rather than the normal $0.25 between the hours of 10 A.M. and 1 P.M. Data have been gathered for demand under other fares as depicted in Figure 2–7.

The data, when graphed, offer strong evidence of a linear demand function during off-peak hours. Since this demand function was not available initially, it is necessary to approximate it from collected data. Fitting a least-squares regression line to the data, we estimate the demand equation as

$$p = -2q + 45 \qquad (2.5)$$

FIGURE 2–7

MBTA Demand Data

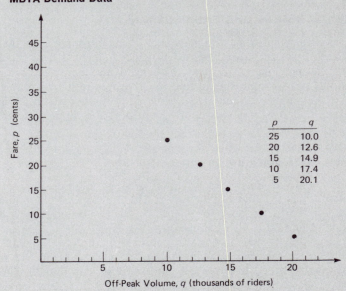

p	q
25	10.0
20	12.6
15	14.9
10	17.4
5	20.1

where $p =$ off-peak fare (cents), and $q =$ off-peak demand (thousands of riders).[2]

If the objective is to maximize the demand for off-peak service, observation of Figure 2–7 would suggest that fares be eliminated, giving an estimated 22,500 passengers during these hours. If, however, the objective is to maximize total revenue during this time period, then the question becomes one of determining the fare necessary to realize this objective. In order to answer this question, an analyst might state total revenue as a function of price and attempt to determine the price or fare which would lead to maximum revenue. As stated earlier, total revenue may be expressed as price per unit times number of units sold, or

$$TR = p \cdot q. \tag{2.6}$$

In its current form, total revenue is stated as a function of two independent variables. If quantity were to be expressed in terms of price, total revenue could be written as a function of only one independent variable, p. This can be accomplished easily by solving Equation (2.5) for q and substituting in Equation (2.6). The resulting objective function is $TR = p(22.5 - p/2)$ or

$$TR = 22.5p - p^2/2. \tag{2.7}$$

---

[2] As demonstrated in Example 3.6 and further discussed in Appendix A.

In this example, the structure for total revenue was apparent, but the exact interrelationships existing between variables had to be approximated through the analysis of empirically derived data.

2.3 DIFFERENTIATION IN ONE EASY LESSON

For those of you who have not been introduced to the concepts of calculus, we will now spend a few pages helping you to "tool-up" for the calculus portions of the text. You need not fear what lies ahead. Newcomers to this topic should find the concepts rather palatable. Old-timers, who may have suffered from a case of mathematical indigestion when taking their first calculus course, will probably appreciate this direct and intuitive approach.

Think of the Derivative as a Slope

As will be illustrated in later sections of this chapter, differential calculus has a fundamental concern with the slope of continuous mathematical functions. Suppose in Figure 2–8 you are interested in finding the slope of line $\overline{pq}$, which is tangent to the function $y = f(x)$ at point a. The slope of this line segment actually represents the *instantaneous slope* of the function for the specific value of x at point a. We refer to this as an instantaneous slope because the tangent slope continually changes for different values of the variable x. Only with linear functions would the tangent slope remain the same for all allowable values of x.

FIGURE 2–8

Instantaneous Slope of $y = f(x)$

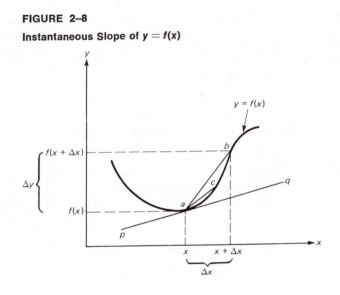

The slope of the tangent line could be determined by several different methods. A carefully constructed tangent line might be drawn using graph paper; the coordinates of any two points on the line could be determined and the slope calculated using the **two-point slope formula**

$$m = \frac{\Delta y}{\Delta x} = \frac{y_2 - y_1}{x_2 - x_1},$$

where Δy (delta y) represents the vertical displacement from point 1 to point 2, and Δx represents the horizontal distance between the two points. An alternative approach would be to identify another point on the curve, such as point b, connect it with the original point a by a straight line, and use the slope of the line segment $\overline{ab}$ as an "approximation" for the actual tangent slope. Obviously this is a poor approximation, but there is a method to our madness. Using the two-point slope formula, we compute the slope of $\overline{ab}$ as

$$m = \frac{\Delta y}{\Delta x} = \frac{f(x + \Delta x) - f(x)}{\Delta x}. \tag{2.8}$$

This is a general formula providing the slope of the straight line connecting any two points on a function which are Δx units apart from each other along the x-axis.

Notice in Figure 2–8 that if the adjacent point is selected closer to point a, as given by point c, the slope of the line segment $\overline{ac}$ becomes a better approximation than the slope of the line segment $\overline{ab}$ to the slope of the tangent line $\overline{pq}$. Recognizing that Δx is the distance along the x-axis separating points a and b, we might state that "in the limit," as Δx approaches zero, the slope of line segment $\overline{ab}$ will come closer and closer to the slope of $\overline{pq}$.

It is this type of reasoning which enables us to generalize a definition for the **derivative** of a continuous mathematical function. The derivative can be thought of as a general equation from which the tangent slope can be determined exactly at any point x on the function. Mathematically, this slope relationship is derived as a "limit" of Equation (2.8). Specifically, the derivative is defined as

$$\frac{dy}{dx} = \lim_{\Delta x \to 0}\left(\frac{f(x + \Delta x) - f(x)}{\Delta x}\right). \qquad (2.9)$$

The dy/dx notation replaces $\Delta y/\Delta x$ to emphasize that the tangent slope at any point on a curve is a measure of the *instantaneous rate of change* in the variable y with respect to a change in x.

Equation (2.9) can be read as saying "in the limit, as the distance along the x-axis separating the two points approaches zero, the slope of the line segment connecting the two points will equal the slope of the tangent at a specific value of x."

Example 2.5

For the function $y = x^2$,

a. Find the general slope equation, or derivative.
b. Find the slope of a tangent to this curve when $x = 1$.

According to Equation (2.9) the derivative can be found by selecting any two points on the curve having coordinates $[x, f(x)]$ and $[x + \Delta x, f(x + \Delta x)]$. Thus, for the function $y = x^2$, the coordinates are, respectively, (x, x^2) and $[x + \Delta x, (x + \Delta x)^2]$. The slope of the line segment connecting these two points is

$$m = \frac{\Delta y}{\Delta x} = \frac{y_2 - y_1}{x_2 - x_1} = \frac{(x + \Delta x)^2 - x^2}{(x + \Delta x) - x}.$$

Simplifying, we get

$$\frac{\Delta y}{\Delta x} = \frac{x^2 + 2x(\Delta x) + (\Delta x)^2 - x^2}{\Delta x}$$

$$= \frac{2x(\Delta x) + (\Delta x)^2}{\Delta x}$$

$$= 2x + \Delta x.$$

Taking the limit as Δx goes to zero, we get

$$\frac{dy}{dx} = \lim_{\Delta x \to 0} [2x + \Delta x]$$

$$= 2x.$$

Thus the derivative, or general slope equation, for the function $y = x^2$ is $dy/dx = 2x$. To determine the slope of the tangent to this function at any point, x, simply substitute the value for x into the derivative expression.

The slope of a tangent to the function when $x = 1$ is $dy/dx = 2(1)$. If a tangent to the curve were constructed at $x = 1$, the *exact slope* of the tangent line would equal $+2$.

The notation $f'(x)$ is often used as an equivalent form for dy/dx. This notation is convenient for specifying the slope of a function when x assumes a particular value. Using the first derivative in Example 2.5, we get

$$f'(0) = 2(0) = 0,$$
$$f'(-1) = 2(-1) = -2,$$

and

$$f'(5) = 2(5) = +10.$$

All specify the exact tangent slopes when $x = 0$, -1, and 5, respectively.

Follow-up Exercises

Determine the formula for the first derivative for each of the following and evaluate at $x = -2$, 0, 2.

1. $y = c$ (constant).
2. $y = x$.
3. $y = c \cdot x^2$.

Rules of Differentiation

The process of finding a derivative is called **differentiation.** Fortunately you do not have to go through the "limit" approach to find derivative expressions. The work has been done for you. Over the years a set of basic rules was developed for finding derivative expressions in a manner similar to that of Example 2.5. If you wish to find the slope expression for a mathematical function, it is simply a matter of applying the rule or rules which are appropriate for the particular functional form.

Table 2–1 provides a list of the basic differentiation rules, and this is followed by examples of their application. You should keep in mind that

TABLE 2–1

Differentiation Rules*

Rule	Function $y = f(x)$	Derivative $\dfrac{dy}{dx} = f'(x) = y'$
1	$y = c$	0
2	$y = x$	1
3	$y = x^n$	nx^{n-1}
4	$y = u(x) \pm v(x)$	$u'(x) \pm v'(x)$
5	$y = c \cdot f(x)$	$c \cdot f'(x)$
6	$y = [u(x)]^n$	$n[u(x)]^{n-1} \cdot u'(x)$
7	$y = u(x)/v(x)$	$\dfrac{v(x) \cdot u'(x) - u(x) \cdot v'(x)}{[v(x)]^2}$
8	$y = u(x) \cdot v(x)$	$u'(x) \cdot v(x) + v'(x) \cdot u(x)$
9	$y = e^{u(x)}$	$e^{u(x)} \cdot u'(x)$
10	$y = c^{u(x)}$	$c^{u(x)} \cdot \ln(c) \cdot u'(x)$
11	$y = \ln[u(x)]$	$\dfrac{1}{u(x)} \cdot u'(x)$

* Functions such as $u(x)$ and $v(x)$ are used to distinguish between different functions having the form $y = f(x)$. c and n are constants. $e = 2.718\ldots$, the base of natural or naperian logarithms (ln).

every mathematical function of the form $y = f(x)$ can be expressed graphically. The derivative allows you to determine the instantaneous slope at any point on the curve.

Example 2.6

Using the rules in Table 2—1, find the derivatives of the functions below (before looking at the answer, try to apply the rule yourself).

a. $y = 10$ 　　　　　 $\dfrac{dy}{dx} = 0$ 　　　　　　　　　　　　　　 [Rule 1]

b. $y = x^2$ 　　　　　 $\dfrac{dy}{dx} = 2x$ 　　　　　　　　　　　　　 [Rule 3]

c. $y = x^{-1/2}$ 　　　 $\dfrac{dy}{dx} = -\frac{1}{2}x^{-3/2}$ 　　　　　　　 [Rule 3]

d. $y = x^4 - 10$ 　　 $\dfrac{dy}{dx} = 4x^3 - 0$

　　　　　　　　　　　 $= 4x^3$ 　　　　　　　　　　　　 [Rules 4, 3, 1]

e. $y = 5x^3 + 2x^2$ 　 $\dfrac{dy}{dx} = 5 \cdot (3x^2) + 2 \cdot (2x)$

　　　　　　　　　　　 $= 15x^2 + 4x$ 　　　　　　　　 [Rules 5, 4, 3]

f. $y = \dfrac{x^4}{7}$ 　　　　 $\dfrac{dy}{dx} = \dfrac{1}{7} \cdot (4x^3)$

　　　　　　　　　　　 $= \dfrac{4x^3}{7}$ 　　　　　　　　　　　 [Rules 5, 3]

g. $y = \dfrac{2x^2}{5x - 1}$ 　　 $\dfrac{dy}{dx} = \dfrac{(5x - 1)[2(2x)] - (2x^2)(5)}{(5x - 1)^2}$

　　　　　　　　　　　 $= \dfrac{10x^2 - 4x}{(5x - 1)^2}$ 　　　　 [Rules 7, 1, 3, 5]

h. $y = (6x^3 + 1)(x^2 - 5)$ 　 $\dfrac{dy}{dx} = (18x^2)(x^2 - 5) + (2x)(6x^3 + 1)$

　　　　　　　　　　　 $= 30x^4 - 90x^2 + 2x$ 　　 [Rules 8, 1, 3, 5]

i. $y = (4x^2 - 1)^3$ 　 $\dfrac{dy}{dx} = 3(4x^2 - 1)^2 \cdot 8x$

　　　　　　　　　　　 $= 24x(4x^2 - 1)^2$ 　　　　 [Rules 6, 1, 3, 5]

j. $y = \left(\dfrac{3}{x+1}\right)^5$ 　 $\dfrac{dy}{dx} = 5\left(\dfrac{3}{x+1}\right)^4 \cdot \dfrac{(x+1)(0) - (3)(1)}{(x+1)^2}$

　　　　　　　　　　　 $= 5\left(\dfrac{3}{x+1}\right)^4 \cdot \dfrac{(-3)}{(x+1)^2}$

　　　　　　　　　　　 $= -\dfrac{1{,}215}{(x+1)^6}$ 　　　　　 [Rules 6, 7, 1, 2]

k. $y = e^x$ 　　　　　 $\dfrac{dy}{dx} = e^x \cdot (1)$

　　　　　　　　　　　 $= e^x$ 　　　　　　　　　　　　 [Rules 9, 2]

l. $y = e^{x^2 - 3}$ 　　 $\dfrac{dy}{dx} = e^{x^2 - 3} \cdot 2x$

　　　　　　　　　　　 $= 2xe^{x^2 - 3}$ 　　　　　　　 [Rules 9, 1, 3]

m. $y = \ln x$ 　　　　 $\dfrac{dy}{dx} = \dfrac{1}{x} \cdot (1)$

　　　　　　　　　　　 $= \dfrac{1}{x}$ 　　　　　　　　　　　　 [Rules 11, 2]

$n.\quad y = \ln(x^2 - 1)$ $\qquad \dfrac{dy}{dx} = \dfrac{1}{x^2 - 1} \cdot (2x)$

$\qquad\qquad\qquad\qquad\qquad = \dfrac{2x}{x^2 - 1}$ [Rules 11, 1, 3]

$o.\quad y = 50(1 - 0.5^x)$ $\qquad \dfrac{dy}{dx} = -50 \cdot (0.5)^x \cdot \ln(0.5) \cdot (1)$

$\qquad\qquad\qquad\qquad\qquad = -50 \cdot (0.5)^x \cdot (-0.69315)$

$\qquad\qquad\qquad\qquad\qquad = (34.6575) \cdot (0.5)^x$ [Rules 10, 1, 2, 5]

Follow-up Exercises

Verify the following:

4. The first derivative of $y = (7 + 4x + x^2)^{-2}$ is $y' = -4(2 + x)(7 + 4x + x^2)^{-3}$.
5. The instantaneous slope for $y = 2(3x^3 - 5x)^2$ at $x = 5$ is 308,000.
6. The instantaneous slope for $y = 1/(2x - 4)$ at $x = 3$ is $-\frac{1}{2}$.
7. The first derivative of $y = \ln(x^3 + 2)^4$ is $y' = 12x^2/(x^3 + 2)$.
8. For $y = e^{2x} \cdot (5 - \ln x^3)^4$, $y' = 2e^{2x} \cdot (5 - \ln x^3)^3 \cdot [5 - \ln x^3 - (6/x)]$.

Higher-Ordered Derivatives

Given a function of the form $y = f(x)$, one can define derivatives of an order higher than $f'(x)$, termed the **first derivative.** For example, the **second derivative** is simply the derivative of the first derivative. Denoted by $f''(x)$, the second derivative represents the instantaneous rate of change in the first derivative with respect to a change in the variable x. Another way of viewing the second derivative is that it represents the rate at which the slope of a function is changing with regard to a change in x. The rules used to find second derivatives are the same as those used in finding first derivatives except that the function differentiated is the first derivative. Third and higher-ordered derivatives can be found in the exact same manner. For instance, the **third derivative** is found by differentiating the second derivative of a function. Intuitive appreciation of the meaning of these derivatives becomes difficult beyond the second derivative.

Example 2.7

Find the first and all higher-ordered derivatives for the function $y = 12x^3 - 2x^2 - 2x + 1$:

$$f'(x) = 36x^2 - 4x - 2$$
$$f''(x) = 72x - 4$$
$$f'''(x) = 72$$
$$f''''(x) = 0.$$

All derivatives higher than the fourth derivative equal zero.

Follow-up Exercises

9.   Find the second derivatives for the functions in Exercises 4, 5, and 7.

10. Find the second and third derivatives for the functions in parts (*l*) and
     (*m*) of Example 2.6.

Later in this chapter we will return to higher-ordered derivatives to demonstrate their usefulness in classical optimization.

A word of caution is in order at this point. By no means have we done a thorough job of treating differentiation. Many important topics have been neglected, including *limits* and *continuity;* hence, even if you have mastered this section, your knowledge of differentiation is partial at best. We hope our limited objectives have been met: for the neophyte, an intuitive understanding of the essence of differentiation, a working knowledge of some basic rules of differentiation, and increased mathematical confidence (It's not so bad after all!); for the "pro," a clear and concise review and a reaffirmation of mathematical maturity (I told you it was easy!).

2.4   SINGLE-VARIABLE OPTIMIZATION

When an objective function can be formulated as a continuous function involving one independent variable, differential calculus easily can identify conditions for optimality, if they exist. This section discusses procedures for determining these conditions.

Stationary Points

Earlier the concepts of relative and global maximum and minimum points were introduced. These are also referred to, collectively, as **extreme points** and they are particularly relevant in identifying conditions for optimality.

Figure 2–9 represents a continuous function similar to that presented earlier. Points *a* and *c* are both relative maxima, while points *b* and *d* are relative minima. Points *c* and *d* are, respectively, the global maximum and minimum over the indicated range of values for x.

One characteristic common to these extreme points is that the slope of the line tangent to the curve at each point is equal to zero. This observation, in fact, leads to the **necessary condition** for identifying extreme points. That is, a necessary condition for an extreme point at $x = x^*$ is that the tangent to the function at $x = x^*$ has a slope equal to zero. Any point which has a tangent slope equal to zero is called a **stationary point.** As will be shown later, stationary points do not have to be extreme points.

You should recall that the first derivative of a function represents a general relationship for the slope of the function at any point on the function. Put another way, the first derivative of a function provides a mathematical expression in x which indicates the instantaneous rate of

FIGURE 2–9

Extreme Points

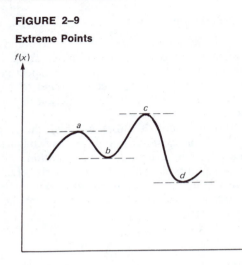

change for the function at any given point. Stationary points, if they exist, can be found by determining the values of x (roots) which satisfy the equation when the first derivative is set equal to zero. Stationary values of x will be distinguished from other values of x by the notation x^*.

Example 2.8

The first derivative of the function

$$y = f(x)$$
$$= 4x^2 + 4x + 2$$

is given by

$$f'(x) = 8x + 4.$$

At $x = 0$, it follows that $f'(0) = +4$. This means that a line which is tangent to the original function at $x = 0$ has a slope equal to $+4$; alternatively, at $x = 0$, y is increasing at the instantaneous rate of four units for each unit increase in the value of x. Similarly, $f'(-2) = -12$; that is, the instantaneous rate of change (slope) at $x = -2$ is -12.

It can be shown easily, by setting the expression for $f'(x)$ to zero and solving for x, that a single stationary point exists at $x^* = -\frac{1}{2}$.

Follow-up Exercises

11. Find the stationary point(s) for the function in part (e) of Example 2.6.
12. Find the stationary point(s) for $y = -x^2 + 5x$.

Determining the Nature of Stationary Points

A variety of situations can be characterized by an instantaneous slope of zero. Figure 2–10 indicates some of the possibilities. Figures 2–10a and 2–10b represent maximum and minimum points, respectively. Over the indicated portion of Figure 2–10a, the function is said to be **concave downward** (or **concave**). In Figure 2–10b, the function is said to be **concave upward** (or **convex**).

Figures 2–10c and 2–10d represent situations in which the slope equals zero, but the conditions for local extreme points are not satisfied. These are both cases where the functions are said to have stationary inflection points. **Inflection points** are points at which the concavity of a function changes from either concave upward to downward, or vice versa. **Stationary inflection points** are points at which the concavity of the function changes *and* the slope equals zero.

FIGURE 2–10

Instantaneous Slopes of Zero

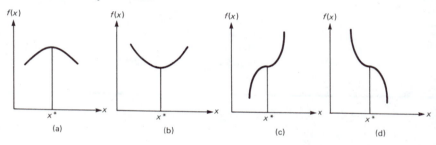

A number of tests can be used to test for the nature of a stationary point—that is, whether it is a relative maximum, a relative minimum, or a stationary inflection point. The tests range from rather intuitive tests which may be computationally cumbersome to tests which are less intuitive but more efficient computationally. We will examine the two most efficient tests.

Second Derivative Test   The second derivative test takes advantage of the fact that if the value of the second derivative is negative at some point, the function is *concave downward* at that point on the curve. This follows because the second derivative is the rate of change of the first derivative, just as the first derivative is the rate of change or slope of the original function; hence, if the rate of change of the slope is negative, the slope becomes less positive or more negative and the curve must be concave downward. If the value of the second derivative is positive, the function is *concave upward* at that point on the curve. Consequently, if a stationary point has been identified and the function is concave upward, the stationary point is a relative minimum; if the concavity is downward, the stationary point must be a relative maximum. To be more precise, if the first derivative equals zero, and the second derivative, $f''(x)$ is defined, then

1. $f(x^*)$ is a relative minimum if $f''(x^*)$ is greater than $(>)0$.
2. $f(x^*)$ is a relative maximum if $f''(x^*)$ is less than $(<)$ 0.
3. The test breaks down or is indeterminate if $f''(x) = 0$.

You should verify for yourself that a *relative* minimum (maximum) is a *global* minimum (maximum) if the second derivative is positive (negative) throughout the relevant range of x.

Example 2.9

Testing the stationary point found at $x^* = -\frac{1}{2}$ in Example 2.8, we get

$$f'(x) = 8x + 4$$
$$f''(x) = 8$$
$$f''(-\tfrac{1}{2}) = 8.$$

Therefore, the function $y = 4x^2 + 4x + 2$ has a relative minimum at $x = -\frac{1}{2}$. The minimum value for y can be verified as $f(-\frac{1}{2}) = 1$.

Example 2.10

The first derivative for the function $y = x^3 + 2x^2 + 5$ is given by

$$f'(x) = 3x^2 + 4x.$$

Setting $f'(x)$ equal to zero and solving for x yields

$$3x^2 + 4x = 0$$
$$x(3x + 4) = 0$$

and

$$x^* = 0, -4/3.$$

In this instance, two stationary points exist. Applying the second derivative test gives

$$f''(x) = 6x + 4$$
$$f''(0) = 6(0) + 4 = 4 > 0,$$

or a relative minimum occurs when $x^* = 0$, and

$$f''(-4/3) = 6(-4/3) + 4 = -4 < 0,$$

or a relative maximum occurs on the function when $x^* = -4/3$. This function is sketched in Figure 2–11.

FIGURE 2–11

Sketch of $y = x^3 + 2x^2 + 5$

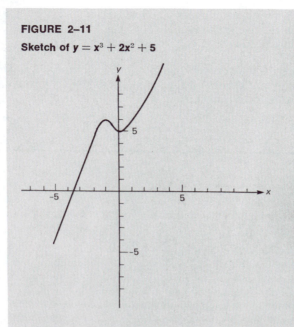

Follow-up Exercises

13. Identify the nature of the stationary point(s) in Exercise 11. Sketch the function.

14. Identify the nature of the stationary point(s) in Exercise 12. Sketch the function.

15. Find the stationary point(s) for and sketch the second-degree polynomial $y = -x^2 + 20x - 100$. Identify the nature of the stationary point(s) and indicate if a global extremum has been found.

Higher-Order Derivative Test   The second derivative test is actually a special case of tests based upon higher-ordered derivatives. As opposed to the second derivative test, the higher-order derivative test will not fail in distinguishing the nature of stationary points. The test procedure is as follows:

1. Find the lowest-ordered derivative for which the value of the derivative is nonzero at the stationary point and denote this derivative as $f^n(x)$ where n is the order of the derivative.

2. If the order of this derivative is even, the stationary point is
   a. A relative maximum if $f^n(x^*) < 0$.
   b. A relative minimum if $f^n(x^*) > 0$.

3. If the order of this derivative is odd, then the stationary point is a stationary inflection point.

Example 2.11

If $y = x^4$, then $f'(x) = 4x^3$. Setting the first derivative equal to zero and solving for x gives $x^* = 0$. Taking the second derivative, we get

$$f''(x) = 12x^2$$

and

$$f''(0) = 12(0)^2 = 0.$$

Since the value of the second derivative equals zero at the stationary point, higher-ordered derivatives must be examined.

$$f'''(x) = 24x$$

and

$$f'''(0) = 24(0) = 0.$$

Again, the value of the third derivative equals zero at the stationary point and the next highest derivative must be examined.

$$f''''(x) = 24$$

and

$$f''''(0) = 24.$$

Since the value of the fourth derivative is nonzero, the nature of the stationary point can be determined. In this case, the order of the first nonzero derivative is 4. Given that n is even, the stationary point is either a relative maximum or minimum. Because $f''''(x^*)$ is greater than zero, it is concluded that the function $y = x^4$ has a relative minimum at $x^* = 0$. This can be seen in Figure 2–12.

FIGURE 2–12

Sketch of $y = x^4$

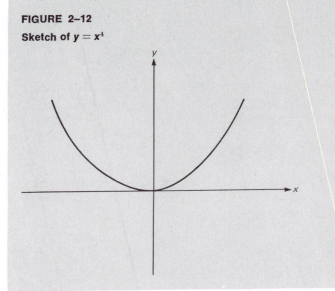

Example 2.12

Given the function $f(x) = (x - 2)^3$, it follows that

$$f'(x) = 3(x - 2)^2(1)$$
$$= 3(x - 2)^2.$$

Setting the first derivative equal to zero, we find the one stationary point at $x^* = 2$. Taking the second derivative, we get

$$f''(x) = 6(x - 2)(1)$$
$$= 6x - 12$$

and

$$f''(2) = 6(2) - 12$$
$$= 0.$$

Since the value of the second derivative equals zero at the stationary point, the third derivative must be examined.

$$f'''(x) = 6$$
$$f'''(2) = 6.$$

Since the order of this derivative is *odd* $(n = 3)$, it is concluded that the function has a stationary inflection point at $x^* = 2$. The function is sketched in Figure 2–13.

FIGURE 2–13

Sketch of $y = (x - 2)^3$

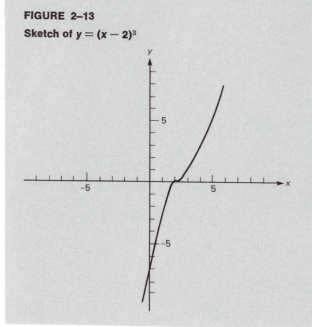

Follow-up Exercise

16. Find the stationary point(s) for and sketch the polynomial of third degree $y = 10 - 4x + 2x^2 + x^3$. Identify the nature of the stationary point(s) and indicate if a global extreme point has been found. Remember the quadratic formula for determining the roots of a quadratic equation? If $ax^2 + bx + c = 0$, then

$$x^* = \frac{-b \pm (b^2 - 4ac)^{1/2}}{2a}.$$

(2.10)

2.5 SINGLE-VARIABLE APPLICATIONS

This section presents a set of applications involving single-variable optimization. The examples include those which were formulated earlier in the chapter.

Example 2.13 *MBTA Continued*

Earlier, a pricing problem was discussed involving the Metropolitan Boston Transit Authority. An objective which involved determining the fare to charge during off-peak hours so as to maximize total revenue during this period was formalized. Total revenue was formulated as a function of the fare charged; the result, Equation (2.7), is repeated for convenience:

$$TR = f(p) = 22.5p - p^2/2.$$

This equation is quadratic in form, and as will be seen later, it graphs as a parabola, concave downward. To determine whether any relative maxima or minima exist, stationary points are first identified. Taking the first derivative of the revenue function with respect to the variable p provides

$$f'(p) = 22.5 - 2p/2$$
$$= 22.5 - p.$$

Setting this equal to zero in order to identify points of zero slope, we get

$$f'(p) = 22.5 - p = 0$$

or

$$p^* = 22.5.$$

Testing the stationary point by means of the second derivative yields

$$f''(p) = -1.$$

Since the value of the second derivative is negative throughout the range of p, it is concluded that there exists a global maximum for total revenue when a fare of 22.5 cents is charged. The revenue function is sketched in Figure 2–14.

FIGURE 2–14

Total Revenue Function for MBTA

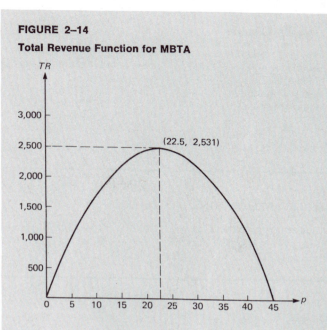

Maximum total revenue is found by substituting $p^* = 22.5$ into the revenue function:

$$TR^* = 22.5(22.5) - (22.5)^2/2$$
$$= 253.125.$$

Can you verify that, in light of the way in which the variables were defined, the maximum total revenue is $2,531.25? Optimal demand during the off-peak hours with a fare of 22.5 cents is determined by substituting this value of p into the demand equation:

$$q^* = 22.5 - p^*/2$$
$$= 22.5 - (22.5)/2$$
$$= 11.25 \text{ (thousand passengers)}.$$

The current demand under "dime-time" is $q = 22.5 - [(10)/2] = 17.5$ (thousand passengers). Thus, total revenue each day for the off-peak period would equal ($0.10) · (17,500) or $1,750. The suggested fare policy would result in an increase of $781.25 in revenues over the current "dime-time" policy.

Follow-up Exercises

17. Thoroughly investigate the implications of the solution just derived. For example, what are the probable effects of using *odd* change fares ($0.22 or $0.23)? What are the implications of selling tokens at two for $0.45? What assumptions are necessary to justify this policy?

How would you go about designing a sampling plan to estimate the demand function? What other implementation issues seem relevant in this problem?

Do you agree with the objective of maximizing off-peak revenues? Would profit make more sense?

18. Formulate the objective function in this problem as a function of q rather than p. Solve for q^*, which leads to maximum total revenue, and compare this with the results of Example 2.13.

Example 2.14 Optimal Advertising Period

Mow-Down Records, Inc., has recently recorded its latest "fad" album: *Love That OR.* The "fad" albums are those which are advertised on local television and are sold by direct mail only. Mow-Down has a number of test cities which it uses as pilot areas for new releases. A medium-sized Eastern city has been selected to test market the latest album, and Mow-Down wishes to determine how many days the advertising campaign should be conducted in order to maximize total profits. From the many campaigns conducted within this city, the company has determined that the proportion of target customers purchasing an album depends upon the length of the promotional campaign. The proportion has been observed to behave empirically according to the function $(1 - e^{-0.02t})$, where t equals the number of days of the campaign.[3] The target market has been estimated at 100,000 persons and the profit margin for each album will be $2, exclusive of advertising expenditures. Current costs for spot advertising on local television are $2,000 per day. Fixed expenses associated with initiating the promotion campaign are $2,500.

Profit can be estimated by computing the gross profit margin less promotion expenses. A necessary component in determining gross profit margin is the number of albums sold. This can be stated in terms of the target market size and response function as

$$\text{Sales (albums)} = 100,000(1 - e^{-0.02t}).$$

Thus,

$$\text{Gross profit margin (dollars)} = (2)(100,000)(1 - e^{-0.02t})$$

or

$$G(t) = 200,000(1 - e^{-0.02t}).$$

Promotion costs are easily stated as

$$C(t) = 2,000t + 2,500.$$

Now, the net profit function can be formulated as

$$
\begin{aligned}
P(t) &= G(t) - C(t) \\
&= 200,000(1 - e^{-0.02t}) - 2,000t - 2,500 \\
&= 197,500 - 200,000e^{-0.02t} - 2,000t.
\end{aligned}
$$

The derivative of the profit function is found to be

$$
\begin{aligned}
P'(t) &= -200,000(-0.02)e^{-0.02t} - 2,000 \\
&= 4,000e^{-0.02t} - 2,000.
\end{aligned}
$$

Setting this to zero, we get

$$e^{-0.02t} = \frac{2,000}{4,000} = \tfrac{1}{2}.$$

---

[3] Recall that $e = 2.718 \ldots$ is the base of natural logarithms. The given function and all estimates can be determined by the methods of Appendix A.

To find the value of t which satisfies the equation, we refer to a table of exponential functions and find that

$$e^{-0.70} = 0.496585$$
$$\doteq \tfrac{1}{2};$$

hence

$$-0.02t \doteq -0.70$$

or

$$t^* \doteq 35 \text{ days.}$$

You should verify by the second derivative test that profits will be maximized on the sale of this album if the promotion campaign runs approximately 35 days.

Can you verify that maximum profits are expected to be $28,185 and that 50.341 percent of the target market is expected to purchase the album? Figure 2–15 graphically portrays the firm's profit function.

FIGURE 2–15

Profit Function for Mow-Down Records, Inc.

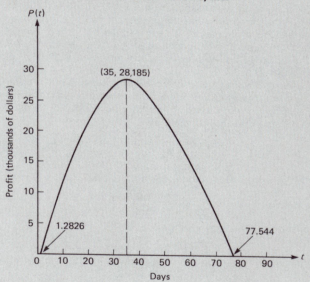

Follow-up Exercises

19. How sensitive are (a) the maximum profit and (b) the optimal length of the promotion campaign to a ±50-percent error in the −0.02 coefficient in the response function?

20. How sensitive are (a) the maximum profit and (b) the optimal length of the promotion campaign to a 50-percent increase in the daily advertising rate?

21. Letting T = market size, v = variable advertising expenditure, c = fixed expense of promotion campaign, m = profit margin per album,

$(1 - e^{-at}) =$ market response function over time, $a =$ constant, and $t =$ length of promotion campaign, show (by derivation) that for a given city the optimal length of a promotion campaign by Mow-Down can be determined by solving for t in the equation

$$e^{-at} = \frac{v}{mTa}.$$

22. Sketch the market response function and interpret its behavior in the context of this application.

Example 2.15 Patrol Sector Design Continued

Earlier we discussed and formulated a problem involving the design of police patrol sectors. The objective was stated in terms of defining the dimensions of the rectangular patrol sector which would minimize the average travel time ($\overline{T}$) for responses to calls for service. Suppose that police planners wish to assign each car to a patrol sector of four square miles and that effective travel speeds in the x and y directions are $v_z = 10$ mph and $v_y = 10$ mph. Substituting these values into Equations (2.3) and (2.4) yields

$$\overline{T} = \frac{1}{3}\left[\frac{x}{10} + \frac{y}{10}\right] \tag{2.11}$$

and

$$x \cdot y = 4. \tag{2.12}$$

Notice that the criterion variable is stated as a function of two independent variables (x and y); however, the dependence between x and y as established by Equation (2.12) allows us to solve for one of the variables in terms of the other (it makes no difference which variable is solved in terms of the other). Solving for x in Equation (2.12) and substituting in Equation (2.11) allows $\overline{T}$ to be expressed in terms of one independent variable:

$$\overline{T} = \frac{1}{3}\left[\frac{(4/y)}{10} + \frac{y}{10}\right]$$

$$= \frac{4}{30y} + \frac{y}{30}.$$

Since the objective is to minimize average travel time, it is necessary to take the first derivative in order to identify any stationary points for the function:

$$f'(y) = -\frac{4}{30y^2} + \frac{1}{30}.$$

Setting the first derivative equal to zero gives

$$\frac{1}{30} = \frac{4}{30y^2}.$$

Multiplying both sides by $30y^2$ and solving for the unknown gives $y^* = \pm 2$. Since a negative dimension is meaningless in this problem, the positive root is the only one of interest. To determine the nature of this stationary point, the second derivative is taken.

$$f''(y) = \frac{8}{30y^3}$$

$$f''(2) = 1/30 > 0.$$

Because this value is greater than zero (and will be for all $y > 0$), it is concluded that a global minimum exists at $y = 2$. The corresponding value for x, from Equation (2.12), is also 2.

Thus, the average response time is minimized if the dimensions of the rectangular patrol sector are 2 miles by 2 miles. The optimal average travel time of 0.133 hour or 8 minutes can be found by substituting the dimensions into Equation (2.11).

Follow-up Exercises

23. You should consider carefully the assumptions underlying this model and the effects violations would have on the structure and solution. To wit: nonrectangular travel, heterogeneity of neighborhoods with regard to density, and the probabilistic nature of travel time. Did you find the assignment of 4 square miles to patrol sectors to be too blithe? What objectives, constraints, or other factors might be introduced in determining the area of a sector?

24. Determine the optimal grid dimensions and travel time for:
    1. $v_x = 10$ mph, $v_y = 20$ mph, and $A = 4$ square miles.
    2. $v_x = 10$ mph, $v_y = 10$ mph, and $A = 6$ square miles.

Example 2.16   Replacement Model

The replacement problem is concerned with determining the optimal point in time at which to replace a capital asset that is characterized both by average capital cost (depreciation) which decreases over time and by operating cost which increases over time. For example, a new automobile is characterized by a depreciation cost which, while high initially, declines over time. All other things equal (styling, prestige, maintenance, costs), one would favor a long replacement period. As time goes on, however, the cost of operating (including maintaining) an automobile increases. This factor tends to shorten the period of ownership if all other things are equal. Because of the specified behavior of the costs, this model is often referred to as the **machine** or **equipment replacement problem.**

This tradeoff in costs can be resolved by minimizing the criterion given by the sum of average capital and operating costs. If $K(t)$ represents the estimated *total* capital cost over the time period t, and $0(t)$ represents the estimated *average* cost of operation (and maintenance) per unit time period over the ownership period t, then

$$C(t) = \frac{K(t)}{t} + 0(t) \tag{2.13}$$

represents the *average cost per unit time period* of owning the asset over the length of time given by t.

To illustrate a simple case: Suppose the particular asset in question has an initial purchase price of P, a salvage value given by S which is independent of age, and an average operating and maintenance cost which increases linearly over time (with intercept "a" and slope "b"), viz.,

and
$$K(t) = P - S \tag{2.14}$$

$$0(t) = a + bt. \tag{2.15}$$

According to Equation (2.13),

$$C(t) = \frac{P-S}{t} + (a + bt).\qquad(2.16)$$

The optimal point in time at which to replace this asset is determined by differentiating $C(t)$ with respect to t, setting $C'(t)$ to zero, and solving for t:

$$C'(t) = \frac{-(P-S)}{t^2} + b$$
$$= 0$$

or

$$t^* = \left(\frac{P-S}{b}\right)^{1/2}.\qquad(2.17)$$

FIGURE 2–16

Average Cost Curves for Replacement Model

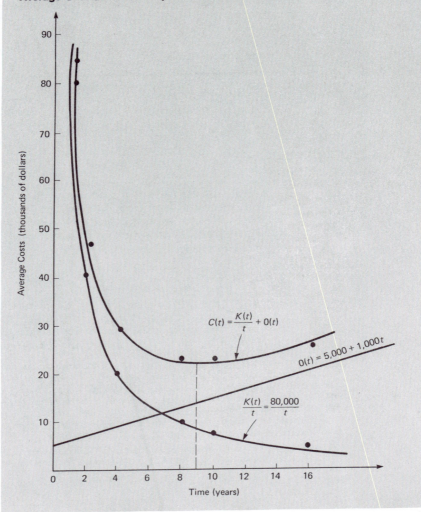

Since $C''(t) = 2(P - S)/t^3 > 0$ for all $t > 0$ and $P > S$, it follows that t^* represents a global minimum. For example, if $P = \$100{,}000$, $S = \$20{,}000$, $a = \$5{,}000$, and $b = \$1{,}000$ per year per year, then $t^* \doteq 8.94$ years and $C(t^*) \doteq \$22{,}889$ per year. (See Figure 2–16.) Note that the total cost over the ownership period is given by the product $t^* \cdot C(t^*)$, or $\$204{,}628$ in the present example.

The model given by Equation (2.13) represents one version among many. Replacement models have been solved which include the treatment of (1) discrete time periods, (2) an infinite time horizon (sequence of machines), and (3) costs expressed as present values. Other extensions have included models which anticipate failures and technological and economic obsolescence.[4]

Follow-up Exercises

25. For the model in the example, find t^* and $C(t^*)$ for the following values of b: 500; 1,500; 2,000. In your judgment, is the decision sensitive to this parameter?

26. Suppose you are given the following cost data for the operation and maintenance of a capital asset:

Year	Cost Each Year (dollars)	Cumulative Cost (dollars)	Average Cost (dollars per year)
1.	6,000		
2.	8,000		
3.	10,000		
4.	12,000		
5.	14,000		

Fill in the last two columns and fit (by the "eyeball" method) a linear function to the last column to show that $0(t) = 5{,}000 + 1{,}000t$ (which you should recognize as the function used in the example). Why would it be logically wrong to fit a function to the first cost column?

**27.[5] Suppose, instead of Equation (2.15), that

$$0(t) = at^b \tag{2.18}$$

where $a > 0$ and $b > 0$ are constants as before.

a. Determine $0'(t)$ and $0''(t)$ to show that $b > 1$ represents the case where operating costs increase at an increasing rate, and $0 < b < 1$ represents the case where operating costs increase at a decreasing rate. Plot $0(t)$ on a graph for the cases $b > 1$, $0 < b < 1$, and $b = 1$.

---

[4] See, for instance, L. O. Kattsoff and A. J. Simone, *Foundations of Contemporary Mathematics, with Applications in the Social and Management Sciences* (New York: McGraw-Hill Book Co., 1967), pp. 374–77; D. Teichroew, *An Introduction to Management Science, Deterministic Models* (New York: John Wiley & Sons, Inc., 1964), pp. 100–104; James E. Shamblin and G. T. Stevens, Jr., *Operations Research: A Fundamental Approach* (New York: McGraw-Hill, Inc., 1974), pp. 98–113.

[5] Double asterisks (**) designate examples and follow-up exercises that are more advanced than others. But don't be intimidated. We think you can handle many of these.

    b. Derive an expression for t^* using Equations (2.14) and (2.18).

    c. Find t^* using the same data as the example, except assume $0(t)$ to be of the form in Equation (2.18) with $a = 5,000$ and $b = 1.2$. Also try $b = 0.8$.

**28. State the expression for $C'(t) = 0$ for models which utilize Equation (2.18) and each of the following exponential capital cost functions:

$$K(t) = P(1 - d^t) \tag{2.19}$$

$$K(t) = P(1 - e^{-dt}) \tag{2.20}$$

where d represents the depreciation factor. For example, $d = 0.9$ would indicate that the salvage value in Equation (2.19), that is, $P(0.9)^t$, decreases by 90 percent per time period. How would you go about solving for t^*? Plot $K(t)$ and $K(t)/t$ for each case. Do the exponential cost functions make more sense than Equation (2.14)?

**29. As you might recall from step six of the paradigm in Chapter 1, *sensitivity analysis* is concerned with the sensitivity of decisions and criteria to errors in estimating parameters and uncontrollable variables.[6] Suppose we were to define $b = \epsilon b'$ where b' represents the actual value of the estimated parameter b and ϵ denotes an error proportion. Using Equation (2.17), derive an expression for $t^*/(t^*)'$ in terms of ϵ where $(t^*)'$ represents the true optimum period. Evaluate and interpret these expressions for $\epsilon = 0.5$ and $\epsilon = 1.5$. Relate these results to your results in Exercise 25 by assuming $b' = 1,000$. Repeat the procedure for $a = \epsilon a'$.

**30. Perform the sensitivity analysis described in Exercise 29 on the model you derived in Exercise 27.

** Example 2.17   *Timing the Sale of an Asset*

    Suppose an investor has an opportunity to invest an amount of capital, C, in a project or asset. The project has the following characteristics: (1) The return on the investment can be estimated by a continuous function, $R(t)$; (2) disinvestment can occur at any time, at which time the investor receives the amount $R(t)$; (3) $R(t)$ is a *monotonically* increasing function, that is, $R'(t) \geq 0$; and (4) the rate of increase of $R(t)$ is decreasing, that is, $R''(t) < 0$, which identifies the function as *concave downward*.

    The investor wishes to determine the optimal length of time, t^*, to hold the asset such that present net worth is maximized.

    The **present value**[7] of the project, when disinvestment occurs at time t and the return $R(t)$ is discounted continuously at rate r, is given by

$$P(t) = R(t) \cdot e^{-rt}. \tag{2.21}$$

---

    [6] Exercises 19 and 20 of this chapter treat this subject informally.

    [7] Present value is a concept which is widely applied to financial criteria over time. The present value of receiving some amount $R(t)$ in t time periods is that *present* amount which when compounded at the investor's opportunity rate of interest exactly yields $R(t)$ in t time periods. For example, if you had $100 to invest at 5 percent per year, in one year your investment would total $105. Thus, the present value to you of receiving $105 one year from now is $100. The act of converting future values to present values is called **discounting.**

Since this project requires an investment of C, a more meaningful criterion is given by the **net present value:**

$$N(t) = P(t) - C$$
$$= R(t) \cdot e^{-rt} - C.$$

Note that C need not be discounted because it represents an outlay in the present $(t = 0)$. Given the objective of determining the value for t which maximizes $N(t)$, we derive the necessary condition that

$$N'(t^*) = R'(t^*) \cdot e^{-rt^*} + R(t^*) \cdot e^{-rt^*} \cdot (-r)$$
$$= 0.$$

Simplifying gives

$$R'(t^*) - rR(t^*) = 0$$

or

$$R'(t^*) = rR(t^*) \tag{2.22}$$

as the necessary condition for an extreme point.
The second derivative is

$$N''(t) = [R'(t) - rR(t)] \cdot e^{-rt} \cdot (-r) + [R''(t) - rR'(t)] \cdot e^{-rt}.$$

Substituting Equation (2.22) for $R'(t)$ in the first bracket simplifies the expression to

$$N''(t) = [R''(t) - rR'(t)] \cdot e^{-rt}.$$

Since $R''(t) < 0$, $r > 0$, $R'(t) \geq 0$, and $e^{-rt} > 0$, it follows that $N''(t) < 0$, which establishes the sufficient condition that t^* represents a global maximum. Note that if $N(t^*) < 0$, then the investment should not be undertaken.

Problems involving the sale of an appreciating asset with the above characteristics include investments in real estate, purchase of works of art, buying of wine from rare vintage years, and the ageing of wines or distilled liquors.

To illustrate, suppose an oenologist has the opportunity to purchase a bottle of Chateau Lafite-Rothchild '49 for $700. A historical analysis based on the sales of similar vintages coupled with an expert judgment of wine market trends results in the following estimate for the return function:

$$R(t) = 500(1 + t^{0.6}).$$

If the investor's opportunity cost (that is, minimum required rate of return including risk) is 8 percent per year based on continuous compounding, then the optimal time to sell can be estimated from Equation (2.22):

$$300t^{-0.4} = 0.08[500(1 + t^{0.6})]$$
$$300t^{-0.4} = 40 + 40t^{0.6}$$
$$300 = 40t^{0.4} + 40t$$
$$t + t^{0.4} - 7.5 = 0.$$

Using Newton's method, we get $t^* = 5.51956$ years.[8] Thus, approximately five and a half years from now the wine can be sold for $R(5.52) \doteq \$1,894$, giving a *net* present value of

---

[8] Newton's method of approximation is an iterative technique for finding the root(s) of an equation of the form $g(x) = 0$. If you need reminding, the root of an equation given by $g(x)$ is the value of x which satisfies $g(x) = 0$. The determination of roots is important primarily for sketching functions and identifying stationary points. For Newton's procedure, see S. B. Richmond, *Operations Research for Management Decisions* (New York: The Ronald Press Company, 1968); Teichroew, *An Introduction to Management Science.*

$$N(5.52) = (1,894) \cdot e^{-0.08(5.52)} - 700$$
$$\doteq 1,218 - 700$$
$$\doteq \$518.$$

In other words, the future sale price of $1,894 has a present value of $1,218 to the investor. The net worth of this investment is determined by subtracting the required outlay of $700; hence, the investor would be $518 richer based on today's dollar. We might note that $1,894 for a bottle of wine is not unrealistic—a recent wine auction in New York City fetched over $9,000 for a single bottle!

Follow-up Exercises

31. Does the revenue function for the wine example satisfy the sufficient condition for maximization?

32. Solve the wine problem if $C = \$500$, $r = 0.08$, and $R(t) = 2,000(1.25 - 0.5^t)$. Determine the optimum sale price and the net present value.

**33. An alternative criterion, also theoretically pleasing, is the maximization of the *internal rate of return*. The internal rate of return is the value of r which satisfies

$$N(r, t) = R(t)e^{-rt} - C = 0.$$

Solving this equation for r gives

$$r = \frac{1}{t} \cdot \ln\left[\frac{R(t)}{C}\right].$$

Prove that the necessary condition for maximum r is

$$\frac{R'(t^*)}{R(t^*)} = \frac{1}{t^*} \cdot \ln\left[\frac{R(t^*)}{C}\right]. \tag{2.23}$$

**34. Solve the wine problem in the example using internal rate of return as the criterion. What is the optimum time period? Optimum rate of return? Does it surprise you that the optimum time period using internal rate of return is different from the optimum time period using net present value?

SELECTED REFERENCES

Childress, Robert L. *Mathematics for Managerial Decisions.* Englewood Cliffs, N.J.: Prentice-Hall, Inc., 1974.

Draper, Jean E., and Klingman, Jane S. *Mathematical Analysis: Business and Economic Applications.* 2d ed. New York: Harper and Row, Publishers, 1972.

Freund, John E. *College Mathematics with Business Applications.* 2d ed. Englewood Cliffs, N.J.: Prentice-Hall, Inc., 1975.

Kattsoff, L. O., and Simone, A. J. *Foundations of Contemporary Mathematics, with Applications in the Social and Management Sciences.* New York: McGraw-Hill Book Co., 1967.

Martin, E. W. *Mathematics for Decision Making—A Programmed Basic Text.* Homewood, Ill.: Richard D. Irwin, Inc., 1969.

Richmond, S. B. *Operations Research for Management Decisions.* New York: The Ronald Press Company, 1968.

Shamblin, James E., and Stevens, G. T., Jr. *Operations Research: A Fundamental Approach.* New York: McGraw-Hill, Inc., 1974.

Teichroew, D. *An Introduction to Management Science, Deterministic Models.* New York: John Wiley & Sons, Inc., 1964.

Theodore, Chris A. *Applied Mathematics: An Introduction.* 3d ed. Homewood, Ill.: Richard D. Irwin, Inc., 1975.

Thierauf, Robert J., and Klekamp, Robert C. *Decision Making through Operations Research.* 2d ed. New York: John Wiley & Sons, Inc., 1975.

ADDITIONAL EXERCISES

35. Find the first and second derivatives for the following functions:

    a. $y = 3x^6$.
    b. $y = 6x^2 - 4x + 10$.
    c. $y = (5x^2 - 1)(x^3 + 3)$.
    d. $y = (1 - x)/x^2$.
    e. $y = (x + 2)^3$.
    f. $y = e^{(5 - x^2)}$.
    g. $y = \ln(x^2 - 5x)$.
    h. $y = (6)^{3x}$.

36. For the following functions, identify all stationary points and determine their nature (relative maxima, minima, or stationary inflection point).

    a. $y = 12x^2 - 6x + 50$.
    b. $y = -6x^4$.
    c. $y = 2(x - 3)^3$.
    d. $y = e^{-5x} - 4x$.
    e. $y = x^3 - 9x^2 - 100$.

37. *Sales Allocation Model*   A book publisher estimates that its profits are directly related to the number of sales representatives ("reps") the company uses. Specifically, profit (p), in thousands of dollars, is related to number of reps (x) by the function

    $$p = -16x^2 + 1{,}600x - 1{,}000.$$

    a. What number of reps will result in maximum profit?
    b. What is the expected maximum profit?
    c. Confirm that the stationary point is a global maximum.

38. *Inventory Model*   A pervasive problem among organizations is determining the appropriate quantities of inventory to keep on hand. A common decision relates to the quantities which should be ordered each time the firm replenishes its inventory (if the inventoried item is supplied by a vendor). These types of models will be addressed specifically in Chapter 11. A firm has determined the following cost function which expresses the annual cost of purchasing, owning, and maintaining its inventory as a function of the size of each order (q).

    $$c = \frac{200{,}000}{q} + 5q + 1{,}000{,}000.$$

    a. Determine the order quantity, q^*, which results in minimum annual inventory cost.

    b.   What is the minimum cost?

    c.   Confirm the nature of this stationary point.

39. *Pricing Model*   The demand function for the product of a particular firm is

$$p = 60{,}000 - 2q,$$

where p = price in dollars and q = number of units demanded. Formulate the total revenue function where revenue, R, is stated as a function of p. What price should be charged so as to maximize total revenue? What is the maximum total revenue?

40. *Pricing Model*   A company estimates the demand, q, for its product to be a function of the price, p, charged. Specifically, the demand function is

$$q = 20{,}000\, e^{-0.05p}.$$

Determine the price which the firm should charge in order to maximize total revenue. What quantity will be demanded at this price? What is the maximum total revenue? Confirm the nature of the stationary point.

41. *Sensitivity Analysis*   In the previous problem, perform a sensitivity analysis on the -0.05 coefficient. How sensitive are the optimal price, optimal order quantity, and total revenue to changes in this coefficient if it can actually fluctuate between -0.02 and -0.10?

42. *Import Tax Model*   The government of a European country is trying to decide on the import tax it should charge on American automobiles. The government realizes that demand for American automobiles will be affected by the tax. It has estimated demand (D) to be related to x, the import tax in dollars, according to the function

$$D(x) = 150{,}000 - 300x.$$

    a.   What tax will result in maximum tax revenues for the country? (Confirm the stationary point as a maximum.)

    b.   How many cars will be expected to be sold at this tax rate?

    c.   What is the maximum revenue?

    d.   If the -300 in the demand equation could be in error by ± 25 percent, what would be the effect on the optimal tax rate and maximum tax revenue?

43. *Charity Campaign Model*   A well-known charity is interested in conducting a television campaign to solicit contributions. The campaign will be conducted in two metropolitan areas. Past experience indicates that the total contributions are a function of the amount of money expended for TV advertisements in each city. Specifically, the charity has determined approximate response functions which indicate the percentage of the population making a donation as a function of the dollars spent on TV advertising. The charity has $100,000 to allocate for advertising in the two cities. Letting x_1 and x_2 represent the number of dollars (in thousands) allocated, respectively, to cities 1 and 2, the charity wants to determine the values which maximize the total donations from the two cities.

	City 1	City 2
Response function	$(1 - e^{-0.04x_1})$	$(1 - e^{-0.08x_2})$
Population	500,000	200,000
Average donation per donor	$1.00	$2.50

(Hint: Take advantage of the fact that $x_1 + x_2 = 100$.) What are the maximum total donations? Confirm the stationary point as a global maximum.

44. *Patrol Car Replacement Model* A police department is attempting to determine an optimal policy for replacing its patrol cars. Each patrol car costs the department $10,000. The car comes fully equipped with special safety features and communications equipment. The department estimates average capital cost and average maintenance cost to be a function of x, number of miles the vehicle is driven. The salvage value of the car in dollars is expressed by the function $S(x) = 7{,}000 - 0.05x$. In other words, the value of the car decreases $3,000 as soon as it is driven off the dealer's lot and further decreases at a rate of $0.05 per mile. The average maintenance cost (dollars per mile) is estimated by the function $0(x) = 0.0000004x + 0.15$. Determine the number of miles a car should be driven prior to replacement if the objective is to minimize the average cost per mile. What is the minimum average cost per mile? Confirm that the stationary point is indeed a minimum.

45. For the replacement model which is described in the preceding exercise, derive an expression for x^* if $S(x) = s - rx$, $0(x) = mx + b$, and the purchase price is P. Compare this result to Equation (2.17). Comments?

46. *Queuing Decision Model* Consider a car-wash queuing system having a single waiting line of automobiles waiting to be washed by a single automated facility. Analysis yields the following cost function:

$$C(x) = \frac{0.5}{x} + \frac{2Ax}{1 - Ax}$$

where $C(x) = $ total cost for queuing system (dollars per hour), $x = $ average time (hours) to wash a car, and $A = $ average arrival rate of cars (cars per hour). The manager wishes to determine the optimal setting for the automated equipment (that is, the average time to wash a car which minimizes total cost). Determine this setting if 20 cars per hour arrive on the average. Verify this solution as the global minimum. What is the optimal cost per hour?

47. *Emergency Response Model* Three towns along a relatively straight coastline are located as indicated below. The populations (in thousands)

of towns A, B, and C are 15, 5, and 7, respectively. The three towns have agreed to support an emergency medical response facility (that is, clinic with paramedics and one vehicle) which will service all three towns. Where should this facility be located if it is desired to minimize the sum of (population) · (distance squared between town and facility) for the three towns? (Hint: Let $x = $ location of facility according to above scale.) Confirm that your solution is a global minimum. Can you think of more desirable surrogate criteria for level of service?

3

Classical Deterministic Models II

CHAPTER 2 focused upon models where some criterion variable is expressed as a function of one independent variable. It would be nice if objective function relationships were always that simple and uninvolved. In most situations, however, such an abstraction oversimplifies the problem. For example, if one attempts to determine the types of variables which influence the demand for the products of a ski-equipment manufacturer, a list of variables might include weather conditions, the quality of the equipment, the price charged for equipment, and advertising expenditures of competing firms. In addition, realistic problems often include constraints on one or more variables. Thus advertising expenditures might be limited by a budget. This is not to imply that single-variable and unconstrained techniques are useless. Rather, the implication is that these techniques may not be adequate for certain situations. Accordingly, the present chapter presents optimization for more than one variable and optimization with constraints.

3.1 TWO-VARIABLE OPTIMIZATION

This section presents the techniques of classical optimization where criterion variables are expressed as functions of two independent variables.

The Criterion "Surface"

With one independent variable, an obective function graphs as a curve in two dimensions. If a criterion variable is expressed as a function of two

65

independent variables, then the graphical representation of the relationship is a "surface" in three dimensions. For example, the function

$$z = f(x, y)$$

or

$$z = 9 - x^2 - y^2/4$$

where $z \geq 0$, $x \geq 0$, and $y \geq 0$ is illustrated in Figure 3–1. Notice that
we focus only on nonnegative values of the three variables. Graphing a
function in three dimensions can be accomplished methodically by observing that, if a value is assumed for one variable in the function, the
three-variable function reduces to a two-variable function which graphs
simply as a curve in two-space.

To illustrate how this function was graphed, if x is assumed to equal
zero, then the original function becomes

$$z = 9 - (0)^2 - y^2/4$$
$$= 9 - y^2/4.$$

FIGURE 3–1

Graphical Representation of a Surface

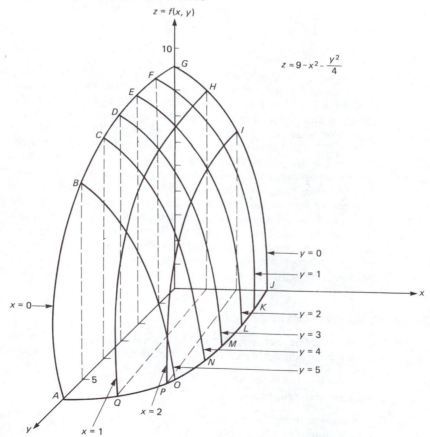

This can be graphed in the zy-plane as a parabola by simply assuming values for y and finding the corresponding values for z. The graphic representation of such a function where one variable is assumed constant is called a **trace.** The trace representing the original function where x = 0 is the curve AG in Figure 3–1. If x is assumed equal to one, the original function reduces to

$$z = 9 - (1)^2 - y^2/4$$
$$= 8 - y^2/4.$$

Graphically, the trace representing this function is the curve QH, which is parallel to the zy-plane and intersects the x-axis at x = 1. One can easily see that if an infinite number of values are assumed for the variable x, the set of associated traces would collectively define the **surface** of the function. Each trace is effectively a "rib," and the composite of all traces forms the shell which represents the function.

Similarly, if values are assumed for the variable y, traces can be graphed parallel to the zx-plane. For example, if y = 0, the original function becomes

$$z = 9 - x^2.$$

Graphically, this trace forms parabola GJ, which is parallel to the zx-plane and cuts through the y-axis at y = 0. Traces FK, EL, DM, CN, and BO can be defined in the same manner by assuming values of 1, 2, 3, 4, and 5, respectively, for the variable y.

Partial Derivatives and Their Meaning

The calculus of multivariate functions, although more involved, is surprisingly similar to that of single-variable functions. The derivative of a single-variable function represents the instantaneous rate of change of the criterion variable with respect to a change in the independent variable. The derivative of a multivariate function also represents the instantaneous rate of change in the criterion variable, but with respect to changes in each of the variables, separately.

The derivative of a multivariate function is termed a **partial derivative.** Partial derivatives can be found with respect to each of the independent variables of a function. For example, given a function of the form

$$z = f(x, y)$$

derivatives can be taken with respect to both x and y. The partial derivative taken with respect to x is denoted as $\partial z/\partial x$, or sometimes as f_x; that taken with respect to y is denoted as $\partial z/\partial y$, or f_y.

The partial derivative taken with respect to x reflects the instantaneous rate of change in z with respect to a change in x only. To determine this effect, other independent variables *cannot* be allowed to fluctuate. If they are allowed to change, the change in z attributable solely to the variable x is difficult to determine. Thus, all other independent variables are assumed constant. The resulting derivative effectively provides a general expression for the instantaneous slope of the family of traces which are parallel to the zx-plane.

In finding $\partial z/\partial y$, x is assumed to be constant. The resulting partial derivative represents the instantaneous rate of change in z with respect to a change in y. Another interpretation is that it gives a general expression for the instantaneous slope of the family of traces parallel to the zy-plane.

The rules for finding partial derivatives are the same as for single-variable functions. The only exception is that the other independent variables must be assumed constant when finding the derivatives. As an illustration, the partial derivative, taken with respect to x of the previously graphed function, is

$$f_x = \frac{\partial z}{\partial x} = -2x.$$

In finding this derivative, the variable y is assumed to be constant and is treated accordingly in applying the derivative rules. As indicated, this represents a general expression for the slope of any trace parallel to the zx-plane. Try verifying this expression by rewriting the equations for traces *GJ, FK, EL, DM, CN,* or *BO* and taking the derivatives of these with respect to x.

The partial derivative with respect to y is

$$f_y = \frac{\partial z}{\partial y} = -y/2.$$

In finding this derivative, x is assumed constant and is treated accordingly. This derivative represents a general expression for the slope of the family of traces parallel to the zy-plane. You can verify this by taking the derivatives of any of the equations representing traces *AG, QH,* or *PI.*

Example 3.1

Given the function $z = 3x^2 - 2xy + 4y^2 + 100$, the partial derivatives are:

$$f_x = 6x - 2y$$
$$f_y = -2x + 8y.$$

Follow-up Exercises

1. Find f_x and f_y for $z = y^2 - x^2$.
2. Find f_x and f_y for $z = (x + y)^3 + (xy/2)$.
3. Find f_x and f_y for $z = \ln(x + 2y) - e^{xy}$.

Example 3.2   Two-Variable Marketing Problem

Assume that annual profits for a television manufacturer can be estimated by the function

$$P(x,y) = 300x + 400y - x^2 - 2y^2 - 2xy$$

where P = profit in \$100's; x = number of franchised retail outlets; and y = advertising expenditures (\$1,000's).

Currently, the firm uses 50 retailers and is spending \$60,000 on advertising. The marginal effect upon profits of adding an additional retailer can be approximated by evaluating

$$f_x = 300 - 2x - 2y.$$

If the partial derivative is evaluated at $x = 50$ and $y = 60$,

$$f_x(50,60) = 300 - 2(50) - 2(60)$$
$$= 80,$$

or profits will increase by approximately \$8,000 with the increase of one retailer—holding advertising expenditures the same. We say "approximately" because the partial derivatives represent tangent slopes to the criterion surface at a particular point. And, as was observed in two dimensions, tangent slopes are continually changing on nonlinear functions.

Similarly, the marginal effect of increasing advertising expenditures by \$1,000 can be estimated by evaluating

$$f_y = 400 - 4y - 2x$$
$$= 400 - 4(60) - 2(50)$$
$$= 60,$$

or profits will increase by approximately \$6,000 with an increase of \$1,000 in advertising expenditures.

Follow-up Exercise

4. Compute total profit when $x = 50$ and $y = 60$. Then compute total profit when $x = 51$ and $y = 60$ and compare with the increase in profits expected in Example 3.2. Also, compute total profit at $x = 50$ and $y = 61$ and compare. Can you explain discrepancies?

Higher-Ordered Partial Derivatives

As with single-variable functions, higher-ordered derivatives can be found for multivariate functions. The interpretation of these derivatives is similar to that for single-variable functions; their importance, as with single-variable functions, is in identifying extreme points.

Second derivatives for a function of the form $z = f(x, y)$ can be of two types: **pure partial derivatives** and **mixed, or cross, partial derivatives.** $\partial^2 z / \partial x^2$ or f_{xx} represents the pure second partial derivative with respect to x. It is found by first determining f_x and then differentiating again with respect to x. From an intuitive standpoint, this derivative offers information about the concavity of traces parallel to the zx-plane. $\partial^2 z / \partial y^2$ or f_{yy} is the second pure partial derivative with respect to y. It is found by first solving for f_y and then differentiating with respect to y. This derivative offers information about the concavity of traces parallel to the zy-plane.

In addition to the two pure second partials, two cross partial derivatives can be found. $\partial^2 z/\partial x \partial y$ or f_{yx} is determined by first finding f_y.[1] This partial derivative is then differentiated with respect to x in order to find the cross partial derivative. The interpretation of this derivative is less intuitive than the pure second derivatives. It represents the rate of change in the slope of traces which are parallel to the zy-plane as the plane shifts incrementally in the x direction.

The other cross partial derivative is found in a similar manner, but by reversing the order of taking the derivatives. In other words, to find $\partial^2 z/\partial y \partial x$ or f_{xy}, f_x is found and is then differentiated with respect to y. The interpretation of this cross partial derivative is that it describes the rate of change in the slope of traces which are parallel to the zx-plane as the plane shifts incrementally in the y direction.

The cross partial derivatives are always equal to one another. In other words, $f_{yx} = f_{xy}$.

Example 3.3

Find all first and second derivatives for the function

$$z = f(x,y) = 5x^3 + 2x^2y + 2y^3 - xy + 100.$$

$$f_x = 15x^2 - 4xy - y.$$
$$f_y = -2x^2 + 6y^2 - x.$$
$$f_{xx} = 30x - 4y.$$
$$f_{yy} = 12y.$$
$$f_{yx} = -4x - 1.$$
$$f_{xy} = -4x - 1.$$

Follow-up Exercises

5. Find all second derivatives for the function in Exercise 1.
6. Find all second derivatives for the function in Exercise 2.
7. Find all second derivatives for the function in Exercise 3.

Conditions for Optimality in Three Dimensions

The process of finding optimum values for functions involving two independent variables is similar to that for single-variable functions. It must be remembered that functions of the form $z = f(x, y)$ are graphically represented by a surface in three dimensions. Relative maximum and relative minimum points can be visualized as the tops of "mounds" or the bottoms of "valleys" on the surface. Figures 3–2 and 3–3 illustrate relative maximum and minimum points, respectively.

---

[1] In the notation f_{yx} the first subscript represents the base with regard to which the first partial derivative was taken and the second subscript is the base of the second derivative.

FIGURE 3–2

Relative Maximum for a Surface

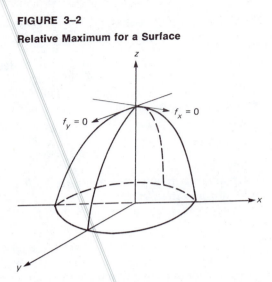

If one examines the conditions at the top of a mound or at the bottom of a valley, it would be found that the slope is zero in all directions. This leads to the **necessary condition** for the existence of a relative maximum or minimum. The first partial derivatives of the criterion function must equal zero:

$$f_x = 0 \quad and \quad f_y = 0. \tag{3.1}$$

This seems logical if one recalls that the first partial derivatives represent expressions for the instantaneous slope of traces which are parallel to the zx-plane and zy-plane. This condition implies that the slopes in both directions must equal zero at a relative maximum or minimum. Any points

FIGURE 3–3

Relative Minimum for a Surface

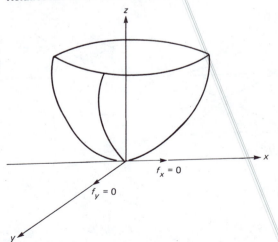

which satisfy the necessary conditions are termed **stationary points,** as before. These stationary points should have coordinates, or locations, specified for *both* of the independent variables.

Once stationary points have been identified, their nature is determined by way of a second derivative test which intuitively investigates the **sufficiency (concavity) conditions** at the stationary point. The conditions for determining the nature of a stationary point located at the point (x^*, y^*, z) require the evaluation of

$$D(x^*, y^*) = f_{xx} \cdot f_{yy} - (f_{xy})^2. \tag{3.2}$$

1. If $D(x^*, y^*) > 0$, then
   a. The stationary point is a relative maximum if *both* $f_{xx}(x^*, y^*)$ and $f_{yy}(x^*, y^*)$ are less than zero.
   b. The stationary point is a relative minimum if *both* $f_{xx}(x^*, y^*)$ and $f_{yy}(x^*, y^*)$ are greater than zero.

2. If $D(x^*, y^*) < 0$, the stationary point is what is referred to as a **saddle-point.** A saddle-point is neither a maximum nor a minimum. It satisfies the necessary conditions for a maximum or a minimum, but the concavity conditions are not satisfied. Figure 3–4 illustrates a saddle-point.

3. If $D(x^*, y^*) = 0$, other techniques are required to determine the nature of the stationary point.[2]

FIGURE 3–4

Saddle-Point

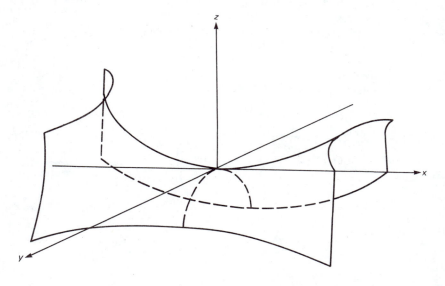

---

[2] For example, see D. Teichroew, *An Introduction to Management Science, Deterministic Models* (New York: John Wiley & Sons, Inc., 1964), pp. 270–72.

Example 3.4

Given

$$z = 4x^2 + 2y^2 - 8x - 2y + 1,$$

find all stationary points and determine their nature.

The first partial derivatives are expressed as $f_x = 8x - 8$ and $f_y = 4y - 2$. It follows that $f_x = 0$ when $x^* = 1$ and $f_y = 0$ when $y^* = \frac{1}{2}$. Thus, the only stationary point on the function occurs when $x = 1$ and $y = \frac{1}{2}$. Finding all second derivatives, we get

$$f_{xx} = 8$$
$$f_{yy} = 4$$
$$f_{xy} = 0$$
$$f_{yx} = 0$$

and computing $D(x^*, y^*)$, we find that

$$D(1, \tfrac{1}{2}) = 8(4) - (0)^2$$
$$= 32.$$

Since $D(x^*, y^*) > 0$, the stationary point is either a relative maximum or a relative minimum. Evaluating the two pure partial derivatives at the stationary point, we find that both are greater than zero, or

$$f_{xx}(1, \tfrac{1}{2}) = 8$$

and

$$f_{yy}(1, \tfrac{1}{2}) = 4;$$

hence, the stationary point is a relative minimum. The value for z at this point is

$$z = 4(1)^2 + 2(\tfrac{1}{2})^2 - 8(1) - 2(\tfrac{1}{2}) + 1$$
$$= -3.5.$$

Follow-up Exercises

8. Prove that $D(x^*, y^*) > 0$ is an impossibility if f_{xx} and f_{yy} are of opposite sign. Would you conclude, therefore, that one only need inspect the sign of either f_{xx} or f_{yy} to determine a relative maximum or minimum when $D(x^*, y^*) > 0$?

9. Confirm that the stationary point given by $x^* = 3$ and $y^* = 4$ represents a relative maximum for the function $z = 2x + 5y + xy - x^2 - y^2 + 10$. Note that you will have to solve two equations simultaneously. Do you remember how? If not, refer to Appendix B at the end of the book.

10. Determine the nature of the stationary point for the function in Exercise 1.

11. Verify that the stationary points for the function

$$f(x_1, x_2) = x_1^2 + 4x_1x_2 - x_1x_2^2$$

are $(-2, 2)$, $(0, 0)$, and $(0, 4)$. Note that the simultaneous equations for the necessary conditions are nonlinear. (See Appendix B.) Identify the nature of each stationary point.

3.2 TWO-VARIABLE APPLICATIONS

In this section we present two examples to illustrate the treatment of models characterized by two independent variables.

Example 3.5   Two-Product Pricing Problem

A firm sells two products for which it has determined the demand functions $q_1 = 110 - 4p_1 - p_2$ and $q_2 = 90 - 2p_1 - 3p_2$, where $q_i =$ demand (in units per day) for the ith product and $p_i =$ price (dollars per unit) of the ith product. The firm wishes to determine the prices it should charge for each product in order to maximize total revenue per day from the two products. Total revenue for the two products is determined by

$$
\begin{aligned}
TR &= p_1 q_1 + p_2 q_2 \\
&= p_1(110 - 4p_1 - p_2) + p_2(90 - 2p_1 - 3p_2) \\
&= 110p_1 - 4p_1^2 - 3p_1 p_2 + 90p_2 - 3p_2^2.
\end{aligned}
\tag{3.3}
$$

To identify any stationary points on the revenue "surface," partial derivatives must be found with respect to p_1 and p_2 and set equal to zero:

$$
\begin{aligned}
f_{p_1} &= 110 - 8p_1 - 3p_2 = 0 \\
f_{p_2} &= -3p_1 + 90 - 6p_2 = 0.
\end{aligned}
$$

Solving the two equations simultaneously for p_1^* and p_2^*, we find that the only stationary point occurs when $p_1^* = p_2^* = 10$. In order to determine the nature of the stationary point, the second derivatives are found and $D(p_1^*, p_2^*)$ is evaluated:

$$
\begin{aligned}
f_{p_1 p_1} &= -8 \\
f_{p_2 p_2} &= -6 \\
f_{p_1 p_2} &= -3 \\
D(10, 10) &= (-8)(-6) - (-3)^2 \\
&= 39 > 0.
\end{aligned}
$$

Since both pure partials are less than zero at $p_1^* = 10$ and $p_2^* = 10$, it is concluded that the stationary point is a relative maximum. In fact, the stationary point is a global maximum because D is greater than zero regardless of the values for p_1 and p_2. The quantities demanded of each product—60 and 40 units per day, respectively—can be found by substituting $p_1 = p_2 = 10$ into each of the original demand equations. Maximum revenue, as determined by substituting back into Equation (3.3), is $1,000 per day.

Follow-up Exercise

12. Suppose that total production cost (dollars per day) for two products is given by the function

$$
C = 4q_1^2 + 2q_2^2 - 80q_1 - 200q_2 + 6,000.
\tag{3.4}
$$

Determine the quantities q_1 and q_2 which result in the minimization of total cost per day. Test the sufficiency condition for minimization. What is the minimum cost?

Example 3.6   Least-Squares Model

The least-squares model is an important and widely used concept in statistics, typically under the subject of regression analysis. This model is the most popular for fitting a curve to a set of data points. This example will illustrate how differential calculus is the tool used to derive the model.

In Example 2.4, concerning the MBTA, a set of data points was presented which reflected demand for transit services under different fares. Whereas the equation of the line fit to the data was presented without proof earlier, this example will derive the relationship by the least-squares technique. As was noted earlier, the data offer strong evidence of a linear demand relationship. The objective is to fit a linear function through these data points and to use the equation of the line to approximate the relationship which exists between price and demand. For the linear function

$$y_c = a + bx \tag{3.5}$$

the least-squares model is concerned with determining the values of a (the y-intercept) and b (the slope) which best approximate the relationship. Note that y_e represents calculated values for y as determined by the estimating equation. Many straight lines can be fit to the data points; some being better than others. The least-squares model defines "best" as the straight line which minimizes the sum of the squared deviations between the *observed* y values and the corresponding *calculated* y values (those lying on the straight line). In Figure 3–5, the least-squares model for three data points identifies the line which minimizes the sum of the squares of the

FIGURE 3–5

Least-Squares Model

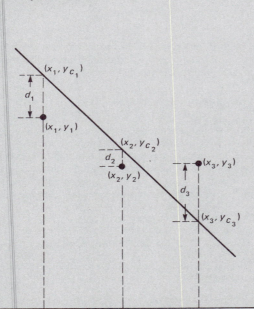

deviations d_1, d_2, and d_3. Mathematically, this criterion is expressed as minimize

$$
\begin{aligned}
S &= d_1^2 + d_2^2 + \cdots + d_n^2 \\
&= \sum_{i=1}^{n} d_i^2 \\
&= \sum_{i=1}^{n} (y_i - y_{c_i})^2 \\
&= \sum_{i=1}^{n} [y_i - (a + bx_i)]^2
\end{aligned}
\tag{3.6}
$$

where n = number of data points;

   d_i = deviation of calculated value of y from observed value of y for ith data point;

   y_i = observed value of y for ith data point;

   y_{c_i} = calculated value of y for ith data point; and

   x_i = observed value of x for ith data point.

TABLE 3–1

Demand Data for MBTA

Price per Ticket	Quantity (1,000 passengers)
25¢	10.0
20	12.6
15	14.9
10	17.4
5	20.1

Using the MBTA data in Table 3–1 and recalling that price (p) was graphed along the y-axis and quantity (q) was graphed along the x-axis, we see that the criterion relationship becomes minimize:

$$
\begin{aligned}
S = f(a,b) \\
= [25 - (a + 10b)]^2 + [20 - (a + 12.6b)]^2 + [15 - (a + 14.9b)]^2 \\
+ [10 - (a + 17.4b)]^2 + [5 - (a + 20.1b)]^2.
\end{aligned}
$$

This criterion relationship can be portrayed graphically as a surface in three dimensions with a value of S determined for every combination of values for a and b. In order to determine the minimum value for S, stationary points must be identified. This is done by finding the first partial derivatives with respect to a and b. (This is not as gruesome as it looks!) Verify that the simplified forms of these partial derivatives are expressed as

$$
\frac{\partial S}{\partial a} = -150 + 10a + 150b;
$$

$$
\frac{\partial S}{\partial b} = -2,000 + 150a + 2,375.08b.
$$

Setting each partial derivative equal to zero and dividing by two, we have identified the following set of simultaneous equations:

$$
5a + \qquad 75b = 75
\tag{3.7}
$$
$$
75a + 1,187.54b = 1,000.
\tag{3.8}
$$

Solving these equations simultaneously leads to the stationary point $a^* = 45$ and $b^* = -2.0$. (Can you verify this result?) To test this point, the following second partial derivatives are found:

$$f_{aa} = +10$$
$$f_{bb} = 2{,}375.08$$
$$f_{ab} = 150.$$

Therefore,

$$D(45, -2.0) = (+10)(2{,}375.08) - (150)^2$$
$$= 1{,}250.8 > 0.$$

Since both f_{aa} and f_{bb} are greater than zero at the stationary point, it is concluded that the sum of the squares of the deviations is minimized when $a = 45$ and $b = -2$, or when the straight line fit to the data has the equation:

$$y_c = 45 - 2x$$

or, in the context of Example 2.4,

$$p = 45 - 2q.$$

Follow-up Exercises

13. Using the above optimization procedure, we can show that the least-squares line of best fit has parameters a and b which are determined by solving simultaneously the following so-called **normal equations:**

$$na + \left(\sum_{i=1}^{n} x_i\right) \cdot b = \sum_{i=1}^{n} y_i \tag{3.9}$$

$$\left(\sum_{i=1}^{n} x_i\right) \cdot a + \left(\sum_{i=1}^{n} x_i^2\right) \cdot b = \sum_{i=1}^{n} y_i x_i. \tag{3.10}$$

Find the indicated sums in Equations (3.9) and (3.10) and verify that they are identical to Equations (3.7) and (3.8).

**14. Derive the normal equations if the criterion relationship is stated in the form

$$\text{Minimize } S = \sum_{i=1}^{n} [y_i - (a + bx_i)]^2.$$

15. Solve Equations (3.9) and (3.10) for a and b and verify the resulting formulas using a textbook in statistics.

3.3 N-VARIABLE OPTIMIZATION

The similarities which have been shown between the procedures of single and bivariate optimization also hold for more than two independent variables. First, it is necessary to identify all stationary points on the objective function. Such points are identified by setting all first partial derivatives equal to zero and solving the resulting system of simultaneous equations. Following the identification of all stationary points, a higher-ordered derivative test must be conducted to determine their nature. As the number of independent variables increases, the computational burden becomes greater and evaluation procedures may change slightly, but the conceptual basis for identifying extreme points is simply a logical extension of that used in the bivariate situation. This section generalizes the procedures of classical optimization for the case of n independent variables.

Stationary Points

Given an objective function involving n independent variables,

$$y = f(x_1, x_2, x_3, \ldots, x_n), \tag{3.11}$$

stationary points are identified by taking the first partial derivative of the function with respect to *each* independent variable. Each of these derivatives should be set equal to zero and the group solved simultaneously to determine the coordinates of any stationary points. In other words, the following system of equations must be solved simultaneously:

$$\frac{\partial f}{\partial x_1} = 0$$

$$\frac{\partial f}{\partial x_2} = 0 \tag{3.12}$$

$$\vdots$$

$$\frac{\partial f}{\partial x_n} = 0.$$

Example 3.7

Given

$$y = f(x_1, x_2, x_3)$$
$$= x_1^2 - 2x_1x_2 + 2x_2^2 + 2x_1x_3 + 4x_3^2 - 2x_3,$$

the conditions for the existence of any stationary points are that

$$\frac{\partial y}{\partial x_1} = 2x_1 - 2x_2 + 2x_3 = 0$$

$$\frac{\partial y}{\partial x_2} = -2x_1 + 4x_2 = 0$$

$$\frac{\partial y}{\partial x_3} = 2x_1 + 8x_3 - 2 = 0.$$

Solving these three equations simultaneously, we see that the only stationary point is identified as having coordinates

$$x_1^* = -1, x_2^* = -\tfrac{1}{2}, x_3^* = \tfrac{1}{2}.$$

Follow-up Exercise

16. Confirm that $(-0.15, 0.25, 0.05)$ is a stationary point for the function given by

$$y = x_1 - 4x_1x_2 - x_2^2 + 5x_3^2 - 2x_2x_3.$$

We might note that the need to solve simultaneous equations causes severe operational difficulties when the equations are nonlinear. In most instances, solutions by this method are not feasible; one of the methods described in Chapter 10 may be appropriate.

Testing Stationary Points

As with single and bivariate situations, determining whether a stationary point is a local maximum or minimum involves higher-ordered derivatives. In particular, one test requires the use of a matrix of second partial derivatives.[3] This matrix, called the **Hessian matrix,** has the form

$$\mathbf{H} = \begin{pmatrix} f_{x_1x_1} & f_{x_1x_2} & f_{x_1x_3} & \cdots & f_{x_1x_n} \\ f_{x_2x_1} & f_{x_2x_2} & f_{x_2x_3} & \cdots & f_{x_2x_n} \\ \cdot & \cdot & \cdot & & \cdot \\ \cdot & \cdot & \cdot & & \cdot \\ \cdot & \cdot & \cdot & \cdot & \cdot \\ f_{x_nx_1} & f_{x_nx_2} & f_{x_nx_3} & \cdots & f_{x_nx_n} \end{pmatrix}.$$

The Hessian matrix is square, the principal diagonal contains the *pure* second partial derivatives, and the remaining elements are *cross* partial derivatives. The matrix is also symmetrical about the principal diagonal since the cross partial derivatives taken with respect to the same two variables are equal.

For an $(n \times n)$ Hessian matrix, a group of n submatrices can be identified. The first of these is the (1×1) matrix consisting of the element in position $(1, 1)$ of the Hessian. Denoting this matrix as $\mathbf{H}_1$, we see that

$$\mathbf{H}_1 = (f_{x_1x_1}).$$

The second submatrix is a (2×2) matrix consisting of the elements found in the upper left-hand corner of the Hessian, or

$$\mathbf{H}_2 = \begin{pmatrix} f_{x_1x_1} & f_{x_1x_2} \\ f_{x_2x_1} & f_{x_2x_2} \end{pmatrix}.$$

The third submatrix is a (3×3) matrix formed from the elements in the first three rows *and* first three columns of the Hessian, or

$$\mathbf{H}_3 = \begin{pmatrix} f_{x_1x_1} & f_{x_1x_2} & f_{x_1x_3} \\ f_{x_2x_1} & f_{x_2x_2} & f_{x_2x_3} \\ f_{x_3x_1} & f_{x_3x_2} & f_{x_3x_3} \end{pmatrix}.$$

_____

[3] Appendix C presents a review of matrix notation.

Proceeding in the same manner, we see that the $(n \times n)$ submatrix is simply the Hessian itself.

The **principal minors** of the Hessian matrix are the **determinants** of the submatrices identified above.[4] These may be denoted by $|\mathbf{H}_i|$, where $\mathbf{H}_i$ represents the ith submatrix. If $(x_1^*, x_2^*, x_3^*, \ldots, x_n^*)$ represents the coordinates of a stationary point for a function involving n independent variables, then the test for extreme points is as follows:

1. Form the Hessian matrix with all partial derivatives evaluated at $(x_1^*, x_2^*, x_3^*, \ldots, x_n^*)$.
2. Evaluate each principal minor of the Hessian matrix.
3. *a.*   If all principal minors are positive, then the Hessian matrix is termed **positive-definite** and the stationary point is a *relative minimum* on the original function.
    b.   If the principal minors alternate in sign, with the odd-numbered minors negative and the even-numbered minors positive, then the Hessian is termed **negative-definite** and the stationary point is a *relative maximum* for the function.
    c.   If neither of the above conditions exists, then the Hessian matrix is **semidefinite** and further analysis in the neighborhood of the stationary point is required to determine its nature.

Example 3.8

Continuing Example 3.7, the Hessian matrix of second partial derivatives is

$$\mathbf{H} = \begin{pmatrix} 2 & -2 & 2 \\ -2 & 4 & 0 \\ 2 & 0 & 8 \end{pmatrix}.$$

The submatrices and corresponding values of the principal minors are:

$$\mathbf{H}_1 = (2) \text{ and } |\mathbf{H}_1| = 2;$$

$$\mathbf{H}_2 = \begin{pmatrix} 2 & -2 \\ -2 & 4 \end{pmatrix} \text{ and } |\mathbf{H}_2| = 4;$$

$$\mathbf{H}_3 = \begin{pmatrix} 2 & -2 & 2 \\ -2 & 4 & 0 \\ 2 & 0 & 8 \end{pmatrix} \text{ and } |\mathbf{H}_3| = 16.$$

Since $|\mathbf{H}_1|$, $|\mathbf{H}_2|$, and $|\mathbf{H}_3|$ are all > 0, we conclude that the stationary point is a relative minimum.

Follow-up Exercises

17.   Verify that this procedure generalizes to include the single and bivariate optimization situations.
18.   Verify by the Hessian matrix approach that the function in Exercise 11 has a *minimum* at $x_1 = -2$ and $x_2 = 2$. Note that the Hessian contains

---

[4] Appendix C also presents a review of minors, cofactors, and determinants.

algebraic expressions in the decision variables *which must be evaluated at the stationary point*. What can you conclude about the stationary point at $x_1 = 0$ and $x_2 = 0$? At $x_1 = 0$ and $x_2 = 4$?

19. Test the nature of the stationary point in Exercise 16.

3.4   OPTIMIZATION WITH CONSTRAINTS

Thus far discussion has focused upon *unconstrained* optimization. This section introduces the subject of **constrained optimization** where an objective function is to be optimized subject to certain constraining or restricting conditions. This situation is the most typical in decision-making settings. Its use has become so widespread that an entire field called **mathematical programming,** to be introduced in subsequent chapters, has evolved. To conceptually illustrate the nature of constrained optimization, we will present an example.

Example 3.9   Product Line Model

A manufacturer of antipollution devices for smokestacks wishes to maximize the firm's profit. The objective function might take the form below, with a product line of *n* devices.

$$\text{Profit} = f(x_i)$$
$$= \sum_{i=1}^{n} (p_i - c_i)x_i - F$$

where p_i = selling price for ith item; c_i = variable costs per unit for ith item; x_i = number of units produced and sold of ith item; and F = fixed expenses. Assuming an operational objective of determining the number of units of each item to produce in order to maximize profits, we see that the decision is fairly obvious. Produce an infinite number of each device so as to become infinitely wealthy. Fortunately, or unfortunately (depending on your point of view), the world of economics is not structured so ideally. Typically, the objective function is not so easy to formulate: Prices and quantities demanded can be related through demand functions, and costs of production and quantities produced can be related through production functions. Even if we assume that the objective function is an accurate representation of the profit relationship, there are usually restrictive conditions which have been neglected in this formulation: There will be limitations upon the amounts of material, labor, and capital resources available for production; demand for the products of the firm will be limited; and items within the product line will compete with one another for input factors, restricting the way in which such resources can be allocated.

Solution by Substitution (Equality Constraints)

If an n-variable objective function is to be optimized subject to $n - 1$ equality constraints, it might be possible to solve for $n - 1$ of the variables in terms of the remaining variable. Should this be the case, the objective function, by a series of substitutions, can be reduced to an unconstrained expression in one independent variable. Indeed, this is the exact procedure that was followed in solving the design for a police patrol sector (Example 2.15).

Example 3.10   Pollution Control Model

An automobile manufacturer is considering the installation of two complementary antipollution devices (catalytic converters) in a new model automobile which is being tested. Configurations of the two devices, in terms of cost of installation, have been tested. Exhaust quality tests and cost analyses uncovered a very strong relationship between each device. A least-squares fit to the data resulted in the criterion function

$$R(x_1, x_2) = -3x_1^2 - 2x_2^2 + 20x_1x_2$$

where $R(x_1, x_2) =$ reduction in pollution particulates per cubic foot of exhaust; $x_1 =$ installation expenditure for the first converter (dollars); and $x_2 =$ installation expenditure for the second converter (dollars).

Prior analysis has established that any installation configuration will satisfy federal and state antipollution guidelines. An edict from "above," however, has established that exactly $100 is to be spent on the installation of either or both converters. At first, management was inclined to minimize installation expenditures subject to the satisfaction of pollution levels. Consumer pressures (and perhaps a social conscience), however, finalized the objective of maximizing

$$R(x_1, x_2) = -3x_1^2 - 2x_2^2 + 20x_1x_2$$

subject to

$$x_1 + x_2 = 100.$$

Solving the constraint for x_1 and substituting this result in the objective function, we reduce the problem to maximizing

$$R(x_2) = -25x_2^2 + 2,600x_2 - 30,000.$$

The original problem, involving an objective function and constraint in two independent variables, has been transformed to an objective function that is stated in terms of one independent variable. Examining this function for stationary points, we see

$$R'(x_2) = -50x_2 + 2,600 = 0$$

or

$$x_2^* = 52.$$

Testing the stationary point, we get

$$R''(x_2) = -50$$

which confirms that R is maximized when $x_2 = 52$. Thus, $48 and $52, respectively, should be expended for the installation of the two catalytic converters. The resulting reduction in pollution particulates per cubic foot of exhaust is 37,600.

**Lagrange Multiplier Method (Equality Constraints)

In many situations, it is either difficult or impossible to solve for one variable in terms of the others in an equality constraint. An alternative and powerful procedure which is widely used for solving constrained optimization problems is the **Lagrange multiplier technique.**

Assume a problem having the form:

Maximize (or minimize)

$$z = f(x, y)$$

subject to

$$g(x, y) = k \tag{3.13}$$

where k is a constant. The Lagrange multiplier method forms a new function composed of the objective function and a linear multiple of the constraint equation. This composite function, called the **Lagrangian function,** has the form

$$L(x, y, \lambda) = f(x, y) - \lambda[g(x, y) - k]. \tag{3.14}$$

The variable λ (lambda) is called the **Lagrange multiplier.** Notice that, since the constraint function, $[g(x, y) - k]$, is required to equal zero, λ can equal any value and the term $\lambda[g(x, y) - k]$ still equals zero. Consequently, as long as the values of x and y satisfy the constraint, the value of the new Lagrangian function is the same as the value of the objective function.

The creation of the Lagrangian function ingeniously transforms the original constrained problem into an unconstrained problem which can be solved by the procedures of n-variable optimization. That is, the determination of stationary points has been translated into the solution of the simultaneous equations

$$\frac{\partial L(x, y, \lambda)}{\partial x} = 0$$

$$\frac{\partial L(x, y, \lambda)}{\partial y} = 0$$

$$\frac{\partial L(x, y, \lambda)}{\partial \lambda} = 0.$$

(Note that the last equation represents the original constraint.)

Due to the dependence between x and y in the constraint, the test for determining the nature of the stationary point is somewhat more involved for the Lagrange multiplier method. The determinant of the following **bordered Hessian matrix** must be determined:

$$\mathbf{H}^B = \begin{pmatrix} 0 & g_x & g_y \\ g_x & L_{xx} & L_{xy} \\ g_y & L_{yx} & L_{yy} \end{pmatrix}$$

where g_x and g_y represent, respectively, the partial derivatives of the left-hand side of the constraint with respect to x and y; L_{xx} and L_{yy} represent the two pure partials of the Lagrangian function; and L_{xy} and L_{yx} represent the cross partials of the Lagrangian function.

By proof, it can be shown that: For $|\mathbf{H}^B| > 0$ the stationary point is a relative *maximum;* for $|\mathbf{H}^B| < 0$ the stationary point is a relative *minimum.*

Example 3.11

Solve the previous problem by the Lagrange multiplier method. Rewriting the problem in the standard form of Equation (3.13), we get

maximize

$$R(x_1, x_2) = -3x_1^2 - 2x_2^2 + 20x_1x_2$$

subject to

$$x_1 + x_2 = 100.$$

The Lagrangian function is

$$L(x_1, x_2, \lambda) = -3x_1^2 - 2x_2^2 + 20x_1x_2 - \lambda[x_1 + x_2 - 100]$$

and the first partial derivatives are

$$\frac{\partial L}{\partial x_1} = -6x_1 + 20x_2 - \lambda = 0$$

$$\frac{\partial L}{\partial x_2} = -4x_2 + 20x_1 - \lambda = 0$$

$$\frac{\partial L}{\partial \lambda} = -x_1 - x_2 + 100 = 0.$$

Solving these three equations simultaneously, we find a stationary point having coordinates $x_1^* = 48$, $x_2^* = 52$, and $\lambda^* = +752$. Testing the stationary point by forming the bordered Hessian matrix, we get

$$\mathbf{H}^B = \begin{pmatrix} 0 & 1 & 1 \\ 1 & -6 & 20 \\ 1 & 20 & -4 \end{pmatrix},$$

and $|\mathbf{H}^B| = 50 > 0$ which, as before, identifies the stationary point as a global maximum.

Interpreting λ

Lambda is much more than an artificial creation allowing for the solution of constrained optimization problems. It has an interpretation which can be very useful in applications. It can be shown for certain conditions that[5]

$$\frac{\partial L(x^*, y^*, \lambda^*)}{\partial k} = \lambda^*; \qquad (3.15)$$

hence, λ^* represents the instantaneous rate of change in the optimal value of the objective function with respect to the constant while all other variables remain fixed. It follows that if λ^* is positive, an increase (decrease) in k results in an increase (decrease) in the optimal value of L according to Equation (3.15). Conversely, for negative λ^*, changes in optimal L move the opposite direction from changes in k.

In most managerial applications the right-hand-side constant, for practical reasons, is restricted to discrete changes. Lambda, therefore, is often interpreted as the *approximate* change in the objective function when the constant in the constraint changes by *one* unit.

To illustrate, we substitute the appropriate values in the Lagrangian function in Example 3.11:

$$\begin{aligned}
L(48, 52, +752) &= -3(48)^2 - 2(52)^2 + 20(48)(52) - (+752)(48 + 52 - 100) \\
&= 37,600 - 752(0). \\
&= 37,600.
\end{aligned}$$

If the 100 increases to 101 in the constraint, then the optimal value of L can be approximated by

$$\begin{aligned}
L(48, 52, +752) &= 37,600 - (752)(48 + 52 - 101) \\
&= 37,600 - (752)(-1) \\
&= 38,352.
\end{aligned}$$

Similarly, if the 100 in the constraint decreases to 99, then the optimal value of L can be approximated by

$$\begin{aligned}
L(48, 52, +752) &= 37,600 - (752)(48 + 52 - 99) \\
&= 37,600 - (752)(+1) \\
&= 36,848.
\end{aligned}$$

Follow-up Exercises

20. You should verify, by reworking the entire problem, that the optimal value of the objective function in Example 3.11 increases by 755.77 if the constraint becomes $x_1 + x_2 = 101$. (Note that this is close to the value of λ^*.)

21. Solve the police sector problem of Example 2.15 on page 55 using the Lagrange multiplier method. Construct the bordered Hessian matrix and test the stationary point. Verbalize the meaning of λ^* in the context of this problem.

---

[5] Willard I. Zangwill, *Nonlinear Programming: A Unified Approach* (Englewood Cliffs, N.J.: Prentice-Hall, Inc., 1969), pp. 66–68.

To reiterate a previous point, interpretation of the impact on the objective function depends on *both* the sign and the magnitude of λ^* *and* the direction of change of the constant in the constraint. Can you verify the characteristics of interpreting λ^* in Table 3–2?

TABLE 3–2

Interpreting λ^* for Equality Constraints
Where $L(x,y,\lambda) = f(x,y) - \lambda[g(x,y) - k]$

Sign of λ^*	Increase in Constant (k)	Decrease in Constant (k)
Positive	Increase in optimal $f(x,y)$	Decrease in optimal $f(x,y)$
Negative	Decrease in optimal $f(x,y)$	Increase in optimal $f(x,y)$

**Generalization of the Lagrange Multiplier Method

The generalization of the technique to n variables and m equality constraints, that is,

optimize

$$z = f(x_1, x_2, \ldots, x_n)$$

subject to

$$g_1(x_1, x_2, \ldots, x_n) = k_1$$
$$g_2(x_1, x_2, \ldots, x_n) = k_2$$
$$\cdot$$
$$\cdot \qquad\qquad\qquad\qquad\qquad (3.16)$$
$$\cdot$$
$$g_m(x_1, x_2, \ldots, x_n) = k_m$$

is a simple, albeit, tedious extension of the two-variable case. In this case, $(n + m)$ simultaneous equations are established from the first partial derivatives of the Lagrangian function

$$L(x_1, x_2, \ldots, x_n, \lambda_1, \lambda_2, \ldots, \lambda_m) = f(x_1, x_2, \ldots, x_n)$$
$$- \sum_{i=1}^{m} \lambda_i[g_i(x_1, x_2, \ldots, x_n) - k_i]. \quad (3.17)$$

The bordered Hessian is also a straightforward extension of the two-variable case, although the same cannot be said for the set of rules which determines the nature of the stationary point.[6]

**Inequality Constraints

The Lagrange multiplier method, although specifically designed for equality constraints, can be applied to the solution of problems characterized by inequality constraints (assuming global optima can be determined).

Consider the problem

---

[6] If you're interested in specifics, see Hamdy A. Taha, *Operations Research: An Introduction* (New York: The McMillan Company, 1971), pp. 617–22.

maximize

$$z = f(\mathbf{X})$$

subject to

$$g(\mathbf{X}) \leq k \tag{3.18}$$

where $\mathbf{X}$ represents the set of independent variables $(x_1, x_2, \ldots, x_n)$. Treating Equation (3.18) as an equality, we form the Lagrangian function in the usual manner; that is,

$$\text{maximize } L(\mathbf{X}, \lambda) = f(\mathbf{X}) - \lambda[g(\mathbf{X}) - k].$$

From a previous section, we know that a *positive* λ^* implies that a *decrease* in k will *decrease* optimal L. Since the left-hand expression in Equation (3.18) *must be less than or equal to k* and the Lagrangian considers $g(\mathbf{X}) = k$, it follows that the *original* problem given by Equation (3.18) implies a *decrease* in k. A decrease in k, however, is undesirable because optimal L will decrease, which is contrary to our desire to *maximize;* hence, the constraint *binds* our solution; that is, maximum L will be achieved at $g(\mathbf{X}) = k$ which implies that the unconstrained stationary point does not satisfy the constraint.

All of this leads us to conclude that, for a *maximization* problem characterized by a ($\leq$) constraint, a *positive* λ^* implies that an increase in k (relaxation of the constraint) is *desirable.*

If λ^* were *negative,* then the decrease in k implied by Equation (3.18) would increase optimal L. This in turn implies that the constraint would *not be binding.* In other words, the problem should be solved by ignoring the constraint. In this case, the Lagrangian solution is termed **pseudo-optimal.**

Reasoning in a similar manner, we see that exactly opposite conclusions are reached for either minimization problems or ($\geq$) constraints. Table 3–3 summarizes these conclusions. (If you're lost, take comfort in the likelihood that you're in the majority; however, before giving up, carefully study Example 3.12, Figure 3–6, and solve Exercises 23 and 24. Then, study the above logic once more.)

TABLE 3–3

Interpreting λ^* for Inequality Constraints Where $L(\mathbf{X}, \lambda) = f(\mathbf{X}) - \lambda[g(\mathbf{X}) - k]$

Optimization Objective	Type of Constraint			
	($\leq$)		($\geq$)	
	$\lambda^* < 0$	$\lambda^* > 0$	$\lambda^* < 0$	$\lambda^* > 0$
Maximize $f(\mathbf{X})$.	(a) Ignore constraint (pseudo-optimal solution)	(b) Constraint binding; *increase k if possible*	(c) Constraint binding; *decrease k if possible*	(d) Ignore constraint (pseudo-optimal solution)
Minimize $f(\mathbf{X})$.	(e) Constraint binding; *increase k if possible*	(f) Ignore constraint (pseudo-optimal solution)	(g) Ignore constraint (pseudo-optimal solution)	(h) Constraint binding; *decrease k if possible*

It is worth reiterating that the preceding discussion relates to optimization problems characterized by a single constraint. The conditions for testing the stationary points of problems having multiple inequality constraints are known as **Kuhn-Tucker conditions,** an advanced subject which will not be treated in this textbook.[7]

Example 3.12   Optimal Advertising Period

In the Mow-Down Records, Inc., problem of Chapter 2 (Example 2.14) the unconstrained objective function was derived as

$$P(t) = 197,500 - 200,000e^{-0.02t} - 2,000t$$

where $P(t)$ represented profits ($) and t was defined as the number of days in the advertising period. The optimal advertising period (t^*) was calculated as 34.6575 days, yielding an expected profit of $28,185.

Now suppose that the original problem included the condition that no more than 30 days of advertising are to be considered. The problem now reads

maximize

$$P(t) = 197,500 - 200,000e^{-0.02t} - 2,000t$$

subject to

$$t \leq 30.$$

Optimizing by the Lagrange multiplier method, we have

$$L(t,\lambda) = 197,500 - 200,000e^{-0.02t} - 2,000t - \lambda(t - 30);$$
$$\frac{\partial L}{\partial t} = 4,000e^{-0.02t} - 2,000 - \lambda = 0;$$
$$\frac{\partial L}{\partial \lambda} = -t + 30 = 0.$$

This gives an optimal solution of $t^* = 30$, $\lambda^* = 196$, and $P^* = \$27,700$. Noting that the problem is of the maximization type, that the constraint is of the ($\leq$) type, and that $\lambda^* > 0$, we see that according to result (b) in Table 3–3 the constraint is binding; hence, k should be allowed above 30 days (if possible) to improve profits. Note that $\lambda^* = 196$ indicates that the instantaneous rate of *increase* in profits is $196 in the direction of *increasing* days. Figure 3–6 graphically portrays this result.

If the constraint were $t \leq 50$, the Lagrangian optimal solution would be $t^* = 50$, $\lambda^* = -528$, $P^* = \$23,900$. (Can you verify this?) A negative λ^* gives us result (a) in Table 3–3, an indication that the constraint is *not* binding. Given this result, the unconstrained problem should be solved, (that is, the Lagrangian solution is pseudo-optimal), which brings us back to $t^* \doteq 35$ and $P^* = \$28,185$.

Finally, for the constraint $t \geq 30$, we would have result (d) in Table 3–3; for $t \geq 50$, result (c) would apply.

---

[7] Ibid.; Teichroew, *An Introduction to Management Science;* and Willard I. Zangwill, *Nonlinear Programming: A Unified Approach* (Englewood Cliffs, N.J.: Prentice-Hall, Inc., 1969).

FIGURE 3–6

Solutions to Mow-Down Records, Inc.

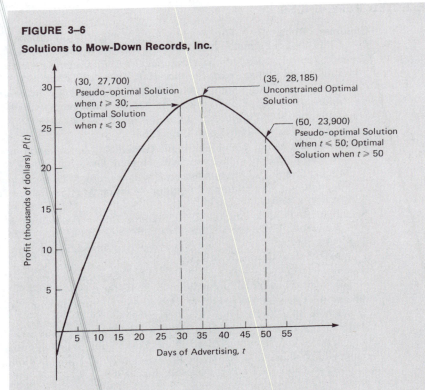

Follow-up Exercises

22. By evaluating $\mathbf{H}^B$, confirm that the stationary point for this problem (when $t \leq 30$) is a maximum.

23. With respect to the advertising problem, confirm that:

   a. The Lagrangian solution when $t \geq 30$ is pseudo-optimal, since $t = 35$ yields a higher profit *and* satisfies the constraint [result (d) in Table 3–3].

   b. The Lagrangian solution when $t \geq 50$ is optimal at $t = 50$, but t should be allowed to decrease if possible [result (c) in Table 3–3].

24. By both the Lagrange multiplier method and by graph, analyze the following problems for *each* of the constraints separately:

minimize

$$Y = x^4$$

subject to

   a. $x \leq 2$
   b. $x \geq 2$.

SELECTED REFERENCES

Childress, Robert L. *Mathematics for Managerial Decisions.* Englewood Cliffs, N.J.: Prentice-Hall, Inc., 1974.

Freund, John E. *College Mathematics with Business Applications.* 2d ed. Englewood Cliffs, N.J.: Prentice-Hall, Inc., 1975.

Gue, Ronald L., and Thomas, Michael E. *Mathematical Methods in Operations Research.* New York: The MacMillan Company, 1968.

Hamming, R. W. *Numerical Methods for Scientists and Engineers.* New York: McGraw-Hill Book Co., 1962.

Hillier, Frederick S., and Lieberman, Gerald J. *Introduction to Operations Research.* 2d ed. San Francisco: Holden Day, Inc., 1974.

McMillan, Claude, Jr. *Mathematical Programming: An Introduction to the Design and Application of Optimal Decision Machines.* New York: John Wiley & Sons, Inc., 1970.

Sivazlian, B. D., and Stanfel, L. E. *Optimization Techniques in Operations Research.* Englewood Cliffs, N.J.: Prentice-Hall, Inc., 1975.

Taha, Hamdy A. *Operations Research: An Introduction.* New York: The MacMillan Company, 1971.

Teichroew, D. *An Introduction to Management Science, Deterministic Models.* New York: John Wiley & Sons, Inc., 1964.

Theodore, Chris A. *Applied Mathematics: An Introduction.* 3d ed. Homewood, Ill.: Richard D. Irwin, Inc., 1975.

Thierauf, Robert J., and Klekamp, Robert C. *Decision Making through Operations Research.* 2d ed. New York: John Wiley & Sons, Inc., 1975.

Zangwill, Willard I. *Nonlinear Programming: A Unified Approach.* Englewood Cliffs, N.J.: Prentice-Hall, Inc., 1969.

ADDITIONAL EXERCISES

25. For the following functions, find *all* first and second partial derivatives.

    a. $y = 5x_1^3 - 2x_1^2 x_2 + 4x_2^2$.
    b. $y = 4x_1^2 - 2x_1 x_2 + 8x_2^2$.
    c. $y = -2x_1^2 - 5x_1 + 6x_2^2 + 6x_2 - 10x_1 x_2$.
    d. $y = 10e^{x_1 x_2}$.
    e. $y = e^{-x_1^2 + x_2^2}$.
    f. $y = 6x_1^2 - 2x_1 x_2 + x_2^2 - 6x_2 x_3 + 2x_3^2$.
    g. $y = 10x_1^2 - 5x_2^2 + 8x_3^2$.

26. For each of the following functions identify any stationary points and determine their nature.

    a. $y = 2x_1^2 - 2x_1 + x_2^2 - x_2$.
    b. $y = -x_1^2 - 2x_2^2 + x_1 + 4x_2 - 2x_1 x_2$.
    c. $y = 5x_1^2 + 20x_1 - 8x_2^2 + 40x_2$.
    d. $y = x_1^2 - 2x_1 x_2^2 + 4x_2^2$.
    e. $y = 2x_1^2 - 16x_1 + 3x_2^2 - 18x_2 + 2x_3^2 - 24x_3$.

27. Suppose that the total revenue function is given by Equation (3.3) and the total cost function is given by (3.4). First express (3.3) in terms of quantities q_i and then determine the quantities which maximize total profit per day. Make sure you test for sufficiency conditions. What is the maximum profit per day? What prices should be charged? Are the results at all questionable? If so, what do you recommend?

28. Using the least squares approach of Example 3.6, determine the equation of the straight line which best fits the following data. What is the minimum value for S?

x	6	4	10
y	4	12	−20

29. The least-squares regression model is not restricted to linear functional forms. Using the same approach as was used in Example 3.6, determine the quadratic function which minimizes the sum of the squares of deviations between actual and predicted values of y for the data below. Note that if you assume a quadratic function to have the form

$$y_c = ax^2 + bx + c,$$

then the criterion, S, becomes a function of a, b, and c.

Verify, using the Hessian matrix, that your values of a^*, b^*, and c^* do result in a minimum value for S. Also, verify that for this "contrived" example, $S^* = 0$.

x	1	−2	2	5	−5
y	11	2	10	−5	−25

30. An analyst has gathered some data and wishes to find a function which gives the "best" fit. It is hypothesized that the variables are related in either a linear or quadratic manner. Determine which functional form is best for the data by deriving least-squares linear and quadratic functions. (See the preceding exercise.) Compare S-values for the two functional forms in order to determine which is "best.

x	1	2	4	6
y	10	7	4	4

31. *Pricing Model* A firm produces three complementary products. Demand functions for each of the three products are expressed below as a function of the prices of the three products.

$$q_1 = 1,000 - 5p_1 - 2p_2 - 3p_3.$$
$$q_2 = 1,500 - 4p_1 - 6p_2 - 2p_3.$$
$$q_3 = 800 - 3p_1 - 3p_2 - 5p_3.$$

In this case q_i is the estimated demand (in units per week) for product i, and p_i is the price of the ith product (in dollars per unit).

a. Determine the prices which should be charged for the three products so as to maximize total revenue (R) from the three products. Verify that you have, in fact, identified a relative maximum. What quantities should be produced if these prices are charged?

b. Suppose that the "production function" is given by

$$C = 2q_1^2 + q_2^2 + 0.5q_3^2 - 200q_1 - 1,000q_2 - 500q_3 + 500,000$$

where C is the total cost (fixed plus variable) of producing q_1, q_2, and q_3 units of products 1, 2, and 3, respectively (in dollars per week). Determine the production quantities which minimize C. Confirm that the stationary point is a minimum. What is minimum C?

32. *Media Mix Model* A national beer producer wants to allocate a $500,-000 advertising budget for the next six months. Advertisements will be

placed on television and in magazines. Profits, in thousands of dollars, are estimated by the function

$$P(x, y) = -x^2 - y^2 + 500x + 1{,}000y$$

where $x =$ thousands of dollars allocated to magazine advertisements and $y =$ thousands of dollars allocated to television advertisements.

a. Assuming full allocation of the budget, determine the allocation which results in maximization of profits using the substitution approach.

b. What are the maximum expected profits? Confirm this stationary point as a maximum.

**33. Solve the preceding exercise using the Lagrange multiplier approach. Interpret the meaning of the value for the Lagrange multiplier. Based on this interpretation, do you suggest an increase or a decrease in the budget? Confirm, using $\mathbf{H}^B$, this stationary point as a maximum.

34. *Agricultural Allocation Model* An analyst for the Department of Agriculture has determined the following profit function based on extensive regression analyses:

$$P(x, y) = 600x + 800y - x^2 - 2y^2 - 2xy$$

where $P(x,y) =$ annual profit in dollars, $x =$ acres of planted soybeans, and $y =$ acres of planted pistachio nuts. Determine the optimal planting decision. Make sure that you confirm the nature of the stationary point. What is the projected maximum annual profit?

35. Suppose that the farm manager for a particular farm wishes to allocate a total of exactly 500 acres to the two cash crops in the preceding exercise. Determine the optimal plantings and annual profit by the:

a. Substitution method.

**b. Lagrange multiplier method. Interpret the meaning of λ^*. Based on this interpretation, do you suggest an increase or a decrease in the acreage allocation to these two plants? Is your suggestion consistent with what one would expect from the decision in Exercise 34?

Don't forget to confirm the nature of the stationary points for parts (*a*) and (*b*).

36. *Portfolio Model* An institutional investor has determined the following function:

$$z = 8x^2 + 4y^2 - 4x - 2y$$

where $z =$ variance in annual return, $x =$ proportion of funds invested in Stock X, and $y =$ proportion of funds invested in Stock Y. Annual return for a stock is defined as $(p_0 - p_1 + d)/p_0$ where p_0 is the price per share at time of purchase, p_1 is the price per share one year after purchase, and d is the dividends paid. Variance, of course, is defined in the statistical sense. For portfolios it represents a measure of risk. Right? Determine the portfolio (that is, value for x and y) which minimizes the variance in annual return given that all funds must be invested in Stock X and/or Stock Y. Use the substitution method and confirm that your optimal portfolio yields minimum variance. What is the minimum variance?

**37. Solve the preceding exercise using the Lagrange multiplier method. Interpret the meaning of λ^*. Confirm the nature of the stationary point using $\mathbf{H}^B$.

38. *Fire Station Location Model* Three towns are located as indicated by the Cartesian coordinate system below. Bond issues for constructing a new fire station which will service all three towns have passed in all three towns. It has been agreed that the station is to be located at a coordinate which minimizes the sum of (tax revenue of town) · (distance squared between town center and location of station) for all three towns. Determine the optimal location of the fire station if tax revenues in thousands of dollars are 200, 100, and 120, respectively, for towns A, B, and C. Let (x, y) represent the location of the fire station. (Hint: The distance between the station and a town is given by the hypotenuse of a right triangle; remember the Pythagorean Theorem?) Confirm that your stationary point is indeed a minimum. Does the surrogate criterion make sense? Why or why not? Can you think of better surrogate criteria?

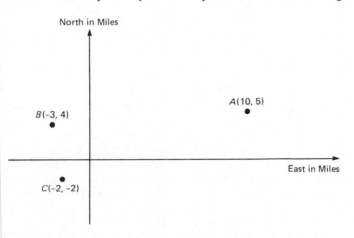

**39. In the preceding exercise, suppose that some powerful politicians have "arranged" that the station is to be located equidistant from towns B and C. Determine the optimal location of the fire station by the Lagrange multiplier method. Apply the appropriate test for the sufficiency condition.

**40. Solve Exercise 32 by the Lagrange multiplier method if:

a. $x + y \leq 500{,}000$.
b. $x + y \geq 500{,}000$.

Relate your results to Table 3–3. In each case, confirm the nature of the stationary point by evaluating $\mathbf{H}^B$.

**41. Solve Example 3.10 on page 82 by the Lagrange multiplier method if:

a. $x_1 + x_2 \leq 100$.
b. $x_1 + x_2 \geq 100$.

Relate your results to Table 3–3. In each case, confirm the nature of the stationary point by evaluating $\mathbf{H}^B$.

4

The Standard Linear
Programming Model

In Chapters 2 and 3, the mathematical objective of maximizing, or minimizing, a constrained, or unconstrained, objective function (criterion) was treated in the classical manner—that is, the objective was effected by implementing the tools of differential calculus. The present chapter introduces *constrained optimization models* which are characterized by both *linear criteria* and *linear constraints*. Although the Lagrange multiplier method can be used to solve linear optimization models (as in Example 5.4*b*), its use is not justified from the standpoint of efficiency. Solution techniques which have been developed for this class of problems fall under the heading of **linear programming.**

4.1 LINEAR OPTIMIZATION MODELS

All linear optimization problems can be characterized by the existence of two or more activities (variables) which compete for limited resources. From the viewpoint of economists, the problem is to determine the "best" allocation of scarce resources to activities. The operational objective of linear programming can be stated succinctly as: Determine the level of each activity (value for each controllable variable) such that a linear criterion is optimized subject to resource limitations and, perhaps, other conditions as expressed by linear constraints.

Economic applications of linear programming have been not only diverse but also eminently successful. Military establishments and the oil industry in particular have made extensive use of this technique. Besides other industries—for example, wood products, metals, automotive, and chemicals—the service and public sectors have increasingly utilized linear programming. The range of applications has been remarkable. For example, financial institutions have used it for portfolio and cash management; industrial firms for food and chemical blending; production departments for scheduling and allocation; marketing departments for media selection in advertising and the distribution of products; and government agencies for such varied uses as solid waste disposal, air and water pollution control, and the study of competitive strategies (game theory). In fact, the technique has found favor, of all places, in the kibbutz system of Israel for the production scheduling of farm products. Of all the tools in operations research, with the possible exception of simulation, *mathematical programming* (of which linear programming is a subset) can be said to have "the sky as the limit" insofar as applications are concerned.

The example which follows will be used to initiate you in the formulation and conceptualization of linear optimization models. Following a discussion on systems of linear inequalities, the example will be solved by graphical techniques. The chapter concludes with a generalized mathematical model for stating linear programming problems and its characteristics, and a set of examples on formulation. So as not to distract you from the essentials of understanding the uses for and statement of linear optimization models, the technique of solution will be deferred until the next chapter.

Example 4.1   Police Patrol Sectors

Returning to the problem on patrol sector design (Examples 2.3 and 2.15 on pages 34 and 55) you might recall that the objective was to determine the dimensions (in miles) of a rectangular patrol sector (*x* and *y*) which minimize the average response time in hours ($\bar{T}$) of a patrol vehicle (Equation 1.1 or 2.3) subject to an area constraint (Equation 1.4 or 2.4). Suppose that travel speeds in the *x* direction and the *y* direction are estimated at 10 mph and 5 mph, respectively, and that the following restraints are imposed on sector design:

1. The perimeter is to be no less than 4 miles.
2. The perimeter is not to exceed 10 miles.
3. The distance in the *y* direction must be *at least* half again as much as the distance in the *x* direction.

Redefining *x*, *y*, and $\bar{T}$ as x_1, x_2, and *z*, respectively, we may state the problem as

minimize

$$z = \frac{1}{30}x_1 + \frac{1}{15}x_2$$

subject to

$$2x_1 + 2x_2 \geq 4 \tag{1}$$
$$2x_1 + 2x_2 \leq 10 \tag{2}$$
$$x_2 \geq 1.5x_1 \tag{3}$$
$$x_1 \geq 0 \tag{4}$$
$$x_2 \geq 0 \tag{5}$$

where the first three constraints correspond, respectively, to the above-stated restraints for the sector and the last two constraints ensure that sector dimensions will not be negative. Note that *both* the objective function and the constraints are *linear in the decision variables,* as required by the linear programming model.

Follow-up Exercise

1. Does the original formulation of the problem (Example 2.3) conform to that for a linear programming model? Why or why not? Would you say that sector constraints in terms of perimeters appear reasonable?

4.2 SYSTEMS OF LINEAR INEQUALITIES

The constraints (1) through (5) in the preceding example illustrate what is called a system of **linear inequalities.**

The Solution Space

In this section we consider graphical implications for such systems. The presence of only two variables allows one to plot an inequality in **two-space,** that is, a graph with two coordinate axes. This procedure makes possible the visualization of what might be termed the **permissible half-space,** or the set of points (x_1, x_2) which satisfies the inequality.

To illustrate this concept, consider the following generalized inequality:

$$a_1x_1 + a_2x_2 \leq b. \tag{4.1}$$

If variable x_2 were to be represented on the vertical axis (ordinate) and variable x_1 on the horizontal axis (abscissa), it makes sense to solve Equation (4.1) in terms of x_2 as a function of x_1. Subtracting a_1x_1 from both sides of the inequality and dividing both sides by a_2, we get[1]

$$x_2 \leq f(x_1)$$
$$x_2 \leq (b/a_2) - (a_1/a_2)x_1. \tag{4.2}$$

Focusing on the equality part ($=$) of Equation (4.2), we see that we have the *slope-intercept* form of a linear function, $y = mx + i,$ where m and i represent the slope and y-intercept, respectively; hence, in this case, b/a_2 represents the y-intercept and $-a_1/a_2$ indicates the slope of the linear function, the plot of which appears in Figure 4–1. (Depending on the signs of a_1 and a_2, the line could be sloped positively.) Note that the permissible half-space includes those points on the line and those points

---

[1] If a_2 were negative, the sense of the inequality would be reversed.

FIGURE 4–1

Permissible Half-Space

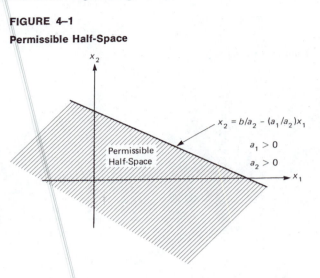

below and to the left of the line. For an inequality of the ($\geq$) type, the permissible half-space would include points on, above, and to the right of the line. If each inequality in a system of linear inequalities in two variables were so plotted in a single diagram, the intersection of all of the permissible half-spaces would indicate the overall permissible region for the system. Typically, this is termed the **solution space** or **feasible region.**

Example 4.2

Continuing Example 4.1, we see that constraints (1) and (2), together with (3), are rewritten below by transposing $2x_1$ to the right side and dividing by 2:

$$x_2 \geq 2 - x_1 \tag{1a}$$
$$x_2 \leq 5 - x_1 \tag{2a}$$
$$x_2 \geq 1.5x_1. \tag{3a}$$

The permissible half-space for each of these constraints is depicted in Figure 4–2. A simple procedure for determining the permissible half-space is to verify whether or not the origin satisfies the constraint. For example, substituting (0, 0) for (x_1, x_2) in constraint (1a) suggests that the origin is not permissible since $0 \geq 2$ violates the constraint; hence, the permissible half-space lies above the line in part (a) of Figure 4–2. (Can you verify the remaining two constraints in this manner?) The nonnegativity constraints have been incorporated automatically by simply graphing the inequalities in the first quadrant. Part (d) of Figure 4–2 indicates the solution space, in the form of a polygon, as the intersection of each of the permissible half-spaces.

FIGURE 4–2

Solution Space for Example 4.2

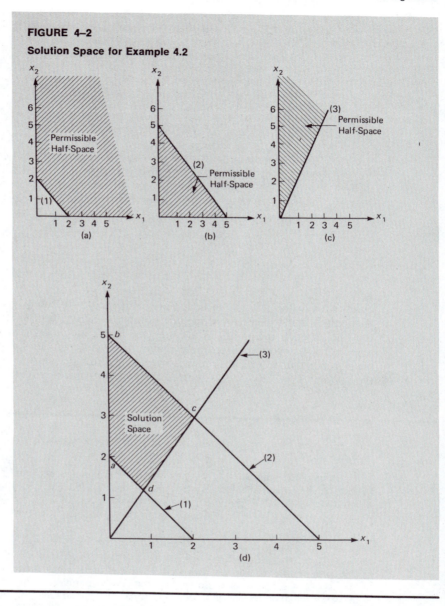

Aberrations in the Solution Space

In some cases, the constraints are formulated in a manner such that there is no common intersection for the permissible half-spaces. For such a case, the *solution space does not exist,* or no points satisfy the constraints. For instance, if the right-hand–side constant of inequality (2) in Example 4.1 were changed to, say, 2, then the solution space for that example would be empty. (You should readily verbalize the inaneness of this inconsistency in the first two constraints.) In linear programming problems there can be a number of explanations for an empty or **null solution space.** Errors in formulating the constraints are highly likely, especially when one considers that real-world applications easily can involve 100 or 200 constraints. Incorrect constraints can be attributed to errors in logic, errors in estimating the parameters (constants), and errors in assigning the correct sense to inequalities. Finally, the situation of no solution space may not always result from errors in formulation. The reality of the problem may be such that no values of the variables simultaneously satisfy the constraints.

FIGURE 4–3

Unbounded Solution Space

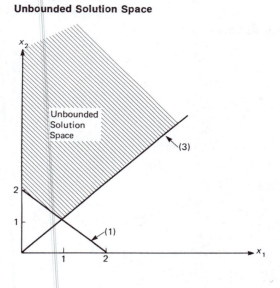

The omission of a constraint, or a group of constraints, in the formulation of a problem can lead to the existence of an **unbounded solution space.** Figure 4–3 illustrates an unbounded solution space for the problem in Example 4.1 when constraint (2) is omitted.

4.3 INCORPORATING THE OBJECTIVE FUNCTION: A GRAPHICAL SOLUTION

The existence of a solution space guarantees an infinite number of solutions, the locations of which can be categorized as (1) the finite number of solutions at the corner points of the polygon—*a, b, c, d* in Figure 4−2d—(2) the infinite number of solutions along the perimeter of the polygon, and (3) the infinite number of solutions within the polygon. The task at hand is to determine, by graphical means, the one solution that is optimal. In some rare cases, an infinite number of solutions may be optimal, as we will subsequently demonstrate.

Douglas Salter
748·8666

Superimposing and Shifting the Objective Function

For two-variable problems, a generalized objective function can be represented by

$$z = c_1 x_1 + c_2 x_2.$$

Notice that, as with the constraints, this function can be represented in the form

$$x_2 = (z/c_2) - (c_1/c_2)\, x_1 \qquad (4.3)$$

where z/c_2 represents the y-intercept and $-c_1/c_2$ the slope. A plot of this function at three different intercept locations (Figure 4–4) clearly illus-

FIGURE 4–4

Plots of Objecting Function Given by Equation (4.3)

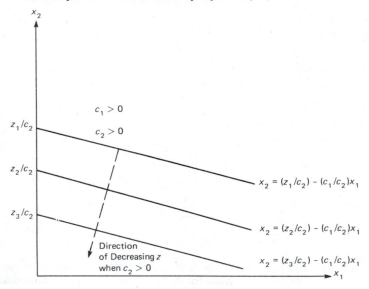

trates that greater intercepts are associated with greater values for the criterion (z) and vice versa; that is,

$$z_1/c_2 > z_2/c_2 > z_3/c_2$$

implies that $z_1 > z_2 > z_3$ for a constant $c_2 > 0$.

Since one is free, within the confines of the solution space, to choose values for x_1 and x_2 which optimize the function, the problem resolves itself into *superimposing a plot of the function (4.3) on the graph of the solution space and shifting the function parallel to itself in a direction which optimizes the criterion (downward for minimization problems and upward for maximization problems when $c_2 > 0$) until the solution space does not permit further shifting.* As will be demonstrated below, the objective function ultimately will pass through a corner point of the polygon;

hence, the optimal solution can be determined by simultaneously solving the two constraints which form the optimal corner point.

Example 4.3

The objective function in Example 4.1 can be restated as

$$x_2 = 15z - (\tfrac{1}{2})x_1$$

and superimposed on a diagram of the solution space, as in Figure 4–5. A tentative objective function can be placed anywhere in the solution space and then shifted in the appropriate direction. In this case, an initial x_2-intercept is chosen arbitrarily at 3 and a line with a slope of $-\tfrac{1}{2}$ is graphed. Since this problem is of the *minimization* type and $c_2 > 0$, the line is shifted *downward* and *parallel* to itself until the solution space *binds*, that is, prevents further shifting. As can be seen, corner point d represents the optimal solution because it both satisfies the constraints and yields the lowest possible x_2-intercept, which is equivalent to the minimum value for the objective function (z).

Optimal values can be read directly from the graph if the level of accuracy is satisfactory. Figure 4–5 indicates values of $x_1 = 0.8$ and $x_2 = 1.2$

FIGURE 4–5

Solution to Police Sector Problem

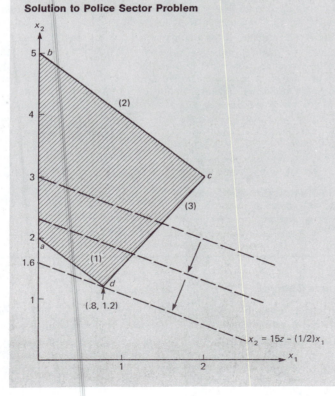

at point d. The optimal value for the x_2-intercept is seen to be 1.6. Recalling that the intercept is given by $15z$ in the linear function, we see that

$$15z = 1.6$$

or

$$z = 8/75.$$

Typically, the procedure for a graphical solution involves sketching a rough graph, determining the optimal point(s), and solving the equations algebraically for the coordinates of the optimal point(s). To illustrate, the optimal corner point, d, is determined by the intersection of constraint lines (1) and (3):

$$x_2 = 2 - x_1 \tag{1}$$
$$x_2 = 1.5x_1. \tag{3}$$

Substituting (3) into (1) and solving for x_1 gives $x_1 = 0.8$; plugging this result back into (3) provides $x_2 = 1.2$; and substituting these two values into the objective function,

$$z = \frac{1}{30}(0.8) + \frac{1}{15}(1.2)$$

yields $z = 8/75$. Thus, a sector which is 0.8 mile by 1.2 miles affords the lowest response time of 8/75 hour, or approximately 6.4 minutes.

Follow-up Exercises

2. Would you expect that the solution always will be constrained by the lower limit on the perimeter of the sector?

3. Solve this problem if the perimeter must be at least 8 miles.

4. Given the general objective function $z = c_1x_1 + c_2x_2$, verify the following characteristics. *Case 1:* $c_1 > 0$ and $c_2 > 0$ make for *negative* slope and *downward* shift for *minimization*. *Case 2:* $c_1 < 0$ and $c_2 > 0$ make for *positive* slope and *downward* shift for *minimization*. *Case 3:* $c_1 > 0$ and $c_2 < 0$ make for *positive* slope and *downward* shift for *maximization*. *Case 4:* $c_1 < 0$ and $c_2 < 0$ make for *negative* slope and *downward* shift for *maximization*. In general, does $c_2 > 0$ imply an upward shift of the objective function for maximization?

5. Find the optimal solution using the solution space of Figure 4–5 for each of the following:

   a. *Maximize* $z = 5x_1 - 15x_2$.
   b. *Maximize* $z = -5x_1 + 15x_2$.
   c. *Minimize* $z = -5x_1 - 15x_2$.

Alternative Optima

Alternative optimal solutions will exist if the objective function is *parallel* to a *binding* constraint. Figure 4–6 illustrates this for a *maximization* problem when $c_2 > 0$. Two points are worth remembering regarding alternative optimal solutions. First, an infinite number of optimal solutions will result. In this particular instance, any point along the line $\overline{bc}$ repre-

FIGURE 4–6

**Alternative Optimal Solutions along $\bar{bc}$
for Maximization Objective ($c_2 > 0$)**

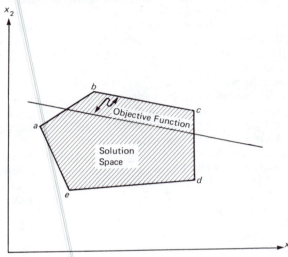

sents an optimal solution. Second, the constraint which is parallel to the objective function must be a binding constraint. For example, if the situation depicted in Figure 4–6 required the *minimization* of the objective function, the optimal solution would be found at point *e*.

If a decision maker is faced with a case of alternative optima, it simply means that more than one combination of values for the decision variables will result in the optimal value for the stated objective. Under such circumstances, the decision maker may select the alternative optimal solution which beneficially affects other criteria (perhaps qualitative).

Follow-up Exercises

6. Graphically solve the following linear programming (LP) problem:

maximize

$$z = 3x_1 + 2x_2$$

subject to

$$3x_1 + 5x_2 \leq 45 \qquad (1)$$
$$6x_1 + 4x_2 \leq 48 \qquad (2)$$

$$x_1, x_2 \geq 0.$$

7. Solve the police sector problem using the data presented in Example 4.1 with the exception that the effective travel speed in both directions is 10 mph (that is, $z = (1/30)x_1 + (1/30)x_2$).

Unbounded Optimal Solution

Earlier in the chapter, the nature of an *unbounded solution space* was illustrated. When such a solution space exists, the optimal value of the objective function may be either bounded or unbounded. In Figure 4–3, for example, an objective function with a negative slope will generate an **unbounded optimal solution** if the objective is to *maximize* the criterion function; in other words, there is no upper limit on the value which the objective function can assume. For the same figure, if the objective were to *minimize* the criterion, then the optimal solution would be *bounded*. Thus you must distinguish carefully between an unbounded solution space and an unbounded optimal solution—the former is a necessary condition for the latter, but the latter will come about *only* if the solution space is unbounded in the direction of the optimal solution.

Unbounded solutions are typically the result of an error in the formulation of the problem. We challenge you to identify a real-world problem having no bound on the objective function. Thus, evidence indicating an unbounded solution should give the analyst cause to review the formulation of the original problem.

Convex Sets

The solution spaces which have been illustrated are examples of **convex sets.** By definition, a convex set is an enclosure such that if any two

FIGURE 4–7

Convex and Nonconvex Sets

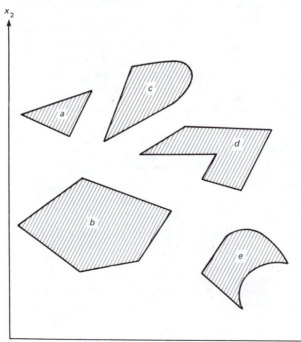

arbitrarily selected points within the set are connected by a straight line, the line will lie entirely within the set.

Figure 4–7 illustrates both convex (*a, b, c*) and nonconvex (*d, e*) sets. The following statements, related to this figure, are of fundamental importance in linear programming.

1. Constraints which are expressed as *linear inequalities* must *necessarily* form a *convex set.* Sets *a* and *b* are illustrations of this statement. You should verify by sketches that the nonconvex set *d* is an impossibility when constructed with linear constraints.

2. Given a linear objective function, regardless of its inclination (slope) or direction of optimization, the optimal solution will always include a *corner* (*extreme*) *point* of a *linear convex set,* as will be demonstrated in the next chapter. You should verify this by determining maxima and minima for various objective functions in sets *a* and *b*. (Can you guess why this result is so important? Hint: Does it help if we can ignore the infinite number of solutions *inside* the convex set?)

3. To further highlight the preceding statements, note that optimal solutions do not necessarily exist at corner points of sets *c* and *e*. Can you illustrate this? Although set *c* is convex, the existence of a curvilinear constraint allows for the possibility of a noncorner point optimal solution.

Example 4.4   Blending Problem

Quantitative Butchers, Inc., is a large-scale distributor of dressed meats which specializes in the hotel market and takes great pride in running a highly technological operation. The president (and head butcher) recently completed a night course entitled "Introduction to Management Science" and immediately took the potential of this new field to heart. As it turned out, he did not have long to wait for his first application. Technological Hotels, Inc., another quantitatively oriented firm, has placed an order for a ground meatloaf (mixed ground beef, pork, and veal) for 1,000 pounds according to the following specifications (based on flavor considerations):

a. The ground beef is to be no less than 400 pounds and no more than 600 pounds.
b. The ground pork must be between 200 and 300 pounds.
c. The ground veal must weigh between 100 and 400 pounds.
d. The weight of ground pork must be no more than one and one half times the weight of veal.

The negotiated contract provides that Technological Hotels will pay Quantitative Butchers $1,200 for supplying the meatloaf. An analysis based on stockyard prices, percent useable meat (excess over waste after dressing), and labor costs indicated that the cost per pound of beef, pork, and veal would be, respectively, $0.70, $0.60, and $0.80. Since the availability of meat poses no problems (otherwise, supply constraints would have to be incorporated), the problem becomes one of maximizing contribution to overhead and profit subject to the specified constraints on flavor proportions and the demand constraint of 1,000 pounds.

Immediately, the president recognized this as a problem in linear programming. (It might be noted here, that our analyst decision maker, the head butcher, earned an "A" in the course.) The following presentation illustrates the solution. Let

$$x_1 = \text{pounds of ground beef;}$$
$$x_2 = \text{pounds of ground pork;}$$
$$x_3 = \text{pounds of ground veal.}$$

At first, the problem appears to consist of three variables, which would make for a rather cumbersome graphical solution. The demand constraint, however, allows for the tacit elimination of any one variable, say x_3; that is,

$$x_1 + x_2 + x_3 = 1,000$$

may be rewritten as

$$x_3 = 1,000 - x_1 - x_2.$$

This expression may be substituted into the objective function and constraints wherever x_3 appears. The complete problem may be stated as

maximize

$$
\begin{aligned}
z &= \text{Revenue} - \text{Variable costs} \\
&= 1,200 - 0.70x_1 - 0.60x_2 - 0.80x_3 \\
&= 1,200 - 0.70x_1 - 0.60x_2 - 0.80(1,000 - x_1 - x_2) \\
&= 400 + 0.10x_1 + 0.20x_2
\end{aligned}
$$

subject to

$x_1 \leq 600$	(1)	condition (a)
$x_1 \geq 400$	(2)	condition (a)
$x_2 \leq 300$	(3)	condition (b)
$x_2 \geq 200$	(4)	condition (b)
$x_3 \leq 400$		condition (c)
$1,000 - x_1 - x_2 \leq 400$		
$x_1 + x_2 \geq 600$	(5)	
$x_3 \geq 100$		condition (c)
$1,000 - x_1 - x_2 \geq 100$		
$x_1 + x_2 \leq 900$	(6)	
$x_2 \leq 1.5x_3$		condition (d)
$x_2 \leq 1.5(1,000 - x_1 - x_2)$		
$1.5x_1 + 2.5x_2 \leq 1,500$	(7)	
$x_1, x_2 \geq 0.$		

Figure 4–8 is a graph for the seven constraints and the objective function. Note that constraints (5) and (6) are **redundant constraints**. Redundant constraints are those which contribute nothing to the determination of the solution space. For graphical solutions, they can be identified readily as those constraints which, if removed from the graph, would result in no change in the solution space. The solution space is given by the polygon *abcde*. The objective function has a slope of $-\frac{1}{2}$ and is maximized at extreme point *b*. The coordinates (500, 300) for point *b* are determined from constraints (3) and (7). The optimal solution, therefore, is to send a meatloaf mixture consisting of 500 pounds of ground beef, 300 pounds of

FIGURE 4–8
Solution to Blending Problem

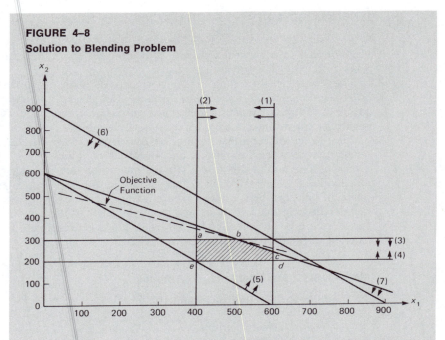

ground pork, and 200 pounds of ground veal. The contribution to overhead and profit is maximized at

$$z = 400 + 0.10(500) + 0.20(300)$$
$$= \$510.$$

Follow-up Exercises

8. What would be the optimal solution if the lower limit on veal were 200
   pounds?

9. What would be the result if at least ten times as much veal as pork
   were specified?

10. Find the optimal solution if veal were to cost $0.30 per pound.

11. Solve Example 4.4 by minimizing cost. Conclusion?

12. Formulate the following:

   a. The three-variable linear programming model (objective function
      and constraints) for Example 4.4. (Hint: There are eight con-
      straints.)

   b. Incorporate a fourth variable, x_4 = pounds of soybean paste. This
      costs $1.20 per pound and must be limited to no more than 100
      pounds in the mixture. Additionally, the mixture is to yield at least
      300 pounds of protein but no more than 110 pounds of fat. Ground
      beef is 28 percent protein and 12 percent fat by weight; ground
      pork is 29 percent protein and 15 percent fat by weight; ground
      veal is 27 percent protein and 10 percent fat by weight; and soy-
      bean paste is 36 percent protein and 8 percent fat by weight.

4.4 THE GENERALIZED LINEAR PROGRAMMING (LP) MODEL

This section reiterates the characteristics of the linear programming (LP) model in a generalized form and analyzes the underlying assumptions.

The linear programming model is concerned with optimizing a *linear objective function* in n decision variables subject to two types of constraints: (1) m **structural constraints** which are *linear,* and (2) n **non-negativity constraints,** one for each decision variable.

The structural constraints are based on the decision variables and reflect the resource limitations and/or other conditions imposed on the problem. The nonnegativity constraints guarantee that each decision variable will be nonnegative. This condition in no way poses an applied problem because, first, almost all applications in economics and management treat variables which assume positive values exclusively, and second, should there be a necessity for allowing negative variables, an algebraic "sleight of hand" can be employed (as illustrated in Section 4.6).

Mathematical Statement of the LP Model

The following symbols are defined:

x_j = jth decision variable.
c_j = Coefficient on jth decision variable in the objective function.
a_{ij} = Coefficient in the ith constraint for the jth variable.
b_i = Right-hand–side constant for the ith constraint.
n = Number of decision variables.
m = Number of structural constraints.

Based on these definitions, the LP model can be stated as optimize (maximize or minimize)

$$z = c_1x_1 + c_2x_2 + \cdots + c_nx_n \qquad (4.4)$$

subject to the structural constraints

$$
\begin{aligned}
a_{11}x_1 + a_{12}x_2 + \cdots + a_{1n}x_n(\leq, \geq, =)b_1 \quad &(1)\\
a_{21}x_1 + a_{22}x_2 + \cdots + a_{2n}x_n(\leq, \geq, =)b_2 \quad &(2)\\
\vdots \qquad\qquad\qquad\qquad\qquad\qquad &\\
a_{m1}x_1 + a_{m2}x_2 + \cdots + a_{mn}x_n(\leq, \geq, =)b_m \quad &(m)
\end{aligned}
\qquad (4.5)
$$

and the nonnegativity constraints

$$
\begin{aligned}
x_1 &\geq 0\\
x_2 &\geq 0\\
&\vdots\\
x_n &\geq 0.
\end{aligned}
\qquad (4.6)
$$

Note that only one sign in ($\leq$, $\geq$, $=$) will pertain to each structural constraint. A more efficient, not to mention elegant, statement of the model can be achieved by employing the summation sign as follows:

optimize

$$z = \sum_{j=1}^{n} c_j x_j \tag{4.7}$$

subject to

$$\sum_{j=1}^{n} a_{ij} x_j (\leq, \geq, =) b_i, \quad i = 1, 2, \ldots, m \tag{4.8}$$

and

$$x_j \geq 0, \quad j = 1, 2, \ldots, n.$$

Follow-up Exercise

13. If the form in Equations (4.7) and (4.8) disturbs you, now is the time to invest effort in familiarizing yourself with the use of summation signs. Because meaningful problems in linear programming are characterized by extensive notation, short-cut symbols are used commonly. As the chapter unfolds, you will find that we rely more and more on the summation sign. With dedication on your part (and clarity on our part), you will become the master of the summation sign. On a separate sheet of paper, start with (4.7) and (4.8) and write them out in the long form, paying close attention to the values which the subscripts assume.

As illustrated graphically, when the number of decision variables is two ($n = 2$), the objective function and constraints plot as **straight lines in two-space;** for three decision variables, the relationships plot as **planes in three-space;** and for n decision variables, although impossible to visualize, the criterion and constraints form what are called **hyperplanes in n-space,** where the intersections of the permissible half-spaces form a convex set (solution space) in n dimensions.

Example 4.5   Product Mix Model

This example is a *dynamic (time-dependent) variation* of the product mix problem. Suppose that a firm has a contract to supply 500 units of product A and 700 units of product B at the end of two time periods, say, quarters.

The objective is to determine how many units should be produced of each product in each time period, subject to labor and raw materials constraints, such that the total of variable and inventory costs is minimized.

Let

$$x_1 = \text{Units made of } A \text{ in Quarter 1.}$$
$$x_2 = \text{Units made of } A \text{ in Quarter 2.}$$
$$x_3 = \text{Units made of } B \text{ in Quarter 1.}$$
$$x_4 = \text{Units made of } B \text{ in Quarter 2.}$$

The variable costs of raw materials and labor vary from one period to the next, as given by Table 4–1.

TABLE 4–1

Variable Costs (dollars per unit)

	Quarter	
Product	1	2
A....................	3	4
B....................	6	5

Units made in the first quarter must be stocked until delivery is made at the end of the second quarter. Without loss of generality assume that carrying costs of inventory are incurred only for one period and are based on the units produced in the first quarter; that is, units produced in the second quarter do not incur inventory costs. A cost analysis indicates that it costs $0.10 per unit per period to inventory product A and $0.20 per unit per period for product B. Furthermore, leftover raw materials from one period to the next cost $0.01 per kilo to store.

The technological data per product and the availability of raw material and labor are given in Table 4–2.

TABLE 4–2

Technological Data and Availabilities

	Per Unit of Product		Availability in Quarter	
	A	B	1	2
Labor (hours)..................	0.5	0.8	350	500
Raw materials (kilos).........	10	7	6,000	4,000

For example, it takes 0.5 hour of labor and 10 kilos of raw material to produce each unit of product A. Note that the same raw material goes into both products and that excess raw material in the first quarter can be inventoried for use in the next quarter. Further assume that unused raw material at the end of the second quarter has been accounted for in the cost of products and that excess labor either has alternative uses or was not commissioned in the first place; that is, the availability figures in Table 4–2 are maxima, so the difference between the labor used and the labor available represents the amount not hired.

The objective function to be minimized is

$z =$ Variable costs $(3x_1 + 4x_2 + 6x_3 + 5x_4)$ + Product inventory costs $(0.1x_1 + 0.2x_3)$
$+$ Raw materials inventory costs $[0.01(6{,}000 - 10x_1 - 7x_3)]$
$= 60 + 3x_1 + 4x_2 + 6.13x_3 + 5x_4.$

Note that the appearance of a constant in the criterion is not part of the generalized LP formulation. In the actual solution to this problem, the constant would be ignored and added in as a "fixed charge" following the solution. Further note that the term $(6{,}000 - 10x_1 - 7x_3)$ represents unused raw material in the first quarter. The constraints are based on

Labor Availability:

$$0.5x_1 \quad\quad\quad + 0.8x_3 \quad\quad\quad \leq 350 \tag{1}$$
$$0.5x_2 \quad\quad\quad + 0.8x_4 \leq 500 \tag{2}$$

Raw Material Availability:

$$10x_1 \quad\quad\quad + \quad 7x_3 \quad\quad\quad \leq \quad 6{,}000 \tag{3}$$
$$10x_2 \quad\quad\quad + \quad 7x_4 \leq \quad 4{,}000 + (6{,}000 - 10x_1 - 7x_3)$$
$$10x_1 + 10x_2 + 7x_3 + \quad 7x_4 \leq 10{,}000 \tag{4}$$

Supply Requirements:

$$x_1 + x_2 \quad\quad\quad\quad\quad\quad = 500 \tag{5}$$
$$x_3 + \quad x_4 = 700 \tag{6}$$

and the nonnegativity conditions $x_j \geq 0, \quad j = 1,2,3,4.$

Note that $0.5x_1$ and $0.8x_3$ represent, respectively, the hours used up in the production of products A and B in the first quarter; hence, constraint (1) states that hours used in Quarter 1 must not exceed the available hours (350). Can you verbalize each of the remaining constraints?

Follow-up Exercises

14. Write down appropriate constraints for the following conditions:

   a. No more than 600 combined units of products A and B can be stored due to a shortage of available space in the warehouse.
   b. At least 200 units but no more than 400 units of product A are to be produced in the first quarter.
   c. The production of product B must equal or exceed the production of product A in each quarter.

**15. Can you reformulate the objective function such that inventory carrying costs are based on average inventories, that is, (beginning inventory + ending inventory)/2? Assume uniform (linear) buildup of product inventories and uniform depletion of the raw material inventory. Note that carrying costs are now incurred in both periods. Compare this new objective function to the previous objective function. Do you think the optimal solution will change?

Underlying Assumptions

The deterministic (nonprobabilistic) nature of the LP model and the linearity assumptions make for certain tacit assumptions in applied problems. Although these assumptions are either met or closely approximated in many applications, the user must be thoroughly familiar with their implications and limitations in order to avoid misusing the LP model. These assumptions, by the way, relate to the issue of validation in our paradigm of Chapter 1.

The following underlying assumptions are a direct result of the characteristics of the LP model:

1. The model is **deterministic.** This means that each coefficient (c_j, a_{ij}, b_i) is fixed and known with certainty. In reality, this would be very unusual. Not only does the estimation of each coefficient require sampling and extrapolation into the future but also, in most cases, the coefficients are random variables with underlying probability distributions. For example, the costs in Table 4–1 and the technological data in Table 4–2 are, most probably, random variables from unknown probability distributions. They would have to be estimated by the arithmetic means of samples based on available (or subjective) data which have been projected into the quarters when production will take place. If you studied sampling theory in a basic statistics course, you should realize that the sample mean, used to estimate the population mean for some parameter in the LP model, is itself a random variable which is subject to fluctuations. In short, the estimation of coefficients in the LP model involves great care. Fortunately, the sensitivity of results to fluctuations in the coefficients can be evaluated by **sensitivity analysis** (Chapter 6) and by advanced programming models known as **parametric** and **stochastic linear programming** (Chapter 10).

2. The model is **proportional.** This condition follows directly from the linearity assumptions for the objective function and constraints. This means that the criterion and the constraints expand or contract proportionally to the level of each activity. For example, doubling the number of units of product B produced in the second quarter (variable x_4) results in a doubling of its cost contribution and a doubling of its labor and material requirements. These conditions represent *constant returns to scale* rather than *economies or diseconomies of scale*. These conditions will not hold if, for instance, the cost coefficients in the objective function or the technological coefficients in the constraints varied as a function of the level for each activity; that is, marginal costs may decrease and production efficiency may increase as the level of output increases. For such problems, linearity assumptions may hold over specific ranges of output, allowing the use of **piecewise linear programming procedures** (Section 4.6); in other special cases, **nonlinear programming algorithms** may be used (Chapter 10).

3. The model is **additive.** The assumption of proportionality guarantees linearity if and only if joint effects or interactions are nonexistent.

This latter assumption implies that the total contribution of all activities (to the criterion or the constraints) is identical to the sum of the contribution for each activity individually. Put another way, "the whole is equal to the sum of its parts." This would not be true if, for example, a company produces two products which compete in the market; the resulting *cross elasticities* would make for interactions which would be reflected by multiplicative terms in the profit function; that is, a change in demand for one will affect the demand for the other and the prices of both. With respect to Example 4.5, increasing the level of product B may affect the labor coefficient of product A (0.5 in Table 4-2) if, in so doing, skilled or experienced labor is diverted from product A. Should this be the case, the model would not be additive. If joint effects are minor, however, a practical solution might be obtained by assuming additivity.

4. The model is **divisible.** This means that fractional levels for the decision variables are permissible, a condition which is evident when one considers that the objective function and constraints were treated as continuous functions in the graphical analysis. Clearly, some problems require integer solutions; for example, how many tankers per month should be leased to transport crude oil from the Middle East to the United States? The decision variables in Example 4.5 are not necessarily restricted to integer values if one assumes the validity of in-process products, that is, products at various stages of production. If the standardized LP model is used for problems requiring integer solutions, then two obvious results are possible: Either the optimal solution will include all integer values for the activities or it will not. The former result is not uncommon and neatly circumvents the problem. The latter result can be treated by "fudging," that is, rounding each fractional answer to the nearest whole number. Great care must be taken in doing so, however, for such a procedure may yield one of two possibilities: (*a*) the resulting solution may not be feasible; that is, it may lie outside the solution space; or (*b*) the resulting solution may not be the optimal *integer* solution. For such cases, **integer programming models** (Chapter 8) may be warranted.

4.5 SCENARIOS AND FORMULATIONS

The implementation of linear programming can be approached in four stages: (1) recognition, (2) formulation, (3) solution, and (4) interpretation. (Can you relate this to the eight-step paradigm of Chapter 1?) For the most part, the solution of linear programming models (Chapter 5) is standardized and readily available in commercial computer packages. Although issues such as large-scale problems and codes which are computationally efficient still present challenges to the operations researcher, the "state of the art" for the solution of such models is more than adequate. The recognition and correct formulation of problems in a linear optimization framework, however, still represent both a formidable challenge and an opportunity for innovation. Of equal importance is the interpretation of results (Chapters 5 and 6), especially in light of the inherent assumptions of the model.

In the examples which follow, it will be assumed that the LP model as a solution to the problem has been recognized. The examples therefore will stress the formulation of the model, a process which includes three distinct mathematical parts: (1) objective function; (2) structural constraints based on resource limitations and/or other conditions imposed on the problem; and (3) nonnegativity constraints. It goes without saying that the correct mathematical statement of the problem is contingent upon the preliminary step of identifying and defining the relevant variables and restrictive conditions.

Example 4.6   Transportation Model

Transportation models are, perhaps, the most extensively used linear models from an economic viewpoint. Oil companies alone literally spend millions of dollars annually to implement these models. This example introduces a simple version of the classical model. A more detailed presentation is left to Chapter 7.

Suppose a chemical company manufactures liquid hydrogen at two different locations in the Northeast and must supply three storage depots in the same geographic region. Table 4–3 provides the relevant data for a given planning horizon.

TABLE 4–3

Transportation Data: Shipping Costs (dollars per 1,000 gallons)

| | Depot | | | Supply |
Plant	1	2	3	(1,000 gallons)
1...........................	30	4	8	50
2...........................	5	10	20	70
Demand (1,000 gallons).........	40	60	20	120

Let

x_1 = Gallons (thousands) shipped from plant 1 to depot 1.
x_2 = Gallons (thousands) shipped from plant 1 to depot 2.
x_3 = Gallons (thousands) shipped from plant 1 to depot 3.
x_4 = Gallons (thousands) shipped from plant 2 to depot 1.
x_5 = Gallons (thousands) shipped from plant 2 to depot 2.
x_6 = Gallons (thousands) shipped from plant 2 to depot 3.

The objective is to minimize transportation costs, as given by

$$z = 30x_1 + 4x_2 + 8x_3 + 5x_4 + 10x_5 + 20x_6$$

such that the **supply constraints**

$$x_1 + x_2 + x_3 \qquad\qquad = 50 \qquad\qquad (1)$$
$$x_4 + x_5 + x_6 = 70 \qquad\qquad (2)$$

the **demand constraints**

$$x_1 \qquad\qquad + x_4 \qquad\qquad = 40 \qquad (3)$$
$$x_2 \qquad\qquad + x_5 \qquad = 60 \qquad (4)$$
$$x_3 \qquad\qquad + x_6 = 20 \qquad (5)$$

and the nonnegativity constraints $x_j \geq 0$, $j = 1, \ldots, 6$ are all met.

Since the total supply available equals the total demand, it is assumed that each plant must produce to its designated capacity. The supply constraints, (1) and (2), indicate that shipments from each plant must equal the designated capacity of the plant. Similarly, the demand constraints, (3) through (5), can be stated as "total shipments from the two plants to each depot must equal the demand at the depot."

A more convenient notational form is achieved by letting x_{ij} represent the shipment from plant i to depot j (note the consistency of this notation with Table 4–3). Thus,

minimize

$$z = 30x_{11} + 4x_{12} + 8x_{13} + 5x_{21} + 10x_{22} + 20x_{23}$$

subject to

$$x_{11} + x_{12} + x_{13} = 50 \qquad (1)$$
$$x_{21} + x_{22} + x_{23} = 70 \qquad (2)$$
$$x_{11} + x_{21} \qquad = 40 \qquad (3)$$
$$x_{12} + x_{22} \qquad = 60 \qquad (4)$$
$$x_{13} + x_{23} \qquad = 20 \qquad (5)$$

and $x_{ij} \geq 0$ for all i and j.

In general, for m origins and n destinations, with s_i supplied by the ith origin and d_j demanded by the jth destination, the problem is to minimize

$$z = \sum_{i=1}^{m} \sum_{j=1}^{n} c_{ij} x_{ij}$$

subject to

$$\sum_{j=1}^{n} x_{ij} = s_i, \quad i = 1, 2, \ldots, m,$$

$$\sum_{i=1}^{m} x_{ij} = d_j, \quad j = 1, 2, \ldots, n,$$

and $x_{ij} \geq 0$ for all i and j, where x_{ij} is defined as before c_{ij} is the cost per unit of transporting from origin i to destination j.

Follow-up Exercises

16. Show that the sum of constraints (1) and (2) is identical to the sum of constraints (3), (4), and (5). Interpret the meaning of this sum. Show that the preceding result holds in general; that is,

$$\sum_i s_i = \sum_j d_j.$$

17. Suppose that the supply and demand constraints were stated in terms of inequalities—($\leq$) and ($\geq$), respectively—rather than in terms of equalities.

   a. Can you reformulate this problem to fit the above mold by adding a "dummy" destination which "picks up" the excess supply when $\sum_i s_i > \sum_j d_j$? Would you say that this dummy represents "unused capacity?"

   b. What "dummy" must be introduced if $\sum_i s_i < \sum_j d_j$? Would you say that this dummy represents "unfulfilled demand?"

Example 4.7 Capital Budgeting Model

In the static version of the capital budgeting (rationing) problem, the decision-making unit—be it a department in a private firm, nonprofit organization, or governmental agency—has various mutually exclusive projects it can undertake in a given time period. Each project is characterized by a derived benefit and an associated cost. The objective is to determine which projects or portions of projects will maximize overall benefit subject to a budgetary constraint.

The following symbols are defined:

x_j = Proportion of the jth project undertaken.
c_j = Return (benefit) associated with the jth project.
a_j = Cost of the jth project.
b = Overall budgetary constraint (dollars available for investing).
n = Number of projects available.

The typical problem is formulated as

maximize

$$z = \sum_{j=1}^{n} c_j x_j$$

subject to

$$\sum_{j=1}^{n} a_j x_j \leq b,$$

$$x_j \leq 1, \quad j = 1, \ldots, n,$$
$$x_j \geq 0, \quad j = 1, \ldots, n.$$

Thus, z is a measure of total return, the first constraint represents the budgetary restriction, and the remaining constraints guarantee that the x_j's will be proportions between zero and one.

In many applications, the x_j's are not allowed to take on fractional values and some projects may not be mutually exclusive.[2] Furthermore, in strictly financial applications, the c_j's typically are expressed in terms of *net present values*. Likewise, the a_j's and b are expressed in present dollars according to the concept of present value.[3]

The problem associated with the selection of projects need not be restricted to the firm. For example, the Department of Health, Education, and

[2] We relax these assumptions in Chapter 8 (Example 8.10).
[3] See footnote 7 on page 59 for a definition of present value.

Welfare (HEW) and the Environmental Protection Agency (EPA) are both confronted with capital budgeting decisions: Which projects should be selected such that overall benefits are maximized and budgetary and other constraints are satisfied? As in all decisions relating to the public sector (on a benefit-cost basis), the most difficult part of the formulation is the definition and quantitative determination of social benefits. Such returns may be classified broadly as *direct and indirect benefits.* For example, antipollution projects under the auspices of the EPA may have direct benefits in terms of cost savings to society, for example, reduced maintenance of buildings and homes and dollar savings relating to the medical treatment of pollution-related illnesses, and indirect benefits as reflected by a better quality of life. Based on these comments and a moment's reflection, one can appreciate the complexities of analyses and value judgments inherent in public welfare applications.

To illustrate, suppose that a team of management scientists, welfare economists, sociologists, and political scientists has analyzed a set of seven long-term projects for HEW as given by Table 4-4. Note that the

TABLE 4-4

Data for HEW Projects

Project	Benefit-Cost Ratio	Present Value of Cost (dollars in millions)
1	1.10	250
2	1.25	400
3	1.40	750
4	1.30	500
5	1.15	450
6	0.90	300
7	1.05	200

return on investment for a project is equal to the benefit-cost ratio minus one. For example, the return on project 1 is 10 percent (that is, $1.10 - 1.00$). What is the return from project 6?

If the total budget is $2 billion ($2,000 million) and the objective is to maximize the sum of *net benefits,* then the usual LP formulation (the "pork barrel" aside) is given by

maximize

$$z = (0.1)(250)x_1 + (0.25)(400)x_2 + (0.40)(750)x_3 + (0.30)(500)x_4 + (0.15)(450)x_5$$
$$+ (-0.10)(300)x_6 + (0.05)(200)x_7$$
$$= 25x_1 + 100x_2 + 300x_3 + 150x_4 + 67.5x_5 - 30x_6 + 10x_7$$

subject to

$$250x_1 + 400x_2 + 750x_3 + 500x_4 + 450x_5 + 300x_6 + 200x_7 \leq 2,000 \quad (1)$$
$$x_1 \leq 1 \quad (2)$$
$$x_2 \leq 1 \quad (3)$$
$$x_3 \leq 1 \quad (4)$$
$$x_4 \leq 1 \quad (5)$$
$$x_5 \leq 1 \quad (6)$$
$$x_6 \leq 1 \quad (7)$$
$$x_7 \leq 1 \quad (8)$$

and $x_j \geq 0$, $j = 1, \ldots, 7$.

Now suppose that other "considerations" must be taken into account: The combined present value of expenses for projects 1 and 7 must exceed $300 million; the combined present value of expenses for projects 3 and 4 must be less than $700 million; and the present value of the amount expended on project 7 must be exactly 40 percent of the amount expended on project 3. These three additional constraints are expressed, respectively, as follows:

$$250x_1 \qquad\qquad\qquad\qquad + 200x_7 \geq 300 \tag{9}$$
$$750x_3 + 500x_4 \qquad\qquad\quad \leq 700 \tag{10}$$
$$200x_7 = (0.4)(750)x_3$$

or

$$-300x_3 \qquad\qquad\qquad + 200x_7 = 0. \tag{11}$$

Follow-up Exercises

18. Do you agree with the interpretation that a fractional value for a project means a smaller version of the project? Is this practical? What underlying assumption in the LP model necessitates the specification of fractional values? (In Chapters 8 and 9 we take up the capital budgeting problem with $x_j = 0$ or 1.)

19. In the context of this problem, what are the implications relating to the assumption of proportionality?

20. Do you have quarrel with the interpretation of "benefits" for this example?

21. Formulate the dynamic capital budgeting problem over m periods for n projects using the following symbols:

    x_{ij} = Proportion of the jth project undertaken in the ith period.
    c_{ij} = Return associated with the jth project in the ith period.
    a_{ij} = Cost of the jth project in the ith period.
    b_i = Budget for the ith period.

    Make sure you stipulate the condition that no more than 100 percent of the jth project can be undertaken across all time periods. Does this make $x_{ij} \leq 1$ for all i and j redundant? Explicitly state the model given the following: $m = 2$, $n = 3$, $c_{11} = 7$, $c_{21} = 4$, $c_{12} = 3$, $c_{22} = 9$, $c_{13} = 2$, $c_{23} = 10$, $a_{11} = 5$, $a_{21} = 2$, $a_{12} = 4$, $a_{22} = 7$, $a_{13} = 2$, $a_{23} = 6$, $b_1 = 9$, and $b_2 = 12$.

Example 4.8   Media Mix Model

The media mix problem is concerned with the allocation of the advertising budget among media (television, radio, magazines, newspapers, and outdoor advertising) such that some criterion is maximized. Typical criteria include—in decreasing order of ease in formulation and increasing order of desirability or importance—total exposure, frequency (impact), reach (coverage), sales, and profits.[4] *Exposure per time period for a given medium* is defined as the product of (1) the number of members of the target group exposed to one insertion in the medium and (2) the number of advertisements in that medium. *Total exposure* then is the sum of exposures across media. *Frequency* is defined as the average number of advertisements seen by each potential consumer during one time period of interest. *Reach* is the total number of target-group consumers exposed to at least one advertisement in a given time period.

Suppose that a trade magazine reports the rated exposure (people per month per dollar of advertising outlay) for each of the above five media, respectively, as 22, 12, 15, 10, and 5. The advertising group of a company is to develop an optimal media mix which is restricted to the following conditions:

1. The total advertising budget is one million dollars.
2. No more than 50 percent of the budget is to be expended on the airwaves (radio and television).
3. No more than 30 percent of the budget is to be expended on any one medium.
4. The rated exposure market segmentation targets indicated in Table 4–5 must be satisfied.

TABLE 4–5

Rated Exposures by Market Segments

Market Segment	Total Exposure Targets (100,000 people per month)		Rated Exposure by Medium* (people per month per dollar)				
	Minimum	Maximum	(1)	(2)	(3)	(4)	(5)
Youth................	25	35	10	5	1	0	1
Women...............	40	—	6	4	7	2	2
College educated........	35	—	3	1	4	5	1

* (1) = Television. (4) = Newspapers.
   (2) = Radio. (5) = Outdoor advertising.
   (3) = Magazines.

Further, let the dollar expenditures ($100,000 per month) be represented by x_1 for television, x_2 for radio, x_3 for magazines, x_4 for newspapers, and x_5 for outdoor advertising. Note that the unit of measure for expenditures (hundred thousand) makes the divisibility assumption quite feasible.

If exposure is assumed to be deterministic, to be constant per dollar of advertising expenditure (proportionality), and to be free of media interaction effects (additivity), then the problem may be formulated as

maximize

$$z = 22x_1 + 12x_2 + 15x_3 + 10x_4 + 5x_5$$

subject to

---

[4] For a more detailed presentation, see David B. Montgomery and Glen L. Urban, *Management Science in Marketing* (Englewood Cliffs, N.J.: Prentice-Hall, Inc., 1969).

$$x_1 + x_2 + x_3 + x_4 + x_5 \leq 10 \tag{1}$$
$$x_1 + x_2 \qquad\qquad\qquad \leq 5 \tag{2}$$
$$x_1 \qquad\qquad\qquad\qquad \leq 3 \tag{3}$$
$$x_2 \qquad\qquad\qquad \leq 3 \tag{4}$$
$$x_3 \qquad\qquad \leq 3 \tag{5}$$
$$x_4 \qquad \leq 3 \tag{6}$$
$$x_5 \leq 3 \tag{7}$$
$$10x_1 + 5x_2 + x_3 \qquad + x_5 \geq 25 \tag{8}$$
$$10x_1 + 5x_2 + x_3 \qquad + x_5 \leq 35 \tag{9}$$
$$6x_1 + 4x_2 + 7x_3 + 2x_4 + 2x_5 \geq 40 \tag{10}$$
$$3x_1 + x_2 + 4x_3 + 5x_4 + x_5 \geq 35 \tag{11}$$

and $x_j \geq 0$, $\qquad j = 1, \ldots, 5$.

Thus, $22x_1$ is the exposure (in hundred thousands per month) provided by the television expenditures, $12x_2$ is the exposure generated by radio, and so on. Similarly, constraint (1) satisfies condition (1), constraint 2) reflects condition (2), constraints (3) through (7) meet condition (3), and constraints (8) through (11) accommodate condition (4).

Follow-up Exercises

22. Do the divisibility, proportionality, and additivity assumptions for this problem seem reasonable? Why or why not?

23. Should there be concern about overlap among market segments? Can you propose how you might avoid this issue in a formulation?

24. Describe how you would formulate the problem if *options* were available within media? As an example, assume that rated exposures are available for three television stations, four radio stations, five magazines, two newspapers, and six billboard locations. How many variables characterize this problem?

25. Describe how you would formulate the problem if *scheduling over time* were required? For example, suppose that monthly allocations to the five media are required over a 12-month planning horizon and that exposures are affected by seasonal factors. How many variables would there be in this time-dependent (dynamic) media mix problem?

**26. Formulate a generalized LP model for the dynamic media mix problem using the following symbols:

x_{jkt} = Expenditure in the kth option of the jth medium in the tth time period.

e_{jkt} = Effectiveness of the kth option of the jth medium in the tth time period.

c_{jkt} = Monetary constraint for the kth option of the jth medium in the tth time period.

b_{jt} = Monetary constraint for the jth medium in the tth time period.

B_t = Overall budgetary constraint in the tth time period.

E_{jktp} = Effectiveness of the kth option of the jth medium in the tth time period for the pth market segment.

U_{tp} = Minimum target for the pth market segment in the tth time period.

V_{tp} = Maximum target for the pth market segment in the tth time period.

P = Number of market segments.

T = Number of periods.

M = Number of media.

n_j = Number of options in the jth medium.

Hint: Multiple subscripting may present a formidable "hurdle" for you in the context of the LP model. Don't let it throw you; it's simply a convenience. For four time periods ($T = 4$), five media ($M = 5$), and three options per medium ($n_1 = n_2 = n_3 = n_4 = n_5 = 3$), the total number of variables is 60 ($4 \times 5 \times 3$).

27. What special problems would be posed by "carry-over" effects among time periods in the dynamic media mix problem?

Example 4.9   Financial Mix Model

Another variation of the mix problem, besides product mix (Example 4.5) and media mix (Example 4.8), is the financial mix problem.

Consider a company which must produce two products over a given production period which is, say, one quarter in length. The company can pay for materials and labor from two sources: company funds and borrowed funds.

The firm faces three decisions: (1) How many units should it produce of product 1? (2) How many units should it produce of product 2? and (3) How much money should it borrow to support the production of the two items? In making these decisions, the firm wishes to maximize the profit contribution subject to the conditions stated below.

1. The company's products are enjoying a *seller's market;* hence, the company can sell as many units of the products as it can produce. Furthermore, the amount the company can produce is small, relative to the overall market; so the amount produced has no effect on market prices. The company, therefore, would like to produce as many units as possible subject to production capacity and financial constraints. The capacity constraints, together with cost and price data, are given in Table 4–6.

TABLE 4–6
Capacity, Price, and Cost Data

Product	Selling Price (dollars per unit)	Cost of Production (dollars per unit)	Required Hours per Unit in Department A	B	C
1	14	10	0.5	0.3	0.2
2	11	8	0.3	0.4	0.1
Available hours per quarter			500	400	200

2. The available company funds during the production period amount to $30,000.
3. A bank will loan up to $20,000 per quarter at an interest rate of 5 percent (0.05) per quarter providing the company's *acid (quick) test ratio* is at least 3 to 1 while the loan is outstanding. Recall that the acid-test ratio is given by the ratio of (1) cash on hand plus accounts receivable to (2) accounts payable.

4. As depicted by Figure 4–9, payments for labor and materials are made at the end of the production period; hence any needed credit is obtained at that point in time. Shipments are made, on credit, at the end of the production period. Finally, sales revenue is received and outstanding liabilities are paid off at the end of the next period.

Let x_1 represent the number of units of product 1 produced, x_2 represent the number of units of product 2 produced, and x_3 represent the amount of money borrowed.

The profit contribution per unit of each product is given by the selling price less the variable cost of production. Total profit is computed by summing the profits from producing the two products *less* the cost associated with any borrowed funds. The objective function is stated as

$$z = (14 - 10)x_1 + (11 - 8)x_2 - 0.05x_3$$
$$= 4x_1 + 3x_2 - 0.05x_3.$$

The production capacity constraints for each department, as given by Table 4–6, are

$$0.5x_1 + 0.3x_2 \leq 500 \qquad (1)$$
$$0.3x_1 + 0.4x_2 \leq 400 \qquad (2)$$
$$0.2x_1 + 0.1x_2 \leq 200. \qquad (3)$$

The funds available for production include both the $30,000 cash that the firm now possesses and any borrowed funds. Consequently, production is

FIGURE 4–9.

Time-Dependent Financial Policies for Example 4.9

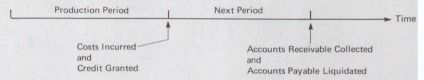

limited to the extent that funds are available to pay for production costs. The constraint expressing this relationship is

$$10x_1 + 8x_2 \leq 30,000 + x_3$$

or

$$10x_1 + 8x_2 - x_3 \leq 30,000. \qquad (4)$$

The borrowed funds constraint, condition (3), is

$$x_3 \leq 20,000. \qquad (5)$$

The constraint based on the acid-test condition is developed as follows:

$$\frac{\text{Cash on hand after production} + \text{Accounts receivable}}{\text{Accounts payable}} \geq 3$$
$$\frac{(30,000 + x_3 - 10x_1 - 8x_2) + 14x_1 + 11x_2}{x_3 + 0.05x_3} \geq 3$$
$$30,000 + x_3 + 4x_1 + 3x_2 \geq 3.15x_3$$
$$4x_1 + 3x_2 - 2.15x_3 \geq -30,000$$
$$-4x_1 - 3x_2 + 2.15x_3 \leq 30,000. \qquad (6)$$

Note that the first term in the denominator, x_3, represents the principal liability and the second term represents the interest payable on that liability. Also note that constraint (6) was altered by multiplying the preceding line by -1. The reason for expressing the right-hand–side constant as a positive number will become clear in the next chapter.

Finally, the nonnegativity constraints are expressed as $x_j \geq 0$, $j = 1, 2, 3$.

Follow-up Exercises

28. Do the decision variables satisfy the divisibility assumptions? What recourse do you have if they do not?

29. What do the additivity and proportionality assumptions imply with regard to Table 4–6?

30. How would you handle the condition that, on the average, only 60 percent of the accounts receivable is collected by the company at the end of the next period?

31. Suppose that labor and material expenses were paid out on a weekly basis. Describe how this might modify the original problem.

32. Modify the example to include an opportunity cost of 3 percent per quarter with the use of company funds.

**33. Can you formulate this problem for a planning horizon of one year (four production periods)? Assume that the cash on hand at the end of a period is augmented by the cash inflows (accounts receivable collected) and depleted by the cash outflows (costs of production, principal repayment, and interest). On the average, 60 percent of accounts receivable is collected one period hence, 30 percent two periods hence, and 9 percent three periods hence (1 percent default).

**34. Modify the preceding problem by incorporating the stipulation that 50 percent of a period's profits must be reserved for dividend payments and capital investment.

**Example 4.10　Solid Waste Management—A Blending Problem[5]

In years past, the problems associated with the disposal of solid wastes (residues) from production processes were considered to be incidental to the problems associated with the production of the primary products. Recently, both the social and economic consequences of solid wastes have forced the explicit consideration of solid waste management. The following example clearly shows that decisions regarding the most efficient manner to produce a set of primary products completely interact with decisions pertaining to the efficient utilization of solid wastes.

A firm produces two primary products, each of which is manufactured through a chemical process which blends three raw materials. Table 4–7 shows how these materials must be blended in order to produce each of the two products. For example, it shows that at least 20 percent of the weight of Product A must be accounted for by Material 1, at least 40 percent by Material 2, and no more than 10 percent by Material 3. Table 4–7 also shows the market prices for each product; it is assumed that the firm, within its normal level of plant operations, can sell as many units of each product as it wants without affecting these prices.

---

[5] Adapted from Albert J. Simone, "A Linear Programming Approach to Solid Waste Management," unpublished paper, University of Cincinnati, 1971.

TABLE 4–7

Product and Price Specifications

Primary Product	Product Specifications	Unit Price
A.........	At least 20% of Material 1 At least 40% of Material 2 No more than 10% of Material 3	$3.00
B.........	At least 10% of Material 1 No more than 30% of Material 3	2.50

In order to guarantee the ready supply of materials, the firm has agreed to purchase certain minimal amounts of each material during each planning period. Moreover, the physical capacities of the firm's manufacturing facilities limit the amount of each material it can handle during the planning period. The upper and lower bounds on the amount of each material that can be processed each period, along with the unit cost of each material, are shown in Table 4–8.

TABLE 4–8

Material Limits and Costs

Material	Minimum (lb.)	Maximum (lb.)	Unit Cost
1.........	2,000	6,000	$2.10
2.........	3,000	5,000	1.60
3.........	4,000	7,000	1.00

The nature of the manufacturing process is such that only a fraction of each material going into each product contributes directly to the primary products. The fraction which is not utilized in the primary products, known as the *coefficient of waste,* can be either (1) recycled (the material's chemical properties have changed as a result of the initial manufacturing operation) into a second related manufacturing process and turned into secondary Products *C* and *D*, or (2) disposed of in part or in total at a specific cost to the firm.

Table 4–9 shows the waste coefficients. For example, 10 percent of the amount of Material 1 initially processed into Product *A* is left over as a residue, while 20 percent of that processed into Product *B* results in a residue.

TABLE 4–9

Waste Coefficients

	Product	
Material	A	B
1..........	0.1	0.2
2..........	0.2	0.2
3..........	0.4	0.5

Assume that secondary Product C can be blended by mixing any amounts of the residues from Materials 1, 2, and 3 derived from Product A with the original (unprocessed) Material 1, as long as the latter is exactly 20 percent of the mix by weight. Similarly, secondary Product D can be blended by mixing any amounts of the residues from Materials 1, 2, and 3 derived from Product B with the original Material 2, as long as the latter is exactly 30 percent by weight of the mix. No waste reduction occurs in the manufacturing process associated with the production of these secondary products. The net revenue per pound (after all associated secondary production expenses) for Products C and D are, respectively, $0.60 and $0.10.

Residue waste materials that are derived from the production of Products A and B and that are not used to manufacture Products C and D must be disposed of. Because the properties of the residue from different material-product combinations differ, the cost of disposing of each residue material not employed in a secondary product differs depending on the primary products from which it was derived. Table 4–10 shows these disposal costs.

TABLE 4–10

Disposal Costs

Material	Unit Cost	
	Product A	Product B
1...........	$0.10	$0.05
2...........	0.10	0.05
3...........	0.20	0.40

The problem facing the firm then, is to decide:

1. How many units of Materials 1, 2, and 3 it should purchase.
2. How much of each material to allocate to primary Products A and B.
3. How much of each material to allocate to secondary Products C and D.
4. How much of each of the residue materials obtained from producing Products A and B should be disposed of immediately rather than recycled into Products C and D.

The firm must make these decisions in such a way that the resulting earnings (total revenue minus total cost) are the largest attainable. This optimal amount of earnings must be obtained without violating the upper and lower limits on material purchases and without deviating from the product specifications on material content. At the same time, the firm must explicitly consider the various waste coefficients; the prices of Products A and B; the unit costs of Materials 1, 2, and 3; the net unit contribution to profit from Products C and D; and the unit cost of disposing of each material-product residue combination. (Try solving this problem by other than analytic means!)

Note that the manufacture of secondary Products C and D is dependent on an *initial commitment* of Materials 1 and 2, respectively, to Products C and D as well as on the residue from the production of primary Products A and B. Thus, secondary product and waste disposal decisions must be made at the same time that primary product decisions are made. From a total systems point of view, the optimal overall policy requires interdependence

TABLE 4–11

Symbols for Material Allocation

	Allocated to Product			
Pounds of Material	A	B	C	D
1...........	x_1	x_2	x_3	—
2...........	x_4	x_5	—	x_6
3...........	x_7	x_8	—	—

of these decisions; that is, the secondary product and/or waste disposal decisions must not be made after the primary product decision has been made.

The adopted notation for the allocation of materials to products is given in Table 4–11. The notation for residues which are allocated to Products C and D is given in Table 4–12. Figure 4–10 summarizes the product–raw materials–residue relationships.

TABLE 4–12

Symbols for Residue Allocation

	Allocated to Product	
Pounds of Residue from	C	D
Material 1—Product A	x_9	—
Material 2—Product A	x_{10}	—
Material 3—Product A	x_{11}	—
Material 1—Product B	—	x_{12}
Material 2—Product B	—	x_{13}
Material 3—Product B	—	x_{14}

Total profit (z) is defined as total revenue (r) minus total material costs (c) minus waste disposal costs (w); that is,

$$z = r - c - w.$$

Total revenue is determined by

$$r = 3.00\,(0.9x_1 + 0.8x_4 + 0.6x_7) + 2.50\,(0.8x_2 + 0.8x_5 + 0.5x_8)$$
$$+ 0.6(x_3 + x_9 + x_{10} + x_{11}) + 0.1\,(x_6 + x_{12} + x_{13} + x_{14})$$

where the first term represents the price of Product A times the number of pounds of Product A produced, the second term represents the price of Product B times the number of pounds produced, the third term represents the net contribution of Product C times the number of pounds of Product C produced, and the last term the net contribution of Product D times the number of pounds produced.[6] Total material cost is given by

$$c = 2.10\,(x_1 + x_2 + x_3) + 1.60\,(x_4 + x_5 + x_6) + 1.00\,(x_7 + x_8)$$

---

[6] Since the waste coefficients for Material 1–Product A, Material 2–Product A, and Material 3–Product A are, respectively, 0.1, 0.2, and 0.4, it follows that x_1 pounds of Material 1, x_4 pounds of Material 2, and x_7 pounds of Material 3 will yield $(0.9x_1 + 0.8x_4 + 0.6x_7)$ pounds of Product A. Right?

FIGURE 4–10

Relationships for Solid Waste Management Problem

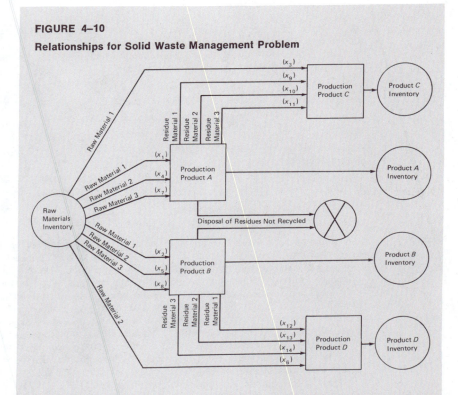

where the first, second, and third terms represent, respectively, the multiplication of the unit costs of Materials 1, 2, and 3 (Table 4–8) and the quantities of Materials 1, 2, and 3 purchased. The waste disposal cost is

$$w = 0.1(0.1x_1 - x_9) + 0.1(0.2x_4 - x_{10}) + 0.2(0.4x_7 - x_{11})$$
$$+ 0.05(0.2x_2 - x_{12}) + 0.05(0.2x_5 - x_{13}) + 0.4(0.5x_8 - x_{14})$$

where each term represents the multiplication of the cost of disposing of a unit (pound) of a given material-product residue and the number of units of the material-product residue left over after all primary and secondary production have taken place.

Substituting the expressions for r, c, and w into the equation for z, multiplying all factors, and collecting all terms, we get the objective function which is to be maximized:

$$z = 0.59x_1 - 0.11x_2 - 1.5x_3 + 0.78x_4 + 0.39x_5 - 1.5x_6 + 0.72x_7$$
$$+ 0.05x_8 + 0.70x_9 + 0.70x_{10} + 0.80x_{11} + 0.15x_{12} + 0.15x_{13} + 0.5x_{14}.$$

From Table 4–8 the linear inequalities which express the least and greatest amounts of each material that can be processed are:

$$x_1 + x_2 + x_3 \geq 2,000 \tag{1}$$
$$x_1 + x_2 + x_3 \leq 6,000 \tag{2}$$
$$x_4 + x_5 + x_6 \geq 3,000 \tag{3}$$
$$x_4 + x_5 + x_6 \leq 5,000 \tag{4}$$
$$x_7 + x_8 \qquad \geq 4,000 \tag{5}$$
$$x_7 + x_8 \qquad \leq 7,000. \tag{6}$$

For example, constraint (1) says that the number of pounds of Material 1 allocated to Products A, B, and C must be at least 2,000.

From Tables 4–7 and 4–9, the constraints which express the material content specifications for Products A and B are

$$0.9x_1 \geq 0.2(0.9x_1 + 0.8x_4 + 0.6x_7)$$

or

$$0.72x_1 - 0.16x_4 - 0.12x_7 \geq 0 \tag{7}$$

$$0.8x_4 \geq 0.4(0.9x_1 + 0.8x_4 + 0.6x_7)$$

or

$$-0.36x_1 + 0.48x_4 - 0.24x_7 \geq 0 \tag{8}$$

$$0.6x_7 \leq 0.1(0.9x_1 + 0.8x_4 + 0.6x_7)$$

or

$$-0.09x_1 - 0.08x_4 + 0.54x_7 \leq 0 \tag{9}$$

$$0.8x_2 \geq 0.1(0.8x_2 + 0.8x_5 + 0.5x_8)$$

or

$$0.72x_2 - 0.08x_5 - 0.05x_8 \geq 0 \tag{10}$$

$$0.5x_8 \leq 0.3(0.8x_2 + 0.8x_5 + 0.5x_8)$$

or

$$-0.24x_2 - 0.24x_5 + 0.35x_8 \leq 0. \tag{11}$$

For example, from Table 4–9, since 10 percent of the amount of Material 1 processed into Product A results in a waste residue, only 90 percent of that amount of Material 1 originally processed into Product A is contained in primary Product A. Thus, if x_1 pounds originally are processed in this way, only $0.9x_1$ will appear in Product A. In the same fashion, the contents of Materials 2 and 3 in Product A will be $0.8x_4$ and $0.6x_7$, respectively. From Table 4–7 it is known that at least 20 percent of the total weight of Product A must be accounted for by Material 1. We also know that the total amount of Product A produced is given by $0.9x_1 + 0.8x_4 + 0.6x_7$. Putting these facts together yields constraint (7). Constraints (8) through (11) are constructed in an analogous manner.

Table 4–9, together with the definition of variables $x_9, \ldots, x_{14}$, requires that the following constraints also must be satisfied:

$$x_9 \leq 0.1x_1 \text{ or } x_9 - 0.1x_1 \leq 0 \tag{12}$$

$$x_{10} \leq 0.2x_4 \text{ or } x_{10} - 0.2x_4 \leq 0 \tag{13}$$

$$x_{11} \leq 0.4x_7 \text{ or } x_{11} - 0.4x_7 \leq 0 \tag{14}$$

$$x_{12} \leq 0.2x_2 \text{ or } x_{12} - 0.2x_2 \leq 0 \tag{15}$$

$$x_{13} \leq 0.2x_5 \text{ or } x_{13} - 0.2x_5 \leq 0 \tag{16}$$

$$x_{14} \leq 0.5x_8 \text{ or } x_{14} - 0.5x_8 \leq 0. \tag{17}$$

For example constraint (12) states that x_9, the number of pounds of Material 1–Product A residue recycled back to Secondary Product C, cannot exceed the Material 1–Product A residue pounds ($0.1x_1$) generated by the production of Product A.

The final two structural constraints give the material content specifications for secondary Products C and D:

$$x_3 = 0.2(x_3 + x_9 + x_{10} + x_{11})$$

or

$$0.8x_3 - 0.2x_9 - 0.2x_{10} - 0.2x_{11} = 0 \tag{18}$$

$$x_6 = 0.3(x_6 + x_{12} + x_{13} + x_{14})$$

or

$$0.7x_6 - 0.3x_{12} - 0.3x_{13} - 0.3x_{14} = 0. \tag{19}$$

For example, constraint (18) says that exactly 20 percent of the total weight of Product C (defined to be the sum of x_3, x_9, x_{10}, and x_{11}) must be accounted for by Material 1.

Finally, the nonnegativity constraints must be satisfied;

$$x_j \geq 0, \quad j = 1, \ldots, 14.$$

The solution to this rather formidable problem will be given in the next chapter (page 179).

Follow-up Exercises

**35. Appropriately modify the example if:

    a. All waste coefficients associated with Material 1 are 0.5.
    b. Fifty percent by weight of original Material 2 must be present in Product D.
    c. The maximum availability of Material 3 is 10,000 pounds.
    d. The unit price of Product A is $5.
    e. All disposal costs associated with Material 3 are $0.70 per pound.

**36. Appropriately modify the example if the production of Product D requires 10 percent by weight of raw Material 1 in addition to the other ingredients previously specified. (Hint: Define a new variable in Figure 4–10.)

**37. Assume that the production of Products C and D results in 5 percent and 10 percent wastes, respectively, of all ingredients in the blends. All wastes of both products either can be combined to produce Product E (which itself has no waste) or can be disposed of at a cost of $0.10 per pound. The net revenue per pound of Product E is $0.20. Appropriately modify

    a. Figure 4–10.
    b. The formulation in the example.

**38. Modify the formulation to include variables which represent the weight of each product which is produced. Specifically, let x_{15} = pounds produced of Product A, x_{16} = pounds produced of Product B, x_{17} = pounds produced of Product C, and x_{18} = pounds produced of Product D.

OMIT.

4.6 SPECIAL ISSUES IN PROBLEM FORMULATION

Many applied problems have characteristics which would render them inconsistent with linear programming formulations. This section presents procedures for overcoming the problems associated with (1) unrestricted variables, (2) nonlinear objective functions, and (3) strict inequalities.

Unrestricted Variables

In Section 4.4 we mentioned that most applications of linear programming in management and economics deal with decision variables which are logically nonnegative. This is a fortunate state of affairs because the mathematical development of the simplex method (next chapter) requires the use of **restricted (nonnegative) variables.** For this reason, of course, we specify the nonnegativity constraints in the generalized statement of the LP problem.

How do we proceed if the formulation of a problem includes **unrestricted variables,** that is, those which are allowed to be either positive or negative? For instance, if a variable represents the change in the level of something, it can be positive, negative, or zero. The answer is surprisingly simple: Express the unrestricted variable as the difference between two nonnegative variables. If x_j is the unrestricted variable, then it would be represented as the difference between the two restricted variables x_j' and x_j'', or

$$x_j = x_j' - x_j''.$$

Thus, wherever x_j appears in a problem the equivalent form $x_j' - x_j''$ is substituted.

Example 4.11

Given the initial LP formulation
maximize

$$z = 5x_1 + 3x_2$$

subject to

$$x_1 + x_2 \leq 25 \tag{1}$$
$$3x_1 - 2x_2 \geq 5 \tag{2}$$

$$x_1 \geq 0$$

x_2 unrestricted,

We express x_2 as $x_2 = x_2' - x_2''$ and substitute into the original formulation of the problem to give
maximize

$$z = 5x_1 + 3(x_2' - x_2'')$$

subject to

$$x_1 + (x_2' - x_2'') \leq 25 \tag{1}$$
$$3x_1 - 2(x_2' - x_2'') \geq 5 \tag{2}$$
$$x_1, x_2', x_2'' \geq 0.$$

It should be noted that due to a condition of linear dependence between the variables x_2' and x_2'', only one of the variables can be positive for a given solution (the other will be zero). In the language of Chapter 5, only one of the two variables can appear in the *basis* for a given solution. Although a proof of this statement is beyond the scope of this text, you can see easily that at most one of the two variables needs to be positive to represent any value of the unrestricted variable. To illustrate, if $x_2 = 5$ in a solution, this would be represented by $x_2' = 5$ and $x_2'' = 0$. If $x_2 = -2$, then $x_2' = 0$ and $x_2'' = 2$. Given the previous statement about linear dependence, what values would be assigned to x_2' and x_2'' if $x_2 = 0$?

Piecewise Linear Functions

Many situations arise in which the structure of linear programming is deemed suitable for modeling either piecewise linear functions or non-linear functions. Piecewise linear approximations of nonlinear relationships are often made with minor losses in accuracy. The objective of these types of transformations is almost always the facilitation of the solution process. It goes without saying that the mathematics of nonlinear functions can become much more complex than for linear functions.

An example of this type of treatment can be illustrated by referring back to the media mix problem (Example 4.8). Typically, the response of audience exposures to advertising expenditures will be nonlinear rather than constant. If the nonlinear function can be estimated *and* approximated by **piecewise linear functions** such that a convex set is formed, then the problem is amenable to the LP formulation. For example, suppose that exposure to television is given by the nonlinear function depicted in Figure 4–11 and approximated by the two dashed linear functions. You should convince yourself that the previous formulation must be modified, first, by replacing (*a*) $22x_1$ by $20x_1' + 2.5(x_1'' - 5)$ in the objective function and (*b*) x_1 by $x_1' + (x_1'' - 5)$ in the constraints and, second, by adding the constraints

$$x_1' \leq 5 \tag{8}$$
$$x_1'' \geq 5. \tag{9}$$

Note that the original five-variable problem has been transformed into a six-variable problem (x_1 was deleted and x_1' and x_1'' have been added). In a similar manner, the above modifications can be extended either to include more linear segments or other media or both.

FIGURE 4–11

Nonlinear Exposure for Television Advertising in Media Mix Problem

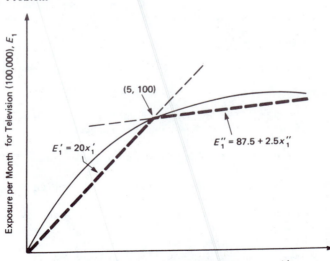

This approach of defining multiple variables based on single variables is valid only if we are attempting to maximize a function which is concave downward or to minimize a function which is concave upward. (Can you reason why?) Otherwise, more advanced procedures using multiple models are required.

Strict Inequality Constraints

You might ask a question related to how *strict* inequalities are handled in linear programming. For instance, what if the amount of money to be expended upon television and radio in Example 4.8 was required to be *less than* 50 percent of the budget? Constraint (2) would then be written as $x_1 + x_2 < 5$.

As you know, the standard form of a linear programming problem requires that constraints be stated as either *weak* inequalities ($\leq$ or $\geq$) or equalities. To overcome this minor problem, you simply substitute a value for the right-hand-side which is within an acceptable tolerance. For instance, the above constraint could be restated as $x_1 + x_2 \leq 4.9999$.

Follow-up Exercises

39. Modify Example 4.11 such that

    a. x_1 is unrestricted.
    b. Both constraints are strict inequalities.

40. Appropriately modify the media mix problem if the function in Figure 4–11 is approximated by three piecewise linear functions as follows: The first segment passes through the origin and coordinate (2, 30); the second segment passes through (2, 30) and (6, 80); and the third segment passes through (6, 80) and (10, 120). What main advantage do you see in having three rather than two segments? What main disadvantage? Interpret the meaning of slopes in these piecewise functions.

SELECTED REFERENCES

Anderson, David R.; Sweeney, Dennis J.; and Williams, Thomas A. *Linear Programming for Decision Making, An Applications Approach.* St. Paul: West Publishing Co., 1974.

Gass, S. I. *Linear Programming: Methods and Applications.* 4th ed. New York: McGraw-Hill, Inc., 1975.

Hadley, G. *Linear Programming.* Reading, Mass.: Addison-Wesley Publishing Co., 1962.

Hillier, Frederick S., and Lieberman, Gerald J. *Introduction to Operations Research.* 2d ed. San Francisco: Holden Day, Inc., 1974.

Hughes, Ann J., and Grawiog, Dennis E. *Linear Programming: An Emphasis on Decision Making.* Reading, Mass.: Addison-Wesley Publishing Co., 1973.

Kim, Chaiho. *Quantitative Analysis for Managerial Decisions.* Reading, Mass.: Addison-Wesley Publishing Co., 1976.

Levin, Richard I., and Lamone, Rudolph P. *Linear Programming for Management Decisions.* Homewood, Ill.: Richard D. Irwin, Inc., 1969.

McMillan, Claude, Jr. *Mathematical Programming: An Introduction to the Design and Application of Optimal Decision Machines.* New York: John Wiley & Sons, Inc., 1970.

Montgomery, David B., and Urban, Glen L. *Management Science in Marketing.* Englewood Cliffs, N.J.: Prentice-Hall, Inc., 1969.

Shamblin, James E., and Stevens, G. T., Jr. *Operations Research: A Fundamental Approach.* New York: McGraw-Hill, Inc., 1974.

Spivey, W. Allen, and Thrall, Robert M. *Linear Optimization.* New York: Holt, Rinehart and Winston, Inc. 1970.

Strum, Jay E. *Introduction to Linear Programming.* San Francisco: Holden Day, Inc., 1972.

Trueman, Richard E. *An Introduction to Quantitative Methods for Decision Making.* New York: Holt, Rinehart and Winston, Inc., 1974.

Wagner, Harvey M. *Principles of Operations Research.* 2d ed. Englewood Cliffs, N.J.: Prentice-Hall, Inc., 1975.

ADDITIONAL EXERCISES

41. Graphically solve the following problems:

a. Maximize

$$z = 6x_1 + 8x_2$$

subject to

$$
\begin{aligned}
x_1 &\geq 2 & (1)\\
x_1 &\leq 8 & (2)\\
x_2 &\geq 2 & (3)\\
x_2 &\leq 6 & (4)\\
2x_1 + 3x_2 &\leq 21 & (5)\\
x_1, x_2 &\geq 0.
\end{aligned}
$$

b. Change the objective function to maximize $z = 6x_1 + 9x_2$.

c. Same as part (*a*) except change (5) to $2x_1 + 3x_2 \leq 8$.

d. Same as part (*a*) except change (5) to $2x_1 + 3x_2 \geq 8$.

e. Same as part (*a*) except change (5) to $2x_1 + 3x_2 \geq 21$ and eliminate (2).

f. Same as part (*d*) except minimize z.

42. Graphically solve the following problems:

a. Minimize

$$z = 12x_1 + 9x_2$$

subject to

$$
\begin{aligned}
x_1 &\leq 10 & (1)\\
x_2 &\leq 8 & (2)\\
x_2 &\geq 3 & (3)\\
2.5x_1 + x_2 &\geq 10 & (4)\\
4x_1 + 3x_2 &\geq 18 & (5)\\
x_1, x_2 &\geq 0.
\end{aligned}
$$

b. Same as part (*a*) except minimize $z = 12x_1 + 3x_2$.

c. Same as part (*a*) except reverse inequality in (5).

d. Same as part (*a*) except eliminate (2).

e. Same as part (*d*) except maximize *z*.

43. *Capital Expansion Model* A company wishes to purchase additional machinery in a capital expansion program. Three types of machines may be purchased: *A, B,* and *C.* Machine *A* costs $15,000 and requires 100 square feet of floor space for its operation. Machine *B* costs $20,000 and requires 150 square feet of floor space. Machine *C* costs $12,000 and requires 125 square feet of floor space. The total budget for this expansion program is $250,000. The maximum available floor space for the new machines is 3,000 square feet.

Given that machines *A, B,* and *C* can produce 150, 210, and 125 pieces per day, the company wants to determine how many machines of each type it should purchase so as to maximize daily output (in units) from the new machines.

a. Explicitly define your decision variables and formulate the LP model.

b. Assess the validity of the four underlying LP assumptions for this problem.

44. *Agricultural Allocation Model* A university has offered a rent subsidy alternative to the families living in the graduate student housing complex. Near the complex are ten acres which can be farmed. The university will allow the residents' organization to farm all or part of this land. Any derived profits can be apportioned to reducing the rent for the graduate families. Families may keep whatever produce they wish for their own use. The university has agreed to buy produce from the students, up to certain limits, for use within the dining services.

The students have agreed to plant lettuce, potatoes, and tomatoes. The table below summarizes for each group over the growing season the projected yield per acre, the demand by the students, the maximum university demand, and estimated profit per unit.

Crop	Yield per Acre	Student Demand	Maximum University Demand	Profit
Lettuce..........	42,000 heads	20,000 heads	100,000 heads	$0.05 per head
Potatoes........	20,000 lb.	50,000 lb.	90,000 lb.	$0.08 per lb.
Tomatoes.......	7,000 lb.	10,000 lb.	40,000 lb.	$0.25 per lb.

Formulate the LP model which would enable the students to determine the number of acres they should allocate to each crop so as to maximize total profit. Assume that student demands are to be exactly satisfied so that profit only applies to crops which are sold to the university over and above student demands.

45. It is logical to assume that the graduate student organization in the previous problem will plant all ten acres. Why? Using this assumption, transform that problem into a two-variable problem and solve for the optimal solution graphically.

46. Modify Exercise 44 to include the following conditions:

a. Lettuce, potatoes, and tomatoes require 1,000, 1,500, and 1,300 gallons of water per acre, respectively, over and above natural rainfall during the growing season. Available water is limited to 12,000 gallons.

    b. Composted manure is to be used for fertilizer. The requirements are 4,200 lb. per acre for lettuce, 3,000 lb. per acre for potatoes, and 8,000 lb. per acre for tomatoes; however, only 40,000 lb. of fertilizer are available overall.

    c. Much as the graduate students and their families enjoy working the farm, the academic demands (and other pleasures) limit total available labor to 52,000 hours over the growing season. Lettuce requires 4,000 hours per acre, potatoes 8,000 hours per acre, and tomatoes 6,000 hours per acre.

    d. Discuss the extent to which you feel the four underlying LP assumptions satisfy this formulation.

47. *Production-Vendor Model* Sniffy Smoke Sensers, Inc., is experiencing a tremendous growth in demand for its household smoke detectors. Sniffy produces both an AC model and a battery-operated model. It has an opportunity to be the exclusive supplier for a major department store chain, The Seers Company. Seers wishes to receive at least 20,000 AC models and 10,000 battery-operated models each week.

Sniffy's unanticipated prosperity has left it short of sufficient capacity to satisfy the Seer's contract over the short run. However, there is a subcontractor who can assist Sniffy by supplying the same types of smoke detectors. Sniffy must decide how many units it will make of each detector and how many units it will buy from the subcontractor. Data below summarize the production, price, and cost parameters.

	Model (hours per unit)		Hours Available per Week
	AC	Battery	
Production Dept..................	0.15	0.10	2,000
Assembly Dept....................	0.20	0.20	4,200
Packaging Dept..................	0.10	0.15	2,500
Total cost per unit..............	$20	$18	

The subcontractor can supply any combination of battery or AC models up to 20,000 units total each week. The cost per unit to Sniffy is $21.50 and $20.00, respectively, for the AC and battery models.

The contract with Seers calls for Sniffy to receive $25.00 for each AC model and $29.50 for each battery model. Formulate the LP model which would allow Sniffy to determine the number of units of each type to produce and to buy so as to maximize total profit. Would you say that divisibility poses a practical problem here? Explain.

48. *Personnel Model* A new Federal Environmental Protection Organization is being formed and there are 2,000 professional and 1,000 nonprofessional positions which need to be filled. Recruiting costs average $1,000 for each professional position and $400 for each nonprofessional position. Typically, these costs are 20 percent higher than average for recruiting women and 30 percent higher for recruiting minorities (men and women). HEW has examined state employment records and has mandated that women should constitute at least 40 percent of new hirings within the agency and minorities at least 50 percent of new hirings. Letting

    x_1 = Number of nonminority women hired as professionals,
    x_2 = Number of nonminority women hired as nonprofessionals,
    x_3 = Number of minority women hired as professionals,
    x_4 = Number of minority women hired as nonprofessionals,

$x_5 =$ Number of nonminority men hired as professionals,
$x_6 =$ Number of nonminority men hired as nonprofessionals,
$x_7 =$ Number of minority men hired as professionals,
$x_8 =$ Number of minority men hired as nonprofessionals,
formulate the LP model which minimizes total recruiting costs in filling the agency's positions. Would you say that divisibility poses a practical problem here? Explain.

49. *Contract Awards Model* An automobile manufacturer wants to award contracts for the supply of four different fuel injection system components. Three contractors have submitted bids on the components; the table below summarizes the prices bid per unit. Where no entry is made, the contractor submitted no bid.

| | Component | | | |
	1	2	3	4
Contractor				
1.........................	$20	$60	$40	—
2.........................	15	75	45	$30
3.........................	—	50	50	25
Demand (units).............	10,000	20,000	6,000	25,000

The demand for a component does not have to be supplied completely by one contractor. In fact, certain contractors have indicated maximum quantities which can be supplied at the bid price. Contractor 1 can supply no more than 4,000 of item 3, contractor 2 no more than 1,000 of item 3, and contractor 3 no more than 15,000 units of item 2.

There is no provision that awards must go to the low bidder. The automobile manufacturer wants to determine how many units of each item should be awarded to each contractor so as to minimize total costs for the four items. Contractor 1 has specified that it requires a minimum award of $200,000 if it is to supply any items at all. The automobile manufacturer wishes to avoid awarding over $1 million in awards to any one company. Formulate the LP model which can solve this problem if x_{ij} is the number of units awarded to contractor i for item j. Would you say that divisibility poses a practical problem here? Explain.

50. *Blending Model* A coffee manufacturer blends four component coffee beans into three final blends of coffee. The table below summarizes the very precise recipes for the final coffee blends, the cost and availability information for the four components, and the wholesale price per pound of the final blends. The percentages in the body of the table indicate the percentage of each component to be used in each blend.

| | Final Blend (percent) | | | Cost per Pound | Maximum Availability Each Week (pounds) |
	1	2	3		
Component					
1.........................	20	35	10	$0.60	40,000
2.........................	40	15	35	0.80	25,000
3.........................	15	20	40	0.55	20,000
4.........................	25	30	15	0.70	45,000
Wholesale price per pound...	$1.25	$1.50	$1.40		

Weekly capacity for the processor's plant is 100,000 pounds, and the company wishes to operate at capacity. There is no problem in selling the final blends, although there is a requirement that minimum production levels of 10,000, 25,000, and 30,000 pounds, respectively, be met for blends 1, 2, and 3. The manufacturer wishes to determine the number of pounds of each component which should be used in each blend so as to maximize total weekly profit. Formulate this as an LP model. (First, explicitly define your decision variables.)

51. *Portfolio Model* Portfolio theory represents an important specialization in the area of finance. An important class of models in this area is based on quadratic programming, as illustrated by Example 10.10. Here we present a simplified scenario.

An endowment fund manager is attempting to determine a "best" investment portfolio. Eight alternative investments are being considered. The table below indicates point estimates for the price per share, the annual growth rate in the price per share, the annual dividend per share,

	Alternative							
	1	*2*	*3*	*4*	*5*	*6*	*7*	*8*
Current price per share....	$100	$20	$50	$75	$150	$220	$115	$40
Past annual growth rate...	0.10	0.08	0.15	0.06	0.05	0.01	0.04	0.02
Past annual dividend per share.................	$1.25	$0.10	$0.25	$2.00	$4.50	$5.00	$2.50	$0.75
Past risk.................	0.08	0.10	0.25	0.08	0.04	0.00	0.02	0.01

and a measure of the risk associated with each investment. In this case risk is defined as the standard deviation in return. Return is defined as (price per share one year hence less current price per share plus dividend per share) ÷ current price per share. The fund has $1 million to invest and it wishes to satisfy the following conditions:

1. The maximum dollar amount to be invested in alternatives 1, 2, and 3 individually is $200,000.
2. At least 25 percent of the total dollar investment should be in alternatives 6, 7, and 8.
3. Total return on investment (including both growth and dividends) should be at least 7 percent.
4. Dividends for the year should exceed $15,000.

a. If the objective is to minimize weighted risk, formulate the LP model for determining the optimal number of shares to purchase of each investment alternative. (Assume that this is a one-year model and that fractional shares of securities may be purchased.)
b. In reality, to what extent do you think the four underlying LP assumptions are violated? Be specific.

52. *Hospital Administration* A local hospital administrator is attempting to determine a work schedule for registered nurses (R.N.'s). The union contract specifies that nurses are to work a normal day of six hours. Nurses may work an additional three hours on an overtime basis (at one and one half their hourly pay rate). R.N.'s are paid an average of $12 per hour. The administrator has determined a daily work schedule in which the day is divided into eight three-hour shifts. The table below indicates the estimated minimum demand for nurses per shift.

				Period				
	1	2	3	4	5	6	7	8
Shift........	12– 3 A.M.	3– 6 A.M.	6– 9 A.M.	9 A.M.– 12 noon	12– 3 P.M.	3– 6 P.M.	6– 9 P.M.	9 P.M.– 12 midnight
Minimum no. of required R.N.'s.....	30	20	40	50	60	50	40	40

Nurses are to start work at the beginning of one of these shifts and end work at the end of the following shift; that is, unless they receive overtime. The contract specifies that any nurses requested to work overtime will receive full payment for three hours of overtime, even if they work less than three hours. Thus, the administrator concludes that overtime, when assigned, should be for the maximum of three hours. The contract also specifies that, on the average, at least 10 percent of all nurses can expect overtime assignments. Let x_t equal the number of nurses reporting to work at the beginning of period t who do not get overtime work and y_t equal the number of nurses reporting to work in period t who do work overtime. Formulate the LP model which will allow the administrator to determine an assignment schedule which meets the shift requirements and contract specifications at a minimum cost.

Does the assumption of divisibility create any difficulty in this problem? What recourse do you have if it does?

53. *Trim Loss (or Cutting Stock) Model* This is a classical LP scenario which includes applications such as paper slitting and textile cutting whereby jumbo reels are cut into smaller reels having various widths. Consider the following situation.

A paper mill produces jumbo reels of paper which are 60 inches wide. The company receives orders for reels which are 12 inches wide, 18 inches wide, 25 inches wide, and 36 inches wide. The manufacturer has received orders for 200, 150, 100, and 50 reels, respectively, of the 12-, 18-, 25-, and 36-inch reels. The firm wishes to determine how to meet these orders so as to minimize total waste.

"Waste" is defined as any leftover portions of a jumbo reel which cannot be used to meet demand. There are two sources of waste: trim loss and surplus. For example, if a jumbo reel is slit into two 25-inch reels, there will be leftover paper (trim loss) having a width of 10 inches. Since there is no use for 10-inch reels (insofar as the outstanding order is concerned), the 10 inches is a measure of waste. Note that this cutting pattern yields two 25-inch reels for each jumbo reel which is cut. Because different cutting patterns can create multiple reels out of jumbo reels, there is a likelihood that surplus or excess will be cut. For example, if 210 12-inch reels result from the cutting process and only 200 are required, then $(210 - 200) \times 12$ is a surplus waste.

There are different ways (patterns) in which a 60-inch reel can be slit. The problem is to determine how many jumbo reels should be slit in each pattern so as to minimize total waste. As a start, determine the different patterns which can be used in slitting a jumbo reel, and note the attendant loss. Only consider patterns which yield waste less than the smallest required width. (There are nine of these.) To help you along, we have filled in the relevant information for the first (arbitrarily selected) pattern. Pattern 1 specifies a jumbo reel is to be split into three

12-inch widths and one 18-inch width, yielding a trim loss of 6 inches per jumbo reel.

Required				Pattern (*j*)					
Width (*i*)	1	2	3	4	5	6	7	8	9
12.........	3								
18.........	1								
25.........	0								
36.........	0								
Trim loss.....	6								

Define x_j as the number of jumbo reels which are to be slit according to pattern j and E_i as the excess (surplus) number of reels of required width i. Formulate the LP model for this problem. What are the implications of divisibility?

54. *Cargo Loading Model*   This class of models addresses decisions concerning the loading of cargo onto vessels, airplanes, trains, spacecraft, and so forth. Here we describe an LP scenario; in Example 8.11 an integer programming approach is presented.

Consider a problem whereby limited quantities of four types of merchandise are available to be loaded into three holds of a freighter. Relevant data are given in the accompanying tables. The dope, of course, is

Freighter Capacities

Hold (*j*)	Weight (tons)	Volume (Cu. ft.)
1. Forward.........	75	4,000
2. Center..........	150	10,000
3. Aft.............	50	7,000

Cargo Data

Merchandise (*i*)	Weight (tons)	Volume (cu. ft. per ton)	Revenue (dollars per ton)
1. Sugar..............	100	48.6	600
2. Rice...............	200	60.0	800
3. Ore................	500	4.1	200
4. Dope..............	50	240.0	300,000

for either research or medicinal purposes. The captain needs to know how much weight of each type of merchandise is to be loaded in each hold such that total revenue is maximized without violating weight and volume constraints. Moreover, the merchandise must be loaded such that the "trim" of the ship is preserved. This means that the ratio of loaded weight in a hold to the weight capacity in that hold must be identical for all three holds. Formulate this problem as an LP model. (Hint: There are 12 variables and 12 structural constraints.)

55. *Diet Model*   The diet problem is another LP "classic." Basically, the objective is to ascertain the quantities of food which should be eaten such that certain nutritional requirements are met at a minimum cost. In recent years, this type of model has been successfully extended and

Food	Measure	Weight (g)	Cost ($/Measure)	Calories	Protein (g)	Fat (g)	Minerals (mg)					Vitamins			
							Iron	Calcium	Phosphorus	Potassium	Sodium	A (units)	B₁ (mg)	B₂ (mg)	C (mg)
Dairy															
Whole milk..........	1 qt.	976	0.40	660	32	40	0.4	1140	930	210	75	1,560	0.32	1.7	6
Ice cream............	1 cup	188	0.35	300	6	18	0.1	175	150	170	140	740	0	0.3	0
Eggs (scrambled or fried)..	2	128	0.15	220	13	16	2.2	60	222	140	338	1,200	0	0.4	0
Cheese (cheddar, American)..........	1 in. cube	17	0.05	70	4	6	0.1	133	128	30	180	230	0	0.1	0
Meat															
Lean ground beef........	3 oz.	85	0.25	185	24	10	3.0	10	158	340	110	20	0	0	0
Broiled chicken........	3 oz.	85	0.12	185	23	9	1.4	10	250	350	50	260	0	0.1	0
Baked flounder........	3.5 oz.	100	0.25	200	30	8	1.4	22	344	585	235	0	0	0	0
Vegetable															
French fried potatoes....	10 pieces	60	0.07	155	1	7	0.7	9	6	510	6	0	0	0	8
Fruit															
Frozen o.j.............	6 oz. can	210	0.30	330	2	0	0.8	69	115	1,315	4	1,490	0.60	0.1	330
Grain															
Converted rice...........	1 cup uncooked	187	0.25	677	14	0	1.6	53	244	300	6	0	0.30	0	0
Min. daily allowance*........				2,400	70	—	10	800	—	—	—	5,000	1.00	1.6	70
Max. daily allowance*.......				2,800	—	—	—	—	—	—	—	40,000	—	—	—

* For healthy men, 35–55 years old, 5′ 9″ height, and 154 lb. weight.

generalized to applications in *food management,* whereby a given population (for example, hospital, university, mental and penal institutions, navy base, and so forth) is to be fed by converting raw food into menu items such that cost is minimized and nutritional, preference, and other constraints are satisfied.[7]

Consider the accompanying nutritional table, where data have been gleaned from Adelle Davis.[8]

Define x_j as the daily weight in grams to be consumed of food j.

a.   Formulate an LP model which minimizes total cost and satisfies the following conditions:

1.   Minimum and maximum daily allowances.
2.   Daily potassium intake should be within $\pm$ 10 percent of daily sodium intake.
3.   Daily calcium intake should be at least two thirds of daily phosphorous intake.

b.   According to Davis, greater amounts of fat in the diet should be accompanied by greater B-vitamin intake. Indicate how you might incorporate this constraint.

c.   Discuss shortcomings of the diet model with respect to its applicability in a food management environment.

---

[7] See, for example, Joseph L. Balintfy, "A Mathematical Programming System for Food Management Application," *Interfaces,* vol. 6, no. 1 (November 1975), pp. 13–31.

[8] *Let's Eat Right to Keep Fit* (New York: Harcourt Brace Jovanovich, Inc., 1970).

5

The Simplex Method

By now you should have a more than fair (masterful?) understanding of the nature and characteristics of the linear programming (LP) model. Specifically, you should feel "comfortable" with the formulation and mathematical statement of the LP model without losing sight of the underlying implications associated with the model. In addition, using graphical techniques, you should have a clear conception of the mathematical properties and operational objective of linear programming. The present chapter continues this exposition by developing the simplex method of solution for LP problems and solving selected scenarios in the previous chapter using a time-shared computer program.

5.1 ON SYSTEMS OF SIMULTANEOUS LINEAR EQUATIONS

Prior to introducing the simplex method, we will consider some characteristics and procedures of solution for systems of simultaneous linear equations. Comprehension of this section will help you to understand the simplex method, as you will soon realize.

Characteristics of Solutions

A linear system of m simultaneous equations in n unknown variables may have *no* solution, a *unique* solution, or an *infinite* number of solutions. If the number of unknown variables is greater than the number of equations ($n > m$), then an infinite number of solutions are possible, but not guaranteed; on the other hand, if $n = m$ or $n < m$, then a necessary, but not sufficient, condition has been established for a single or unique solution.

To illustrate, consider the following system of two equations $(m = 2)$ and three unknown variables $(n = 3)$:

$$x_1 + x_3 = 10 \qquad (1)$$
$$x_2 + x_3 = 5. \qquad (2)$$

Note that *any* two variables can be solved for in terms of the remaining variable. For example, x_1 and x_2 can be expressed in terms of x_3 as

$$x_1 = 10 - x_3 \qquad (1)$$
$$x_2 = 5 - x_3. \qquad (2)$$

You should be able to verify that choosing *any* value for x_3 provides unique values for x_1 and x_2; hence, this system has an infinite number of solutions. In general when $n > m$, *any* m variables can be expressed in terms of the *remaining* $(n - m)$ variables; since an infinite number of arbitrary values can be assigned to the remaining variables, the system has an infinite number of possible solutions.

Now consider a system where $n = m$:

$$5x_1 + x_2 = 10 \qquad (1)$$
$$10x_1 + 2x_2 = 40. \qquad (2)$$

Convince yourself that the equations do not yield a solution (the two lines are parallel). If the right-hand–side constant in (2) were changed to 20, then the system would have an infinite number of solutions, since (1) and (2) would be equivalent. Finally, if the coefficient of x_1 in (2) were 5 instead of 10, then the system would have a unique solution at $x_1 = -4$ and $x_2 = 30$.

When $n < m$, the solution procedure is tedious and a unique solution is not likely. A solution for the n unknown variables is determined by selecting n equations from among the m available; that is, we discard $(m - n)$ equations for any one potential solution. Since the number of potential solutions using this procedure is the number of combinations of m taken n at a time, a unique solution results if and only if the potential solutions are identical.

The above illustrations are meant to provide a superficial review of solutions to simultaneous equations with emphasis upon (1) the relationship between m and n and (2) the nature of the coefficients and right-hand–side constants. If you need further review of this material, read Appendix B before going on to the next section.

A Method of Solution

Essentially the simplex method is a procedure for solving linear simultaneous equations. In Appendix B at the end of the book we solve several sets of simultaneous equations using the **elimination-substitution technique.**

As you are probably aware, a number of procedures exist for solving systems of linear equations. Rather than providing a treatise on all methods, we will focus on one particularly appealing approach which is utilized by the simplex procedure.

Two fundamental properties characterize simultaneous equations which are linear:

1. The validity of the equality is not violated if the same algebraic operation is performed on both sides of the equation, for example, both sides of an equation can be divided or multiplied by a constant.
2. Any one equation can be replaced by the sum of itself and a linear multiple of any other equation without altering the validity of, or losing information in, the system. That is "equals can be added to equals."

Example 5.1

Given the system

$$5x_1 + 4x_2 = 24 \tag{1}$$
$$2x_1 + 5x_2 = 13, \tag{2}$$

you should have little difficulty in convincing yourself that replacing Equation (1) by ten times itself gives the equivalent system

$$50x_1 + 40x_2 = 240 \tag{1a}$$
$$2x_1 + 5x_2 = 13. \tag{2}$$

Similarly, equation (2a) below can be created by adding Equations (1a) and (2):

$$50x_1 + 40x_2 = 240 \tag{1a}$$
$$52x_1 + 45x_2 = 253. \tag{2a}$$

The resulting system is equivalent to (1) and (2). If you are skeptical, separately solve systems (1)–(2) and (1a)–(2a) by elimination-substitution and compare the solution values for x_1 and x_2.

These two fundamental properties can be used to transform linear equations into equivalent equations which are used for solution by the **identity matrix method.** To illustrate the end result of this method, consider the initial system given in Example 5.1,

$$5x_1 + 4x_2 = 24 \tag{Initial}$$
$$2x_1 + 5x_2 = 13,$$

and its equivalent or final form for solution:

$$1x_1 + 0x_2 = 4.0 \tag{Final}$$
$$0x_1 + 1x_2 = 1.0.$$

By inspection it is apparent that the only set of values uniquely satisfying this final system (and consequently the initial system) is $x_1 = 4$ and $x_2 = 1$.

The transformations in proceeding from the initial system to the final system are often called **row operations.** If, as above, there is a unique solution to an $(m \times m)$ system of simultaneous equations, then the identity matrix method systematically utilizes row operations on the original system of equations to produce a new system of equations with a particular property.[1] The desired end result is to transform the original system of equations into an equivalent system for which the resulting matrix of variable coefficients is in the form of an **identity matrix:**

$$I = \begin{pmatrix} 1 & 0 & \cdots & 0 \\ 0 & 1 & \cdots & 0 \\ \cdot & \cdot & \cdot & \cdot \\ \cdot & \cdot & \cdot & \cdot \\ \cdot & \cdot & \cdot & \cdot \\ 0 & 0 & \cdots & 1 \end{pmatrix}$$

Once this is achieved, the solution can be read directly from the right-hand–side constants.

As will be illustrated in Example 5.2, the most efficient process for performing this transformation of the original system is to create the identity matrix one column at a time. In each instance the column element which is equal to "one" should be created first, followed by the remaining "zero" elements in the column.

Example 5.2

We now solve the system of Example 5.1 by the identity matrix method. For your convenience, the algebraic operations are indicated in the right margin. To avoid confusion in the algebraic expressions, Equation (i) is denoted as (e_i).

$$5x_1 + 4x_2 = 24 \qquad (e_1)$$
$$2x_1 + 5x_2 = 13. \qquad (e_2)$$

Dividing (e_1) by 5 forces the coefficient of x_1 to 1:

$$1x_1 + 0.8x_2 = 4.8 \qquad (e_3 = e_1/5)$$
$$2x_1 + 5x_2 = 13. \qquad (e_2)$$

Moving down the first column, we find a zero coefficient can be obtained for x_1 in the second equation by multiplying (e_3) by -2 and adding the resultant equation to (e_2):

$$1x_1 + 0.8x_2 = 4.8 \qquad (e_3)$$
$$0x_1 + 3.4x_2 = 3.4. \qquad (e_4 = e_2 - 2e_3)$$

For the second column, dividing (e_4) by 3.4 yields the required coefficient for x_3:

$$1x_1 + 0.8x_2 = 4.8 \qquad (e_3)$$
$$0x_1 + 1x_2 = 1.0. \qquad (e_5 = e_4/3.4)$$

---

[1] An $(m \times m)$ system is one having m equations and m variables, and is conceptualized as a **matrix** or tableau. For convenience and by convention, the equations and unknown variables correspond to rows and columns, respectively. Thus, the coefficients 5 and 2 represent the first column of the system in Example 5.1.

Multiplying (e_5) by -0.8 and adding this result to (e_3) produces the desired coefficient of zero for x_2 in (e_6):

$$1x_1 + 0x_2 = 4.0 \qquad (e_6 = -0.8e_5 + e_3)$$
$$0x_1 + 1x_2 = 1.0. \qquad (e_5)$$

Thus, x_1 and x_2 equal the right-hand–side constants in (e_6) and (e_5), respectively.

Follow-up Exercises

By the identity matrix method, solve the following systems:

1. Example 1 in Appendix B, page 739.
2. Example 3 in Appendix B, page 740.

5.2 STANDARD FORM OF THE LP MODEL

In Section 4.3 we should have convinced you that a unique optimal solution to an LP problem, if it exists, will be found at a corner point. Realizing that the coordinates of a corner point are determined by solving simultaneous equations, we see that the inequalities in an LP formulation *must be converted to equalities.*

A preliminary step required by the simplex method is the transformation of the problem to the so-called **standard form** such that the following three conditions are met:

1. The structural constraints are expressed as equalities.
2. The right-hand–side constants in the structural constraints are nonnegative.
3. All the variables are nonnegative.

Condition (1) is required so that the identity matrix method of solution in the previous section can be applied; the rationale for the other two conditions will become evident in Sections 5.3 and 5.4.

Given an LP problem having m structural constraints of the ($\leq$) type; (mixed constraints will be considered in Section 5.6) that is,

optimize

$$z = c_1x_1 + c_2x_2 + \cdots + c_nx_n,$$

or

$$z = \sum_{j=1}^{n} c_jx_j,$$

subject to

$$a_{11}x_1 + a_{12}x_2 + \cdots + a_{1n}x_n \leq b_1$$
$$a_{21}x_1 + a_{22}x_2 + \cdots + a_{2n}x_n \leq b_2$$
$$\vdots \qquad \vdots \qquad \vdots \qquad \vdots \qquad \vdots$$
$$a_{m1}x_1 + a_{m2}x_2 + \cdots + a_{mn}x_n \leq b_m,$$

or

$$\sum_{j=1}^{n} a_{ij}x_j \leq b_i, \qquad i = 1, \ldots, m,$$

and

$$x_j \geq 0, \qquad j = 1, \ldots, n,$$

the standard form is expressed as

optimize

$$z = \sum_{j=1}^{n} c_j x_j$$

subject to

$$\sum_{j=1}^{n} a_{ij}x_j + S_i = b_i, \qquad i = 1, \ldots, m, \qquad (5.1)$$

and

$$x_j \geq 0, \qquad j = 1, \ldots, n, \qquad S_i \geq 0, \qquad i = 1, \ldots, m,$$

where S_i is termed the **slack variable** for the ith constraint. In other words, since the left-hand side of the constraint must be less than or equal to the right-hand–side constant, the inequality can be converted to an equality by adding an additional variable to the left-hand side which picks up the "slack." Note that the slack variables do not appear in the objective function as they contribute nothing to the criterion.

Example 5.3

Suppose the LP problem is to

maximize

$$z = 7x_1 + 10x_2$$

subject to

$$5x_1 + 4x_2 \leq 24 \qquad (1)$$
$$2x_1 + 5x_2 \leq 13 \qquad (2)$$
$$x_1, x_2 \geq 0.$$

The standard form is expressed as

maximize

$$z = 7x_1 + 10x_2$$

subject to

$$5x_1 + 4x_2 + S_1 \qquad = 24 \tag{1}$$
$$2x_1 + 5x_2 \qquad + S_2 = 13 \tag{2}$$
$$x_1, x_2, S_1, S_2 \geq 0.$$

Note that slack variables represent unused resources when right-hand–side constants represent available resources. For example, if $5x_1$ and $4x_2$ represent, respectively, tons of raw material utilized in the production of Products 1 and 2, and 24 represents available supply of raw material, then a value of 2 for S_1 would mean that 2 tons of raw material (of the 24 available) were not used.

Condition (2) of the standard form requires the right-hand–side constants, (b_i), to be nonnegative. Should there be a negative b_i, it is a simple matter to multiply both sides of the inequality by a minus one (-1). Note that doing so reverses the sense of the inequality.

Condition (3) requires all variables to be nonnegative. In effect this condition was imposed in the generalized form of the LP model of Section 4.4 by specifying nonnegativity constraints. Decision variables which are unrestricted in sign can be handled by the method of Section 4.6.

Follow-up Exercise

3. Suppose that the original problem of Example 5.3 had a (-24) right-hand–side constant for constraint (1) and x_2 unrestricted. Express the standard form.

5.3 OVERVIEW OF SIMPLEX METHOD

The transformation of the LP problem having m ($\leq$) constraints to the standard form results in a constraint system of m equations in $(n + m)$ unknown variables. (Note that the original n variables have been augmented by the m slack variables.) Since the system of linear equations has more unknowns than equations, an infinite number of solutions are possible. (Do you remember why?)

Basic Feasible Solutions

Assuming there is a feasible solution, we will see that the simplex method reduces the number of solutions which need to be considered from an infinite number to a finite subset of solutions which contains the optimal solution(s). This first step is accomplished by setting *any* n unknown variables to zero and solving for the remaining m unknown variables. The number of ways of selecting m variables from among $(n + m)$ variables is given by the combination formula:

$$\begin{pmatrix} \text{Total number of variables} \\ \text{Number of equations} \end{pmatrix} = \begin{pmatrix} n + m \\ m \end{pmatrix}$$

$$= \frac{(n + m)!}{(n + m - m)!m!} = \frac{(n + m)!}{n!m!} ; \qquad (5.2)$$

hence, Equation (5.2) provides the maximum number of solutions which need to be considered.

This finite subset of solutions can be reduced further by considering strictly nonnegative $(x_j \geq 0)$ *starting* solutions, or feasible solutions. The remarkable result here is that the optimal solution is contained within this last subset of solutions. This is guaranteed by a theorem in linear programming which states:

> A closed convex set bounded from below has an optimal solution at an extreme point.

Since the system of linear inequalities forms a convex set which is bounded from below (as guaranteed by the third condition of the standard form, or all $x_j \geq 0$), the above theorem applies to the LP formulation.[2] In two dimensions, this is equivalent to stating that the optimal solution is at a corner point of the solution space as illustrated in Figure 4–7.

The m variables chosen for a solution are said to constitute a **basis;** hence, they are termed **basic variables,** as opposed to the remaining n **nonbasic variables,** which are set equal to zero.

Given a starting basic solution, the simplex method systematically searches the feasible extreme points. These **basic feasible solutions** are selected so as to improve the objective function at each iteration until no further improvement is possible, at which point the optimal solution has been found.

To illustrate these points, the problem presented in Example 5.3 will be solved graphically, by enumeration, and by the Lagrange multiplier method.

The graphical solution is shown in Figure 5–1. As can be seen, the convex solution space is given by *ABCD* and the optimal solution is at $x_1 = 4$ and $x_2 = 1$ (Point *C*).

Solution by Enumeration

In solving the problem by enumeration, the maximum number of solutions (corner points) which need to be considered is given by Equation (5.2). The general procedure involves (1) the determination of each of

---

[2] Another theorem in linear programming guarantees that linear inequalities form a convex set, a result which is developed visually in Section 4.3.

FIGURE 5–1

Graphical Solutions to Example 5.3

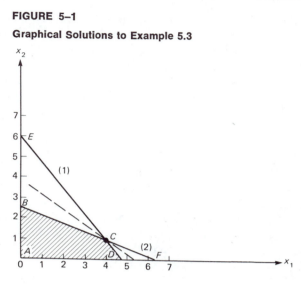

these solutions, (2) the identification of a subset of feasible solutions, and (3) the selection of the optimal solution from the feasible subset.

Example 5.4a

In Example 5.3, there were two decision variables ($n = 2$) and two constraints ($m = 2$); hence, the maximum number of solutions which must be determined is

$$\binom{4}{2} = \frac{4!}{2!2!} = \frac{4 \cdot 3 \cdot 2 \cdot 1}{2 \cdot 1 \cdot 2 \cdot 1} = 6.$$

Table 5–1 provides the six solutions and their characteristics.

Note that every solution must be examined to determine the optimal solution. Any one solution is effected by selecting the two (n) nonbasic vari-

TABLE 5–1

Solution by Enumeration

Solution Number	Basis	Values of Basic Variables	Value of Objective Function	Corner Point in Figure 5–1	Comment
1	(S_1, S_2)	(24.0,13.0)	0.0	A	Feasible
2	(S_1, x_1)	(−8.5,6.5)	45.5	F	Infeasible
3	(S_1, x_2)	(13.6,2.6)	26.0	B	Feasible
4	(S_2, x_1)	(3.4,4.8)	33.6	D	Feasible
5	(S_2, x_2)	(−17.0,6.0)	60.0	E	Infeasible
6*	(x_1, x_2)	(4.0,1.0)	38.0	C*	Feasible

* Optimal feasible solution.

ables which are to be set to zero. The other two variables, therefore, constitute a basis, the solution of which can be determined by solving the two (m) simultaneous equations in two (m) unknowns. For example, Solution 4 is determined by setting S_1 and x_2 to zero and solving for S_2 and x_1 in

$$5x_1 \qquad = 24 \qquad\qquad (1)$$
$$2x_1 + S_2 = 13. \qquad\qquad (2)$$

Two of the solutions (2 and 5) are infeasible because of violations in the non-negativity constraints; hence, the optimal solution (Solution 6) is selected from among the set of feasible solutions. Note that the feasible solutions (A,B,C,D) represent corner points of the solution space in Figure 5–1.

Follow-up Exercises

4. Solve the following problem by enumeration:

   Maximize

   $$z = 8x_1 + 5x_2$$

   subject to

   $$2x_1 + 3x_2 \leq 600 \qquad\qquad (1)$$
   $$5x_1 + 4x_2 \leq 1{,}000 \qquad\qquad (2)$$
   $$x_1, x_2 \geq 0.$$

   Verify your results by solving the problem graphically.

5. Solve the police sector problem (Example 4.1, page 95) by enumeration. Treat the ($\geq$) constraints by *subtracting* an additional variable, E_i, from the left-hand side. Check your results against Figure 4–5 and Example 4.3.

**Solution by the Lagrange Multiplier Method

Solution by enumeration can be viewed as a special case of solution by the Lagrange multiplier method (p. 83). In this case, the total number of constraints is given by the number of structural constraints (m) plus the number of nonnegativity constraints (n). Since the optimal solution for the n decision variables must occur at an extreme point, a total of n out of the $(m + n)$ constraints must be satisfied in an equality sense. Once again, the number of candidates for an optimal solution is given by Equation (5.2).

Example 5.4b

To illustrate this approach, first label $x_1 \geq 0$ as constraint (3) and $x_2 \geq 0$ as (4) in Example 5.3. Now suppose constraints (1) and (4) are selected for solution. It follows that the Lagrangian function is given by

$$L(x_1, x_2, \lambda_1, \lambda_4) = 7x_1 + 10x_2 - \lambda_1(5x_1 + 4x_2 - 24) - \lambda_4(x_2 - 0)$$

and the first-order conditions by

$$\frac{\partial L}{\partial x_1} = 7 \quad - 5\lambda_1 \qquad = 0$$

$$\frac{\partial L}{\partial x_2} = 10 \quad - 4\lambda_1 - \lambda_4 = 0$$

$$\frac{\partial L}{\partial \lambda_1} = -5x_1 - 4x_2 + 24 = 0$$

$$\frac{\partial L}{\partial \lambda_4} = \qquad - x_2 \qquad = 0.$$

Solving for the variables and the multipliers, we get $\lambda_1^* = 7/5$, $\lambda_4^* = 4.4$, $x_1 = 4.8$, and $x_2 = 0$, which is recognized as Solution 4 in Table 5–1. Based on Table 3–3, $\lambda_1^* > 0$ implies that constraint (1) binds the solution (Case *b*) and $\lambda_4^* > 0$ implies that constraint (4) does not bind the solution (Case *d*). Agree?

Follow-up Exercises

6. Verify Solutions 5 and 6 in Table 5–1 by the Lagrange multiplier method. Relate the values of λ^* to policies in Table 3–3.
7. Using the bordered Hessian matrix, verify that Solution 6 corresponds to a maximum stationary point. What result do you get when you apply the same test to Solution 5?

A moment's reflection and calculation with Equation (5.2) should convince you that solution by enumeration or by the Lagrange multiplier method is impractical; for example, the production mix problem of Example 4.5 would require the examination of 210 solutions, and the solid waste problem of Example 4.10 (which is small-scale compared to actual applications) has over 9 billion possible solutions. Assuming it takes a computer 0.1 second to generate each solution, we find 9 billion solutions would require more than nine years of continuous CPU time! As will be demonstrated next, the simplex method usually converges on the optimal solution rapidly.

5.4 SIMPLEX METHOD OF SOLUTION: ($\leq$) CONSTRAINTS

The simplex method of solution is an iterative calculating procedure for the LP problem which avoids infeasible solutions and improves the objective function at each iteration. The method of solution is essentially identical to the identity matrix method presented in Section 5.1; it differs only in the criteria which guide the procedure for row operations to find the optimal solution.

By setting up the equations in a tabular format, a more efficient **tableau form** for expressing and solving (both by hand and by computer) the standard LP model can be achieved.

Tableau Form

In order to consolidate every equation in the LP model, the objective function is added to the constraints in the standard form, Equation (5.1), as follows:

$$1z - c_1 x_1 - c_2 x_2 - \cdots - c_n x_n - 0S_1 - 0S_2 - \cdots - 0S_m = 0$$
$$0z + a_{11}x_1 + a_{12}x_2 + \cdots + a_{1n}x_n + 1S_1 + 0S_2 + \cdots + 0S_m = b_1$$
$$0z + a_{21}x_1 + a_{22}x_2 + \cdots + a_{2n}x_n + 0S_1 + 1S_2 + \cdots + 0S_m = b_2$$

$$0z + a_{m1}x_1 + a_{m2}x_2 + \cdots + a_{mn}x_n + 0S_1 + 0S_2 + \cdots + 1S_m = b_m.$$

Note that z is now treated in the same manner as the other variables in the problem. Its role as a dependent variable becomes obscured by its inclusion as just another variable in a system of simultaneous equations. An equivalent representation is given by the following tableau form:

	Criterion Value	Decision Variables			Slack Variables			Right-hand–side Constants
	z	x_1	x_2 $\cdots$	x_n	S_1 S_2	$\cdots$	S_m	b_i
z-equation	1	$-c_1$	$-c_2$ $\cdots$	$-c_n$	0 0	$\cdots$	0	0
Constraint equations	0	a_{11}	a_{12} $\cdots$	a_{1n}	1 0	$\cdots$	0	b_1
	0	a_{21}	a_{22} $\cdots$	a_{2n}	0 1	$\cdots$	0	b_2
	$\cdot$	$\cdot$	$\cdot$ $\cdot$	$\cdot$	$\cdot$ $\cdot$	$\cdot$	$\cdot$	$\cdot$
	0	a_{m1}	a_{m2} $\cdots$	a_{mn}	0 0	$\cdots$	1	b_m

Solution Procedure

The following steps generalize the simplex method of solution:

1. **Select a convenient starting basis of m variables which is feasible.** Recalling that variables *outside* the basis are set to zero and that the appearance of an *identity matrix* for the coefficients of variables in a system of linear simultaneous equations makes for a convenient solution (Example 5.2), it can be seen from the tableau that S_1, S_2, . . . , S_m represent a convenient starting basis with an immediate solution of b_1, b_2, . . . , b_m, respectively.

Example 5.5

Incorporating the objective function in the system of equations given by the standard form of Example 5.3 results in the following format:

$$1z - 7x_1 - 10x_2 - 0S_1 - 0S_2 = 0$$
$$0z + 5x_1 + 4x_2 + 1S_1 + 0S_2 = 24$$
$$0z + 2x_1 + 5x_2 + 0S_1 + 1S_2 = 13.$$

In tableau form this is expressed as:

Basis	z	x_1	x_2	S_1	S_2	b_i
—	1	−7	−10	0	0	0
S_1	0	5	4	1	0	24
S_2	0	2	5	0	1	13

For the sake of convenience, the variables in the basis are indicated in the first column of the tableau. The selection of S_1 and S_2 for the basis is equivalent to setting x_1 and x_2 to zero; hence, the system of three equations is reduced to

$$1z + 0S_1 + 0S_2 = 0 \tag{0}$$
$$0z + 1S_1 + 0S_2 = 24 \tag{1}$$
$$0z + 0S_1 + 1S_2 = 13 \tag{2}$$

which provides an immediate solution of $z = 0$, $S_1 = 24$, and $S_2 = 13$. Note that the first solution is at the origin (point A) in Figure 5–1.

Two important points must be understood: First, the appearance of an identity matrix in the tableau *underneath z and the variables in the basis* immediately provides the right-hand–side (RHS) constants as the solution; second, the RHS constants must be *nonnegative* in order to guarantee a feasible solution.[3]

The next solution is initiated by replacing a variable in the basis with a variable outside the basis such that the value of z is improved.

2.   **Select an entering variable by applying the "optimality criterion":** Select the *non*basic variable which has the *best per unit contribution* to the objective function. For *maximization* problems, select the value having the *most negative* coefficient in the z equation of the tableau; for minimization problems, select the value which is *most positive*.[4] In case of a *tie,* arbitrarily select one of the tied variables.

3.   **Select the leaving variable and the amount of the entering variable by applying the "feasibility criterion":** Determine the *maximum* amount of the entering variable which can be brought in for each potential leaving variable in the basis such that the value of the leaving variable

---

[3] See condition (2) of the standard form in Section 5.2.

[4] If this seems the opposite from what you would expect, recall that the c_j coefficients in the tableau are opposite in sign from the original formulation of the problem.

is forced to zero; select as the leaving variable the one corresponding to the *smallest* of the maximum amounts. This value represents the amount of the entering variable.

Example 5.6

Continuing the previous example, we select x_2 as the entering variable because it has the most negative coefficient (-10) of the nonbasic variables in the z equation of the tableau; this is equivalent to the best per unit contribution in the original objective function which is to be maximized; that is, each unit of x_2 *increases* z by 10.

Because there are two constraint equations, only two variables are allowed in the basis; hence either S_1 or S_2 must leave; that is, one or the other must be set to zero. The feasibility criterion allows for the maximum entry of x_2 such that variables which remain in the basis do not violate the nonnegativity condition. Consider the two constraints

$$5x_1 + 4x_2 + S_1 \qquad = 24 \qquad (1)$$
$$2x_1 + 5x_2 \qquad + S_2 = 13. \qquad (2)$$

Since x_1 is not in the basis, it may be ignored ($x_1 = 0$). Solving for S_1 and S_2, we get

$$S_1 = 24 - 4x_2 \qquad (1a)$$
$$S_2 = 13 - 5x_2. \qquad (2a)$$

If S_1 were to be selected as the leaving variable it must be set to zero; this would give, from Equation (1a), a value of 24/4, or 6, for x_2. If S_2 were to be selected, then from Equation (2a) it follows that $x_2 = 13/5$, or 2.6. Note, however, that a value of 6 for x_2 would cause S_2 to be negative based on (2a), which results in an infeasible solution; hence, the *maximum* value that can be assigned to x_2 such that one of the variables leaves the basis (S_2) while the remaining variable does not become negative (S_1) is 2.6 The next solution, therefore, is

$$x_2 = 2.6$$
$$S_1 = 24 - 4(2.6)$$
$$= 13.6$$

$$x_1 = 0$$
$$S_2 = 0$$
$$z = 7(0) + 10(2.6)$$
$$= 26,$$

which is recognized as Solution 3 in Table 5–1 and Point B in Figure 5–1.

Based on the above, the feasibility criterion can be operationalized more effectively as:

a.   Calculate the ratios $r_1, r_2, \ldots, r_m$ by dividing the RHS constants by the corresponding constraint coefficients of the entering variable; that is,

$$r_i = b_i / a_{ij}^* \qquad (5.3)$$

where b_i is the ith RHS constant in the tableau, a_{ij}^* is the coefficient of the *corresponding* (ith) constraint for the *entering* variable, x_j, and r_i is the *maximum* amount allowed for the entering variable by the ith constraint.

b. Select the leaving variable as the one in the basis corresponding to the *minimum* r_i where $r_i \geq 0$; the amount of the entering variable is given by this r_i.

In the preceding example,

$$r_1 = 24/4$$
$$r_2 = 13/5.$$

Since r_2 is minimum, the basic variable associated with the second constraint (S_2) is selected as the leaving variable. The allowable amount for the entering variable x_2 is precisely $13/5$.

Because *zero* or *negative* a_{ij}^* imply that an infinite amount of the entering value can be assigned (Can you show this?), their corresponding ratios are simply ignored whenever they appear.

4. **Modify the tableau to reflect the new solution.** The objective is to force an identity matrix immediately underneath z and the *new* set of basic variables by performing *row operations* as in Example 5.2.

Example 5.7

The original tableau of Example 5.5 is modified by including row numbers and an r_i column. The new tableau is shown below.

Basis	z	x_1	x_2	S_1	S_2	b_i	Row No.	r_i
I	1	-7	-10*	0	0	0	(0)	—
S_1	0	5	4	①	0	24	(1)	$24/4 = 6.0$
S_2	0	2	⑤	0	①	13	(2)	$13/5 = 2.6$*
II	1	-3*	0	0	2	26	(0)	—
S_1	0	⟨17/5⟩	0	①	$-4/5$	68/5	(1)	$13.6/3.4 = 4.0$*
x_2	0	2/5	①	0	1/5	13/5	(2)	$2.6/0.4 = 6.5$

*The asterisks at the end of the r_i column identify S_2 and S_1 as the leaving variables. The asterisk above the -10 identifies x_2 as the entering variable and the asterisk above the -3 identifies x_1 as the entering variable.

In order to follow the movement of the identity matrix, each unity element is identified by the symbol □ . Since the column corresponding to z always remains intact, we omit the symbol for its unity element. Note that the portion of the identity matrix in the constraint equation section is associated only with basic variables and that a one must be located at each intersection of the row and column corresponding to the basic variables, *with zeros elsewhere in that column.* Thus, the columns under S_1 and S_2 in Tableau I have all zero's except for the one's at the $S_1 - S_1$ and $S_2 - S_2$ intersections; likewise for the columns under x_2 and S_1 (the new basis) in Tableau II.

In Tableau I, the asterisk (*) above the -10 in the z equation identifies x_2 as the entering variable according to the optimality criterion; the asterisk following the 2.6 in the r_i column identifies S_2 as the leaving variable according to the feasibility criterion; hence, in the new basis, x_2 will replace S_2. The constraint coefficient corresponding to the intersection of the S_2 row and the x_2 column is circled, ⑤, and termed the **pivot element.** The row associated with the leaving variable S_2, or the row corresponding to minimum r_i, is termed the **pivot equation** or **key row.** The column for the entering variable is labeled the **key column.**

Tableau II is generated by creating the new identity matrix for the new set of basic variables by row operations. The objective in transforming from Tableau I to Tableau II is to force an identity matrix format on the key column, as follows:

a. In Tableau I, divide the pivot equation, Row (2), by the pivot element 5. This gives Row (2) in Tableau II. Note that unity has been forced in the $x_2 - x_2$ intersection.
b. To force the necessary zero in Row (1) of the key (x_2) column, multiply Row (2) of Tableau II by -4 and add it to Row (1) in Tableau I. This gives Row (1) in Tableau II.
c. To force the necessary zero in Row (0) of the key column, multiply Row (2) of Tableau II by 10 and add it to Row (0) of Tableau I. This gives the new Row (0) in Tableau II.

Now, note the following: First, the identity matrix plus the fact that the nonbasic variables (x_1 and S_2) are equal to zero make the RHS (right-hand–side) constants the solutions for the respective basic variables (S_1 and x_2); second, in Row (0), the zero values for x_1 and S_2 coupled with zero coefficients for S_1 and x_2 provide the RHS constant as the solution to z. In other words, essentially we have created the following system of equations:

$$1z + 0S_1 + 0x_2 = \quad 26 \tag{0}$$
$$0z + 1S_1 + 0x_2 = 68/5 \tag{1}$$
$$0z + 0S_1 + 1x_2 = 13/5. \tag{2}$$

Consequently, at the second iteration, the solution is

$$z = 26$$
$$S_1 = 68/5$$
$$= 13.6$$
$$x_2 = 13/5$$
$$= 2.6$$
$$x_1 = 0$$
$$S_2 = 0.$$

5. **Repeat the steps (2) through (4) until no further improvement is possible in the objective function.** Note that, for a maximization problem, no further improvement is possible when the coefficients in Row (0), the z equation, are all zero or positive.

Example 5.8

Continuing the previous problem, we see that Tableau II indicates that x_1 is the entering variable (optimality criterion) and S_1 is the leaving variable (feasibility criterion). The new pivot equation is (1) and the new pivot element is 17/5. The next tableau follows:

Basis	z	x_1	x_2	S_1	S_2	b_i	Row No.	r_i
III	1	0	0	15/17	22/17	38	(0)	
x_1	0	☐1	0	5/17	−4/17	4	(1)	
x_2	0	0	☐1	−2/17	5/17	1	(2)	

Since no coefficients in Row (0) are negative, improvement (increase) in the objective function is not possible. The optimal solution, at the third iteration, is

$$z = 38$$
$$x_1 = 4$$
$$x_2 = 1$$
$$S_1 = 0$$
$$S_2 = 0.$$

Note that the simplex method sequentially evaluated z at the points A, B, and C of Figure 5–1, which represent three of the possible six solutions in Table 5–1.

Example 5.9

To further reinforce the simplex procedure, the following problem is solved step by step:

maximize

$$z = 3x_1 + 10x_2 + 4x_3 + 6x_4$$

subject to

$$2x_1 + 2x_2 + 5x_3 + x_4 \le 50 \quad (1)$$
$$x_1 - 2x_2 + x_3 + 5x_4 \le 40 \quad (2)$$
$$10x_1 + 5x_2 + 2x_3 + 4x_4 \le 150 \quad (3)$$
$$x_1, x_2, x_3, x_4 \ge 0$$

Basis	z	x_1	x_2	x_3	x_4	S_1	S_2	S_3	b_i	Row No.	r_i
			*								
I	1	-3	-10	-4	-6	0	0	0	0	(0)	—
S_1	0	2	②	5	1	☐1	0	0	50	(1)	$50/2 = 25*$
S_2	0	1	-2	1	5	0	☐1	0	40	(2)	—
S_3	0	10	5	2	4	0	0	☐1	150	(3)	$150/5 = 30$
					*						
II	1	7	0	21	-1	5	0	0	250	(0)	—
x_2	0	1	☐1	5/2	1/2	1/2	0	0	25	(1)	$25 \div 1/2 = 50$
S_2	0	3	0	6	⑥	1	☐1	0	90	(2)	$90/6 = 15*$
S_3	0	5	0	$-21/2$	3/2	$-5/2$	0	☐1	25	(3)	$25 \div 3/2 = 50/3$
III	1	15/2	0	22	0	31/6	1/6	0	265	(0)	
x_2	0	3/4	☐1	2	0	5/12	$-1/12$	0	35/2	(1)	
x_4	0	1/2	0	1	☐1	1/6	1/6	0	15	(2)	
S_3	0	17/4	0	-12	0	$-11/4$	$-1/4$	☐1	5/2	(3)	

* Denote leaving and entering variables.

To aid you in following the row operations from Tableaus I to II and from Tableaus II to III, try following Table 5–2 (if you can stand it).

For example, Row (0) of Tableau II was determined by multiplying Row (1) of Tableau II by 10 and adding the resulting equation to Row (0) of Tableau I.

To reiterate a previous point, the new tableau is determined from the previous tableau by forcing a one in the pivot element and zeros elsewhere in the column of the entering variable.

Note that, in Tableau I, r_2 is undefined because the corresponding co-efficient of the entering variable is negative ($a_{22} = -2$). Since all of the co-

TABLE 5–2

Row Operations for Example 5.9

New Row i in Tableau k ($R_i T_k$)	Was Determined by ($=$)	The Indicated Row Operations
$R_1 T_2$	$=$	$R_1 T_1 / 2$
$R_0 T_2$	$=$	$10 R_1 T_2 + R_0 T_1$
$R_2 T_2$	$=$	$2 R_1 T_2 + R_2 T_1$
$R_3 T_2$	$=$	$-5 R_1 T_2 + R_3 T_1$
$R_2 T_3$	$=$	$R_2 T_2 / 6$
$R_0 T_3$	$=$	$R_2 T_3 + R_0 T_2$
$R_1 T_3$	$=$	$(-1/2) R_2 T_3 + R_1 T_2$
$R_3 T_3$	$=$	$(-3/2) R_2 T_3 + R_3 T_2$

efficients in Row (0) of Tableau III are greater than or equal to zero, the optimal solution is given by the RHS constants:

$$z = 265$$

$$x_1 = 0$$

Basis $\begin{cases} x_2 = 35/2 \\ x_4 = 15 \\ S_3 = 5/2 \end{cases}$ $\begin{array}{l} x_3 = 0 \\ S_1 = 0 \\ S_2 = 0. \end{array}$

You should verify that with $S_1 = 0$ and $S_2 = 0$, the implication is that constraints (1) and (2) are binding; that is, constraints associated with these slack variables are satisfied as strict equalities; conversely, a positive value for a slack variable ($S_3 = 5/2$) indicates that the constraint associated with the slack variable is satisfied as an inequality; that is, the RHS constant of constraint (3) could be 5/2 less without affecting the optimal solution.

Follow-up Exercises

8. Solve Exercise 4 by the simplex method.
9. By both the simplex method and a graphical solution, verify that the optimal solution to the problem below is $x_1 = 50$, $x_2 = 20$, $S_2 = 30$, and $z = 19$. Note that the basis contains three variables.

Maximize

$$z = 0.3x_1 + 0.2x_2$$

subject to

$$\begin{array}{rl} 6x_1 + & 6x_2 \leq 420 \\ 3x_1 + & 6x_2 \leq 300 \\ 4x_1 + & 2x_2 \leq 240 \end{array}$$

$$x_1, x_2 \geq \quad 0.$$

5.5 INTERPRETATION OF COEFFICIENTS

In Section 5.4 we concentrated primarily on the mechanics and mathematical justification for the simplex method. In this section we will attempt to provide a greater understanding of the interpretation and meaning of the data provided in a simplex tableau. This will be reinforced by the interpretation of an example within an applications context.

In Examples 5.4 through 5.8 the following problem was solved:

maximize

$$z = 7x_1 + 10x_2$$

subject to

$$5x_1 + 4x_2 \leq 24 \tag{1}$$
$$2x_1 + 5x_2 \leq 13 \tag{2}$$

$$x_1, x_2 \geq \quad 0.$$

Suppose that x_1 and x_2 represent, respectively, the number of containers of beef and pork that are to be transported by air freight from a packing house in Chicago to a wholesaler in Boston. Normally, meat is distributed by refrigerated trucks; a strike by independent truckers, however, has created a meat crisis in the Northeast which can be alleviated only by air freight. (This actually happened in February 1974.) The objective is to determine the amount of each meat to ship (the wholesaler will accept any mix) such that the profit contribution of the shipment is maximized subject to weight and volume constraints. Table 5–3 provides the relevant information in a form which is consistent with the formulation of the problem. For your convenience, Tableau II is reproduced below.

TABLE 5–3

Data for Air Cargo Problem

Meat Type	Profit Contribution ($100 per container)	Volume (cu. yd. per container)	Weight (1,000 lb. per container)
1(beef)	7	5	2
2(pork)	10	4	5
Availabilities		24	13

Basis	z	x_1	x_2	S_1	S_2	b_i	Row No.	r_i
II	1	−3*	0	0	2	26	(0)	—
S_1	0	17/5	0	1	−4/5	68/5	(1)	13.6/3.4 = 4.0*
x_2	0	2/5	1	0	1/5	13/5	(2)	2.6/0.4 = 6.5

* Denote entering and leaving variables.

Algebraic Interpretation of Simplex Procedure

As demonstrated earlier in the chapter, the identity matrix procedure for solving simultaneous equations transforms an original system of equations into an equivalent system. Examining Tableau II, we see that the information contained within can be written alternatively in equation form as

$$1z \quad - 3x_1 + 0x_2 + 0S_1 + \quad 2S_2 = 26 \quad (0)$$

$$0z + (17/5)x_1 + 0x_2 + 1S_1 - (4/5)S_2 = 68/5 \quad (1)$$

$$0z + \quad (2/5)x_1 + 1x_2 + 0S_1 + (1/5)S_2 = 13/5. \quad (2)$$

Recall that the nonbasic variables x_1 and S_2 were set equal to zero in this second solution. After substituting these values of zero into the equation, we find the values $z = 26$, $S_1 = 68/5$, and $x_2 = 13/5$ can be read directly from the right-hand–side constants. Notice once again that the coefficients on these variables form the columns of a (3×3) identity matrix.

The simplex procedure uses a "marginal analysis" approach to determine if a better solution exists. The essential question being asked is "What are the marginal effects of introducing one unit of a nonbasic variable into the solution?" The effects can be categorized as those which *influence the objective function* and those which *influence the current basic variables*. The marginal effects can be seen readily by rewriting the previous system of equations as follows:

$$z = \quad 26 + \quad\quad 3x_1 - \quad\quad 2S_2 \tag{0}$$

$$S_1 = 68/5 - (17/5)x_1 + (4/5)S_2 \tag{1}$$

$$x_2 = 13/5 - \quad (2/5)x_1 - (1/5)S_2. \tag{2}$$

This revised system of equations expresses the value of z and the values of the current basic variables in terms of those currently not in the solution (x_1 and S_2). The first equation can be interpreted as saying that the current value of z is 26, but if one unit of x_1 is created, z will increase by 3; if one unit of S_2 is introduced, z will decrease by 2. Thus, the coefficients of x_1 and S_2 can be thought of as representing **marginal rates of change** in the objective function. The effects upon the basic variables are read from the next two equations. Equation (1) implies that S_1 has a value of $68/5$, that increasing x_1 by one unit will reduce S_1 by $17/5$, and that increasing S_2 by one unit will increase S_1 by $4/5$. A similar interpretation can be given for Equation (2) in terms of the basic variable x_2. The coefficients of x_1 and S_2 in these equations represent **marginal rates of substitution** between basic variables and nonbasic variables which are *candidates* for entrance into the solution (basis).

In summary, the marginal effects of introducing any nonbasic variable into the basis can be found by observing the column of coefficients for that variable in Equations (0), (1), and (2).

Generalized Interpretation of Tableau Elements

We now consider a generalized interpretation of the basis column, RHS constants (b_i column), r_i column, Row (0), and Row (1) through Row (m)—but first, a note of warning. The algebraic interpretation in the previous section can be helpful in understanding the elements in a simplex tableau; however, to avoid confusion in interpreting marginal effects, keep in mind that the coefficients of the variables in the algebraic formulation are opposite in sign from the coefficients in the tableau.

Basis Column   This column contains the m basic variables whose values have been determined by setting all other variables to zero and by solving simultaneously the set of m constraint equations. Note should be made that the basic variables are those corresponding to the columns of an identity matrix in the constraint equation section of the tableau. For this reason, the row in which a basic variable is indicated contains a one (1) in the column representing that basic variable.

b_i **Column**   The right-hand–side constant for Row (0) always represents the current value of the objective function. The right-hand–side constants for the remaining m rows—Row (1)–Row (m)—represent the values of the m basic variables in the solution. The values, of course, correspond to the variables listed in the Basis column.

r_i **Column** r_i values indicate the maximum amount of the entering variable permitted by the ith constraint. Another way of viewing these values is that they represent the number of units of the entering variable required to drive the corresponding basic variable to a value of zero.

Row (0)   The coefficients in this row represent the marginal effects upon the value of the objective function of entering a unit of the variable represented by each column. The coefficients are the negative of the actual marginal effect. Consequently, a given coefficient can be interpreted as the decrease (positive value) or increase (negative value) of introducing one unit of the column variable. Interpreted from an alternative perspective, these coefficients reflect the *opportunity gain* (positive value) or *opportunity loss* (negative value) of *not* including one unit of the column variable.

We might note that, because of the identity matrix, Row (0) values for basic variables always equal zero. This is just as well since the analyst is most concerned with the marginal effects of nonbasic variables.

As we will demonstrate in Chapter 6, the coefficients directly underneath the slack variables in Row (0) of the *final* tableau represent so-called **shadow prices.** The shadow price associated with S_i is the amount by which the optimal value of the objective function would change if the RHS constant of the ith constraint were increased by one unit, *providing the same variables remain in the optimal basis*. Since many ($\leq$) constraints represent limited resources in LP problems, shadow prices are often thought of as representing the economic value of having an additional unit of a given resource.

Row (1) through Row (m)   The coefficient values for the last m rows represent the previously mentioned marginal rates of substitution. For any given column, the coefficients represent the marginal changes expected in the existing basic variables by introducing a unit of the column variable. As with the coefficients of Row (0), the coefficients are of a sign opposite to their actual effect upon the basic variable. That is, a negative coefficient implies an *increase* in the corresponding basic variable; a positive coefficient implies a *decrease*.

Interpretation of Air Cargo Problem

Let us now turn to an interpretation of Tableau II within the context of the application.

Present Solution   Since columns z, x_2, and S_1 have the form of a (3×3) identity matrix (the z column will always appear the same) x_2 and S_1 are identified as the basic variables in this solution. Since a one (1) appears in Row (1) of column S_1, the variable S_1 is placed in this row of the basis column. Similarly, the appearance of a one (1) in Row

(2) of the x_2 column requires the presence of x_2 in this row of the Basis column.

The corresponding values in the b_i column indicate that $z = 26$, $S_1 = 68/5$ and $x_2 = 13/5$. This solution suggests that 2.6 containers of pork should be shipped at a profit of $2,600.

A value of $68/5$ for S_1 indicates a slack of $68/5$ in the first constraint; that is, 13.6 cubic yards of unused volume remain in the cargo hold when 2.6 containers of pork are shipped. (Can you verify this directly from the first constraint?)

Since x_1 and S_2 are not in the basis, their values are zero in this solution. This means that no shipments are recommended for beef and that there is no slack in constraint (2). This latter result implies that the shipment of 2.6 containers of pork exhausts fully the 13-ton capacity of the cargo hold.

Implications for Improvement If a better solution exists, it can be determined by looking at Row (0). The -3 under x_1 indicates that shipping one unit (container) of beef will *increase* profits by three units ($300). Similarly, the 2 under S_2 implies that bringing in a unit (1,000 pounds) of slack weight (that is, displacing 1,000 pounds of cargo) will result in a two unit ($200) reduction in the objective function. Consequently, a better solution exists and it can be found by introducing x_1 (shipping units of beef).

Examination of Rows (1) and (2) for the x_1 column indicates the marginal effects on the current basic variables of introducing one unit of x_1. The first, $17/5 = 3.4$, means that the introduction (shipment) of one unit (container) of beef would displace 3.4 cubic yards of unused volume. According to Table 5–3 each unit of beef requires 5 cubic yards, so why the inconsistency? Bear with us. According to the coefficient immediately below $17/5$, each unit of beef additionally will displace $2/5$ unit of pork. Since the removal of $2/5$ unit of pork will free 1.6 cubic yards of space ($2/5$ unit times 4 cubic yards per unit), the *effective* space requirement for each *additional* unit of beef is only 3.4 cubic yards ($5 - 1.6$). Why will the inclusion of one unit of beef in the shipment displace $2/5$ unit of pork? Because the weight constraint is *binding,* which means that the inclusion of beef must be accompanied by the removal of pork. From Table 5–3, beef and pork require 2,000 pounds per unit and 5,000 pounds per unit, respectively. Therefore, $2/5$ unit of pork must be removed for each unit of beef included in order to completely exhaust the weight constraint, that is, in order for S_2 (a nonbasic variable) to remain at zero.

Why is the *marginal* increase in profits only three units when a profit contribution of seven units is indicated in the original objective function? The inclusion of one unit of beef results in the displacements of $2/5$ unit of x_2 (pork) and $17/5$ units of S_1 (volume capacity), which gives a marginal change in the original objective function of 3, that is, $7 - (2/5)(10) - (17/5)(0)$.

Finally, the r_i values indicate the number of units of x_1 which are required to drive the existing basis values to zero. The r_1 value of 4.0 in Row (1) indicates that, with the addition of the fourth unit of beef, S_1

or excess volume in the cargo hold will be eliminated. Similarly, the 6.5 in Row (2) indicates that 6.5 units of beef could be introduced before eliminating shipments of pork. Can you verify that the introduction of 6.5 units of beef would be impossible? Why?

Interestingly, an examination of Row (0) in the final tableau of Example 5.8 indicates that 15/17 and 22/17 represent, respectively, the shadow prices associated with constraints (1) and (2). Thus, if it were possible to increase the volume constraint from 24 to 25 cubic yards, the optimal profit would increase by 15/17; similarly, a relaxation of the weight limitation to 14,000 pounds would increase optimal profit by 22/17. If it was equally costly to create either an additional cubic yard of volume or an additional 1,000 pounds of weight capacity, which would you create? Once again, we emphasize (and prove in Chapter 6) that the interpretation of a shadow price is contingent upon the preservation of the present optimal basis.

5.6 SIMPLEX METHOD OF SOLUTION: MIXED CONSTRAINTS

In the standard form of LP problems characterized by ($\leq$) constraints, the inequalities were converted to equalities by adding slack variables to the left sides. Furthermore, the slack variables made for a convenient starting basis in the simplex method.

Converting LP Model to Standard Form

For problems including ($\geq$) constraints, the left-hand side of the inequation must be at least equal to the RHS constant; hence, the inequality can be forced into the form of an equation by subtracting a **surplus variable** from the left side. Doing so, however, precludes the use of a surplus variable in the starting basis, for the coefficient of -1 yields an infeasible (negative) solution; hence, it is necessary to *add* to the left-hand side yet another variable, termed an **artificial variable,** which can be used in the starting basis. Finally, in order to guarantee the elimination of the artificial variable from the final solution, a very heavy penalty is assigned to the artificial variable in the objective function. This takes the form of a very large *negative* coefficient in the objective function of *maximization* problems and a very large *positive* coefficient for *minimization* problems. While other methods are available, this so-called **method of penalties** remains the most popular.

Problems containing *equality constraints* can be treated in several ways. One method is to reduce the number of original variables by solving the equalities for selected variables and substituting the results in the inequalities and the objective function. Thus a problem having n real variables and m_3 equality constraints can be converted into a problem having $n - m_3$ real variables and m_3 fewer constraints. This approach has the shortcoming that eliminated variables may turn up negative in the final solution, since their explicit removal bypasses the nonnegativity restrictions.

A second approach for treating a problem with m_3 equality constraints involves selecting any m_3 real variables for the original basis; however, because basic variables are allowed to appear in only one equation (Can you verify this from the simplex tableau?), the chosen variables must be eliminated from all *other* equations plus the objective function.

A third, more convenient method, is to simply add an artificial variable to the left-hand side of every equality restriction. The method of penalty will guarantee, should a solution exist, that the artificial variable will not appear in the final solution.[5] This technique will be utilized in our development of the simplex method.

Based on the above, the generalized objective function of Equation (4.7) is expressed as

$$z = \sum_{j=1}^{n} c_j x_j \pm \sum_{i=m_1+1}^{m} M A_i \qquad (5.4)$$

where A_i is the artificial variable for the ith constraint, M is the penalty (a very large number) assigned to artificial variables in the objective function,[6] m_1 is the number of ($\le$) constraints, and m is the total number of constraints. If z is to be maximized, $(-M)$ must be used; for minimization problems $(+M)$ is used. (Do you see the logic?)

Constraints of the ($\le$) type are treated as before,

$$\sum_{j=1}^{n} a_{ij} x_j + S_i = b_i, \qquad i = 1, \ldots, m_1. \qquad (5.5)$$

Constraints of the ($\ge$) type are written in the standard form as

$$\sum_{j=1}^{n} a_{ij} x_j - E_i + A_i = b_i, \qquad i = m_1 + 1, \ldots, m_1 + m_2 \qquad (5.6)$$

where E_i is the excess (surplus) variable for the ith constraint and m_2 is the number of ($\ge$) constraints. Finally, equality constraints are expressed as

$$\sum_{j=1}^{n} a_{ij} x_j + A_i = b_i, \qquad i = m_1 + m_2 + 1, \ldots, m. \qquad (5.7)$$

Table 5–4 summarizes the nomenclature for the standard form of the problem.

----

[5] Should the problem not have a solution, at least one artificial variable will appear in the final basis with a positive value. See Example 5.13.

[6] Because of this choice of letter, the method of penalties is also known as the **M-technique.**

TABLE 5-4

Nomenclature for Standard Form of LP Problems

Constraint Type	Number	Type of Supplemental Variable	No. of Supplemental Variables
$\leq$	m_1	Slack (S_i)	m_1
$\geq$	m_2	Surplus (E_i) and Artificial (A_i)	$2m_2$
$=$	m_3	Artificial (A_i)	m_3
Total........	m		$m_1 + 2m_2 + m_3$

Note that the **supplemental variables** now include three types: slack, surplus, and artificial. Furthermore, the total number of variables (T) is given by the sum of **real variables** (x_j's) and supplemental variables, or

$$T = n + (m_1 + 2m_2 + m_3)$$
$$= n + m + m_2. \tag{5.8}$$

Generating Tableaus

As before, the first step in applying the simplex method is the conversion of the LP model to the standard form. Thereafter, the generation of tableaus follows readily, with some minor modifications.

Example 5.10

Given the problem

minimize

$$z = 2x_1 + 4x_2$$

subject to

$$x_1 + 5x_2 \leq 80 \tag{1}$$
$$4x_1 + 2x_2 \geq 20 \tag{2}$$
$$x_1 + x_2 = 10 \tag{3}$$
$$x_1, x_2 \geq 0,$$

the standard form is expressed as

minimize

$$z = 2x_1 + 4x_2 + MA_2 + MA_3$$

subject to

$$x_1 + 5x_2 + S_1 = 80 \tag{1}$$
$$4x_1 + 2x_2 - E_2 + A_2 = 20 \tag{2}$$
$$x_1 + x_2 + A_3 = 10 \tag{3}$$
$$x_1, x_2, S_1, E_2, A_2, A_3 \geq 0.$$

Note that the *minimization* of z requires *positive M*'s in the objective function. Expressing the system of equations in tableau form gives:

Basis	z	x_1	x_2	E_2	S_1	A_2	A_3	b_i	Row No.	r_i
I	1	-2	-4	0	0	$-M$	$-M$	0	(0)	—
S_1	0	1	5	0	$\boxed{1}$	0	0	80	(1)	
A_2	0	4	2	-1	0	$\boxed{1}$	0	20	(2)	
A_3	0	1	1	0	0	0	$\boxed{1}$	10	(3)	

Carefully note that surplus variables (E_i) cannot appear in the starting basis, since infeasible solutions would result; for example, including E_2 in the starting basis above would yield $E_2 = -20$. This was the purpose for introducing artificial variables. The *starting basis, therefore, will always consist of slack and artificial variables*—S_1 A_2, and A_3 in the present example.

Further note that Row (0) of Tableau I is inconsistent because basic variables A_2 and A_3 have *nonzero* coefficients. Because of this the RHS constant does not give the correct value of z; that is, the starting basis dictates that $A_2 = 20$ and $A_3 = 10$, which should give $z = 30M$. It is worth repeating that Row (0) gives a direct solution to z as the RHS constant if and only if the coefficients of the basic variables are zero, as dictated by the identity matrix; the coefficients of the *nonbasic* variables need not be zero because those variables, themselves, have values of zero. The upshot of this observation is that *Row (0) must be modified, by row operations, to yield coefficients of zero for the artificial variables.*

Tableau II is generated by replacing Row (0) of Tableau I by the sum of itself plus M times Row (2) plus M times Row (3):

Basis	z	x_1	x_2	E_2	S_1	A_2	A_3	b_i	Row No.	r_i
II	1	$\overset{*}{-2 + 5M}$	$-4 + 3M$	$-M$	0	0	0	$30M$	(0)	—
S_1	0	1	5	0	$\boxed{1}$	0	0	80	(1)	$80/1 = 80$
A_2	0	$\textcircled{4}$	2	-1	0	$\boxed{1}$	0	20	(2)	$20/4 = 5*$
A_3	0	1	1	0	0	0	$\boxed{1}$	10	(3)	$10/1 = 10$

Recall that the optimality criterion for *minimization* problems identifies the entering variable as the one having the *largest positive coefficient* in Row (0) of the tableau, which is equivalent to the greatest *marginal reduction* in the objective function. Consequently, x_1 is the first variable to enter the basis, since the coefficient $(-2 + 5M)$ is larger than any other coefficient (remember that M is a very large positive number).

From Tableau II on, the procedure is the same as before except for one item: *For minimization problems, the optimal solution has been found when all coefficients in Row (0) are either zero or negative.*

Basis	z	x_1	x_2	E_2	S_1	A_2	A_3	b_i	Row No.	r_i
III	1	0	$-3+M/2$ *	$-1/2+M/4$	0	$1/2-5M/4$	0	$10+5M$	(0)	—
S_1	0	0	$9/2$	$1/4$	①	$-1/4$	0	75	(1)	$75 \div 9/2 =$ $16\,2/3$
x_1	0	①	$1/2$	$-1/4$	0	$1/4$	0	5	(2)	$5 \div 1/2 = 10$
A_3	0	0	⟨$1/2$⟩	$1/4$	0	$-1/4$	①	5	(3)	$5 \div 1/2 = 10*$
IV	1	0	0	1 *	0	$-1-M$	$6-M$	40	(0)	—
S_1	0	0	0	-2	①	2	-9	30	(1)	—
x_1	0	①	0	$-1/2$	0	$1/2$	-1	0	(2)	—
x_2	0	0	①	⟨$1/2$⟩	0	$-1/2$	2	10	(3)	$10 \div 1/2 = 20*$
V	1	0	-2	0	0	$-M$	$2-M$	20	(0)	—
S_1	0	0	4	0	①	0	-1	70	(1)	
x_1	0	①	1	0	0	0	1	10	(2)	
E_2	0	0	2	①	0	-1	4	20	(3)	

In Tableau III, r_2 and r_3 were tied; arbitrarily, A_3 was chosen to leave, although x_1 could have left instead. In Tableau IV, r_1 and r_2 were ignored because they were negative. (Why?) The final solution, from Tableau V, is

$$z = 20$$
$$S_1 = 70 \qquad x_2 = 0$$
$$x_1 = 10 \qquad A_2 = 0$$
$$E_2 = 20 \qquad A_3 = 0.$$

Follow-up Exercises

10. In Example 5.10, break the tie in Tableau III by selecting x_1 as the leaving variable and continue the problem.

11. Solve the police sector problem (Example 4.1), page 95, by the simplex method. Relate each step to your solution by enumeration in Exercise 5 of this chapter.

5.7 ABERRATIONS IN SOLUTIONS

Four typical contingencies may arise in the solution of an LP problem: alternative optimal solutions, unbounded solutions, nonexisting feasible solutions, and degeneracy. As with most contingencies, you (the user) may never encounter any of these in actual practice. We feel, however, that it is better to understand the nature of and prepare for any eventuality —rather than "punting."

Alternative Optimal Solutions

In the previous chapter it was indicated (Figure 4–6 on page 103) that an *infinite* number of alternative optima will exist if the *objective function is parallel to a binding constraint.*[7] Example 5.11 illustrates the detection of such a condition in the simplex tableau.

Example 5.11

Consider the problem

maximize

$$z = x_1 + 2x_2$$

subject to

$$2x_1 + 4x_2 \leq 9 \tag{1}$$
$$3x_1 + x_2 \leq 12 \tag{2}$$

$$x_1, x_2 \geq 0.$$

As can be seen, the objective function is parallel to constraint (1). You should easily verify by a sketch that (1) is also a binding constraint. The simplex solution follows.

Basis	z	x_1	x_2	S_1	S_2	b_i	Row No.	r_i
I	1	−1	*−2	0	0	0	(0)	—
S_1	0	2	④	[1]	0	9	(1)	9/4*
S_2	0	3	1	0	[1]	12	(2)	12
II	1	*0	0	1/2	0	9/2	(0)	—
x_2	0	1/2	[1]	1/4	0	9/4	(1)	9/2
S_2	0	(5/2)	0	−1/4	[1]	39/4	(2)	39/10*
III	1	0	0	1/2	0	9/2	(0)	—
x_2	0	0	[1]	3/10	−1/5	3/10	(1)	
x_1	0	[1]	0	−1/10	2/5	39/10	(2)	

---

[7] By definition, a binding constraint has no slack or surplus, that is, is satisfied in the equality sense.

Tableau II gives the optimal solution as $S_2 = 9.75$, $x_2 = 2.25$, and $z = 4.5$. Note, however, that *nonbasic* variable x_1 has a *coefficient of zero in Row (0)* of the optimal tableau (Tableau II). This means that the inclusion of x_1 in the basis will have no effect on z, *implying that an alternative optimal solution exists.* In other words, a new solution having $x_1 > 0$ will yield the same optimal value of z. Tableau III enters x_1 at the expense of S_2 to give an alternative optimal solution of $x_1 = 3.9$, $x_2 = 0.3$, and $z = 4.5$. (Note that the nonbasic variable S_2 now has a zero coefficient in the z row). Thus, any one of the infinite number of feasible points along constraint (1) will yield an optimal solution.

Computationally, the family of alternative optima can be determined as *weighted averages* of the *basic* (that is, corner point) alternative optima:

$$x_{aj} = \sum_{i=1}^{k} w_i x_{ij}, \quad j = 1, \ldots, n \tag{5.9}$$

where

$x_{aj} = $ Alternative optimum value for variable j.
$x_{ij} = i$th *basic* alternative optimum value for variable j.
$w_i = $ Weight for ith basic alternative optimum.
$k = $ Number of basic alternative optima.

Recall from your basic course in statistics that two conditions must hold with respect to weights in a weighted average:

$$0 \leq w_i \leq 1$$
$$\sum_{i=1}^{k} w_i = 1.$$

In the present example, $k = 2$, $x_{11} = 0$, $x_{21} = 3.9$, $x_{12} = 2.25$, and $x_{22} \doteq 0.3$; hence,

$$x_{a1} = \quad 0w_1 + 3.9w_2$$
$$x_{a2} = 2.25w_1 + 0.3w_2.$$

The following family of alternative optima is generated for arbitrarily selected values of w_1 and w_2:

w_1	w_2	x_{a1}	x_{a2}
0.0..........	1.0	3.900	0.300
0.2..........	0.8	3.120	0.690
0.5..........	0.5	1.950	1.275
0.8..........	0.2	0.780	1.860
1.0..........	0.0	0.000	2.250

Follow-up Exercises

12. Verify that the above family of alternative optima yields the same maximum value for z.

13. Determine the basic alternative optima for the problem

maximize

$$z = 3x_1 + 2x_2$$

subject to

$$3x_1 + 5x_2 \leq 60 \tag{1}$$
$$6x_1 + 4x_2 \leq 48 \tag{2}$$
$$x_1, x_2 \geq 0.$$

Generate a family of optimal solutions.

14. How many basic alternative optima (extreme points) are possible with two decision variables (that is, what values are possible for k when $n = 2$)? What values are possible for k when $n = 3$? (Hint: Conceptualize the problem graphically.)

Unbounded Solutions

The relationship between an *unbounded solution space* and a *bounded* or *unbounded solution* was treated in Chapter 4. To refresh your memory (or to give your thumb a rest), we repeat a salient point: An unbounded solution space will yield an unbounded solution if and only if the optimization of the objective function is in the direction of the unbounded portion of the solution space. Otherwise, the solution is bounded. Example 5.12 illustrates the nature of the simplex calculations for both cases.

Example 5.12

Optimize

$$z = -2x_1 + x_2$$

subject to

$$5x_1 - x_2 \leq 20 \tag{1}$$
$$x_1 \qquad \leq 5 \tag{2}$$
$$x_1, x_2, \geq 0.$$

As previously indicated, a negative or zero coefficient ($a_{ij} \leq 0$) in *a less than or equal to* structural constraint for a particular variable (x_j) implies that an infinite amount of that variable can be introduced into the solution without violating that constraint. In our present problem, assigning infinity to x_2 does not violate constraints (1) or (2). Figure 5–2 illustrates the un-

FIGURE 5–2

Unbounded Solution Space with Bounded and Unbounded Solutions

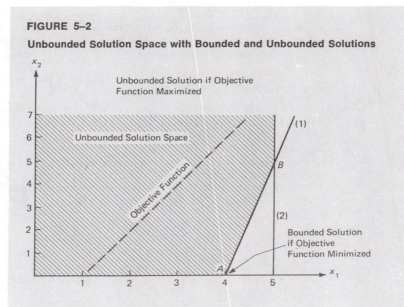

bounded solution *space* for this problem. The starting tableau is given below.

Basis	z	x_1	x_2	S_1	S_2	b_i	Row No.	r_i
—	1	2	−1	0	0	0	(0)	—
S_1	0	5	−1	1	0	20	(1)	
S_2	0	1	0	0	1	5	(2)	

Now suppose the problem is to *maximize z*. The (−1) value associated with x_2 in Row (0) of the tableau indicates that the introduction of one unit of x_2 would increase the current value of z by one. Since all of the marginal rates of substitution are less than or equal to zero for column x_2, an infinite number of units can be introduced without driving any of the current basic variables to zero (Remember the interpretation given in Section 5.5?); consequently, the value of z will have no bound ($z = \infty$). If the problem were to *minimize z*, no longer would it be desirable to enter x_2. The problem then has a *bounded solution* (point A in Figure 5–2) because x_1, the variable to be entered, is bounded.

In general, having *all* negative or zero marginal rates of substitution in a column represents a *necessary* condition for an unbounded optimal solution, but the *sufficient* condition must be established by determining the desirability of entering the unbounded variable as reflected by the *sign* of its coefficient in Row (0). This leads to the conclusion that an LP problem has an unbounded optimal solution if at any iteration (tableau) the variable chosen to *enter* the basis has all zero or negative marginal rates of substitution.

Follow-up Exercises

15. Change the objective function to $z = -10x_1 + x_2$ and use the original constraints. Analyze the problem both graphically and by the simplex method for the case which minimizes z.

16. Change the objective function to $z = 2x_1 - x_2$ and use the original constraints. Analyze the problem both graphically and by the simplex method for the two cases of minimizing and maximizing z. Note that, graphically, minimization implies shifting the z function upward. Why?

17. By graph and simplex tableaus analyze each of the following variations of Example 5.12:

   a. Maximize
   $$z = -2x_1 + x_2$$
   subject to
   $$5x_1 - x_2 \geq 20 \tag{1}$$
   $$x_1 \leq 5 \tag{2}$$
   $$x_1, x_2 \geq 0.$$

   b. Reverse the inequality in constraint (2) of part a.
   c. Maximize
   $$z = -2x_1 + x_2$$
   subject to
   $$5x_1 + x_2 \geq 20 \tag{1}$$
   $$x_1 \leq 5 \tag{2}$$
   $$x_1, x_2 \geq 0.$$

   d. Minimize z in part c.

No Feasible Solution

A problem has no feasible solution if its solution space is empty. Example 5.13 illustrates the detection of this condition by the simplex method.

Example 5.13

Maximize
$$z = 2x_1 + 3x_2$$
subject to
$$x_1 + x_2 \leq 10 \tag{1}$$
$$x_1 + x_2 \geq 20 \tag{2}$$
$$x_1, x_2 \geq 0.$$

Constraints (1) and (2) are clearly inconsistent (show this by graph). The simplex method provides the following.

Basis	z	x_1	x_2	E_2	S_1	A_2	b_i	Row No.	r_i
I	1	$-2-M$	*$-3-M$	M	0	0	$-20M$	(0)	—
S_1	0	1	①	0	☐1	0	10	(1)	10*
A_2	0	1	1	-1	0	☐1	20	(2)	20
II	1	1	0	M	$3+M$	0	$30-10M$	(0)	—
x_2	0	1	☐1	0	1	0	10	(1)	
A_2	0	0	0	-1	-1	☐1	10	(2)	

Note that the lack of negative coefficients in Row (0) of Tableau II implies that the optimal solution has been reached. A positive value for the artificial variable ($A_2 = 10$), however, indicates that constraint (2) has not been satisfied; hence, the solution is not feasible.

When an artificial variable appears in the final solution (basis) at a positive level, the problem has no feasible solution. Should the artificial variable appear at a zero level, the solution would be optimal and feasible, although the problem may have either a redundant constraint or basic feasible solutions which are degenerate (see below).

Follow-up Exercises

Solve the following problems and draw conclusions based on your results.

18. Maximize

$$z = x_1 + 2x_2 + 3x_3$$

subject to

$$2x_1 + x_2 + x_3 \leq 1 \qquad (1)$$
$$5x_1 + 7x_2 + 4x_3 \geq 15 \qquad (2)$$
$$5x_1 + 7x_2 + 4x_3 \geq 2 \qquad (3)$$
$$x_1, x_2, x_3 \geq 0.$$

19. Change the RHS constant of (2) to 4.

Degeneracy

A degenerate basic solution is one in which one or more basic variables has a value of zero. This can happen when a tie occurs for the leaving variable in the previous iteration. The variable arbitrarily selected to leave the basis will be forced to zero by the amount chosen for the entering variable according to the feasibility criterion. The tied variable which remains in the basis, however, will also drop to a zero level. At this point, one of three things can happen: (1) the solution will be temporarily degenerate; (2) the solution will be a degenerate optimal solution; or (3) the optimal solution, if it exists, will not be reached due to cycling.

The first case was demonstrated in Example 5.10. In Tableau III, x_1 and A_3 were tied for the "honor" of leaving variable and the latter was selected arbitrarily. Accordingly, x_1 dropped to a zero level in the degenerate solution of Tableau IV. Degeneracy proved to be temporary, however, as indicated by the optimal solution of Tableau V.

The danger of degeneracy is the potential for cycling or returning to a previously generated intermediate (nonoptimal) solution. If this were to happen, then the simplex algorithm "stalls" in its attempt to reach the optimal solution. The algorithm loops repetitively through a subset of non-optimal (basic) solutions without changing the value of the objective function. Improved solutions are always indicated by Row (0) values, but the minimum r_i value is always equal to zero. Advanced procedures, not to be treated here, have been developed to overcome this rare problem—although, simply returning to the point where the r_i values were originally tied and selecting another of the tied variables for removal often resolves the cycling problem.

Follow-up Exercise

20. Solve the following both graphically and by the simplex method:

maximize
$$z = 2x_1 + 6x_2$$

subject to

$$x_1 + 2x_2 \leq 20 \tag{1}$$
$$2x_1 + 3x_2 \leq 30 \tag{2}$$
$$x_2 \leq 10 \tag{3}$$
$$x_1, x_2 \geq 0.$$

5.8 **SHORT TABLEAUS

For those of you who thrive on efficiency, we now illustrate a method which reduces the computational burden (and the computer storage space required by the tableau) associated with the use of the simplex procedure. A solid understanding of the simplex method, as presented thus far, is prerequisite to your understanding and taking full advantage of the efficiencies offered by this method.

This procedure reduces the size of the simplex tableau which is carried along during the solution process. Such a reduction is possible because for each basic solution we need only consider the effects associated with introducing nonbasic variables. Therefore, why carry the identity matrix associated with the basic variables? Let us treat it as a "phantom" identity matrix, remembering that it should be included but that it is easier not to explicitly recompute it at each iteration.

The shortened tableau will include columns for each nonbasic variable and a column for the basic variable which exits. This latter column simply facilitates the computational procedure; it is not essential to include it if you thoroughly understand the simplex procedure.

Example 5.14

The solution to Example 5.9 using the short tableau follows.

Basis	x_1	x_2	x_3	x_4	S_1	b_i	r_i
I	-3	$\overset{*}{-10}$	-4	-6	0	0	
S_1	2	②	5	1	1	50	$50/2 = 25*$
S_2	1	-2	1	5	0	40	—
S_3	10	5	2	4	0	150	$150/5 = 30$

Basis	x_1	S_1	x_3	x_4	S_2	b_i	r_i
II	7	5	21	$\overset{*}{-1}$	0	250	
x_2	1	1/2	5/2	1/2	0	25	$25 \div 1/2 = 50$
S_2	3	1	6	⑥	1	90	$90/6 = 15*$
S_3	5	$-5/2$	$-21/2$	3/2	0	25	$25 \div 3/2 = 50/3$

Basis	x_1	S_1	x_3	S_2		b_i	
III	15/2	31/6	22	1/6		265	
x_2	3/4	5/12	2	$-1/12$		35/2	
x_4	1/2	1/6	1	1/6		15	
S_3	17/4	$-11/4$	-12	$-1/4$		5/2	

If you compare these tableaus with the original tableaus you will find them very similar. A few comments are necessary, though, for clarification. In each tableau the column representing the departing basic variable is filled only *after* the minimum ratio, r_i^*, is identfied. In Tableau I the minimum ratio of 25 identified S_1 as the departing variable. Because the column elements associated with S_1 change with the new solution, the corresponding column of the "phantom" identity matrix is added in for purposes of moving to the next tableau. Notice that in Tableau II, x_2 has replaced S_1 in the basis and the new S_1 column has replaced the x_2 column among the nonbasic variables. The simplex arithmetic is exactly the same as with the full-scale tableau in that basic row operations are performed to transform the column elements for the entering basic variable (x_2) into the appropriate identity matrix column (notice that this involves a movement of the new S_1 column after its computation).

Follow-up Exercises

21. Try solving Example 5.14 on your own and check your tableau entries against ours.
22. Use the short form in solving the problem given in Example 5.3.
23. Use the short form in solving the police sector problem and compare your results to those found in Exercise 11.

5.9 COMPUTERIZED SOLUTIONS

In actual applications, the solution of LP problems by hand calculation is unheard of, as the availability of efficient computer codes for the simplex method is widespread. Most computer manufacturers, OR consulting firms, and commercial time-sharing vendors provide "canned" programs based on variations of the simplex method which are more efficient than the standard simplex method regarding storage and computational requirements (not to mention more complex). This being the case, the recognition, formulation, and interpretation of LP problems present the challenges, insofar as the general user is concerned.[8]

In Chapter 4, six scenarios were presented and their LP formulations were developed. This section presents solutions to two scenarios and provides some interpretations. The next chapter will consider interpretations further, especially in terms of the sensitivity of the optimal solution to errors in estimating the parameters (coefficients and RHS constants).

Product Mix Model—Example 4.5

Appendix 5A illustrates the input and output using a particular time-shared computer program for the product mix problem of Chapter 4 on page 109.

Both the input and the output should be self-explanatory. Note that the user must add in the constant 60 in the objective function *following* the solution, as no provision is made for a constant in the generalized objective function. Thus, the minimum total cost for the two-quarter planning horizon is $5,084.75 plus $60, or $5,144.75. To achieve this minimum cost, the firm should produce: in the first quarter, all 500 units of product A and 75 units of product B; in the second quarter, the remaining 625 units of product B (note the rounding error).

The slack associated with the first constraint ($S_1 = 40$) indicates that only 310 hours of labor will be utilized in the first quarter, that is, 350 hours are available, of which 40 will not be utilized. Similarly, $S_3 = 475$

---

[8] As mentioned previously, the problems encountered in large-scale mathematical programming continue to represent a formidable challenge to specialists in operations research.

implies that of the 6,000 kilos of raw material that are available in the first quarter, 475 kilos need not be used. Finally, $S_4 = 100$ suggests that 9,900 kilos of raw material, from the available 10,000, will be used over the planning horizon.

The shadow prices corresponding to the six constraints are 0, -1.41, 0, 0, 3.00, and 6.19, respectively. Note that a shadow price of zero is consistent with the existence of slack in a constraint; for example, since 40 hours of labor are unused in the first quarter, increasing the labor availability above 350 offers no reduction in optimal cost.

The shadow price of -1.41 associated with the second constraint implies that each additional hour above 500 (up to a point) decreases optimal cost by $1.41 (conversely, each reduction of one available hour in the second quarter increases optimal total cost by $1.41). Can you interpret the shadow prices 3.00 and 6.19?

You should verify readily that the total cost breaks down as follows:

Variable costs.....................................	$5,075.00
Product inventory costs.........................	65.00
Raw materials inventory costs..................	4.75
Total......................................	$5,144.75

How important are the inventory costs relative to the variable costs of production? Do you think that the production decision (values for x's) would change if inventory costs were to be ignored in the formulation?

Solid Waste Management, a Blending Problem—Example 4.10, page 123

Appendix 5B indicates a maximum profit of $6,135.86 after only 28 iterations. (Recall that this problem had over 9 billion corner-point solutions.) The quantities for the real variables in the basis dictate the pounds of each material and residue which go into the four products, as defined by Tables 4–11 and 4–12. Note that the optimal solution is degenerate ($x_6 = 0$).

Purchases of materials include 6,000 pounds for Material 1 ($x_1 + x_2 + x_3$), 5,000 pounds for Material 2 ($x_4 + x_5 + x_6$) and 4,000 pounds for Material 3 ($x_7 + x_8$).

Variables x_9 through x_{14} indicate the pounds of residue which are to be allocated to the secondary products based on specific material-product combinations. The residue which is to be disposed of for any given combination is determined by subtracting the allocated residue in the optimal solution from the waste residue (as given by the product of the waste coefficient and the optimal material-product allocation). For example, the residue of Material 1 from the production of Product A is given by $0.1x_1$ or 330.667 pounds; of this, 330.667 pounds (variable x_9) are to be allocated to the production of product C; hence, no residue from this material-product combination will be disposed of. Can you verify that all residue from the production of Product A (1,322.66 pounds) will be allocated to the production of Product C and that all residue from the production of Product B (2,381.32 pounds) will be disposed of?

Because constraint types are input into the program sequentially by *type* of constraint, the constraint numbers in the computer run do not coincide with the constraint numbers in the problem formulation of Chapter 4. The accompanying table provides the correspondence:

Constraint No. in the Formulation	Corresponding Constraint No. in the Computer Solution
1	12
2	1
3	13
4	2
5	14
6	3
7	15
8	16
9	4
10	17
11	5
12	6
13	7
14	8
15	9
16	10
17	11
18	18
19	19

An examination of the slack and surplus variables of Appendix 5B indicates the following: The minimum amount of Material 3 ($S_3 = 3,000$) and the maximum amounts of Materials 1 and 2 ($E_{12} = 4,000$; $E_{13} = 2,000$) are used; none of the Product B residues is completely utilized ($S_9 \doteq 473$; $S_{10} = 405$; $S_{11} = 1,504$); more than 20 percent of Material 1 is used in Product A, or about 1,786 pounds above the minimum required ($E_{15} \doteq 1,786$); and the amount of Material 1 in Product B is about 1,389 pounds above the minimum required ($E_{17} \doteq 1,389$).

The following weights of each product are produced:

$$
\begin{aligned}
\text{Product } A &= 0.9x_1 + 0.8x_4 + 0.6x_7 & \doteq 5{,}952 \text{ pounds.} \\
\text{Product } B &= 0.8x_2 + 0.8x_5 + 0.5x_8 + & \doteq 5{,}014 \text{ pounds.} \\
\text{Product } C &= x_3 + x_9 + x_{10} + x_{11} & \doteq 1{,}653 \text{ pounds.} \\
\text{Product } D &= x_6 + x_{12} + x_{13} + x_{14} & \doteq 0 \text{ pounds.}
\end{aligned}
$$

Follow-up Exercises

Using a computerized LP program, solve and completely analyze the following problems:

24. Example 4.6   Transportation Model
25. Example 4.7   Capital Budgeting Model

SELECTED REFERENCES

Anderson, David R.; Sweeney, Dennis J.; and Williams, Thomas A. *Linear Programming for Decision Making, An Applications Approach*. St. Paul: West Publishing Co., 1974.

Gass, S. I. *Linear Programming: Methods and Applications*. 4th ed. New York: McGraw-Hill, Inc., 1975.

Hadley, G. *Linear Programming*. Reading, Mass.: Addison-Wesley Publishing Co., 1962.

Hillier, Frederick S., and Lieberman, Gerald J. *Introduction to Operations Research*. 2d ed. San Francisco: Holden Day, Inc., 1974.

Hughes, Ann J., and Grawiog, Dennis E. *Linear Programming: An Emphasis on Decision Making*. Reading, Mass.: Addison-Wesley Publishing Co., 1973.

Kim, Chaiho. *Quantitative Analysis for Managerial Decisions*. Reading, Mass.: Addison-Wesley Publishing Co., 1976.

Levin, Richard I., and Lamone, Rudolph P. *Linear Programming for Management Decisions*. Homewood, Ill.: Richard D. Irwin, Inc., 1969.

McMillan, Claude, Jr. *Mathematical Programming: An Introduction to the Design and Application of Optimal Decision Machines*. New York: John Wiley & Sons, Inc., 1970.

Montgomery, David B., and Urban, Glen L. *Management Science in Marketing*. Englewood Cliffs, N.J.: Prentice-Hall, Inc., 1969.

Shamblin, James E., and Stevens, G. T., Jr. *Operations Research: A Fundamental Approach*. New York: McGraw-Hill, Inc., 1974.

Spivey, W. Allen, and Thrall, Robert M. *Linear Optimization*. New York: Holt, Rinehart and Winston, Inc. 1970.

Strum, Jay E. *Introduction to Linear Programming*. San Francisco: Holden Day, Inc., 1972.

Trueman, Richard E. *An Introduction to Quantitative Methods for Decision Making*. New York: Holt, Rinehart and Winston, Inc., 1974.

Wagner, Harvey M. *Principles of Operations Research*. 2d ed. Englewood Cliffs, N.J.: Prentice-Hall, Inc., 1975.

ADDITIONAL EXERCISES

28. Solve the following system of equations using the identity matrix method:

$$5x_1 + 2x_2 - x_3 = 15$$
$$3x_1 - 2x_2 \quad\;\; = 16$$
$$x_1 + \;\; x_2 + x_3 = \;\; 3.$$

29. For each of the following phenomena, summarize the way in which you become aware of it when solving graphically and when solving by the simplex method.

    a. Alternative optimal solutions.
    b. No feasible solution.
    c. Unbounded solution.
    d. Redundant constraints.

30. *a.* Solve the following problem using the simplex method:

Maximize

$$z = 7x_1 + 5x_2$$

subject to

$$5x_1 + 3x_2 \le 50$$
$$4x_1 - 2x_2 \le 30$$

$$x_1, x_2 \ge 0.$$

    b. Verify your solution by solving graphically and relate tableaus to specific corner points.

31. *a.* Solve the following problem by the simplex method:

Minimize

$$z = 4x_1 + 2x_2 + x_3$$

subject to

$$x_1 + x_2 + x_3 \le 40$$
$$2x_1 + x_2 + .5x_3 \ge 10$$

$$x_1, x_2, x_3 \ge 0.$$

    b. What is your conclusion?

32. *a.* Solve the following problem by the simplex method:

Maximize

$$z = 3x_1 + 5x_2$$

subject to

$$6x_1 - 4x_2 \ge 24$$
$$-4x_1 + 2x_2 \le 12$$

$$x_1, x_2 \ge 0.$$

    b. Verify your solution by solving graphically.
    c. What is your conclusion?
    d. By the simplex method, solve the problem if z is to be minimized. Confirm graphically.

33. Consider the following simplex tableau for a maximization problem.

Basis	z	x_1	x_2	x_3	S_1	S_2	b_i
—	1	0	-2	-3	1	0	18
x_1	0	1	-1/2	3	-1/2	0	20
S_2	0	0	2	1	2	1	18

    a. How many constraints and what types were there in the original formulation?

    b. Verbally interpret all tableau elements in the x_2 column. Do the same for elements in the x_3 column.

34. *a.* Determine the shadow prices in the optimal solution to Exercise 30 and interpret their meaning.

    b. Change the RHS constant in the first constraint to 51 and determine optimal z. Is the change in optimal z consistent with the shadow price?

35. Consider an LP model with 20 real variables (x's), 10 constraints of the ($\leq$) type, 15 constraints of the ($\geq$) type, and 5 constraints of the ($=$) type. Suppose all constraints are in standard form.

    a. What is the total number of variables?

    b. How many solutions are possible by enumeration?

    c. Is each solution to part (*b*) equivalent to a corner point of the solution space? Explain.

    d. Describe the manner in which the simplex method realizes efficiencies in solving this problem.

36. Consider the following tableau, where the letters *a* through *o* represent specific numerical values.

Basis	z	x_1	x_2	S_1	S_2	b_i
—	1	a	b	c	d	e
?	0	f	g	h	i	j
?	0	k	l	m	n	o

    a. Suppose this were a starting tableau and $f < 0$, $g > 0$, $k = 0$, and $l > 0$. Conclusion?

    b. Assuming the indicated ranges of values immediately preceding, fill in the following cells with "yes" or "no" in answer to the question "unbounded optimal solution?"

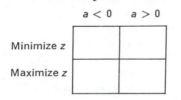

	$a < 0$	$a > 0$
Minimize z		
Maximize z		

    c. If this were a final tableau with x_1 and S_1 in the basis and $b = 0$, then what could you conclude? Explain.

    d. If x_1 and S_2 were in the basis (in the first and second rows, respectively), then what would be the meaning of $g > 0$? $g < 0$? Express an appropriate algebraic relationship relating x_1 to the nonbasic variables.

    e. Again if x_1 and S_2 were in the basis, then what must be true about the values of f, k, i, and n?

    f. Is it possible to have $j < 0$ or $o < 0$? Explain.

g. If this were an intermediate tableau for a minimization problem and x_1 and S_2 are in the basis, then what must be true about values for a, b, c, and d?

h. Same as part (g) except the tableau is final. Is it possible to have a positive shadow price associated with a ($\leq$) constraint in a minimization problem? Explain.

**37. The optimality criterion which has been used relies on the *marginal* change in z for a one-unit increase in the nonbasic variable under consideration. Define a new optimality criterion which selects the entering variable as the one yielding the best *total* improvement in z. (Hint: This means that the maximum amount for the nonbasic variable under consideration must be determined according to the feasibility criterion.) Apply this new optimality-feasibility criterion to the solution of the problem in Example 5.3 and relate the tableaus to specific corner points in Figure 5–1. What advantages and disadvantages do you foresee for this new criterion?

**38. Solve the following problem using the short tableau procedure.

Maximize

$$z = x_1 + 3x_2 + 4x_3 + 2x_4$$

subject to

$$
\begin{aligned}
x_1 + x_2 + x_3 + x_4 &\leq 100 \\
2x_1 + x_2 &\geq 20 \\
x_2 + 2x_3 - x_4 &\leq 80
\end{aligned}
$$

$$x_1, x_2, x_3, x_4 \geq 0.$$

**39. Solve the following problem using the short tableau procedure.

Minimize

$$z = 4x_1 + 3x_2 + x_3$$

subject to

$$
\begin{aligned}
2x_1 + 5x_2 - x_3 &\geq 30 \\
4x_1 + x_2 + 2x_3 &\geq 25
\end{aligned}
$$

$$x_1, x_2, x_3 \geq 0.$$

**40. Using a computerized LP program, solve one of the following models from Chapter 4:

a. Exercise 43.
b. Exercise 44.
c. Exercise 46.
d. Exercise 47.
e. Exercise 48.
f. Exercise 49.
g. Exercise 50.
h. Exercise 51.
i. Exercise 52.
j. Exercise 53.
k. Exercise 54.
l. Exercise 55.

APPENDIX 5A   COMPUTER SOLUTION TO PRODUCT MIX MODEL

linear programming
***** ***********

to run this program a file space
must be identified.

what is the name of your file
?ex45

do you wish to read from your file

    (yes = 1, no = 2)
?2

are you an expert on this program

    (yes = 1, no = 2)
?2

supply the following information by
entering five integer numbers on one line
separated by commas.

    (1) type: (max = 1) (min = 2)

no. of:

    (2) real variables
    (3) <= constraints
    (4) >= constraints
    (5)   = constraints
?2,4,4,0,2

constraint input
········ ·····

the right-hand-side constant and coefficient values will be
requested for each constraint. to enter the coefficient
values, type the variable no. and the coeff. value,
separated by a comma. zero coeff. need not be entered.
exit to next constraint by entering 0,0

constraint no.   1   (<= type)

right-hand side
?350

APPENDIX 5A (*continued*)

coefficients

?1, .5

?3, .8

?0, 0

constraint no.   2   (< = type)

right-hand side
?500

coefficients
?2, .5

?4, .8

?0, 0

constraint no.   3   (< = type)

right-hand side
?6000

coefficients
?1, 10

?3, 7

?0, 0

constraint no.   4   (< = type)

right-hand side
?10000

coefficients
?1, 10

?2, 10

?3, 7

?4, 7

constraint no.   5   (= type)

right-hand side
?500

coefficients
?1, 1

?2, 1

?0, 0

APPENDIX 5A (continued)

constraint no.   6   (= type)

right-hand side
?700

coefficients
?3,1

?4,1

?0,0

objective function input
....

enter the variable number and the coefficient value in
a similar manner.

?1,3

?2,4

?3,6.13

?4,5

do you wish to change any data?

   (yes=1, no=2)
?2

there are more than 10 columns in your tableau, therefore
if you wish a printout of tableaus, they will not be in formatted form.
do you wish a print out of
0 = no tableaus
1 = last tableau only
2 = 1st and last
3 = all tableaus
?0

APPENDIX 5A (concluded)

objective function minimized at   5084.7461

    5 iterations required

basic variables
. . . .

variable number	quantity of this variable	variable type	associated with constraint number
1	500.00000	real	
3	75.00000	real	
4	624.99976	real	
5	40.00000	slack	1
7	474.99976	slack	3
8	100.00328	slack	4

do you want shadow prices?

   (yes = 1, no = 2)
?1

shadow prices
. . . .

associated with constraint	shadow price
1	0.0
2	-1.4125
3	0.0
4	0.0
5	3.0000
6	6.1875

do you want a sensitivity analysis?

   (yes = 1, no = 2)
?1

APPENDIX 5B   COMPUTER SOLUTION TO SOLID WASTE
MANAGEMENT MODEL

objective function maximized at   6135.8633

   28 iterations required

basic variables

variable number	quantity of this variable	variable type	associated with constraint number
1	3306.66992	real	
2	2362.66016	real	
3	330.66602	real	
4	2976.00220	real	
5	2023.99487	real	
6	0.0	real	
7	991.99951	real	
8	3007.99805	real	
9	330.66675	real	
10	595.18946	real	
11	396.70883	real	
23	2999.99707	slack	3
29	472.53174	slack	9
30	404.79785	slack	10
31	1503.99634	slack	11
15	3999.99951	surplus	12
16	2000.00000	surplus	13
18	1785.59888	surplus	15
20	1388.79785	surplus	17

Postoptimality Analysis and the Dual Problem

IN DISCUSSING the decision-making paradigm in Chapter 1, we indicated that validation and interpretation are on-going processes. Having formulated and solved an LP problem, the analyst must next perform the extremely crucial phase of postoptimality analysis, often referred to as **sensitivity analysis.** This chapter discusses sensitivity analysis, revisits the concept of shadow prices, and presents an alternative and useful approach to formulating LP problems called the **dual problem.**

6.1 THE NATURE OF SENSITIVITY ANALYSIS

The Rationale

Rarely are the parameters (c_j's, a_{ij}'s, and b_i's) in any linear programming problem known with certainty. They are often, at best, estimates of the actual values of the relevant parameters. For example, rated exposures per dollar of advertising expenditure for media mix models (Example 4.8) usually are estimates of actual exposure rates determined by marketing research studies based on statistical sampling. The available labor hours per quarter in Example 4.9 (Financial Mix Model) are estimates which do not reflect the uncertainties associated with absenteeism or personnel transfers and the required labor hours per unit are only point estimates of universe (true) averages. Likewise, profit contributions used in objective functions fail to portray the uncertainties associated with unit selling prices and variable expenses such as wages, raw materials, and shipping. The point is that many of these parameters (constants) cannot be determined with certainty because of either measurement difficulties or probabilistic behavior (especially over time).

Even with such uncertainties initial estimates must be made in order to solve the problem. In the typical business firm, accounting and marketing information systems often provide this type of information. Adherence to good sampling, estimating, and forecasting procedures (see Appendix A at the end of the book) will tend to secure more viable and informative data. For example, we might estimate expected (mean) demand for a particular type of service using a mathematical forecasting model which also provides information on the standard deviation and the associated probability distribution.

Once the problem has been solved using the "assumed" values, the analyst (and the decision maker) should question how the resultant LP solution (the optimal basis and value of the objective function) would be affected if the parameters took on values other than those used in the initial formulation. The term "sensitivity analysis" has been used to describe this form of postoptimality analysis. If this analysis reveals that the optimal basis and value of the objective function are only slightly affected by significant changes in the parameters, then the solution would be judged to be *insensitive*. If, however, the basis and/or objective function do vary significantly with rather minor changes in the parameters, then the solution can be characterized as *sensitive*.

This chapter is largely devoted to the manner in which sensitivity analysis is conducted on one parameter at a time. Consideration of simultaneous variations in parameters is more realistic, but the methodology of such an analysis is beyond the scope of this text. In presenting sensitivity analysis we first use an intuitive approach (where possible) to facilitate your anticipating the effects of changes in parameters. A belief in the tenet "a picture is worth a thousand words" moves us next to present graphical analysis followed by a methodology based on the simplex tableau. As you will see, the elegance and power of sensitivity analysis becomes evident when one considers the undesirable alternative of completely reworking the problem to determine the sensitivity of the optimal solution (the "brute force" approach).

The Linear Equation Revisited

Equation (6.1) represents the equation for a straight line in two dimensions:

$$a_1 x_1 + a_2 x_2 = b. \tag{6.1}$$

Recalling the discussion in Chapter 4, you should verify that the slope of this line is given by the formula

$$m = -a_1/a_2 \tag{6.2}$$

and the x_2-intercept is given by the formula

$$k_2 = b/a_2. \tag{6.3}$$

Figure 6–1 graphically portrays the situation when a_1, a_2, and b are all greater than zero.

Sensitivity analysis in linear programming is concerned with changes in

FIGURE 6–1

Linear Equation

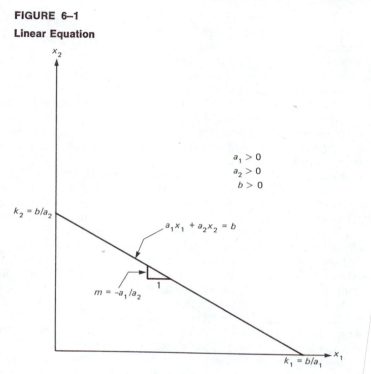

$a_1 > 0$
$a_2 > 0$
$b > 0$

$k_2 = b/a_2$

$a_1 x_1 + a_2 x_2 = b$

$m = -a_1/a_2$ 1

$k_1 = b/a_1$

FIGURE 6–2

Response* When *b* Increases to *b'

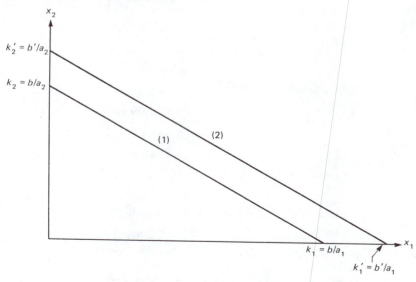

$k_2' = b'/a_2$

$k_2 = b/a_2$

(1)   (2)

$k_1 = b/a_1$

$k_1' = b'/a_1$

the parameters of linear equations. To prepare you for later discussions, it will be useful to present first the graphic responses of straight lines to changes in the constants. If, for example, the right-hand side (b) of Equation (6.1) *increases* to b', the slope of the line ($-a_1/a_2$) is not influenced but the x_2-intercept increases to (b'/a_2) and the x_1-intercept (b/a_1) increases to (b'/a_1). Thus, the line remains parallel to itself but moves outward from the origin as in line (2) of Figure 6–2. Can you verify what happens if b·decreases?

If a_1 *increases* to a_1' (all other parameters remaining constant) the slope of our equation becomes more negative, the x_1-intercept decreases, and the x_2-intercept remains stationary. Line (2) in Figure 6–3 demonstrates

FIGURE 6–3

Response When a_1 Increases to a_1'

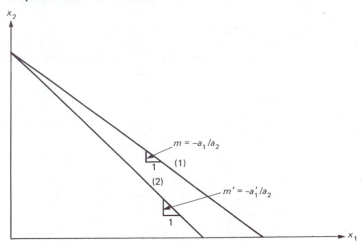

this clockwise change in the orientation of line (1). A *decrease* in a_1 results in a less negative (or more positive) slope and no change in the x_2-intercept.

Finally, verify for yourself that if a_2 *increases,* the slope becomes less negative (a counterclockwise change) and the x_2-intercept decreases. Similarly, verify that the exact opposite changes occur if a_2 *decreases.*

Follow-up Exercises

1. For the equation $4x_1 + 8x_2 = 24$, verify graphically the effects discussed in the last section by allowing each parameter to change by $\pm$ 50 percent of its original value.

2. Do the effects described in the last section hold for negative a_j values? Change the equation in Exercise 1 to $-4x_1 + 8x_2 = 24$ and test to see the effects from allowing the parameters to change.

6.2 SENSITIVITY ANALYSIS—OBJECTIVE FUNCTION COEFFICIENTS (NONBASIC VARIABLES)

The Air Cargo Problem Revisited

In Section 5.5 on page 160, we discussed the solution to an air cargo problem. In the current section we will refer to this problem with one minor modification. Assume the profit contribution for beef is 20 ($100's) per container shipped instead of the original 7. The problem is reformulated below where x_1 and x_2 represent, respectively, the number of containers of beef and pork which are to be shipped.

Maximize

$$z = 20x_1 + 10x_2$$

subject to

$$5x_1 + 4x_2 \leq 24 \qquad \text{(Volume)}$$
$$2x_1 + 5x_2 \leq 13 \qquad \text{(Weight)}$$
$$x_1, x_2 \geq 0.$$

The original and final tableaus for this problem are presented below for convenience of reference.

Basis	z	x_1	x_2	S_1	S_2	b_i	Row No.	r_i
I (Initial)	1	-20*	-10	0	0	0	(0)	
S_1	0	5	4	1	0	24	(1)	24/5*
S_2	0	2	5	0	1	13	(2)	13/2
II (Final)	1	0	6	4	0	96	(0)	
x_1	0	1	4/5	1/5	0	24/5	(1)	
S_2	0	0	17/5	$-2/5$	1	17/5	(2)	

* Denotes entering or leaving variable.

The final solution recommends the shipment of 4.8 containers of beef and no pork. The maximum profit for this shipment is 96 ($100's). Notice that with this shipment the volume capacity is totally utilized; however, the weight of the shipment falls 3.4 (1,000's) pounds short ($S_2 = 17/5$) of the plane's capacity. Figure 6–4 illustrates the graphic representation of the optimal solution (point c).

General sensitivity analysis for this problem is concerned with identifying the ranges over which parameters can fluctuate and still retain x_1 and

FIGURE 6–4

Air Cargo Optimal Solution

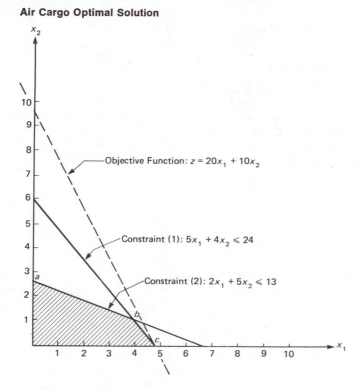

S_2 in the basis. That is, what kinds of changes will cause a revision of the present decision to ship all beef, limited by the aircraft's volume? From a graphical perspective, we wish to determine the ranges of variation in the parameters within which the optimal solution remains at point c. In this section, the parameter of interest is the objective function coefficient for the nonbasic variable x_2 (that is, $c_2 = 10$).

Intuitive Approach

In a problem of this scale, intuition can be useful in anticipating expected effects. The nonbasic variables in the optimal solution to the present problem are S_1 and x_2. Since it is meaningless to consider the change in the profit associated with a slack variable (its objective function coefficient is fixed at zero), our attention should be directed to the contribution from x_2 (pork). Relative to the profit contribution for beef ($c_1 = 20$), the contribution of 10 for pork is less favorable. We would expect that if the 10 were to decrease, then pork would be even less desirable and our decision to ship as much beef as possible would be reinforced; however, if the contribution were to increase for pork, we might expect that at some higher profit contribution pork would become a desirable commodity to ship. Thus, intuition would lead us to conclude that the existing solution is *insensitive* to decreases in the contribution of pork but *sensitive* to an increase, beyond some point.

Graphical Approach

Specifically, we are questioning the effects on $(-c_1/c_2)$ of changes in c_2. Graphically the slope of the objective function is $(-20/10)$. If c_2 decreases, then the x_2-intercept will increase for a given x_1-intercept or the slope will become more negative (the objective function can be thought of as rotating clockwise in its orientation from z to z' in Figure 6–5a). This type of rotation reinforces the decision at point c and

FIGURE 6–5

Sensitivity to c_2

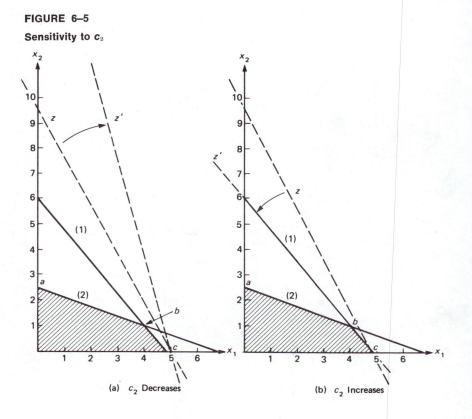

(a) c_2 Decreases

(b) c_2 Increases

matches our intuitive statement that the solution is insensitive to decreases in the profit contribution of pork.

If, however, the contribution from pork (c_2) increases, then the slope of the objective function becomes less negative or reorients itself in a counterclockwise manner. In Figure 6–5b, if c_2 increases to 16, then the objective function will become parallel to constraint (1) and we would have alternative optimal solutions along the line segment $\overline{bc}$. If c_2 increases beyond 16 and remains less than 50, then the slope of the objective function becomes less negative than that of constraint (1) but more negative than that for constraint (2), and a new optimal solution will be found at point b. This corner point recommends a policy of introducing one container of pork and reducing the shipment of beef to four containers (note also that this solution fully utilizes both the volume and weight capacities). Consequently, the graphical analysis agrees with our intuitive analysis. The solution at point c is insensitive to decreases in c_2 but sensitive to increases. The decision maker would now have a rule that states: Ship only beef until the price of pork reaches 16; then ship pork and beef until the price of pork goes above 50; then ship only pork.

Follow-up Exercises

By graphical and algebraic means, verify the following:

3. If $c_2 = 16$, then alternative optima exist along segment $\overline{bc}$.
4. If $16 < c_2 < 50$, then the optimal solution is at point b.
5. If $c_2 = 50$, then alternative optima are given along $\overline{ab}$.
6. If $c_2 > 50$, then the optimal solution is at point a.

Simplex Approach

The analysis for nonbasic variables is relatively easy given simplex tableaus. Essentially, we are to determine over what range of variation in c_2 will the existing basis remain optimal. First define the contribution on c_2 as $c_2 = 10 + \Delta$, where 10 equals the original contribution plus some change, delta (Δ). If this newly defined value for c_2 is used, Row (0) in the *initial* simplex tableau will appear as shown below.

Basis	z	x_1	x_2	S_1	S_2	b_i	Row No.	r_i
I (Initial)	1	-20	$-(10+\Delta)$	0	0	0	(0)	

We have already pointed out that in sensitivity analysis there is no need to completely rework the problem with new parameters. In this instance we are interested in knowing how the addition of Δ influences the *final* tableau. The key is remembering how Row (0) values are updated from tableau to tableau. If you think about this for a moment (or a little longer) you will remember that Row (0) values are determined solely by the row operation of adding multiples of other rows to Row (0). Refer to the original and final tableaus presented earlier for this problem (page 194). The Row (0) coefficient for x_2 has changed from -10 to $+6$ in going from the initial to the final tableau (or $+16$ has been added). If the original Row (0) coefficient had been $-(10 + \Delta)$, then the simplex algorithm would result in the coefficient $-(10 + \Delta) + 16$, or $(6 - \Delta)$, in the final tableau.

Basis	z	x_1	x_2	S_1	S_2	b_i	Row No.	r_i
II (Final)	1	0	$(6 - \Delta)$	4	0	96	(0)	
x_1	0	1	4/5	1/5	0	24/5	(1)	
S_2	0	0	17/5	$-2/5$	1	17/5	(2)	

Without redoing the entire problem, we have shown that the only effect of changing the objective function contribution on a nonbasic variable is to change the Row (0) coefficient for that variable in the final tableau. The question still remains, though, by how much can c_2 change while maintaining the same optimal solution? Recall that, in a *maximization* problem, the solution is optimal as long as all Row (0) coefficients are greater than zero. In this problem, the existing basis will remain optimal as long as

$$6 - \Delta > 0$$

or

$$\Delta < 6.$$

In other words, this solution will remain optimal as long as $c_2 < 16$. If $\Delta > 6$ or $c_2 > 16$, then the Row (0) coefficient for x_2 becomes negative and x_2 would enter the solution. (What situation would we have if $\Delta = 6$ or $c_2 = 16$?) Note that the inequality would have been reversed if this problem had been of the minimization type. (Why?)

Follow-up Exercises

7. Determine the variable which leaves the basis, the number of units of x_2 which will enter, and the resulting values of other basic variables if $\Delta = 8$. Does this agree with our graphical analysis?

8. For Example 5.9 on page 158, determine the ranges over which the contributions on x_1 and x_3 can independently fluctuate and have the existing basis remain optimal.

9. It does not take the inventive student too long to develop a quick scheme for conducting sensitivity analysis on objective function contributions for nonbasic variables. How inventive are you?

6.3 SENSITIVITY ANALYSIS—OBJECTIVE FUNCTION COEFFICIENTS (BASIC VARIABLES)

Intuitive Approach

Continuing the air cargo example, we find that the basic variables in the optimal solution are x_1 and S_2. As before, we ignore the slack variable and concern ourselves with the range over which the contribution on beef (c_1) can fluctuate before our decision of exclusive beef shipments changes. On an intuitive level we would expect that increases in the profit contribution for beef would reinforce the decision to ship beef only; however, we might expect that if the profit contribution were to decrease on beef, a point might be reached whereby beef becomes less attractive as a shippable commodity and we might consider the substitution of pork. Thus, we would expect the optimal basis to be *insensitive* to increases but *sensitive* to decreases in c_1.

We might note at this point (so as to not lead you astray) that the *insensitivity* signal for this example is intuitively correct only because a single decision variable is in the optimal basis. The results for the objective function coefficients will often be counterintuitive; that is, upper and lower limits will exist. The reason for this will become clear in the next two approaches.

Graphical Approach

The slope of the objective function is $(-c_1/c_2)$ or $(-20/10)$. If c_1 increases while c_2 remains constant, then the slope becomes more negative or rotates in a clockwise direction. As seen in Figure 6–6, this reinforces point c as optimal. (Note that if the optimal solution had been at point b, then a large enough increase in c_1 would result in a new optimum at point c.) On the other hand, a decrease in c_1 results in a less negative slope. If c_1 decreases sufficiently, then the slope of the objective function will become the same as that of constraint (1). If c_1 decreases beyond this level, point b will become the new optimal corner point. Further decreases will result eventually in an optimal solution at point a.

𝕯𝖔𝖚𝖌𝖑𝖆𝖘 𝕾𝖆𝖑𝖙𝖊𝖗
748·8666

FIGURE 6–6

Sensitivity to c_1

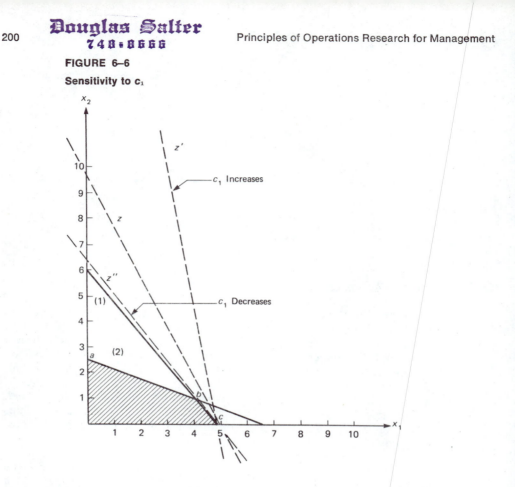

Simplex Approach

Sensitivity analysis on objective function coefficients is slightly more involved for basic variables. To conduct sensitivity analysis on c_1 we begin in the same manner as with nonbasic variables. If we define $c_1 = 20 + \Delta$, Row (0) of the initial tableau changes accordingly.

Basis	z	x_1	x_2	S_1	S_2	b_i	Row No.	r_i
I (Initial)	1	$-(20 + \Delta)$	-10	0	0	0	(0)	

You should be able to verify that in going from the initial to the final tableaus of the original problem, $+20$ was added to the original Row (0) coefficient of x_1 to force the final value of zero. Thus, if the initial Row (0) coefficient had been $-(20 + \Delta)$, then the final tableau would appear as below.

Basis	z	x_1	x_2	S_1	S_2	b_i	Row No.	r_i
II (Final)	1	$-\Delta$	6	4	0	96	(0)	
x_1	0	1	4/5	1/5	0	24/5	(1)	
S_2	0	0	17/5	$-2/5$	1	17/5	(2)	

If you examine this tableau carefully, you should realize that it is not in the format required for reading-off the optimal solution. The Row (0) elements for basic variables should always equal zero. Because this is not true for x_1, row operations must be performed in order to create the desired condition. Multiplying Row (1) by Δ and adding to Row (0), produces the following tableau.

Basis	z	x_1	x_2	S_1	S_2	b_i	Row No.	r_i
II (Final)	1	0	$6 + (4/5)\Delta$	$4 + (1/5)\Delta$	0	$96 + (24/5)\Delta$	(0)	
x_1	0	1	4/5	1/5	0	24/5	(1)	
S_2	0	0	17/5	$-2/5$	1	17/5	(2)	

This tableau indicates how the change in the objective function contribution for x_1 affects the optimal tableau. Notice that Δ appears in Row (0) for the nonbasic variables x_2 and S_1. In addition, the appearance of the Δ term in the b_i column shows the effect of a change in c_1 on the current value of the objective function.

Again, the question is over what range of values for Δ is the current solution still optimal? The variable x_2 would not become a candidate for entrance into the solution as long as

$$6 + (4/5)\Delta > 0$$

or

$$\Delta > -7.5.$$

If Δ becomes less than -7.5 (the contribution from beef becomes less than 12.5), then the Row (0) coefficient for x_2 would be less than zero, and x_2 would be identified as the new entering variable. S_1 would not be considered as a candidate for entrance as long as

$$4 + (1/5)\Delta > 0$$

or

$$\Delta > -20.$$

If Δ becomes less than -20 (the contribution from shipping beef becomes less than zero), then S_1 would become the new variable to enter the basis. (Seems to make sense, doesn't it?)

Since we are concerned with the range of variation over which the present all-beef solution remains optimal, it is necessary to compare the Δ values leading to the entrance of the nonbasic variables.

Figure 6–7 represents a sketch of the two allowable ranges which were

FIGURE 6–7

Allowable Changes in c_1

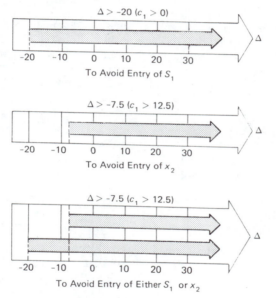

determined by separately considering the nonentry of variables x_2 and S_1. Entry into the basis of variable S_1 can be avoided by values of $\Delta > -20$, but in order to avoid the entry of x_2, Δ must be greater than -7.5; hence, the present solution will remain optimal as long as $\Delta > -7.5$ or $c_1 > 12.5$.

In this example, the optimal solution is insensitive to increases in c_1. As previously mentioned, however, for many problems the optimal solution is sensitive to variations in both directions (see the follow-up exercises). Thus, care must be taken in examining Δ-values for basic variables.

In summary, sensitivity analysis for the coefficients of basic variables requires a translation of the change (Δ) from the initial to the final tableau. This will lead ultimately to a nonzero Row (0) coefficient for a basic variable which subsequently must be removed by a row operation. The latter operation always will create a Δ term in Row (0) for some or all of the nonbasic variables. It is at this stage that the allowable ranges of variation are determined. Again, the beauty is that these ranges of allow-able values can be determined without reworking the entire problem using trial-and-error values for the parameters.

Follow-up Exercises

11. Conduct a sensitivity analysis on the objective function contributions for the basic variables in this problem as originally solved in Chapter 5, pages 156 to 158.

12. Within what ranges can the coefficients of x_2 and x_4 in the objective function vary such that the solution of Example 5.9 (page 158) remains optimal?

6.4 SENSITIVITY ANALYSIS—RIGHT-HAND–SIDE CONSTANTS

This form of sensitivity analysis is concerned with the range over which the right-hand–side (b_i) of a constraint can fluctuate such that the optimal solution remains feasible. Because intuition is only marginally helpful in this case, we proceed directly to a graphical analysis.

Graphical Approach

In the air cargo problem, the constraints represented volume and weight restrictions for the airplane. As discussed in Section 6.1, a change in the right-hand–side constant of a linear equation in two variables causes changes in the x_1-intercept and x_2-intercept but no change in the slope of the line. Let us focus upon the right-hand side of constraint (1), the 24 cubic yards of volume. In the optimal solution, the volume constraint is binding and there is slack in the weight constraint. Should the volume decrease, Figure 6–8 indicates that the constraint moves toward the origin. If the volume decreases sufficiently, then constraint (1') indicates the point where constraint (2) would no longer form a binding edge on the area of feasible solutions. Notice that the basic variables remain the same but their values are changing. That is, for any decrease in volume, the decision is still to ship only beef. This result holds even after constraint (2) becomes redundant. The optimal value of the objective function decreases with the decrease in volume as indicated by the movement of z to z'.

If the volume increases, then the outward movement of constraint (1) will lead eventually to a change of basic variables if it moves beyond constraint (1″). Beyond this point constraint (2) becomes totally binding, constraint (1) is redundant, and the optimal solution occurs at point d. The basic variables for solutions in this range are x_1 and S_1; the increased values for x_1 and z are easily computed as $x_1 = 13/2$, $z'' = 130$.

The following observation will be useful in understanding the simplex

FIGURE 6–8

Sensitivity to b_1

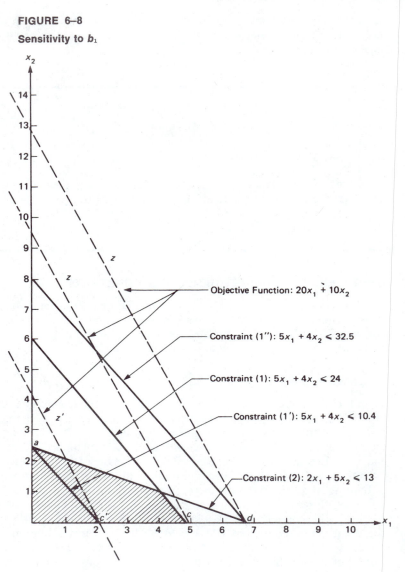

Objective Function: $20x_1 + 10x_2$

Constraint (1''): $5x_1 + 4x_2 \leqslant 32.5$

Constraint (1): $5x_1 + 4x_2 \leqslant 24$

Constraint (1'): $5x_1 + 4x_2 \leqslant 10.4$

Constraint (2): $2x_1 + 5x_2 \leqslant 13$

analysis. The original optimal basis included x_1 and S_2. What happens to S_2 as constraint (1) moves outward? It becomes smaller. At (1''), S_2 equals zero, and any further movement will lead to negative slack if the current basis remains. As you know, however, a negative value is not permissible for any variable, as an infeasible solution would result. This is the essence of sensitivity analysis on the right-hand–side constants. By how much can they vary before the existing solution is no longer feasible? Notice again, however, that as long as the existing solution remains feasible, it also remains optimal (although z changes) as the coefficients in Row (0) are unchanged.

Simplex Approach

As with the objective function coefficients, we redefine the right-hand side of constraint (1) as:

$$b_1 = 24 + \Delta,$$

where Δ represents the change in value of the original b_1. The initial tableau follows.

Basis	z	x_1	x_2	S_1	S_2	b_i	Row No.	r_i
I (Initial)	1	−20	−10	0	0	0	(0)	
S_1	0	5	4	1	0	$24 + \Delta$	(1)	
S_2	0	2	5	0	1	13	(2)	

Now, pay very close attention! We would like to know what the final tableau would look like had we started with Δ on the right-hand side of constraint (1). Again it is not necessary to rework the entire problem. If you think of the b_i-column in the manner below, Δ can be thought of as having a column of coefficients exactly like those for S_1.

b_i
$0 + 0\Delta$
$24 + 1\Delta$
$13 + 0\Delta$

└─── This column identical to column under S_1 in initial tableau above.

Since the same row operations are performed on both the left-hand and right-hand sides of the equations, Δ will have the same column of coefficients in the final tableau as S_1. Or, the final tableau would appear as below (refer back to the final tableau on page 194).

Basis	z	x_1	x_2	S_1	S_2	b_i	Row No.	r_i
II (Final)	1	0	6	4	0	$96 + 4\Delta$	(0)	
x_1	0	1	4/5	1/5	0	$24/5 + (1/5)\Delta$	(1)	
S_2	0	0	17/5	−2/5	1	$17/5 − (2/5)\Delta$	(2)	

What values can Δ assume for this solution to remain feasible? These values can be determined by solving for the Δ's which allow x_1 and S_2 to remain positive, or

$$x_1 = 24/5 + (1/5)\Delta \geqslant 0 \text{ as long as } \Delta \geqslant -24$$

and

$$S_2 = 17/5 - (2/5)\Delta \geqslant 0 \text{ as long as } \Delta \leqslant 8.5.$$

We can say, then, that this solution will remain feasible as long as

$$-24 \leqslant \Delta \leqslant 8.5$$

or

$$0 \leqslant b_1 \leqslant 32.5.$$

That is, the current solution (ship beef only) will remain feasible (and optimal) as long as there is *some* cargo space but no more than 32.5 cubic yards. Again, the result agrees with the graphical analysis.

The key to this analysis is identifying a "sister variable" to the Δ which has been added to the right-hand side of the constraint under study (that is, a variable which has the same column of coefficients as Δ). This sister variable always will be the slack or artificial variable which originally had been added to the constraint.

Finally, suppose that $\Delta = 6$ for b_1 (that is, the new value of b_1 is 30). Since this value is within the permissible range, the above basis remains feasible; however, the *values* of the basic variables change according to the derived relationships. Thus, $x_1 = (24/5) + (1/5)(6) = 6$ and $S_2 = (17/5) - (2/5)(6) = 1$. What we are trying to say is that permissible changes in Δ related to right-hand–side constants result in the *same* set of basic variables but with *different* values. This was not the case for permissible Δ's associated with objective function coefficients; in that case, neither the mix nor the values of basic variables changed (optimal z, however, did change).

Shadow Prices

In Section 5.5 we defined the **shadow price** associated with the ith constraint as the amount by which the optimal value of the objective function would change if b_i were increased by one unit.

Now note the Row (0) coefficient on Δ (the 4) for the b_i-column in the preceding tableau. *Over the range of variability permissible for Δ,* the 4 is a measure of the marginal value of the resource associated with the first constraint (volume). That is, an increase of 1 cubic yard of space ($\Delta = 1$) would increase profit by 4 to 100 ($100's); 2 additional cubic yards ($\Delta = 2$), or 26 cubic yards, would increase profit to 104 ($100's); and a decrease of 3 cubic yards ($\Delta = -3$) would decrease profit to 84 ($100's). This 4 is termed a shadow price because it represents the foregone profit (the price we pay) for not having an extra cubic yard of space in the cargo hold.

Finally, note that the shadow price associated with the ith constraint necessarily appears in Row (0) underneath the slack or artificial variable associated with that constraint. (Why?)

Follow-up Exercises

15. Perform sensitivity analysis on the right-hand side of constraint (2). Also, what is the marginal effect (shadow price) upon the value of optimal z over the permissible range of values for Δ?

16. Do the same for the right-hand–side constants in Example 5.9 (page 158).

6.5 SENSITIVITY ANALYSIS—MINIMIZATION AND MIXED CONSTRAINTS

To further reinforce the simplex approach for performing sensitivity analysis, we now solve a problem which is characterized by both a *minimization* objective and *mixed* constraints. We continue Example 5.10 on page 167 by reproducing below the initial and final tableaus. Carefully note that the initial tableau is given by Tableau II, not Tableau I. (Do you remember why?)

Example 6.1

Basis	z	x_1	x_2	E_2	S_1	A_2	A_3	b_i	Row No.	r_i
		*								
II (Initial)	1	$-2+5M$	$-4+3M$	$-M$	0	0	0	$30M$	(0)	—
S_1	0	1	5	0	1	0	0	80	(1)	80
A_2	0	4	2	-1	0	1	0	20	(2)	5*
A_3	0	1	1	0	0	0	1	10	(3)	10
V (Final)	1	0	-2	0	0	$-M$	$2-M$	20	(0)	—
S_1	0	0	4	0	1	0	-1	70	(1)	
x_1	0	1	1	0	0	0	1	10	(2)	
E_2	0	0	2	1	0	-1	4	20	(3)	

* Denotes entering and leaving variables.

Objective Function Coefficients (Nonbasic Variables)

Inspection of the final tableau indicates that x_2 is the relevant nonbasic variable. Since the original objective function (ignoring the artificial variables) was

$$z = 2x_1 + 4x_2,$$

the revised objective function becomes

$$z = 2x_1 + (4 + \Delta) x_2.$$

The entry under x_2 in Row (0) of Tableau II would now appear as $(-4 - \Delta + 3M)$. In the row operations which carried us from Tableau II to Tableau V, the entry under x_2 in Row (0) changed from $(-4 + 3M)$ to -2; hence, $(-2) - (-4 + 3M)$ or $(2 - 3M)$ must have been added to the initial entry. To our new initial tableau entry of $(-4 - \Delta + 3M)$ we add, therefore, $(2 - 3M)$ to arrive at our new final tableau entry of $(-2 - \Delta)$.

For our current basis to remain optimal, the Row (0) entry in the final tableau for x_2 must remain *negative* (remember that this is a *minimization* problem); that is,

$$-2 - \Delta < 0$$

or

$$\Delta > -2.$$

Having specified that $c_2 = 4 + \Delta$, we see that $c_2 > 2$ for our current basis to remain optimal.

Objective Function Coefficients (Basic Variables)

Letting $c_1 = 2 + \Delta$, or

$$z = (2 + \Delta) x_1 + 4x_2,$$

we see then that the entry under x_1 in Row (0) of Tableau II becomes $(-2 - \Delta + 5M)$. Since $(2 - 5M)$ must be added to arrive at the final tableau value (can you show this?), the following tableau results.

Basis	z	x_1	x_2	E_2	S_1	A_2	A_3	b_i	Row No.	r_i
V (Final)	1	$-\Delta$	-2	0	0	$-M$	$2 - M$	20	(0)	—
S_1	0	0	4	0	1	0	-1	70	(1)	
x_1	0	1	1	0	0	0	1	10	(2)	
E_2	0	0	2	1	0	-1	4	20	(3)	

The existence of an entry $(-\Delta)$ under x_1 (a basic variable) in Row (0) makes for an inconsistency which must be removed (look at the column under x_1 and state why). Multiplying Row (2) by Δ and adding to Row (0) gives the following.

Basis	z	x_1	x_2	E_2	S_1	A_2	A_3	b_i	Row No.	r_i
V	1	0	$-2+\Delta$	0	0	$-M$	$2-M+\Delta$	$20+10\Delta$	(0)	

For the current solution to remain optimal, the range of Δ must be such that neither x_2 nor A_3 is allowed to enter the basis; that is,

$$-2 + \Delta < 0$$
$$\Delta < 2$$

and

$$2 - M + \Delta < 0$$
$$\Delta < M - 2.$$

Recalling that M is a very large penalty, we see clearly that only the range $\Delta < 2$ insures that neither variable enters the basis. Consequently, c_1 must be less than 4 for the current solution to remain optimal.

Right-Hand–Side Constants

For constraint (3) we let $b_3 = 10 + \Delta$. The relevant parts of the new initial and final tableaus are given below.

Basis	... A_3	b_i
(Initial)	0	$30M + 0\Delta$
S_1	0	$80 \quad + 0\Delta$
A_2	0	$20 \quad + 0\Delta$
A_3	1	$10 \quad + 1\Delta$

Basis	... A_3	b_i
(Final)	$2 - M$	$20 + (2 - M)\Delta$
S_1	-1	$70 - \quad 1\Delta$
x_1	1	$10 + \quad 1\Delta$
E_2	4	$20 + \quad 4\Delta$

Notice in the initial tableau that the column of coefficients on Δ in the b_i column has identical coefficients to the A_3 column; hence, whatever operations have been performed on the A_3 column must necessarily be performed on the Δ column. Applying this principle immediately gives the right-hand side of the final tableau.

For the optimal basis to remain feasible, the allowable range for Δ must be such that no basic variable is allowed to assume a negative value; that is,

$$S_1 = 70 - \Delta \geqslant 0 \text{ as long as } \Delta \leqslant 70;$$
$$x_1 = 10 + \Delta \geqslant 0 \text{ as long as } \Delta \geqslant -10;$$
$$E_2 = 20 + 4\Delta \geqslant 0 \text{ as long as } \Delta \geqslant -5.$$

Figure 6–9 indicates the three regions corresponding to these allowable Δ ranges; hence, the above optimal solution remains feasible as long as

$$5 \leqslant b_3 \leqslant 80 \text{ (that is, } -5 \leqslant \Delta \leqslant 70).$$

FIGURE 6–9

Allowable Changes in b_3

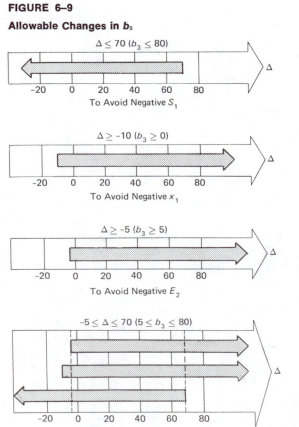

$\Delta \leq 70 \ (b_3 \leq 80)$

To Avoid Negative S_1

$\Delta \geq -10 \ (b_3 \geq 0)$

To Avoid Negative x_1

$\Delta \geq -5 \ (b_3 \geq 5)$

To Avoid Negative E_2

$-5 \leq \Delta \leq 70 \ (5 \leq b_3 \leq 80)$

To Avoid Any Negative Basic Variables

Now carefully note the following. If b_3 were really 50 and not 10 (that is, $\Delta = 40$), what would be the optimal solution? From the above final tableau (realizing that Δ is within the allowable range), we have

$$S_1 = 70 - \Delta = 70 - 40 = 30;$$
$$x_1 = 10 + \Delta = 10 + 40 = 50;$$

and

$$E_2 = 20 + 4\Delta = 20 + 4(40) = 180.$$

Since

$$z = 2x_1 + 4x_2,$$

the optimal value of the objective function is

$$z = 2(50) + 4(0)$$
$$= 100.$$

(If you're really with us) you might have realized that the immediately preceding final tableau in its present form is not consistent with our result of 100; that is,

$$z = 20 + (2 - M)\Delta.$$

It becomes apparent, therefore, that *the original coefficient in the objective function for* A_3 *(that is,* $+M$*) must be added to the coefficient on* Δ. This gives the correct value

$$\begin{aligned} z &= 20 + 2\Delta \\ &= 20 + 2(40) \\ &= 100. \end{aligned}$$

It follows that the shadow price associated with the third constraint is given by the coefficient of 2 on Δ, or by the pure number in Row (0) under A_3 in the final tableau.

In general, *the shadow price associated with a constraint of the* $(\geq)$ *or* $(=)$ *type equals the pure number in Row (0) immediately under the corresponding artificial variable in the final tableau.* Its interpretation is identical to the case with a $(\leq)$ type constraint.

Follow-up Exercises

17. By the simplex procedure, show that the allowable range for b_1 is above 10 and for b_2 is below 40.

18. Validate the five sensitivity solutions for Example 6.1 by the graphical approach.

19. Can you state a general rule for determining the allowable range associated with the objective function coefficients of nonbasic variables? (Hint: Take care to distinguish between maximization and minimization objectives.)

20. Perform sensitivity analyses on the c_j's and b_i's for the police sector problem in Exercise 11 of Chapter 5.

Example 6.2

In actual practice sensitivity analysis typically is performed by the computer program which solves the original problem. Figure 6–10 illustrates computer output for the product mix problem of Example 4.5 which was presented in Section 5.9.

Sensitivity analyses on the coefficients of the objective function indicate the current solution remains optimal if the following conditions hold *independently* of one another: (1) the variable cost of Product A in the second quarter (c_2) is *above* $2.29 per unit; (2) the variable cost of Product A in the first quarter (c_1) is *below* $4.71 per unit; (3) the cost coefficient for Product B in the first quarter (c_3) is *above* $5.00; and (4) the cost coefficient for Product B in the second quarter (c_4) is *below* $6.13. These results indicate that a reasonable amount of error in estimating these coefficients (within approximately 57 percent for c_1, 42 percent for c_2, 19 percent for c_3, and 23 percent for c_4) will *not* alter the present optimal decision. If the analyst is

FIGURE 6–10

Product Mix Model

sensitivity analysis

．．．．．．．．．．．．．．．．．．

objective function

．．．．．．．．．．．．．．．．．．

*** nonbasic variables ***

variable	delta	limit
2	−1.70625	2.29375

*** basic variables ***

variable	lower delta	upper delta	lower limit	upper limit
4	************	1.13000	************	6.13000
1	************	1.70625	************	4.70625
3	−1.13000	************	5.00000	************

right-hand-side constants

．．．．．．．．．．．．．．．．．．．．

constraint no.	lower delta	upper delta	lower limit	upper limit
1	−40.00000	************	310.00000	************
2	−40.00000	59.99999	460.00000	559.99999
3	−474.99976	************	5525.00024	************
4	−100.00328	************	9899.99672	************
5	−500.00000	10.00032	0.00000	510.00032
6	−75.00000	14.28613	625.00000	714.28613

1 = do you wish to alter any data and run again
2 = do you wish to terminate the program
3 = do you wish to run a new problem
?2

stop
time 9.07 secs.

Note: The asterisks indicate no upper or lower limit.

uncertain about the degree of error associated with any or all of the coefficients, greater care in estimation may be warranted (of course, the cost of greater accuracy must be weighed against the expected improvement in the criterion).

Lower and upper limits for b_i's are indicated also. For example, a labor availability in the first quarter below 310 hours would make the present optimal solution infeasible (the asterisks indicate *no* upper limit). Can you interpret the remaining limits in the context of the problem?

6.6 OTHER FORMS OF POSTOPTIMALITY ANALYSIS

The types of sensitivity analyses which can be performed are not restricted to those we have presented. The analytical burden does become more severe, though, with other types. The important consideration for the decision maker is an awareness of the full potentialities of the solution procedures which are being employed.

Other forms of sensitivity analysis include analysis of changes in the structural coefficients (a_{ij}'s) for the system of constraints. Graphically, a change in an a_{ij} coefficient results in a change in the slope of the related constraint. The analysis by the simplex method varies both in form and degree of difficulty depending upon whether the a_{ij} value is associated with a basic or nonbasic variable.

In addition, postoptimality analysis can be used to examine simultaneous variations in the parameters and structural variations in the LP model. For instance, it is possible to determine the impact on the optimal solution if a constraint which was originally omitted needs to be included in the model. Similarly, it is possible to determine the effects of adding a new variable to the problem.

If it is revealed that an optimal solution is extremely sensitive to variations in a particular parameter, then the decision maker should weigh the costs and benefits associated with acquiring a better estimate of the parameter. For example, if the optimal decision in a media mix problem is particularly sensitive to the estimated television exposures per dollar of advertising budget, the decision maker might weigh the costs and associated benefits of having an additional marketing research survey conducted to determine a better estimate of this parameter. The benefits would take the form of the opportunity costs associated with making a nonoptimal decision and the costs would be any direct and indirect costs associated with acquiring the improved estimate.

Follow-up Exercises

21. Graphically examine the effects of changes in the a_{ij} coefficients in the air cargo problem. Allow each parameter to change by $\pm$ 50 percent of its original value.

22. For the air cargo problem, determine the ranges of ($-c_1/c_2$) for optimal solutions at each of the corner points a, b, and c.

6.7 THE DUAL PROBLEM

Duality is the state of being made up of two distinct but related parts. The concept represents the possibility of an intriguing universal state which has been proposed and debated in diverse disciplines. For example, philosophers speak of mind and matter as underlying all known phenomena; theologians propose the underlying principles of good and bad, and the doctrine that man has both a physical and a spiritual nature; and chemists have proved that every definite compound consists of two parts having opposite electrical activity. Well, management scientists are not to be outdone, for every LP problem has a related problem called the **dual problem.**

The dual problem is formulated from information contained in the original problem, often referred to as the **primal problem,** and when solved, the dual provides all essential information about the solution to the original problem. Three uses of duality motivate the treatment of the dual problem and underscore its usefulness in the theory of linear programming: (1) the dual problem is often easier to solve than the original problem; (2) the dual can be extremely useful in performing the types of postoptimality analyses previously discussed; and (3) the dual can be applied more efficiently to the solution of certain types of models (for example, the transportation algorithm in Chapter 7 and project scheduling in Chapter 14).

The Canonical Primal

The dual problem can be formulated when the original problem is a maximization or minimization type and when it contains any mix of constraint types. Typically if the primal problem is to be maximized, then the dual will be a minimization problem and vice versa. Unfortunately, the degree of variation in the form of the primal problem leads to a complicated set of transformation rules which are often difficult to remember even for those who work with linear programming on a regular basis. If all primal problems had the same basic structure, then the rules would be fewer and simpler for all concerned.

Fortunately, any primal LP problem can be formulated in a standard form referred to as the **canonical form.** The canonical form is a maximization problem with all constraints of the ($\leq$) type and all variables satisfying the nonnegativity condition, or

maximize

$$z_c = \sum_{j=1}^{n} c_j x_j$$

subject to

$$\sum_{j=1}^{n} a_{ij} x_j \leq b_i \qquad\qquad i = 1, 2, \ldots, m$$

$$x_j \geq 0. \qquad\qquad j = 1, 2, \ldots, n.$$

To convert any primal LP problem to the canonical primal form one may have to select from among a set of three transformation rules. Let us illustrate these by example.

Example 6.3

Consider the following primal problem (Examples 5.10 and 6.1):

minimize

$$z = 2x_1 + 4x_2$$

subject to

$$x_1 + 5x_2 \leq 80 \tag{1}$$
$$4x_1 + 2x_2 \geq 20 \tag{2}$$
$$x_1 + x_2 = 10 \tag{3}$$

$$x_1, x_2 \geq 0.$$

Transformation rule 1: A function will be minimized if one maximizes the negative of the function. Thus, the objective function above will be minimized if you maximize the canonical objective function

$$z_c = -z = -2x_1 - 4x_2.$$

Transformation rule 2: An equality constraint can be replaced by two inequality constraints of opposite sense. Constraint (3) can be replaced by the two constraints (3a) and (3b).

$$x_1 + x_2 \leq 10 \tag{3a}$$
$$x_1 + x_2 \geq 10. \tag{3b}$$

Transformation rule 3: Constraint inequalities can be reversed by multiplying both sides of the inequality by minus one. Constraints (3b) and (2) can be converted to ($\leq$) types by multiplying both sides by (-1), or

$$-x_1 - x_2 \leq -10 \tag{3b'}$$
$$-4x_1 - 2x_2 \leq -20. \tag{2'}$$

If you are concerned about the negative b_i values on the right-hand side of the resulting constraints, good observation. (If you weren't concerned, go back to sleep!) The simplex method requires that all right-hand-side constants be nonnegative. At this time we are only concerned with formulation. If we were to solve by the simplex method we could simply reconvert the constraint to its original inequality sense.

The statement of the original primal problem in canonical primal form is given below:

maximize

$$z_c = -2x_1 - 4x_2$$

subject to

$$x_1 + 5x_2 \leq 80 \tag{1}$$
$$-4x_1 - 2x_2 \leq -20 \tag{2'}$$
$$x_1 + x_2 \leq 10 \tag{3a}$$
$$-x_1 - x_2 \leq -10 \tag{3b'}$$

$$x_1, x_2 \geq 0.$$

Follow-up Exercises

23. State the canonical form of the police sector problem (Example 4.1) on page 95.

24. State the canonical form of Example 4.6 (Transportation Model) on page 114.

The Dual of the Canonical Primal

If the primal problem is of the canonical form stated in the last section, then the dual can be generalized as

minimize

$$z_d = \sum_{i=1}^{m} b_i y_i$$

subject to

$$\sum_{i=1}^{m} a_{ij} y_i \geq c_j \qquad\qquad j = 1, 2, \ldots, n$$

$$v_i \geq 0 \qquad\qquad i = 1, 2, \ldots, m$$

where y_i represents the ith **dual variable.** The dual problem is stated in terms of the primal problem in the following manner:

a. The canonical primal is a maximization problem and the dual is a minimization problem.
b. The canonical primal has all $(\leq)$ constraints and the dual has all $(\geq)$ constraints.
c. All variables in the canonical primal and dual are nonnegative.
d. For every variable in the primal there is a corresponding constraint in the dual (therefore, the dual has n constraints).
e. For every constraint in the primal there is a corresponding dual variable (therefore, the dual has m variables).
f. The objective function contribution for the jth variable of the canonical primal is the right-hand–side constant for the jth dual constraint.
g. The ith right-hand–side constant in the canonical primal is the objective function contribution for the ith dual variable.
h. The column of technological coefficients (a_{ij}'s) associated with variable j of the canonical primal becomes the row of coefficients for the jth constraint of the dual.

Example 6.4   Air Cargo Problem

The air cargo problem as revised for this chapter is repeated below:

maximize

$$z = 20x_1 + 10x_2$$

subject to

$$5x_1 + 4x_2 \leq 24 \qquad\qquad (1)$$
$$2x_1 + 5x_2 \leq 13 \qquad\qquad (2)$$

$$x_1, x_2 \geq 0.$$

Notice that this problem already is in the canonical form; that is, the dual of this problem will be a minimization type, it will have two $(\geq)$ constraints corresponding to the two variables in the primal, it will have two dual variables corresponding to the two ($\leq$) constraints in the primal, the objective function contributions for the two dual variables will equal the right-hand–side constants for the two primal constraints, the right-hand–side constants for the two dual constraints will equal the objective function contributions for the two primal variables, and the rows of technological coefficients for the two dual constraints will correspond to the columns of technological coefficients for the two primal variables, respectively. This last characteristic is equivalent to stating that the matrix of technological coefficients in the dual is simply the transpose of the corresponding matrix in the canonical primal.

Following these guidelines, we can state the dual problem as:

minimize

$$z_d = 24y_1 + 13y_2$$

subject to

$$5y_1 + 2y_2 \geq 20$$
$$4y_1 + 5y_2 \geq 10$$

$$y_1, y_2 \geq 0.$$

Example 6.5

We now state the dual of the canonical primal problem of Example 6.3.

Canonical Primal Problem:

maximize

$$z_c = -2x_1 - 4x_2$$

subject to

$$\begin{aligned} x_1 + 5x_2 &\leq 80 & (1) \\ -4x_1 - 2x_2 &\leq -20 & (2) \\ x_1 + x_2 &\leq 10 & (3') \\ -x_1 - x_2 &\leq -10 & (3'') \end{aligned}$$

$$x_1, x_2 \geq 0$$

Dual Problem:

minimize

$$z_d = 80y_1 - 20y_2 + 10y_3' - 10y_3''$$

subject to

$$y_1 - 4y_2 + y_3' - y_3'' \geq -2$$
$$5y_1 - 2y_2 + y_3' - y_3'' \geq -4$$

$$y_1, y_2, y_3', y_3'' \geq 0$$

Now, refresh your memory on the topic of unrestricted variables in Section 4.6 on page 129. By defining $y_3 = y_3' - y_3''$ the above dual problem can be stated as:

Alternative Dual Problem:

minimize

$$z_d = 80y_1 - 20y_2 + 10y_3$$

subject to

$$y_1 - 4y_2 + y_3 \geq -2$$
$$5y_1 - 2y_2 + y_3 \geq -4$$
$$y_1, y_2 \geq 0$$
$$y_3 \quad \text{unrestricted.}$$

After noting that constraint (3') and (3'') in the canonical primal were the result of equality constraint (3) in the primal, we see that *an unrestricted dual variable corresponds to an equality constraint in the primal problem.*

Follow-up Exercises

25. Formulate the dual problem for the police sector problem (Exercise 23).
26. a. Formulate the dual problem for the transportation model (Exercise 24).
    b. Try stating a general expression for the dual objective function given m origins each with supply s_i and n destinations each with demand d_j. Let u_i represent the dual variable associated with supply constraint (i) and v_j represent the dual variable associated with demand constraint (j).
    c. Try stating a general expression for the dual constraints.

Primal-Dual Properties

An important point for you to keep in mind is that the solution to either the primal or dual problem provides the solution to the other (which we will illustrate). Other significant properties include the following.

Property 1 (Fundamental Inequality of Duality Theory) If x_1, x_2, . . . , x_n is any feasible solution to the maximization problem and y_1, y_2, . . . , y_m is any feasible solution to the minimization problem, then $c_1x_1 + c_2x_2 + \cdots + c_nx_n \leq b_1y_1 + b_2y_2 + \cdots + b_my_m$. In other words, the value of the objective function for the maximization (canonical primal) problem will always be less than or equal to the value of the objective function for the minimization (dual) problem.

Property 2 If feasible solutions exist for both the primal and dual problems, then both problems have a finite optimal solution for which the values of the objective functions are equal. A peripheral relationship is such that if the primal problem has an unbounded solution, then the dual has no feasible solution. (Can you reason this out?)

Property 3 The optimal values for the dual variables are read from the optimal tableau of the primal problem as Row (0) coefficients for the respective *artificial* and/or *slack variables*. (If the optimal tableau for the *canonical* primal problem is available, then only slack variables are relevant.) The optimal values for the primal variables can be read from the optimal tableau of the dual problem as the *negative* of the Row (0) coefficients associated with the respective *surplus variables*. A useful corollary (as you will see in Section 7.4) is that the optimal value for a dual slack or surplus variable is equivalent to the Row (0) coefficient of the corresponding primal variable in the optimal tableau.

Property 4 (Complementary Slackness)   If a constraint is satisfied as a strict *inequality* (slack exists) in the optimal solution to the primal problem, then the corresponding dual variable will equal zero. Similarly, if in the optimal solution to the dual problem a constraint is satisfied as a strict inequality, then the corresponding primal variable will equal zero.

Example 6.6

The solution to the dual of the air cargo problem (Example 6.4) follows.

Basis	z_d	y_1	y_2	E_1	A_1	E_2	A_2	c_j	Row No.	r_i
I	1	$9M-24$ *	$7M-13$	$-M$	0	$-M$	0	$30M$	(0)	
A_1	0	5	2	-1	1	0	0	20	(1)	$20/5=4$
A_2	0	④	5	0	0	-1	1	10	(2)	$10/4=2.5$*
II	1	0	$-17M/4+17$	$-M$	0	$5M/4-6$ *	$-9M/4+6$	$30M/4 + 60$	(0)	
A_1	0	0	$-17/4$	-1	1	⑤/4	$-5/4$	$30/4$	(1)	$\dfrac{30/4}{5/4}=6$*
y_1	0	1	$5/4$	0	0	$-1/4$	$1/4$	$10/4$	(2)	—
III (Final Dual)	1	0	$-17/5$	$-24/5$	$24/5-M$	0	$-M$	⑨⑥	(0)	
E_2	0	0	$-17/5$	$-4/5$	$4/5$	1	-1	⑥	(1)	
y_1	0	1	$8/20$	$-1/5$	$1/5$	0	0	④	(2)	

Basis	z_p	x_1	x_2	S_1	S_2	b_i	Row No.	r_i
II (Final Primal)	1	0	⑥	④	0	⑨⑥	(0)	
x_1	0	1	$4/5$	$1/5$	0	㉔/5	(1)	
S_2	0	0	$17/5$	$-2/5$	1	$17/5$	(2)	

* Denotes entering or leaving variable.

The final tableau for the primal has been repeated for purposes of comparison. Looking at the table below, we see that Property 1 was satisfied in as much as the value of the primal objective function was always less than or equal to that of the dual. Both problems have finite optimal solutions

Iteration	z_p	z_d
1.............	0	$30M$
2.............	96	$(30/4)M + 60$
3.............		96

with the same optimal value of 96 (Property 2). As indicated by Property 3, the value of y_1 is read from the optimal primal tableau as the Row (0) coefficient for the slack variable S_1 ($y_1 = 4$). Since the second primal constraint is satisfied as a strict inequality, Property 4 states that the second dual variable should equal zero ($y_2 = 0$). This is confirmed by the Row (0) coefficient for the slack variable S_2 in the optimal primal tableau and by the absence of y_2 in the optimal basis of the final dual tableau.

Reading the solution of the primal from the final dual tableau, we see that Property 3 indicates that the value for x_1 is the negative of the Row (0) coefficient for the surplus variable E_1 in the optimal dual tableau (that is, the negative of $-24/5$). Since the second dual constraint is satisfied as a strict inequality, the second primal variable should equal zero according to Property 4. This is verified in the optimal dual tableau by the Row (0) coefficient for the surplus variable E_2 and by the absence of x_2 in the optimal basis of the primal problem. Note that, according to the corollary of Property 3, the Row (0) coefficient for x_2 in the primal tableau (6) is equal to the optimal value for the corresponding surplus variable in the dual problem ($E_2 = 6$).

Shadow Prices—One More Time

On reading Property 3, you should have realized that *the optimal value for a dual variable is the shadow price associated with the corresponding constraint*. Do you see why this makes sense? Since the right-hand–side constant in a constraint of the primal problem is the coefficient of the corresponding dual variable in the objective function of the dual problem, a one-unit change in that right-hand–side constant (if feasible) corresponds to an *optimal* change in the objective function given by the value of the corresponding *optimal* dual variable. To illustrate, if the RHS constant of constraint (1) in the air cargo problem is increased by one unit to 25 cubic yards, profit would increase by 4 ($100's) as you can verify by noting that $y_1 = 4$ in Example 6.6 and that the new dual objective function (see Example 6.4) is given by

$$z_d = (24 + 1) y_1 + 13y_2.$$

Note that this result is identical to the result given in the "Shadow Price" subsection of Section 6.4.[1]

_____

[1] We might note that the optimal values of the Lagrange multipliers (λ_i's) in Example 5.4b are, in fact, the optimal values of the dual variables. Based on the definitions of shadow prices and Lagrange multipliers, do you agree that these are one and the same?

Follow-up Exercises

27. Solve the dual problem associated with Example 5.10 on page 167 and identify the solution to the primal problem. (Before solving the dual, write down the expected solution from the final tableau of the primal.) Relate optimal values of dual variables to shadow prices.

28. Given the following primal problem, formulate and solve the dual problem. Write down the optimal solution to the primal and verify that it is correct. (Could you have stated the dual directly from *this* primal?)

Minimize

$$z = 32x_1 + 34x_2$$

subject to

$$3x_1 + x_2 \geq 5$$
$$2x_1 + 4x_2 \geq 6$$

$$x_1, x_2 \geq 0.$$

29. Based on your solution to the police sector problem (Exercise 11 in Chapter 5 on page 169) state the optimal solution for the dual variables and z_d in Exercise 25 of this chapter.

30. Under what conditions in the primal is it possible to have a negative optimal value for a dual variable?

31. How can you tell that nonoptimal iterations in the dual represent infeasible solutions in the primal?

The Dual and Its Implications

If you are harboring the thought that duality is redundant (not to mention "slippery"), let us reassure you that you are wrong. Its power and value have been amply demonstrated both by insightful theoretical developments and by efficient empirical applications.

One of the important attributes of the dual is the computational efficiency that it affords when the original problem has a large number of constraints and relatively few variables. As an example, if an original problem has 20 real variables, 50 constraints of the ($\geq$) type, and 30 constraints of the ($\leq$) type, then the initial simplex tableau will contain 150 variables (20 real, 50 surplus, 50 artificial, and 30 slack) and 81 rows (80 constraints plus the z row) of elements. Including the z columns and RHS columns, the matrix of elements which must be computed for each tableau is (81×152), or 12,312 elements. With 50 artificial variables in the initial basis, it is likely that this problem would require at least 50 iterations beyond the initial tableau (presuming a feasible, nondegenerate solution). On the other hand, for all $c_j > 0$, the equivalent dual problem will have a tableau which is (21×122) or 2,562 elements (agree?) which need to be computed at each iteration (a 79 percent reduction). And, it is quite possible that the number of iterations required to reach the optimal solution for the dual will be much fewer than for the primal problem.

In many large-scale LP problems, the solution process places considerable strain upon the computer in terms of core requirements as well as computation time required to converge to the optimal solution. Consequently, if the primal problem involves a large number of variables (say 100) and a significantly larger number of constraints (say 1,000), then serious consideration should be given to solving the dual problem rather than the primal.

In addition to computational efficiency, the theory of the dual is particularly well-suited to performing certain types of sensitivity analyses. Our objective, however, is not to explore this area any further than to enlighten you as to the existence of this potentiality. If you recall for a moment the transpose nature of the primal-dual relationships you should be able to convince yourself of the equivalence between performing sensitivity analysis on the objective function coefficients of one problem and the right-hand–side values of the other. Furthermore, the advantages which accrue from using the dual go beyond the types of sensitivity analyses which we demonstrated. The dual is useful in studying the effects of changes in the technological coefficients, the addition of new variables, and the addition of new or supplemental constraints. Moreover, as mentioned at the beginning of this chapter, the decision maker may be concerned about the simultaneous variation in the structure and/or parameters of an LP problem. The analyses presented in this chapter focused only upon *independent* variation of parameters. Although the analysis of simultaneous variation is much more involved than of independent variation, the dual greatly facilitates the process.

A final advantage of duality theory is its efficient application to the solution of certain widely implemented models, as we will demonstrate in Chapter 7 (transportation model) and Chapter 14 (PERT-CPM model).

SELECTED REFERENCES

Anderson, David R.; Sweeney, Dennis J.; and Williams, Thomas A. *Linear Programming for Decision Making, An Applications Approach.* St. Paul: West Publishing Co., 1974.

Gass, S. I. *Linear Programming: Methods and Applications.* 4th ed. New York: McGraw-Hill, Inc., 1975.

Hadley, G. *Linear Programming.* Reading, Mass.: Addison-Wesley Publishing Co., 1962.

Hillier, Frederick S., and Lieberman, Gerald J. *Introduction to Operations Research.* 2d ed. San Francisco: Holden Day, Inc., 1974.

Hughes, Ann J., and Grawoig, Dennis E. *Linear Programming: An Emphasis on Decision Making.* Reading, Mass.: Addison-Wesley Publishing Co., 1973.

Kim, Chaiho. *Quantitative Analysis for Managerial Decisions.* Reading, Mass.: Addison-Wesley Publishing Co., 1976.

Levin, Richard I., and Lamone, Rudolph P. *Linear Programming for Management Decisions.* Homewood, Ill.: Richard D. Irwin, Inc., 1969.

McMillan, Claude, Jr. *Mathematical Programming: An Introduction to the*

Design and Application of Optimal Decision Machines. New York: John Wiley & Sons, Inc., 1970.

Montgomery, David B., and Urban, Glen L. *Management Science in Marketing.* Englewood Cliffs, N.J.: Prentice-Hall, Inc., 1969.

Shamblin, James E., and Stevens, G. T., Jr. *Operations Research: A Fundamental Approach.* New York: McGraw-Hill, Inc., 1974.

Spivey, W. Allen, and Thrall, Robert M. *Linear Optimization.* New York: Holt, Rinehart and Winston, Inc., 1970.

Strum, Jay E. *Introduction to Linear Programming.* San Francisco: Holden Day, Inc., 1972.

Trueman, Richard E. *An Introduction to Quantitative Methods for Decision Making.* New York: Holt, Rinehart and Winston, Inc., 1974.

Wagner, Harvey M. *Principles of Operations Research.* 2d ed. Englewood Cliffs, N.J.: Prentice-Hall, Inc., 1975.

ADDITIONAL EXERCISES

32. Briefly discuss reasons why an analyst would conduct postoptimality analysis for a linear programming problem.

33. For the following LP problem,

    maximize

    $$z = 10x_1 + 6x_2$$

    subject to

    $$x_1 + x_2 \leq 40$$
    $$3x_1 + 2x_2 \geq 30$$
    $$2x_1 + 3x_2 \leq 90$$

    $$x_1, x_2 \geq 0.$$

    a. Solve the problem graphically.
    b. Intuitively analyze and suggest the anticipated effects of increases and decreases in the objective function coefficients for x_1 and x_2.
    c. Graphically verify the sensitivity of the optimal basis to changes in the two objective function contributions.

34. For the problem in Exercise 33:

    a. By the simplex method determine the range for each RHS constant within which the current optimal basis remains feasible.
    b. Confirm your results in part (*a*) by graphical means.
    c. Determine each shadow price.
    d. Interpret the meaning of each shadow price and note the range in the corresponding RHS constant over which this interpretation is valid.
    e. Using the appropriate shadow price, predict optimal z if:

        1. b_1 changes from 40 to 43.
        2. b_1 changes from 40 to 35.
        3. b_1 changes from 40 to 50.
        4. b_2 changes from 30 to 40.
        5. b_3 changes from 90 to 60.

f. Graphically confirm your answers to part (e).
g. Based on your analysis in part (a), predict the new values for x_1, E_2, and S_3 for the change indicated in part (e-2). Graphically confirm these changes.

35. For the problem in Exercise 33:

a. State the canonical primal problem.
b. State the dual problem.
c. Solve the dual problem by the simplex method.
d. Identify specific primal-dual properties by comparing the optimal dual tableau to the optimal primal tableau which was determined in Exercise 34, part (a).
e. Relate optimal values for dual variables to the shadow prices found in Exercise 34, part (c). Conclusion?

36. For the following LP problem:

maximize

$$z = 4x_1 + 2x_2 + x_3 + 3x_4$$

subject to

$$2x_1 + x_2 \qquad + x_4 \leq 4$$
$$2x_1 - x_2 + 2x_3 \qquad \leq 3/2$$
$$3x_1 + 2x_2 + x_3 + 2x_4 \leq 8$$

$$x_1, x_2, x_3, x_4 \geq 0,$$

the final simplex tableau is given below.

Basis	z	x_1	x_2	x_3	x_4	S_1	S_2	S_3	b_i
(Final)	1	1/2	1	1/2	0	0	0	3/2	12
x_4	0	3/2	1	1/2	1	0	0	1/2	4
S_1	0	1/2	0	-1/2	0	1	0	-1/2	0
S_2	0	2	-1	2	0	0	1	0	3/2

a. Determine the permissible ranges over which the objective function coefficients x_1, x_2, and x_3 can vary such that the basis above continues to be optimal.
b. Do the same for x_4.
c. Is the value of optimal z altered as the objective function coefficients vary? Do the values change for the decision variables?

37. In the previous problem:

a. Conduct a sensitivity analysis for each of the right-hand–side constants.
b. What are the shadow prices associated with each constraint?
c. Over what ranges in the right-hand–side constants are these shadow prices valid?
d. Without reworking the problem, predict optimal z, x_4 S_1, and S_2 if:

1. b_3 changes from 8 to 9.5.
2. b_3 changes from 8 to 40.
3. b_3 changes from 8 to 6.

38. For the primal problem in Exercise 36:

   a. State the dual problem.
   b. Read the optimal solution to the dual problem from the optimal tableau in Exercise 36.
   c. Relate optimal values for dual variables to the shadow prices found in Exercise 37, part (b).
   d. Solve the dual problem in part (a) and read from the final tableau the solution to the primal problem.

39. For the following LP problem:

   minimize

   $$z = 5x_1 + 6x_2 + 7x_3$$

   subject to

   $$x_1 + x_2 + x_3 = 1,000$$
   $$x_1 \leq 300$$
   $$x_2 \geq 150$$
   $$x_3 \geq 200$$

   $$x_1, x_2, x_3 \geq 0,$$

   the final simplex tableau is given below.

Basis	z	x_1	x_2	x_3	A_1	S_2	E_3	A_3	E_4	A_4	b_i
(Final)	1	0	0	0	$(6 - M)$	-1	0	$-M$	-1	$(1 - M)$	5,900
E_3	0	0	0	0	1	-1	1	-1	1	-1	350
x_1	0	1	0	0	0	1	0	0	0	0	300
x_2	0	0	1	0	1	-1	0	0	1	-1	500
x_3	0	0	0	1	0	0	0	0	-1	1	200

   a. Conduct a sensitivity analysis on the objective function coefficients for x_1, x_2, and x_3.
   b. To which of these three parameters is the optimal basis most sensitive?

40. In the previous problem:
   a. Conduct a sensitivity analysis for each of the right-hand–side constants.
   b. To which of these parameters is the optimal basis most sensitive?
   c. What are the shadow prices associated with each constraint and over what ranges in RHS constants are their interpretations valid?
   d. Without reworking the problem, predict optimal z, x_1, x_2, and x_3 if

      1. b_1 changes from 1,000 to 900.
      2. b_1 changes from 1,000 to 1,200.
      3. b_1 changes from 1,000 to 350.

**41. For the primal problem in Exercise 39:

   a. State the canonical primal problem.
   b. State the dual problem.
   c. Read the optimal solution to the dual problem from the optimal tableau in Exercise 39.

    d.   Confirm your answer to part (*c*) by solving the dual problem in part (*b*).

    e.   Relate optimal values for dual variables to the shadow prices found in Exercise 40, part (*c*).

**42. Formulate the dual problem given the following primal:

minimize

$$z = 10x_1 + 5x_2$$

subject to

$$
\begin{aligned}
x_1 + x_2 &\ge 10 \\
x_1 &\ge 4 \\
x_2 &\ge 6 \\
x_1 + 3x_2 &= 15 \\
x_1 &\ge 0
\end{aligned}
$$

$$x_2 \text{ unrestricted.}$$

7

Specialized Linear Models

ALL LINEAR PROGRAMMING PROBLEMS can be solved by the simplex method; however, certain classes of LP problems, due to their specialized structure, lend themselves to solution by other techniques which are computationally more efficient than the simplex method. Generally, these types of linear problems can be represented by so-called **network models.** The **transportation model** and the **assignment model** represent two important subclasses which we will treat in this chapter. Network representations per se will be deferred until Chapters 9 and 14.

7.1 THE TRANSPORTATION MODEL

Generalized Form and Characteristics

In Chapter 4 we introduced an example of the classical transportation problem (Example 4.6). The classical transportation problem involves the shipment of some homogeneous commodity from various **origins** or sources of supply to a set of **destinations** each demanding specified levels of the commodity. It is assumed that allocation of the commodity from each origin is unrestricted with the exception of the amount available. This means that each origin can theoretically ship all, part, or none of its supply to any of the destinations. The assumption of a homogeneous commodity implies no difference in commodity characteristics among origins. The goal is to allocate the supply available at each origin in such a way as to optimize a criterion while satisfying the demand at each destination. The usual objective function is to minimize the total transportation cost or total weighted distance or to maximize the total profit contribution from the allocation.

As we will subsequently demonstrate through examples, the structure of the classical transportation model is comprehensive enough to include the solution of problems which have nothing to do with the shipment of commodities. The twin features of flexibility and significant computational advantages are what make the transportation model such an important class of linear models.

The data for Example 4.6 are repeated in Table 7–1 for convenience. The body of the matrix contains unit shipping costs (dollars per 1,000 gallons) between each plant (origin) and each depot (destination). The right-hand column indicates the supply available at each plant and the last row indicates the demand at each depot. Using the double-subscripted

TABLE 7–1

Transportation Data for Example 4.6

	Depot or Destination			Supply	
Plant or Origin	1	2	3	(1,000 gallons)	
1	$30	4	8	50	
2	5	10	20	70	
					120
Demand (1,000 gallons)	40	60	20	120	

variables x_{ij} to represent the number of commodity units (thousands of gallons) shipped from plant i to depot j, the LP statement of the problem is

minimize

$$z = 30x_{11} + 4x_{12} + 8x_{13} + 5x_{21} + 10x_{22} + 20x_{23}$$

subject to

$$
\begin{array}{llllll}
x_{11} + & x_{12} + & x_{13} & & & = 50 & \text{(Plant 1)} \\
& & & x_{21} + & x_{22} + & x_{23} = 70 & \text{(Plant 2)} \\
x_{11} & & & + & x_{21} & = 40 & \text{(Depot 1)} \\
& x_{12} & & + & x_{22} & = 60 & \text{(Depot 2)} \\
& & x_{13} & & + & x_{23} = 20 & \text{(Depot 3)}
\end{array}
$$

$$x_{ij} \geq 0 \text{ for all } i \text{ and } j.$$

In general, for m origins and n destinations, the problem is to

minimize

$$z = \sum_{i=1}^{m} \sum_{j=1}^{n} c_{ij} x_{ij}$$

subject to

$$\sum_{j=1}^{n} x_{ij} = s_i \qquad i = 1, \ldots, m$$

$$(7.1)$$

$$\sum_{i=1}^{m} x_{ij} = d_j \qquad j = 1, \ldots, n$$

$$x_{ij} \geq 0 \qquad\qquad \text{for all } i \text{ and } j,$$

where x_{ij} = number of units shipped from origin i to destination j; c_{ij} = cost of shipping one unit from origin i to destination j; s_i = units available at the ith origin; and d_j = units demanded at the jth destination.

It is also assumed that total supply and total demand are equal to one another, or

$$\sum_{i=1}^{m} s_i = \sum_{j=1}^{n} d_j \qquad\qquad (7.2)$$

Later in the chapter a procedure for handling imbalance between total supply and total demand will be demonstrated.

Solution Procedures

The basic steps for solving transportation problems are the same as those in the simplex method. The differences involve the manner in which the steps are operationalized. An initial basis is identified and it is examined to determine if it is optimal. If it is not optimal a new variable enters the basis and the optimality check is repeated as in the simplex method.

The various techniques for solving transportation models are collectively termed **transportation methods.** In order to use the transportation method, you should be aware of two requirements. First, the transportation method requires that total supply and total demand be equal ("balanced"). If you think about it for a moment, this requirement is the same as the equality conditions created by adding slack and surplus variables. Second, the basis in the transportation method will never contain *more than* $(m + n - 1)$ basic variables where m, again, equals the number of origins and n, the number of destinations. This is due to the inherent redundancy in transportation constraints. Because of the equality between total supply and demand, once $(m + n - 1)$ constraints have been satisfied, the remaining constraint is automatically satisfied. In the example above, if we knew that Plants 1 and 2 had shipped their 120 (1,000 gallons) and that Depots 1 and 2 had received delivery of 40 and 60 (1,000 gallons), respectively, Depot 3 *must* have received the remaining 20 (1,000 gallons).

Of the various optimization procedures for solving the transportation model, we will present two: stepping stone and MODI. As you will see, differences among procedures reflect differences in efficiency rather than differences in substance.

Example 7.1   Yew Haw Trucking Company

A national truck rental firm, Yew Haw Trucking Company, is planning for a heavy demand of rental trucks during the month of June. An inventory of its trucks (all 16-foot vans) combined with projections for demand indicate that three eastern metropolitan areas will be short of the number of trucks required to satisfy expected demands. Three other metropolitan areas have surpluses of trucks above the number expected to be needed during this period. It should be noted that these projections reflect anticipated movements of trucks between now and the first day of June.

In an effort to prepare for the period of heavy demand, company officials wish to relocate trucks from those metropolitan areas expected to have surpluses to those having shortages. Drivers can be hired to drive the

TABLE 7–2

Cost, Supply, and Demand Data for Yew Haw Trucking Company

Origin (Surplus Area)	Destination (Shortage Area)			Supply (Surplus of Trucks)
	1	2	3	
1	$ 50	100	100	110
2	200	300	200	160
3	100	200	300	150
Demand (shortage of trucks)	140	200	80	420 / 420

trucks between cities, and the company would like to redistribute its trucks at a minimum cost. The costs (in dollars) of driving a truck between cities are provided in Table 7–2, as well as the surplus and shortage figures for each metropolitan area. Conveniently, the total surplus (supply) and total shortage (demand) are equal at 420 trucks.

Follow-up Exercises

1. Formulate the linear programming model for Yew Haw Trucking Company.

2. The discussion above implies that the optimal solution to any transportation model will contain, *at most*, $m + n - 1$ *decision variables* in the basis because of redundancy in the constraints. How is redundancy indicated in a simplex solution? Solve the LP model in Exercise 1 by the simplex method to verify the claims made about the optimal basis.

7.2 SELECTED APPLICATIONS OF THE TRANSPORTATION MODEL

The transportation model is among the most extensively implemented OR models, especially for planning purposes. As already mentioned, one primary reason for this is the major computational advantages which accrue when solving this model. This feature is especially important for large-scale applications which otherwise might go unsolved.

A second important reason for the popularity of this model is the existence of widespread "ready-made" (classical) applications in the real world relating to the distribution of commodities (which, of course, is where the model inherits the name "transportation"). To our knowledge, not one facet of distribution channels (for example, plants to regional warehouses to wholesale outlets to retail outlets) has escaped the analytical benefits of this type of modeling.

A third major reason for the importance of this model is the flexibility of application to problems other than the classical type. For example, variations of the model have been used for production scheduling and inventory control; the scheduling of meals, freighters, and airplanes; the assignment of machines to jobs and personnel to tasks; and a myriad of other applications, including the solutions to product mix, plant location, traveling salesperson, international trade, and contract award problems.

In this section, we present and formulate three problems of the non-classical transportation type. At the end of the chapter other exercises will be presented (for you to formulate).

Example 7.2   Caterer Problem

The caterer problem is a classical formulation in linear programming. Here we present the problem in a transportation framework.

Suppose a caterer must supply clean napkins in the amounts 1,000; 700; 800; 1,200; and 1,500 for the next 5 days, respectively. The caterer has three alternatives for supplying napkins in any given day: (1) purchase new napkins at a cost of $1.00 each; (2) utilize previously soiled napkins which have been cleaned by a 2-day service at a cost of $0.10 each; or (3) utilize previously soiled napkins which have been cleaned by a 1-day (next-day) service at a cost of $0.20 each.

The transportation data in Table 7–3 have been determined by treating the demand for each day as a "destination" and the purchases and soiled napkins for each day as "origins." Note that, in the extreme, the caterer could purchase the entire set of 5,200 napkins; hence, the theoretical supply for Origin 1 is 5,200. The supplies for the remaining origins are simply the number of napkins soiled (or required) on a specific day which could be utilized in subsequent days of the planning horizon. Napkins soiled on the fifth day do not represent an origin because they cannot be reused in this planning horizon.

Because the total supply of napkins (8,900) exceeds the total demand for napkins (5,200), a total of 3,700 available napkins will not be utilized.

TABLE 7–3

Data for Caterer Problem

Origin (Source of Napkins)	Destination (Demand for Day)						Supply
	1	2	3	4	5	Dummy	
1 (Purchases)	$1.00	1.00	1.00	1.00	1.00	0	5,200
2 (Soiled Day 1)		0.20	0.10	0.10	0.10	0	1,000
3 (Soiled Day 2)			0.20	0.10	0.10	0	700
4 (Soiled Day 3)				0.20	0.10	0	800
5 (Soiled Day 4)					0.20	0	1,200
Demand	1,000	700	800	1,200	1,500	3,700	8,900 / 8,900

To satisfy Equation (7.2), the condition of equality between total supply and total demand, a **dummy destination** is established with a requirement of 3,700 napkins.

The cost of "transporting a napkin from Origin 1 to any of the destinations" (that is, the cost of purchasing a single napkin for use in any given day) is $1. For origin 2, napkins soiled in Day 1, the cost of providing napkins for use in Day 2 is $0.20 per napkin and for use in any of the other days is $0.10 per napkin. Costs for the other cells follow similarly. Note that costs in the dummy cells necessarily must be zero. (Can you reason why?)

If x_{ij} represents the number of napkins provided from supply alternative i (Origin i) to satisfy the demand of Day j (Destination j or the dummy), c_{ij} represents the cost per napkin for the given (i, j) combination, s_i represents the available napkins from supply alternative i, d_j represents the required napkins for Day j or the dummy, m represents the number of available supply alternatives (five origins), and n represents the number of days for which there is demand (six destinations), then the transportation formulation given by Equation (7.1) holds exactly.

Follow-up Exercises

3. Can you determine a way in which the supply column values may be reduced in Table 7–3? What effect does this have on demand at the dummy destination?

4. Suppose that on the day just prior to the beginning of the planning horizon the caterer has available 400 clean napkins and 200 soiled napkins. Add two more origins and construct a new table.

5. Formulate the LP model (objective function and constraints) for the caterer problem.

6. Why is this model (single planning horizon) not relevant for the case where the planning horizon represents one cycle in a continuous (infinite) process?

Example 7.3 Committee Assignments

Suppose that m members of a college faculty are to be assigned to n standing committees according to their preferences for the coming academic year. Let x_{ij} = one if the ith person is assigned to the jth committee; zero otherwise; c_{ij} = preference score (low score implies high preference) of the ith person for the jth committee; s_i = number of committees served by the ith person; and d_j = number of members required by the jth committee.

Given these definitions, you should readily verify that the mathematical statement of the model is exactly equivalent to Equation (7.1). Note that each faculty member becomes an "origin" which can "supply" either zero or one "unit" to satisfy committee ("destination") demands. The objective is to maximize the cumulative preference of the faculty or to *minimize* the cumulative preference score.

If any one faculty member is to serve on one and only one committee and if assignments are to be made uniformly such that each committee has approximately the same number of members, then the model becomes

minimize

$$z = \sum_{i=1}^{m} \sum_{j=1}^{n} c_{ij} x_{ij}$$

subject to

$$\sum_{j=1}^{n} x_{ij} = 1, \quad i = 1, \ldots, m \qquad \text{(one committee per person)}$$

$$\sum_{i=1}^{m} x_{ij} = [m/n], \quad j = 1, \ldots, n \qquad \text{(uniform number per committee)}$$

$$x_{ij} = 0 \text{ or } 1.$$

For example, if $m = 50$ and $n = 8$, then the integer part of the ratio of m to n is $[m/n] = 6$. Since two faculty members are now left over (that is, total supply exceeds total demand by two units), *an imbalance has been created which can be rectified by creating a "dummy" committee* with a requirement of two.

This results in a new column of the table for transportation data with a demand of two and "costs" (preferences) of zero for each individual (origin). In effect, this represents the addition of the following constraint:

$$\sum_{i=1}^{m} x_{i9} = 2. \quad \text{(dummy committee)}$$

Following the solution, the two members assigned to the dummy committee can be given their top preferences on the other committees.

We might note that this 450-variable (50×9) problem can be solved

---

[1] Some critics would entirely agree with the use of "dummy" in this context.

easily by computer in a transportation context. As a 0–1 integer programming problem, however, the methods (computerized) discussed in Chapters 8 or 9 would fail to find an optimal solution in an acceptable time span.

Follow-up Exercises

7. How would you scale the c_{ij}'s? (See Example 1.5 and Exercise 4 on page 17.) Justify your answer based on your "knowledge" of scale considerations.

8. Let x_{ijk} represent the assignment variable for individual i from department k on committee j. Suppose there are six college departments and that committee 1 requires representation from each department. If c_{ijk}, s_i, and d_j are defined as before, state the mathematical formulation of this model. Is this a transportation model? Can you think of a scheme for avoiding the subscript "k" given that m_1 members are in department 1, m_2 members are in department 2, and so forth?

Example 7.4   Production Scheduling and Inventory Control

The transportation model can be applied to the problem of scheduling production and controlling inventory over several time periods.[2] The typical case is the manufacturer with a seasonal sales pattern; production can remain completely stable (thereby absorbing seasonal fluctuations with inventory buildups and depletions), production can vary to meet the sales pattern (no inventories), or production can follow some midground approach between these two extremes.

The most straightforward formulation involves a tradeoff between overtime costs and inventory holding costs. In this formulation, for each time period, such as a month, we define regular and overtime capacity in units, such as production hours. We also estimate (by the methods of Appendix A) the unit costs of regular and overtime production and the cost per time period of holding a unit in inventory.

The transportation formulation identifies regular and overtime production capacities in each period as "origins" and demands for each period as "destinations." The cost associated with each cell is determined as the sum of production cost per unit and the cost of holding a unit in inventory (if any). The decision variables are defined in terms of production quantities in a given period manufactured by a given method (regular or overtime) for delivery in the present or some future period.

For example, consider a four-period model with projected (or contracted) demands of 40, 60, 75, and 60 units in Periods 1, 2, 3, and 4, respectively. The costs are $4.00 per unit for regular time, $6.00 per unit for overtime, and $1.50 for holding a unit in inventory for one period. For simplicity, we assume that these costs are identical in each period. Furthermore, in each period, regular production capacity is 50 units and overtime production capacity is 20 units. Table 7–4 illustrates the transportation data for this example.

---

[2] Transportation models involving allocations over time are known as **multi-stage transportation models.** Such models also can be solved (less efficiently) by dynamic programming (Chapter 9).

TABLE 7–4

Transportation Data for Example 7.4

Origin (Source of Production)	Destination (Demand in Period)					Supply (Production Capacity)
	1	2	3	4	Dummy	
1 Regular Period 1	$4.00	$5.50	$7.00	$ 8.50	?	50
2 Overtime Period 1	6.00	7.50	9.00	10.50	?	20
3 Regular Period 2		4.00	5.50	7.00	?	50
4 Overtime Period 2		6.00	7.50	9.00	?	20
5 Regular Period 3			4.00	5.50	?	50
6 Overtime Period 3			6.00	7.50	?	20
7 Regular Period 4				4.00	?	50
8 Overtime Period 4				6.00	?	20
Demand	40	60	75	60	45	280 / 280

To illustrate the calculation of costs, consider Origin 3. The first cell is infeasible because it is impossible to produce in Period 2 for delivery in Period 1 (assuming backordering is not allowed). The cost in the second cell is simply the cost per unit of regular production ($4). The cost of $5.50 in the third cell represents the cost of producing a unit on regular time in Period 2 for delivery in Period 3, or $4.00 plus the cost of holding the unit for one period ($1.50)—and so forth.

Since total supply is greater than total demand, a dummy destination is created to pick up the slack. Each dummy in this case represents unused production capacity. An interesting question concerns the cost values to assign to the dummy column. Although it may be tempting to uniformly assign zero, that would infer an ability to hold regular production costs completely variable. That is, it would be equivalent to assuming that workers can be sent home when not needed at no cost to the company. The zero assumption may be valid for overtime, but if workers remain on the job for 40 hours per week with or without something to do, the dummy cost for an origin associated with regular production may better be estimated as the cost per unit of regular production ($4). Alternatively, if product costing is based on direct labor plus raw materials plus overhead, then dummy regulars should be costed as a proportion of $4.

We now define the following symbols for the general statement of this model (don't panic):

x_{ijk} = Production units in period i for period j using method k ($k = 1$ for regular time and $k = 2$ for overtime).

c_{ijk} = cost (production plus inventory) per unit produced in i for j by method k.

p_{ik} = Production cost per unit in period i using method k.

h_i = Cost of holding a unit in inventory in period i.

d_j = Number of units demanded in period j.

s_{ik} = Capacity units in period i for method k.

n = Number of time periods in the planning horizon.

The mathematical statement of the LP model becomes

minimize

$$z = \sum_{i=1}^{n} \sum_{j \geq i}^{n} \sum_{k=1}^{2} c_{ijk} x_{ijk}$$

subject to

$$\sum_{i=1}^{j} \sum_{k=1}^{2} x_{ijk} \geq d_j, \qquad j = 1, \ldots, n \text{ (demand requirements)}$$

$$\sum_{j=i}^{n} x_{ij1} \leq s_{i1}, \qquad i = 1, \ldots, n \text{ (regular time capacity)}$$

$$\sum_{j=i}^{n} x_{ij2} \leq s_{i2}, \qquad i = 1, \ldots, n \text{ (overtime capacity)}$$

$$x_{ijk} \geq 0 \text{ over all } i, j, \text{ and } k.$$

Note that j must always be greater than or equal to i. (If not, what would x_{321} imply?) In a transportation context, the requirement in any given period represents a destination and the regular time and overtime production in any given period *each* represent an origin. Typically, the sum of the capacities is greater than the total demand; that is,

$$\sum_{i=1}^{n} \sum_{k=1}^{2} s_{ik} \geq \sum_{j=1}^{n} d_j,$$

which requires the stipulation of a dummy demand to "pick up" the *excess* production capacity; hence, the problem has $n + 1$ destinations and $2n$ origins.

Finally, assuming linear production costs (with no setup cost), the unit cost for any given cell of the transportation table is determined from either

$$c_{ijk} = p_{ik} + \sum_{t=i+1}^{j} h_t, \qquad\qquad j > i,$$

or

$$c_{ijk} = p_{ik}, \qquad\qquad j = i.$$

Note the subscripting on the holding cost summation; for example, a unit produced in period 3 for period 5 incurs two periods of holding costs (the fourth and fifth).

Also note that this formulation assigns a cost of zero to excess production capacity. In Exercise 9b we ask you to relax this restriction.

Follow-up Exercises

9. *a.* Construct a transportation table for the following data: $n = 5$, $d_1 = 10$, $d_2 = 12$, $d_3 = 15$, $d_4 = 10$, $d_5 = 13$, $p_{11} = 100$, $p_{21} = 110$, $p_{31} = 120$, $p_{41} = 130$, $p_{51} = 140$, $p_{12} = 1.5p_{11}$, $h_i = 10$, for all i, $s_{11} = 10$, $s_{21} = 10$, $s_{31} = 6$, $s_{41} = 10$, $s_{51} = 8$, and $s_{12} = 0.5s_{11}$.
   Assume that excess regular time production capacity is costed at 60 percent of regular time production cost. Excess overtime production capacity is costed at zero.

   **b.* Express this problem according to an LP format.

   **c.* Use a computerized simplex routine to solve the problem in part (b) or a transportation routine (if available) to solve the problem in part (a).

   **d.* For the solution in part (c), what is the breakdown in *optimal* total cost among inventory cost, regular time production cost, overtime production cost, and excess capacity cost?

10. Solve Example 7.4 using a computerized simplex or transportation package. Use regular time production costs for the appropriate dummies. What is the optimal cost breakdown?

**11. Suppose m_i represents the maximum inventory allowed in period l. Can you formulate an appropriate constraint set? Does the transportation model apply now?

7.3 ALGORITHM FOR THE TRANSPORTATION MODEL

Based on your study of the first two sections, you should have a clear understanding of the structure and generality of the transportation model. We now turn to the details of a computational procedure for solving transportation problems.

Special Structure

To illustrate what we mean by special (mathematical) structure in transportation problems, consider the initial simplex tableau shown below for the LP model associated with Table 7–1.

Basis	z	x_{11}	x_{12}	x_{13}	x_{21}	x_{22}	x_{23}	A_1	A_2	A_3	A_4	A_5	b_i	Row No.	r_i
I	1	-30 $+2M$	-4 $+2M$	-8 $+2M$	-5 $+2M$	-10 $+2M$	-20 $+2M$	0	0	0	0	0	240M	(0)	
A_1	0	1	①	1	0	0	0	1	0	0	0	0	50	(1)	$50/1 = 50$*
A_2	0	0	0	0	1	1	1	0	1	0	0	0	70	(2)	
A_3	0	1	0	0	1	0	0	0	0	1	0	0	40	(3)	
A_4	0	0	1	0	0	1	0	0	0	0	1	0	60	(4)	$60/1 = 60$
A_5	0	0	0	1	0	0	1	0	0	0	0	1	20	(5)	

This tableau illustrates the structural characteristics which lead to more efficient solution procedures. If you focus upon the a_{ij} coefficients, you will notice that they are all zero or one. In addition, all of the right-hand–side constants are nonnegative whole numbers. You will later see that these properties guarantee that any basic feasible solution contains variables which have nonnegative integer values. In addition, you should observe that each column for the decision variables, x_{ij}, contains two a_{ij} values equal to one and the remainder equal to zero.[3]

Suppose we were to go on to the next solution. The first tableau indicates that x_{12} will enter the basis and A_1 will leave. Now generate the next tableau on your own. Did it seem a little easier than usual? You should have discovered that forcing the identity column under x_{12} was fairly simple. In fact with the exception of computing the new Row (0) values, all other new rows (if they need to be computed) can be computed by adding or subtracting the pivot equation to the old row. You will always find that the *pivot element* is one, requiring no change in the pivot equation.

If you continue to solve by the simplex method, you will observe that the revised a_{ij} values will always equal 0, +1, or −1. This property eliminates the need to use row operations of multiplication or division; even on computers this can allow for substantial savings in the time required to solve problems. This problem, however, still requires five simplex iterations before reaching the optimal solution. For large-scale problems the number of iterations, coupled with the size of each tableau, makes the solution process overly tedious and expensive. Fortunately, special computational procedures have been developed which exploit the special structure of this type of linear programming problem.

Tabular Format

The transportation method uses a tabular format for displaying problem data and solution information, as generalized in Table 7–5. Note that there is one row for each origin and one column for each destination. The objective function coefficients are contained in the subcells at the intersection of each row and column. In addition the last column and the last row contain, respectively, the capacities of each origin and the requirements for each destination. These are the right-hand sides for the constraints and are often referred to collectively as **rim requirements.** Finally, values for the decision variables are indicated as entries in the main cells. (For keglers, this tabular format has a "striking" similarity to a bowling scoresheet.)

Developing the Starting Solution

Although there is latitude in selecting the initial solution in the simplex method, the simplest procedure is to start with an initial basis containing

---

[3] These characteristics simplify the matrix manipulations of computerized routines by guaranteeing that the minors (see Appendix C) of the matrix of coefficients (a_{ij}) are all ± 1 or 0. This is known as the **unimodular property** of the Matrix **A.**

TABLE 7–5

Generalized Table for Transportation Method

Origin	Destination				Supply
	1	2	$\cdots$	n	
1	x_{11} $\quad c_{11}$	x_{12} $\quad c_{12}$	$\cdots$	x_{1n} $\quad c_{1n}$	s_1
2	x_{21} $\quad c_{21}$	x_{22} $\quad c_{22}$	$\cdots$	x_{2n} $\quad c_{2n}$	s_2
$\vdots$	$\vdots$	$\vdots$	$\vdots$	$\vdots$	$\vdots$
m	x_{m1} $\quad c_{m1}$	x_{m2} $\quad c_{m2}$	$\cdots$	x_{mn} $\quad c_{mn}$	s_m
Demand	d_1	d_2	$\cdots$	d_n	$\sum_{j=1}^{n} d_j$ $\quad \sum_{i=1}^{m} s_i$

slack and artificial variables.[4] The transportation method allows for greater discretion in arriving at an initial solution providing that $(m + n - 1)$ basic variables are selected. The advantage of such discretion is that one can surely select an initial basis which is closer to the optimal basis than the initial basis arrived at by the simplex method. This can lead to fewer iterations in reaching the optimal solution.

The **Northwest Corner Method** is a popular (but unthinking) technique for arriving at an initial solution. The scheme is to start in the upper left-hand cell (northwest corner) and assign units from Origin 1 to Destination 1. Assignments are continued in such a way that the supply at Origin 1 is completely allocated before moving on to the remaining origins. The same type of sequential allocation applies to assignments made to destinations. The demand for Destination 1 is satisfied before making allocations to Destination 2, and so forth. This pattern of assignments leads to a sort of staircase arrangement of assignments. The decision rule for making allocations to each relevant cell is based on selecting the minimum of the unused supply for the row and the unsatisfied demand for the column, or in considering an assignment to cell (i,j):

---

[4] Other adaptations of the simplex method not discussed in this book permit initial solutions that are closer to the optimum.

$$x_{ij} = \min\,(s_i - s_i',\, d_j - d_j') \tag{7.3}$$

where $s_i' = $ the sum of previous allocations from Origin i
and $d_j' = $ the sum of previous allocations to Destination j.

Example 7.5 Northwest Corner Method for Yew Haw Trucking Company

To illustrate the Northwest Corner Method, we develop an initial solution for Example 7.1.

1. The capacity of 110 trucks at Origin 1 is less than the 140 units demanded at Destination 1. Consequently, all of the capacity at Origin 1 is allocated to cell (1,1). (See Table 7–6.)
2. The exhaustion of the supply at Origin 1 leads to Origin 2. The 160 units available at Origin 2 are compared with the 30 remaining trucks required at Destination 1. This leads to the assignment of 30 trucks to cell (2,1).
3. The assignment in (2) leaves 130 trucks available at Origin 2 and the requirements of Destination 1 satisfied. Moving to the needs of Destination 2, we see that a comparison of the 200 trucks required with the 130 remaining at Origin 2 results in the assignment of 130 units to cell (2,2).
4. Having exhausted the capacity of Origin 2, we find the 150 units available at Origin 3 are compared with the 70 units still required at Destination 2. This leads to an assignment of 70 units to cell (3,2).
5. The remaining 80 units at Origin 3 exactly equals the demand at Destination 3. Thus, 80 units are assigned to cell (3,3).

The complete initial solution appears in Table 7–6. It indicates that 110

TABLE 7–6

Northwest Corner Method

Origin	Destination 1	Destination 2	Destination 3	Supply
1	50 110	100	100	110
2	200 30	300 130	200	160
3	100	200 70	300 80	150
Demand	140	200	80	420 / 420

trucks should be delivered from the city representing Origin 1 to the city representing Destination 1, 30 from Origin 2 to Destination 1, 130 from Origin 2 to Destination 2, 70 from Origin 3 to Destination 2, and 80 from Origin 3 to Destination 3. Total cost for this redistribution is summarized in the accompanying table.

Basic Variable	Value		Unit Delivery Cost		Contribution to Total Cost
x_{11}	110	$\times$	50	=	$ 5,500
x_{21}	30	$\times$	200	=	6,000
x_{22}	130	$\times$	300	=	39,000
x_{32}	70	$\times$	200	=	14,000
x_{33}	80	$\times$	300	=	24,000
					$88,500

Simplicity and speed are the primary advantages of the Northwest Corner Method; however, a complete disregard for objective function coefficients is its principal disadvantage. (Not once during the allocation process were we concerned with delivery cost.) For this reason, a variety of alternative techniques have been proposed for obtaining an initial solution. Each of these has as its major goal a starting basis from which fewer iterations are required to reach the optimal solution. Invariably, the tradeoff involves greater time spent in identifying the initial solution but less time in progressing to the optimal solution. One popular alternative is an "eyeball" approach which sequentially seeks the low-cost cells while satisfying row and column constraints. We will now illustrate this **Least Cost Method** by example.

Example 7.6   Least Cost Method for Yew Haw Trucking Company

Table 7–7 illustrates the initial solution for the trucking example by the Least Cost Method. To start, the least cost element in the table is identified ($c_{11} = 50$) and the maximum feasible amount is allocated to the corresponding cell ($x_{11} = 110$). Since Row 1 is satisfied, it is crossed out.

The next lowest cost element *among feasible cells* is located ($c_{31} = 100$) and the maximum feasible amount is entered ($x_{31} = 30$). This eliminates Column 1. The next lowest cost element of 200 is given by either c_{23} or c_{32}. Arbitrarily selecting the former gives $x_{23} = 80$ and the elimination of Column 3. The solution is completed by entering 80 and 120 in cells (2,2) and (3,2), respectively, to satisfy the requirements of Destination 2. The total cost for this solution is $72,500, which is lower than the solution given by the Northwest Corner Method.

TABLE 7–7

Least Cost Method

Origin	Destination 1	Destination 2	Destination 3	Supply
1	50 / 110	100	100	110
2	200	300 / 80	200 / 80	160
3	100 / 30	200 / 120	300	150
Demand	140	200	80	420 / 420

The primary problem with the Least Cost Method is that the selection of one low-cost cell may block a better cell because of row and column constraints. **Vogel's Approximation Method (VAM)** attempts to overcome this problem by computing a type of *opportunity cost* or penalty associated with each assignment.

The procedure is to find the two lowest cost cells for each row and column. Subtracting the smaller of these costs from the other produces a Vogel number for each row and column. We select the *largest* Vogel number, and make the first assignment to the corresponding *lowest* cost cell; as before, we assign the maximum amount for the corresponding decision variable, as limited by row and column constraints. Ties can be broken arbitrarily. After each assignment, the Vogel numbers are recomputed based on the remaining rows and columns. The procedure is repeated until all assignments have been made.

Example 7.7   Vogel's Approximation Method for Yew Haw Trucking Company

If we apply VAM to the Yew Haw problem we obtain the accompanying Vogel numbers:

$$\text{Row 1: } 100 \ (c_{12}) - 50 \ (c_{11}) = 50$$
$$2: 200 \ (c_{23}) - 200 \ (c_{21}) = 0$$
$$3: 200 \ (c_{32}) - 100 \ (c_{31}) = 100$$

$$\text{Column 1: } 100 \ (c_{31}) - \ 50 \ (c_{11}) = \ 50$$
$$2: 200 \ (c_{32}) - 100 \ (c_{12}) = 100$$
$$3: 200 \ (c_{23}) - 100 \ (c_{13}) = 100.$$

Since three Vogel numbers are tied for the maximum of 100, we arbitrarily select the first in the list (corresponding to Row 3) and assign 140 trucks to x_{31}. Note that the subscript "31" is based on the lowest cost in Row 3, or c_{31}. The value of "140" is determined using Equation (7.3), that is, the minimum of 150 and 140. Can you explain the rationale?

In the next pass, Column 1 is ignored (its demand has been satisfied) and the Vogel numbers for Columns 2 and 3 remain unchanged:

$$\text{Row 1: } 100 \ (c_{13}) - 100 \ (c_{12}) = \quad 0$$
$$2: 300 \ (c_{22}) - 200 \ (c_{23}) = 100$$
$$3: 300 \ (c_{33}) - 200 \ (c_{32}) = 100$$
$$\text{Column 2: } \qquad \ldots \qquad = 100$$
$$3: \qquad \ldots \qquad = 100.$$

Arbitrarily selecting the first 100 in the list (Row 2) results in an assignment of 80 trucks from Origin 2 to Destination 3 ($x_{23} = 80$). Since all but one of the column constraints have now been satisfied, all the remaining trucks at Origins 1, 2, and 3 must be assigned to Destination 2, and the initial solution is:

$$x_{12} = 110$$
$$x_{22} = \ 80$$
$$x_{23} = \ 80$$
$$x_{31} = 140$$
$$x_{32} = \ 10$$
$$z = \$67{,}000.$$

As would be expected the cost of the initial solution given by VAM ($67,000) is considerably lower than the costs given by the Northwest Corner Method ($88,500) and by the Least Cost Method ($72,500).

Follow-up Exercise

12. Develop initial solutions by the Northwest Corner Method, the Least Cost Method, and VAM for the problem given in Table 7–1 (Example 4.6). Compare objective function values and weigh improvements against differences in "grunt" work.

In general, VAM gives good initial solutions and is well-suited to computer implementation. Generally, the increased computational burden of VAM over the Northwest Corner Method is trivial when implemented by computer. Additionally, more sophisticated variations exist for VAM, for example, calculating secondary Vogel numbers for breaking ties by subtracting the next lowest cost from the next-to-next lowest cost.

No method for initial solutions guarantees optimality nor has any one been consistently better than the others. The various approaches simply guarantee the generation of a starting feasible basis. We now turn to a simplex-based procedure for determining the optimal solution.

Stepping Stone Algorithm

Given a starting feasible basis, the **stepping stone algorithm** is a popular method for optimally solving transportation models. The approach parallels the simplex method almost exactly. Both methods employ marginal analysis to determine the effects of introducing new variables into the existing basis. The equivalent of the Row (0) values in a simplex tableau are first computed for each nonbasic variable. If an improved solution is possible, a new variable enters the basis, replacing one of the original basic variables, and the new solution is developed. This procedure is continued until no further improvement is possible. We present the algorithm by way of example.

Example 7.8   Stepping Stone Algorithm for Yew Haw Trucking Company

Starting with the initial solution for the trucking example given by the Northwest Corner Method (Example 7.5), we outline the solution algorithm with the steps indicated below.

Step 1: *Determine the Improvement Index for Each Nonbasic Variable (Cell).* As mentioned previously, the idea is to determine the effects upon the existing solution of introducing one unit of a nonbasic variable (that is, a variable not currently in the basis). To illustrate (see Table 7–8) we focus upon cell (1, 2) which by virtue of having an empty cell indicates that no trucks are being shipped from Origin 1 to Destination 2. The question we want to ask is what tradeoffs with the existing basic variables (that is, those in solution) would be required if one truck is delivered from Origin 1 to Destination 2? If one truck is allocated to cell (1, 2), 111 trucks would be designated for delivery from Origin 1. Since this exceeds its capacity,

TABLE 7–8

Closed Path for Cell (1, 2)

Origin	Destination 1	Destination 2	Destination 3	Supply
1	⊖1 ← 50 110	⊕1 100	100	110
2	⊕1 200 → 30	⊖1 300 130	200	160
3	100	200 70	300 80	150
Demand	140	200	80	420 420

an adjustment is necessary *with existing basic variables*. A reduction by one in deliveries from Origin 1 to Destination 1 to 109 trucks reestablishes balance in the supply constraint for Origin 1. The reduction by one truck in cell (1, 1), however, results in an undershipment to Destination 1. This can be compensated for by increasing the deliveries in cell (2, 1) to 31. As expected (Will this ever end?), this allocation results in an overshipment from Origin 2. Finally, if deliveries in cell (2, 2) are reduced to 129, overall balance is restored. That is, the *rim requirements* (row and column constraints) are satisfied. The series of required exchanges are indicated in Table 7–8 by the closed path of directed arrows.

Now that the required tradeoffs or adjustments have been identified for the entry of x_{12}, the important question is the resulting effect on the current value of the objective function. This can be determined easily by noting that for each cell (*ij*) receiving an increased allocation of one unit, costs increase by the corresponding cost coefficient (c_{ij}). Similarly, costs decrease by the value of the cost coefficient wherever allocations have been reduced by one unit. These effects are summarized in the accompanying table.

Cell (i, j)	Change in x_{ij} (Δx_{ij})	Change in Total Cost ($c_{ij} \cdot \Delta x_{ij}$)
(1, 2).................	+1	+100
(1, 1).................	−1	− 50
(2, 1).................	+1	+200
(2, 2).................	−1	−300
Net change.....................................		− 50 (Improvement Index, I_{12})

Thus, the delivery of one truck from Origin 1 to Destination 2 would lead to a $50 reduction in total costs.

This marginal change in the objective function (−$50) is equivalent to the effect of the Row (0) value of x_{12} in the simplex method, and is referred to as the **improvement index** for cell (1,2).

If we had the simplex tableau which corresponds to the starting basis in front of us, the column corresponding to x_{12} would appear as below (the rows corresponding to the basic variables might be interchanged). Do you remember from Chapter 5 why the signs are reversed on the Row (0) value and the column of marginal rates of substitution?

Basis	···	x_{12}	···	Row No.
—	···	50	···	(0)
x_{11}	···	1	···	(1)
x_{21}	···	−1	···	(2)
x_{22}	···	+1	···	(3)
x_{32}	···	0	···	(4)
x_{33}	···	0	···	(5)

Now is the time to state a rule (for those of you who have a leaning toward the "kitchen-counter" or "cook-book" approach to quantitative courses) which will identify the required exchanges resulting from introducing a nonbasic variable.

To determine the required exchanges with the existing basis from introducing a unit to an unoccupied cell, trace a **closed path** which begins at the unoccupied cell of interest, moves *alternately* in horizontal and vertical directions pivoting only on occupied cells, and terminates on the unoccupied cell. A (+1) is assigned to the unoccupied cell (indicating an increase of one unit) and succeeding corner points on the path are alternately assigned (−1) and (+1) values. The pluses and minuses indicate the required adjustments. It is important to understand that if the basis contains $(m + n - 1)$ variables (occupied cells), there is *one* unique path that can be traced which satisfies the rim requirements.

The direction taken in tracing the closed path (clockwise or counterclockwise) makes no difference. The procedure is a bit more tricky than

TABLE 7–9

Closed Path for Cell (1, 3)

Origin	Destination			Supply
	1	2	3	
1	(−1) ← 50 ← 100 (+1) 100			
	110			110
2	(+1) ← 200 → (−1) 300 200			
	30	130		160
3	100 (+1) ← 200 → (−1) 300			
		70	80	150
Demand	140	200	80	420 / 420

merely jumping from the cell of interest to *any* occupied cell in the same row or column. It is necessary to go to *the* occupied cell which will allow you to trace a closed path, and not lead to a "dead end." For example, if in starting with cell (1, 2) you next decided to jump to cell (3, 2) and thereafter to cell (3, 3), you would be "stuck." If you find yourself in this predicament and do not see any easy way out, then go back to the cell of interest and "go the other way."

As a demonstration of one more path, Table 7–9 indicates the closed path and corresponding adjustments to basic variables for cell (1, 3). You should verify that the improvement index for cell (1, 3) is −150.

The paths for each unoccupied cell in this initial solution and their associated improvement indices are summarized in the accompanying table. (Check these out to test your understanding.)

Nonbasic Cell (i,j)	Closed Path	Improvement Index (I_{ij})
(1,2).............	$(1,2) \rightarrow (1,1) \rightarrow (2,1) \rightarrow (2,2) \rightarrow (1,2)$	$-\ 50$
(1,3).........	$(1,3) \rightarrow (1,1) \rightarrow (2,1) \rightarrow (2,2) \rightarrow (3,2) \rightarrow (3,3) \rightarrow (1,3)$	-150
(2,3).............	$(2,3) \rightarrow (2,2) \rightarrow (3,2) \rightarrow (3,3) \rightarrow (2,3)$	-200^*
(3,1).............	$(3,1) \rightarrow (3,2) \rightarrow (2,2) \rightarrow (2,1) \rightarrow (3,1)$	0

Step 2: If a Better Solution Exists, Determine Which Variable (Cell) Should Enter the Basis. An examination of the improvement indices indicates that the introduction of three of the four nonbasic variables would lead to a reduction in total delivery costs. *For minimization problems the existence of any negative improvement index implies that a better solution exists;* otherwise, the optimal solution has been determined. As with the optimality criterion in the simplex method, we will select the variable (cell) to enter the basis as the one which leads to the greatest marginal improvement in the objective function.[5] In our example cell (2,3), or x_{23}, is selected for entrance.

Step 3: Determine the Number of Units to Assign the Incoming Variable (and Determine the Departing Basic Variable). This step is performed by returning to the closed path associated with the incoming cell. Figure 7–1

FIGURE 7–1

Closed Path for Cell (2, 3)

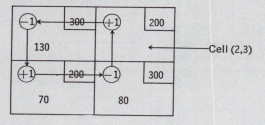

is a section of the starting table showing the closed path for cell (2, 3). Since each unit assigned to x_{23} decreases total cost by $200 (according to the improvement index), we would like to allocate as many deliveries as possible from Origin 2 to Destination 3. For every unit introduced in cell (2, 3), the quantities contained in cells (2, 2) and (3, 3) will decrease by one unit. We will simply introduce exactly enough units to drive *one* of the existing cells to zero (which preserves the $m + n - 1$ allocations) without allowing others to become negative (which preserves feasibility). The only candidates for going to zero are those cells in a minus position along the path. The variable which leaves the basis is always the one having the smallest quantity or value.[6] Since the tradeoff is one for one, its value also indicates

---

[5] As in the simplex method, *any* nonbasic variable which offers an improvement in z can be selected for entry.

[6] It is possible to have more than one variable leave the basis. If so, degeneracy results—a condition we treat later in the chapter.

the maximum amount which can be entered of the incoming variable. In our example the value of 80 associated with cell (3, 3) is the smallest in a minus position on the path; hence, x_{23} is assigned 80 units and x_{33} (the leaving variable) is assigned a value of zero. (What would happen to the values of the basic variables if 81 units were introduced?)

You should be able to relate the procedures of this step to the procedure of computing the minimum positive r_i ratio in the simplex method. It is exactly the same.

Step 4: *Develop the New Solution, and Return to Step 1.* This is the easy part! Again referring to the closed path for the incoming variable, add the quantity determined in Step 3 to all cells in a plus position and subtract it from those in a minus position. Table 7–10 presents the new solution. Rather than multiplying the new values of all basic variables times their corresponding unit costs to compute the new value of the objective function, we can subtract from the previous value of the objective function the total reduction in costs from entering the new variable, or

$$z = \$88,500 - 80\ (\$200)$$
$$= \$88,500 - \$16,000$$
$$= \$72,500.$$

The solution to this problem is completed in Tables 7–10 through 7–12. Closed paths and improvement indices for unoccupied cells are summarized for your convenience.

Since all of the improvement indices are greater than or equal to zero,

TABLE 7–10

Second Iteration for Trucking Example

Origin	Destination 1	Destination 2	Destination 3	Supply
1	50 110	100	100	110
2	200 30	300 50	200 80	160
3	100	200 150	300	150
Demand	140	200	80	420 / 420

$$z = \$72,500$$

Cell	Closed Path	I_{ij}
(1,2)	$(1,2) \rightarrow (1,1) \rightarrow (2,1) \rightarrow (2,2) \rightarrow (1,2)$	-50^*
(1,3)	$(1,3) \rightarrow (1,1) \rightarrow (2,1) \rightarrow (2,3) \rightarrow (1,3)$	$+50$
(3,1)	$(3,1) \rightarrow (3,2) \rightarrow (2,2) \rightarrow (2,1) \rightarrow (3,1)$	0
(3,3)	$(3,3) \rightarrow (2,3) \rightarrow (2,2) \rightarrow (3,2) \rightarrow (3,3)$	$+200$

TABLE 7–11

Third Iteration for Trucking Example

Origin	Destination 1	Destination 2	Destination 3	Supply
	Destination			
1	50 / 60	100 / 50	100	110
2	200 / 80	300	200 / 80	160
3	100	200 / 150	300	150
Demand	140	200	80	420 / 420

$z = \$70{,}000$

Cell	Closed Path	I_{ij}
(1,3)	$(1,3) \to (1,1) \to (2,1) \to (2,3) \to (1,3)$	+50
(2,2)	$(2,2) \to (1,2) \to (1,1) \to (2,1) \to (2,2)$	+50
(3,1)	$(3,1) \to (3,2) \to (1,2) \to (1,1) \to (3,1)$	−50*
(3,3)	$(3,3) \to (2,3) \to (2,1) \to (1,1) \to (1,2) \to (3,2) \to (3,3)$	+150

TABLE 7–12

Fourth (and Final) Iteration for Trucking Example

Origin	Destination 1	Destination 2	Destination 3	Supply
	Destination			
1	50	100 / 110	100	110
2	200 / 80	300	200 / 80	160
3	100 / 60	200 / 90	300	150
Demand	140	200	80	420 / 420

$z = \$67{,}000$ (optimum)

Cell	Closed Path	I_{ij}
(1,1)	$(1,1) \to (3,1) \to (3,2) \to (1,2) \to (1,1)$	+50
(1,3)	$(1,3) \to (1,2) \to (3,2) \to (3,1) \to (2,1) \to (2,3) \to (1,3)$	+100
(2,2)	$(2,2) \to (2,1) \to (3,1) \to (3,2) \to (2,2)$	0
(3,3)	$(3,3) \to (2,3) \to (2,1) \to (3,1) \to (3,3)$	+200

the solution presented in Table 7–12 is optimal. It indicates that the redistribution of trucks can be achieved at a minimum total cost if 110 trucks are delivered from the city represented by Origin 1 to the city represented by Destination 2, 80 each from Origin 2 to Destinations 1 and 3, 60 from Origin 3 to Destination 1, and 90 from Origin 3 to Destination 2. The total (optimal) cost for the redistribution is $67,000.

Does the improvement index for cell (2, 2) of the final tableau stimulate any brainwaves? Improvement indices equal to zero in an optimal solution indicate the same thing as they did in the simplex method—**alternative optimal solutions.**

Follow-up Exercises

13. Solve the trucking example for the initial solution given by the Least Cost Method (Example 7.6). Comments?

14. Solve the trucking example for the initial solution given by VAM (Example 7.7). Comments?

15. Find the alternative optimal solution for Yew Haw. Check this solution against the solution found by VAM (Example 7.7). Conclusions? What are the implications of this solution for management? How many all-integer alternative optimal solutions are there?

16. Select one of your initial solutions in Exercise 12 and solve the problem by the stepping stone method.

Stepping Stone Method v. Simplex Method

By now the similarities between the stepping stone method and the simplex method must be apparent. There is indeed a one-for-one correspondence between the steps of these solution procedures. In addition, you should recognize the relative efficiencies offered by the transportation method. In the simplex method successive solutions are generated by computationally burdensome row (matrix) operations which include addition, subtraction, multiplication, and division. Additionally, the simplex procedure further taxes us (and computers) by augmenting the variable set with slack, surplus, and artificial variables. By contrast, the transportation method strictly utilizes the more efficient operations of addition and subtraction (except for the trivial multiplication in evaluating z) and works exclusively with the original set of decision variables (except, perhaps, for the addition of a dummy variable).[7]

Furthermore, given integer s_i and d_j, the resulting x_{ij} *must necessarily be integers* since only additions and subtractions are required. This feature, coupled with the speed of the transportation method, allows the solution

---

[7] We will consider the computational implications of dummy variables later in the chapter.

of some large-scale integer programming (Chapter 8) and dynamic programming (Chapter 9) problems in the real world which otherwise would be computationally infeasible.

OMIT

7.4 ALTERNATIVE TRANSPORTATION METHOD

In this section we will illustrate how the simplex-based stepping stone method can be made more efficient by utilizing concepts from the dual of the transportation problem.

The Dual Transportation Model[8]

The dual problem of the primal transportation model possesses properties which can improve the efficiency of solving these types of problems. It can be shown easily that the dual problem for the transportation model given by Equation (7.1) is

maximize

$$z_d = \sum_{i=1}^{m} s_i u_i + \sum_{j=1}^{n} d_j v_j \qquad (7.4)$$

subject to

$$u_i + v_j \le c_{ij} \text{ for all } i, j \qquad (7.5)$$

$$u_i, v_j \text{ unrestricted.}$$

In Example 6.5 on page 217 we demonstrated that for each equality constraint in a primal problem there exists a corresponding dual variable which is unrestricted. Consequently, the m supply constraints and n demand constraints in the transportation model lead to the unrestricted variables u_i and v_j, respectively, in the dual problem. (Note that we have defined the two classes of dual variables to distinguish between the supply constraints and the demand constraints of the primal problem.)

If an allocation is made between Origin i and Destination j (that is, $x_{ij} > 0$), then the marginal or Row (0) contribution for the basic variable x_{ij} must be zero. This implies, according to Property 3 of Section 6.7, that there must be no slack in the corresponding dual constraint, or

$$u_i + v_j = c_{ij}. \qquad (7.6)$$

Stated very simply, when any allocation is made between Origin i and Destination $j(x_{ij} > 0)$, the sum of the dual variables associated with the constraints for the particular origin and destination (u_i and v_j) will equal the objective function contribution c_{ij}; if an allocation is not made ($x_{ij} = 0$), then the sum of the dual variables is less than c_{ij}.

---

[8] You might find it useful to review Section 6.7 before proceeding. Did you solve Exercise 26 in Chapter 6 (page 218)?

Example 7.9

Given the solution in Table 7–13, we would like to determine the cor-

TABLE 7–13

Sample Solution

Origin	Destination 1	Destination 2	Destination 3	Supply
1	5 60	10 30	15	90
2	1	20 70	30 80	150
Demand	60	100	80	240 240

responding values of the dual variables. The following equations reflect the property given by Equation (7.6) for the four basic variables:

Basic Variable	Corresponding Dual Constraint
x_{11}	$u_1 + v_1 = 5$
x_{12}	$u_1 + v_2 = 10$
x_{22}	$u_2 + v_2 = 20$
x_{23}	$u_2 + v_3 = 30.$

Note that this system involves four equations and five unknown variables. The reason for fewer equations than dual variables is the one redundant constraint which is characteristic of transportation problems.

To solve for values of the dual variables, we arbitrarily assign a value of zero to one of them. Indirectly this declares one of the primal constraints as redundant and allows us to solve for the dual variables associated with the remaining $m + n - 1$ constraints. Letting $u_1 = 0$, verify that the dual variables have the following values: $v_1 = 5$; $v_2 = 10$; $u_2 = 10$; and $v_3 = 20$.

Primal-dual properties provide the foundation for a much more efficient method of computing improvement indices. The method, referred to as the Modified Distribution (MODI) method, eliminates the need to trace closed paths for *each* nonbasic variable as in the stepping stone method.

Follow-up Exercises

17. Write the dual of the Yew Haw problem and verify that it has the form of Equations (7.4) and (7.5).

Derive Equations (7.4) and (7.5) starting with the primal problem given by Equation (7.1). Is your result consistent with Exercise 26 in Chapter 6 (page 218)?

MODI Algorithm

The MODI method is nothing more than the stepping stone algorithm with a "souped-up" technique for computing improvement indices. The basis for the MODI method is the dual formulation of the transportation model.

This method provides a tabular approach to determining the values of the dual variables associated with any solution to a transportation problem. Once the values of the dual variables have been identified, the improvement index for any nonbasic variable can be computed using the equation

$$I_{ij} = c_{ij} - u_i - v_j. \tag{7.7}$$

The justification for Equation (7.7) is based on primal-dual Property 3 in Section 6.7; that is, the slack associated with a specific (i,j) dual constraint (as given by I_{ij}) equals the negative of the Row (0) coefficient in the simplex tableau for the corresponding primal variable (x_{ij}). Thus, I_{ij} represents the change in the value of the objective function (z) which would result by introducing one unit of the nonbasic variable x_{ij}.

Example 7.10

To illustrate, we modify Table 7–13 by including a column for u_i values and a row for v_j values as in Table 7–14. Rather than writing and solving the system of equations as was done in Example 7.9 we assign an arbitrary value to any u_i or v_j and place it in the appropriate row or column. As we did in Example 7.9, let $u_1 = 0$ and place this value in the first row of the u_i column. Now for each *basic* cell, (i,j), $u_i + v_j$ must equal c_{ij}, according to Equation (7.6). Using the arbitrary value for u_1, we can proceed sequentially through each *basic* cell by identifying at each step the value for another dual variable (u_i or v_j). For instance, from Equation (7.6),

$$c_{12} = u_1 + v_2$$

or

$$v_2 = 10 - 0.$$

This gives an entry of ten in the second column of the v_j row. Can you verify the remaining assignments in Table 7–14?

TABLE 7–14

MODI Transportation Table

Origin	Destination 1	2	3	Supply	u_i
1	5 60	10 30	15	90	0
2	1 	20 70	30 80	150	10
Demand	60	100	80	240 / 240	
v_j	5	10	20		

Having found the values for all u_i and v_j, we use Equation (7.7) to determine the improvement index for each nonbasic cell.

Cell	I_{ij}
(1,3).................	$15 - 0 - 20 = -5$
(2,1).................	$1 - 10 - 5 = -14*$

For this solution, improvement (assuming a minimization objective) is possible and x_{21} would enter the solution.

Once a cell is designated for entrance, its closed path must be identified to determine the necessary exchanges with the current basic variables and the amount to enter of the incoming variable.

Follow-up Exercises

19. Using the MODI method, recompute the improvement indices associated with the initial solution in Yew Haw (given under Table 7–9).

20. Using the MODI method (and any initial solution you wish), solve the problem below:

minimize

$$z = 20x_{11} + 15x_{12} + 5x_{21} + 10x_{22} + 20x_{31} + 5x_{32}$$

subject to

$$
\begin{aligned}
x_{11} + x_{12} &= 75 \\
x_{21} + x_{22} &= 125 \\
x_{31} + x_{32} &= 100 \\
x_{11} + x_{21} + x_{31} &= 200 \\
x_{12} + x_{22} + x_{32} &= 100 \\
x_{ij} &\geq 0.
\end{aligned}
$$

7.5 SPECIAL CONSIDERATIONS IN SOLVING TRANSPORTATION PROBLEMS

In this section we consider some special cases in solving transportation problems: unequal total supply and total demand, degeneracy, maximization of the objective function, and certain restrictions and extensions.

Unbalanced Conditions

Imbalance between total supply and total demand is the rule rather than the exception. Since the transportation method requires equality between total supply and total demand, a procedure which is equivalent to adding slack variables in the simplex method can be used to ensure balance for problems characterized by unbalanced conditions.

If total supply exceeds total demand, then a **dummy destination** can be added to the transportation table with an artificial demand exactly equal to the surplus supply. Tables 7–3 and 7–4 represent this case. Although dummy costs typically are assigned values of zero, care must be exercised not to automatically apply this policy. As discussed in Example 7.4, the context of a problem might warrant the assignment of other dummy costs.

If total supply is less than total demand, then a **dummy origin** is introduced which has a capacity exactly equal to the excess demand. As in the previous case, objective function contributions of zero are often assigned to all allocations from the dummy origin. In so doing, however, the implication is that there is no preference (and associated penalty) for which destination will have unfulfilled demand.

Follow-up Exercises

21. Solve the caterer problem given by Table 7–3.
22. Solve the caterer problem for the table you constructed (or will construct) in Exercise 4.
23. Solve the production scheduling-inventory control problem (Table 7–4) using dummy costs of zero. If alternative optima exist, explain their economic implications.
24. Solve the same problem as Exercise 23 using regular time costs for regular production in the appropriate dummy cells. Compare this solution to the solution in Exercise 23. If alternative optima exist, explain their economic implications.
25. Solve the problem in Exercise 9 using 60% of regular time costs in the appropriate dummy cells.

Degeneracy

With the simplex method, the unlikely possibility of cycling was the only concern of degeneracy. In the transportation model, degeneracy is of much greater importance because a degenerate solution produces an inability to compute improvement indices for all nonbasic variables (cells).

Degeneracy occurs when the basis contains less than $(m + n - 1)$ basic variables. This condition can arise either in developing the initial solution or at some intermediate solution. The first situation might arise when using the Northwest Corner Method. If an allocation results in the simultaneous exhaustion of the capacity for an origin and the fulfillment of the remaining demand at a destination, you will end up with fewer than $m + n - 1$ basic variables. Table 7–15 portrays a situation where the initial assignment exhausts the capacity of Origin 1 and satisfies the demand at Destination 1. The resulting solution has only 3 basic variables.

TABLE 7–15

Degeneracy in Initial Solution

Origin	Destination 1		Destination 2		Destination 3		Supply
1	75	5	ϵ	10		8	75
2		4	60	15	65	12	125
Demand	75		60		65	200	200

This can be resolved by using another approach (Least Cost Method or VAM) for finding an initial basis which contains $(m + n - 1)$ variables or by adding an artificial allocation, ϵ, to one of the unoccupied cells.[9] Epsilon (ϵ) is assumed to be an infinitesimally small quantity which would never actually be allocated. Its presence, though, allows for $(m + n - 1)$ basic variables and the ability to continue with the solution process. Epsilon should be considered as an occupied cell and modified in the same manner as other occupied cells. In some instances ϵ may drop out in later solutions; in others it may be a part of the final solution.

Degeneracy occurs in an intermediate solution when the values of more than one basic variable go to zero with the entrance of a new variable. This occurs, as in the simplex method, whenever there is a tie for the *leaving* variable (Step 3 of the stepping stone algorithm). For example,

---

[9] The placement of ϵ cannot be in just *any* unoccupied cell; it has to be placed in either the column or the row associated with the cell which simultaneously fulfilled the supply and demand constraint.

assume that in the partial table below the unoccupied cell has been selected for entrance. Introducing 80 units will result in two of the three

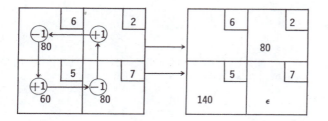

basic variables going to zero. If degeneracy occurs at any intermediate
solution, then introduce ϵ to one of the two cells which dropped out of the
basis and continue as before.[10]

Follow-up Exercises

26. Solve the transportation problem given below starting with the Northwest Corner Method.

Origin	Destination 1	Destination 2	Supply
1	5	4	25
2	2	7	45
3	3	6	30
Demand	75	25	100 / 100

27. Solve the committee assignment problem (Example 7.3) for three committees and ten faculty members and the following data (a computer
package would help):

---

[10] If more than two cells drop out of the basis (say, k), then occupy $k - 1$ cells
with epsilons.

Individual	Dispreferences for Committee			Committees to Be Served
	1	2	3	
1................	0.5	0.7	0.1	1
2................	0.8	0.2	0.4	1
3................	0.0	0.8	0.9	1
4................	0.6	0.5	0.5	1
5................	0.9	0.0	0.5	1
6................	0.2	0.1	0.7	1
7................	0.1	0.6	0.0	1
8................	0.5	0.3	0.8	1
9................	0.0	0.7	1.0	1
10................	1.0	0.5	0.0	1
Committee membership......	3	3	4	10

28. Solve the committee assignment problem (Example 7.3) by modifying the data in Exercise 27 such that the third committee requires a membership of three.

29. Solve the committee assignment problem (Example 7.3) by modifying the data in Exercise 27 such that only the first eight faculty members are available to satisfy the committee requirements of ten.

Maximization Problems

As with the simplex method, the only difference between solving minimization and maximization problems is in the interpretation of the improvement indices. Improvement in a maximization problem is indicated by the existence of any positive indices in the stepping stone or MODI algorithms. For initial solutions, the Least Cost Method becomes the Greatest Contribution Method and VAM is based upon the highest and next highest values, again using highest resultant Vogel numbers. Otherwise the procedures are exactly the same.

Follow-up Exercises

30. Suppose the dollar figures in Table 7–1 represent profit contributions. Solve this problem so as to maximize the total profit contribution.

31. Find the optimal allocation of trucks for Yew Haw if the contributions in Table 7–2 represent profits.

Restrictions and Extensions

For many problems, restrictions are imposed on routes $(x_{ij}$'s$)$. These can take the form of exclusions or constraints of the $(\leq, =, \geq)$ type. Routes can be excluded for reasons of managerial discretion or infeasibility of assignment. For instance, in Tables 7–3 and 7–4, excluded routes were simply crossed out. (Why?) In a computer package, excluded cells can be treated by costing them in a manner which makes them undesirable for allocations, that is, by making the unit contribution $+M$ for minimization problems and $-M$ for maximization problems (as in the simplex method), where M is a very large number.

Constraints can specify constant values for certain variables or impose upper or lower bounds (or both) on x_{ij}. If it was specified that $x_{ij} = b$, then the problem can be solved by reducing both s_i and d_j by b, crossing out cell (i, j), and proceeding as before. If it was specified that $x_{ij} \geq b$, then the problem can be solved by reducing both s_i and d_j by b, proceeding as before, and adding b to whatever solution value was obtained for x_{ij}. The case $x_{ij} \leq b$ requires more complex considerations which we will not treat.[11]

Extensions to the transportation method include (1) the treatment of nonhomogeneous goods, (2) the incurrence of setup costs when using a given route, (3) variation of objective function coefficients as a given function of the size of x_{ij}; and (4) structural coefficients in the supply constraints. Case (1) can be treated by various ad hoc procedures, including the use of a weighted average for c_{ij}; cases (2) and (3) can be solved using mathematical programming methods such as dynamic programming (Chapter 9) and separable programming (Chapter 10), and case (4) can be solved using the generalized transportation method.[12]

Follow-up Exercises

32. Solve the Yew Haw problem (Table 7–2) if $x_{22} = 20$.

33. Solve the Yew Haw problem (Table 7–2) if $x_{31} \geq 70$.

**34. Can you solve the production scheduling-inventory control problem (Example 7.4) using dummy costs of zero if the maximum inventory allowed is 35 units per period? (Show that the Northwest Corner Method is infeasible because of an inventory level of 40 units in Period 2.)

---

[11] If you dare see G. B. Dantzig, *Linear Programming and Extensions* (Princeton, N.J.: Princeton University Press, 1963) or M. Simonnard, *Linear Programming*, trans. W. S. Jewell (Englewood Cliffs, N.J.: Prentice-Hall, Inc., 1966).

[12] A version of case (2) will be illustrated as Example 8.9. For the generalized transportation method see Hamdy A. Taha, *Operations Research: An Introduction* (New York: Macmillan Publishing Co., 1971), or G. Hadley, *Linear Programming* (Reading, Mass.: Addison-Wesley Publishing Co., 1962).

7.6 SENSITIVITY ANALYSIS FOR TRANSPORTATION PROBLEMS

The motivation for sensitivity analysis was well-established in Chapter 6. In this section, we illustrate sensitivity analysis (in the framework of the transportation method) on objective function coefficients for nonbasic and basic variables, supplies, and demands.

Objective Function Coefficients (Nonbasic Variables)

As you know, the optimal solution (for a minimization problem) has been found when $I_{ij} \geq 0$ for all nonbasic variables (cells). In this case, we are interested in determining the amount by which the coefficient c_{ij} for a nonbasic variable can change for the current solution to remain optimal. We accomplish this easily by utilizing Equation (7.7) on the *final* tableau, as illustrated next.

Example 7.11

The final computational tableau (MODI method) for the Yew Haw problem is given by Table 7–16. Can you verify the u_i and v_j using (7.6)? For non-

TABLE 7–16

Final MODI Tableau for Yew Haw

Origin	Destination 1	2	3	Supply	u_i
1	50	100 / 110	100	110	0
2	200 / 80	300	200 / 80	160	200
3	100 / 60	200 / 90	300	150	100
Demand	140	200	80	420 / 420	
v_j	0	100	0		

basic cell (1, 1), as in the simplex method, we define $c_{11} = 50 + \Delta$. The current solution remains optimal as long as $I_{11} > 0$, or by utilizing Equation (7.7) as long as

$$c_{11} - u_1 - v_1 > 0$$

or

$$50 + \Delta - 0 - 0 > 0,$$

or

$$\Delta > -50.$$

In other words, the current solution remains optimal if $c_{11} > 0$; otherwise, a new optimal basis would result.

For cell (2,2), we define $c_{22} = 300 + \Delta$ and get:

$$I_{22} > 0$$

or

$$300 + \Delta - 200 - 100 > 0$$

or

$$\Delta > 0.$$

Thus, if $c_{22} > 300$, the current solution remains optimal. Since $c_{22} = 300$ for this problem, it follows that an alternative optimal solution exists.

Follow-up Exercises

35. Verify that $c_{13} > 0$ and $c_{33} > 100$ for the current solution in this example to remain optimal. What happens if $c_{33} = 100$?

36. Perform a sensitivity analysis on the objective function coefficients of nonbasic variables for Example 4.6 (Table 7–1).

Objective Function Coefficients (Basic Variables)

Again utilizing Equation (7.7), we can easily conduct sensitivity analysis on the objective function coefficients for basic variables.

Example 7.12

Given the final tableau (Table 7–16) for Yew Haw, let us examine the range over which the $200 delivery cost for basic route (2, 1) can vary and still allow the existing basis to remain optimal. Defining $c_{21} = 200 + \Delta$, we substitute the new coefficient into the final tableau, as illustrated in Table 7–17. This new value for c_{21} causes some adjustments in certain u_i and v_j values. For example, since $I_{ij} = c_{ij} - u_i - v_j = 0$ for all basic variables, either u_2 or v_1 must be *increased* by Δ in order for I_{21} to remain equal to zero. Increasing v_1 to $0 + \Delta$, or Δ, requires a readjustment of other u_i and v_j values.[13] Applying Equation (7.7) to the remaining basic variables results in the changes which appear in Table 7–17. To determine the impact of the change in c_{21} upon the nonbasic variables, their improvement indices are

---

[13] Just as well, we could have selected to increase u_2 to $200 + \Delta$. It doesn't matter. Try it.

TABLE 7-17

Modified Final MODI Tableau for Yew Haw

Origin	Destination 1		Destination 2		Destination 3		Supply	u_i
1		50		100		100	110	$0 - (\Delta)$
			110					
2	80	$200 + \Delta$		300	80	200	160	200
3	60	100	90	200		300	150	$100 - (\Delta)$
Demand	140		200		80		420 / 420	
v_j	$0 + (\Delta)$		$100 + (\Delta)$		0			

recomputed using the new (u_i, v_j) values. The new indices are computed below. Verify that the current basis will remain optimal as long as $-100 < \Delta < 0$, or $100 < c_{21} < 200$.

Cell	I_{ij}
(1, 1).........	$50 - (-\Delta) - (\Delta) = 50$
(1, 3).........	$100 - (-\Delta) - (0) = 100 + \Delta$
(2, 2)....	$300 - (200) - (100 + \Delta) = -\Delta$
(3, 3)......	$300 - (100 - \Delta) - 0 = 200 + \Delta$

Follow-up Exercises

37. Complete the sensitivity analysis on the objective function coefficients for the other basic variables in Yew Haw.

38. Perform a sensitivity analysis on the objective function coefficients of basic variables in Example 4.6 (Table 7–1).

Supplies and Demands (RHS Constants)

As demonstrated in Chapter 6, the dual variable associated with the *i*th constraint is a **shadow price**; that is, u_i is the relative implicit contribution of one additional unit from Origin *i* and v_j is the relative implicit contribution of one additional unit to Destination *j*. Note that this economic interpretation is entirely consistent with the dual objective function given by Equation (7.4). For example, an increase of one unit in the supply of

Origin 2 from s_2 to $(s_2 + 1)$ and a simultaneous decrease of the unit in the supply of Origin 1 from s_1 to $(s_1 - 1)$ imply a change in the optimal value of the objective function (Δz) given by $(u_2 - u_1)$.

Based on the above, the changes in the optimal value of the objective function for various cases are given by the relationships below.

Case 1 Simultaneous *increase* of one unit in the supply of Origin p and *decrease* of one unit in the supply of Origin q. *Change in* z:

$$\Delta z = u_p - u_q \tag{7.8}$$

Change in basic x_{ij}: Trace "dead-end" path for unit $(\pm)$ adjustments in basic x_{ij} to reflect new s_p and s_q.

Case 2 Simultaneous *increase* of one unit in the demand by Destination p and *decrease* of one unit in the demand by Destination q. *Change in* z:

$$\Delta z = v_p - v_q \tag{7.9}$$

Change in basic x_{ij}: Trace "dead-end" path for unit $(\pm)$ adjustments in basic x_{ij} to reflect new d_p and d_q.

Case 3 Simultaneous *increases* of one unit in the supply of Origin p and the demand by Destination q. *Change in* z:

$$\Delta z = u_p + v_q \tag{7.10}$$

Change in basic x_{ij}: Trace "closed" path for unit $(\pm)$ adjustments in basic x_{ij} as if one unit were *removed* from cell (p, q).

Case 4 Simultaneous *decreases* of one unit in the supply of Origin p and the demand by Destination q. *Change in* z:

$$\Delta z = -u_p - v_q \tag{7.11}$$

Change in basic x_{ij}: Trace "closed" path for unit $(\pm)$ adjustments in basic x_{ij} as if one unit were *added* to cell (p, q).

Case 5 *Increase* of one unit in the supply of Origin p. *Change in* z:

$$\Delta z = u_p - \max_i u_i \tag{7.12}$$

Change in basic x_{ij}: Trace "dead-end" path for unit $(\pm)$ adjustments in basic x_{ij} by creating *oversupply* at the Origin associated with max u_i.

Case 6 *Increase* of one unit in the demand by Destination p. *Change in* z:

$$\Delta z = v_p - \max_j v_j \tag{7.13}$$

Change in basic x_{ij}: Trace "dead-end" path for unit $(\pm)$ adjustments in basic x_{ij} after allocating *unsatisfied demand* to the destination associated with max v_j.

Case 7 *Decrease* of one unit in the supply of Origin *p*. *Change in* z:

$$\Delta z = -u_p - \max_j v_j \tag{7.14}$$

Change in basic x_{ij}: Trace "dead-end" path for unit ($\pm$) adjustments after allocating *unsatisfied demand* to the destination associated with max v_j.

Case 8 *Decrease* of one unit in the demand by Destination *p*. *Change in* z:

$$\Delta z = -v_p - \max_i u_i \tag{7.15}$$

Change in basic x_{ij}: Trace "dead-end" path for unit ($\pm$) adjustments in basic x_{ij} after allocating *oversupply* to the origin associated with max u_i.

For each case above, values for the dual variables must be obtained from a *nondegenerate optimal* tableau. We now illustrate some of these by example.

Example 7.13

Case 1: In Table 7–16, suppose $s_1 = 111$ and $s_2 = 159$. From Equation (7.8), $\Delta z = 0 - 200 = -200$. The "dead-end" path begins with a $+1$ adjustment in basic cell (1, 2) to reflect the new supply (increase of 1 in s_1) and continues with $\pm$ unit adjustments in basic variables such that all s_i and d_j are satisfied (*if feasible*). We term this type of path "dead-end" because it never returns to the originating cell. In this case, it is given by (1, 2) $\rightarrow$ (3, 2) $\rightarrow$ (3, 1) $\rightarrow$ (2, 1) which results in the following *adjusted* basic variables: $x_{12} = 111$, $x_{32} = 89$, $x_{31} = 61$, and $x_{21} = 79$.[14] As you can verify easily, the new optimal value for z has decreased by 200.

Case 4: Supply $s_2 = 159$ and $d_2 = 199$. Then, according to Equation (7.11), $\Delta z = -200 - 100 = -300$. The "closed" path begins and ends with the addition of one fictitious unit of flow to cell (2, 2): (2, 2) $\rightarrow$ (3, 2) $\rightarrow$ (3, 1) $\rightarrow$ (2, 1) $\rightarrow$ (2, 2). The adjusted basic variables are $x_{32} = 89$, $x_{31} = 61$, and $x_{21} = 79$. Note that $x_{12} = 110$ and $x_{23} = 80$ remain unchanged. The new solution is optimal and satisfies the new set of supplies and demands.

Case 5: Suppose $s_3 = 151$. From Equation (7.12), $\Delta z = 100 - 200 = -100$ where $u_2 = \max u_i$. Oversupply, therefore, will be created at Origin 2; that is, only 159 trucks will be sent from Origin 2. Do you see the logic? If a truck is not to be sent (which is to say that a truck is to be sent to a dummy destination with an assumed cost of zero), then utilize the extra unit at Origin 3 with a relative cost of \$100 ($u_3 = 100$) and reduce by one truck the shipment from the origin which gives us the maximum possible relative cost reduction (that is, \$200 for Origin 2 since $u_2 = 200$); hence, the optimal z will decrease

---

[14] This path could also begin with a -1 adjustment in basic cell (2, 1) in order to satisfy $s_2 = 159$. The same path, in reverse, would result. Try it. Note that a -1 adjustment in basic cell (2, 3) would not work. Why? Because all s_i and d_j would not be satisfied by a path originating in this cell. Try it.

by \$100. The adjusted basic variables are $x_{31} = 61$ and $x_{21} = 79$; that is, the dead-end path runs between cells (3, 1) and (2, 1).

Follow-up Exercises

39. Using Table 7–16, evaluate Cases 2, 3, 6, 7, and 8 for $p = 1$ and $q = 2$.
40. Evaluate all eight cases for the optimal solution to Example 4.6 (Table 7–1) given that $p = 2$ and $q = 1$.

7.7 ASSIGNMENT MODEL

A special case of the transportation model is the **assignment model.** Just as the special structure of the transportation model allowed for more efficient solution procedures than the simplex method, the characteristics of the assignment model allow its solution by more efficient procedures than the transportation method.

Assumptions and General Form

An assignment problem is one where the objective is to optimally allocate n origins or activities to n destinations or needs. Unlike the transportation model, a resource must be allocated *totally* or uniquely to a given task. The typical example includes the assignment of n persons or machines to n different jobs in such a way as to minimize (or maximize) some objective function. Other examples include the assignment of sales personnel to sales districts in order to maximize sales effectiveness, the assignment of airline crews to flights in order to minimize costs, the assignment of rescue units to rescue tasks in order to minimize total combined time to complete all rescue tasks, the assignment of boats or planes to charter trips in order to maximize total profit, the assignment of social workers to welfare cases in order to maximize the number of cases closed within a specified period, and the assignment of snowplow crews to areas of a city so as to optimize transportation mobility.

The mathematical statement of the assignment model is

minimize (maximize)

$$z = \sum_{i=1}^{n} \sum_{j=1}^{n} c_{ij} x_{ij} \qquad (7.16)$$

subject to

$$\sum_{j=1}^{n} x_{ij} = 1, \qquad i = 1, \ldots, n, \qquad (7.17)$$

$$\sum_{i=1}^{n} x_{ij} = 1, \qquad j = 1, \ldots, n, \qquad (7.18)$$

$$x_{ij} = 0 \text{ or } 1. \qquad (7.19)$$

Notice from Equation (7.19) that the decision variables are assigned values of either zero or one. Zero is assigned to x_{ij} if resource i is *not* allocated to task j; x_{ij} is assigned a value of one if resource i is assigned to task j. Constraint set (7.17) assures that each resource can be assigned to one task only. Constraint set (7.18) ensures that each task is assigned one and only one of the resources. Other characteristics worth noting are that the number of resources is equal to the number of tasks and the right-hand–side constants are all equal to one. In the context of the transportation model given by Equation (7.1), it follows that $m = n$ and $s_i = d_j = 1$ for the assignment model.

Solution Methods

Five general categories of solution methods, from least to most efficient, can be identified: (1) total enumeration, (2) 0–1 programming, (3) simplex method, (4) transportation method, and (5) special-purpose algorithms.

Total enumeration of the $n!$ solutions can be dismissed at the outset as too costly for problems of meaningful size; for example for $n = 20$ over 2.4×10^{18} solutions must be examined. Algorithms associated with 0–1 programming are impractical (costly) for problems having more than, say, 100 variables and 50 constraints.[15] An assignment problem with only $n = 25$ (that is, 625 variables and 50 constraints) already is beyond the capabilities of these procedures.

The simplex method is a reasonable computational alternative, although severe degeneracy is guaranteed since half (n) of the variables in the basis will be zero. This implies redundancy in half of the constraints. Still, the accessibility of simplex-based computer packages which are capable of solving large problems and the certainty of an integer (0–1) solution are persuasive factors for using the simplex method if more efficient computerized procedures are not available.

Since the assignment model is a special case of the transportation model, the transportation method can be used as a method of solution. As you know, this alternative is more efficient than the simplex method, although severe degeneracy makes for an "unclean" solution.

Finally, the ultimate is to use a special-purpose algorithm which has been designed to exploit the special structure of the assignment model. Among the most popular of the special-purpose algorithms is the **Hungarian method,** an iterative technique which utilizes opportunity costs. We will not, however, devote space to a discussion of this technique. Our concern is simply to create awareness of the structural characteristics and areas of application of this model.

---

[15] Zero-one programming includes a set of algorithms for solving linear programming problems having decision variables restricted to values of zero or one. We present this topic in Chapter 8.

Example 7.14   Court Scheduling

In recent years, OR/MS specialists have become increasingly involved in applications relating to the criminal justice system.[16] One factor which interferes with the administration of justice is court congestion. To illustrate a simplified version of the problem, suppose that a district court is attempting to assign four judges to four court dockets. The objective is to minimize the total time required to complete all of the cases on the four dockets. Based upon the composition of the cases scheduled on each docket and given district court records to indicate the ability of judges to process different types of cases, it is possible to estimate the number of days that it would take each judge to clear each docket. These data are displayed in Table 7–18.

TABLE 7–18

Estimated Days to Clear Docket

	Docket			
Judge	1	2	3	4
1..............	14	13	17	14
2..............	16	15	16	15
3..............	18	14	20	17
4..............	20	13	15	18

Follow-up Exercises

41. Formulate the LP model for this problem.
42. Solve the LP model using a computerized package.
43. Construct the table for solving this problem by the transportation method.
44. By the transportation method, determine the assignment which yields the minimum total time to clear the four dockets.
45. Mathematically, why is the committee "assignment" problem (Example 7.3) *not* an assignment model?

---

[16] It's a good thing!

SELECTED REFERENCES

Anderson, David R.; Sweeney, Dennis J.; and Williams, Thomas A. *Linear Programming for Decision Making, An Applications Approach*. St. Paul: West Publishing Co., 1974.

Dantzig, G. B. *Linear Programming and Extensions*. Princeton, N.J.: Princeton University Press, 1963.

Gass, S. I. *Linear Programming: Methods and Applications*. 4th ed. New York: McGraw-Hill, Inc., 1975.

Hadley, G. *Linear Programming*. Reading, Mass.: Addison-Wesley Publishing Co., 1962.

Hillier, Frederick S., and Lieberman, Gerald J. *Introduction to Operations Research*. 2d ed. San Francisco: Holden Day, Inc., 1974.

Hughes, Ann J., and Grawiog, Dennis E. *Linear Programming: An Emphasis on Decision Making*. Reading, Mass.: Addison-Wesley Publishing Co., 1973.

Kim, Chaiho. *Quantitative Analysis for Managerial Decisions*. Reading, Mass.: Addison-Wesley Publishing Co., 1976.

Levin, Richard I., and Lamone, Rudolph P. *Linear Programming for Management Decisions*. Homewood, Ill.: Richard D. Irwin, Inc., 1969.

McMillan, Claude, Jr. *Mathematical Programming: An Introduction to the Design and Application of Optimal Decision Machines*. New York: John Wiley & Sons, Inc., 1970.

Montgomery, David B., and Urban, Glen L. *Management Science in Marketing*. Englewood Cliffs, N.J.: Prentice-Hall, Inc., 1969.

Shamblin, James E., and Stevens, G. T., Jr. *Operations Research: A Fundamental Approach*. New York: McGraw-Hill, Inc., 1974.

Simonnard, M. *Linear Programming*. Translated by W. S. Jewell. Englewood Cliffs, N.J.: Prentice-Hall, Inc., 1966.

Spivey, W. Allen, and Thrall, Robert M. *Linear Optimization*. New York: Holt, Rinehart and Winston, Inc., 1970.

Strum, Jay E. *Introduction to Linear Programming*. San Francisco: Holden Day, Inc., 1972.

Taha, Hamdy A. *Operations Research: An Introduction*. New York: Macmillan Publishing Co., 1971.

Trueman, Richard E. *An Introduction to Quantitative Methods for Decision Making*. New York: Holt, Rinehart and Winston, Inc., 1974.

Wagner, Harvey M. *Principles of Operations Research*. 2d ed. Englewood Cliffs, N.J.: Prentice-Hall, Inc., 1975.

ADDITIONAL EXERCISES

46. *Contract Award Problem*   The Department of the Army wishes to award supply contracts to companies who supply hair nets. The "Modern" Army is experiencing (hair) growing pains and it has reached a compromise in which recruits may retain their lengthy locks provided they wear hair nets while on duty. The Army has agreed to supply the nets. Three suppliers have submitted sealed bids which quote the price per case of nets (delivered) to four regional locations. The bids are summarized below. Also shown are estimates of the maximum number of cases each supplier can provide and the regional requirements. Note that suppliers 1 and 2 have not quoted bids for regions 4 and 3, respectively.

	Region				Max. Supply
Supplier	1	2	3	4	(Cases)
1.................	$25	$28	$20	—	1,000
2.................	20	30	—	$29	1,300
3.................	23	18	25	32	1,200
Required number of cases.................	800	1,000	600	800	

Suppliers may receive contracts to provide all or part of the needs of any region. Given the objective of minimizing the cost of providing the hair nets:

a. Formulate this as a linear programming problem.
b. Is this in the mathematical form of a transportation model?
c. Cite two different ways in which you might handle the two unquoted bids in the LP formulation.

47. For the previous problem:

a. Find an initial basic feasible solution using the Northwest Corner Method.
b. Continue from this initial solution to determine the contract awards which will result in minimum total cost.

48. Cap and Gown Enterprises (C&G) has contracted to provide caps and gowns for graduation ceremonies for four local colleges. College A will have ceremonies Friday night, graduating 700 students; College B will hold ceremonies Saturday morning, graduating 600 students; College C will hold ceremonies Saturday night, graduating 700 students; and College D will hold ceremonies Sunday afternoon graduating 500 students. C&G currently has 400 sets of caps and gowns. It wishes to minimize the cost of providing graduation dress for the four schools. C&G can have Friday night's caps and gowns cleaned and ready for Saturday night's ceremonies at a cost of $2.50 per set. Saturday morning's sets can be cleaned at the same price for Sunday morning. New cap and gown sets cost $50.

a. Formulate this problem as a transportation model by setting up a table identifying all origins and destinations and appropriate costs.
b. Solve this problem by the transportation method.

49. *Media Mix* A manufacturer of clothing is interested in developing an advertising campaign which will reach four different age-groups. Advertising campaigns can be conducted within TV, radio, and periodicals. The following table indicates the estimated cost per exposure in each age group according to the medium employed. In addition, maximum ex-

Media	Age Groups				Max. Exposure (millions)
	13–18	18–22	22–35	35 & over	
TV..........................	$0.10	$0.08	$0.09	$0.11	30
Radio......................	0.05	0.07	0.08	0.10	15
Periodicals.................	0.15	0.09	0.08	0.08	18
Minimum number of exposures (millions).........	18	8	12	10	

posure levels desired within each medium as well as minimum desired exposures within each age group are identified.

Formulate this problem as a transportation model and solve as follows:

a. Generate initial solutions by the three methods which were illustrated in the chapter. Which method gives the least cost?
b. Select the best initial solution from the preceding part and solve the problem by the transportation method of your choice.
c. Solve this problem if the policy is to provide at least 4 million exposures through TV in the 22–35 age group.

50. For the preceding problem:

    a. Formulate the LP model which will determine the number of exposures which should be sought for each age group in each medium so as to minimize total advertising costs.

    ***b.* Formulate the dual problem and interpret the dual variables.

51. *Processing Welfare Applications* A state welfare agency hires some social workers on a part-time basis in order to get through particularly busy periods. One activity for which these persons are hired is the review and evaluation of welfare applications. During the coming month the agency projects a need to hire part-timers. Workers are paid on a piecework basis according to the type of application reviewed and the experience of the social worker. Five social workers have been contacted to determine their interest in employment for the coming month. Each has provided an estimate of the maximum number of welfare applications they would be willing to evaluate this month (the agency makes certain that the number of applications is within the capability of the social worker).

    The table summarizes the cost per application per social worker, the maximum number of applications per social worker, and the number of applications which must be evaluated of each type.

Type of Application	Social Worker					Number of Applications
	1	2	3	4	5	
Aid to individuals..................	$10	$12	$11	$12	$10	125
Aid to families with dependent children.................	8	9	8	10	8	90
Benefits for the elderly..........................	7	9	6	8	8	60
Maximum number of applications per social worker......................	60	40	80	75	65	

Defining x_{ij} as the number of applications of type i assigned to social worker j:

    a. Formulate the objective function and constraint set if the objective is to minimize the total cost of processing the 275 applications.

    b. Set this problem up as a transportation model and solve by the transportation method.

    c. Solve this problem if the third social worker is to process at least 50 "Aid to Individuals" applications.

52. *Public Works* Boston has five locations around the city in which sand and salt stockpiles are maintained for winter icing and snow storms. For most major storms, all salt and sand is distributed from these five shelters to five different city zones. In fact, there is usually a need for additional sand and salt; however, it is currently impractical to gain access to additional stores which are maintained at a central depot in time to be of benefit (officials keep their fingers crossed that the city will not be hit by back-to-back storms).

    The Director of Public Works, a M.B.A. graduate with a public service inclination, wishes to determine the best way to allocate the salt and sand supplies during a storm. Her criterion is to minimize the time required to meet the needs of the five zones. In the absence of reliable time estimates (especially during storms) she has decided to use the flow-distance criterion computed by multiplying volume transported times distance. The table summarizes the distances (miles) between the sand and salt shelters and the center of each zone. Note that because of either department policy or geographical restrictions (natural barriers), shelters

	Zone					
Shelter	1	2	3	4	5	Truckloads Available
1...................	1.2	—	2.2	—	—	200
2...................	3.8	4.5	5.2	2.3	3.2	250
3...................	—	6.4	—	4.2	1.8	150
4...................	2.9	3.1	5.2	4.1	3.8	300
5...................	1.5	—	4.0	6.1	2.2	100
Truckloads demanded......	150	200	300	175	175	

1, 3, and 5 do not supply all five zones. If x_{ij} is defined as the number of truckloads allocated from shelter i to zone j:

a. Solve this problem by the transportation method.
b. Do you agree with the chosen criterion? What other surrogates might be chosen?

53. *Plant Distribution* A company is engaged in a plant distribution study. The plant has five main work centers at which end items are assembled. Each center uses, among others, a common part. The part is stored in bins at three locations within the plant. Although alternative locations are being considered for the bins, the production manager wishes to determine the best way in which to allocate parts from the existing bins to the five work centers. The criterion selected to evaluate the current layout is a measure of volume of parts multiplied times the distance over which the parts are moved.

The table summarizes the distances (in feet) between each bin and each work center, the number of parts available in each bin, and the number required at each work center.

	Work Center					
Bin	1	2	3	4	5	Parts Available
1......................	25	40	75	20	60	1,500
2......................	50	40	65	25	30	2,000
3......................	25	50	70	40	80	1,000
Parts required...............	1,000	1,500	800	900	300	

If the objective is to minimize the weighted measure of volume times distance then:

a. Formulate this problem as a transportation model and solve by the transportation method.
b. Solve this problem if exactly 200 parts must be delivered to work center 3 from bin 1.

54. *Sales Force Assignment* A company wishes to assign four "reps" to four sales districts. Management officials have estimated the total sales (in $1,000's) each rep would generate if assigned to the different districts for one year. These are summarized here.

	District			
Sales Representative	1	2	3	4
1......................	50	25	78	64
2......................	43	30	70	56
3......................	60	28	80	66
4......................	54	29	75	60

a. By the transportation method, determine the assignment which maximizes total sales.

b. How would your solution change if rep 3 cannot be assigned to either district 2 or district 4?

55. *Police Patrol Assignment* Sin City's police chief wishes to allocate five tactical patrol units to five precincts which have recently been experiencing large increases in crime incidence. The five teams are different with respect to number of officers, years of experience, and mode of operation. Crime analysts have estimated the number of "Index" (serious) offenses expected in each precinct during the coming month. Based upon the demographic and crime incidence characteristics of each precinct, analysts have also determined a *crime deterrence factor* which represents the portion of anticipated crimes expected to be deterred as a result of the tactical unit's efforts. The table summarizes these factors.

Crime Deterrence Factors

	Precinct				
Team	1	2	3	4	5
A.................	0.25	0.28	0.40	0.22	0.30
B.................	0.35	0.18	0.32	0.26	0.34
C.................	0.22	0.26	0.29	0.24	0.32
D.................	0.36	0.40	0.44	0.38	0.42
E.................	0.18	0.24	0.15	0.22	0.20

The estimated number of Index offenses for the next month are summarized for each precinct as follows: 400 for Precinct 1; 500 for Precinct 2; 450 for Precinct 3; 600 for Precinct 4; and 575 for Precinct 5.

The chief wishes to allocate the five teams in such a way as to minimize the *expected* number of Index offenses for the five precincts during the coming month.

a. Formulate the objective function and constraints for this model.

b. Find a computerized LP or transportation package and solve this problem.

**c.* In another text, look up the "Hungarian Method" for solving assignment problems. Upon reviewing the procedure, solve this problem.

56. *Solid Waste Disposal* A major U.S. city has three incinerator sites for processing solid waste. There are six garbage collection areas within the city. The city wants to determine the least cost method of disposing of their trash. Costs are broken into two components. Each incinerator is characterized by an operating cost, c_j, which is the cost of processing each ton of waste. There is also the cost, t_{ij}, which expresses the cost of transporting each ton of waste from collection area i to incinerator j. Each collection area generates w_i tons of waste per month and each incinerator has a processing capacity of p_j tons per month.

    a. Define decision variables and formulate a generalized LP model for this problem.

    b. The accompanying table summarizes the transportation costs per ton of waste. Also indicated are values for w_i and p_j. Incinerator sites 1, 2, and 3 have variable operating costs of $75, $60, and $80 per ton, respectively. Formulate the LP model for these data. (Note: We have purposely reversed rows and columns in the table; we don't want you to get lazy.)

Incinerator Site	Collection Area						Capacity per Month (Tons)
	1	2	3	4	5	6	
1.............	$60	$50	$70	$40	$45	$55	4,000
2.............	75	30	45	55	80	70	5,500
3.............	40	50	25	60	50	35	3,000
Tons generated per month............	500	750	1,500	1,000	1,800	1,200	

    c. Solve this problem by the transportation method.

    d. Perform sensitivity analyses for the costs associated with the first incinerator site.

***e.* Suppose that the six collection areas represent potential collection areas which are being considered for purchase by the city. At least four must be purchased. The monthly interest charges to finance the purchases for collection areas 1 through 6 would be, respectively, $50, $75, $60, $85, $100, $70. Appropriately modify the formulation in part (*b*). (Hint: Define a new set of decision variables, $y_i = 0$ if area *i* is not selected; 1 otherwise, $i = 1, \ldots, 6$.) Is this formulation still a transportation model? Explain.

57. An optimal solution to a transportation problem with a minimization objective is presented in the accompanying table.

Origin	Destination			Supply
	1	2	3	
1	(22) 16	26	(24) 18	46
2	(8) 14	(6) 22	18	14
3	(15) 12	24	16	15
Demand	45	6	24	75 / 75

    a. Verify that the optimal solution has been found.

    b. Conduct sensitivity analysis on the objective function coefficients for all nonbasic variables.

    c. Conduct sensitivity analysis for the objective function contributions for all basic variables.

***d.* Conduct sensitivity analysis for Cases 1 through 8 for $p = 3$ and $q = 2$.

8

Integer and Zero-One Programming

DURING our discussions of linear programming, some of you may have been concerned about the assumption of divisibility. The implication of this assumption was "that fractional levels for decision variables are permissible. . . ." The consequences of this assumption are that final solutions to LP problems may recommend the production of fractional units of products, the investment in a portion of a project, or the assignment of fractional units of workers to jobs.

The issue of noninteger solutions was briefly addressed in Section 4.4. For the most part, you were probably left with the impression that the issue was not too serious and that simply rounding the noninteger solution would provide a close approximation to the optimal integer solution. This approach may produce the desired results for some problems. In general, however, one of two consequences will occur when one forces an integer solution by rounding an optimal LP solution: The solution either will become infeasible (that is, the solution "falls" outside the solution space) or will be nonoptimal (that is, one or more other integer solutions give better results.[1]

Because of the nontrivial scale of many empirical problems which require integer solutions, a body of knowledge called **integer programming** has evolved. This chapter presents integer programming and the more specialized area of zero–one programming. The theory of integer programming will be kept to a minimum; instead, emphasis will be on specific

---

[1] In some cases it can be shown that rounding always gives infeasible results. See Fred Glover and David C. Sommer, "Pitfalls of Rounding in Discrete Management Decision Problems," *Decision Sciences,* vol. 6, no. 2 (April 1975), pp. 211–20.

issues in problem formulation, extensive examples where integer programming has been applied, solution approaches, computational experiences, and an overall assessment of the real-world potential for integer programming models.

8.1 THE NATURE OF INTEGER PROGRAMMING PROBLEMS

This section elaborates on some characteristics of integer programming, revisits the air cargo problem first presented in Chapter 5, and discusses the cost of requiring indivisibility.

Characteristics of Integer (Linear) Programming

Integer (linear) programming is a form of mathematical programming. It is really a special case of linear programming where all (or some) variables are restricted to nonnegative integer values. When all variables are restricted to being integer, the problem is said to be a **pure integer programming problem.** If only selected variables are restricted to being integer and the remaining variables are not, the problem is said to be a **mixed integer programming problem.** A special case of integer programming is the situation where integer variables are restricted to values of either zero or one. When all variables in a problem are 0–1 in nature, it is said to be a **zero–one (0–1) programming problem.**

If you think back to Chapter 7, you should recognize that the transportation and assignment models are both examples of integer programming models. As long as the s_i and d_j values in a transportation problem are integer, an all-integer optimal solution is guaranteed. The transportation problem is an example of a pure integer programming problem. Similarly, the typical assignment problem is an example of a 0–1 programming problem. If an integer programming problem has the special structural characteristics of these models, the specialized solution procedures presented in Chapter 7 are appropriate.

A variety of specialized solution methods have been proposed for solving integer programming problems. In general, these methods all attempt to capitalize upon the special structure of each type of problem. In our overview of these solution methods, attention will be focused more extensively upon techniques developed for pure integer programming problems.

Realizing that integer programming problems are special cases of linear programming problems, you should agree that the optimal noninteger solution to an integer programming problem will always be better than or equal to the optimal integer solution. In fact, if an integer programming problem is solved by the simplex method and an all-integer optimal basis results, then you have found the optimal integer solution. Both linear programming and integer programming problems start with the same area of feasible solutions. However, the integer requirement of the latter problem is more restrictive and is likely to cause a reduction in the feasible solution space. It will never result in an increased set of feasible solution points. *Thus, the optimal solution to an integer programming problem can never be better than its noninteger counterpart.*

Example 8.1   Air Cargo, Again

The reduction in the feasible solution space can be illustrated by referring back to the air cargo problem originally presented in Section 5.5 and modified in Section 6.2. The modified problem, as rewritten using an integer programming format, has the form

maximize

$$z = 20x_1 + 10x_2$$

subject to

$$5x_1 + 4x_2 \leq 24 \,(\text{Volume})$$
$$2x_1 + 5x_2 \leq 13 \,(\text{Weight})$$

$$x_1, x_2 = \text{nonnegative integers,}$$

where x_1 and x_2 represent, respectively, containers of beef and pork which are to be shipped in a cargo plane subject to volume and weight constraints. Note that the only difference between LP formulations and pure integer programming formulations is the replacement of the nonnegativity condition $(x_j \geq 0)$ by the condition of nonnegative integers.

The optimal LP solution recommended the shipment of 4.8 containers of beef (x_1) and no containers of pork (x_2). The maximum profit was $96 (100's). This solution assumes that 0.8 of a container can be shipped, which in reality is not possible. The problem is, in fact, an integer programming problem, and we are restricted to shipping whole containers of meat; we might, therefore, suggest that simple *rounding* of the noninteger solution will provide the optimal integer solution. However, by rounding x_1 up to 5, verify that the volume constraint is violated and the solution $(x_1 = 5, x_2 = 0)$ is infeasible. Rounding down to $x_1 = 4$, the solution $(x_1 = 4, x_2 = 0)$ is feasible and integer but, unfortunately, nonoptimal $(z = 80)$. As will be shown graphically, the optimal integer solution occurs at $x_1 = 4$ and $x_2 = 1$ with a resulting profit of $90 (100's). The message gained from this example is that, although simple rounding of optimal noninteger solutions is appealing, optimal or feasible results are not necessarily achieved (note that another variable entered the basis). Moreover, the complexity exhibited in rounding noninteger solutions in small problems can become overwhelming in large-scale problems. It is also important to note that without exhaustive enumeration of all combinations of integer-valued solutions or some other way to assure optimality, rounding offers no signal that the optimal solution has been found.

Graphical Perspective

For problems involving two decision variables, a graphical approach lends itself very well to finding optimal integer solutions. Figure 8–1 portrays the solution to the air cargo problem. The optimal noninteger solu-

FIGURE 8–1

Graphical Solution to Air Cargo Problem

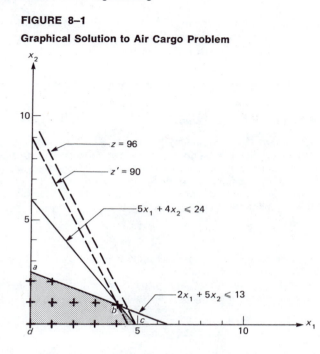

tion occurs at point c. Notice that **lattice marks** $(+)$ have been used to identify the feasible integer solution points. Since the optimal solution found at point c is noninteger, the objective function, z, must be moved parallel to itself toward the origin until it intersects a feasible integer solution point. The first such point is point b which occurs at $x_1 = 4$, $x_2 = 1$. The difference in values for z between the optimal noninteger and optimal integer solutions is often referred to as the **cost of indivisibility.** The difference—in this example $96 - 90 = \$6(100\text{'s})$—represents the opportunity cost of not being able to assign noninteger values to basic variables in the optimal solution.

8.2 ISSUES IN PROBLEM FORMULATION

Many managerial problems are inherently integer programming problems. Others are not necessarily integer but possess *special characteristics which can be modeled accurately only through the use of integer variables.* In this section we will discuss some of these special conditions and the manner in which they can be modeled. In Section 8.3 resolution of these issues will be illustrated in the formulation of selected applications.

Mutually Exclusive Constraints

For some problems, a set of mutually exclusive constraints exists. For example, a research and development program might be approved if available scientific personnel are used from one of two laboratory facilities but not from both laboratories. This is an example of the simplest case of mutually exclusive constraints—"either-or" constraints.

Example 8.2   Either-Or Constraints

The Checkerboard Round Company has bushels of corn (x_1), barley (x_2), and wheat (x_3) which they can blend into either hog food or breakfast cereal. However, due to differences in sanitation requirements and general public image, the firm feels it should be in either one business or the other. Let us assume that (1) is a constraint associated with the production of hog food and (2) is a similar constraint for breakfast cereal:

$$5x_1 + 2x_2 - 3x_3 \leq 50 \tag{1}$$
$$2x_1 - 4x_2 - \ x_3 \leq 30. \tag{2}$$

Constraints (1) or (2) would be operative only if it was decided to produce hog food or breakfast food, respectively.

To model this situation a new 0–1 variable, y, is introduced in the following manner to replace the original constraints:

$$5x_1 + 2x_2 - 3x_3 \leq 50 + yM \tag{1'}$$
$$2x_1 - 4x_2 - \ x_3 \leq 30 + (1 - y)M. \tag{2'}$$

M is defined as an arbitrarily large constant. The variable y is assigned an objective function coefficient of zero. With y being restricted to a value of either zero or one, the effect is as follows:

a. If $y = 1$, then the second constraint (2') reverts to its original form (2) and becomes a binding constraint. With M chosen sufficiently large, the right-hand side of constraint (1') becomes so large that any values of x_1, x_2, and x_3 satisfying constraint (2') will easily satisfy (1'), making (1') essentially redundant.

b. If $y = 0$, then the first constraint (1') reverts to its original form (1) and becomes binding; constraint (2') becomes redundant.

Note that the inclusion of y makes this a four-variable mixed integer problem: x_1, x_2, and x_3 are the original nondiscrete decision variables and y is a zero-one discrete variable which mathematically satisfies the either-or constraint.

If there are m_1 mutually exclusive less-than-or-equal-to constraints, then the term y_iM is added to the right-hand side of each. Each y_i is a 0–1 variable. To assure that only one of the m_1 constraints will be binding, an additional constraint of the form

$$\sum_{i=1}^{m_1} y_i = m_1 - 1$$

is added.

Example 8.3 m_1 Mutually Exclusive Constraints

Given the four mutually exclusive constraints

$$x_1 + x_2 + x_3 \leq 5$$
$$2x_1 - x_2 + x_3 \leq 10$$
$$4x_1 - x_2 - x_3 \leq 12$$
$$5x_1 - x_2 \qquad \leq 6,$$

four 0–1 variables must be added in the manner below in order to assure that only one of the constraints will be binding.

$$x_1 + x_2 + x_3 \leq 5 + y_1 M$$
$$2x_1 - x_2 + x_3 \leq 10 + y_2 M$$
$$4x_1 - x_2 - x_3 \leq 12 + y_3 M$$
$$5x_1 - x_2 \qquad \leq 6 + y_4 M$$
$$y_1 + y_2 + y_3 + y_4 = 3$$
$$y_i = 0 \text{ or } 1, \text{ for } i = 1,2,3,4.$$

m_1 Constraints, k of Which Must Be Binding

Some problems may require that a subset of constraints must hold in the solution to the problem. Assume that of m_1 less-than-or-equal-to constraints, k of these must be binding. As with the treatment of mutually exclusive constraints, a 0–1 variable will be multiplied times an arbitrarily large constant, M, for each constraint. To assure that only k of the m_1 constraints are binding, the constraint below should be added to the set.

$$\sum_{i=1}^{m_1} y_i = m_1 - k$$

If in Example 8.3 we desire that three of the four constraints be binding, the first four constraints are treated as before, but the last constraint is replaced by

$$y_1 + y_2 + y_3 + y_4 = 4 - 3$$
$$= 1.$$

This type of situation might arise in a problem having multiple criteria. In Chapter 1, we discussed the problems of multiple criteria and the concept of satisficing. A firm may establish satisfactory or minimum expected levels for a group of criteria such as net profit, gross sales, market share, and rate of return on investment. In determining whether to make a capital investment, management may specify that the minimum satisfactory levels for a given number of these criteria must be attained.

Interdependent Variables

In some problems, a mutual dependence may exist between projects. An example might be a project such as building a second floor that requires the first floor project to precede it.

Example 8.4   Dependent Projects

Let us define x_j as a 0–1 variable representing the acceptance ($x_j = 1$) or rejection ($x_j = 0$) of project j. If project 3 cannot be accepted unless project 2 has been accepted, then this restriction can be accounted for by including the constraint

$$x_3 \leq x_2$$
or
$$-x_2 + x_3 \leq 0.$$

If projects 2 and 3 must be undertaken together or not at all, then the condition can be represented by the constraint

$$x_2 - x_3 = 0.$$

Fixed Charge Problems

In our discussions of linear programming, any problems involving minimization of costs assumed that fixed costs are constant and need not be explicitly accounted for in the formulation of the LP model. Such was the case in Example 4.5 (Product Mix Model). Many problems involve a fixed charge element which cannot be realistically modeled by linear programming. The conversion of the original problem to a mixed integer programming problem allows for variations in fixed charges and related effects upon variable costs.

Example 8.5   Economies of Scale

Economies of scale are well-recognized within production systems. A product mix problem may contain the alternatives of using different types of machinery to produce an item. A more expensive machine which provides for a more automated production process may result in lower variable production costs per unit at higher levels of output than a less expensive machine designed to operate at lower levels of output. The typical rule-of-thumb is that higher fixed cost configurations lead to the tradeoff of lower per unit variable cost.

Suppose a company is considering the alternative of using three different production processes in order to satisfy production requirements for a given item. Let x_j be the number of units produced using process j; k_j be the fixed cost associated with operating process j; and c_j be the variable production cost per unit for process j. Although we will assume that other constraints exist in the problem, our concern here is to demonstrate how to represent the *fixed cost element*. If the objective is to minimize total costs, the total cost for each process would be represented by the equations

$$C_j = \begin{cases} k_j + c_j x_j & \text{if } x_j > 0 \\ 0 & \text{if } x_j = 0. \end{cases}$$

In order to represent this situation we introduce the 0–1 variable y_j which assumes a value of one if process j is used ($x_j > 0$) and a value of zero if process j is not used ($x_j = 0$). The objective function becomes

$$\text{minimize } z = (k_1 y_1 + c_1 x_1) + (k_2 y_2 + c_2 x_2) + (k_3 y_3 + c_3 x_3).$$

Note that the expression for z actually represents the C_j condition, from above. Can you see the logic behind this?

The other concern is to assure ourselves that each y_j will take on the appropriate value. That is, y_j must equal zero or one, only, and must equal one whenever $x_j > 0$. We assure the assignment of these discrete values by the constraint sets

$$y_j \leq 1 \text{ for } j = 1,2,3,$$
$$y_j \geq 0 \text{ for } j = 1,2,3,$$

and y_j is an integer for all j.

Some solution algorithms simply require the identification of variables as being 0–1 in nature, but others require the type of explicit formulation of constraints shown above in order to insure that certain integer variables will be 0–1.

To make sure $y_j = 1$ when $x_j > 0$, three constraints of the form

$$x_j \leq M y_j$$

or

$$x_j - M y_j \leq 0$$

are necessary. M, as before, is a constant having a value much larger than any value possibly assumed by x_j. The only way in which x_j can assume a value greater than zero is for y_j to equal one. Verify that if x_j is greater than zero and $y_j = 0$, then there is a contradiction. Also, notice that when $x_j > 0$ and $y_j = 1$ the above constraint is satisfied but is in no way *binding* (presuming M has been assigned a large enough value).

Follow-up Exercises

In this section we have discussed the manner in which special conditions that arise in problem formulation can be handled by integer programming. The conditions treated are by no means exhaustive of all that you might encounter. Try your luck on the following problems, not all of which have been discussed in the previous section.

1. If there are two either-or constraints which are of a ($\geq$) nature, does the formulation change from the way in which ($\leq$) constraints were treated in this section? If so, demonstrate by example.

2. Given the following mutually exclusive constraints, reformulate them so as to assure the condition of mutual exclusiveness (that is, that one and only one constraint will hold).

$$x_1 + x_2 + x_3 \leq 40$$
$$2x_1 - x_2 + x_3 \geq 20$$
$$x_1 \qquad\quad -x_3 \geq 15$$

3. Of a set of projects being considered for investment purposes, three projects are interrelated. If x_j is a 0–1 variable representing the rejection or acceptance of project j,

   a. Formulate the condition that assures at least two of the three projects must be accepted.

   b. Formulate the conditions that assure either all three projects are accepted or all three are rejected.

8.3 SELECTED APPLICATIONS

In this section, we offer examples of problems which lend themselves to formulation as integer programming problems. A number of the formulation issues discussed in Section 8.2 are illustrated by these applications.

Example 8.6 Public Transportation

The Department of Transportation (DOT) is experimenting on a pilot basis with personalized public transportation. One concept under consideration is the use of small, nonpolluting, six-passenger computer-controlled vehicles for transporting workers between their homes and jobs. Fares would be competitive with the costs of using an automobile. The benefits are fairly obvious: custom, door-to-door transportation, less vehicular congestion, lowered risk of accidents, and lowered pollution.

A pilot program based within a small midwestern city is proposing the experimental use of two such vehicles (each vehicle has a capacity of six) in different zones of the city. DOT analysts have located 16 citizens interested in participating in the pilot project. Each has filled out and returned a questionnaire designed to gather information pertinent to their participation in the project. Data include such items as home location, location of employment, time employee must be at work, and time employee leaves work. The data from the questionnaires were used to generate an index of compatibility which reflects the degree to which each individual's location and schedule attributes match those for the two vehicles. Table 8–1 indicates the indices, which range from a low value of one (1) to a maximum value of compatibility of ten (10). DOT officials want to maximize cumulative compatibility in making assignments of applicants to vehicles. Additionally, they wish to ensure that at least two females are assigned to each route. Applicants 3,5,9,10,11, and 15 are females.

This problem can be formulated as a 0–1 integer program. Let us define the variable x_{ij} to represent the assignment of applicant i to route j. If $x_{ij} = 1$, then the assignment is made; if $x_{ij} = 0$, then it is not. The objective function is formulated by multiplying each variable by its respective index of compatibility, or

$$\text{maximize } z = 3x_{11} + 8x_{12} + 7x_{21} + 8x_{22} + \cdots + 8x_{16.1} + 10x_{16.2}.$$

TABLE 8–1

Indices of Compatibility

Applicant	Vehicular Route 1	Vehicular Route 2
1..................	3	8
2..................	7	8
3..................	9	4
4..................	10	6
5..................	8	·8
6..................	3	9
7..................	5	6
8..................	3	4
9..................	1	9
10..................	8	8
11..................	1	3
12..................	9	6
13..................	10	7
14..................	4	4
15..................	7	8
16..................	8	10

Three types of structural constraint sets are necessary. One set must ensure that an applicant is assigned to, at most, one vehicle. The first and last of these 16 constraints are shown below for applicants 1 and 16, respectively.

$$x_{11} + x_{12} \leq 1 \qquad (1)$$

$$\vdots \qquad \qquad \vdots$$

$$x_{16,1} + x_{16,2} \leq 1. \qquad (16)$$

The next set of structural constraints assures that no more than six applicants will be assigned to a vehicle. These capacity constraints for vehicles 1 and 2, respectively, have the form

$$x_{11} + x_{21} + \cdots + x_{16,1} \leq 6 \qquad (17)$$
$$x_{12} + x_{22} + \cdots + x_{16,2} \leq 6. \qquad (18)$$

The final set of structural constraints guarantees that at least two females are assigned to each route:

$$x_{31} + x_{51} + x_{91} + x_{10,1} + x_{11,1} + x_{15,1} \geq 2 \qquad (19)$$
$$x_{32} + x_{52} + x_{92} + x_{10,2} + x_{11,2} + x_{15,2} \geq 2. \qquad (20)$$

Finally, we stipulate the conditions for 0–1 integers: $x_{ij} = 0$ or 1 for all i and j.

Follow-up Exercises

4. The condition $x_{ij} = 0$ or 1 for all i and j implies the use of a 0–1 programming algorithm for solving this problem. If instead we had specified

x_{ij} = nonnegative integers for all i and j, then an integer programming algorithm would be implied. Can you state why an integer programming procedure would yield 0–1 solutions for all x_{ij} in this problem?

5. Generalize the statement of this problem using summation notation if m applicants apply for n vehicular routes. Let c_{ij} = the index of compatibility between applicant i and route j; b_j = capacity of vehicle j; and w_j = minimum number of women for vehicle j. Assume that the first m_1 applicants in the table are women. What relationship must hold between all w_j and m_1 for a feasible solution to be realized?

6. If the stipulation for women were to be dropped, then this problem can be conceptualized as a transportation model. State the data for this revised problem in the form of a transportation tableau.

7. How might you go about constructing a compatibility index? Does the use of this index in the objective function present a problem in scaling?

Example 8.7   Fire Equipment Positioning

Emergency response systems have received considerable attention by operations researchers in recent years. One area of concern is the positioning of emergency response units within a city. Units, in this instance, may refer to fire fighting units, ambulance units, or police patrol units. Questions which have been addressed include the *prepositioning* of units prior to the beginning of a tour of duty and the *repositioning* of remaining units when certain units become unavailable.

Assume that a city has eight fire stations which service 22 fire districts within the city. Figure 8–2 indicates relative locations of the fire stations and fire districts. Analysis of historical response time data has led to the identification of fire stations which can respond to fires in each fire district

FIGURE 8–2

Fire Station and Fire District Locations

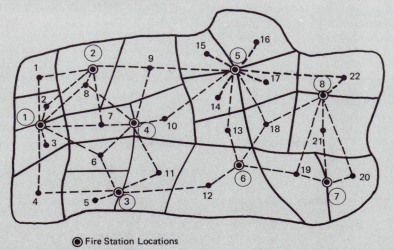

⊙ Fire Station Locations

within a predetermined maximum allowable average response time. The branches of Figure 8–2 indicate the districts which each fire station can service within the average allowable response time. The absence of a branch between any station and fire district implies that the station cannot respond within the allowable time.

The Board of Fire Commissioners is interested in considering if some of the existing fire stations can be closed; that is, can the city get by with less than the existing eight stations and, if so, which can be eliminated? One way to look at it is to find the smallest set of fire stations required to *cover* all fire districts. "Cover" in this instance means that at least one fire station would be able to respond to all fire districts within the maximum allowable average response time. Problems of this type are called **set-covering problems.**

This problem can be formulated as a 0–1 problem. Let x_j be a 0–1 variable defined for each fire station location, where $x_j = 1$ if a fire unit is positioned at fire station j and $x_j = 0$ if a fire unit is not. The objective is to minimize the number of stations, which is formulated as

$$\text{minimize } z = x_1 + x_2 + x_3 + x_4 + x_5 + x_6 + x_7 + x_8.$$

The constraint set simply involves one constraint for each fire district which assures coverage of that district. For example, a constraint which assures coverage of district 1 is

$$x_1 + x_2 \geq 1. \tag{1}$$

The constraint for district 8 is

$$x_1 + x_2 + x_4 \geq 1. \tag{8}$$

Follow-up Exercises

8. Complete the formulation of the fire station problem.

9. Examination of Figure 8–2 should reveal that units *must* be located at certain fire stations, such as station 5. Show how this observation as well as other related redundancies allow the original formulation to be simplified considerably.

10. Because of higher incidence of fires within certain districts, it may be required that more than one fire unit be available to service these districts. How will this type of requirement affect the formulation of this type of problem?

11. Discuss other issues of fire unit response which this simplified scenario fails to address. Also, discuss other criteria which might be considered in this problem.

Example 8.8 Political Campaign Tour

The campaign manager for a presidential candidate is planning a campaign tour to the capitals of four states believed to be critical to winning. Leaving from Washington, D.C., the candidate wants to visit each capital and then return to Washington. Because of rapidly diminishing balances in campaign coffers, as well as investigative reporters interested in efficient use of public campaign funds, the campaign manager wishes to minimize transportation costs of the trip for the candidate and his traveling staff.

Finding the minimum cost tour is a classic **traveling salesman (sales representative)** problem which can be formulated as a 0–1 integer programming problem. The decision variable x_{ij} equals one if the tour includes a leg in which there is travel *from* city i *to* city j and x_{ij} equals zero if there is no trip from city i to city j. The objective is to minimize either travel cost or travel distance, where c_{ij} is defined as the cost (or distance) associated with traveling from city i to city j.[2] This leads to the general form of the objective function:

$$\text{minimize } z = \sum_{i=1}^{n} \sum_{j=1}^{n} c_{ij} x_{ij} \qquad (1)$$

where n equals the *total number* of cities (including the starting point). For example, $n = 5$ for the campaign tour above. A value of $x_{ij} = 1$ when $i = j$ makes no sense. (Do you see why?) In order to prevent the assignment of a value of one to these variables, they may be excluded in the formulation or assigned extremely large cost coefficients in the objective function.

The constraint set typically consists of three types of constraints. The first assures that each city is visited exactly one time:

$$\sum_{\substack{i=1 \\ i \neq j}}^{n} x_{ij} = 1 \quad \text{for } j = 1, 2, \ldots, n. \qquad (2)$$

For example, the constraint for city 3 in a five-city problem would read

$$x_{13} + x_{23} + x_{43} + x_{53} = 1.$$

The second subset of constraints assures that there is exactly one departure from each of the n cities:

$$\sum_{\substack{j=1 \\ j \neq i}}^{n} x_{ij} = 1 \quad \text{for } i = 1, 2, \ldots, n. \qquad (3)$$

The constraint

$$x_{21} + x_{23} + x_{24} + x_{25} = 1,$$

for example, ensures this condition for city 2.

If no other constraints were to be specified, this problem would have the exact form of the *assignment model* discussed in Chapter 7. However, there can be values for the decision variables which satisfy constraint sets (2) and (3) but which do not fulfill the travel objectives. The formulation, as it now stands, allows for **subtours.** Figure 8–3 illustrates one subtour solution to a five-city problem which is to originate and terminate at city 1. Note that this solution represents a valid mathematical solution to the problem specified by constraint sets (2) and (3). Since a complete tour is not accomplished, however, it represents a meaningless (real-world) solution. Consequently, it is necessary to include a third constraint set which prohibits subtours such as those illustrated in Figure 8–3.

To prevent two-city subtours we simply specify that if there is travel from city i to city j, then there cannot be travel from j to i. For example, to

---

[2] Sequencing, scheduling, routing, and traveling sales representative problems are all examples of so-called **combinatorial problems.**

FIGURE 8-3

**Two-City and Three-City Subtours
for Five-City Problems**

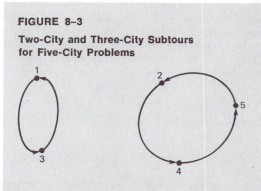

prevent a subtour between cities 1 and 3, we formulate this constraint.

$$x_{13} + x_{31} \leq 1.$$

To prevent three-city subtours, two constraints must be constructed for *each combination* of three cities. For example all three-city subtours among cities 2, 4, and 5 can be prevented by specifying the following two constraints:

$$x_{24} + x_{45} + x_{52} \leq 2$$
$$x_{25} + x_{54} + x_{42} \leq 2.$$

Note that the first of these two constraints eliminates the subtour indicated in Figure 8-3. Can you sketch the second constraint? Further note that the first constraint implies travel from city 2 to city 4 to city 5 and back to city 2. Algebraically, you should confirm that it does not matter where one begins in a circular subtour. For example, write down the constraint preventing travel from city 4 to city 5 to city 2 and back to city 4, and mathematically compare this to the first constraint above.

Now carefully consider the following: For a tour involving five cities only two-city subtours need to be prevented to eliminate the possibility of all subtours. If all two-city subtours are eliminated, then all three-city subtours are automatically eliminated in a five-city problem, as guaranteed by constraint sets (2) and (3). In Figure 8-3, for example, if the subtour between city 1 and city 3 is eliminated by the appropriate constraint, then the indicated three-city subtour is not possible. Furthermore for a five-city problem, four-city subtours are not possible because one-city subtours ($x_{ij} = 1$ for $i = j$) are disallowed. Finally the number of two-city subtours in a five-city problem is given by combinations of five taken two at a time, or ten. Since a single constraint eliminates a given two-city subtour, it follows that ten constraints are required to eliminate all subtours in a five-city problem.

Finally, the conditions for nonnegative integers must be specified: $x_{ij} =$ nonnegative integers for all i and j. Why is it unnecessary to specify these as 0-1 conditions?

Interestingly, this type of model is applicable not only to political campaigns and traveling sales representatives but also to truck routings and production scheduling. For example, a series of products may need to be scheduled on a common production facility so as to minimize setup costs. Consider soap making at a company such as Procter and Gamble where Tide, Oxydol, Dreft, Cheer, and other brands are made. The cost of switching from white Tide to white Oxydol is low, higher from Tide to blue Cheer, and still higher from Cheer to Tide. By conceptualizing each soap as a "city" and the facility as the "salesrepresentative," it follows that the above model can be applied.

Finally, as Exercise 13 illustrates, LP formulations of the traveling sales-representative problem become large as the number of cities increases. For this reason, special-purpose algorithms have been developed for solving this problem.

Follow-up Exercises

12. Answer the following:

    a. In a six-city tour, why need we only eliminate two-city and three-city subtours?

    b. In a seven-city tour, why need we only eliminate two-city and three-city subtours?

    c. In an eight-city tour, all two-city, three-city, and four-city subtours must be eliminated. Write down the necessary constraints to eliminate all subtours among cities 2,5,6, and 8. (Hint: Six constraints are needed to eliminate all subtours among four specific cities.)

    d. How many two-city, three-city, and four-city subtours are possible in an eight-city tour? How many constraints are needed to eliminate all of these two-city, three-city, and four-city subtours? How many total constraints in an eight-city problem? How many variables?

    e. How many variables and constraints must be specified in a seven-city problem? A six-city problem?

**13. Let k represent the number of cities in a subtour. Write general algebraic expressions for the following.

    a. For an n-city problem, what values of k must be considered?

    b. How many constraints are needed to eliminate all subtours among k specific cities?

    c. How many constraints are needed to eliminate all k-city subtours given n total cities?

    d. How many constraints are needed to eliminate all subtours given n total cities?

    e. For the number of cities below indicate the number of variables and total number of constraints in the model. How might you describe the rate of increase in the size of the model relative to the rate of increase in the number of cities? If you were to enumerate all possible solutions, how many must you consider?

        1. $n = 5$
        2. $n = 10$
        3. $n = 20$
        4. $n = 40$

14. Given the estimated transportation costs for each pair of cities in Table 8–2, completely formulate the five-city campaign tour problem. Does it matter what number you label Washington, D.C.? How many five-city tours are possible?

15. Suppose the presidential candidate wishes to visit city 5 directly after city 3. How is this represented in the model? Does this result in any simplification of the model?

TABLE 8–2

Transportation Costs ($100's)

		To City			
From City	1	2	3	4	5
1..................	—	22	34	10	25
2..................	22	—	15	56	48
3..................	34	15	—	45	24
4..................	10	56	45	—	9
5..................	25	48	24	9	—

Note: City 1 is Washington, D.C.

16. Because of the good press coverage and the support expected in cities 4 and 2, the presidential candidate wants to visit city 5 directly after a visit to either 4 or 2. (City 5 is believed to be the city of weakest support.) How can this constraint be represented in the model?

Example 8.9   Conditional Transportation Problem

In Chapter 7 the transportation model was considered. In its classical application there are m origins or sources of supply and n destinations or points of demand. Each origin, i, has an available supply, s_i, and each destination, j, has demand, d_j. The objective is to determine how many units (x_{ij}) should be shipped from each origin to each destination in order to satisfy the supply and demand constraints at a minimum transportation cost.

The conditional transportation problem is an extension of the transportation problem. It is representative of a group of problems involving setup costs and the selection of an optimal set of sources to meet the required demands. The group includes plant and warehouse location, promotion programs, and product line expansion.

In the plant location problem, m possible sites are being considered as supply points. The objective is to choose the sites, and the amounts to be shipped from each site to each demand point, in order to minimize total costs. Costs can include variable unit transportation cost (t_{ij}) and manufacturing cost (c_i), as well as fixed overhead costs (f_i) which depend on the supply sites selected.

The formulation of this problem requires the introduction of a 0–1 variable:

$$y_i = \begin{cases} 1 & \text{if site } i \text{ is selected} \\ 0 & \text{if site } i \text{ is not selected.} \end{cases}$$

The objective is to minimize the sum of fixed overhead costs, transportation costs, and manufacturing costs:

$$\text{minimize } z = \sum_{i=1}^{m} f_i y_i + \sum_{i=1}^{m} \sum_{j=1}^{n} (t_{ij} + c_i) x_{ij}.$$

Capacity constraints differ from those used in the transportation model. For each proposed site, there will be a constraint of the form

$$\sum_{j=1}^{n} x_{ij} \leq s_i y_i \qquad\qquad i = 1, \ldots, m$$

or

$$\sum_{j=i}^{n} x_{ij} - s_i y_i \leq 0, \qquad\qquad i = 1, \ldots, m.$$

If site i is not selected, then $y_i = 0$, and shipments will be prohibited from the site. The demand constraints for each destination remain unchanged and are of the form

$$\sum_{i=1}^{m} x_{ij} \geq d_j, \qquad\qquad j = 1, \ldots, n.$$

The usual 0–1 constraints also must be added:

$$y_i = 0 \text{ or } 1, \qquad\qquad i = 1, \ldots, m.$$

In addition, nonnegativity constraints must be applied to all x_{ij}. If x_{ij} are restricted to nonnegative integers, then the following is specified: $x_{ij} =$ nonnegative integers for all i and j. If all x_{ij} are divisible (for example, units of tons or gallons), then the usual nonnegativity condition is specified: $x_{ij} \geq 0$ for all i and j. In the latter case, the existence of both integer (y_i) and noninteger (x_{ij}) variables makes for a mixed integer programming problem.

Follow-up Exercises

17. Suppose each destination was allowed to receive shipments from no more than r origins. How would this affect the formulation?

18. Suppose each origin could ship to no more than p destinations. How would the formulation be affected?

19. Formulate the plant location problem for the case where two sites and four demand points are under consideration. The fixed costs associated with sites 1 and 2 are $60,000 and $50,000, respectively. Other pertinent data are provided in Table 8–3 (all costs have been discounted to the present).

TABLE 8–3

Data for Plant Location Problem

Supply Point	Demand Point 1	2	3	4	Capacity per Planning Period
1	1.00 3.00	1.20 2.00	1.10 3.00	0.50 1.00	20,000
2	0.75 5.00	0.60 3.00	2.00 2.00	1.05 4.00	25,000
Demand per planning period	10,000	5,000	7,000	12,000	34,000 45,000

Note: The first entry in each cell represents unit transportation cost (dollars per unit) for the given route; the second entry represents unit manufacturing cost (dollars per unit) at each plant.

Example 8.10   Capital Budgeting

Capital budgeting problems are of obvious managerial importance. You have seen a capital budgeting problem formulated as a linear programming model (Example 4.7). In Chapter 9 we present another variation using a dynamic programming model (Example 9.3). The very nature of these problems makes them particularly amenable to integer programming formulations because of the "go,no-go" nature of the implied decisions.

Example 4.7 on page 116 involved the selection from among seven long-term HEW projects. In the formulation of this problem we assumed that divisibility was possible and that HEW could invest in fractional portions of the seven projects. The decision variables, x_j, were defined as the portions of each project, j, that would be undertaken; hence, they were continuous in the range from zero to one. In most capital budgeting problems these decision variables must be restricted to either zero or one, implying either total investment or no investment.

Follow-up Exercises

20.   Reformulate Example 4.7 using 0–1 values for all x_{ij}.
21.   Reformulate the preceding exercise with the following additional considerations.
      a.   Projects 1 and 3 must be undertaken together, if at all.
      b.   At most, four projects may be undertaken.
      c.   Projects 4 and 5 are mutually exclusive (that is, if one is undertaken, the other cannot be undertaken).
      d.   Projects 6 and 7 are dependent (that is, project 7 cannot be undertaken unless project 6 is undertaken).

Example 8.11   Knapsack Problem

The **knapsack problem** is a classical OR allocation problem which has a wide range of applications. In the classical problem a knapsack is to be filled with a selection from n possible items. The available quantity of each item is limited to one unit and each item has attributes of weight and relative benefit. The problem is to select which of the n items should be packed in the knapsack in order to maximize the total benefit contributed by the items without violating a specified maximum weight. If $x_j = 1$, then item j is selected for inclusion in the knapsack; otherwise, $x_j = 0$.

The formulation of this combinatoric problem as an integer programming model has been motivated because of the large number of potential solutions. For problems involving n possible items, the number of different combinations of items which may be selected for inclusion in the knapsack is 2^n. For a problem involving 10 items, there are 1,024 different combinations of items; for 15 items there are over 30,000 different combinations; and for 30 items we get more than 1 billion combinations (of course, these are not all feasible).

Variations on the classical problem allow for additional constraints and the inclusion of more units of item j. **Cargo-loading problems,** of which the air cargo problem at the beginning of this chapter is a specific example, are knapsack problems.

Follow-up Exercises

22. Given that c_j is a measure of benefit for item j, w_j is the weight of item j, and W is the maximum allowable weight, formulate the *classical* knapsack problem.

23. In addition to the definitions in the preceding exercise, suppose v_j is the volume taken up by item j, V is the maximum allowable volume, and x_j is the number of units selected of item j. Formulate the cargo-loading problem.

8.4 SOLUTION METHODS

A variety of solution approaches are available for solving integer programming problems. Some of these are generalized for all types of integer programming structures; others are tailored to the special structure of certain integer programming problems (such as pure 0–1 problems). In this section we will describe three of the more widely used algorithms for solving the generalized integer programming problem. Additionally, we will overview some of the more specialized approaches.

"Brute-Force" Approach

One intuitive approach would suggest total enumeration of all feasible integer combinations of the pertinent decision variables. With small-scale problems having relatively few decision variables, this approach can be effective. However, for most realistic problems, the number of feasible combinations becomes overwhelming. For example, in a traveling sales representative problem involving travel to m different cities (not including the originating city) and return to the originating city, the number of different tours (not all necessarily feasible, of course) is $(m!)$. For $m = 10$, the number of tours exceeds 3.6 million and for $m = 20$, the number exceeds 2 quintillion! For problems of this magnitude, many years of fast computer time would be required. It is easy to see why complete enumeration of combinatorial problems is to be discouraged. We now turn to a technique which enumerates only a small proportion of possible solutions.

Branch-and-Bound Algorithm

The branch-and-bound algorithm is suited for pure integer, mixed integer, and 0–1 problems. It uses, as its starting point, the optimal simplex solution to the "unintegerized" version of the original problem. If this solution does not satisfy the integer requirements, then the original problem is partitioned into a subset of problems which are more constrained than the original problem. By relying on the simplex algorithm, we sharply reduce the feasible area for potential optima as compared with total enumeration. Also, aside from the special searching procedures of the branch-and-bound method, no new solution algorithm is required. As discussed earlier in the chapter, the optimal integer solution can be no better than the optimal solution to the straight (unintegerized) LP problem. Thus, the optimal value of the objective function in the continuous version of the problem provides an upper (lower) *bound* on the optimal value for the integer version in a maximization (minimization) problem.

Example 8.12

Perhaps the easiest way to understand the nature of the branch-and-bound method is to illustrate by example. The graphical representation of the following integer programming problem is shown in Figure 8–4:

FIGURE 8–4

Graphical Solution to Example 8.12

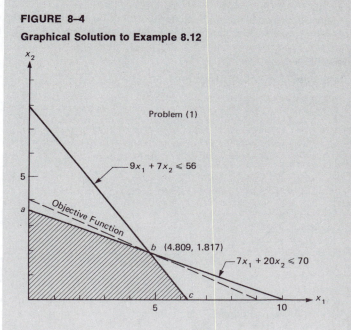

Maximize

$$z = 40x_1 + 90x_2$$

subject to

$$9x_1 + 7x_2 \leq 56$$
$$7x_1 + 20x_2 \leq 70$$

$$x_1, x_2 = \text{nonnegative integers.}$$

Note that the optimal simplex solution occurs at point *b* with neither variable assuming an integer value ($x_1 = 4.809$, $x_2 = 1.817$, and $z = 355.890$).

The branch-and-bound algorithm focuses upon one of the noninteger decision variables (the choice is arbitrary). For instance we might focus upon $x_1 = 4.809$. It stands to reason that the optimal integer solution will have an

integer value assigned to x_1 such that $x_1 \leq 4$ or $x_1 \geq 5$. The noninteger region between $x_1 = 4$ and $x_1 = 5$ is not feasible in the integer version of the
problem. Consequently, the branch-and-bound algorithm *branches* from the
original problem, or partitions it into two further constrained problems which
eliminate this noninteger area. Figure 8–5 illustrates the graphic representation of these two problems. For the sake of reference, we will number the
original problem as problem (1) and descendant problems as problems (2),
(3), and so forth.

Solving each of the newly formed problems by the simplex method as if
they were continuous (noninteger) problems yields the following solutions:

Problem (2)	Problem (3)
$z = 349.000$	$z = 341.390$
$x_1 = 4.000$	$x_1 = 5.000$
$x_2 = 2.100$	$x_2 = 1.571$

Again, neither solution is all-integer, but both have led to integer values for
x_1. Since we excluded no feasible integer solution points in creating these

FIGURE 8–5

Partitioned Descendants from Problem (1)

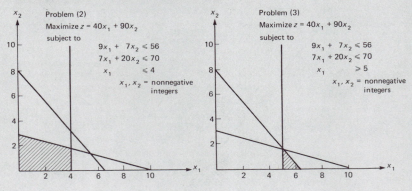

two problems, the values of 349.000 and 341.390 act as upper bounds for any
feasible integer solutions. That is, integer values of four or less for x_1 cannot
possibly result in a z value greater than 349.000 and values of five or
more for x_1 cannot exceed 341.390 for z.

The branch-and-bound algorithm works on the principle of searching
problem subsets to find feasible solutions, but discarding (not searching)
subsets that cannot produce results superior to those already attained.
Continuing the analysis, we could partition from either problem (2) or problem (3) in an effort to integerize x_2. However, the "potential" associated with
partitioning from problem (2) is more promising. This is because the upper
bound on any descendant problem which further constrains problem (2)
is $z = 349.000$, whereas the best that can be expected from descendants of
problem (3) is $z = 341.390$. Thus, the next step begins with problem (2) by
adding the constraints $x_2 \leq 2$ (problem 4) and $x_2 \geq 3$ (problem 5). In this
subset of problems the noninteger area between $x_2 = 2$ and $x_2 = 3$ is excluded, since $x_2 = 2.1$ in the solution to Problem (2).

Figure 8–6 summarizes the remaining steps leading to the identification of the optimal integer solution. In problem (4) an all-integer solution is identified with an objective function valued at 340. In problem (5), the other descendant problem from problem (2), the optimal solution is not integer. However, since any descendant problems cannot produce z values greater than 327.120, we can discard problem (5) and its descendants from further considerations.

One might be inclined to conclude that the optimal integer solution has been found. However, there is potentially a better solution from one of the descendants of problem (3). The value of $z = 341.390$ is greater than the

FIGURE 8–6

Summary of Branch-and-Bound Solution

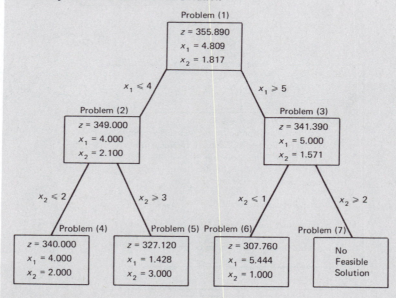

340 found in problem (4). Therefore, it is necessary to partition problem (3) into problems (6) and (7) by adding the constraints $x_2 \leq 1$ and $x_2 \geq 2$, respectively. As can be seen in Figure 8–6, the results for these two problems are inferior to the solution found in problem (4). Any descendants from problem (6) would have optimal values for z no greater than 307.76 and any descendants of problem (7) would be infeasible. Thus, the optimal integer solution is $x_1 = 4$, $x_2 = 2$, and $z = 340$.

The branch-and-bound procedure can be summarized by the flow diagram of Figure 8–7. Study it carefully and trace through the subsets of problems in Figure 8–6 to verify that this is the procedure we used.

FIGURE 8–7

The Branch-and-Bound Procedure

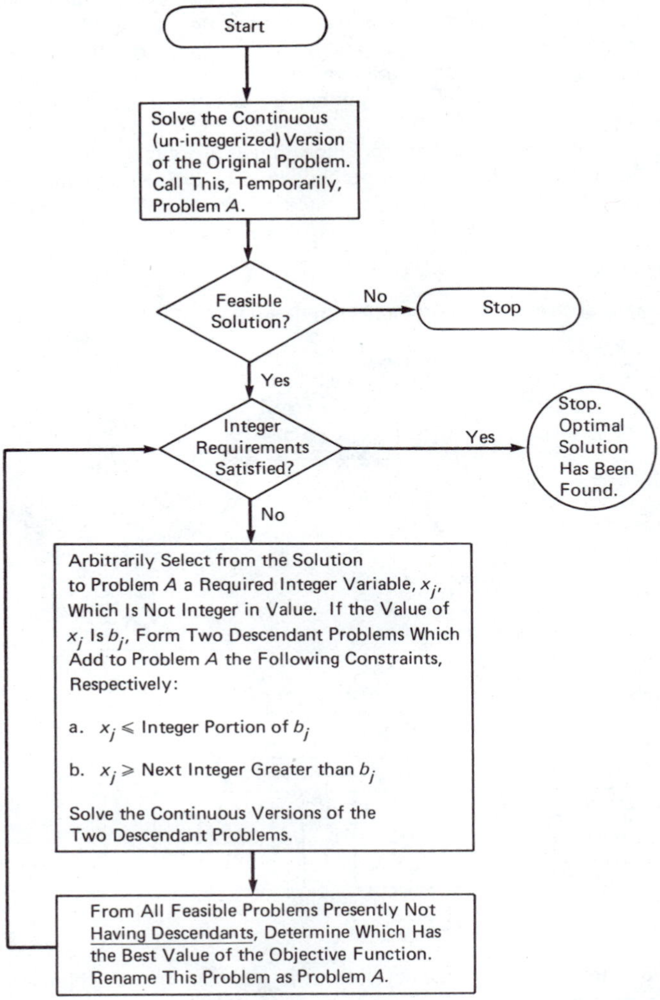

As mentioned earlier, the branch-and-bound algorithm is suited for both pure and mixed integer problems. Referring to Figure 8–6, we see that had x_1 been the only required integer variable, the optimal solution would have been that found in problem (2) with $z = 349.000$, $x_1 = 4$, and $x_2 = 2.100$.

In summary, the branch-and-bound algorithm provides for an intelligent search of the feasible solution space. As opposed to the brute-force approach of complete enumeration, the search is restricted to partial enumeration of promising integer solution points. However, you should not be misled to the conclusion that branch-and-bound algorithms always can produce optimal solutions with computational ease. *Relative ease*, yes, but not absolute ease; a 99.9-percent reduction of 2 quintillion potential solutions is still a big number. We will reconsider this issue in Section 8.5.

Follow-up Exercises

24. State the objective function and constraints, and graph the solutions to problems (4), (5), (6), and (7) in Example 8.12 (Figure 8–6).

25. Solve Example 8.12 by the branch-and-bound procedure if x_2 is required to be integer and x_1 is not.

26. Solve Example 8.12 by selecting x_2 in problem (1) as the variable which causes descendants.

27. Solve the problem below by:

   a. Rounding the simplex solution (note that this is not obvious).
   b. Graphical means.
   c. Branch-and-bound method.

Maximize

$$z = 8x_1 + 20x_2$$

subject to

$$x_1 + 3x_2 \le 9$$
$$9x_1 + 7x_2 \le 56$$

$$x_1, x_2 = \text{nonnegative integers.}$$

28. Solve the air cargo problem by the branch-and-bound method.

29. Solve the following problems using a computerized simplex or (better yet) a branch-and-bound package which is available to you.

   a. Exercise 20.
   b. Exercise 21.
   c. Example 4.9 on page 121.

Gomory's Cutting Plane Algorithm

Another popular technique for solving either pure or mixed integer programming problems is Gomory's cutting plane algorithm. This technique begins, as with the branch-and-bound algorithm, with the optimal solution to the continuous version of the problem. If the optimal solution does not satisfy the integer requirements of the problem, new constraints are formulated and added to the problem. These constraints represent planes (in two-space) or hyperplanes (in *n*-space) which effectively "cut away" portions of the feasible solution space while assuring that no feasible integer solution points are eliminated.

The principle behind the use of these cutting planes can be tied back to our discussions of linear programming. In Chapter 4 we concluded that at least one of the optimal solutions to an LP problem occurs at a corner point of the feasible solution space. The simplex algorithm provides a systematic search of corner points until it identifies the one which is optimal. Since all corner points are not necessarily integer, the cutting plane method attempts to pare down the feasible solution space such that it contains integer corner points. If this is accomplished, then application of the simplex method will result in the identification of the optimal integer solution.

For two-variable problems, the procedure can be shown by graphical representation. Figure 8–8 illustrates an area of feasible solutions ($abcd$)

FIGURE 8–8

Area of Feasible Solutions for Maximization Problem

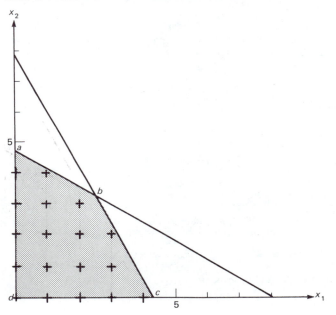

for a maximization problem. Aside from the origin, none of the other corner points are all-integer. The cutting plane method reduces the area of feasible solutions to "force" integer corner points. Figure 8–9 illustrates the extreme case in which all corner points are forced to integer coordinates. Three cutting planes (1, 2, and 3) have been added which slice into the solution space, thereby eliminating the shaded portions of the original area of feasible solutions. No feasible integer-valued points have been eliminated. The boundaries of the reduced area of feasible solutions are often said to make up a **convex hull.** This is the smallest convex set necessary to include all of the feasible integer solution points.[3]

---

[3] See Section 4.3 for the definition of a convex set.

Application of the simplex method would now lead directly to the optimal integer solution.

We will not present the mechanics of how cutting plane equations are developed; rather, we will offer some feeling for how the procedure works.[4] First, cutting planes are developed in order to force the noninteger-valued variables to integer values. If a starting solution involves a number of noninteger variables, then generally one variable is selected to provide the basis for developing a new constraint (cutting plane). Once this constraint has been identified, it can be added to the original constraint set

FIGURE 8–9

Convex Hull

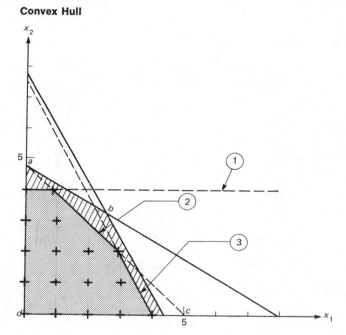

and the entire problem can be re-solved by the simplex method. Or, an advanced simplex procedure, called the **dual simplex method,** can be used to incorporate the constraint in the final tableau of the previous solution and allow the optimal solution of the larger problem to be found without starting from scratch.

It should be mentioned that it is usually not necessary to add enough cutting planes to reduce the solution space all the way down to its convex hull. Depending on the objective function for the problem in Figure 8–9,

[4] For detailed treatments see Harvey M. Wagner, *Principles of Operations Research,* 2d ed. (Englewood Cliffs, N.J.: Prentice Hall, Inc., 1975); Claude McMillan, Jr., *Mathematical Programming* (New York: John Wiley & Sons, Inc., 1970); or Narendra Paul Loomba and Efraim Turban, *Applied Programming for Management* (New York: Holt, Rinehart and Winston, 1974).

it might take as little as one cutting plane to reach the optimal integer solution.

Compared with the branch-and-bound algorithm, several significant differences are evident. Thinking in terms of a two-dimensional situation, both methods add new constraints or cutting planes to the original problem. The cutting planes in the branch-and-bound method are always perpendicular to one of the coordinate axes, whereas this is not necessarily the case with Gomory's cutting planes. Also, Gomory's planes always result in a reduction of the original area of feasible solutions without any exclusion of feasible integer-valued points. Conversely, the branch-and-bound algorithm often defines solution spaces which exclude feasible integer-valued points. Can you reason why?

Implicit Enumeration

Implicit enumeration is a technique for solving 0–1 problems. Since procedures exist for converting any integer programming problem into a 0–1 problem, implicit enumeration is more generally applicable than we might first believe. For realistic problems, we dismissed complete enumeration of all integer solution values as a procedure having appeal only to the dedicated masochist. Implicit enumeration, like branch-and-bound, only enumerates a subset of all possible combinations of variables.

The primary difference between implicit enumeration and branch-and-bound is that whereas branch-and-bound evaluates complete solutions (utilizing the simplex method), implicit enumeration builds from partial solutions. The building is in the fashion of a tree where whole branches can be dismissed from further consideration. The partial solution simply means the assignment of zero or one to a subset of the decision variables.

Given a partial assignment, an analysis of the constraint set, objective function, and unassigned decision variables can lead to the elimination of certain subsets of solutions. These subsets might be infeasible, or a lower (upper) bound on the objective function indicates they are not promising. Thus, certain sets of solution points associated with completion of a partial solution can be ignored and are said to be "implicitly enumerated." An example will be helpful in providing better understanding.

Example 8.13

Study for a moment the following 0–1 problem.

Minimize

$$z = 2x_1 + 5x_2 + 3x_3 + 4x_4$$

subject to

$$-4x_1 + x_2 + x_3 + x_4 \geq 0 \qquad (1)$$
$$-2x_1 + 4x_2 + 2x_3 + 4x_4 \geq 4 \qquad (2)$$
$$x_1 + x_2 - x_3 + x_4 \geq 1 \qquad (3)$$

$$x_1, x_2, x_3, x_4 = 0 \text{ or } 1.$$

Table 8–4 presents an enumeration of all possible solutions (not all feasible). With four different 0–1 variables there are 2^4, or 16, combinations of values for the four decision variables.

TABLE 8–4

Complete Enumeration of Solution Values for Example 8.13

Solution	x_1	x_2	x_3	x_4
1	0	0	0	0
2	0	0	0	1
3	0	0	1	0
4	0	0	1	1
5	0	1	0	0
6	0	1	0	1
7	0	1	1	0
8	0	1	1	1
9	1	0	0	0
10	1	0	0	1
11	1	0	1	0
12	1	0	1	1
13	1	1	0	0
14	1	1	0	1
15	1	1	1	0
16	1	1	1	1

Since this problem is of the minimization type and since all c_j values are greater than zero, the best possible solution would be an assignment of values of zero to all decision variables leading to a value of $z = 0$. However, this solution is infeasible because of the violation of constraints (2) and (3). Because we are interested in minimizing z, making an assignment of $x_1 = 1$ is a reasonable place to start since it has the smallest c_j value. For this partial assignment, however, constraints (1) and (2) are violated. More importantly, although the violation of constraint (2) can be rectified with certain choices for the remaining decision variables, this is not so for constraint (1). That is, when $x_1 = 1$, constraint (1) can never be satisfied. (Do you see why?) Thus, all solutions which allow $x_1 = 1$ can be ignored. In Table 8–4 you can observe that we have excluded by implicit enumeration solutions 9 through 16 due to their infeasibility. By this one elimination, we have reduced the combinations by 50 percent (2^4 to 2^3).

We now know that x_1 *must equal zero* in the optimal solution. If we next assign a value of one to x_2, then the partial solution ($x_1 = 0$, $x_2 = 1$) is feasible. Because this is a minimization problem, the only reasonable completion of this partial solution is an assignment of the values $x_3 = x_4 = 0$, leading to a value of $z = 5$. Assigning a value of one to either or both of these variables would lead to values of z which are greater than five. We have, by implicit enumeration, eliminated from consideration solutions 6 through 8 in Table 8–4 because their objective function values are inferior to an existing solution.

Follow-up Exercises

30. Determine the optimal solution to Example 8.13 by implicit enumeration.
31. Solve Example 8.13 by the branch-and-bound method. Compare to implicit enumeration.

This brief discussion illustrates the manner in which the implicit enumeration process works. A variety of specialized procedures have been developed to facilitate implicit enumeration. As in our treatment of cutting plane methods, our purpose here is to intuitively explain their rationale.

Other Solution Methods

A variety of other solution approaches have been proposed for solving integer programming problems. Some are heuristic procedures (rule-of-thumb with no guarantee of optimality) and others combine characteristics of branch-and-bound, cutting plane, or implicit enumeration methods. Characteristics of the three techniques discussed in this section have been integrated with heuristic methods and with other forms of mathematical programming such as dynamic programming. In almost every case, these hybrid approaches have, as their primary objective, the more efficient solution of large-scale integer programming problems. As we will demonstrate in Chapter 16, the solution of realistic combinatorial problems involves a tradeoff between solution quality and solution cost as measured by the computational burden. Although optima are desirable, they may be unattainable or terribly costly.

8.5 INTEGER PROGRAMMING: AN ASSESSMENT

The major "hang-up" with integer programming problems is not their formulation but their efficient solution. Experiences in using various solution procedures can be best described as inconsistent and disappointing. Each method has its advantages and disadvantages. What works well for one problem may fail miserably with a very similar problem. A number of authors have stated that the selection of the best solution algorithm is an art, but it is an art form which few have mastered in real-world applications. Some experiences associated with these solution procedures are shared below.

Cutting Plane Algorithms

Cutting plane algorithms (such as Gomory's) can be computer-coded rather easily. Although they supposedly will converge to the optimal solution in a finite number of iterations, this finite number is often too large to make for efficient solution, even with computers. One problem with these procedures is their sensitivity to round-off errors. Computers must use decimal arithmetic with simplex-related solution procedures because of the inherent fractional values which arise in computing solutions. The double precision arithmetic feature available on many computer codes is only a partial solution to this problem. The problem is further compounded by the large number of cutting planes which must be added for combinatorial problems which "mushroom."

Another observation is that cutting plane algorithms often "stall" in a manner similar to the cycling phenomenon in linear programming. The objective function, rather than maintaining the same value from iteration to iteration as was the case of cycling, reaches plateaus in its improvement. Many cutting planes tend to be added with relatively small changes in the value of the objective function. This expensive feature is common in large-scale problems (and frequently occurs in smaller problems). In order to avoid these plateaus in objective function improvement (which may require thousands of iterations to pass through), integer programming experts have suggested ways of "tricking" the algorithm out of these zones.

Cutting plane algorithms have been inconsistent in their success. They are often extremely sensitive to the form of the integer programming problem. Simply rearranging the order of constraints may significantly change the number of cutting planes required to converge to the optimal solution. These algorithms have also been known to have difficulty in solving problems which have large a_{ij} and b_i values.

A final criticism of cutting plane methods is that they are based upon a dual method (dual-simplex). This technique starts with an infeasible solution and remains infeasible until the optimal solution has been found. If the method fails to converge to the optimal solution or if it is too costly to allow complete convergence, then the user is left with no "near-optimal" or "good" feasible solution.

Semienumerative Approaches

Branch-and-bound procedures have been effective in solving "small" problems; however, if problems are "large" (say, more than 50 variables and 25 constraints) or if the initial simplex solution is a significant "distance" from the optimal integer solution, then the number of iterations required may be prohibitively large. The examples we used to illustrate solution procedures are deceptive because of their small size. But problem size is not the only determinant of solution complexity. Certain problems permit "large branches" to be "pruned," whereas others have to go all the way out to the "tips." In comparison with cutting plane algorithms, however, a benefit of branch-and-bound methods is that failure to converge to the optimum within a specified time (cost) allocation still leaves the user with a *feasible solution* which may be of some value.

A major computational advantage of implicit enumeration is that it is based upon integer arithmetic. Thus, fixed point arithmetic features can be used in coding the algorithm, thereby eliminating rounding problems. Moreover, the memory requirement for 0–1 problems may be less for implicit enumeration approaches than for simplex-related methods. (Can you offer reasons why?) Converting a general integer programming problem to its 0–1 equivalent, however, results in the addition of many variables. Unfortunately, memory capacity and processing time can become critical in such situations.

A Caveat

The state-of-the-art in solving integer programming problems is changing, and the future may yield improved solution methods which bring the technology of integer programming closer to successful large-scale applications. We would be remiss, however, if you were left with the impression that the present state of the art is "rosy." This is well-illustrated by the following quote from one of the prototype articles of R. E. D. Woolsey. This sage of real-world pragmatism entitled his article "A Candle to Saint Jude, or Four Real-World Applications of Integer Programming."[5]

> In most of the standard texts of MS/OR, integer programming is treated just as any other mathematical programming technique. The fact that most of the algorithms proposed are extremely difficult to use in practice is simply ignored. To be blunt, the difference between theory and practice in integer programming can only be marked by the thousands of dollars spent getting these algorithms to converge in an economic amount of time; because the Management Scientist says that the algorithm will "converge in a finite number of steps" is no guarantee that the company might not be bankrupted by the expense first. Thus, many of those who actually solve problems turn to heuristic methods [Chapter 16] to get good starting solutions, followed by some kind of branch-and-bound scheme to take every possible advantage of problem structure. But these methods are often given short shrift in OR/MS texts and journals due to their "inelegance." One recalls the remark of Marshall Joffre upon seeing one of the world's last cavalry charges in WWI: "It is magnificent, but is it war?"

SELECTED REFERENCES

Anderson, David R.; Sweeney, Dennis J.; and Williams, Thomas A. *Linear Programming for Decision Making, An Applications Approach*. St. Paul: West Publishing Co., 1974.

Hillier, Frederick S., and Lieberman, Gerald J. *Introduction to Operations Research*. 2d ed. San Francisco: Holden Day, Inc., 1974.

Kim, Chaiho. *Quantitative Analysis for Managerial Decisions*. Reading, Mass.: Addison-Wesley Publishing Co., 1976.

---

[5] *Interfaces*, vol. 2, no. 2 (February 1972).

Loomba, Narendra Paul, and Turban, Efraim. *Applied Programming for Management*. New York: Holt, Rinehart and Winston, Inc., 1974.

McMillan, Claude, Jr. *Mathematical Programming: An Introduction to the Design and Application of Optimal Decision Machines*. New York: John Wiley & Sons, Inc., 1970.

Plane, Donald R., and McMillan, Claude, Jr. *Discrete Optimization*. Englewood Cliffs, N.J.: Prentice-Hall, Inc., 1971.

Taha, Hamdy A. *Integer Programming: Theory, Applications, and Computations*. New York: Academic Press, 1975.

Wagner, Harvey M. *Principles of Operations Research*. 2d ed. Englewood Cliffs, N.J.: Prentice-Hall, Inc., 1975.

ADDITIONAL EXERCISES

32. *Disaster Airlift* The International Red Cross is preparing to send emergency supplies into a small Central American country which has incurred extensive damage from an earthquake. Red Cross executives have received initial reports of the extent of the damage and emergency needs, and they wish to assure that the first planeload of supplies will provide the maximum immediate benefit.

Major constraints pertain to the weight and volume restrictions of the plane. The plane which will be used has a weight capacity of 30,000 pounds and a volume capacity of 6,000 cubic feet. Table 8–5 presents a listing of the emergency supplies being considered for shipment, the weight and volume of the shipping container for each item, the average number of people whose needs can be satisfied per container, and the relative value assigned to each item for this particular disaster. Although the criterion to be used in selecting items for shipment is difficult to quantify, the Red Cross uses an index of benefit computed by multiplying the number of persons served per container by the relative value assigned to each item. The index of benefit is shown as the last column in the table.

TABLE 8–5

Technological Data for Disaster Airlift

Item No.	Item	Weight per Container	Volume per Container	Persons Served	Relative Value	Index of Benefit
1	Blood	100 lb.	20 ft.³	150	5	750
2	Medical drugs	200 lb.	30 ft.³	2,500	3	7,500
3	Other medical supplies	150 lb.	50 ft.³	100	1	100
4	Food	50 lb.	8 ft.³	100	2	200
5	Water	75 lb.	6 ft.³	150	4	600

One can see that the use of this criterion could lead to an allocation which excludes items of high priority. Other constraints must be specified in order to assure that items of high priority are shipped in adequate quantity. For example, at least 40 containers of blood, 10 containers of medical drugs, and 100 containers of water must be shipped on this first plane.

a. Defining x_j as the number of containers shipped of item j, formulate this as an integer programming problem.

**b.* Find the optimal solution.

33. *Court Scheduling*   A court clerk wants to schedule the two district courts within a city. Depending upon the hours of operation and number of judges available, each court is characterized by an estimated number of judge-hours. Three categories of hearings may be scheduled into each court. The clerk has estimates of the number of judge-hours required to process a hearing, which varies depending on the court.

During the coming month there will be 800 and 1,000 judge-hours available in courts 1 and 2, respectively. The clerk wishes to determine the number of hearings of each type to schedule for each court. In doing so, at least 25 type-1, 70 type-2, and 30 type-3 hearings are scheduled. Because of the usual backlog of type-1 hearings, the number scheduled of types 2 and 3 should not constitute more than 75 percent of the total hearings scheduled for the month.

The estimated judge-hours per court per type of hearing are given below.

	Hearing Type		
	1	2	3
1..................	20	2	12
2..................	18	3	13

a. If x_{ij} is defined as the number of hearings of type i scheduled in court j, formulate the integer programming problem which will allow for scheduling the greatest number of hearings during the coming month.

**b.* Find the optimal solution.

34. *Capital Expansion*   Mac, Don, and Al's, a well-established hamburger chain, is planning for an expansion. They wish to open a chain of large steak-houses over the next five years. Ten potential cities have been explored; construction costs as well as annual (before tax) profit figures have been estimated for each site.

Cities	Construction Cost	Estimated Annual Profit
Northeast		
Boston......................	$250,000	$75,000
New York....................	300,000	90,000
Baltimore...................	225,000	60,000
South		
Atlanta.....................	200,000	55,000
New Orleans.................	275,000	80,000
West		
Los Angeles.................	250,000	85,000
San Francisco...............	260,000	50,000
Midwest		
St. Louis...................	175,000	45,000
Chicago.....................	200,000	55,000
Cincinnati..................	180,000	40,000

Mac, Don, and Al have appropriated $1.8 million for construction in this first phase of expansion. They have also specified some restrictions in allocating the funds. At least one steak-house *must* be built in each the South and the West. At least two must be built in the East. In the Midwest, there is concern for equal treatment. Consequently, steak-houses should be built in all three of the cities or in none of them.

   a. If the objective is to maximize total annual profit, formulate the 0–1 problem which would allow for an optimal selection of sites for expansion.

***b.* Find the optimal solution.

35. *Aircraft Purchase* Trans Oriental Pacific (TOP) Airlines is considering a capital expansion. Their objective is to purchase new aircraft for their Pacific runs. TOP is considering the purchase of Boeing 747s, DC-10s, and Lockheed 1011s. The budget for new purchases is $100 million. Boeing 747s cost $5 million, DC-10s cost $4 million, and Lockheed 1011's cost $3.8 million. On the average, each type of plane is expected to generate annual after-tax profits of $200,000, $175,000, and $185,000, respectively. Projected demands for air service require the purchase of at least two Boeing 747s and either three or more Lockheed 1011s or four or more DC-10s. TOP has also allocated $5 million per year for additional personnel hirings to support the operation of the new aircraft. Each 747 requires $180,000, each DC-10 $140,000, and each Lockheed 1011 $160,000 in new hirings.

    Currently, available maintenance facilities allow 600 days of maintenance per year for the new purchases. Each 747 requires 40 days of annual maintenance, each DC-10 requires 35 days, and each 1011 requires 45 days. It is possible, however, to increase the available annual maintenance to 1,000 days. To accomplish this the maintenance facilities would have to be expanded at a capital cost of $3 million, which would come out of the budget for new purchases.

   a. Explicitly define your decision variables and formulate this model.

***b.* Find the optimal solution.

36. A firm is considering investing in a number of projects. Let $x_j = 1$ if the firm invests in project j and $x_j = 0$ if it does not. Write the constraints which would assure that:

   a. For six possible projects, not less than three should be invested in.
   b. Projects 3, 4, and 5 are mutually exclusive.
   c. Project 4 cannot be invested in unless project 2 is.
   d. Projects 1, 2, and 6 are dependent upon each other. Either all three are invested in or none is.
   e. Project 5 can be invested in only if projects 3 and 4 have been allocated funds.

37. *Solid Waste Disposal Revisited* Reread Exercise 56 at the end of Chapter 7. Overcome by smoke and public outcry, the city council has proposed the development of two new landfill areas. Four sites are being considered for purchase by the city; only two will be purchased. Based upon a projected ten-year period of use for each landfill area selected, monthly capacities have been estimated (in tons). As in Chapter 7, variable costs include both transportation and operating costs at the sites. The city comptroller has provided a monthly amortization estimate (based

upon anticipated purchase price) for each proposed site. The estimated transportation costs and other data are summarized in the accompanying table.

Landfill Site	Collection Area						Capacity per Month (Tons)	Operating Cost per Ton	Amortized Cost per Month
	1	2	3	4	5	6			
1........	$70	$60	$65	$50	$40	$55	7,000	$40	$5,000
2........	80	55	40	75	60	50	5,000	50	4,000
3........	50	60	45	70	50	40	4,500	55	3,500
4........	40	70	55	60	55	30	6,000	45	4,500
Estimated tons per month.....	500	750	1,500	1,000	1,800	1,200			

The objective is to determine the two sites to purchase and the number of tons to be transported from each collection area to each site so as to minimize the sum of monthly amortization, transportation, and operating costs.

a. Formulate this problem as a mixed integer programming problem.
**b.* Find the optimal solution.

38. *Job Retraining Model* A certain branch of the Armed Services has instituted a plan whereby a recruit must work at three different jobs during a two-year "hitch," where each job is to last eight months. Whenever a recruit changes from one job to another, a certain number of days is involved in retraining for the new job. In general, this retraining time is a function of the immediately preceding job. The table indicates estimated retraining times (days) in shifting from one job to another. The

From Job	To Job			
	Civilian	A	B	C
Civilian...............	—	20	10	5
A.................	0	—	8	1
B.................	0	15	—	4
C.................	0	17	6	—

"brass" wants to know the job sequence which minimizes retraining time.

a. Solve this problem by enumeration.
b. Formulate this problem as a 0–1 programming model. What general class of problems does this model fall under?

39. *"Super Sunday"* Super Sunday, the once-a-year TV extravaganza focused upon the activities of the NFL Super Bowl, has almost become a tradition. CBS has received the TV contract for this year's family festivities. Producers have identified 12 potential camera locations within the stadium. They have also identified 25 stadium areas which may require camera coverage during the pregame, game, and postgame activities. The accompanying table indicates each camera location and the stadium areas which the camera can cover.

Camera Location	Stadium Areas
1	1,3,4,6,7
2	4,7,8,12
3	2,5,9,11,13
4	1,2,18,19,21
5	3,6,10,12,14
6	8,14,15,16,17
7	18,21,24,25
8	2,10,16,23
9	1,6,11
10	20,22,24,25
11	2,4,6,8
12	1,6,12,17

CBS executives are concerned about costs for the production. Consequently, they have set an objective of minimizing the number of camera locations. In seeking this objective they want at least one camera to be available to cover each stadium area. Camera location 9 is the "blimp," and executives have decided that the blimp *will* be used because of viewer expectation and fascination with the shots from this location. Stadium areas 1 and 2 are locker room locations. The viewer interest in football personalities has led the executives to request that at least two camera locations be available to cover each of these areas.

a. Formulate the 0–1 programming problem which will allow for determining the minimum number of cameras needed for coverage.

b. In which locations are cameras required? Why? Which constraints does this eliminate in the formulation?

**c.* Find the optimal solution.

**40. *Travel Budget Allocation* The dean of the College of Business Administration at a university in the northeast is seeking assistance in allocating the travel budget for the coming academic year. A total of n requests have been received from faculty members who wish to travel for professionally related reasons. Most requests are for travel to professional meetings for the purpose of presenting research papers, chairing a session, participating as a discussant, recruiting, or simply attending for the purpose of professional development. Other reasons for travel include attendance of special seminars, and so forth. The dean has developed a set of weighted priorities for travel requests which accounts for an assessment of the professional development associated with the activity and the recognition and peripheral benefits which might be derived from the activity by the university and the college.

There are not sufficient funds for all n requests. And there are other constraints which must be satisfied in allocating the total budget. For instance, the dean has decided upon certain minimum and maximum dollar allocations of the budget to each department based upon the number of faculty members in each department. Thus, the total travel expense for each department is not to exceed the amount allocated to the department. Each department decides if there is a maximum number of trips any member can make. In addition each department can specify maximum dollar expenditures for each faculty member.

Assume that the dean wishes to maximize the cumulative benefit (cumulative priority) from allocating the budget.

a. Formulate the general form of this model as 0–1 problem if:

x_{ijk} = 0–1 variable associated with granting the ith travel request of faculty member j in department k.

p_{ijk} = Priority assigned to the ith request of faculty member j in department k.

c_{ijk} = Estimated cost associated with the corresponding request.

n_k = Number of faculty members in department k.

l_k = Minimum travel budget allocated to department k.

m_k = Maximum travel budget allocated to department k.

b = Total budget for college.

t_k = Maximum number of trips for any member of department k.

d_k = Maximum dollar expenditure by any member of department k.

r_{jk} = Number of requests by member j of department k.

s = Number of departments.

b. How would the problem change if the objective was to maximize overall faculty activity (or total number of trips)?

41. *Telephone Operator Scheduling* The New England Telephone Company is preparing for the influx of summer residents into a local resort and it wishes to determine the number of summer employees who should be hired to handle the added switchboard volume. Analysts have projected the number of operators needed during hourly intervals of each day. These are listed here.

Period	Time	Operators Needed
1.........	7 A.M. – 8 A.M.	5
2.........	8 A.M. – 9 A.M.	8
3.........	9 A.M. –10 A.M.	8
4.........	10 A.M. –11 A.M.	10
5.........	11 A.M. –12 noon	12
6.........	12 noon – 1 P.M.	16
7.........	1 P.M. – 2 P.M.	16
8.........	2 P.M. – 3 P.M.	14
9.........	3 P.M. – 4 P.M.	14
10.........	4 P.M. – 5 P.M.	15
11.........	5 P.M. – 6 P.M.	11
12.........	6 P.M. – 7 P.M.	13
13.........	7 P.M. – 8 P.M.	12
14.........	8 P.M. – 9 P.M.	14
15.........	9 P.M. –10 P.M.	13
16.........	10 P.M. –11 P.M.	12
17.........	11 P.M. –12 midnight	10
18.........	12 midnight–1 A.M.	8
19.........	1 A.M. – 2 A.M.	6

There is no need to be concerned with the 2 A.M.–7 A.M. period because of a permanent night staff which works between 11 P.M. and 7 A.M. The figures in the previous table reflect the additional operators needed for the 7 A.M.– 2 A.M. period.

There are 14 shifts which can be used to meet the summer demand. These shifts have been established by the company through the years. The shifts are listed here. The company has considerable flexibility with its scheduling. Summer help, mainly college students, can be called on an hour's notice to report to work. Thus, split shifts (such as shift 3) are sometimes used.

Shift	Time Period
1..............	10 A.M. –6 P.M.
2..............	7 A.M. –3:30 P.M.
3..............	10 A.M. –1 P.M. *and* 4 P.M.–8 P.M.
4..............	10 A.M. –1 P.M. *and* 6 P.M.–10 P.M.
5..............	9:30 A.M.–5:30 P.M.
6..............	11 A.M. –7 P.M.
7..............	12 noon –8 P.M.
8..............	1 P.M. –9 P.M.
9..............	4 P.M. –10 P.M.
10..............	5 P.M. –11 P.M.
11..............	6 P.M. –12 midnight
12..............	7 P.M. – 1 A.M.
13..............	8 P.M. –2 A.M.
14..............	8 A.M. –11 A.M. *and* 5 P.M.–9 P.M.

The company wishes to determine how many operators should be hired for each shift so as to satisfy the demands during the summer. The objective is to minimize the total number of operators used during the periods of concern. (Assume that operations beginning a shift on a half hour are not available to cover the full one hour period.)

    a. Formulate this as an integer programming problem.

**b. Find the optimal solution.

42. *Diet Model Revisited* With respect to the diet problem presented as Exercise 55 on page 139:

    a. Modify the formulation such that the meal includes at least 100 grams of *one* of the meat items and can exceed 250 grams for only one dairy product.

**b. Find the optimal solution.

**43. If an efficient integer programming computerized package is available to you, solve the following problems:

    a. Example 8.6.
    b. Exercise 8.
    c. Exercise 14.
    d. Exercise 19.
    e. Exercise 56*e* in Chapter 7, page 273.

**44. If you have access to an LP computer package, simulate the branch-and-bound procedure by solving the following pure integer programming problem.

Maximize

$$z = 4.5x_1 + 3x_2 + 5x_3$$

subject to

$$
\begin{aligned}
x_1 + x_2 + x_3 &\geq 10 \\
3x_1 + 2x_2 \quad\quad &\leq 35 \\
2x_1 \quad\quad + 3x_3 &\leq 28
\end{aligned}
$$

$$x_1, x_2, x_3 = \text{nonnegative integers.}$$

Construct a figure of the type illustrated in Figure 8–6.

**45. If you have access to an LP computer package, simulate the branch-and-bound procedure by solving the following mixed integer programming problem.

Minimize

$$z = 10x_1 + 12x_2 + 9x_3 + 6x_4$$

subject to

$$
\begin{aligned}
x_1 + 4x_2 \quad\quad - x_4 &\geq 16 \\
x_1 + x_2 + x_3 \quad\quad &\geq 20 \\
2x_1 \quad\quad + 3x_3 + x_4 &\geq 36
\end{aligned}
$$

$$
\begin{aligned}
x_1, x_2, x_3 &= \text{nonnegative integers} \\
x_4 &\geq 0.
\end{aligned}
$$

Construct a figure of the type illustrated in Figure 8–6.

**46. For the following 0–1 programming problem:

Minimize

$$z = 4x_1 + 3x_2 + 5x_3 + 4x_4$$

subject to

$$
\begin{aligned}
x_1 + x_2 + x_3 + x_4 &\geq 2 \\
x_1 - x_2 \quad\quad + 2x_4 &\geq 1 \\
x_2 + x_3 - 2x_4 &\geq -1
\end{aligned}
$$

$$x_1, x_2, x_3, x_4 = 0, 1.$$

a. Completely enumerate all solutions (feasible and infeasible).
b. Solve this problem by implicit enumeration.

9

Dynamic Programming

DYNAMIC PROGRAMMING is a recursive approach to optimization problems which has found wide and increasing applicability. By a **recursive optimization procedure** we mean one which *optimizes on a step-by-step basis utilizing information from the preceding steps.* In short, we "optimize as we go." Recall that in the mathematical programming algorithms, optimization also was achieved on a step-by-step basis, but it was iterative rather than recursive; that is, each step represented a unique solution which was nonoptimal. In dynamic programming, a single step is sequentially related to the preceding steps, is not in itself a solution to the problem, but does contain information which identifies a segment of the optimal solution.

Because of these features, dynamic programming is most often applied to problems requiring a sequence of interrelated decisions. Many time-dependent (dynamic) processes are characterized by sequential decision problems which need to be solved; hence the term **dynamic programming.** Other applications which are particularly well-suited to dynamic programming involve interrelationships rather than time-dependencies per se, although time dependencies are a common basis for expressing interrelationships among variables. A more apt term for dynamic programming, therefore, might be *recursive optimization.*

As you proceed in the chapter, we believe that you will be struck by the simplicity and elegance of this procedure. The actual formulation and implementation of such problems, however, are difficult and often "slippery," primarily because the approach uses principles rather than an algorithm. We begin by orienting you to some basic concepts and terminology utilizing a simple example and follow with computational procedures applied to the simple example and other realistic problems; presentations and model formulations for additional scenarios; and an assessment of the contributions, potentialities, and shortcomings of recursive optimization.

9.1 FUNDAMENTALS

We begin by defining terminology and stating principles which are fundamental to dynamic programming, all of which are then illustrated using two computational procedures, forward and backward.

Terminology and Principles

The fundamental approach of dynamic programming involves (1) the breaking down of a multistage problem into its subparts, steps, or *single* **stages,** a process called **decomposition;** (2) making decisions one at a time, or recursively, at *each stage,* according to a specific optimization objective; and (3) combining the results at each stage to solve the entire problem, a process called **composition.** The act of composition results in a set of sequential decision rules called a **policy.** For example, dynamic programming would optimize an *n*-variable problem by decomposing it into a series of *n* stages (each variable a stage), assigning an optimal value to each variable, and combining the results from each stage to generate the overall solution to the problem.

At each stage, the decision rule is determined by a criterion or objective function, called the **recursive equation,** which utilizes Bellman's famous **principle of optimality:**

> An optimal set of decision rules has the property that, regardless of the *i*th decision, remaining decisions must be optimal with respect to the outcome which results from the *i*th decision.

Note that, if this were not so, the entire policy could not possibly be optimal. Think it over! The movement from one stage to another, or the decision made in any one stage, affects the **state** (a specified measurable condition) of the system which, most often, is determined by mathematical equations termed **transformation functions.** For example, the recursive equation for an *n*-variable optimization problem is based, at each stage, on the objective function contribution of the stage variable plus the optimal contributions of all preceding variables; the state of the system preceding and following any given stage is based on the slacks and surpluses associated with constraints; and the transformation functions are determined from the constraints themselves.

Basically, that is all there is to it. We now present a simple example to illustrate the implementation of these concepts and, we hope, their subsequent clarification.

Computational Procedures

Two basic computational approaches have been developed. The **forward computational procedure,** or **forward recursion,** is illustrated first using the classical shortest route problem. Subsequent examples will further reinforce forward recursions. In Section 9.5 some of the same problems will be solved using the **backward computational procedure,** or **backward recursion.**

Example 9.1 Shortest Route Problem

Figure 9–1 illustrates a **network** which represents the "stagecoach" version of the shortest route problem. The objective is to determine the path from the origin (I) to the destination (VIII) which minimizes the sum of the numbers along the **directed arcs** of the path. A directed arc is a line segment with an arrow to show the direction of travel between two **nodes.** Nodes are identified by Roman numerals and are used to represent the beginning and ending of directed arcs. Typically, the number associated with each arc represents the distance, time, or cost of "traveling" along that particular segment of the "journey." The terms "traveling" and "journey" are used loosely because many important applications and variations of the shortest route model are unrelated to travel, for example, project scheduling and equipment replacement decisions.

Simple observation and counting indicates the existence of five distinct paths through the network, the optimal path given by I–II–VI–VIII with a total

FIGURE 9–1

Shortest Route Problem: Forward Recursion

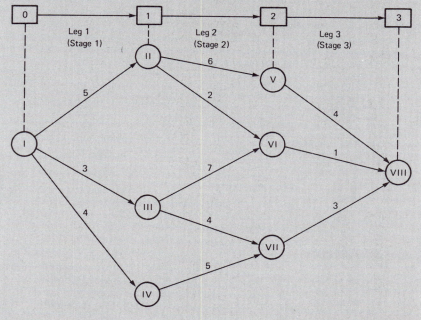

"distance" of 8. In typical applications, the number of paths is too great to solve by enumeration; hence, there is a real need for procedures which efficiently solve this type of problem. Dynamic programming is one such procedure, although other more efficient procedures exist for this particular type of problem.

Dynamic programming decomposes this problem into three stages, one for each leg of the journey. Note that nodes are useful in identifying where one is located prior to or following the completion of a leg of the journey. For example, if path III–VI is followed, the location prior to leg 2 is node III and the location at the completion of this leg is node VI. Node VI in this instance would be the location prior to the beginning of leg 3. Thus, the end point for one leg corresponds to the starting point for the next leg of the journey.

Given where one is located following any leg of the trip, it is simple to illustrate how a decision is made utilizing a recursive equation in the context of Bellman's principle of optimality. Consider the third leg of the trip and the only end point for this portion of the trip (node VIII). The decision to be made at this stage is "from which immediately preceding node shall we travel?" Traveling from nodes V, VI, or VII increases our travel distance by 4, 1, and 3, respectively. For our decision at this point in the journey, we must add each of these distances to its respective *optimal policy* (route) through leg 2. Thus, the shortest path through the first two legs which ends at node V has a length of 11 (or 5 + 6). If node V is chosen as the starting point for leg 3, the minimum total distance for the entire trip is 15 (or 4 + 11). Likewise, the shortest path through the first two legs which ends at node VI has a length of 7 (5 + 2 is less than 3 + 7). If node VI is chosen as the starting point for leg 3, the minimum total distance for the trip is 8 (1 + 7). Verify for yourself that if node VII is the starting point, the minimum total distance is 10 (3 + 7). It follows that the optimal policy for "this leg" is to travel from node VI to node VIII, and the optimal distance is 8.

Note that we adhered to the *principle of optimality* in that best decisions were identified regardless of the route chosen for leg 2 of the journey. Furthermore, the basic criterion for the decision was based on the following *additive recursive equation:*

Cumulative distance through leg 3 = Distance for leg 3 + best cumulative distance through leg 2.

By sequentially applying the principle of optimality beginning with the first leg and ending with leg 3, overall minimization of travel distance can be achieved. The calculations for each leg are shown in the accompanying illustration of Stages 1 through 3.

Carefully relate the headings for each table to Figure 9–1. The rows in each table correspond to the end points for that leg of the trip (verify this for each table by checking against Figure 9–1). The columns correspond to the decision alternatives for that leg. In our example, given an end point for a leg of the journey, we must decide the best (optimal) node from which to begin the leg. This decision, as already illustrated, is based on the recursive equation.

For the first leg, nodes II, III, and IV are the possible end points and node I is the only available starting point; hence, there is only one column of recursive-equation calculations for this stage, and whatever the results, the best decision for each row will be "start leg 1 at node I." Note that the

Stage (Leg) 1: Cumulative distance through stage 1
= Distance for stage 1 + Optimal cumulative distance
through stage 0.

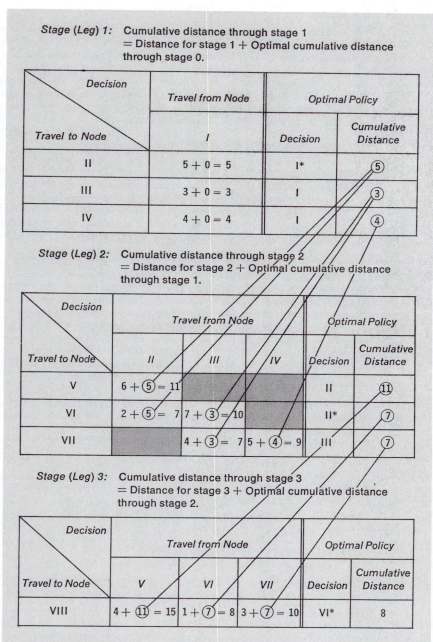

Decision / Travel to Node	Travel from Node	Optimal Policy	
	I	Decision	Cumulative Distance
II	$5 + 0 = 5$	I*	⑤
III	$3 + 0 = 3$	I	③
IV	$4 + 0 = 4$	I	④

Stage (Leg) 2: Cumulative distance through stage 2
= Distance for stage 2 + Optimal cumulative distance
through stage 1.

Decision / Travel to Node	Travel from Node			Optimal Policy	
	II	III	IV	Decision	Cumulative Distance
V	$6 + ⑤ = 11$			II	⑪
VI	$2 + ⑤ = 7$	$7 + ③ = 10$		II*	⑦
VII		$4 + ③ = 7$	$5 + ④ = 9$	III	⑦

Stage (Leg) 3: Cumulative distance through stage 3
= Distance for stage 3 + Optimal cumulative distance
through stage 2.

Decision / Travel to Node	Travel from Node			Optimal Policy	
	V	VI	VII	Decision	Cumulative Distance
VIII	$4 + ⑪ = 15$	$1 + ⑦ = 8$	$3 + ⑦ = 10$	VI*	8

optimal cumulative distance through the preceding stage (leg 0) is zero for the decision alternative which ends at node I.

Consider the second row in the table for leg 2. If node VI is the end point and we decide to reach it by traveling from node II, the distance traveled over leg 2 will be 2 (according to Figure 9–1). To this distance we must add the minimum cumulative distance for leg 1 when node II is the end point for that leg of the trip. This is found under the optimal cumulative distance column in the row corresponding to node II in the *preceding table* (for leg 1). Given this decision, the total distance traveled *through* leg 2 would equal (2 + 5), or 7, as given by the recursive equation. Similarly, if we decide to start leg 2 at node III and complete it at node VI, the respective figures are (7 + 3 = 10). Since travel from IV to VI is not possible, the corresponding cell is not filled. Examining the row corresponding to node VI, we see that the optimal decision for an arrival at node VI is "travel from node II" (that is, 7 is less than 10 and we are minimizing). The remaining calculations are determined in a similar manner.

The optimal policy for leg 3 of the trip is "travel from VI to VIII." This being the last leg of the trip, the associated cumulative distance of 8 represents the shortest distance for the entire journey. *We now work backward through the tables to define the shortest route.* Having identified node VI as an optimal point on the shortest route (in the table for leg 3), we turn to the table for leg 2 and find that node II is the optimal starting point corresponding to VI as the ending node for leg 2. Given that travel from II to VI is optimal for leg 2, we identify node I as the best decision for the row corresponding to node II in the table for leg 1. This gives I–II–VI–VIII as the shortest path. For convenience, points along the optimal path are identified by (∗). *Note once again that by applying the principle of optimality at each successive leg of the journey, the optimal solution for the entire network emerges.*

Now, carefully "store" the following. In the terminology of dynamic programming, each leg represents a *stage*. For each stage there will be a corresponding computational table. The decision made in any one stage affects the *state* (condition) of the system. The condition of the system for the stagecoach problem is defined in terms of one's location in the network.[1] Since nodes define locations, it follows that nodes represent states in this example. An *entering state* and a *leaving state* are always associated with each stage. In this chapter, the rows for a specific table will always represent alternative *leaving states* for that stage.

Follow-up Exercises

1. Verify the remaining entries in each table.
2. Change the distance of arc II–VI to 5 and completely solve for the shortest route using dynamic programming.
3. By dynamic programming, determine the *longest route* in Figure 9–1.

---

[1] As you might recall, this version of the shortest route problem was called the stagecoach version. It gets its name from the fact that we have arbitrarily designated legs along a journey which can be traveled by a *stage*coach (hence, the equivalence of legs and stages). Furthermore, beginning and ending points for each stage (the nodes) can be represented by the locations (states in the United States) on a map. For general dynamic programming solutions to shortest and longest route problems, see Exercises 43 and 44, pages 349 and 350.

9.2 STRUCTURE OF DYNAMIC PROGRAMMING

In this section, we present a system of notation for dynamic programming which allows us to clearly and uniquely specify the structure of dynamic programming. If you have been diligent (by solving the follow-up exercises and understanding what you did), you should be in an excellent frame of mind to understand the present section; otherwise, study the previous material once again.

System of Notation

Although the implementation of dynamic programming is conceptually simple, the system of notation which is necessary for the formulation of such models can be tough going; however, as you know by now, without the precision of mathematical notation, it is extremely cumbersome to formulate and solve complex mathematical problems.

FIGURE 9–2

Decomposed System

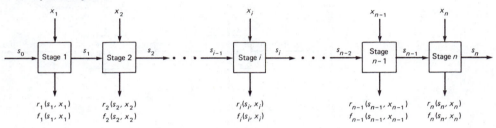

The following symbols are defined:

$$i = \text{Stage number.}$$
$$n = \text{Number of stages.}$$
$$x_i = \text{Decision variable in Stage } i.$$
$$s_i (s_{i-1}, x_i) = \text{State of the system } following \text{ Stage } i.[2]$$
$$r_i(s_i, x_i) = \text{Return or result associated with a particular state-decision}$$
$$\text{combination } (s_i, x_i) \text{ in Stage } i.$$
$$f_i(s_i, x_i) = \text{Value of criterion as given by recursive equation for a particular state-decision combination } (s_i, x_i) \text{ in Stage } i.$$
$$f_i^*(s_i) = \text{Optimal value of criterion as given by recursive equation for a particular state } (s_i) \text{ in Stage } i.$$

The decomposition of a problem according to a dynamic programming format is illustrated in Figure 9–2. In the shortest route problem, we stated that the stages correspond to the legs of the trip. Prior to Stage 1 the system is in its initial state (s_0). In the shortest route problem, the state of the system corresponds to one's location; hence, the initial state (s_0) is being located at node I. A starting value, $f_0\ (s_0, x_0)$, for the recur-

[2] In this notation, the parenthetic expression represents an *argument*. Thus, the value of s_i is a function of the values of s_{i-1} and x_i.

sive function must be specified also. The criterion in the shortest route problem is "distance traveled" and the starting value for this criterion is zero (no distance covered yet). A decision in Stage 1 (x_1) transforms the system into a different state (s_1) and yields a value for the criterion given by $f_1(s_1, x_1)$. In the forward recursion of the shortest route problem the decision in Stage 1 was to move to node II from node I, yielding a value for the distance criterion of 5 units traveled. The procedure continues in this manner sequentially until the last stage, Stage n, is completed. Figure 9–3 summarizes the optimal decomposition of the shortest route problem by the forward recursive approach.

To simplify the notation somewhat, the arguments associated with states, returns, and the criterion will be dropped; that is, the forms s_i, r_i, f_i, and f_i^* will be used instead of those depicted above. Keep in mind, however, that the state of the system following a stage (s_i) is a function of the state preceding the stage (s_{i-1}) and of the decision made in that

FIGURE 9–3

Decomposition of Shortest Route Problem (Forward Recursion)

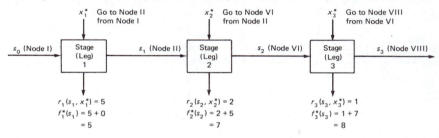

stage (x_i). Likewise, the return and recursive equation in any given stage are functions of the state-decision combinations (rows and columns in our computational examples). Finally, the optimal value for the criterion, f_i^*, in Stage i, is a function of the leaving state for that stage (s_i).

Recursive Equations and Transformation Functions

For any specific leaving state-decision combination in any stage (Stage i), the value for the criterion is given by the general **recursive equation**

$$f_i = G(r_i, f_{i-1}^*) \qquad (9.1)$$

where G represents some functional form. Carefully note that the optimal value of the criterion in the preceding stage is itself a function of *its* leaving state; that is, f_{i-1}^* is really $f_{i-1}^*(s_{i-1})$. In general, the optimal value of the criterion in Stage i is defined by selecting the permissible value of x_i which optimizes f_i:

$$f_i^* = \text{optimal } [f_i]. \qquad (9.2)$$
$$\text{all } x_i$$

By "all x_i" we mean the set of values for x_i which is allowed by constraints, bounds, or other conditions (for example, integer restrictions).

Alternatively, by combining Equations (9.1) and (9.2) we have the **optimal recursive equation:**

$$f_i^* = \underset{\text{all } x_i}{\text{optimal}} \, [G(r_i, f_{i-1}^*)]. \tag{9.3}$$

In Example 9.1 the recursive Equations (9.1) and (9.3) were *additive,* or

$$f_i = r_i + f_{i-1}^* \tag{9.4}$$

and

$$f_i^* = \underset{\text{all } x_i}{\text{min}} \, [r_i + f_{i-1}^*]. \tag{9.5}$$

The optimal recursive equation given by Equation (9.5) is the most commonly presented recursive equation in dynamic programming.[3] In Example 9.5, a multiplicative recursion will be illustrated.

With reference to the computational tables of the shortest route problem, in Stage i we represented the state of the system (s_i) by the location of a node (a row in the table), a decision (x_i) by the location of a node from which one was to travel (a column in the table), a return (r_i) by the "distance" between those two nodes, a criterion value (f_i) by the sum of r_i and the optimal cumulative distance through the preceding stage (f_{i-1}^*), and the optimal criterion value (f_i^*) by the best cumulative distance through the stage (as determined by the lowest number in each row of the table and entered in the last column). Each f_i was entered in its appropriate cell in the table (the cell corresponding to the intersection of the selected s_i, x_i). For example, in the table for Stage 2 of Example 9.1, when $s_2 = \text{VI}$ and $x_2 = \text{III}$, it follows that $r_2 = 7$, $f_1^* = 3$, $f_2 = 10$, and $f_2^* = 7$. In the table for Stage 3 with $s_3 = \text{VIII}$ and $x_3 = \text{V}$, then $r_3 = 4$, $f_2^* = 11$, $f_3 = 15$, and $f_3^* = 8$.

In general, the transformation of a state through a stage, which we term **stage transformation,** can be depicted by

$$s_{i-1} = T(s_i, x_i) \tag{9.6}$$

where T is a functional form for the transformation called the **transformation function.** In Example 9.1 stage transformations were achieved by visual inspection of the network rather than by equations of the type given by Equation (9.6). Now make note of the following:

1. That the solution process successively determines

    $$(\text{Set of } f_1^*) \rightarrow (\text{Set of } f_2^*) \rightarrow \cdots \rightarrow (\text{Set of } f_n^*).$$

2. That, given some ending state (s_n), its corresponding f_n represents the optimal value of the criterion for the entire system $(f_3^* = 8$ in Example 9.1).

3. That (given s_n) the optimal policy for the system is successively determined by finding

    $$x_n^* \rightarrow x_{n-1} \rightarrow \cdots \rightarrow x_1^*$$

---

[3] This form satisfies two necessary conditions for optimization termed separability and monotonicity; for example, see G. L. Nemhauser, *Introduction to Dynamic Programming* (New York: John Wiley & Sons, Inc., 1966); otherwise, the problem may not be decomposable.

through *backward stage transformations*.[4] Thus, in Example 9.1, the determination of

$$(\text{Set of } f_1^*) \longrightarrow (\text{Set of } f_2^*) \longrightarrow (\text{Set of } f_3^*)$$
$$(5,3,4) \longrightarrow (11,7,7) \longrightarrow (8)$$

allowed the identification of

$$x_3^* \longrightarrow x_2^* \longrightarrow x_1^*$$
$$\text{VI} \longrightarrow \text{II} \longrightarrow \text{I}.$$

Finally, we draw your attention to the significance of the wording for the scale at the top of Figure 9–1. The values along the scale are consciously varied to represent the subscript *i*. In a forward recursion, *i* represents the number of stages along the solution route (legs in our example) *already completed*.

9.3 MORE COMPUTATIONAL EXAMPLES

To further reinforce concepts and computational procedures, two more examples (with categorical or discrete x_i's and s_i's) will be formulated and solved. The first, a variation on the capital budgeting problem (see Examples 4.7 and 8.10) illustrates an allocation process with *alternative optimal solutions*. The second, an inventory problem, represents a variation on the transportation formulation of Example 7.4, illustrates the inclusion of *exogeneous variables* and an *infinite time horizon,* and treats a *nonlinear criterion. Sensitivity analysis* in dynamic programming is illustrated in both examples.

Example 9.2 Capital Budgeting Model

The comptroller of a company has $5 million for capital investment to allocate among three divisions. Each division was asked to submit new project proposals together with relevant cost and revenue data. Based on the proposals, the comptroller constructed Table 9–1 by discounting all future cash flows (costs and revenues) and expressing them in terms of net present values.[5] For example, Project *C* requires a present outlay of $2 million and yields a net (after subtracting the initial capital outlay and the discounted future costs) present value of $2 million. As can be seen, not every division proposed the same number of projects. Note that the first project for each division represents a decision not to select a project from that division. Furthermore, projects across divisions are independent. To avoid morale problems in the divisions, however, no more than one project can be selected from any one division. Alternatively, the projects for any one division can be treated as being mutually exclusive.

---

[4] For this reason, s_{i-1} rather than s_i is to the left of the equal sign in Equation (9.6).

[5] Discounting is both theoretically appropriate as a criterion and widely employed. If you're hazy or unaware of these concepts, you may want to read Example 2.17.

TABLE 9–1

Capital Investment Data (millions of dollars)

	Capital Outlay (c)	Net Present Value of Benefits (r)
Division 1		
Project A	0	0
Project B	1	2
Project C	2	2
Project D	3	2
Division 2		
Project E	0	0
Project F	3	3
Division 3		
Project G	0	0
Project H	1	1
Project I	2	3

The dynamic programming approach decomposes this problem into three stages ($n = 3$), one for each division. The decision variable in the ith stage (x_i) represents adoption of the particular project which is under consideration in Division i. The result associated with each stage (r_i) is defined in terms of the net present value for the project under consideration in that division. Working with a *forward recursion,* the state of the system and recursive function (criterion) are defined as follows:

s_i = *Cumulative* capital outlay available for allocation through Stage i (or for Divisions 1, 2, . . . , i);

f_i^* = *Cumulative* optimal net present value generated by Divisions 1, 2, . . . , i.

Assuming independence of projects across divisions, the recursive equation is additive and given by

$$f_i = r_i + f_{i-1}^*. \tag{9.7}$$

In words, total net present value after the selection of a project in Division i (f_i) equals the net present value for that project (r_i) plus the optimal total net present value through the preceding division (f_{i-1}^*).

The selection of a particular project (a decision) in Stage i uniquely transforms the state of the system according to

$$s_i = s_{i-1} + c_i$$

where c_i represents the capital outlay required by the selected project (based on the decision x_i) in Division i. In words, total capital outlay through Division i equals total capital outlay through Division $i - 1$ plus selected capital outlay in Division i. For consistency with Equation (9.6), the *transformation function* is expressed as

$$s_{i-1} = s_i - c_i. \tag{9.8}$$

The computational tables follow. Note that f_0^* is necessarily zero since there is no return prior to investment in the first project. More importantly, note that the structure of the tables is identical to those in Example 9.1; that is, *rows represent possible states leaving a stage and columns represent alternative decisions.*

Stage 1: $f_1 = r_1 + f_0^*$.

s_1 \ x_1	A	B	C	D	x_1^*	f_1^*
0	0 + 0 = 0				A* ₁	0
1	0 + 0 = 0	2 + 0 = 2			B*	2
2	0 + 0 = 0	2 + 0 = 2	2 + 0 = 2		B, C	2
3	0 + 0 = 0	2 + 0 = 2	2 + 0 = 2	2 + 0 = 2	B, C, D	2
4	0 + 0 = 0	2 + 0 = 2	2 + 0 = 2	2 + 0 = 2	B, C, D	2
5	0 + 0 = 0	2 + 0 = 2	2 + 0 = 2	2 + 0 = 2	B, C, D	2

Stage 2: $f_2 = r_2 + f_1^*$.

s_2 \ x_2	$\vec{E}$	F	x^*	f_2^*
0	0 + 0 = 0		E	0
1	0 + 2 = 2		E	2
2	0 + 2 = 2		E	2
3	0 + 2 = 2	3 + 0 = 3	F*	3
4	0 + 2 = 2	3 + 2 = 5	F*	5
5	0 + 2 = 2	3 + 2 = 5	F	5

Stage 3: $f_3 = r_3 + f_2^*$.

s_3 \ x_3	G	H	I	x_3^*	f^*
0	0 + 0 = 0			G	0
1	0 + 2 = 2	1 + 0 = 1		G	2
2	0 + 2 = 2	1 + 2 = 3	3 + 0 = 3	H, I	3
3	0 + 3 = 3	1 + 2 = 3	3 + 2 = 5	I	5
4	0 + 5 = 5	1 + 3 = 4	3 + 2 = 5	G, I	5
5	0 + 5 = 5	1 + 5 = 6	3 + 3 = 6	H, I*	6

Carefully note that the computation of any f_i requires a *stage transformation* using Equation (9.8) in order to determine f_{i-1}^*. For instance, consider the allocation of $4 million through Stage 3 (that is, $s_3 = 4$). The selection of Project I gives a return of 3 and requires an outlay of 2 (see Table 9–1); hence, according to Equation (9.8) $2 million are available ($s_2 = 4 - 2$) for allocation through Stage 2. If $2 million are available through Stage 2, then (looking at the table for Stage 2) the best policy through Stage 2 yields a total net present value of $2 million ($f_2^* = 2$). This gives, according to the recursive equation, an entry of $3 + 2$ in the ($s_3 = 4$, $x_3 = 1$) cell of the table for Stage 3. Further note that certain cell entries are *infeasible*. Can you explain why?

Since $5 million are available for allocation to all three divisions, a unique end state of $s_3 = 5$ is defined for the last table, with an associated overall optimal net present value of $6 million ($f_3^* = 6$ when $s_3 = 5$). Because the optimal policy allows the selection of Projects H or I in Division 3 it immediately becomes evident that alternative optimal policies (solutions) exist.

Figure 9–4 illustrates the backward stage transformations for determining the optimal policies. Thus, if Project H is selected, its capital outlay of $1 million ($c^* = 1$ from Table 9–1) reduces the available capital outlay to $4 million ($s_2 = 4$) for the two other divisions. The table for Stage 2 indicates that the optimal policy for $s_2 = 4$ is the selection of Project F. The outlay for this project is $3 million ($c_2 = 3$), which only leaves $1 million for Division 1 ($s_1 = 1$). According to the table for Stage 1, Project B should be selected if only $1 million is allocated to that division. Alternatively, the selection of Projects I, F, and A would yield the same optimal net present value of $6 million.

Do you realize that the state variable for this problem represents the *slack* in the budgeting constraint? For example, $s_2 = 4$ means that $4 million are available to the first two divisions after the allocation of $1 million for Division 3 has been made.

Note that it would not have been necessary to generate the first five rows of the third table ($s_3 = 0, \ldots, 4$) in that the terminal condition ($s_3 = 5$) was known beforehand. We included these rows in order to illustrate briefly *sensitivity analysis* in dynamic programming. For example, if only $4 million

FIGURE 9–4

Backward Stage Transformations for Determining Optimal Policies for Capital Budgeting Model

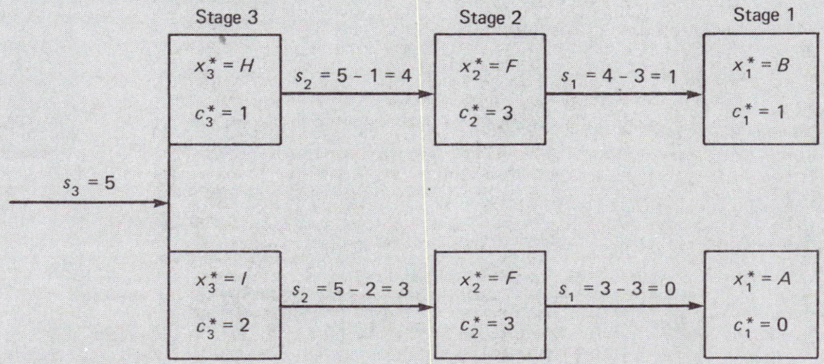

were available for capital outlays, the optimal net present value would be $5 million with the selection of Projects B, F, and G or Projects B, E, and I or Projects C, E, and I.

Follow-up Exercises

4. Draw a figure such as Figure 9–3 for this example.
5. What is the optimal policy and net present value if only $3 million are available for capital outlays? Based on this and the results when $4 million are available, can you make a recommendation?
6. Formulate this problem as an integer (0–1) programming model.
**7. Solve the model formulated in the preceding exercise using an algorithm from Chapter 8. Which approach (dynamic programming or integer programming) do you prefer and why?

Example 9.3　Production-Inventory Model

A manufacturing firm wishes to prepare a production-inventory schedule over n periods (quarters) for an expensive low-volume product which has been contracted. Due to time and labor constraints, the number of items produced during the tth period (x_t) cannot exceed a maximum capacity for that period (K_t). The demand in the tth period (d_t) can be met both by production in that period and by the *ending* inventory (s_{t-1}) from the previous period, although the latter cannot exceed the storage capacity (S). In other words, items can be produced in one period and carried over in inventory (at a cost) for consumption in a subsequent period. For simplicity we assume that the beginning inventory for the horizon, s_o, is zero and no ending inventory is desired $(s_n = 0)$. Furthermore, we assume that negative inventories (that is, backorders or lost sales) are not allowed. The cost per period of holding an item in inventory is given by h_t and the total cost of producing x_t items in period t is given by some production function $C_t(x_t)$.

An integer programming formulation for this problem is given by

minimize

$$z = \sum_{t=1}^{n} [C_t(x_t) + h_t \cdot s_t]$$

subject to

$$
\left.
\begin{aligned}
s_1 &= x_1 - d_1 \\
s_t &= s_{t-1} + x_t - d_t \qquad t = 2, 3, \ldots, n-1 \\
s_n &= 0
\end{aligned}
\right\} \tag{1}
$$

$$x_t \le K_t \qquad\qquad t = 1, \ldots, n \tag{2}$$

$$s_t \le S \qquad\qquad t = 1, \ldots, n \tag{3}$$

x_t, s_t nonnegative integers.

Ideally, the cost criterion is expressed in terms of present value. Constraint set (1) ensures the appropriate accounting identity among beginning inventory, ending inventory, production, and demand. (Can you verbalize these?)

Constraint sets (2) and (3) account for production and storage constraints. For notational convenience, s_t is treated as a decision variable along with x_t, although in reality it represents the surplus associated with constraints which meet demand. (Could you express this problem without the use of s_t?)

If the production and inventory costs were stationary (constant over time) and if $C_t(x_t)$ were linear, an integer programming algorithm (Chapter 8) could be used to solve this type of model. Suppose, however, that the total cost function for production ($\$1,000$) is estimated as

$$C_t(x_t) = \begin{cases} (12 + t) - 6x_t + x_t^2, & 0 < x_t \le 5 \\ 0, & x_t = 0 \end{cases} \quad t = 1, \ldots, n. \qquad (9.9)$$

Clearly, a linear formulation is inappropriate. Note that a setup cost is incurred which is a function of the period and that the function is U-shaped with a minimum total cost at three units. Dynamic programming, however, is uniquely suited to solve this type of *nonlinear optimization problem*.

Letting each time period represent a stage (that is, Quarter 1 is Stage 1, Quarter 2 is Stage 2, and so forth), we define the following symbols:

$x_i \equiv$ Number of units produced in Quarter i.
$s_i \equiv$ *Ending inventory* in Quarter i, or *leaving state* for stage i.
$r_i \equiv$ Production cost plus inventory holding cost in Quarter i.
$f_i^* \equiv$ Optimal cumulative cost through the first i quarters.

Since the ending inventory for a period must equal the beginning inventory for that period plus the amount produced in that period less the demand in that period (that is, $s_i = s_{i-1} + x_i - d_i$), it follows that the *transformation function* is given by

$$s_{i-1} = s_i - x_i + d_i. \qquad (9.10)$$

The "return" for Stage i is given by

$$r_i = \text{Production Cost} + \text{Inventory holding cost}$$
$$= C_i(x_i) + h_i \cdot s_i$$

where $C_i(x_i)$ is defined by Equation (9.9). Thus, for $x_i = 0$,

$$r_i = h_i \cdot s_i \qquad (9.11)$$

and, for $0 < x_i \le 5$,

$$r_i = 12 + i - 6x_i + x_i^2 + h_i \cdot s_i. \qquad (9.12)$$

Note that the holding cost of inventory for any period is based on the ending inventory for that period. Furthermore, note that states and stage returns are influenced by the *exogeneous variable* d_i; that is, demand represents an influence from outside the production-inventory system.

As in the preceding examples, the *optimal recursive equation* is additive:

$$f_i^* = \min_{x_i = 0, \ldots, K_i} [r_i + f_{i-1}^*]. \qquad (9.13)$$

Note that x_i is restricted to integer values between 0 and K_i inclusive.

Consider the data presented in Table 9–2 for a four-quarter model ($n = 4$) in which maximum production and inventory capacities are five and three, respectively (that is, $K_t = 5$ for all t and $S = 3$). For convenience, production costs have been tabulated in Table 9–2 according to Equation (9.9).

TABLE 9–2

Data for Example 9.3*

Period (t)	Stage (i)	Production Costs, $C_i(x_i)$ When x_i Equals						Holding Cost per Unit (h_i)	Demand (d_i)
		0	1	2	3	4	5		
1.......... 1		0	8	5	4	5	8	1	2
2.......... 2		0	9	6	5	6	9	1	2
3.......... 3		0	10	7	6	7	10	2	3
4.......... 4		0	11	8	7	8	11	2	3

* All costs in $1,000; all demands in units.

Utilizing Equation (9.11) or (9.12) to determine r_t (with the aid of Table 9–2) and Equation (9.10) to calculate the relevant s_{i-1} for determining f_{i-1}^* in the table for the preceding stage, you should be able to verify (after some tedium) the results below. (Can you verbalize the computations for any given cell in the context of this application?)

As usual, each column for a particular table represents a specific decision alternative for that stage and each row represents a possible leaving state for that stage. In this example, each row represents a possible ending inventory for that time period.

Note that infeasible cells are a direct result of the avoidance either of negative inventories $(s_{i-1} < 0)$ or of excessive storage $(s_{i-1} > 3)$. For example, the cell given by $s_2 = 1$ and $x_2 = 5$ in Stage 2 is infeasible because according to the transformation function, the ending inventory in Quarter 1 would be negative; that is, $s_1 = s_2 - x_2 + d_2 = 1 - 5 + 2 = -2$. Furthermore, you should confirm that the stipulation of a beginning inventory of zero for Period 1 (that is, $s_o = 0$) results in only four feasible cells for Stage 1.

Since the ending inventory for the planning horizon is to be zero, then $s_4 = 0$ and the overall minimum cost (from the table for Stage 4) is $20,000 for the year (that is, $f_4^* = 20$ is the cumulative cost for Periods 1 through 4). The optimal policy in Stage 4 (Period 4) indicates a production of 3 units. This means that, given the delivery of 3 units in this period $(d_4 = 3)$ and no ending inventory $(s_4 = 0)$, 0 units must be left in inventory at the end of the third period. In other words, according to Equation (9.10), $s_3 = 0 - 3 + 3 = 0$. Entering the table for Stage 3 at $s_3 = 0$, the optimal policy dictates the production of three units $(x_3^* = 3)$ in Period 3. Continuing in this manner, the entire optimal production schedule of 3, 3, 0, and 4 units for Periods 4, 3, 2, and 1, respectively, can be determined. Can you verify directly from the tables that ending inventories for Periods 1, 2, 3, and 4 are 2, 0, 0, and 0, respectively? (Look at the s_i's for the optimal rows.)

Since s_4 represents the ending inventory for the planning horizon, a sensitivity analysis based on ending inventory can be carried out easily. For instance, an ending inventory of 3 units for Period 4 would call for a production schedule of 4, 0, 4, and 5 units in Periods 1, 2, 3, and 4, respectively, with an optimal cost of $33,000.

Finally, the treatment of time periods as stages gives dynamic programming the powerful capability of both performing sensitivity analysis on the planning horizon (value of n) and treating *infinite time horizons*. The latter is possible (in a forward recursion) if the system achieves an "effective"

Stage 1: $f_1 = r_1 + f_0^* = C_1(x_1) + 1 \cdot s_1 + 0.$

s_1 \ x_1	0	1	2	3	4	5	x_1^*	f_1^*
0			$5+0+0=5$				2	5
1				$4+1+0=5$			3	5
2					$5+2+0=7$		4*	7
3						$8+3+0=11$	5	11

Stage 2: $f_2 = r_2 + f_1^* = C_2(x_2) + 1 \cdot s_2 + f_1^*.$

s_2 \ x_2	0	1	2	3	4	5	x_2^*	f_2^*
0	$0+0+7=7$	$9+0+5=14$	$6+0+5=11$				0*	7
1	$0+1+11=12$	$9+1+7=17$	$6+1+5=12$	$5+1+5=11$			3	11
2		$9+2+11=22$	$6+2+7=15$	$5+2+5=12$	$6+2+5=13$		3	12
3			$6+3+11=20$	$5+3+7=15$	$6+3+5=14$	$9+3+5=17$	4	14

Stage 3: $f_3 = r_3 + f_2^* = C_3(x_3) + 2 \cdot s_3 + f_2^*$.

s_3 \ x_3	0	1	2	3	4	5	x_3^*	f_3^*
0	0+0+14 = 14	10+0+12 = 22	7+0+11 = 18	6+0+7 = 13			3*	13
1		10+2+14 = 26	7+2+12 = 21	6+2+11 = 19	7+2+7 = 16		4	16
2			7+4+14 = 25	6+4+12 = 22	7+4+11 = 22	10+4+7 = 21	5	21
3				6+6+14 = 26	7+6+12 = 25	10+6+11 = 27	4	25

Stage 4: $f_4 = r_4 + f_3^* = C_4(x_4) + 2 \cdot s_4 + f_3^*$.

s_4 \ x_4	0	1	2	3	4	5	x_4^*	f_4^*
0	0+0+25 = 25	11+0+21 = 32	8+0+16 = 24	7+0+13 = 20			3*	20
1		11+2+25 = 38	8+2+21 = 31	7+2+16 = 25	8+2+13 = 23		4	23
2			8+4+25 = 37	7+4+21 = 32	8+4+16 = 28	11+4+13 = 28	4, 5	28
3				7+6+25 = 38	8+6+21 = 35	11+6+16 = 33	5	33

steady state (that is, the process essentially becomes time independent) beyond some finite horizon or if the objective function is bounded. For example, steady state for our inventory model essentially occurs at some finite horizon if all costs are discounted to time zero. The treatment of unbounded horizons is also possible either in the case of stationary cycles in the processes (for example, periodic quarterly demands such as 2, 2, 3, 3, 2, 2, 3, 3, . . .) or by the use of more advanced mathematical procedures.[6]

Follow-up Exercises

8. Draw a figure for this example such as Figure 9–3.

9. With respect to the computational tables:

   a. Why must $0 \le s_i \le 3$ and $0 \le x_i \le 5$ for each table? Do these *bounds* on s_i and x_i reflect constraints in the integer programming formulation?

   b. Confirm that an ending inventory of 3 units for the planning horizon results in an optimal production schedule of 4 units in Period 1; 0 units in Period 2; 4 units in Period 3; and 5 units in Period 4.

   c. Confirm that ending inventories for the schedule in Part (b) are 2, 0, and 1 units for Periods 1, 2, and 3, respectively, according to the following two methods. *Method 1:* Fill in the table below using simple algebra.

t	Beginning Inventory	Production	Demand	Ending Inventory
1.......				
2.......				
3.......				
4.......				

   Method 2: Look up s_i's in the computational tables for rows giving the optimal production schedule.

   d. From the table for Stage 4, $f_4^* = \$33,000$ when $s_4 = 3$. Confirm this figure by summing up production and inventory costs for the four periods.

10. From the table for Stage 3, $f_3^* = \$13,000$ for the optimal production policy. Confirm that this represents the sum of production and inventory costs for the first three periods.

11. Extend the forward recursion to five periods, given that demand is 5 units in Period 5 and holding cost is 2. Assess the change in the optimal production-inventory schedule.

12. Solve the production-inventory problem if the beginning inventory for Period 1 is 2 units.

**13. Formulate and solve a production-inventory dynamic programming model which allows shortages (that is, negative inventories). Use a

---

[6] As discussed in R. E. Bellman, *Dynamic Programming* (Princeton, N.J.: Princeton University Press, 1957) and Nemhauser, *Introduction to Dynamic Programming.*

shortage cost of 1 ($1,000) per item per period. Assume that items must be backordered; that is, the total order of ten items must be filled by the end of the four periods. Explicitly state the new recursive equation.

9.4 ADDITIONAL SCENARIOS AND FORMULATIONS

In this section we describe and formulate a police patrol application and a reliability problem which utilizes a multiplicative (rather than additive) recursive equation.

Example 9.4   Allocation of Police Patrol Teams

Efficient allocation of scarce resources is the name of the game in most enterprises. The public sector is no exception. Within the public sector the allocation of emergency response resources is an area of vital concern. Given limited personnel (police, fire fighters, ambulance drivers, and so forth) and support equipment (patrol cars, fire trucks, ambulances, or rescue trucks), how do you deploy these resources in order to achieve as close as possible the objectives of the emergency response function? Dynamic programming has been one means of providing answers to these types of allocation problems.

Larsen developed a dynamic programming model which has as its objective the optimal allocation of police patrol cars to geographic areas or beats.[7] The model allows police administrators to articulate specific policy objectives which can, in turn, be input directly into the model. These objectives represent multiple criteria which are considered by the model in its allocation of patrol cars. One criterion is chosen for optimization and the remaining criteria are satisfied through constraints. For example, given desired levels (hours) of preventive patrol during a tour of duty, desired frequencies of patrol of a beat, acceptable travel times to reported incidents, and/or minimum numbers of patrol units per geographic area, the model provides the police administrator with the necessary numbers of patrol units which meet all of these policy objectives.

A simplified illustration of the application of dynamic programming to police patrol allocations follows. You will be asked to formulate and solve this example in a follow-up exercise. Assume that a police administrator wishes to allocate *all* 12 patrol teams of two officers to four precincts. A departmental policy prescribes that at least one two-officer team must be assigned to each precinct, but no more than four teams to any one precinct. The primary objective in allocating the 12 teams is to minimize the expected number of serious crimes among the four precincts during an eight-hour

---

[7] Richard C. Larsen, *Models for the Allocation of Urban Police Patrol Forces*, Technical Report No. 44, M.I.T. Operations Research Center, Cambridge, Mass., 1969.

tour of duty. Statisticians within the department have estimated expected numbers of serious crimes for these four precincts as a function of the number of patrol teams assigned. These are presented in Table 9–3.

The optimal allocation of police officers can be determined by dynamic programming. The problem can be solved as a four-stage model in which each stage represents a precinct; the state variable represents the total number of two-officer teams available for allocation to i precincts; the decision variable is the number of teams allocated at each stage (precinct);

TABLE 9–3

Estimated Serious Crimes per Tour of Duty

Number of Two-Officer Teams	Precinct			
	1	2	3	4
1....................	20	40	8	36
2....................	18	38	4	34
3....................	16	36	2	32
4....................	12	30	1	25

and the return function represents the total expected number of serious crimes.

Follow-up Exercises

14. For a forward recursion:

    a. Carefully define x_i, r_i, s_i, and f_i.
    b. State the recursive equation for f_i and the optimal recursive equation for f_i^*.
    c. State the transformation function.
    d. Solve the problem.
    e. What does sensitivity analysis imply?

15. Formulate the police patrol problem as an integer program. (*Hint:* Define $x_{ij} = 1$ if i teams are assigned to precinct j; 0, otherwise.)

**16. Solve the preceding exercise (if you have an integer-programming package available). Compare results to the dynamic programming solution. In what respect does dynamic programming offer a clear advantage?

17. What is the optimal solution if the departmental policy requires *at least* two teams but no more than four per precinct?

18. Solve the last exercise if there are 14 teams available. Compare values of the objective function.

Example 9.5   Reliability Model

Since the inceptions of large-scale military and space programs and the concurrent growth of the electronics industry, reliability models have enjoyed a great deal of attention from mathematicians, engineers, and operations researchers. To capture the essence of these models, consider the problem of designing an electronic device with four components which are aligned in series. "In series" means that the components are arranged one after the other, as in the first column of Figure 9–5. Failure of any of the components means failure for the entire electronic device. The problem is to determine the number of parallel units for each component (that is, the number of units of a given type of component, which includes the working unit plus backup units of the same type) such that reliability is maximized subject to a cost constraint and a limit of 3 units per component. (See Figure 9–5). *Reliability* is defined as the probability that the device does not fail over a particular planning horizon.

FIGURE 9–5

Design for Electronic Device

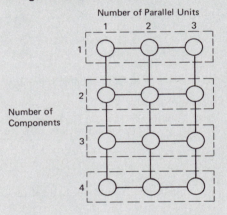

If, in our example, two units represent a particular component (that is, the original component plus a backup), then the failure of the first unit results in the second unit switching in automatically (we assume the switching process is completely reliable). It follows that by increasing the reliability of each component, the reliability of the device itself increases.

Suppose that the probabilities of *failure* for *each unit* of Components 1, 2, 3, and 4 are 0.2, 0.5, 0.4, and 0.3, respectively. Now consider a design which specifies two parallel units for the first component. In order for Component 1 to fail, each of its two parallel units must fail (we assume independence among parallel units). The probability of this occurrence, according to the elementary multiplication rule of probability, given by Equation (A.7) on page 706 is $(0.2) \cdot (0.2)$ or 0.04; hence, the reliability of the first component (r_1) when two parallel units are used is $(1.0 - 0.04)$ or 0.96. Table 9–4 provides cost (c_i) and reliability (r_i) calculations for each of the possible alternatives for each component (x_i).

To illustrate the calculation of reliability for the entire device, consider the decision of two units for Component 1 $(x_1 = 2)$, one unit for Component 2 $(x_2 = 1)$, and three units each for Components 3 and 4 $(x_3 = 3$ and $x_4 = 3)$.

TABLE 9–4

Reliability (r_i) and Cost (c_i) Data*

Component Number (i)		Number of Parallel Units (x_i)		
		1	2	3
1				
	c_1.............	3	4	5
	r_1.............	0.80	0.96	0.99
2				
	c_2.............	1	2	3
	r_2.............	0.50	0.75	0.88
3				
	c_3.............	2	4	5
	r_3.............	0.60	0.84	0.94
4				
	c_4.............	1	2	2
	r_4.............	0.70	0.91	0.97

* Costs expressed in units of $1,000; reliabilities expressed to two significant digits.

The entire device fails if any one of its components fails. In other words, the device continues to operate so long as *all* of the components continue operation. The reliability of the system, therefore, is given by $(0.96) \cdot (0.50) \cdot (0.94) \cdot (0.97)$, or approximately 0.44.

The objective then is to maximize the product of component reliabilities $(r_1 \cdot r_2 \cdot r_3 \cdot r_4)$ subject to a cost constraint of, say, $10,000.[8] In general, this problem is formulated as

maximize

$$z = \prod_{i=1}^{n} r_i(x_i)$$

subject to

$$\sum_{i=1}^{n} c_i(x_i) \leq b$$

$$x_i \leq u_i, \qquad i = 1, \ldots, n,$$
$$x_i \geq 1, \qquad i = 1, \ldots, n,$$

x_i positive integer,

where n represents the number of components, b denotes the budget, u_i stipulates the upper limit on parallel units for the ith component, and where it is understood that component reliabilities (r_i's) and costs (c_i's) are func-

---

[8] A shorthand notation for product forms (comparable to Σ for summation) is the use of the symbol Π. In general, $\prod_{i=1}^{n} f_i(x) = f_1(x) \cdot f_2(x) \cdot \ldots \cdot f_n(x)$.

tions of the number of parallel units per component (x_i's). Note that both the objective function and budget constraint are *nonlinear*.

Letting the components correspond to stages in a forward recursion, you should have no difficulty (by now) in understanding the following transformation function and **multiplicative recursive equation:**[9]

$$s_i = \text{Available funds for Components } 1, 2, \ldots, i$$
$$= s_{i-1} + c_i$$

or

$$s_{i-1} = s_i - c_i$$

and

$$f_i^* = \text{Optimal reliability for Components } 1, 2, \ldots, i$$
$$= \max(r_i \cdot f_{i-1}^*). \tag{9.14}$$
$$x_i = 1,2,3$$

Follow-up Exercises

19. Get out your electronic calculator and determine the optimal design for the device in the preceding example by partially (intelligently) enumerating all of the feasible designs.
20. Determine the optimal design by dynamic programming.
21. Draw conclusions based on a sensitivity analysis of the budget.

---

[9] A necessary condition for the decomposition of multiplicative recursive equations is that the r_i be nonnegative real numbers; otherwise, optimization will not be achieved.

9.5 BACKWARD RECURSIONS

Up to this point the presentation has treated forward recursions exclusively. In this section we illustrate backward recursions and assess their use.

Computational Examples

Backward recursions are best illustrated by example. First we rework the stagecoach problem of Example 9.1. Then we follow with a workforce planning model which illustrates the solution procedure for continuous (rather than discrete) decision variables and states of nature.

Example 9.6   Shortest Route Problem Using Backward Recursion

The network in Figure 9–6 is identical to the network in Figure 9–1, except for the order in which legs are examined and stages are identified.

FIGURE 9–6

Shortest Route Problem: Backward Recursion

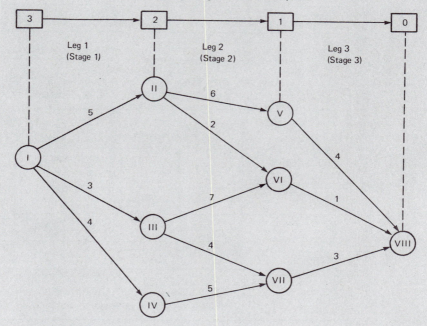

Number of Legs (Stages) Yet to Be Completed

As can be seen, *the backward procedure reverses the numbering of stages.* Now, the stage number refers to the number of legs (stages) *yet to be completed.* The computational tables, therefore, begin with the destination (Stage 1) and work *backward* to the beginning (Stage 3) of the journey, as indicated below.

By necessity, the leaving states (nodes) for each stage differ from the forward recursion. In other words, *the leaving state for a particular stage now represents the node from which we travel.* Also note that the decision at each stage is couched in terms of "to which point shall we travel?" How did we phrase this question in the forward procedure?[10] Otherwise, the backward recursion is identical to the forward recursion (but for the reversal of direction, of course).

---

[10] "From which point shall we travel?"

Stage 1 (Leg 3): Cumulative distance through stage $1 =$ Distance for stage 1 + Optimal cumulative distance through stage 0

Leaving State, s_1 (Travel from Node)	Travel to Node VIII	Optimal Policy Decision	Optimal Policy Cumulative Distance
V	$4 + 0 = 4$	VIII	④
VI	$1 + 0 = 1$	VIII*	①
VII	$3 + 0 = 3$	VIII	③

Stage 2 (Leg 2): Cumulative distance through stage $2 =$ Distance for stage 2 + Optimal cumulative distance through stage 1

Leaving State, s_2 (Travel from Node)	Travel to Node V	Travel to Node VI	Travel to Node VII	Optimal Policy Decision	Optimal Policy Cumulative Distance
II	$6 + ④ = 10$	$2 + ① = 3$		VI*	③
III		$7 + ① = 8$	$4 + ③ = 7$	VII	⑦
IV			$5 + ③ = 8$	VII	⑧

Stage 3 (Leg 1): Cumulative distance through stage $3 =$ Distance for stage 3 + Optimal cumulative distance through stage 2

Leaving State, s_3 (Travel from Node)	Travel to Node II	Travel to Node III	Travel to Node IV	Optimal Policy Decision	Optimal Policy Cumulative Distance
I	$5 + ③ = 8$	$3 + ⑦ = 10$	$4 + ⑧ = 12$	II*	8

Follow-up Exercises

22. Verify the entries in each cell of each table.
23. Solve Exercise 2 using the backward recursion.
24. Solve Exercise 3 using the backward recursion.
25. Consider the capital budgeting problem of Example 9.2 in the context of a backward recursion. Define s_i as the total capital outlay available

for allocation when i divisions remain unallocated (that is, with i more divisions to go). Note that the transformation function given by Equation (9.8) does not change. For example, if $i = 2$, then $s_1 = s_2 - c_2$ says that the available capital when one division remains unallocated equals the available capital when two divisions remain unallocated less the cost for the allocation in Stage 2. Define f_i as the cumulative net present value when i divisions remain to be allocated. Mathematically, the recursive equation for f_i is identical to Equation (9.7). Now, if we preserve the same correspondence as before with respect to stage number and division number (that is, the decision in Stage 1 relates to Division 1, and so forth), then you should convince yourself that the three computational tables in the example also represent a backward recursion!

**26. For the production-inventory model of Example 9.3, redefine Period 4 as Stage 1, Period 3 as Stage 2, Period 2 as Stage 3, and Period 1 as Stage 4. Now define

$s_i \equiv$ amount of *beginning* inventory for the period associated with Stage i (that is, beginning inventory with i periods *to go*)

and

$f_i^* \equiv$ Optimal cost for Stage i (that is, optimal cumulative cost over the *last* i periods in the planning horizon).

As before, s_i is the state of the system leaving Stage i, which is represented by rows in the table for Stage i. The transformation function and return function for Stage i will change; however, the form of f_i^* as given by Equation (9.13) remains the same.

a. Confirm that $s_{i-1} = s_i + x_i - d_i$.
b. Confirm that Equation (9.11) is replaced by

$$r_i = h_i \cdot (s_i - d_i)$$

and Equation (9.12) is replaced by

$$r_i = [12 + (n - i + 1)] - 6x_i + x_i^2 + h_i \cdot (s_i + x_i - d_i).$$

(Hint: The one-to-one correspondence between Quarter t and Stage i is determined from $t = n - i + 1$.)
c. Solve this problem by a backward recursion.
d. By sensitivity analysis, determine the optimal policy if beginning inventory for Quarter 1 is two units. What is the advantage of a backward recursion over a forward recursion with respect to sensitivity to beginning inventory in Quarter 1 (See Exercise 12.)
e. In words, compare forward and backward recursions with respect to sensitivity to number of periods in the planning horizon? Ending inventory for the planning horizon?

**Example 9.7 Workforce Planning Model

Up to this point, optimization at each stage (for each subproblem) has been accomplished by the process of *enumeration* with the aid of tables. This procedure is feasible when the decision variable (x_i) and state variable (s_i) for each stage are finite and discrete. If these variables are discrete but can take on an infinite number of values, *integer programming* (Chapter 8) techniques *may* be appropriate for finding the optimal policies at each stage. If x_i and s_i are *continuous,* however, the appropriate procedures include (1) *classical calculus* (Chapter 2) for unconstrained subproblems, (2) *Lagrangian functions* (Chapter 3) for subproblems with equality constraints, (3) *Kuhn-Tucker conditions* (not treated in this text) for subproblems with inequality constraints, (4) *linear programming* (Chapter 4 through 6) for subproblems with linear criteria and linear constraints, and (5) other *mathematical programming* and *search procedures* (Chapter 10), depending on the characteristics of the problem. If optimization for any given stage is not possible, then *heuristic procedures* (Chapter 16) represent the only recourse.

To illustrate a procedure which utilizes classical calculus, consider the problem of scheduling a workforce over four quarters ($n = 4$) for an organization. Each quarter has a projected demand for labor in hours. Assuming that the labor requirements must be met and that overtime is not allowed, management is faced with the cost tradeoff of hiring-firing on the one hand and idle labor on the other. The objective is to propose a workforce schedule which (1) meets requirements for labor of 30,000, 40,000, 35,000, and 50,000 hours in Quarters 1, 2, 3, and 4 respectively, and (2) minimizes the sum of costs associated with changes in the workforce and idle labor over the planning horizon of four quarters.

Suppose that the workforce level prior to Quarter 1 stands at 32,000 hours and that an analysis indicates a cost of $6 per hour for idle labor and a cost associated with workforce changes (hours) equal to 1 percent of the square of the change.

Working with a backward recursion to facilitate the stage transformations we define the following:

d_i = Demand in Stage i.[11]
x_i = hours of workforce hired ($x_i > 0$) or fired ($x_i < 0$) in Stage i.
s_i = Workforce level (hours) with i more quarters to go.
r_i = Costs (dollars) of idle time and hiring-firing in Stage i.

The transformation function and recursive equation follow easily from the definitions

$$s_{i-1} = s_i + x_i \tag{9.15}$$

and

$$f_i = \min_{x_i \geq d_i - s_i} [r_i + f_{i-1}^*]$$

or

$$f_i = \min_{x_i \geq d_i - s_i} [6(s_{i-1} - d_i) + 0.01x_i^2 + f_{i-1}^*]. \tag{9.16}$$

Substituting Equation (9.15) into (9.16) gives

$$f_i^* = \min_{x_i \geq d_i - s_i} [6(s_i - d_i) + 6x_i + 0.01x_i^2 + f_{i-1}^*]. \tag{9.17}$$

Note that the condition which requires meeting the demand for labor in each quarter is expressed as

$$s_{i-1} \geq d_i \tag{9.18}$$

___
[11] Note that $d_1 = 50,000$, $d_2 = 35,000$, $d_3 = 40,000$, and $d_4 = 30,000$.

or substituting Equation (9.15) into Equation (9.18) as

$$x_i \geq d_i - s_i. \tag{9.19}$$

Further note that the unit of measurement for the decision variable (hours) and the availability of part-time labor make x_i and s_i continuous variables.

Stage 1:

$$f_1 = 6(s_1 - 50,000) + 6x_1 + 0.01x_1^2 + 0 \tag{9.20}$$

The requirement of 50,000 hours in Stage 1 (Period 4) and the non-optimality of having idle labor in the last period dictate that

$$x_1^* = 50,000 - s_1; \tag{9.21}$$

that is, hire as much as you need to reach the requirement. Note that an optimal policy necessarily specifies that s_1 never exceed the maximum requirement of 50,000. Plugging Equation (9.21) into (9.20) gives the optimal recursion in Stage 1 as

$$f_1^* = 0.01(50,000 - s_1)^2. \tag{9.22}$$

Stage 2:

$$f_2 = 6(s_2 - 35,000) + 6x_2 + 0.01x_2^2 + 0.01(50,000 - s_1)^2 \tag{9.23}$$

Substituting Equation (9.15) into (9.23) we can express f_2 strictly in terms of s_2 and x_2, or

$$f_2 = 6(s_2 - 35,000) + 6x_2 + 0.01x_2^2 + 0.01(50,000 - s_2 - x_2)^2. \tag{9.24}$$

To find the optimal policy in Stage 2, we take the partial derivative of f_2 with respect to x_2, set it to zero, and solve for x_2, giving

$$x_2^* = 24,850 - 0.5s_2. \tag{9.25}$$

The second-order condition identifies x_2^* as a global minimum. The crucial question now is "Does x_2^* satisfy the constraints imposed by Equation (9.19)?" The answer is yes, as found by plugging Equation (9.25) in (9.19) and given that $s_2 \geq 40,000$ according to Equation (9.18); hence, (9.25) represents the optimal policy in Stage 2 and the optimal recursion is given by

$$f_2^* = 12,439,550 - 497s_2 + 0.005s_2^2 \tag{9.26}$$

after substituting Equation (9.25) into (9.23) and simplifying.

Stages 3 and 4 proceed in the same manner to arrive at

$$x_3^* = 40,000 - s_3 \tag{9.27}$$
$$f_3^* = 16,560,000 - 800s_3 + 0.01s_3^2 \tag{9.28}$$
$$x_4^* = 19,850 - 0.5s_4 \tag{9.29}$$

and

$$f_4^* = 16,380,000 - 794(s_4 + x_4) + 0.02s_4x_4 + 0.01s_4^2 + 0.02x_4^2. \tag{9.30}$$

Note that Equation (9.27) satisfies (9.19) strictly, which should indicate to you that the stationary point in Stage 3 did not satisfy (9.19).

Given that $s_4 = 32,000$, we successively evaluate Equations (9.29), (9.27), (9.25), and (9.21), making use of (9.15), to get $x_4^* = 3,850$, $x_3^* = 4,150$, $x_2^* = 4,850$, and $x_1^* = 5,150$; that is, hire 5,150; 4,850; 4,150; and 3,850 hours of labor in Quarters 1, 2, 3, and 4, respectively. Given an optimal hiring-firing policy in each stage, the workforce levels for Quarters 1, 2, 3, and 4 are 35,850; 40,000; 44,850; and 50,000, respectively. The optimal cost, as given by Equation (9.30), is $915,550 over four quarters.

Follow-up Exercises

27. Verify Equations (9.25) through (9.30).
28. What is the optimal policy and associated cost if the initial labor force is 40,000? 50,000?
29. Formulate and solve the workforce problem by defining x_i as *workforce level* with i more quarters to go. Which approach is easier?
30. Illustrate the difficulty of stage transformations when using a forward recursion for this problem.
**31. Since optimization in any given stage is subject to a constraint, the workforce planning model can be solved using Lagrange multipliers. Illustrate this approach by differentiating the Lagrangian function for Stage 2.

     Based on the sign of λ, interpret whether or not the constraint binds (see Table 3–3).

On Selecting A Procedure: Forward or Backward Recursion?

The analyst's decision regarding the use of forward or backward recursions will be determined by personal preference, by the difficulty of effecting stage transformations for the particular application, by the type of sensitivity analysis desired, or by the specification of initial or final states. Transformations of state which occurred in the stage decisions for the shortest route problem were straightforward in either the forward direction or the backward direction; however, for many other applications, especially time-dependent processes, the backward procedure facilitates the conceptualization and computation of transformations (as suggested by Exercise 30). For this reason, there is a decided preference in the literature for backward recursions (much to the dismay of beginning students).

9.6 ASSESSMENT

This section concludes our treatment of dynamic programming by assessing its good points, bad points, and future prospects.

Advantages

1. The process of breaking down a complex problem into a series of interrelated subproblems often provides insight into the nature of the problem. This advantage of dynamic programming is especially evident for sequential types of processes (for example, production smoothing and scheduling on an on-going basis or control of a chemical process), some of which can be solved only by dynamic programming.
2. Because dynamic programming is an approach to optimization rather than a technique, it has a flexibility which allows application to other types of mathematical programming problems. Essentially, each term or variable in the objective function is assigned a stage, the decision at

each stage is based on the level or value for that variable, and the amount of unused or used resource (right-hand–side constant) for a constraint is represented by a state variable. Integer programming problems and linear programming problems can be solved in this manner, the former using tabular form (Example 9.2) and the latter using a nontabular (continuous) form. The approach can be used to solve nonlinear integer programs (Example 9.5), nonlinear continuous programs (Example 9.7), and other optimization problems characterized by nonconvex or discontinuous functions. Additionally, dynamic programming is applicable to either deterministic or stochastic processes and to adaptive processes (for example, feedback-control systems in the making of steel).[12]

3. The computational procedure in dynamic programming allows for a "built-in" form of sensitivity analysis based on state variables and on the variable represented by the stages. For example, the final tableaus for the capital budgeting model (Example 9.2) and the reliability model (Example 9.5) allow for examination of the sensitivity of the solution to the budget; the final tableau of the production-inventory model (Example 9.3) related sensitivity of the solution to the level of ending inventory; the final optimization equation for x_4^* in the workforce planning model (Example 9.7) readily allows for an examination of solution sensitivity to the beginning level of workforce; and the extension of the number of stages in the forward versions of the production-inventory model and the workforce planning model allows the treatment of varying planning horizons. This latter capability also opens the way to the treatment of unbounded planning horizons, especially under the circumstances of a present value criterion or stationary cycles.

4. Finally, dynamic programming achieves computational savings over complete enumeration. For example, complete enumeration of a problem with two variables ($n = 2$) and ten alternatives per variable requires the examination of 10^2 or 100 solutions; an increase to four variables ($n = 4$) generates 10^4 or 10,000 solutions; for six variables ($n = 6$) the number of possible solutions is 10^6 or 1,000,000. In short, difficulty in enumeration increases exponentially as the number of variables increases linearly. In contrast, the number of stages in dynamic programming would increase from two to four to six, which essentially represents a linear increase in computational difficulty. As the size of the problem increases, the disparity in calculations between the two approaches becomes pronounced.

Disadvantages

1. Although dynamic programming is conceptually more powerful than its sister techniques in mathematical programming, the high degree of expertise, insight, and "art" which is required in the efficient formulation of complex problems (especially with regard to the

---

[12] *Probabilistic dynamic programming* treats states as random variables, as illustrated in Chapter 15, Exercise 46, and Chapter 17, Exercise 45.

specification of transformations) has to be considered a disadvantage in that it limits its usage.

2. A further disadvantage is the lack of a general algorithm akin to, say, the simplex method. This is not an inconsequential problem as it restricts the availability of generalized computer codes which are necessary for widespread and inexpensive implementation of dynamic programming. Some progress has been made, however, in classifying applications by type and developing computational procedures which, while not identical, have structures which are similar.[13]

3. The most formidable shortcoming of dynamic programming is the so-called curse of **dimensionality.** This problem is encountered when a particular application is characterized by multiple states (termed a multidimensional state vector). For such formulations, the storage capacity and computational capabilities of computers can be taxed severely. To illustrate, consider a discrete three-stage problem ($n = 3$) which has ten decision alternatives per stage (ten columns in a tableau excluding the optimal policy columns), and one state variable with 100 alternatives (rows). The number of storage cells required per matrix (tableau) would be $(10) \cdot (100)$ or 1,000.[14] The addition of second and third state variables, each with 100 alternatives, would increase the required number of cells to 100,000 and 10 million, respectively.[15] Thus, storage requirements increase geometrically as the dimensions of the state variable increase linearly. Computation time will increase roughly by the same magnitude. Although more efficient computational procedures (by using, believe it or not, the Lagrange multiplier techniques of Chapter 3) and increased computer capabilities will tend to compensate for these effects, "breakthroughs" will be required to relegate them to the status of minor problems.

Potentialities

Dynamic programming procedures and concepts have had a significant impact both in the development of other academic areas (for example, Markov processes, game theory, trajectories, and numerical analysis) and in the successful solution of certain applied problems (for example, inventory replenishment, production scheduling, equipment replacement and maintenance, and chemical control processes). Its scope is broad and

[13] Allocation processes (Examples 9.2 and 9.5), dynamic processes (Examples 9.3 and 9.7), multistage production processes, feedback-control processes, network processes, and Markov processes (Chapter 15). For details see R. E. Bellman and S. E. Dreyfus, *Applied Dynamic Programming* (Princeton, N.J.: Princeton University Press, 1962) and N. P. Loomba and E. Turban, *Applied Programming for Management* (New York: Holt, Rinehart and Winston, Inc., 1974).

[14] An efficiently written computer program would carry only one full matrix for calculations in the current stage and one additional matrix to store the optimal decision for each stage. The number of cells in the computational matrix can be reduced even further with an additional dosage of ingenuity. Any ideas?

[15] This last figure is already beyond the high-speed core capabilities of any electronic computer extant. Although other forms of storage can be used (for example, magnetic tape or disk), the required access times would be prohibitive.

its areas of application are being extended continually. If significant future progress were to be made in achieving standardization and in overcoming the problem of dimensionality, then we would not be facetious in characterizing dynamic programming as "supertechnique."

SELECTED REFERENCES

Bellman, R. E. *Dynamic Programming.* Princeton, N.J.: Princeton University Press, 1957.

Bellman, R. E., and Dreyfus, S. E. *Applied Dynamic Programming.* Princeton, N.J.: Princeton University Press, 1962.

Denardo, E. V. *Dynamic Programming: Theory and Application.* Englewood Cliffs, N.J.: Prentice-Hall, Inc., 1975.

Hadley, G. F. *Nonlinear and Dynamic Programming.* Reading, Mass.: Addison-Wesley Publishing Co., 1964.

Loomba, N. P., and Turban, E. *Applied Programming for Management.* New York: Holt, Rinehart and Winston, Inc., 1974.

Nemhauser, G. L. *Introduction to Dynamic Programming.* New York: John Wiley & Sons, Inc., 1966.

Wagner, H. M. *Principles of Operations Research.* Englewood Cliffs, N.J.: Prentice-Hall, Inc., 1975.

ADDITIONAL EXERCISES

The **structure** of a dynamic programming (*DP*) problem is identified by the following:

1. Definition of stage and number of stages.
2. Identification of decision variables.
3. Definition of state variable and statement of transformation function.
4. Statement of return function (algebraic or tabular).
5. Statement of optimal recursive equation.

32. *Fire Station Allocation* Planners for a city are to recommend the "best" allocation of fire stations to three districts. Anywhere from zero to three stations can be located in a district. Not surprisingly, the number of stations located in a district has a bearing on the annual property damage caused by fires for that district. The table below reflects this relationship. Differences among districts are due to factors such as population, residential-commercial mix, socioeconomic makeup, and quality of construction. A budget constraint restricts the total number of allocations to five stations.

Annual Property Damage (millions of dollars)

District	Number of Stations per District			
	0	1	2	3
1.............	2.0	0.9	0.3	0.2
2.............	0.5	0.3	0.2	0.1
3.............	1.5	1.0	0.7	0.3

   a. Identify the *DP* structure for this problem. Do you have "quarrel" with the criterion? Explain.

   b. Determine the optimal allocation by *DP*.

      c. What would be the effect on the criterion of a total allocation of four stations? How should these stations be allocated?

33. Suppose that the budgetary restriction for the preceding problems is given by

$$3x_1 + x_2 + 2x_3 \leq 9 \text{ (millions of dollars)},$$

which reflects differential costs across districts. (x_j is the number of stations allocated to district j). Answer each part of the preceding exercise. As before, assume an upper limit of three stations per district.

34. For the firestation scenario of the preceding two exercises, suppose that we wish to minimize

$$z = 2(0.5)^{x_1} + (0.5)^{x_2} + 2(0.6)^{x_3} \text{ (property damage in millions of dollars)}$$

subject to

$$3x_1 + x_2 + 2x_3 \leq 9 \text{ (budget in millions of dollars)}$$
$$x_j = 0,1,2, \ldots \text{ all } j,$$

where x_j is the number of fire stations allocated to district j. Other than that imposed by the budget, assume no upper limit on the number of stations that can be assigned to a district.

    a. Identify the *DP* structure for this problem.
    b. Determine the optimal allocation and value of the criterion by *DP*.
    c. Explore the implications of an \$8 million budget and a \$7 million budget.

35. *Research Funds Allocation* An agency in the Department of Health, Education, and Welfare (HEW) has \$6 million for allocation to three cancer research clinics. In general, the greater the size of a grant for a particular clinic, the greater will be the subsequent savings of lives over a specified planning horizon. By consensus, experts have provided the following data.

Savings in Lives over the Next Decade (millions)

Clinic	Funds Allocation (millions of dollars)						
	0	1	2	3	4	5	6
1.............	5	7	10	15	25	40	60
2.............	10	15	20	24	27	30	32
3.............	1	10	15	20	30	35	45

Note that funds are allocated in increments of \$1 million.

    a. Identify the *DP* structure for this problem.
    b. Determine the optimal allocation by *DP*.
    c. What would be the effects on the criterion and on the allocation if only \$5 million were available?
    d. What would be the effects if each clinic must receive a minimum of \$1 million?

36. *Cargo-Loading Model* A manned (womanned?) lunar space vehicle is to be loaded with three types of geological kits for purposes of experimentation. At least one kit, but no more than four kits, of each type must be loaded. In general, the more kits of a certain type the better, since a greater quantity of experimental information can be gathered. Unfortunately, the payload of the vehicle limits the total weight of the experi-

mental kits to 250 pounds (volume is not restrictive). Relevant data are given in the table below.

Measure of Experimental Value

Type of Kit	Weight per Kit (lb.)	Number of Kits Loaded			
		1	2	3	4
1................	20	4	7	9	10
2................	50	6	7	8	9
3................	30	3	6	8	9

a. Identify the *DP* structure for this problem.
b. Determine the optimal loading by *DP*. (Hint: You should be efficient in specifying leaving states for each stage, lest you have 251 rows in a tableau. For example, you need only consider four leaving states in stage 2).
c. What is the value of s_o and what does it represent?

37. Consider the following nonlinear integer program:

maximize
$$z = 3x_1 - x_2 + 2x_2^2$$
subject to
$$2x_1 + 3x_2 \leq 10$$
$$x_1, x_2 = 0,1,2, \ldots$$

a. Identify its *DP* structure.
b. Solve this problem by *DP*.
c. Solve this problem for a RHS constant of 8.

38. Solve the problem in the preceding exercise for each case below.

a. Add the constraint $x_1 \geq 1$.
b. Add the constraints $x_1 \geq 1$ and $x_1 \leq 3$.
c. Add the constraints $x_1 \geq 3$ and $x_2 \geq 2$.
d. What would be the implication of adding another constraint of the type $a_1x_1 + a_2x_2 \leq b$?

39. *Feedlot Optimization* A simplified feedlot optimization problem is concerned with the amounts of a certain type of ration (x_t) which a feedlot operation is to feed an animal over a planning horizon ($t = 1, 2, \ldots, T$) such that the profit contribution per animal is maximized.[16]

A feedlot purchases animals from livestock growers when the animals reach a certain age or weight. While in the feedlot, animals are fed a special diet for T time periods, after which they are sold to a slaughterhouse. The variable cost of the ration per time period is a function of the amount in the ration, as indicated by $c_t(x_t)$ in the accompanying table:

x_t (lb.)	$c_t(x_t)$ ($)
150....................	20
200....................	30
250....................	35

[16] For a more realistic (and more complex) formulation see C. F. Meyer and R. J. Newett, "Dynamic Programming for Feedlot Optimization," *Management Science*, vol. 16, no. 6 (1970), pp. B410–26.

The weight of an animal at the end of period t is given by its weight at the end of the preceding period plus the weight gain during period t. The weight gain during period t is a function of the amount of feed in period t, as indicated by $g_t(x_t)$:

$g_t(x_t)$ (lb.)	x_t (lb.)
50......................	150
70......................	200
80......................	250

Higher weight gains during a period tend to be associated with higher operating costs (for example, maintenance costs, veterinary costs, and so forth). Moreover, these costs increase over time, as given by the function

$$m_t(x_t, t) = 0.01t \cdot g_t(x_t),$$

where $m_t(x_t, t)$ represents these operating costs. Any other costs are considered fixed.

The feedlot purchases animals initially weighing 500 pounds and sells them after three periods at a weight of 700 pounds. The operator wishes to determine a feeding schedule such that total feeding cost is minimized.

a.   Identify the *DP* structure for this problem.

b.   Determine the optimal decision and value of the criterion by *DP*. (Hint: In a forward recursion, the three leaving states for stage 1 are 550, 570, and 580; the three leaving states for stage 2 are 620, 630, and 650; and the leaving state for stage 3 is 700.)

40.   Suppose that the feedlot operator in the preceding exercise is willing to consider all possible ending weights (that is, weight at the end of three periods).

a.   Generate *DP* tableaus. (Hint: The number of leaving states for stages 1, 2, and 3 are, respectively, 3, 6, and 9.)

b.   Determine optimal contribution to profit and overhead for each ending state if the feedlot pays $0.40 per pound for an animal and receives $0.50 per pound after three time periods. What optimal ending weight and feeding schedule do you recommend?

**41. *Replacement Model*   Consider the following variation for the general class of models first presented as Example 2.16 on page 56. An expensive capital asset (for example, printing press, freighter, airplane, and so forth) is characterized by a purchase price at the *beginning* of period i (P_i) which increases over time, a salvage value at the *beginning* of period j (S_j) which decreases over time, and an operating cost *during* period t (C_t) which increases over time. Based on past experience, the following functions have been determined.

$$\begin{aligned}
P_i &= 2 + 0.1i & &\text{(millions of dollars)}, \\
S_j &= P_i \cdot (0.8)^{j-i}, \quad j > i & &\text{(millions of dollars)}, \\
C_t &= 0.05 + 0.01t, \quad i \le t < j & &\text{(millions of dollars)}.
\end{aligned}$$

Thus, the total cost for an asset which is purchased at the beginning of period i and replaced at the beginning of period j is given by

$$TC_{ij} = P_i - S_j + \sum_{t=i}^{j-1} C_t, \quad j > i.$$

For example, if the asset is purchased at the beginning of period 3 $(i = 3)$ and replaced at the beginning of period 5 $(j = 5)$, then

$$TC_{35} = P_3 - S_5 + \sum_{t=3}^{4} C_t$$

$$= P_3 - P_3 \cdot (0.8)^{5-3} + (C_3 + C_4)$$
$$= P_3[1 - (0.8)^2] + C_3 + C_4$$
$$= [2 + 0.1(3)](1 - 0.64) + [0.05 + 0.01(3)] + [0.05 + 0.01(4)]$$
$$= 0.998.$$

a. For a planning horizon of four years, compute a table for TC_{ij}. Note that the table has four rows $(i = 1, 2, 3, 4)$ and four columns $(j = 2, 3, 4, 5)$.

b. Identify the *DP* structure for this problem. (Hint: Let each stage represent a point-in-time at the beginning of a year. A backward recursion may be easier to conceptualize.)

c. Solve this problem by *DP*.

**42. Solve the preceding replacement model after discounting all TC_{ij} (that is, express the cost criterion in present value terms). Use an interest rate of 10 percent per year.

**43. *Generalized Shortest and Longest Routes through a Network: Forward Recursion* Let stage i represent node i; let x_i represent the node "from which we travel" when located at node (in stage) i; let s_i represent the

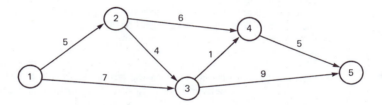

node "to which we travel" when in stage i; let r_i represent the "distance between node i and node s_i"; and define $f_i = r_i + f_{x_i}^*$. To find $f_{x_i}^*$ go back to stage x_i and state i. As usual, label the columns in your tableau as x_i and the rows as s_i. (This isn't as bad as it seems. Just maintain visual contact with the network.)

a. By *DP* find the shortest route through this network.

b. By *DP* find the longest route through this network.

**44. *Generalized Shortest and Longest Routes through a Network: Backward Recursion* Let stage i represent node $(n - i + 1)$, where n is the total number of nodes; let x_i represent the node "to which we travel" when located at the node corresponding to stage i; let s_i represent the node "from which we travel" when in stage i; let r_i represent the distance between the node represented by stage i and node s_i; and define $f_i = r_i + f_{n-x_i+1}^*$. To find $f_{n-x_i+1}^*$ go back to stage $(n - x_i + 1)$ and state $(n - i + 1)$; that is, go back to the stage for node x_i and the state corresponding to the node associated with stage i. As usual, label the columns in your tableau as x_i and the rows as s_i. (This isn't as bad as it seems. Just maintain visual contact with the network.)

  a. By *DP* find the shortest route through the network in Exercise 43.
  b. By *DP* find the longest route through the network in Exercise 43.

**45. *Solar Energy Installation* An experimental solar energy system for resi-
       dential heating consists of three major components: solar collector made
       up of plate glass which is oriented toward the sun; water tank for storing
       thermal energy; and a piping-control system for regulating flows, pressure,
       and temperature.
           Suppose that three surface areas for the collector are under considera-
       tion: 500, 600, and 700 square feet. Engineering tests show that the area
       of the collector directly affects its ability to increase average ambient
       (outdoor) temperatures. The 500 square-foot collector increases ambient
       temperature by a factor of 6; the 600 square-foot collector by a factor of
       7; and the 700 square-foot collector by a factor of 8. For example, given
       an average ambient temperature of 30° F, the 600 square-foot collector
       has the capability of sending water into the storage tank which is heated
       to 210° F (30 × 7). Over the life of a typical home (estimated at 40
       years), the amortized cost of the collector is $.50 per square foot per
       year.
           Two choices are available for the size of the storage tank: 800 gallons
       and 1,000 gallons. Generally, the larger tanks have a greater ability to
       store thermal energy for use during the nightime or during cloudy
       weather. The effective heat retention of the smaller tank is 0.7, and that
       of the larger tank is 0.8. For example, the larger tank is capable of ef-
       fectively maintaining the water at 168° F when the collector delivers
       water at 210° F (210 × 0.8). The amortized cost of the storage facility is
       $0.15 per gallon per year.
           Two choices also are available for the piping and control system. These
       are amortized at $50 per year and $100 per year. The efficiency factor for
       the cheaper alternative is 0.4 and that for the more expensive alternative
       is 0.5. For example, if the effective temperature of water in a tank is
       168° F, then an efficiency factor of 0.5 means that the effective tempera-
       ture which can be delivered to the residence is 84° F (168 × 0.5).
           The effective delivery temperature is important because it determines
       the average cost of supplying conventional heat to supplement the solar
       system. For a 2,000 square-foot residence which is heated to 70° F, the
       average annual cost of the conventional heating system has been estimated
       by the following relationship:

$$h = 150 + 10(70 - \text{Effective delivery temperature}).$$

       Note that effective delivery temperatures above 70° F reduce h below
       $150 per year. Moreover, if a calculation yields $h < 0$, then h should be
       set to zero.

  a. Identify the *DP* structure for this problem.
  b. Determine the optimal design by *DP*. (To simplify the problem,
      round off the effective delivery temperature to the nearest 10° F.)

10

Overview of Other
Mathematical Programming
Methods

THE MATHEMATICAL PROGRAMMING MODELS and techniques presented in Chapters 2 through 9 have proven to be of significant value to decision makers. Because one of our goals is to survey the OR field, this text would not be complete without a brief overview of some additional areas of mathematical programming. In this chapter we first discuss the emerging area of **goal programming.** Thereafter, other mathematical programming methods are overviewed: **parametric linear programming, stochastic programming,** and **nonlinear programming.**

GOAL PROGRAMMING

Up to now we have presented mathematical techniques which can, under specified assumptions, determine values for decision variables which optimize a single quantifiable objective function (which may be a surrogate for the true objective in the problem). As discussed in Chapter 1, multiple goals (criteria or objectives) may exist for any given problem. These goals may be of different dimensions (maximize profits v. maximize market share); they may be difficult to quantify (maximize customer satisfaction); and they may conflict with one another (minimize hospital costs v. maximize hospital service). The second of these is an issue unto itself, but if we assume that multiple objectives are quantifiable, a relatively new technique, **goal programming (GP),** shows great promise.

Introduction

Goal programming is primarily a variation of linear programming. Recent extensions, however, include quadratic objective functions. First

351

identified by Charnes and Cooper, the technique of goal programming was extended and refined by Ijiri.[1] Lee has provided one of the first comprehensive presentations of the topic and has been a pioneer in identifying areas of application.[2]

Goal programming is a form of linear programming which allows for consideration of a single goal or multiple goals. The goals may or may not be of the same dimension or unit of measurement. In addition, goal programming allows for consideration of conflicting goals. If multiple goals exist, the decision maker must specify an ordinal ranking of goals. The goal programming solution method operates in a way which addresses lower-priority goals only after higher-priority goals have been satisfied as best as possible. This forces decision makers into giving careful consideration to the relative importance of their goals. For example, in postoptimality analysis the decision maker is provided the opportunity to assess the effects of changing the priorities of multiple goals or of increasing or decreasing the number of goals.

Whereas linear programming identifies from the set of feasible solutions the point which *optimizes* a single objective, goal programming identifies the point which satisfies *best* either the single goal or set of goals in the problem. Given the number of goals, the priority structure specified by the decision maker, and the inevitable competition among goals, the best solution is often one which satisfices. (Remember this concept from Chapter 1?) With multiple goals, all goals usually cannot be realized exactly. Goal programming attempts to minimize the deviations from these goals with consideration given to the hierarchy of stated priorities.

In linear programming, goals can be stated individually as constraints. Suppose a hospital has a goal of adding 50 new rooms over the next two years and another goal of keeping capital expenditures during the same period below $1 million. These two goals could be specified as constraints in an LP model. If other capital commitments made it impossible to realize the goal of 50 new rooms, then the LP result would simply indicate no feasible solution. The goal programming treatment of this same situation, however, would provide a solution which, depending upon the order of priorities, gives the hospital administrator information concerning possible tradeoffs between rooms and budget. The infeasibility of meeting both goals has not changed, but a solution would be identified which minimizes the deviations from specified goals.

Example 10.1   Media Mix, Single Goal

In Example 4.8 we presented an LP formulation of a media mix problem. Here we examine a simplified version of this problem: the amounts of money

---

[1] Y. Ijiri, *Management Goals and Accounting for Control* (Chicago: Rand McNally, 1965).

[2] Sang Lee, *Goal Programming for Decision Analysis* (Philadelphia: Auerbach Publishers, Inc., 1972).

to allocate for television and radio advertisements. Rated exposures per thousand dollars of advertising expenditure are 10,000 and 7,500, respectively, for television and radio. If the advertising budget for the next campaign is $100,000 and no more than 70 percent of the budget can be expended on television, then the LP formulation for maximizing total advertising exposures is

maximize

$$z = 10{,}000x_1 + 7{,}500x_2$$

subject to

$$x_1 + x_2 \le 100$$
$$x_1 \quad\;\; \le\;\; 70$$

$$x_1, x_2 \ge\;\; 0$$

where $x_1 =$ thousands of dollars spent on TV advertising and $x_2 =$ thousands of dollars spent on radio advertising.

Now, presume that management has set a target goal of 1 million exposures for the advertising campaign; that is, they would be satisfied if their campaign reaches 1 million exposures. The LP approach would be to include this goal as a constraint having the form

$$10{,}000x_1 + 7{,}500x_2 \ge 1{,}000{,}000.$$

You should be able to verify that there is no feasible solution to this revised problem.

The GP formulation of the same problem is

minimize

$$z = d^- + d^+$$

subject to

$$10{,}000x_1 + 7{,}500x_2 + d^- - d^+ = 1{,}000{,}000 \qquad (1)$$
$$x_1 + \quad x_2 \qquad\qquad\qquad \le 100 \qquad (2)$$
$$x_1 \qquad\qquad\qquad\qquad \le 70 \qquad (3)$$

$$x_1, x_2, d^-, d^+ \ge\;\; 0.$$

The two nonnegative variables d^- and d^+ are referred to as **deviational variables.** They represent, respectively, the amount by which the exposure goal is *underachieved* (d^-) or *overachieved* (d^+). The objective function contains the deviational variables only and not the decision variables x_1 and x_2. Linear dependency between the deviational variables assures that only one of the two can assume a positive value for any solution (that is, it is impossible to have both underachievement and overachievement of a goal). If the goal is achieved exactly, then both deviational variables will equal zero. If the goal cannot be achieved (where LP would indicate no feasible solution), then goal programming will attempt to achieve it as closely as possible.

As the problem was originally stated, the decision maker is interested in achieving the exposure goal exactly. Thus, both deviational variables are included in the objective function. If overachievement of the exposure goal was acceptable, then only d^- would be included in the objective function. The concern would be the minimization of the degree of underachievement of the exposure goal. Conversely, if underachievement is acceptable for a given goal, then only $d+$ would be included in the objective function.

In this formulation, no preference or priority has been assigned to either underachievement or overachievement of the single goal in the problem. In the next section we will present examples with multiple goals; these problems require the decision maker to rank order the goals according to priorities.

Follow-up Exercises

1. Explain why it would be logically incorrect to

   a. Maximize $z = d^- + d^+$.
   b. Maximize $z = d^- - d^+$.
   c. Minimize $z = d^- - d^+$.

2. Modify z in the example if the decision maker finds overachievement of the goal to be desirable. Need you modify constraint (1)? Explain.

3. Reformulate Example 10.1 if management wishes to spend as close as possible to the $100,000 budget subject to (a) expenditures of less than $70,000 on television and (b) achievement of a total exposure above 1.2 million. (Hint: Define the deviational variables in terms of overachievement and underachievement of the budget.)

Formulation Issues

The underlying assumptions and formulation of a GP model are similar to that of an LP model. Critical to the formulation is the specification of a goal structure by the decision maker. Two types of variables will be a part of any formulation: **decision variables** and **deviational variables.** Two classes of constraints may be formulated for a problem: **system constraints** which are not directly related to goals and **goal constraints** which are directly related to goals. In Example 10.1, the first constraint would be considered a goal constraint and the two budget constraints represent system constraints.

With goal constraints, it is conceivable that the ultimate solution may result in either the underachievement or overachievement of the particular goal. For this reason, *both* types of deviational variables should be included as a part of each goal constraint. This is true even if only one of the deviational variables appears in the objective function. Furthermore, *in all cases,* goal constraints are of the equality ($=$) type.

The objective function is always minimized and must be composed of deviational variables only. When more than one goal exists:

a. More than one set of deviational variables may be associated with any goal.
b. Multiple goals must be assigned ordinal **priority factors** (that is, they must be rank ordered).

c. When deviational variables are at the same priority level, **differential weights** may be assigned to the variables in the objective function.

The following examples illustrate these issues for multiple-goal problems.

Example 10.2   Media Mix, Multiple Goals

In the previous example, assume that management has agreed that the campaign cannot be judged successful if total exposures are under 750,000. The campaign would be viewed as superbly successful if 1 million exposures occurred. In this example, management has rank ordered four goals it wishes to achieve, arranged from highest to lowest priority:

1. Minimize the underachievement of the exposure goal of 750,000 exposures.
2. Avoid expenditures of more than $100,000.
3. Avoid expenditures of more than $70,000 for television advertisements.
4. Minimize the underachievement of the goal of 1 million exposures.

The GP formulation of the revised problem is
minimize

$$z = P_1 d_1^- + P_2 d_2^+ + P_3 d_3^+ + P_4 d_4^-$$

subject to

$$10,000x_1 + 7,500x_2 + d_1^- - d_1^+ = 750,000 \tag{1}$$
$$x_1 + x_2 + d_2^- - d_2^+ = 100 \tag{2}$$
$$x_1 + d_3^- - d_3^+ = 70 \tag{3}$$
$$10,000x_1 + 7,500x_2 + d_4^- - d_4^+ = 1,000,000 \tag{4}$$

$$x_1, x_2, d_1^-, d_1^+, d_2^-, d_2^+, d_3^-, d_3^+, d_4^-, d_4^+ \geq 0,$$

where

d_1^- = Amount by which total exposures fall short of 750,000.
d_1^+ = Amount by which total exposures exceed 750,000.
d_2^- = Amount by which total expenditures fall short of $100 thousand.
d_2^+ = Amount by which total expenditures exceed $100 thousand.
d_3^- = Amount by which television expenditures fall short of $70 thousand.
d_3^+ = Amount by which television expenditures exceed $70 thousand.
d_4^- = Amount by which total exposures fall short of 1 million.
d_4^+ = Amount by which total exposures exceed 1 million.
P_k = Priority factor with rank k.
x_j = $1,000s expended on jth medium ($j = 1$ for TV and $j = 2$ for radio).

Notice that deviational variables have been added to the two budgetary constraints; they have become goal constraints.

In the objective function, deviational variables are implicitly weighted by ordinal priority factors (P_k). That is, P_k simply serves to identify the priority level (rank) for the goal which it "weighs," where $k = 1$ represents the highest priority, $k = 2$ represents the next highest priority, and so forth. These factors may be thought of as being preemptive in the sense that the goal associated with P_k must be satisfied as best as possible before considering the goal associated with P_{k+1}. Mathematically, the relationship between these factors can be stated as $P_k >>> P_{k+1}$ where $(>>>)$ implies that P_k is "much greater" than P_{k+1}. Note, however, that the ordinal nature of P_k does not require the assignment of a numeric value.

In the objective function the highest priority (P_1) is associated with d_1^- which represents the underachievement of the 750,000 exposure goal. Also, there is concern for exceeding both the total budget and the television budget, with the former having a higher priority (P_2) than the latter (P_3); consequently, d_2^+ and d_3^+ are included in the objective function with respective priority factors of P_2 and P_3. The variables d_2^- and d_3^- are not included in the objective function because of management's apparent lack of concern for spending less than budgeted amounts. The lowest priority goal is to minimize the underachievement of the exposure goal of 1 million; thus, the inclusion of d_4^- and its priority factor given by P_4.

Follow-up Exercises

4. Modify z in Example 10.2 if goals 3 and 4 have the same priority.
5. Suppose the priorities of the four goals in Example 10.2 were reversed. Reformulate the problem by

   a. Redefining the deviational variables.
   b. Changing the subscripts of the P_k's in z.
   Which approach requires less effort to reformulate?

6. Modify Example 10.2 if the condition in goal 3 is stated as a system constraint rather than as a goal constraint. In other words, eliminate goal 3 as a goal.

Example 10.3   Media Mix, One More Time

Continuing the previous example, assume that the two most important audiences for the company are persons 18 to 21 years of age and persons 25 to 30 years of age. Table 10–1 presents estimates of the numbers of individuals in the two age groups expected to be exposed to advertisements per $1,000 of expenditure.

Management has established a goal of reaching at least 250,000 persons in each of the two age groups, and ranks the achievement of these targets as the fifth most important goal. In addition, management realizes and wishes to account for the fact that the purchasing power of the 25 to 30 age group is twice the purchasing power of the 18 to 21 age group. The modified problem is formulated below.

TABLE 10–1

Exposures per $1,000

Age	Television	Radio
18–21 years..............	2,500	3,000
25–30 years..............	3,000	1,500

Minimize

$$z = P_1 d_1^- + P_2 d_2^+ + P_3 d_3^+ + P_4 d_4^- + P_5 d_5^- + 2P_5 d_6^-$$

subject to

$$
\begin{aligned}
10{,}000x_1 + 7{,}500x_2 + d_1^- - d_1^+ &= 750{,}000 & (1)\\
x_1 + x_2 + d_2^- - d_2^+ &= 100 & (2)\\
x_1 + d_3^- - d_3^+ &= 70 & (3)\\
10{,}000x_1 + 7{,}500x_2 + d_4^- - d_4^+ &= 1{,}000{,}000 & (4)\\
2{,}500x_1 + 3{,}000x_2 + d_5^- - d_5^+ &= 250{,}000 & (5)\\
3{,}000x_1 + 1{,}500x_2 + d_6^- - d_6^+ &= 250{,}000 & (6)
\end{aligned}
$$

$$x_1, x_2, d_1^-, d_1^+, d_2^-, d_2^+, d_3^-, d_3^+, d_4^-, d_4^+, d_5^-, d_5^+, d_6^-, d_6^+ \geq 0,$$

where (in addition to the previous definitions)

d_5^- = Amount by which total exposures in the 18 to 21 age category fall short of 250,000.

d_5^+ = Amount by which total exposures in the 18 to 21 age category exceed 250,000.

d_6^- = Amount by which total exposures in the 25 to 30 age category fall short of 250,000.

d_6^+ = Amount by which total exposures in the 25 to 30 age category exceed 250,000.

P_5 = Priority factor with rank 5.

In the objective function both d_5^- and d_6^- (underachievement of exposure targets for the two markets) have the same priority factor; however, d_5^- and d_6^- have been assigned *differential weights* of 1 and 2, respectively, to account for the relative purchasing power of persons in the two age groups. These differentials imply that management perceives underachievement of the exposure goal in the 25 to 30 group to be twice as "costly" as underachievement in the other group. Also note that two sets of deviational variables $(d_5^-, d_5^+$ and $d_6^-, d_6^+)$ are associated with goal 5.

Follow-up Exercises

7. What modification is necessary in Example 10.3 if the purchasing power differential is to be ignored?

8. Why would it be wrong to assign a priority factor of P_6 to d_6^- in the objective function of Example 10.3?

9. Does the number of goal constraints always equal the number of goals? Explain.

10. Reformulate Example 10.3 by accounting for relative purchasing power between the two age groups as follows: Eliminate the use of differential weights; make goal 5 the exposure target for the 25 to 30 age group; make goal 6 the exposure target for the 18 to 21 age group; and identify goal 6 as having lower priority than goal 5.

11. Suppose that management specifies a goal of keeping budget overruns for the campaign below $5,000. Assume this goal to have the second highest priority, with goals 2 through 5 in the original formulation becoming goals 3 through 6. Define: d_7^- = amount of budget overrun short of $5,000 and d_7^+ = amount of budget overrun in excess of $5,000. With respect to Example 10.3:

a. Appropriately modify z.
b. Add a goal constraint exclusively in terms of deviational variables.
c. Rewrite the constraint in part b using the decision variables x_1 and x_2.

Example 10.4 University Admissions

As noted in other chapters, educational planning has received increasingly more attention by OR/MS analysts. Let us illustrate how a much simplified university admissions planning problem can be examined with goal programming.

A small midwestern university is attempting to reach admission decisions for next year. It wants to determine the numbers of in-state and out-of-state students to admit to each of its three colleges—Arts and Sciences (A&S), Business Administration (BA), and Engineering (E). Each of the three colleges has quotas for the coming year of 1,500; 400; and 200 new students, respectively, and the university has an enrollment goal of 2,000 new students. The university also has benchmark goals that 75 and 25 percent of new students come, respectively, from in-state and out-of-state. Furthermore, the university hopes that 40 percent of the new students will be women and that 1,300 new students will be added to the dormitories. Flexible living arrangements have allowed the elimination of dorm quotas for men and women. Table 10–2 indicates historical dorm percentages which have been

TABLE 10–2

Dorm Percentages by Residency and Sex

Residence	Men	Women
In-state	0.50	0.60
Out-of-state	0.80	0.95

fairly stable over time. The admissions office has estimated the maximum numbers of applicants it expects to meet the minimum requirements for admission to the various programs. These are listed in Table 10–3.

TABLE 10–3

Maximum Number of Students Meeting Minimum Admission Requirements

Students	A&S	BA	E
In-state men	800	400	200
In-state women	400	100	10
Out-of-state men	300	100	50
Out-of-state women	150	50	5

University administrators have rank ordered the following goals which are to be considered in making the admission decisions.

1. Exactly achieve the university admissions goal of 2,000 new students.
2. Achieve the college quotas (with preference given to achieving the goal for Business first, Engineering second, and A&S last).
3. Minimize the underachievement of the goal of 75-percent in-state admissions.
4. Minimize the overachievement of the goal of 25-percent out-of-state admissions.
5. Minimize the underachievement of the housing goal of 1,300 students.
6. Minimize the underachievement of the 40-percent goal for women.
7. Restrict the overachievement of the housing goal to 50 students.

If we let

x_1 = Number of in-state men admitted to A&S,
x_2 = Number of in-state men admitted to Business,
x_3 = Number of in-state men admitted to Engineering,
x_4 = Number of in-state women admitted to A&S,
x_5 = Number of in-state women admitted to Business,
x_6 = Number of in-state women admitted to Engineering,
x_7 = Number of out-of-state men admitted to A&S,
x_8 = Number of out-of-state men admitted to Business,
x_9 = Number of out-of-state men admitted to Engineering,
x_{10} = Number of out-of-state women admitted to A&S,
x_{11} = Number of out-of-state women admitted to Business,
x_{12} = Number of out-of-state women admitted to Engineering,

then the formulation of the problem is given by

minimize

$$z = P_1(d_1^- + d_1^+) + 3P_2(d_3^- + d_3^+) + 2P_2(d_4^- + d_4^+) + P_2(d_2^- + d_2^+) + P_3d_5^- + P_4d_6^+ \\ + P_5d_7^- + P_6d_8^- + P_7d_9^+$$

subject to

$$
\begin{array}{lr}
x_1 & \leq 800 \quad (1) \\
x_2 & \leq 400 \quad (2) \\
x_3 & \leq 200 \quad (3) \\
x_4 & \leq 400 \quad (4) \\
x_5 & \leq 100 \quad (5) \\
x_6 & \leq 10 \quad (6) \\
x_7 & \leq 300 \quad (7) \\
x_8 & \leq 100 \quad (8) \\
x_9 & \leq 50 \quad (9) \\
x_{10} & \leq 150 \quad (10) \\
x_{11} & \leq 50 \quad (11) \\
x_{12} & \leq 5 \quad (12)
\end{array}
$$

$$x_1 + x_2 + x_3 + x_4 + x_5 + x_6 + x_7 + x_8 + x_9 + x_{10} + x_{11} + x_{12} + d_1^- - d_1^+ = 2,000 \quad (13)$$
$$x_1 \quad\quad + x_4 \quad\quad + x_7 \quad\quad + x_{10} \quad\quad + d_2^- - d_2^+ = 1,500 \quad (14)$$
$$x_2 \quad\quad + x_5 \quad\quad + x_8 \quad\quad + x_{11} \quad\quad + d_3^- - d_3^+ = 400 \quad (15)$$
$$x_3 \quad\quad + x_6 \quad\quad + x_9 \quad\quad + x_{12} + d_4^- - d_4^+ = 200 \quad (16)$$
$$x_1 + x_2 + x_3 + x_4 + x_5 + x_6 + d_5^- - d_5^+ = 0.75(x_1 + x_2 + \cdots + x_{12})$$

or

$$0.25x_1 + 0.25x_2 + 0.25x_3 + 0.25x_4 + 0.25x_5 + 0.25x_6 - 0.75x_7 - 0.75x_8 \\ - 0.75x_9 - 0.75x_{10} - 0.75x_{11} - 0.75x_{12} + d_5^- - d_5^+ = 0 \quad (17)$$
$$x_7 + x_8 + x_9 + x_{10} + x_{11} + x_{12} + d_6^- - d_6^+ = 0.25(x_1 + x_2 + \cdots + x_{12})$$

or

$$-0.25x_1 - 0.25x_2 - 0.25x_3 - 0.25x_4 - 0.25x_5 - 0.25x_6 + 0.75x_7 + 0.75x_8$$
$$+ 0.75x_9 + 0.75x_{10} + 0.75x_{11} + 0.75x_{12} + d_6^- - d_6^+ = \quad 0 \quad (18)$$

$$0.5x_1 + 0.5x_2 + 0.5x_3 + 0.6x_4 + 0.6x_5 + 0.6x_6 + 0.8x_7 + 0.8x_8 + 0.8x_9$$
$$+ 0.95x_{10} + 0.95x_{11} + 0.95x_{12} + d_7^- - d_7^+ = 1,300 \quad (19)$$

$$x_4 + x_5 + x_6 + x_{10} + x_{11} + x_{12} + d_8^- - d_8^+ = 0.40(x_1 + x_2 + \cdots + x_{12})$$

or

$$-0.40x_1 - 0.40x_2 - 0.40x_3 + 0.60x_4 + 0.60x_5 + 0.60x_6 - 0.40x_7 - 0.40x_8$$
$$- 0.40x_9 + 0.60x_{10} + 0.60x_{11} + 0.60x_{12} + d_8^- - d_8^+ = \quad 0 \quad (20)$$

$$d_7^+ + d_9^- - d_9^+ = \quad 50 \quad (21)$$

$$\text{all } x_j \text{ and } d_i \geq \quad 0.$$

A few aspects of this formulation should be noted. First, constraints (1) through (12) are system constraints while (13) through (21) are goal constraints. Also, the second highest priority goal involves three subgoals. In the objective function, the deviational variables associated with these subgoals have been assigned the same priority factor, but they have been weighted differently by arbitrarily chosen differential weights (the highest of which is assigned to the most important subgoal). These subgoals might have been handled by simply assigning each a different priority factor. Either approach is acceptable. A final observation relates to the last constraint which consists of deviational variables only. The deviational variable d_7^+ represents the degree of overachievement of the housing goal of 1,300 students. This constraint is specifically established in order to restrict this overachievement to no more than 50 students.

Follow-up Exercises

12. With respect to Example 10.4:

    a. Verify the system constraints using Table 10–3.
    b. Define the deviational variables, $d_i^{-,+}$, and verify each goal constraint.
    c. Verify the objective function.

13. Indicate changes in the formulation if the three subgoals of goal 2 were to be made goals 2, 3, and 4 (with the other goals appropriately renumbered).

14. What other method might have been used to represent the goal restricting overachievement of the housing goal to 50 students?

15. Is there interdependence between goals 3 and 4 which would allow for simplification of the formulation? If so, what are the simplifications in the model?

16. Ms. W. Lib, the Affirmative Action Officer, has questioned the low ranking given to goal 6. Indicate changes in the formulation if the priorities associated with goals 6 and 3 are switched.

17. Describe how you would incorporate considerations relating to minority students classified by ethnic or racial characteristics.

18. What other goals might a university or college consider in making admissions decisions?

10.2   GOAL PROGRAMMING SOLUTION METHODS

A complete exposition of GP solution methods is not consistent with the overview nature of this chapter. To give you an intuitive feel for these procedures, however, we will illustrate graphical solutions and describe simplex-based solutions.

Graphical Solutions

If you remember the graphical approach to solving LP problems, then you will find that procedure very similar to the one used in goal programming. As with LP, graphical solutions are restricted to situations in which there are two real decision variables. For problems suitable to graphical analysis, we need to satisfy the following five conditions:

1. Make certain that all constraints include real variables.[3]
2. Graph all system constraints (those not involving deviational variables) and identify the corresponding area of feasible solutions. If no system constraints exist, then the area of feasible solutions is the entire northeast quadrant.
3. Graph the straight lines corresponding to the goal constraints, labeling the deviational variables.
4. Within the area of feasible solutions identified in step (2), determine the point or points which satisfy the highest priority goal.
5. Sequentially consider the remaining goals and the points which satisfy them to the greatest extent possible. Make certain that a lower priority goal is not achieved by reducing the degree of achievement of higher priority goals.

Example 10.5   Product Mix Problem

Consider a simple product mix problem in which a firm produces two products. Each product must be processed through two departments which have available, respectively, 30 and 60 hours of capacity per day. Each unit of Product 1 requires 2 hours in Department 1 and 6 hours in Department 2. Each unit of Product 2 requires 3 hours in Department 1 and 4 hours in Department 2. Management has rank ordered (from highest to lowest priority) the following goals which it would like achieved in determining the daily product mix:

1. Minimize the underachievement of management's goal of joint total production of 10 units.
2. Minimize the underachievement of management's goal of producing 7 units of Product 2.
3. Minimize the underachievement of management's goal of producing 8 units of Product 1.

---

[3] Goal constraints may sometimes be stated in terms of deviational variables only. In these situations, they must be restated in terms of the real variables prior to proceeding with the graphical analysis.

If we define $x_j =$ units produced of product j and $d_i^{-,+} =$ underachievement $(-)$ or overachievement $(+)$ associated with goal i, then the formulation of this problem is

minimize

$$z = P_1 d_1^- + P_2 d_2^- + P_3 d_3^-$$

subject to

$$
\begin{array}{lll}
2x_1 + 3x_2 & \leq 30 & \text{(1)} \\
6x_1 + 4x_2 & \leq 60 & \text{(2)} \\
x_1 + x_2 + d_1^- - d_1^+ & = 10 & \text{(3)} \\
x_2 + d_2^- - d_2^+ & = 7 & \text{(4)} \\
x_1 + d_3^- - d_3^+ & = 8 & \text{(5)}
\end{array}
$$

$$x_1, x_2, d_1^-, d_1^+, d_2^-, d_2^+, d_3^-, d_3^+ \geq 0.$$

In this problem, constraints (1) and (2) are system constraints. Constraints

FIGURE 10–1

Graphical Solution to Product Mix Goal Programming Problem

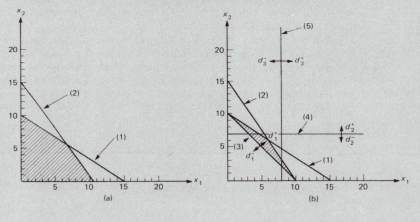

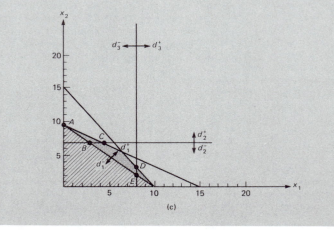

(3) through (5) are goal constraints. Figure 10–1a illustrates the area of feasible solutions associated with the two system constraints. In Figure 10–1b, the lines associated with the goal constraints have been added and the deviational variables have been identified. The area of feasible solutions has been modified in this figure to exclude that area representing under-achievement of the total production goal of 10 units. This was the goal of greatest importance. In Figure 10–1c the second goal has been accounted for by setting d_2^- to zero. The set of points which satisfies the system con-straints and represents fulfillment of the first two goals is represented by area ABC. The final goal is to minimize the underachievement of the goal of producing 8 units of Product 1. The optimal solution occurs at C where d_3^- is minimized as best as possible. We could move to points D or E where d_3^- would equal zero; however, this movement would increase d_2^-, sacrificing the achievement of a higher priority goal.

In the optimal solution daily production equals 7 units of Product 2 and 4.5 units of Product 1. There is overachievement of the joint production goal equal to $(11.5 - 10)$ 1.5 units, exact achievement of the production goal of 7 units of Product 2, and underachievement of the production goal for Product 1 of $(8 - 4.5)$ 3.5 units.

Follow-up Exercises

19. Where would the optimal solution occur if goals 2 and 3 were reversed in their priority?

20. In the above problem, assume that the marginal profits associated with each unit of Products 1 and 2 are, respectively, $2 and $5. Determine the optimal solution if the first two goals remain the same as in the original statement but the third is replaced by a goal which is to achieve a daily profit of $60.

Example 10.6   Graphical Solution to Example 10.2

The media mix problem in Example 10.2 is restated below. All four constraints are goal constraints. Verify for yourself in Figure 10–2 that the optimal solution occurs at point F.

Minimize

$$z = P_1 d_1^- + P_2 d_2^+ + P_3 d_3^+ + P_4 d_4^-$$

subject to

$$
\begin{array}{llr}
10{,}000x_1 + 7{,}500x_2 + d_1^- - d_1^+ = & 750{,}000 & (1) \\
x_1 + \quad x_2 + d_2^- - d_2^+ = & 100 & (2) \\
x_1 \qquad + d_3^- - d_3^+ = & 70 & (3) \\
10{,}000x_1 + 7{,}500x_2 + d_4^- - d_4^+ = & 1{,}000{,}000 & (4)
\end{array}
$$

$$x_1, x_2, d_1^-, d_1^+, d_2^-, d_2^+, d_3^-, d_3^+, d_4^-, d_4^+ \geq \qquad 0.$$

FIGURE 10–2

Graphical Solution to Example 10.2

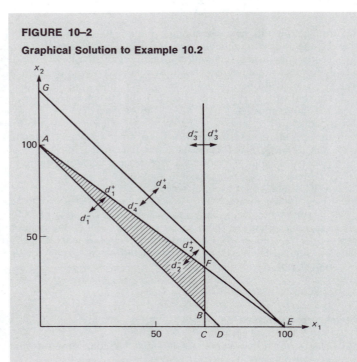

Follow-up Exercises

21. In Example 10.6, interpret fully the optimal solution. How could manage-ment realize its goal of 1 million exposures? Point B requires less ex-penditures, but why is it nonoptimal?

22. Solve Example 10.1 graphically.

23. Solve graphically and compare:

    a. Example 10.3
    b. Exercise 10

24. Solve Exercise 11 graphically. Note that the last constraint, which is constructed of deviational variables only, must be rewritten in terms of the real variables x_1 and x_2.

Simplex-Based Solutions

When a GP problem consists of more than two decision variables, non-graphical procedures must be utilized. Some procedures modify the initial GP formulation in a manner which allows the use of existing simplex computer programs.[4] Another procedure modifies the simplex algorithm itself.[5] In either case, both procedures are simplex-based.

To describe the latter approach in brief, a modified simplex tableau is formulated much in the same manner as with LP. A row is established for each system constraint and each goal constraint, and a column is established for all variables including decision variables, deviational variables, and slack, surplus, or artificial variables where they are required. Slack, surplus, and artificial variables would be introduced for system constraints (nongoal constraints). Slack and surplus variables would be assigned objective function contributions of zero as in the simplex method. Artificial variables would be assigned contributions of $+M$ where $M >>> P_1$. This simply implies that artificial variables are introduced only for the purpose of generating the initial basic feasible solution, and they must be costed in the objective function as significantly less desirable than the deviational variables associated with the goal of highest priority.

In the simplex method the single objective function is embodied in Row (0). The simplex criterion for determining whether there is a better solution requires examination of this row. In the GP solution method multiple criterion rows are established: one for each preemptive priority level in the problem. These rows are usually arranged in order of priority. In moving from one solution to the next, one seeks to satisfy as best as possible the criterion for the achievement of the highest priority goal, followed by the next highest, and so on. Since *goal programming problems are always stated as minimization problems,* the criterion row associated with the highest priority goal is examined for any *positive* coefficients. The entering variable is selected as the column having the largest positive coefficient. If all coefficients are eventually driven to nonpositive values, then that goal has been achieved and attention is then directed to the criterion row associated with the next highest priority goal. Precautions must be taken while moving from iteration to iteration to assure that the levels of achievement for higher priority goals are not sacrificed in an effort to better achieve lower priority goals.

Assessment

Goal programming is a mathematical programming technique which exhibits great potential for handling decision problems involving multiple (often conflicting) goals or objectives. The technique is, relatively speaking, still in its infancy, and there are a number of areas in which research is needed. One of these is sensitivity (postoptimality) analysis. Sensitivity analysis can be conducted on parameters to a limited extent, but the effort required is considerably greater than with linear programming. A key to improvement in this process would be a better understanding of duality

[4] See A. Charnes and W. W. Cooper, *Management Models and Industrial Applications of Linear Programming* (New York: John Wiley & Sons, Inc., 1961) and D. B. Field, "Goal Programming for Forest Management," *Forest Sciences,* vol. 19, no. 2 (1973), pp. 125–35.

[5] For specifics, see A. J. Hughes and D. E. Grawoig, *Linear Programming: An Emphasis on Decision Making* (Reading, Mass.: Addison-Wesley Publishing Co., 1973) and Lee, *Goal Programming.*

theory as it relates to goal programming. If it were possible to explicitly specify the dual of a GP problem, then it might be possible to achieve the degree of power and flexibility associated with postoptimality analysis of the LP model.

10.3 ADVANCED LINEAR PROGRAMMING

As you know by now, linear models play a prominent role in OR/MS. Accordingly, we have given them their proper share of attention: standard linear programming (Chapters 4 through 6), transportation models (Chapter 7), integer programming (Chapter 8), and goal programming (Chapter 10). In this section we complete the treatment of linear models by briefly describing **parametric linear programming, stochastic programming,** and additional algorithms (computational procedures) which are commonly used.

Parametric Linear Programming

Parametric LP is a form of systematic postoptimality (sensitivity) analysis which automatically allows selected parameters (b_i's and c_j's) to be varied continuously over specified ranges. The output from this analysis shows the optimal solution as a function of these changes.

To be more specific, consider the usual objective function for LP,

$$z = c_1x_1 + c_2x_2 + \ldots + c_nx_n,$$

and its parametric LP equivalent for varying objective function contributions (c_j's):

$$z(\Delta) = (c_1 + k_1\Delta)x_1 + (c_2 + k_2\Delta)x_2 + \ldots + (c_n + k_n\Delta)x_n.$$

In this case, $z(\Delta)$ indicates that the criterion is a function of Δ, the **ranging parameter.** Note that the case $\Delta = 0$ yields the original objective function. The k_j's represent *relative rates of change* when the (c_j) parameters are to be varied *simultaneously*. If a selected k_j is set equal to unity and the remaining k_j's are set equal to zero, then the analysis only varies the selected objective function contribution. This is equivalent to varying a selected c_j *independently* of the other c_j's.

Typical computer programs require specific input values for each k_j and a range of values for Δ. A simplex-based procedure is then utilized to provide optimal values of z as a function of Δ, $z^*(\Delta)$, and optimal values of decision variables as a function of Δ, $x_i^*(\Delta)$.

Example 10.7   Air Cargo Problem Re-Revisited

In Chapter 6 we performed extensive sensitivity analyses on the following problem:

maximize

$$z = 20x_1 + 10x_2$$

subject to

$$5x_1 + 4x_2 \leq 24 \quad \text{(Volume)}$$
$$2x_1 + 5x_2 \leq 13 \quad \text{(Weight)}$$
$$x_1, x_2 \geq 0$$

where x_1 and x_2 represent, respectively, the number of containers of beef and pork to be shipped by air cargo; z is in terms of profit in \$100; the first constraint represents 24 cubic yards of volume capacity for the aircraft; and the last constraint represents 13,000 pounds of weight capacity.

The parametric LP equivalent for varying profit contributions simply involves a rewrite of z:

$$z(\Delta) = (20 + k_1\Delta)x_1 + (10 + k_2\Delta)x_2.$$

If we assume independence between variations in the two profit contributions, then to vary c_1 between 20 and 30 requires the specification of $k_1 = 1$, $k_2 = 0$, and $0 \leq \Delta \leq 10$. To vary c_2 between 10 and 25, we specify $k_1 = 0$, $k_2 = 1$, and $0 \leq \Delta \leq 15$. If increases in marginal pork profit are only possible at the expense of corresponding decreases in marginal beef profits, then $k_1 = -1$, $k_2 = 1$, and Δ may be varied as desired.

Parametric LP formulations for right-hand-side constants are stated analogously:

$$a_{i1}x_1 + a_{i2}x_2 + \ldots + a_{in}x_n \quad (\leq, =, \geq) \quad b_i$$

becomes

$$a_{i1}x_1 + a_{i2}x_2 + \ldots + a_{in}x_n \quad (\leq, =, \geq) \quad b_i + k_i\Delta.$$

Follow-up Exercises

25. In the air cargo problem, state the parametric equivalent of z if marginal profit gains in beef are double the corresponding declines in marginal pork profit.

26. State the parametric LP model of the air cargo problem for each of the following cases:

    a. Independence between volume and weight and sensitivity based on increases in volume capacity of up to 16 cubic yards.

    b. Same Δ as in part (a), but where 1 cubic yard of additional volume yields 500 pounds of additional weight capacity.

27. Either by the methods of Chapter 6 or by a parametric LP computer program which is available to you, fill in the following table for sensitivity of the air cargo solution to changes in

    a. Profit contributions where $k_1 = 0$, $k_2 = 1$, and $-10 \leq \Delta \leq 50$.

    **b. Capacities where $k_1 = 1$, $k_2 = 0.5$, and $0 \leq \Delta \leq 50$.

Optimal z	Optimal x_1	Optimal x_2	Δ
.	.	.	.
.	.	.	.
.	.	.	.

Stochastic Programming

The specification of deterministic parameters represents one of the key underlying assumptions of the general LP model introduced in Chapter 4. Subsequently, sensitivity analysis was developed as a means to acknowledge uncertainty in the estimation of parameters. If one or more parameters in an LP model are directly treated as random variables from specified probability distributions, then stochastic programming procedures are required for solving the model.[6]

A simple approach to solving LP models with random variables for parameters is the specification of expected values (means) for each probabilistic parameter, followed by the implementation of the usual (deterministic) simplex solution. Unfortunately, it can be shown that this procedure will usually yield fallacious optimal solutions. For this reason, only stochastic programming procedures can guarantee the correct optimal solution (assuming, of course, that the data are correct).

Three approaches are common in stochastic programming: The first two seek an equivalent (but enlarged) deterministic version of the stochastic model which is then solved either by the simplex method (if the resulting model is linear) or by one of the nonlinear methods discussed in Sections 10.4 and 10.5 (if the resulting model is nonlinear); the third approach, termed **chance-constrained programming,** formulates a deterministic version of the stochastic model by incorporating what are called chance constraints (without enlarging the original problem). Significant increases in computational burden characterize the first two approaches, whereas conceptual problems in interpreting the optimal solution typify the third approach.

In general, as with all OR models, users must weigh the potential benefits associated with using more sophisticated models against the likely increase in costs which such models engender.

Extensions of the Simplex Algorithm

The widespread use of linear programming has promoted the development of simplex-based procedures which more efficiently solve either large-scale problems or problems with special structure. The transportation method is a good illustration of the latter. In this section we describe three popular extensions (from many available) of the simplex method.

The **revised simplex method** is geared to computer implementation by carrying tableau information more efficiently and by effecting calculations using matrix algebra. The short tableau in Section 5.8 (without the column for the basic variable which exists) illustrates the necessity of storing only the coefficients associated with nonbasic variables. These two extensions allow the efficient solution of problems having in the neighborhood of 4,000 constraints and several times that number of variables.

The **dual simplex method** essentially applies the simplex method to the equivalent dual problem without directly specifying the dual. It offers

---

[6] A review of probability theory is provided in Appendix A.

computational efficiencies for problems having a large number of artificial variables. Additionally, this method considerably simplifies the process of sensitivity analysis.

The **decomposition method** applies the revised simplex method to large-scale multidivisional problems. Multidivisional problems are those which can be decomposed into separate divisions or subproblems for individual optimization. Thereafter, the separate optimal solutions can be synthesized into an overall optimal solution. A large corporation with many autonomous divisions represents a typical arena for this approach.

10.4 NONLINEAR PROGRAMMING

Although nonlinear objective functions and constraints are considered in the classical optimization techniques of Chapters 2 and 3, in the brief treatment of piecewise linear functions in Section 4.6, and in dynamic programming, our focus on mathematical programming models has been characterized by linear objective functions and linear constraint relationships. This "linearization of the world" has been a useful presumption in that many relationships are indeed linear, or if not, they can be approximated well by linear functions. There are, however, many problems in which the objective function and/or constraints cannot be reasonably represented as linear. We can all think of situations in which the assumption of "constant returns to scale" is not a valid one, such as production relationships, sales response functions, and inventory cost relationships. To deal with these types of problems, a body of mathematical programming techniques, falling under the general classification of **nonlinear programming (NLP),** has evolved.

Concepts and Issues

The general form of a nonlinear programming problem can be stated as:

maximize (minimize)

$$z = f(x_1, x_2, \ldots, x_n)$$

subject to

$$g_1(x_1, x_2, \ldots, x_n) \quad (\leq, =, \geq) \quad b_1$$
$$g_2(x_1, x_2, \ldots, x_n) \quad (\leq, =, \geq) \quad b_2$$
$$\vdots \qquad\qquad\qquad\qquad \vdots$$
$$g_m(x_1, x_2, \ldots, x_n) \quad (\leq, =, \geq) \quad b_m$$
$$x_1, x_2, \ldots, x_n \geq 0$$

where *at least* one of the functions $f(x_1, x_2, \ldots, x_n)$ or $g_i(x_1, x_2, \ldots, x_n)$ is nonlinear.

The generalized problem allows for a great variety of nonlinear programming forms. A problem may consist of:

1. A linear objective function and a constraint set with some or all of the constraints nonlinear.
2. A nonlinear objective function and a linear constraint set.
3. A nonlinear objective function and a constraint set with some or all of the constraints nonlinear.

Compared to linear programming, a number of issues tend to complicate the solution process.

Our discussions in Chapter 2 developed the concept of *local* versus *global* extreme points. This was never a problem in linear programming; however, in NLP problems it can be very difficult to distinguish between the two. We noted in Chapter 4 that the constraints in any LP model form a *convex set;* this allowed the identification of global optimal solutions in terms of extreme (corner) points. Unfortunately, NLP models are often characterized by nonconvex constraint sets. For example, in Figure 10–3, the constraint set consists of both a linear and a nonlinear constraint. Note that if the objective function is linear with slope as indicated and of the maximization type, we encounter a situation where point B can be viewed as a local maximum, but the global maximum occurs at point A. This is easy enough to see graphically; however, for other than simple models, NLP algorithms often have difficulty in making these distinctions.

Thus, one of the attractive features of linear programming is that the linear (convex) constraint set always results in a corner point optimal solution which is selected from a set of basic feasible solutions. These basic feasible solutions always consist of m basic variables, where m equals the number of constraints. On the other hand, in nonlinear programming, optimal solutions may occur at corner points, at other boundary points on the area of feasible solutions, or at interior points within the area of feasible solutions. In addition, the number of basic variables cannot be generalized as in LP.

FIGURE 10–3

Nonconvex Constraint Set with Local and Global Optima

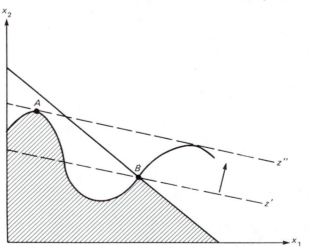

Example 10.8 Corner Point Optimal Solution

Consider the following NLP problem consisting of a linear constraint set and a nonlinear objective function:

maximize

$$z = 20x_1 + 6x_2 + x_1x_2 - 0.25x_1^2 - 0.5x_2^2$$

subject to

$$2x_1 + x_2 \leq 80 \tag{1}$$
$$x_1 + 2x_2 \leq 80 \tag{2}$$
$$x_1 + x_2 \leq 50 \tag{3}$$
$$x_1, x_2 \geq 0.$$

As can be seen in Figure 10–4, the objective function has been graphed for three values of z. These so-called **contour lines** indicate all points which

FIGURE 10–4

Corner Point Optimal Solution

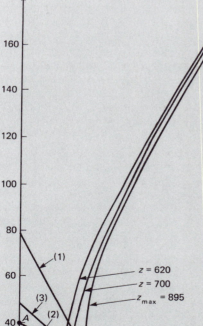

result in the same value for z. In this example the maximum occurs at the corner point C (30, 20), where the contour line associated with $z = 895$ is tangent to the constraint set ($ABCDE$).

Example 10.9   Boundary Point Optimal Solution

In the following NLP problem, the objective function is a quadratic form which graphs as a circle.[7] The constraint set is again linear.

Minimize

$$z = x_1^2 + x_2^2 - 14x_1 - 6x_2 + 58$$

subject to

$$x_1 + x_2 \le 25 \tag{1}$$
$$2x_1 + x_2 \ge 20 \tag{2}$$
$$2x_1 + 3x_2 \ge 36 \tag{3}$$

$$x_1, x_2 \ge 0.$$

FIGURE 10–5

Boundary Point Optimal Solution

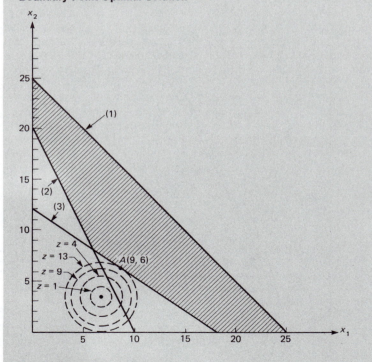

---

[7] The objective function can be rewritten as $z = (x_1 - 7)^2 + (x_2 - 3)^2$. This conforms to the quadratic form $(x - a)^2 + (y - b)^2 = c^2$, which represents a circle with center at (a, b) and radius of c.

Note in Figure 10–5 that the objective function is minimized at a value of 13 at point *A*, which is a boundary point on the area of feasible solutions, but not a corner point.

Follow-up Exercise

28. In the last example, verify that the objective function is minimized at an *interior* point within the area of feasible solutions if the constraint set is revised to be

$$2x_1 + x_2 \geq 10$$
$$2x_1 + 4x_2 \geq 20$$
$$x_1 + x_2 \leq 25$$
$$x_1, x_2 \geq 0.$$

Convex Programming

Convex programming is concerned with a class of nonlinear programming problems which are characterized by structural features that facilitate the solution process. Convex programming problems involve the maximization of a *concave* (or the minimization of a *convex*) objective function subject to a group of constraints which form a convex set of feasible

FIGURE 10–6

Concave and Convex Functions

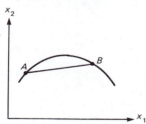

(a) Strictly Concave Function

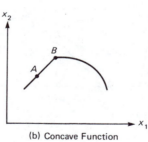

(b) Concave Function

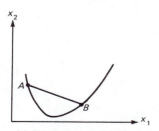

(c) Strictly Convex Function

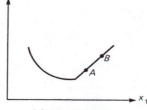

(d) Convex Function

solutions. These structural properties facilitate the process of differentiating between global and local extreme points.

In Chapter 2 we illustrated concave and convex functions. We now offer more precise definitions. Referring to Figure 10–6a, a function is said to be **strictly concave** if the line segment connecting any two points on the function lies entirely *below* the function itself. A function is said to be **concave** (but not strictly concave) if the line segment lies either on the function or entirely below it. This situation occurs whenever there are any linear segments on the function, as in Figure 10–6b. Similarly, a function is **strictly convex** (Figure 10–6c) if the line segment connecting any two points on the function lies entirely *above* the function and **convex** (Figure 10–6d) if the line segment lies either on or above the function.

It is the concavity (convexity) of the objective function, coupled with a *convex set* of feasible solutions (as illustrated in Figure 4–7), which leads to a reduction in the difficulty often associated with distinguishing global extreme points from local extreme points. These properties simply imply that when an algorithm has found a *local optimum* within the area of feasible solutions, it has, in fact, found the *global optimum*.

In actual practice, concavity-convexity conclusions regarding functions and sets in *n*-space are based on mathematical procedures. To illustrate these concepts, however, consider Figure 10–7, which graphically il-

FIGURE 10–7

Local and Global Maxima

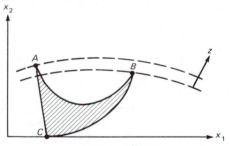

(a) Nonconvex Set

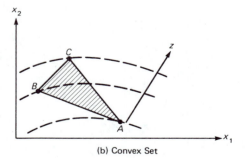

(b) Convex Set

lustrates two variations for a problem requiring maximization. In Figure 10–7a the concave objective function is to be maximized over the non-convex set of feasible solutions ABC. If we assume that maximization of z is in the direction indicated, then the potential confusion at point B on the part of solution algorithms becomes evident. An examination of any feasible point in the vicinity of point B would lead one to the conclusion that at the very least there is a local maximum at point B. Observation of this simple graphic situation, however, indicates that the global maximum occurs at point A. In Figure 10–7b, the concave objective function is to be maximized over a convex set of feasible solutions. Until point C is reached, an examination of any candidate point for the global maximum would reveal that there is at least one neighboring point in the convex set which has a greater value for the objective function.

Quadratic Programming

Quadratic programming problems represent a special class of convex programming problems having a quadratic objective function and a linear constraint set. From the standpoint of solution methods, these problems are relatively simple compared with other nonlinear programming forms. This is because the form of the quadratic programming problem is not too different from the standard linear programming problem. The only difference is the inclusion of some second-order terms in the objective function.[8]

A generalized statement of the quadratic programming problem is

minimize

$$z = \sum_{j=1}^{n} c_j x_j + \sum_{j=1}^{n} \sum_{k=1}^{n} c_{jk} x_j x_k$$

subject to

$$\sum_{j=1}^{n} a_{ij} x_j \ (\leq, =, \geq)\ b_i \qquad i = 1, \ldots, m$$

$$x_j \geq 0 \qquad\qquad j = 1, \ldots, n.$$

Example 10.8, which resulted in a corner point optimal solution, is a quadratic programming problem. The strong similarity with the LP model has led to solution procedures which, with some modifications, utilize the simplex method to derive optimal solutions to quadratic programming problems.

---

[8] A second-order term is one for which the sum of the exponents on all variables is 2. For example, $3x_1^2$ and $6x_1 x_2$ are both second-order terms.

Example 10.10   Portfolio Model

A classical example of a quadratic programming problem is the investment portfolio selection model as formulated by Markowitz.[9] It is widely held that most investors are concerned primarily with two attributes of the investment: *return* on the investment and *risk*. Typically there is an inverse relationship between return and risk. An investor can often increase *expected* return by accepting greater risk in the investment, and vice versa.

Most portfolio models focus on determining the amount of funds to commit to each security (stock or bond) from among a set of specified securities. The objective in the Markowitz model is to minimize some measure of the risk associated with the portfolio while assuring some minimum return on the total investment. Return on a security over a specified period of time is defined as net proceeds (final market price minus initial market price plus dividends or interest) divided by initial market price. For example, if you bought a stock now for $100, sold it a year from now for $105, and received dividend payments amounting to $3, then your return would be 0.08 (or 8 percent per year). Risk is related to the variability in the value of the investment. Specifically, Markowitz uses the "variance" in the return on investment as the measure of risk. Typically, individual returns within a set of investments exhibit statistical dependence; that is, over time the returns for any two securities may exhibit positive or negative correlation. For this reason, investors often seek diversification in their portfolios. To account for the risk associated with nondiversification, the covariance in the returns between pairs of investments is used.[10]

If we let

x_j = Proportion of available capital invested in alternative j,
s_j^2 = Variance in the return for investment j,
$s_{i,j}^2$ = Covariance between returns of investments i and j,
r_j = Expected return on investment j,
r_m = Minimum desired return on portfolio,
n = Number of securities,

then the Markowitz model can be generalized as the following quadratic programming problem:

minimize

$$z = x_1^2 s_1^2 + x_2^2 s_2^2 + \cdots + x_n^2 s_n^2 + \tfrac{1}{2}(x_1 x_2 s_{1,2}^2 + x_1 x_3 s_{1,3}^2 + \cdots + x_{n-1} x_n s_{n-1,n}^2)$$

subject to

$$x_1 + x_2 + \cdots + x_n = 1.0 \tag{1}$$
$$r_1 x_1 + r_2 x_2 + \cdots + r_n x_n \geq r_m \tag{2}$$

$$x_1, x_2, \ldots, x_n \geq 0.$$

The ($\tfrac{1}{2}$) coefficient preceding the covariance terms in the objective function compensates for the duplication of these terms in the expansion. Note that

[9] Harry M. Markowitz, *Portfolio Selection: Efficient Diversification of Investments*, Cowles Foundation Monograph, No. 16 (New York: John Wiley & Sons, 1959).

[10] Covariance is a measure which is related to the coefficient of correlation. See Section A.6 in Appendix A at the end of the book.

constraint (1) specifies that all available funds must be invested. Further note that the objective function represents a weighted variance for the portfolio.

Follow-up Exercises

29. Reformulate the objective function if the returns are all statistically independent.
30. Can you bypass constraint (1) by specifying "cash" as an investment alternative? What would be its return and risk?
31. Formulate a portfolio model which maximizes return subject to a risk constraint. Do you foresee problems in solving this model? Explain.

10.5 SOLUTION METHODS FOR NONLINEAR PROGRAMMING PROBLEMS

In Chapters 2 and 3 we introduced classical optimization procedures for nonlinear objective functions. The calculus was found to be useful in addressing unconstrained problems involving relatively few variables. In addition we discussed the *Lagrange multiplier method* as a means of handling constrained optimization problems having equality constraints. In practice, these techniques become very inefficient in solving nonlinear programming problems of any size.

We also mentioned the *Kuhn-Tucker conditions* for solving problems where some or all constraints have the form of inequalities. The Kuhn-Tucker conditions are a set of equations (often nonlinear) which must be solved simultaneously. These conditions are of theoretical significance in that they provide a set of *necessary conditions* for extreme points in constrained optimization problems. In problems possessing certain properties they may in fact be *sufficient conditions*. Convex programming problems are an example of where this is true. Like the Lagrangian method, however, the Kuhn-Tucker approach suffers from computational inefficiency. In large-scale problems, solutions are essentially impossible.

In this section we will overview some of the more popular approaches to solving nonlinear programming problems. A detailed discussion of these techniques is beyond the scope of the text. Those of you interested in a more in-depth treatment are urged to consult references cited at the end of the chapter.

Separable Programming

In Section 4.6 we discussed the extension of linear programming in which nonlinear relationships are approximated by piecewise linear functions. Under certain conditions, this approach can be very useful in solving nonlinear programming problems. When this approach is applied to convex programs, it is referred to as **separable programming.** If the nonlinear relationships in a problem are "separable," then they may be approximated by a group of linear functions. For a function to be separable it implies that any nonlinear function of the form

$$f(x_1, x_2, \ldots, x_n)$$

can be rewritten in an equivalent form

$$f_1(x_1) + f_2(x_2) + \ldots + f_n(x_n)$$

where the equivalent function involves additive relationships (linear or nonlinear) expressed in terms of each different variable in the original function. The nonlinear component functions in the new relationship are each approximated by a series of linear segments in a manner similar to that illustrated in Section 4.6.

It should be apparent that one of the advantages of approximating nonlinear relationships with linear approximations is that the problem becomes linearized; thus, it lends itself to solution by simplex-based methods. One must always be aware, however, of the error which is introduced by using these approximations. The extent of the error can be reduced by increasing the number of linear segments used to represent the nonlinear functions, but the computational burden also increases.

Gradient Methods

Gradient methods represent another approach to solving certain types of nonlinear programming problems. The **gradient** of a function is the vector of partial derivatives associated with the function. Given the function

$$f(x_1, x_2, \ldots, x_n),$$

the gradient is defined as

$$\nabla \mathbf{f} = \begin{pmatrix} \dfrac{\partial f}{\partial x_1} \\ \dfrac{\partial f}{\partial x_2} \\ \cdot \\ \cdot \\ \cdot \\ \dfrac{\partial f}{\partial x_n} \end{pmatrix}.$$

For example, given the function

$$f(x_1, x_2, x_3) = x_1 x_2 + x_1 x_3 + 2 x_2 x_3 - x_1^2 - x_2^2 - x_3^2$$

the gradient is

$$\nabla \mathbf{f} = \begin{pmatrix} \partial f/\partial x_1 \\ \partial f/\partial x_2 \\ \partial f/\partial x_3 \end{pmatrix} = \begin{pmatrix} x_2 + x_3 - 2x_1 \\ x_1 + 2x_3 - 2x_2 \\ x_1 + 2x_2 - 2x_3 \end{pmatrix}.$$

When the gradient is evaluated at any point—$(x_1, x_2, \ldots, x_n)$—it indicates the direction of steepest ascent along the function *from that point*. For the previous function, the gradient evaluated at $x_1 = 1$, $x_2 = 2$, $x_3 = 1$ is

$$\nabla \mathbf{f} = \begin{pmatrix} 1 \\ -1 \\ 3 \end{pmatrix}.$$

From the point $(1, 2, 1)$ the projection of the vector $\begin{pmatrix} 1 \\ -1 \\ 3 \end{pmatrix}$ results in the steepest possible ascent along the function. If you envision the function in terms of a set of contours, then the gradient vector projects itself in a direction which is perpendicular to the slope contour at the point being evaluated.

For maximization problems, gradient methods are somewhat analogous to mountain climbing. Just as there are different routes which may be taken in climbing a mountain, there are different gradient approaches for "searching" the surface of a mathematical function. If you follow the direction of the gradient vector, you might think of yourself standing at the bottom of a mountain and looking for the direction of steepest ascent. Having identified this direction, you proceed for a distance in this direction, stopping at a second point. From the new location, you survey the various grades and select the direction of steepest ascent in which to move to a third location. If you continue this pattern, then eventually you should reach the "top of the mountain" (maximum of the function).

Example 10.11   Gradient Solution-Unconstrained Problem

To illustrate a gradient approach consider the following concave function for which we wish to identify the global maximum:

$$y = 2x_1 + 5x_2 + x_1 x_2 - x_1^2 - x_2^2 + 10.$$

The gradient for this function is

$$\nabla \mathbf{y} = \begin{pmatrix} 2 + x_2 - 2x_1 \\ 5 + x_1 - 2x_2 \end{pmatrix}.$$

Arbitrarily, we begin the search from the origin: $x_1 = x_2 = 0$. It should be pointed out that any point can be selected as the starting point.

If we evaluate the gradient at our starting point we find that

$$\nabla \mathbf{y} = \begin{pmatrix} 2 \\ 5 \end{pmatrix}.$$

This vector implies that from the point $x_1 = x_2 = 0$, the instantaneous rate of increase in y is $+2$ units for each unit increase in x_1 and $+5$ units for each unit increase in x_2. From the standpoint of moving in the direction of the gradient, the next question is how far do we move? What we would like to do is move along the gradient as long as the value of y increases. Thus, we are concerned essentially with determining the optimal *step size, t**. Co-ordinates of points along the projection of the gradient can be defined as a function of the **step size** (*t*) by the following relationship:

$$\mathbf{x}' = \mathbf{x} + t\nabla \mathbf{y}$$

where $\mathbf{x}'$ is the vector of coordinates for the new point and $\mathbf{x}$ is the vector of coordinates for the original point.

In our example,

$$\mathbf{x}' = \begin{pmatrix} x_1' \\ x_2' \end{pmatrix}$$

$$= \begin{pmatrix} 0 \\ 0 \end{pmatrix} + t \begin{pmatrix} 2 \\ 5 \end{pmatrix}$$

or

$$x_1' = 0 + 2t \tag{1}$$

and

$$x_2' = 0 + 5t. \tag{2}$$

If we substitute these relationships for the new coordinates of x_1 and x_2 into the original function, then y becomes a function of the variable t. And, as can be seen below, it is a simple matter to differentiate the function with respect to t to determine the value of t which maximizes y:

$$y = 2x_1 + 5x_2 + x_1 x_2 - x_1^2 - x_2^2 + 10$$
$$= 2(2t) + 5(5t) + (2t)(5t) - (2t)^2 - (5t)^2 + 10$$
$$= 29t - 19t^2 + 10$$

$$\frac{dy}{dt} = 29 - 38t.$$

By setting this first derivative equal to zero, we find that y will be maximized at $t^* = 0.763$, or the optimal step size is 0.763. Substituting into (1) and (2), we can identify the coordinates of the new point to be

$$x_1' = 0 + 2(0.763)$$
$$= 1.526$$

and

$$x_2' = 0 + 5(0.763)$$
$$= 3.815.$$

Having reached the point (1.526, 3.815), where the value of y is 21.07, we determine the direction of steepest ascent from this point by evaluating the gradient at (1.526, 3.815):

$$\nabla \mathbf{y} = \begin{pmatrix} 2.763 \\ -1.104 \end{pmatrix}.$$

Moving along this vector, coordinates of potential stopping points are given by

$$\mathbf{x}' = \begin{pmatrix} 1.526 \\ 3.815 \end{pmatrix} + t \begin{pmatrix} 2.763 \\ -1.104 \end{pmatrix}$$

or

$$x_1' = 1.526 + 2.763t$$

and

$$x_2' = 3.815 - 1.104t.$$

Again, to determine the optimal step size, these expressions for x_1' and x_2' are substituted into the original equation to yield

$$y = f(t)$$
$$= -11.903t^2 + 8.853t + 21.066.$$

Differentiating as before, t^* is found to equal 0.372; the coordinates of the new stopping point are (2.554, 3.404), with a value of y equal to 22.71. Table 10–4 summarizes the first four iterations.

TABLE 10–4

Iterations for Gradient Solution

Iteration	t^*	(x_1, x_2)	y
0.........................		(0.00,0.00)	10.00
1.........................	0.763	(1.53,3.82)	21.07
2.........................	0.372	(2.55,3.40)	22.71
3.........................	0.762	(2.78,3.97)	22.96
4.........................	0.374	(2.93,3.91)	22.99

This problem is the same as Exercise 9 in Chapter 3. By observation, it is apparent that the gradient approach is converging toward the global optimal point (3, 4), where y is maximized at a value of 23. It is worth noting that, given a nonconcave function which has stationary points, the gradient method would converge on a local maximum (which may or may not be the global maximum).

The process of minimizing a function by gradient techniques is not unlike the process of searching the floor of a valley for its lowest point. Since the projection of the gradient corresponds to increases in the value of the function, it follows that the negative of the gradient provides the direction of decreases along the function. New coordinates, therefore, must be defined according to $x' = x - t\nabla y$; otherwise, the procedure is identical to that outlined in Example 10.11.

The preceding simple example illustrates the general idea of gradient approaches for unconstrained problems. For constrained optimization, the constrained problem is converted into an equivalent unconstrained problem by constructing the Lagrangian function. The new function is then searched for a saddle point. (A saddle point is illustrated in Figure 3–4.)

The multiplicity of gradient methods essentially represents an effort to speed convergence on the optimal solution and to improve stopping rules.

In many instances gradient techniques simply attempt to get "as close as possible" to the optimal solution. Gradient approaches may cycle around the optimal solution point, requiring tremendous numbers of iterations to identify it exactly. To deal with the tradeoff between precision and computational burden, most techniques use a stopping rule which compares changes in the values of either the independent variables or the criterion variable between successive solutions. If the change is within a pre-specified tolerance, then the search terminates.

Problems which are multimodal or which have pronounced *ridges* cause further difficulty for gradient methods. Many iterations may be executed with relatively little improvement, only to find that one is considerably distant from the optimal solution.

Follow-up Exercises

32. Confirm iterations 3 and 4 in Table 10–4.

33. What would be the last iteration in Table 10–4 if the algorithm is to stop whenever:
    a. The criterion changes by less than 1 percent?
    b. Both decision variables change by less than 1 percent?
    From the standpoint of actual decisions, which rule do you prefer and why?

34. Carry out iterations starting with the coordinate (4, 5). Stop the computational procedure by applying the stopping rule in part (a) of the preceding exercise.

35. Verify that the gradient approach converges to the point (1, −5) when minimizing

$$y = 4x_1^2 + 2x_2^2 - 8x_1 - 2x_2 + 1.$$

This problem was solved by classical methods in Example 3.4, page 73.

Other Methods

As with LP models, many specialized procedures have been developed for solving NLP models with special structure. Three of these procedures are particularly common. **Branch-and-bound** procedures can be used to solve convex programming problems having variables which are pure or mixed-integer. These procedures are similar to that described in Section 8.4. The **Sequential Unconstrained Minimization Technique (SUMT)** converts a convex programming problem into a sequence of unconstrained optimization problems by combining the objective function and constraints into a single function. Then each individual problem in the sequence may be solved by, say, classical or gradient methods. **Geometric Programming** applies to certain formidable problems having nonlinear (power) terms in the objective function and the constraints. This procedure utilizes the dual to transform the problem into an equivalent problem having a concave objective function and linear constraints. This latter problem then can be solved by one of the available procedures for solving convex programs having linear constraints.

Assessment

Many other techniques have been proposed for solving nonlinear programming problems. In most instances, they have been developed to exploit specific structural properties of problems. Indicative of this are the large groups of solution methods proposed for convex programming problems and quadratic programming problems. These methods are usually compared with one another on the basis of convergence properties and computational burden. Unfortunately, no solution method is uniformly efficient in solving all types of nonlinear programming problems. Although the outlook for the development of such a solution technique is uncertain, considerable progress has been made in refining solution methodologies for classes of NLP problems.

As with integer and dynamic programs, a word of caution is in order: The level of efficiency in solving medium and large-scale NLP problems is not that impressive. Users must constantly ask questions regarding the cost-benefit tradeoff of requiring an optimal solution. In many instances, prohibitive costs will force the user to turn to the techniques described in Chapter 16.

SELECTED REFERENCES

Charnes, A., and Cooper, W. W.   *Management Models and Industrial Applications of Linear Programming.* New York: John Wiley & Sons, Inc., 1961.

Gue, Ronald L., and Thomas, Michael E.   *Mathematical Methods in Operations Research.* New York: The Macmillan Company, 1968.

Hughes, A. J., and Grawoig, D. E.   *Linear Programming: An Emphasis on Decision Making.* Reading, Mass.: Addison-Wesley Publishing Co., 1973.

Ijiri, Y.   *Management Goals and Accounting for Control.* Chicago: Rand McNally, 1965.

Lee, Sang M.   *Goal Programming for Decision Analysis.* Philadelphia: Auerbach Publishers, Inc., 1972.

Loomba, Narenda Paul, and Turban, Efraim.   *Applied Programming for Management.* New York: Holt, Rinehart and Winston, Inc., 1974.

McMillan, Claude, Jr.   *Mathematical Programming: An Introduction to the Design and Application of Optimal Decision Machines.* New York: John Wiley & Sons, Inc., 1970.

Sivazlian, B. D., and Stanfel, L. E.   *Optimization Techniques in Operations Research.* Englewood Cliffs, N.J.: Prentice-Hall, Inc., 1975.

Taha, Hamdy A.   *Operations Research: An Introduction.* New York: The Macmillan Company, 1971.

Wagner, Harvey M.   *Principles of Operations Research,* 2d ed. Englewood Cliffs, N.J.: Prentice-Hall, Inc., 1975.

Zangwill, Willard I.   *Non-Linear Programming: A Unified Approach.* Englewood Cliffs, N.J.: Prentice-Hall, Inc., 1969.

ADDITIONAL EXERCISES

36. Given the following goal programming problem:

Minimize

$$z = P_1 d_1^- + P_2 d_2^- + P_3 d_3^- + P_4 d_3^+$$

subject to

$$
\begin{array}{lr}
4x_1 + 2x_2 & \leq 64 & (1) \\
2x_1 + 3x_2 & \leq 48 & (2) \\
5x_1 + 6x_2 + d_1^- - d_1^+ = 60 & (3) \\
x_1 \quad\quad + d_2^- - d_2^+ = 8 & (4) \\
x_2 + d_3^- - d_3^+ = 6 & (5)
\end{array}
$$

$$x_1, x_2, d_1^-, d_1^+, d_2^-, d_2^+, d_3^-, d_3^+ \geq 0.$$

a. Solve graphically.
b. Solve graphically if the right-hand side of constraint (4) equals 20.
c. Solve the original problem if the objective function is

$$z = P_1(d_1^- + d_1^+) + P_2 d_2^- + P_3 d_3^- + P_4 d_3^+.$$

37. Given the following goal programming problem:

Minimize

$$z = P_1(d_1^- + d_1^+) + P_2 d_{2|}^- + P_3 d_3^+$$

subject to

$$
\begin{array}{lr}
2x_1 + 4x_2 & \geq 20 & (1) \\
5x_1 + 3x_2 & \geq 30 & (2) \\
x_1 & \geq 3 & (3) \\
x_1 + x_2 + d_1^- - d_1^+ = 12 & (4) \\
x_2 + d_2^- - d_2^+ = 4 & (5) \\
x_1 \quad\quad + d_3^- - d_3^+ = 6 & (6)
\end{array}
$$

$$x_1, x_2, d_1^-, d_1^+, d_2^-, d_2^+, d_3^-, d_3^+ \geq 0.$$

a. Solve graphically.
b. Solve the original problem graphically if there is an added constraint $(x_2 + d_4^- - d_4^+ = 12)$ and an added term in the objective function $(P_4 d_4^-)$.

38. Solve Exercise 36 if x_1 and x_2 are restricted to nonnegative integer values. What does this restriction imply about the values of the deviational variables?

39. Solve Exercise 37 if x_1 and x_2 are restricted to nonnegative integer values. What does this restriction imply about the values of the deviational variables?

40. *Product Mix Problem*   Example 4.5 involved a product mix decision. In addition to the information given in that problem regarding constraints, assume that management has specified the following goals (in order of preference):

1. The total number of units produced of Product *A* during the two periods must be exactly 500 units.
2. The total number of units produced of Product *B* during the two periods must be exactly 700 units.
3. The amount by which total costs exceed $5,000 is to be minimized.

Formulate this as a goal programming problem.

41. *Personnel Model* Exercise 48 on page 135 in Chapter 4 involved recruiting for a new federal agency. Formulate this as a goal programming model if the management has specified the following goals (in order of preference):

1. Minimize the amount of overexpenditure for recruiting purposes if the budget is $2.5 million.
2. Minimize the underachievement of the goal that women constitute at least 40 percent of new hirings.
3. Minimize the underachievement of the goal that minorities constitute at least 50 percent of new hirings.
4. Restrict the overexpenditure for recruiting costs to $250,000.

42. *Portfolio Model* Exercise 51 on page 137 in Chapter 4 involved determining the best investment portfolio for an endowment fund.
   a. Formulate this as a goal programming model if the fund manager has specified the following goals (in order of preference):

   1. Minimize the underachievement of the goal of a 7 percent return on investment.
   2. Minimize the overachievement of the goal that the weighted risk of the portfolio equal 5.5 percent.
   3. Minimize the underachievement of the goal of $15,000 in annual dividends.
   4. Minimize the underachievement of the goal that 25 percent of the total investment be in alternatives 6, 7 and 8 (combined).
   5. Restrict the overachievement of the immediately preceding goal to 5 percent (that is, joint investment no more than 30 percent of total investment).
   6. Restrict the overachievement of the weighted risk goal to 1 percent.

   b. Discuss advantages and disadvantages of this model v. the model of Exercise 51 in Chapter 4 and the model presented in Example 10.10.

43. *Cargo Loading* Good old Hugh Moore is retired on Nantucket and spends his summers driving an ice cream truck which he purchased two years ago. Recently, Hugh completed a college-by-mail course entitled "Management Science for the Elderly." This gave him the idea to ask his progressive supplier, the O.R. Ice Cream Company to advise all of its 10,000 drivers as to the best mix of ice cream products to put on their trucks each week. The accompanying table indicates (for Hugh's operation) the possible products, their volume, profit margin, minimum weekly demand (based upon past experience), and maximum weekly demand.

Item	Volume (ft.^{3})	Profit Margin	Minimum Demand	Maximum Demand
Popsicles (doz.)...................	0.25	$0.36	40 doz.	80 doz.
Cones (doz.)......................	0.30	0.24	24 doz.	64 doz.
Sandwiches (doz.)................	0.20	0.30	32 doz.	56 doz.
Cups (doz.).......................	0.25	0.30	36 doz.	76 doz.
Sundaes (doz.)...................	0.30	0.60	16 doz.	48 doz.
Pints.............................	0.05	0.10	96	240
Quarts...........................	0.10	0.22	96	200
Half-gallons......................	0.20	0.50	120	280

Hugh's truck has a volume capacity of 128 ft.³ In deciding upon the mix of products to carry, Hugh has specified the following goals (in order of importance):

1. Minimize the underachievement of making $300 in profit each week.
2. Minimize the underachievement of meeting the expected minimum demand for each item (differentially weighted according to relative profit margin).
3. Fill the truck exactly to capacity.
4. Minimize the overachievement of carrying no more than the maximum expected weekly demand for each item (differentially weighted according to relative volume of the items).

Formulate the goal programming model for this problem.

44. *Forest Management* Consider the following simplified forest management problem for a small national forest. In the next fiscal year 20,000 acres are to be allocated in a manner which comes as close as possible to meeting a set of four specified goals. Goals relate to the four uses which this particular forest can be put to: backpacking, hunting, special habitats for timber wolf, and timber cutting. Each acre of forest can accommodate 1,000 visitor-days for backpacking, 100 visitor-days for hunting, two wolves, and 12,000 cubic feet of timber. The operating cost per year associated with each type of land use differs because of the nature of supervision, types of personnel, and so on. Per acre annual operating costs are estimated as $15 for backpacking, $20 for hunting, $5 for wolves, and $4 for timber cutting. Operating expenses for these activities, however, *must* be paid for out of revenue from leasing timber land to the lumber companies. Each acre designated for timber cutting is leased for $240 per year. Goals, in order of importance, have been dictated by "top brass" in the Department of Interior:

1. Minimize the overachievement of cutting 6 million cubic feet of timber (because of pressure from environmentalists).
2. Minimize the underachievement of 700,000 visitor-days for hunting (the hunting lobby is strong in Washington).
3. Exactly achieve the goal of sustaining 20,000 wolves (the head administrator owns a pet wolf).
4. Minimize the overachievement of 5 million visitor-days for backpacking (a backpacking lobby does not exist).

Formulate the goal programming model for this problem.

45. *Product Pricing* A firm sells three complementary products. It wishes to determine the prices it should charge for each of the three products so as to maximize joint total revenue. Analysts have estimated that demand for each product is a function of the prices of all three products. Specifically, the demand functions are

$$q_1 = 1,000 - 3p_1 - 1.5p_2 - p_3$$
$$q_2 = 500 - p_1 - 2p_2 - 1.5p_3$$
$$q_3 = 2,000 - 2p_1 - p_2 - 4p_3$$

where q_i is the quantity (units) demanded of product i and p_i is the price (per unit) charged for product i. Management has specified that because of the nature of the three items (a customer will often buy all three) the combined price should not exceed $125. Due to cost considerations, the minimum prices which should be charged for the three products are $25, $40, and $15, respectively. In addition, market research has indicated customer ill will is created if the price of product 2 is more than twice the price of product 1.

Formulate (only) the quadratic programming problem which would allow the firm to determine the optimal prices it should charge.

46. *Car Pooling*   A total of m people have filled out a questionnaire for the purpose of becoming part of a car pool. Items on the questionnaire included name, address, sex, occupation, location of work, time work begins, and time work ends. Based on this information, analysts have determined a compatibility index between person i and person k, c_{ik}, for all possible pairs of persons. A large value for this index implies incompatibility. Let K and L represent, respectively, the minimum number and maximum number of people in a car pool.

a.   Formulate a generalized 0–1 quadratic programming model given that n car pools are specified.

b.   Do we have a size problem in solving this model? (Hint: Determine the number of terms in the objective function and the number of decision variables if $m = 100$ and $n = 20$.)

**47.   Given the function

$$y = -x_1^2 + x_1 - 2x_1x_2 - 2x_2^2 + 4x_2,$$

use the gradient approach (starting at $x_1 = x_2 = 0$) to search for a relative maximum at $x_1 = -1$ and $x_2 = 3/2$.

**48.   Given the function

$$y = 2x_1^2 + 3x_2^2 + 2x_3^2 - 16x_1 - 18x_2 - 24x_3,$$

use the gradient approach (starting at $x_1 = x_2 = x_3 = 0$) to search for a relative minimum on the function. Verify that the gradient approach converges to a relative minimum at $x_1 = 4$, $x_2 = 3$, and $x_3 = 6$.

11

Inventory Models

IN THIS CHAPTER we present a few traditional inventory models in isolation; continue these ideas to produce a set of inventory control decision rules (that is, design an inventory control *system*); present a somewhat different approach to inventory control, materials requirements planning (MRP); and briefly review some management science questions which result.

11.1 THE NATURE OF INVENTORY

An **inventory** may be thought of as a list of some category of materials, machines, persons, money, or information for some organizational unit at some point in time. Inventories are "added to" and "depleted from"; if the addition and depletion processes are stopped, what remains is inventory. Alternatively, an inventory can be conceived as a useable resource which is idle.

We all know that manufacturing firms typically "take inventory" once a year; included is the counting and valuation of all goods—raw materials, work-in-process, and finished goods. Similarly, retail firms count their stocks; and universities, hospitals, police departments, and other public or semipublic organizations take periodic inventories of equipment. Inventories of money tend to be verified more often through reconciliation of bank statements, petty cash funds, or cash registers. Formal analyses of personnel inventories are less frequent, but enlightened personnel departments in large organizations do indeed maintain accurate personnel inventory data. However, personnel and money increasingly are both being conceived and controlled as inventories. Information inventories are a bit more abstract, but nonetheless, information is added and depleted from records (information inventories) ranging from lists to massive computer files.

Most inventory models are concerned with finding the best way to add and deplete inventories. Before turning our attention to these, however, there are a few basic questions that need to be answered: (1) What is the function of an inventory? (2) What is the nature of the inventory environment? (3) What are inventory-related criteria?

Inventory Function

The primary function of a material inventory is to *decouple* successive stages in the production-distribution-consumption chain. Raw material inventories permit production decisions to be made independently from supplier procurement decisions. Work-in-process inventories permit material conversion activities to be individually optimized. This is a critical point: If some component part requires one hour of work on machine A and two hours on machine B (per unit), then allowing an inventory to build between A and B can permit both machines to run at optimal efficiency. The alternative (no inventory) is to run machine A at 50 percent of its capacity.

The same decoupling exists in distribution inventories, where variability in customer demand levels are absorbed as much as possible by inventories rather than by production. This dampens "shocks" which otherwise would be received directly by production. For example, if the normal demand for some item is 100 units per month, but in one month demand is 110 and the following month demand is 90, the rate of production can be held at a constant 100 by absorbing the fluctuations in inventory.

The decoupling concept applies equally well to nonmanufacturing inventories. Retail inventories are maintained to support customer demand, variability in demand, purchasing practices (for example, quantity discounts), and variability in replenishment times. The stock and characteristics of university classrooms permit (and dictate) the ability to offer class schedules. Savings and checking accounts decouple income from spending (borrowing and credit can be considered in the same way). Dams permit water usage to be more independent of rainfall. Food supplies permit meal preparation to be decoupled from shopping. Personnel inventories permit smoother and more rapid organizational change because every need does not require a hiring decision. Finally, information inventories are the most abstract, since information "demands" tend to be less predictable; all of the issues raised in step four of the decision-making paradigm are critical to the makeup of information inventories.

Inventory Environments

Before presenting some classical inventory models, we find it useful to overview possible inventory environments and to note the two predominant decisions addressed by inventory models: (1) In what quantity should the inventory be replenished? (2) When should the replenishment begin?

We distinguish in this chapter between **vendor** (purchasing) inventory models and **production** inventory models. Vendor models are those in which the inventoried item is purchased from suppliers outside the company. Production models are those in which the user of the item produces the replenishment supply.

Another distinction made in inventory analyses is the treatment of demand for an item as **deterministic** or **stochastic.** In a small number of cases, deterministic demand is reasonable, as when demand is contractual or otherwise relatively stable. In most cases, however, demand must be treated as a random variable. This requires, of course, the specification of an appropriate probability distribution for demand.

The time delay between the initiation of a replenishment order and the receipt of the items is called the **lead time.** Lead time, as with demand, can be either deterministic or stochastic. If both the demand during the lead time period and the lead time period are known with certainty, then the development of an inventory model is straightforward; however, any uncertainty associated with lead time period or lead time demand makes for a more complex analytic model. As will be seen in Section 11.5, the use of buffer quantities of the inventoried item (referred to as **safety stocks**) is one approach to protecting against such uncertainties.

Order launching refers to the release of an order, either for production or purchase, and relates to the key question of when the order should be initiated. Classical ordering policies are of two types. **Fixed-order quantity systems,** to which we devote most of our attention, are those in which a perpetual inventory record is maintained. The records are reviewed on a continuous basis until the inventory level reaches a predetermined level referred to as the **reorder point.** At this time, an order is launched for a fixed replenishment quantity. The second type of ordering policy is the **periodic review system.** Rather than maintaining a continuous review of the inventory level, periodic checks are made, usually at fixed time intervals. The quantity on hand is compared with the desired inventory level and the difference between the two is ordered. Whereas the order quantity is always the same in fixed-order quantity systems, the order quantity is variable with this system. Many variations on these two basic alternatives exist. For example, it is possible to periodically review, estimate the probability of a stockout if an order is not placed until the next review, and then order in fixed (or varying) quantities.

The echelon structure of the inventory system also must be specified. A **single-echelon system** is one where inventories directly service ultimate demand. Examples include the clothing inventories of a small independent retailer who services consumers, the hospital which inventories blood, and the manufacturer who ships to customers directly from the factory. Alternatively, **multiechelon systems** move the inventoried item through various "levels" or "stocking points." This occurs whenever a stocking point serves as a warehouse for one or more other stocking points. For example, inventories for a major department store might be characterized as two-echelon if inventories at regional warehouses service inventories at retail stores. Note that each of these could be treated independently as single-echelon systems. Doing so, however, generally results in suboptimization. Because of their analytic complexity, multiechelon systems will not be treated in this textbook.

Another issue which must be considered includes the treatment of **single versus multiple items.** Generally, it is desirable to view an inventory in terms of multiple items; that is, most organizations carry not one but many separate items in inventory. An approach which seeks to optimize the inventory policy for each separate item generally fails to optimize the overall inventory policy for the organization, as issues relating to storage, capital, dependencies among items, and other constraints have been ignored. The general modeling approach for multiple items is mathematical programming, heuristic methods, or simulation.

The treatment of shortages also must be explicit. Shortages are either allowed or not allowed. If allowed, then it must be specified whether or not **backordering** (fulfilling the shortage at a later date) is allowed. If backordering is not possible, then a **lost sales environment** is assumed. In some cases, a mixture of backordering and lost sales may be appropriate.

Finally, the planning horizon of interest must be specified for modeling purposes. This means that the model must consider either a **finite discrete-time horizon** or an **infinite continuous-time horizon.** The classic models in this chapter treat an infinite time horizon. The case of a finite time horizon has been illustrated both in the transportation chapter (Example 7.4) and in the dynamic programming chapter (Example 9.3). An advantage of discrete-time models over continuous-time models is their ability to treat items which are either *perishable* or *salvable*.

Cost Criteria

Proper management of inventory resources is obvious merely from the pervasiveness of these inventories. It is similarly apparent from a macroeconomic point of view. The U.S. business investment in physical materials inventory often approximates more than $200 billion. For General Motors alone, this investment runs about $4 billion. The annual opportunity cost for GM alone at a nominal 5 percent is $200 million.

One straightforward inventory criterion is minimization of cost; however, an understanding of inventory functions highlights inventory benefits as well as costs. A more appropriate criterion, therefore, might be overall return on investment to the firm. Unfortunately, this criterion is difficult to assess as it relates to the inventory decision; hence we must specify surrogate criteria. A discussion of all inventory surrogate criteria is beyond our scope. Included are issues such as speculative buying, product life cycles, and asset management.

In determining an optimal inventory policy, the criterion function is most often one of cost. Classical inventory analysis identifies four major cost components. Depending on the structure of the inventory environment, some or all of these cost components may be included in the objective function.

The first cost component is the **purchase cost** for vendor supply environments or **direct production costs** in the case of items produced by the user. In either situation the unit cost may be constant for all replenishment quantities or it may vary with the quantity purchased or produced. Vendors frequently offer discounts or price breaks if the user purchases quantities which exceed some specified quantity. Similarly, unit costs may decrease as larger production runs are made due to economies of scale.

The second cost component is **setup or ordering cost.** This cost is incurred whenever an inventory is replenished. Generally, it is independent of the quantity replenished. Ordering cost is the term used for purchasing or vendor models. In this context it is primarily clerical and administrative in nature; that is, it is the cost which is incurred for activities from the time the replenishment supply is requested to the time that the order is received, paid for, and placed in inventory. Typical elements are the costs associated with processing and expediting the purchase order, follow-up, transportation, receipt, inspection, location of the items, and payment for the order. In production models, the term "setup cost" is frequently used to include the same types of clerical and administrative costs; in addition, they include the costs of labor and materials used in setting up machinery for the production run.

The third cost component is **carrying (holding) cost.** This cost is proportional to the amount of inventory and the time over which it is held. It essentially represents the explicit and implicit costs of maintaining and owning the inventory. A significant component of carrying cost is the *opportunity cost* associated with owning the inventory. Although estimating procedures vary from firm to firm, this cost often reflects the rate of return which the company might expect to earn on the money invested in inventory. Out-of-pocket costs which are normally accounted for include the cost of storage space (rent or cost of ownership), handling costs (including warehouse personnel, forklift trucks, and other equipment), insurance and taxes, allowances for depreciation, quality deterioration, obsolescence, and costs of administering inventory and maintaining records.

The fourth inventory cost component accounts for the explicit and implicit costs of being out of stock when items are requested. These **shortage costs** are computed differently depending upon whether or not backordering is possible. When backordering is permitted, explicit costs are incurred for overtime, special clerical and administrative efforts, expediting, and special transportation. When the unavailable item is a finished good, there is often an implicit cost reflecting loss of goodwill. This is a difficult cost to measure since it supposedly accounts for lost future sales. In other cases, it may not make sense to cost the "lost sale." For example, how would you cost unavailable blood which results in loss of life? If the item is a raw material being used in a production process, then the shortage cost would also reflect costs of expediting, idle machines, and extra labor. When backordering is not permitted, the primary costs reflect lost immediate and future sales, or in the case of raw materials inventory, the cost of idle facilities, disrupted schedules, and lost sales.

The shortage cost may be computed in different ways, depending on the situation. In some instances the cost may be a fixed amount regardless of the number of units short or the period of time over which the shortage exists. An example would be when the cost consists only of the added administrative and clerical expenses associated with processing a backorder. In other situations, shortage costs vary as a function of the number of units short and/or the length of time over which there is a shortage. In some cases, explicit penalty clauses may be written into supply agreements which link costs to these two variables. Our models in this chapter are of the latter type.

11.2 CLASSIC ECONOMIC ORDER QUANTITY (EOQ) VENDOR MODEL

In this section we develop the classic deterministic economic order quantity (EOQ) model for vendor supply of inventory items. It is the simplest of the inventory models and will be followed in later sections by other deterministic models which are of greater complexity, and which relax the initial set of assumptions. In all cases, the objective is to find the optimum order quantity (Q^*) and the optimum reorder point (R^*).

Model Assumptions

The following assumptions are made in this model:

1. Demand per time period (D) is known with certainty and is at a constant (linear) rate.
2. Lead time (t_L) is known with certainty and equals zero.
3. Stockouts are not permissible.
4. Replenishment is instantaneous (that is, the entire order is received in one batch).
5. Order quantities (Q) are always the same size and are not restricted to being discrete.
6. Unit cost for items is constant (no discounts).
7. Single-item, single-echelon inventories are assumed.
8. Infinite planning horizon is assumed.
9. Demand, lead time, and costs are stationary (that is, remain fixed over time).

These assumptions lead to the type of inventory behavior depicted in Figure 11–1. Note that deterministic demand and deterministic lead time allow for the placement of orders in such a way that the new supply arrives at the instant the old stock is used up. In other words, for t_L fixed

FIGURE 11–1

Inventory Behavior: Classic EOQ Model

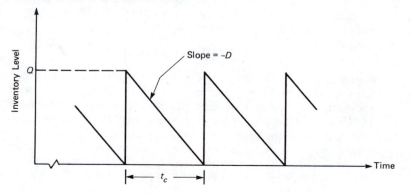

at zero and for constant D, the reorder point R is determined automatically when inventory reaches zero. Each sawtooth portion of Figure 11–1 represents the behavior of inventory during an **inventory cycle,** which requires time t_c.

The assumptions in this model are questionable in regard to how closely they approximate reality. This model, however, provides a framework for the analysis of more complex models. In addition, situations do exist in which this model provides significant inputs for inventory policy.

Model Development

In addition to Q, R, D, t_c, and t_L, the following symbols are defined: C_h = holding cost per unit of item per time period (exclusive of fixed costs), and C_o = ordering cost per order. Although the classic EOQ model can be developed so as to minimize total annual inventory costs, we will generalize the model for any time period by developing the cost function for one inventory cycle (since all inventory cycles are assumed to be identical for deterministic models). Once this is accomplished, the total cost function for any time period of concern can be found by multiplying the cost per cycle by the number of cycles in the time period.

As stated above, the criterion to be minimized (total cost) is the sum of the cost components discussed previously. Since no shortages are allowed under the assumptions of this model, no shortage cost will be incurred. And since unit purchase costs are assumed constant, this cost cannot be affected by inventory policy. Consequently, the pertinent variable costs per time period are ordering cost plus carrying cost.

Since one order is placed per cycle, the *ordering cost per cycle* is C_o. Ordering cost per time period is computed as

Ordering cost per time period = (Number of orders per time period)
$$\times \text{(Order cost per order)}$$
$$= \text{NC}_0.$$

However, the *number of orders per time period* can be defined as

N = (Units of item demanded per time period) ÷ (Units of item per order)
    = D/Q.

In other words, if 500 units are demanded per month and 250 units are in each order, then two orders per month must be placed. Thus, the *ordering cost per time period* is given by

$$f_1(Q) = (D/Q)C_o. \tag{11.1}$$

Carrying cost per inventory cycle is computed as (average number of units in inventory) × (number of time periods per inventory cycle) × (holding cost per unit of item per time period). Observation of Figure 11–1 should lead you to the conclusion that the average number of units in inventory during any inventory cycle equals $Q/2$. More rigorously, the average inventory over an inventory cycle is given by the area under the inventory curve divided by the length of the inventory cycle. The area of one triangle in Figure 11–1 is one half the base times the height, or $\frac{1}{2} t_c Q$.

Dividing this result by t_c yields $Q/2$.[1] Therefore, carrying cost per cycle equals $(Q/2) \cdot (t_c) \cdot (C_h)$. Noting that $t_c = Q/D$ (Can you show this?), it follows that the carrying cost per cycle may be expressed as $(Q^2/2D) \cdot C_h$. Multiplying this by the number of cycles per time period ($N = D/Q$) gives the *carrying cost per time period:*

$$f_2(Q) = (D/Q) \cdot (Q^2/2D) \cdot (C_h) \qquad (11.2)$$
$$= (Q/2)C_h.$$

Total cost per time period now can be defined as

$$C(Q) = f_1(Q) + f_2(Q)$$
$$= (D/Q)C_o + (Q/2)C_h. \qquad (11.3)$$

Figure 11–2 indicates the behavior of ordering cost, carrying cost, and their sum as a function of Q. The order quantity Q^* which minimizes

FIGURE 11–2

Inventory Costs: Classic EOQ Model

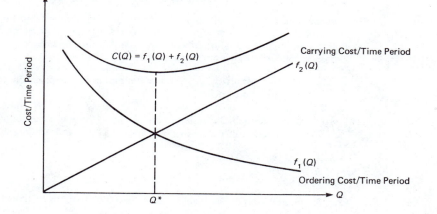

total cost is determined by differentiating $C(Q)$ with respect to Q. This procedure yields the classic *EOQ* formula:[2]

$$Q^* = \sqrt{2DC_o/C_h}. \qquad (11.4)$$

Based on the assumption of zero lead time and the geometry of Figure 11–1, you should confirm that Q^* should be ordered whenever the in-

---

[1] Note that the area under the inventory curve for one cycle is in terms of (units of item) · (time periods). Dividing this area by the number of time periods per cycle then leaves us with (units of item) as average inventory.

[2] Note that the process of differentiation assumes that $C(Q)$ is a continuous function; hence, D and Q cannot be restricted to integer values: If D and Q are large integer numbers, however, then Equation (11.4) should yield an optimal solution to the nearest unit. For an EOQ model which assumes integrality, see G. Hadley and T. M. Whitin, *Analysis of Inventory Systems* (Englewood Cliffs, N.J.: Prentice-Hall, Inc., 1963), pp. 40–42.

ventory level drops to zero (that is, $R^* = 0$). In other words, assuming instantaneous replenishment at the moment an order is placed, it would never pay to launch an order prior to the point where the inventory curve touches the time axis, as an unnecessary carrying cost would be incurred.

Follow-up Exercises

1. Critique the assumptions made in the classic EOQ model.

2. Verify that the stationary point defined by Equation (11.4) is a universal minimum by finding the first and second derivatives.

3. Articulate reasons for the tradeoff (inverse) relationship which exists between ordering cost and carrying cost.

4. Mathematically verify

    a. That per time period ordering costs and carrying costs are equal when operating with an EOQ policy; that is, that $f_1(Q^*) = f_2(Q^*)$.
    b. That optimal cost is given by $C^*(Q) = \sqrt{2C_o C_h D}$.

5. The equation $N = D/Q$ implies a direct and obvious relationship between N (number of orders per time period) and Q. Thus, the optimal EOQ policy can be stated alternatively by defining the optimal number of orders to place during each time period.

    a. Show that $N^* = \sqrt{DC_h/(2C_o)}$ by substituting the expression for Q^* into the equation above.
    b. Formulate total cost, Equation (11.3), in terms of N instead of Q. Having defined $C(N)$, determine N^* by (1) equating ordering cost $f_1(N)$ with carrying cost $f_2(N)$; (2) finding $C'(N)$ and setting it equal to zero.
    c. Graphically sketch $f_1(N)$, $f_2(N)$, and $C(N)$.

**6. Confirm that $Q/2$ is the average inventory as follows:

    a. Functionally state the level of inventory with respect to time for any given cycle. Use Figure 11.1 as a reference.
    b. Determine average inventory from

$$\bar{L} = \frac{\int_0^{t_c} L(t)dt}{t_c}.$$

Example 11.1   Metrobus, Inc.

Metrobus, Inc., is a city-owned transit company which operates a fleet of 400 buses. The fleet includes buses used for public transit as well as school buses. Buses used in public transit average close to 400 miles per day, seven days a week. School buses also amass considerable mileage, though not nearly as much as public transit buses. Metrobus is interested in establishing an inventory policy for bus tires which minimizes the sum of annual ordering and carrying costs. All buses use the same type of tire and the annual requirements are estimated at 5,000 tires. Ordering cost per order is $125 and the cost of carrying a tire in inventory for one year is estimated at $20. For practical purposes lead time is zero, as the supplier will deliver on the day an order is placed. Note that the basic unit of measurement for a time period is one year in this case.

Applying Equation (11.4), we see that the order quantity which minimizes total inventory cost per year is

$$Q^* = \sqrt{2DC_o/C_h}$$
$$= \sqrt{2(5,000)(125)/20}$$
$$= \sqrt{62,500}$$
$$= 250.$$

You should confirm that the annual carrying and ordering cost total $5,000 for this optimal policy, that is, that $C(Q^*) = 5,000$.

The optimal number of orders each year is

$$C(Q^*) = \left(\frac{D}{Q}\right) C_o + \left(\frac{Q}{2}\right) C_n$$

$$= \left(\frac{5000}{250}\right) 125 + \left(\frac{250}{2}\right) 20$$

$$= \$5000$$

$$N^* = \frac{D}{Q^*}$$
$$= \frac{5,000}{250}$$
$$= 20.$$

The length of the inventory cycle is 0.05 year; that is,

$$t_c^* = \frac{Q^*}{D}$$
$$= \frac{250}{5,000}$$
$$= 0.05$$

or

$$t_c^* = 1/N^*$$
$$= 1/20.$$

This means that the time between any two successive order arrivals (or order placements) is approximately 2.5 weeks.

Follow-up Exercises

7. Determine Q^*, $C(Q^*)$, N^*, t_c^*, and R^* for Metrobus, Inc., for each of the three environments below.

   a. $D = 4,000$ and no other changes.
   b. $C_h = 2$ and no other changes.
   c. $C_o = 250$ and no other changes.

   Sketch inventory behavior. Are changes in optimal policy logical given the indicated changes in the parameters? In actual practice, what would you do about the fact that Q^* is noninteger?

8. If Metrobus must order tires by the dozen, compare the costs of purchasing in lots of 240 (20 dozen) v. 252 (21 dozen). Are the total costs "significantly" different from those of the EOQ model?

9. Solve Example 11.1 if the basic time period is one month. Make appropriate adjustments for demand and costs. Conclusion?

10. A processor of raw sugar for health food stores processes 4.5 million tons of sugar cane per year. Ordering costs per order are estimated at $5,000 (including shipping cost) and carrying costs per ton per year are estimated at $2.25. The fixed lead time is 0 days. What is the EOQ for this company? What is the total inventory cost per year? Sketch inventory behavior.

11. Assume that in Exercise 10 the supplier of sugar cane pays for shipping and gets the best price by shipping in tankers at full capacity. Cargo ships are available with capacities of 100,000 tons or 200,000 tons. The supplier has agreed to sell to the processor at the same price provided that the purchases are in quantities of 100,000 or 200,000 tons. The processor saves $4,000 per order on shipping costs. What are the total costs under the two alternatives? Which size shipment should the processor accept? If the supplier gives the processor the option of unrestricted order quantities with payment of shipping charges (Exercise 10) versus the option of the above with no payment of shipping charges, then what should the processor choose?

11.3 EXTENSIONS OF CLASSIC EOQ VENDOR MODEL

In this section we present EOQ models for vendors which relax the assumptions of zero lead time and no shortages.

EOQ with Lead Time

One of the assumptions of the classic EOQ model is zero lead time. We now consider the case where lead time is greater than zero. As before it is assumed that lead time is deterministic and stationary. The case of probabilistic lead time is taken up in Section 13.5.

Figure 11–3 illustrates two situations wherein lead time is either less than optimal cycle time $(t_L < t_c^*)$ or greater than optimal cycle time $(t_L > t_c^*)$. Note the following:

1. The optimal reorder quantity Q^* is unaffected by the magnitude of the lead time, which means that Equation (11.4) is still relevant.
2. The optimal reorder point R^* must be determined such that the replenishment arrives exactly at the beginning of a new cycle.

First consider the case when $t_L < t_c^*$. Demand during the lead time is $t_L \cdot D$, which is less than Q^* because $Q^* = t_c^* \cdot D$ and $t_L < t_c^*$; that is, $t_L \cdot D$ is necessarily less than $t_c^* \cdot D$. This means that we simply place an order when inventory level drops to $R^* = t_L \cdot D$, thereby guaranteeing that replenishment arrives exactly at the end of the *current* cycle.

Now consider the case where $t_L > t_c^*$. Lead time demand is still $t_L \cdot D$; however, this demand is now greater than Q^*. Right? In this case it is not possible to reorder at an inventory level which will exactly absorb lead time demand. How then is lead time demand satisfied? Both by the amount of inventory on hand when an order is launched (that is,

FIGURE 11–3

Reorder Points for Lead Times Greater Than Zero

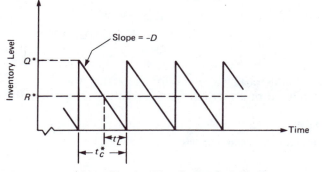

(a) Lead Time Less Than Optimal Cycle Time

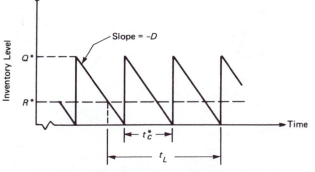

(b) Lead Time Greater Than Optimal Cycle Time

by R^*) and by the replenishments (from previous orders) which arrive *during* the lead time under consideration. Thus

Lead time demand $= R^* +$ (Replenishments which arrive during lead time)

$$t_L \cdot D = R^* + [t_L/t_c^*] \cdot Q^*$$

or

$$R^* = t_L \cdot D - [t_L/t_c^*] \cdot Q^* \qquad (11.5)$$

where $[t_L/t_c^*]$ represents the integer part of the quotient t_L/t_c^*, that is, the number of complete cycles during a lead time. Note that $[t_L/t_c^*] = 0$ when $t_L < t_c^*$, in which case Equation (11.5) is simply the result we got for case (*a*) in Figure 11–3.

If the lead time is 0.02 year (7.3 days) for Example 11.1, then from Equation (11.5) the order for 250 tires should be placed whenever inventory drops to

𝕯𝖔𝖚𝖌𝖑𝖆𝖘 𝕾𝖆𝖑𝖙𝖊𝖗
748ᵢ8666

$$R^* = (0.02) \cdot (5{,}000) - [0.02/0.05] \cdot (250)$$
$$= 100 - 0$$
$$= 100 \text{ tires.}$$

If the lead time is 0.08 year (29.2 days), however, then

$$R^* = (0.08) \cdot (5{,}000) - [0.08/0.05] \cdot (250)$$
$$= 400 - (1) \cdot (250)$$
$$= 150.$$

Figure 11–4 illustrates these results. Note that for the case where $t_c = 0.02$, the release of an order when inventory drops to 100 within any

FIGURE 11–4

Inventory Behavior for Metrobus, Inc.

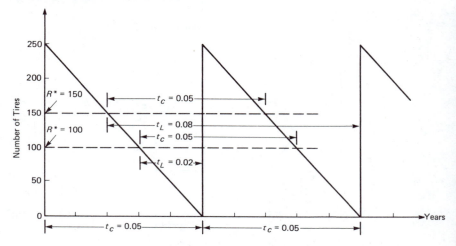

cycle results in the receipt of that order at the end of the *same* cycle; however, for the case where $t_c = 0.08$, the release of an order when inventory drops to 150 within any cycle results in the receipt of that order at the end of the *next* cycle.

Follow-up Exercises

12. Sketch inventory behavior for Metrobus, Inc. if the lead time is

    a. 15 days.
    b. 45 days.

13. Sketch inventory behavior for Exercise 10 if the lead time is

    a. 7 days.
    b. 31 days.

EOQ with Backorders

We now present a more general case of the classic EOQ model discussed in Section 11.2. In this model we allow shortages of inventory which can be backordered. As before all demands must be met ultimately; hence, at the moment of replenishment, all backorders are satisfied prior to meeting new demands. These backorders, however, incur a shortage cost. Why might a vendor allow backorders? When backorders are allowed, the assumption of unaffected demand requires that all demand will be met. By delaying purchases, however, part of each incoming order is immediately allocated to backordered demand. Consequently, fewer orders may be made resulting in lower ordering costs, and average inventory levels *may* be lower resulting in reduced carrying costs. This trade-

FIGURE 11–5

Inventory Behavior: Classic EOQ with Backorders

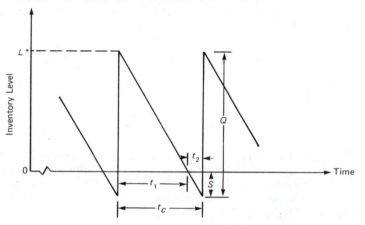

off between ordering and carrying costs on the one hand and backordering costs on the other hand is often exploited, particularly by the home furnishings industry.

Figure 11–5 portrays the inventory behavior for this model. We define the following variables in addition to those defined in Section 11.2: $S =$ maximum number of units short; $C_s =$ shortage cost per unit per time period; $L^* =$ maximum inventory level; $t_1 =$ time within a cycle during which inventory is held; and $t_2 =$ time within a cycle during which a shortage exists.

In this model, the decision variables are Q, the order quantity, and S, the maximum shortage. The order cost component is the same as earlier, or

$$f_1(Q, S) = (D/Q)C_o.$$

Carrying cost is determined as in the classic model. The carrying cost per cycle is based on the triangle in Figure 11–5 with t_1 as base:

$$(L^*/2) \cdot t_1 \cdot C_h. \tag{11.6}$$

Using relationships of similar triangles, we see that

$$\frac{t_1}{L^*} = \frac{t_1 + t_2}{Q}$$

or

$$t_1 = \frac{(t_1 + t_2)(L^*)}{Q}.$$

But, the time of one complete cycle, $t_1 + t_2$, can be expressed equivalently as Q/D. Thus,

$$t_1 = \frac{(Q/D)(L^*)}{Q}$$

$$= \frac{L^*}{D}. \tag{11.7}$$

Since the maximum inventory level L^* can be stated as $Q - S$, we can combine Equations (11.6) and (11.7) to compute the carrying cost per cycle as

$$\frac{(Q - S)^2}{2D} \cdot C_h.$$

Multiplying by the number of cycles per period, D/Q, we find total carrying cost per period is

$$f_2(Q, S) = \frac{(Q - S)^2}{2Q} \cdot C_h. \tag{11.8}$$

The final cost component is the shortage cost. This is determined in a manner similar to that used for carrying cost. Shortage cost per cycle is given by (average number of units short) × (time short per cycle) × (shortage cost per unit per time period). Based on the triangle below the time axis in Figure 11–5, the shortage cost per cycle is

$$(S/2) \cdot t_2 \cdot C_s. \tag{11.9}$$

Again by similar triangles,

$$\frac{t_2}{t_1 + t_2} = \frac{S}{Q}$$

or

$$t_2 = \frac{S}{Q}(t_1 + t_2).$$

Since $(t_1 + t_2) = Q/D$, as before, it follows that

$$t_2 = \frac{S}{Q} \cdot \frac{Q}{D} = \frac{S}{D}.$$

Combining this result with Equation (11.9) gives a shortage cost per cycle of

$$\frac{S^2 C_s}{2D}.$$

Multiplying by the number of cycles, D/Q, we see that shortage cost per time period is given by

$$f_3(Q, S) = \frac{S^2 C_s}{2Q}. \tag{11.10}$$

Combining the three cost components, we see that the total variable cost function for this model can be expressed as

$$C(Q, S) = \frac{D}{Q} C_o + \frac{(Q - S)^2}{2Q} C_h + \frac{S^2 C_s}{2Q}. \tag{11.11}$$

Taking partial derivatives of Equation (11.11) with respect to Q and S and solving for the stationary point, we find that the optimal order quantity is

$$Q^* = \sqrt{\left(\frac{2DC_o}{C_h}\right) \cdot \left(\frac{C_h + C_s}{C_s}\right)} \tag{11.12}$$

and the maximum shortage quantity is

$$S^* = \sqrt{\frac{2C_o DC_h}{C_h C_s + C_s^2}}. \tag{11.13}$$

Example 11.2 Cracked Block Associates

An Alaskan distributor of antifreeze is attempting to establish an optimal inventory policy. The clientele is relatively unchanging and demand is approximately constant throughout the year. Because of limited competition, there is less concern with shortages than other businesses might experience. Any unsatisfied demand can be backordered. Annual demand for antifreeze is 600,000 cases, ordering cost per order is $100, carrying cost per case per year is $0.25, and backorder cost per case per year is $2. Using Equation (11.12) we see that the optimal order quantity is approximately

$$Q^* = \sqrt{[2(600,000)(100)/0.25] \cdot [(0.25 + 2.00)/2.00]}$$
$$= 23,238 \text{ cases}.$$

Based on Equation (11.13) the maximum shortage is approximately

$$S^* = \sqrt{\frac{2(100)(600,000)(0.25)}{(0.25)(2.00) + (2.00)^2}}$$
$$= 2,582 \text{ cases}.$$

Follow-up Exercises

14. For Example 11.2 compute

    a. The annual ordering, carrying, and shortage costs under the optimal policy.

    b. The time between orders (that is, the cycle time).

    c. The proportion of demand which must be backordered each year.
    d. The time per cycle over which shortages exist.
    e. The maximum inventory level.
    f. The number of orders per year.

15. A major distributor of Tree-Worn Tennis balls is enjoying its best year ever. Tennis has taken over as the country's fastest growing participant sport. Retailers are pleading for more tennis equipment. The boom in indoor tennis clubs has resulted in an almost constant rate of demand for balls and equipment throughout the year. Annual demand of Tree-Worn balls for this distributor is 300,000 dozens. Ordering cost per order is estimated at $40, carrying cost per dozen per year at $0.20, and shortage cost per dozen per year at $0.50. Determine the order quantity, Q^*, and maximum allowable shortage, S^*, which result in the minimization of variable costs. What are the component costs under this policy? What is the time between orders? What proportion of annual demand must be backordered each year? What is the maximum inventory level? What proportion of the time do backorders exist? How many orders per year are placed?

16. Suppose that backorders are allowed for Metrobus, Inc. (Example 11.1) at a cost of $100 per tire per year. Determine Q^*, S^*, and component costs for this policy. Compare to Q^* and component costs in Example 11.1.

17. Based on the logic behind Equation (11.5), it can be shown that the optimal reorder point for the backorder model is given by

$$R^* = t_L D - [t_L/(t_1 + t_2)] Q^* - S^*. \qquad (11.14)$$

Determine R^* for Example 11.2 if the lead time is

    a. 2 days.
    b. 10 days.
    c. 35 days.

18. Show that Q^* in Equation (11.12) approaches Q^* in Equation (11.4) as the backorder cost approaches infinity. What happens to S^* as backorder cost approaches infinity? Do you conclude that the classic model in Section 11.2 is a special case of the EOQ model with backorders?

**19. Verify Equations (11.12) and (11.13) by finding partial derivatives of (11.11) and setting them equal to zero.

**20. Verify that the stationary point as expressed by Equations (11.12) and (11.13) is a global minimum for the cost function (11.11).

11.4 OTHER DETERMINISTIC MODELS

So far we have developed deterministic EOQ models for vendors which included backorders versus no backorders and lead times versus no lead times. In this section we conclude the treatment of deterministic models by a brief overview of other models and the explicit development of a quantity discount model for vendors.

Overview

Other deterministic models which have been treated in the literature include, but are not restricted to, the following:

1. Vendor EOQ model with lost sales.
2. Periodic review models.
3. EOQ models with discrete demands and order quantities.
4. Multi-item EOQ models with resource constraints.
5. Production EOQ models.
6. Production models with discrete time periods over finite time horizons.
7. Quantity discount models.

Interestingly, the EOQ model with lost sales yields the same optimal decision rule for Q^* and R^* as the classic EOQ model, as long as inventory is to be stocked in the first place. Similarly, deterministic periodic review models provide identical optimal decisions as deterministic reorder point (EOQ) models.

EOQ models with discrete D and Q require a marginal or difference equation type of analysis, as the calculus does not apply. Generally, the development of the model and the decision rules which result are more complex for the discrete case than for the continuous case. For this reason, "fudging" (rounding) the results of the continuous model is the typical approach to solving the discrete model, which works well if demand is high and unit costs are low.

Environments with multiple items subject to resource constraints are more typical of reality. Unfortunately, these models are difficult to solve. Typical constraints include limits on inventory levels, space, and capital. If the inventory costs of separate items are additive, then objective functions can be constructed easily based on single-item models; otherwise, complex interactions among items must be specified. Classical optimization with Lagrange multipliers (Chapter 3) and nonlinear mathematical programming techniques (Chapter 10) are the usual approaches to solving these types of models.

The production EOQ model is a classic model which is rarely used in actual practice, although it is often developed in textbooks which treat the topic of inventory models. Mathematical programming approaches, particularly dynamic programming and integer programming, have proven more successful in actual practice. For instance, the dynamic programming model of Example 9.3 takes into consideration a finite planning horizon, discrete time periods, discrete units for items, resource constraints, nonlinear and dynamic production costs, dynamic inventory costs, and fixed costs of production. The transportation model of Example 7.4 includes these same features except for nonlinearities and fixed costs. In Section 11.6 we discuss an alternative approach to production scheduling and inventory control.

Single Quantity Discount

All models presented thus far have assumed that the unit purchasing cost is constant. This allowed us to ignore purchasing costs in the objective functions, thereby simplifying the methods of solution. Frequently, however, suppliers offer discounts if buyers purchase in large quantities. The motivation for doing so is straightforward. In vendor models, the supplier moves more inventory forward in the distribution channel and lowers carrying costs if buyers purchase in larger quantities. Whoever pays for the transportation of the items can potentially benefit from lower unit shipping costs. Moreover, by purchasing a large lot size, the buyer is trading off lowered purchasing and ordering costs (fewer orders) with higher carrying costs.

Several different discount structures are possible. In this section we illustrate a total cost comparison for a single discount problem; in the next section we generalize this procedure.

If a company is offered a single quantity discount, then one approach is to compare the total cost for the best inventory policy without the discount to the total cost if the discount is accepted. Total cost per time period is defined as the sum of ordering cost per time period, carrying cost per time period, shortage cost per time period, and purchasing cost per time period, or

$$TC\,(Q,\,S,\,P) = C(Q,\,S) + D \cdot P \qquad\qquad (11.15)$$

for the backorder model and

$$TC\,(Q,\,P) = C(Q) + D \cdot P \qquad\qquad (11.16)$$

for the no-shortage model, where $C(Q)$ is defined by Equation (11.3), $C(Q,\,S)$ is defined by Equation (11.11), D is demand per time period, P is purchase cost per unit of item, and $D \cdot P$ represents the purchasing cost per time period.

Example 11.3 Metrobus, Inc.—Revisited

Suppose that the supplier of tires to Metrobus (Example 11.1) has made an offer in which a discount of 2 percent off the normal cost of $100 per tire will be applied if Metrobus purchases in quantities of 1,000 or more. Metrobus officials wish to analyze this proposal to see if it is worth their while. Analysts have decided to compare total costs under the current EOQ policy with those which would exist under the discount situation.

Recalling that $D = 5,000$ tires per year, $Q^* = 250$ tires, $C_o = \$125$ per order, and $C_h = \$20$ per tire per year, we see that

$$TC(Q^*,\,P) = (D/Q^*)C_o + (Q^*/2)C_h + D \cdot P$$
$$TC(250,100) = (5,000/250)(125) + (250/2)(20) + (5,000)(100)$$
$$= 505,000.$$

This means that an EOQ ordering policy with no discount incurs a cost of $505,000 per year.

Under the discount policy, $P = 98$ and Q is set to the minimum lot size which qualifies for a discount ($Q = 1,000$).[3] This reduces the ordering cost, increases the carrying cost, and reduces the purchasing cost:

$$TC(1,000, 98) = (5,000/1,000)(125) + (1,000/2)(20) + (5,000)(98)$$
$$= 500,625.$$

If total annual cost is the primary criterion, then there is an apparent savings of $4,375 per year. Comparing individual cost components between the two models it can be seen that the increased carrying costs associated with buying the larger quantity, although not offset by the decrease in the ordering cost, is more than balanced by savings in the purchasing cost.

Follow-up Exercises

21. Using the formula for TC, prove to yourself that any order quantity greater than 1,000 will result in increased costs.
22. In Example 11.3 the discount offer was acceptable to Metrobus on a cost basis. In fact, Metrobus would have accepted the offer had there been less of a discount. The **indifference discount** is the discount per unit which equates total costs under the EOQ policy with those under the discount offer. Solve for the indifference discount, d, in the Metrobus example by redefining TC for the discount policy in terms of d and equating with the EOQ cost of $505,000.
23. Assume in Exercise 10 that the sugar processor has been offered a 1-percent discount on the purchasing cost of $100 per ton if purchases are in quantities of 100,000 tons or more. Should the processor accept the offer on the basis of total cost comparisons?
24. What is the indifference discount for the preceding exercise?
25. *Backorder Case* Compare annual ordering, carrying, shortage, purchasing, and total costs for the vendor in Example 11.2 if a discount of 0.2 percent is offered on the per case purchase cost of $20 for purchases of 100,000 cases or more. What Q and S do you recommend? Sketch inventory behavior. *Note:* If Q is fixed at a particular discount level, then optimal S must be determined by differentiating Equation (11.11) with respect to S. This procedure yields $S = QC_h/(C_s + C_h)$. Can you show this?

---

[3] Assuming that carrying cost is unaffected, the lower P simply has the effect of shifting the total cost curve downward by a constant amount. Since $Q = 1,000$ is greater than $Q^* = 250$, it follows that further increases in Q result in higher total costs; that is, we would not wish to move further to the right when located to the right of the minimum point in a convex curve such as in Figure 11–2.

Multiple Quantity Discounts

Often suppliers offer a progression of discrete discounts to buyers, each discount corresponding to a larger minimum purchase quantity. To simplify the presentation, assume a vendor model with no shortages and a constant carrying cost per unit per year.[4] This means that the purchasing price is not an element in the determination of Q^* according to Equation (11.4). Moreover, changes in the purchasing price have no effect on $C(Q)$. It follows, therefore, that decreases in the purchasing price of items do nothing but lower the vertical orientation of the total cost function. In other words, total inventory cost for any order quantity Q is less when the unit purchasing cost is lower. This is demonstrated in Figure 11–6, where based on Equation (11.16) it follows that $TC(Q, P_1) > TC(Q, P_2) > TC(Q, P_3)$ for any Q when $P_1 > P_2 > P_3$.

Assume in Figure 11–7 that a supplier will sell at price P_1 unless the buyer agrees to purchase in quantities of Q_1 or more units, in which case P_2 is the selling price. Similarly, if the buyer agrees to buy in quantities of Q_2 or more units, the lower price P_3 applies. If the objective is to

FIGURE 11–6

Total Inventory Cost per Period; Multiple Quantity Discounts

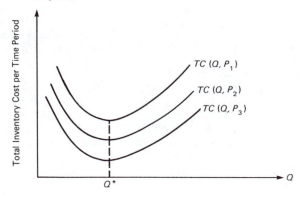

minimize the total inventory cost per time period, then it is apparent that this is achieved when the order size is Q_2 units and the price is P_3. Note that Q^* is not permissible at price P_3 since $Q^* < Q_2$.

The result in this illustration cannot be generalized; that is, the lowest total inventory cost will not always be associated with the policy of purchasing the minimum allowable quantity at the lowest price offered. In general, the minimum cost solution is found by first computing Q^*. (Remember that Q^* is independent of purchasing price, provided that ordering cost and unit carrying cost remain the same.) Next, compute the total inventory cost for Q^* and the appropriate unit purchasing price for that order size, $TC(Q^*, P^*)$. The only way in which total cost might be lower is if the buyer purchases the minimum quantity corresponding to a unit purchasing price which is *lower* than P^*. Total costs under

---

[4] In reality, carrying cost per unit per year may decrease as the unit cost decreases. The reason for this is that a major part of carrying cost reflects the opportunity cost associated with having an investment in inventory, where the value of the investment is directly related to the unit cost of the item. See Exercise 31 for the treatment of variable carrying cost.

FIGURE 11–7

Total Inventory Costs: Two Price Discounts

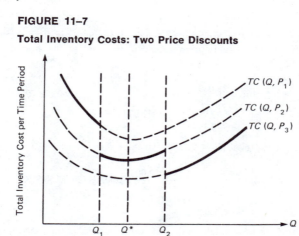

these lower price alternatives must be compared to $TC(Q^*, P^*)$ to determine the best policy.

Example 11.4 Term Papers, Inc.

A certain successful entrepreneur purchases high-quality term papers ("guaranteed A") from an even bigger entrepreneur for resale to unethical students. Annual demand is 25,000 papers, carrying cost is $2.50 per paper per year, and ordering cost is $100 per order. Students, being as desperate as they are, never backorder. The purchase price is normally a stiff $30 per paper; however, the supplier will sell at a 1-percent discount if the buyer purchases in lots of at least 5,000 papers and a 1.5-percent discount if the buyer purchases in lots of 10,000 papers or more.

Given the parameters, the economic order quantity at any price is

$$Q^* = \sqrt{\frac{2DC_0}{C_h}}$$

$$= \sqrt{\frac{2(25,000)(100)}{2.50}}$$

$$= \sqrt{2,000,000}$$

$$\doteq 1,414 \text{ papers.}$$

Since Q^* is not large enough to qualify for a quantity discount, the regular price of $30 applies (that is, $P_1 = 30$). Thus, according to Equations (11.16) and (11.3),

$$TC(1,414, 30) = \frac{25,000}{1,414}(100) + \frac{1,414}{2}(2.50) + (25,000)(30)$$

$$= 1,768 + 1,768 + 750,000$$

$$= 753,536.$$

The only possibilities for lower total cost would occur if the firm purchased the minimum quantity at each price break. Total cost at the first discount level ($P_2 = 29.70$) is

$$TC(5{,}000, 29.70) = \frac{25{,}000}{5{,}000}(100) + \frac{5{,}000}{2}(2.50) + (25{,}000)(29.70)$$
$$= 500 + 6{,}250 + 742{,}500$$
$$= 749{,}250.$$

At the other discount level ($P_3 = 29.55$), we have

$$TC(10{,}000, 29.55) = \frac{25{,}000}{10{,}000}(100) + \frac{10{,}000}{2}(2.50) + (25{,}000)(29.55)$$
$$= 250 + 12{,}500 + 738{,}750$$
$$= 751{,}500.$$

From the standpoint of annual total cost, term papers should be bought in lots of 5,000 units at a price of $29.70 per paper.

Follow-up Exercises

26. Sketch the total cost curves for this example.

27. Determine the optimal decision if carrying cost is $8 per paper per year. Sketch the total cost curves and compare to the original example.

28. For Metrobus, Inc. (Example 11.3) suppose that demand remains the same ($D = 5{,}000$) but ordering cost increases to $250 per order and holding cost decreases to $10 per tire per year. The normal price of a tire is still $100, but the following discounts apply: $P = 98$ if $250 \leq Q < 500$; $P = 97$ if $500 \leq Q < 1{,}000$; $P = 96$ if $1{,}000 \leq Q < 2{,}000$; and $P = 95$ if $Q \geq 2{,}000$. Determine the optimal policy. Sketch the total cost curves. Compare cost components (ordering, holding, and purchasing) for each Q which you considered.

29. A regional automotive parts wholesaler purchases catalytic converters from the manufacturer for distribution to regional dealers and automotive repair shops. Annual demand is constant at 100,000 units, carrying cost is $30 per unit per year, and ordering cost is $250 per order. Without discounts, the purchase price is $200 per converter. Assume that backorders are not allowed. The manufacturer offers a 2-percent discount for orders of at least 1,000 converters, a 3-percent discount for orders of at least 5,000, and a 3.5-percent discount for orders of at least 10,000. Determine the ordering policy which minimizes total cost per year. Sketch the total cost functions. Compare cost components (ordering, holding, and purchasing) for each Q which you considered.

30. *Backorder Case* Suppose that backorders are allowed in the preceding exercise. For given Q, optimal S must be determined from $S = QC_h/(C_s + C_h)$, as discussed in Exercise 25. Determine the optimal policy. Sketch the total cost functions. Compare cost components (ordering, holding, shortage, and purchasing) for each Q which you considered. Compare the optimal policy and total cost to that obtained in the preceding exercise.

**31. *Variable Carrying Cost* Suppose that carrying cost varies proportionally to the price paid for the item; $C_h = h \cdot P$ where h is the carrying cost proportion. For example, if $h = 0.20$ per time period (that is, carrying cost is 20 percent of the price), then $C_h = \$20$ per unit per time period when $P = \$100$ per unit and $C_h = \$10$ per unit per time period when $P = \$50$ per unit. For this case, you should realize that the total cost curves of Figure 11–7 have their minima at different values of Q. Can you reason out why $Q_3^* > Q_2^* > Q_1^*$ for curves where $P_1 > P_2 > P_3$? Moreover, the shape of each curve is different because the $C(Q)$ component differs. It can be shown, however, that the curves never intersect. It follows that Q^* must be calculated for every price which is considered.

a. Outline a step-by-step methodology for determining the optimal policy where C_h is variable. *Hint:* Step 1 is the calculation of Q^* for the *lowest* price. If this Q^* is allowable, then the optimal policy has been found; otherwise, go on to the next lowest price. When the first allowable Q^* has been determined, then $TC(Q^*, P^*)$ must be compared to each TC corresponding to the minimum purchase quantity for prices lower than P^*.

b. Solve Example 11.4 if the carrying cost percentage is $8\frac{1}{3}$ percent per year. Compare results.

c. Solve Exercise 28 if $h = 0.10$. Compare results.

d. Solve Exercise 29 if $h = 0.15$. Compare results.

11.5 STOCHASTIC INVENTORY MODELS[5]

Until this section all models have assumed that demands and lead times are deterministic. Although deterministic models often provide useful approximations to stochastic environments, models which directly incorporate uncertainties are more appropriate, particularly when variances are high. This section first overviews stochastic models and then presents in detail an EOQ model with probabilistic demands.

Overview

When we speak of stochastic inventory models we refer to models which treat demands or lead times (or both) as random variables with specific probability distributions. As in the deterministic case, many models have been developed. A classic model is the single-period model with probabilistic demand, whereby a single stocking decision is made for one time period for an item which is either perishable or salvable (that is, has a salvage value at the end of the period). Examples include the stocking of newspapers, magazines, food items, and blood.[6] Multiperiod periodic review models with stochastic demand represent another important class of models, with the usual variations relating to types of

---

[5] This section requires knowledge of the concepts in Sections A.1 and A.2 of Appendix A beginning on page 702.

[6] We present this model in Exercise 34 in Chapter 17.

probability distributions, cost structures, the nature of shortages, and the treatment of lead times.[7]

Needless to say, the incorporation of stochastic demand increases the level of modeling complexity. In many cases, particularly when both demands and lead times are probabilistic, closed-form solutions are not possible. This means that decision rules based on mathematical formulas are not available. This problem is particularly acute when dependencies exist both among items in a multi-item environment and among lead times (as when more than one order is outstanding).

Approaches to solving stochastic models include dynamic programming (Chapter 9), simulation (Chapter 13), Markov processes (Chapter 15), decision analysis (Chapter 17), and classical methods (for example, mathematical statistics and calculus). In the remainder of this section we develop by classical methods two order point models with stochastic demand, fixed lead time, and an infinite continuous-time horizon. In Chapter 13 we incorporate stochastic lead time and solve by simulation.

EOQ with Stochastic Demand: Model 1

We now consider the same model as in Section 11.2, except for allowing both stochastic demand and backorders. One naïve approach to dealing with this situation is to determine the order quantity Q by Equation (11.4) and to set the reorder point R at a level equal to the expected (average) demand during the lead time. Unfortunately, lead time demand rarely equals its expected value and, as seen in Figure 11–8, the possibility exists of shortages.

To protect against uncertainties, organizations often provide **safety (buffer) stocks** of inventory which act as a buffer against unexpected increases in lead time demand or lead time period. The approach of the model in this section first determines the economic order quantity Q^*

FIGURE 11–8

Inventory Behavior: Constant Lead Time-Stochastic Demand

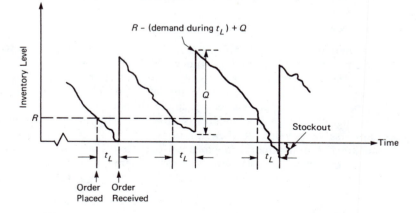

---

[7] This model is treated in Exercise 45 in Chapter 15.

as given by Equation (11.4). Then, the appropriate level of safety stock is determined by minimizing the sum of (1) the expected carrying cost per time period associated with holding the safety stock and (2) the expected shortage cost per time period. (Can you reconcile the tradeoff relationship between these two cost components?) The following symbols are defined:

$\underline{d}_L$ = Random variate for discrete demand during fixed lead time t_L.
$\bar{d}_L$ = Mean (average) demand during lead time.
$f(d_L)$ = Probability mass function for lead time demand.
R = Reorder point.
C_h = Holding cost per unit per time period.
$\bar{D}$ = Mean demand per time period.
Q^* = Order quantity given by Equation (11.4).
C_p = Penalty cost per unit backordered (independent of the length of the backorder period).

All other assumptions in Section 11.2 are assumed to hold. Moreover, we assume a nonnegative expected safety stock (that is, $R \geq \bar{d}_L$) and no more than one order outstanding at any point in time.

Given the objective of minimizing the per time period sum of expected safety stock carrying cost and expected shortage cost, the cost function can be established as a function of R:

$C(R)$ = (Expected safety stock carrying cost per time period) + (Expected backordering cost per time period)

$$= C_h(R - \bar{d}_L) + C_p\left(\frac{\bar{D}}{Q^*}\right)\sum_{d_L > R}(d_L - R)f(d_L). \tag{11.17}$$

Note that $(R - \bar{d}_L)$ represents the expected safety stock. Further note that whenever lead time demand exceeds the reorder point a stockout occurs. Thus, the *summation* expression in Equation (11.17) represents the expected shortage in units per inventory cycle. $(\bar{D}/Q^*)$ indicates the expected number of orders (cycles) per time period or, accordingly, the expected number of times during a time period that a stockout is possible.

By finding the derivative of Equation (11.17) with respect to R, it can be shown that $C(R)$ will be minimized when

$$\sum_{d_L > R^*} f(d_L) = \frac{Q^* C_h}{C_p \bar{D}}$$

or

$$P(d_L > R^*) = \frac{Q^* C_h}{C_p \bar{D}}. \tag{11.18}$$

As in Section (11.2) this procedure assumes that the cost function is continuous. In this case it is not continuous, since d_L is assumed discrete.[8]

---

[8] Continuous demand requires the use of integral calculus for expressing cumulative probabilities. See Hadley and Whitin, *Analysis of Inventory Systems,* and M. Starr and D. Miller, *Inventory Control: Theory and Practice* (Englewood Cliffs, N.J.: Prentice-Hall, Inc., 1962).

For large demands, however, the approximation is reasonable. Additionally it is unlikely that Equation (11.18) will be satisfied as an equality because of discrete d_L. For this reason, the decision rule is to set the reorder point at the lowest value R^* which satisfies

$$P(d_L > R^*) \leq \frac{Q^*C_h}{C_p\bar{D}}. \tag{11.19}$$

Note that $P(d_L > R^*)$ represents the cumulative probability that d_L is greater than R^*, which is the same as $1 - P(d_L \leq R^*)$, the complement of the cumulative distribution function (CDF) at R^*, or $1 - F(R^*)$. Thus,

$$1 - F(R^*) \leq \frac{Q^*C_h}{C_p\bar{D}}$$

or R^* is the smallest value for which

$$F(R^*) \geq 1 - \frac{Q^*C_h}{C_p\bar{D}}. \tag{11.20}$$

Example 11.5   Gotham City Hospital Blood Bank

The management of blood is an important area within health care delivery systems. Blood banks have been developed which perform the functions of procurement, storage, processing, and distribution of blood. The uncertainties associated with both supply and demand usually result in the maintenance of relatively large buffer stocks. Blood bank inventory models are complex, for several reasons:

. . . (1) both supply and demand are random; (2) approximately 50 percent of all bloods demanded, "crossmatched," and held for a particular patient are eventually found not to be required for that patient; (3) blood is perishable, the present legal lifetime being 21 days in most areas; and (4) each blood bank typically interacts with a number of other banks.[9]

Assume that GCH is in the process of studying the inventory policies of its blood bank. It is interested in determining the optimal buffer stock to maintain. Needless to say, the assumptions of the model developed in the previous section need to be "stretched" to apply to the blood bank environment; however, assume that the analysts agree that the assumptions are close enough to use the model for a quick "benchmark" solution. The model is to be applied to the entire inventory of blood used by the hospital. Subsequently, further analyses can be conducted for each "type" of blood.

Mean annual demand is 160,600 units of blood (based on 365 days). Lead time for receiving replenishment supplies from the regional cooperative blood bank is deterministic and equal to two days. The carrying cost of blood is estimated at $2.25 per unit per year. Ordering cost is estimated at $63

---

[9] John B. Hennings, "Blood Bank Inventory Control," *Management Science,* vol. 19, no. 6 (February 1973), p. 637.

per order. Based on Equation (11.4), Q^* is approximately 3,000 units of blood per order.

GCH has worked out a loan arrangement with a private blood bank in Gotham City whereby if GCH incurs a temporary shortage of blood, it can immediately borrow units at a cost of $1.50 per unit. The agreement also specifies the replacement of the borrowed blood units when GCH receives its next replenishment supply.

Lead time demand (that is, demand for *any* two-day period) is stochastic. It is characterized reasonably well by the empirical distribution in Table 11–1. According to Equation (A.12) in Appendix A on page 710, the mean of this distribution is 880.[10]

TABLE 11–1

Lead Time Demand: GCH

Class Intervals for Lead Time Demand	Lead Time Demand (d_L)	Probability $f(d_L)$	Cumulative Probability $F(d_L)$
790 but under 810...............	800	0.02	0.02
810 but under 830...............	820	0.05	0.07
830 but under 850...............	840	0.07	0.14
850 but under 870...............	860	0.18	0.32
870 but under 890...............	880	0.36	0.68
890 but under 910...............	900	0.18	0.86
910 but under 930...............	920	0.07	0.93
930 but under 950...............	940	0.05	0.98
950 but under 970...............	960	0.02	1.00

In order to determine the optimal reorder point R^* we first compute

$$1 - \frac{Q^*C_h}{C_p\overline{D}} = 1 - \frac{3,000(2.25)}{1.50(160,600)}$$
$$= 1 - 0.0280$$
$$= 0.9720.$$

We conclude that the lowest value of R satisfying Equation (11.20) is $R^* = 940$. In other words, according to Table 11–1, R must be 940 for the cumulative probability to exceed 0.9720, or $F(940) \geq 0.9720$. Thus, 3,000 units of blood should be ordered whenever inventory drops below 940 units. Since the expected lead time demand is 880, the recommended buffer stock is

$$R^* - \overline{d}_L = 940 - 880$$
$$= 60 \text{ units.}$$

Follow-up Exercises

32. Why is Equation (11.17) inappropriate for the case where a negative safety stock is allowed?

---

[10] Note that 880 is mean demand per two days. Per day the mean demand is 440, which when multiplied by 365 days gives $\overline{D} = 160,600$ units per year.

33. Show why it is necessary that demand during a lead time must not exceed order quantity (that is, $d_L \leq Q^*$) in order to satisfy the assumption that no more than one order is to be outstanding at any point in time. Is it possible for d_L to exceed Q^* in Example 11.5? Why is the model given by Equation (11.17) not appropriate when more than one order is outstanding?

34. Estimate the probability of a blood shortage while an order is outstanding for Example 11.5. What reorder point should be established if this probability is to be approximately zero?

35. Fill in the table below for Example 11.5. Does the policy $Q^* = 3,000$ and $R^* = 940$ yield minimum $C(R)$?

R	Expected Safety Stock Carrying Cost per Year	Expected Number of Units Short per Cycle	Expected Shortage Cost per Year	C(R)
880				
900				
920				
940				
960				

36. Determine the recommended order quantity, reorder point, and buffer stock for Example 11.5 if

a. $C_p = 3$.
b. $C_p = 0.50$.
c. $\bar{D} = 250,000$.
d. $C_h = 5$.

**37. Suppose that demand for blood is Poisson (see Section A.3) with $\lambda = 500$ units *per day*. Note that $\bar{D}$ now differs from before, but all other parameters remain unchanged. Take care that the lead time is still two days. What order quantity, reorder point, and buffer stock do you recommend? What is the probability of a stockout while an order is outstanding? Hint: Use the normal curve as an approximation to the Poisson cumulative probability $F(d_L)$, where the mean and variance are given by Equations (A.25) and (A.26) in Appendix A.

38. For Example 11.1 (Metrobus, Inc.) suppose that $C_o = \$125$ per order and $C_h = \$20$ per tire per year, as before, but demand is stochastic according to the following probability distribution for a five-day lead time:

d_L	60	64	68	72	76	80	84
$f(d_L)$	0.15	0.20	0.40	0.10	0.08	0.05	0.02

Determine Q^*, R^*, and expected buffer stock if the penalty cost is $5 per tire backordered. (Base the calculation of $\bar{D}$ on a 365-day year.)

**EOQ with Stochastic Demand: Model 2

The model which is developed in the preceding section is based on a *partial* cost tradeoff: expected buffer stock carrying cost per time period

v. expected shortage cost per time period. Moreover, Q^* is determined independently from the specified objective function $C(R)$. These two simplifications result in a model which is rather easy to solve; however, it suffers from the fact that it does not give an optimal policy in the sense of minimizing the expected *total* inventory cost.

The model developed in this section minimizes the following approximation to the expected total inventory cost per time period:

$C(Q, R)$ = (Expected ordering cost per time period) + (Expected carrying cost per time period) + (Expected backordering cost per time period)

$$= C_o(\bar{D}/Q) + C_h(\frac{Q}{2} + R - \bar{d}_L) + C_p(\bar{D}/Q) \cdot \sum_{d_L > R} (d_L - R) f(d_L),$$

(11.21)

where all symbols have been defined in the preceding sections. The logic behind the expected ordering cost per time period is identical to that of the classic EOQ model. The expected backordering cost per time period is identical to that of the preceding model. The expected carrying cost per time period, however, is only an approximation to the exact carrying cost per time period.

If we assume that the number of units backordered is negligible, then the expected physical inventory when an order arrives is the safety stock $(R - \bar{d}_L)$. At this time, the expected physical inventory immediately rises by the amount Q to $(R - \bar{d}_L + Q)$, as indicated in Figure 11–9. We label this the beginning of a cycle. The ideal cycle ends when the physical inventory drops to the safety stock, at which time the next order of Q units arrives. It follows that average inventory is simply the expected safety stock $(R - \bar{d}_L)$ plus $Q/2$, as expressed in Equation (11.21). An exact (but complex) solution for carrying cost would take into consideration the likelihood that physical inventory reaches a level of zero *prior* to the arrival of an order, as illustrated at the end of the third cycle in Figure 11–8.

FIGURE 11–9

Behavior of Idealized Inventory with No Backorders

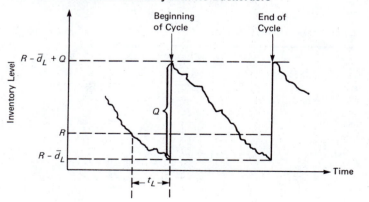

Finding partial derivatives with respect to both Q and R and setting these to zero leads to

$$Q^* = \sqrt{\frac{2D[C_o + C_p \sum\limits_{d_L > R} (d_L - R^*) \cdot f(d_L)]}{C_h}} \tag{11.22}$$

and

$$F(R^*) \geq 1 - \frac{Q^* C_h}{C_p \bar{D}}, \tag{11.23}$$

which when solved simultaneously yield Q^* and R^*. Note that Equations (11.20) and (11.23) are the same. The algorithmic procedure outlined below can be used to solve for Q^* and R^*.

1. A trial value is established for Q by using the classic EOQ formula,
   $$\sqrt{2DC_o/C_h}.$$
2. The value for Q found in step (1) is substituted into Equation (11.23) to find a corresponding value of R.
3. A new value for Q is computed by substituting the value of R into Equation (11.22).
4. R is recomputed from Equation (11.23) using the most recent value of Q.
5. Steps (3) and (4) are repeated until the values of Q and R have converged (sometimes to within some predetermined tolerance).

The algorithm usually converges within a few steps with trial values of Q getting larger at each iteration.

Example 11.6 Simultaneous Determination of Q and R

Assume an inventoried item having the following characteristics: $C_o = 100$, $C_h = 50$, $C_p = 2.50$, $\bar{D} = 36,500$, and average lead time demand equals 500 with a distribution as indicated in Table 11–2.

TABLE 11–2

Lead Time Demand Distribution

d_L	$f(d_L)$	$F(d_L)$
460	0.020	0.020
470	0.060	0.080
480	0.130	0.210
490	0.165	0.375
500	0.250	0.625
510	0.165	0.790
520	0.130	0.920
530	0.060	0.980
540	0.020	1.000

1. Computing a trial value of Q, we get

$$Q = \sqrt{\frac{2(36,500)(100)}{50}}$$
$$= 382.10.$$

2. Substituting $Q = 382.1$ into Equation (11.23), we get

$$F(R) \geq 1 - \frac{(382.1)(50)}{(2.50)(36,500)}$$
$$\geq 1 - 0.209$$
$$\geq 0.791.$$

The smallest R for which $F(R) \geq 0.791$ is $R = 520$.
3. Substituting $R = 520$ into Equation (11.22), we get

$$Q = \sqrt{\frac{2(36,500)\{100 + 2.5[(530 - 520)(0.060) + (540 - 520)(0.020)]\}}{50}}$$
$$= 386.85.$$

4. Substituting $Q = 386.85$ into Equation (11.23) results in $F(R) \geq 0.7880$, implying $R = 510$.
5. Recomputing Q using Equation (11.22) yields $Q = 388$.

You should verify that beyond this step, computed R values will not change; neither, then, will computed Q values. Thus, the algorithm has converged to optimal values of $R^* = 510$ and $Q^* = 388$. The safety stock implied by this solution is $R - \bar{d}_L = 510 - 500 = 10$ units.

Follow-up Exercises

39. Determine the optimal policy for the GCH blood bank (Example 11.5) using Model 2. Compare total inventory cost per year for both models based on Equation (11.21).
**40. Solve Exercise 37 using Model 2. Compare the two models based on the total inventory cost per year, as given by Equation (11.21).
41. Solve Exercise 38 using Model 2. Compare $C(Q, R)$ for each model.

11.6 INVENTORY CONTROL SYSTEMS

Up to this point, we have largely devoted our attention to the development of inventory models in isolation. It must be understood that the application of these concepts typically involves the design of decision rules to carry out the actions indicated by the models: a computerized set of decision rules to "do the routine things routinely."

For many inventory environments, there are far too many items for individual attention (perhaps thousands, tens of thousands, or even hundreds of thousands). Under these circumstances, the potential cost savings of scientific approaches to inventory management far outweigh the cost of implementing the models. What is needed is a computerized set of decision rules which can monitor individual demand forecasts and stock status, and thereafter issue replenishment orders at "good" times for "good" quantities.

In this section we introduce the concept of a basic inventory control system, and follow with brief discussions of two systems which are available commercially.

Schematic of Basic Inventory Control System

The schematic in Figure 11–10 illustrates a simplified inventory control system for a single product in a vendor environment. First, available data can be used for forecasting and estimating the necessary parameters and uncontrollable variables (for example, forecast of demand; probability distribution for demand, costs, and lead time). Appendix A discusses some statistical procedures relating to this issue. We might note that estimates and forecasts based on statistical methodologies should be

FIGURE 11–10

Basic Inventory Control System

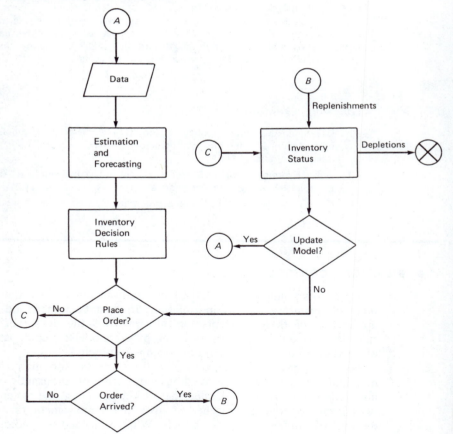

revised subjectively by the manager if necessary. For example, a portion of future demand may be known with certainty if it is contractual.

Next, a specific model generates the decision rules. For a reorder point type model, this means the determination of Q^* and R^*. The issue of which model to use can be resolved by a validation procedure which utilizes simulation. For example, each model under consideration can be applied to a set of historical data (if available). Criteria relating to performance (for example, costs, stockouts, average inventory levels, and so forth) then can be compared in order to select the "best" model. Similarly, the performance of the model which is selected by this procedure can be compared to the actual performance of whatever inventory policy was in use during the historical period. This serves to validate the model if it outperforms the previous policy by a wide enough margin to justify any increases in the cost of implementation. A segment of this validation process should also include sensitivity analysis, particularly with respect to the estimation of parameters which are risky, for example, backordering or penalty costs.

The remaining flows in the figure should be self-explanatory. Note however, that the model should be updated at some point in time. In effect, this procedure overcomes the assumption of stationariness. The signal to update the model might be given periodically (for example, every six months) or it might be based on a decision rule which monitors predicted performance v. actual performance. Chapter 18 discusses control systems in more detail.

IMPACT

IMPACT is an inventory control system available through IBM as a software computer package. It is particularly appropriate for vendor environments (for example, wholesalers and retailers).

IMPACT develops a forecast for each item under control (using exponential smoothing), examines the probability of a stockout before the next review period, compares this probability to a predefined safety stock level, and makes a tentative decision on whether or not to order. The system computes order quantities and safety stocks for each item based on EOQ logic. Additionally it takes into consideration quantity discounts, freight rates, volumes, weights, and the concept of "balance." Given a multi-item environment and joint ordering, it is generally desirable to order as many items as possible in a single order from the same supplier. This policy reduces the number of orders and increases the potential for quantity discounts. IMPACT balances all items such that, given the realization of perfect forecasts, all items from the same supplier would be ordered at the same point in time.

The IMPACT system is only one example of an inventory control system, but it does illustrate the change in orientation toward scientific inventory control. Companies using systems such as IMPACT enjoy personnel savings, lower inventories, fewer stockouts, and other favorable measures of inventory surrogate criteria. More importantly, formal inventory control systems free creative personnel, such as buyers, for duties more in line with the fundamental objectives of the firm, (for example, product line studies and special purchasing opportunities). One wholesale grocer reduced backroom inventories at its retail stores to about zero; increased turnover to the extent that a 400-percent increase in volume over a six-year period required only a 60-percent increase in inventory and a 10-percent increase in the number of items carried; took advantages of more discounts and special deals; was able to easily adapt to transient conditions such as warehouse additions and significant volume changes; and did all of this with no increase in the number of buyers. On the cost side, the inventory control system used (IMPACT) accounted for approximately 10 to 15 hours of IBM 360/30 computer time per month. The rental rate on that machine at the time was approximately $50 per hour, so the monthly cost can be estimated at $500 to $750.

Material Requirements Planning (MRP)

MRP is the best central focus for production planning and inventory control in a complex manufacturing environment. The goal of this system is basically the same as that in order point systems: a set of decision rules to do the routine things routinely so that managerial effort can be utilized more meaningfully. The means to that end, however, are dramatically different.

The notion of MRP as the "Copernican" approach was developed by Joseph Orlicky of IBM Corporation; it clearly focuses attention on the differences between MRP and order point systems. Just as Copernicus found that the earth revolves around the sun rather than vice versa, the MRP view is that inventory control in the manufacturing environment is a misnomer. Inventories exist only to support production schedules, and there is no such thing as a desired inventory level to be replenished.

The most important underpinning to MRP is the distinction between *dependent demand* and *independent demand*. The latter, where demand must be estimated or forecasted, is assumed by order point systems. Dependent demand, on the other hand, occurs because of internal decision making, can be calculated exactly, and is not well-approximated by forecasting models. Once a production plan for the assembly of end items has been established, the exact demand for the component parts which are necessary to support the assembly plan can be calculated. For example, if a furniture plant were to assemble 600 chairs of a particular kind every six weeks, then the weekly demand for the chair seats would be 0, 0, 0, 0, 0, 600. The average weekly demand is 100; it can be shown, however, that the resultant 95-percent safety stock level would equal 343 units. These 343 units would be unneeded for five weeks out of six and *insufficient* for the sixth week!

The simple fact is that demand for component parts is usually not a random process. The furniture firm sells chairs not chair seats; the demand for seats is completely determined by (dependent upon) assembly needs. We do not need a safety stock of chair seats when we are not assembling chairs. Moreover, the Copernican analogy is even more relevant when one considers how the order point approach would operate in this example. If there were an inventory of chair seats that was being depleted by chair assembly, then 600 units would be withdrawn in week

6. This draw might reduce the inventory substantially below the reorder point, and interpretation of that low inventory might lead to a rush replenishment order. But, we will not *need* any more seats until week 12.

The superiority of an MRP system over an order point system can be nicely illustrated by the approach of a restaurant to meal planning. In an order point system, the chef would review the pantry inventory levels daily before deciding on replenishments. Any item which fell below the reorder point would be added to the shopping list in the amount given by the economic order quantity. A sample rule might be: Buy ten 50-pound sacks of Uncle Ben's rice whenever the inventory gets below 100 pounds.

The MRP approach would plan the meals to be offered during the week, which is equivalent to what is called the *master production schedule*. The set of meals (finished products) would then be *exploded* into the necessary ingredients (components or raw materials) by looking in the chef's cookbook (in manufacturing, the "cookbook" is called a *bill of materials*). The result would be a list of required ingredients and their necessary amounts. These *gross requirements* would then be compared to pantry inventories to determine the *net requirements* for the shopping list (economic order quantities could still be purchased). Additionally, the MRP system tells the chef when and in what amounts each ingredient is needed, which is called *time phasing*.

There should be no doubt in your mind that the MRP system would result in fewer stockouts and lower inventories. For example, consider an item such as poultry spice. If the inventory level fell below the reorder point immediately following the Christmas holidays, then the reorder point system would order more poultry spice even though the next large requirement for turkey in the "master production schedule" were not until Thanksgiving. A less severe case of the same phenomenon occurs when rice is replenished even though no meal with rice is planned during the next week. For planned meals using either a much larger than usual quantity of an ingredient or an ingredient not normally stocked, the order point system again will be inferior to the MRP system.

In concluding, it is useful to note that the benefits of MRP are not without costs. Forecasts, master production schedules, and bills of materials need to be precise. Large data bases require extensive data maintenance, and concomitant procedural changes are usually called for day-to-day. MRP can lead to substantial returns. This is particularly true if the final product is made up of complex assemblies, lead times for components and/or raw materials are long, and the manufacturing cycle for the finished product is long.

SELECTED REFERENCES

Buckhan, J., and Koenigsberg, E. *Scientific Inventory Management.* Englewood Cliffs, N.J.: Prentice-Hall, Inc., 1963.

Buffa, E. S., and Taubert, W. H. *Production-Inventory Systems: Planning and Control.* Rev. ed. Homewood, Ill.: Richard D. Irwin, Inc., 1972.

Greene, J. H. *Production and Inventory Control.* Rev. ed. Homewood, Ill.: Richard D. Irwin, Inc., 1974.

Hadley, G., and Whitin, T. M. *Analysis of Inventory Systems*. Englewood Cliffs, N.J.: Prentice-Hall, Inc., 1963.

Naddor, E. *Inventory Systems*. New York: John Wiley & Sons, Inc., 1966.

Orlicky, J. *Material Requirements Planning: The New Way of Life in Production and Inventory Management*. New York: McGraw-Hill Book Co., Inc., 1975.

Starr, M., and Miller, D. *Inventory Control: Theory and Practice*. Englewood Cliffs, N.J.: Prentice-Hall, Inc., 1962.

Wagner, H. M. *Statistical Management of Inventory Systems*. New York: John Wiley & Sons, Inc., 1962.

ADDITIONAL EXERCISES

42. *Energy Inventories* A southern power company has recently made the publicly unpopular decision to resume burning coal. Although environmentalists have been lobbying to block this action, the Southern Regional Power Consortium approved the proposal that 20 percent of the energy requirements be generated using coal. The remaining 80 percent will originate from a combination of petroleum, nuclear, and hydroelectric sources.

    Energy demands tend to be relatively constant year-round because of the stability of the climate. Consequently, company analysts have projected a requirement of 10,000 tons of coal per day, or 3,650,000 tons per year. They are attempting to determine an optimal ordering policy which would lead to the minimization of total inventory costs. The supplier of their coal, Smokiest Mountain Coal Company, has quoted a delivered price of $60 per ton. Carrying costs are estimated at $5 per ton per year and ordering costs at $500 per order. Assuming that lead time is deterministic and constant at two days, determine:

    a. The economic order quantity.
    b. The optimal reorder point.
    c. The optimal number of orders to place each year.
    d. The minimum annual inventory costs.

    What happens if lead time doubles to four days?

43. For Exercise 42, assume that the coal is shipped by train and that it must be purchased by the carload. Thus, coal must be purchased in units of 40 tons (the capacity per jumbo hopper car).

    a. Determine the minimum cost order quantity and reorder point given this constraint.
    b. What is the optimal number of orders to place each year?
    c. What are the total annual inventory costs under this policy?
    d. What is the cost to the power company of the added restriction when compared with part (*d*) in Exercise 42.

44. By now we are all comfortable with sensitivity analysis. Company analysts admit that carrying costs can actually fluctuate between $4 and $7. Similarly, ordering cost per order can fluctuate between $350 and $700 per order. If the parameters assume their extreme values, analyze the effects of these fluctuations *independently* by determining the effects on the

    a. EOQ.
    b. Optimal reorder point.

    c.   Number of orders.
    d.   Total annual cost.

To which of these parameters do Q^*, N^*, and total cost seem to be most sensitive?

**45.   Again referring to the initial data in Exercise 42, estimate the effect on Q^* and total cost of instantaneous changes in C_o and C_h by:

    1.   Independently finding the derivatives of the expressions for Q^* and $C(Q^*)$ with respect to C_o and C_h.
    2.   Evaluating these derivatives when all parameters assume the values given in Exercise 42.

      Interpret the meaning of these derivatives. Would you say that Q^* and $C(Q^*)$ are very sensitive to changes in C_o and C_h? Explain.

46.   Smokiest Mountain Coal Company has offered the power company a 0.5 percent discount (one half of one percent) if they will order in quantities of 100,000 tons or more.

    a.   What are total annual costs under the discount?
    b.   Should the power company accept the offer?
    c.   What is the indifference discount (see Exercise 22)?

47.   Smokiest Mountain Coal Company has offered the power company a progression of discount possibilities. The offer is summarized here.

Purchase Price	Minimum Purchase Quantity
$60.00	No minimum
59.50	100,000 tons
59.00	125,000 tons
58.75	150,000 tons

    a.   Determine the optimal order quantity and reorder point for the power company.
    b.   What is the minimum total annual inventory cost?

48.   Assume that lead time is deterministic and equal to two days in Exercise 42. However, assume that lead time demand is stochastic with a mean of 20,000 tons and a distribution as given.

Class Intervals for Lead Time Demand (tons)	Lead Time Demand (d_L)	$f(d_L)$
16,500 but less than 17,500	17,000	0.02
17,500 but less than 18,500	18,000	0.08
18,500 but less than 19,500	19,000	0.20
19,500 but less than 20,500	20,000	0.40
20,500 but less than 21,500	21,000	0.20
21,500 but less than 22,500	22,000	0.08
22,500 but less than 23,500	23,000	0.02

    The power company recognizes the penalty associated with incurring shortages. When a shortage of coal occurs oil must be substituted at an effective additional cost of $1 per ton short. This $1 reflects additional costs associated with arranging and operating at higher levels of capacity at the oil-burning facilities. A company policy specifies that when replenished supplies of coal arrive following a shortage, the coal-burning facilities will reciprocate by operating at higher capacity so as to replace the energy units provided during the shortage (assume this is done at a negligible additional cost).

    a.   Determine the optimal order quantity and optimal reorder point.
    b.   What is the suggested buffer stock?
    c.   Rework parts (*a*) and (*b*) above if the penalty cost is \$0.25 per ton short.

**49.   *a.*   *Simultaneously* compute Q^* and R^* for the data given in Exercise 48.
    b.   What should the safety stock be for this policy?
    c.   Based on Equation (11.21), compare the expected cost per day for this model to the expected cost per day for the policy in Exercise 48. Conclusion?
    d.   Compare the expected annual cost of the policy in part (*a*) to what the expected annual cost would be for the policy given in Exercise 42. Comment on the meaning of this difference.

50. Suppose that for the scenario in Exercise 48, the shortage cost is based not only on the amount short but also on the length of time over which the shortage exists, that is, \$1 per ton per day.

    a.   Explicitly state why the model which was used in Exercise 48 is inappropriate.
    b.   Determine the optimal policy and associated cost using the deterministic backorder model as an approximation. In which direction does this model bias Q^* and R^*?
    c.   Modify the policy in part (*b*) to account for the discounts indicated in Exercise 47.
   **d.   Modify the policy in part (*c*) if the carrying cost is 10 percent of the purchase price.

51. *Financial Management* Inventory models have been applied in arenas not usually thought of as involving inventory concepts. One such area is that of financial management. Any of you who have taken a finance course should readily concede that cash on hand is an inventoried item. Financial managers regularly deal with the problem of determining the optimal level of cash to keep on hand.

    A variation on this treatment involves a company which has regular cash needs during a time period. The problem is to determine the optimal amount of new funds to obtain from borrowing. The objective is to minimize the costs of going to the market for funds and the opportunity cost associated with "carrying" the funds. Let

    $Q =$ Amount of cash obtained from each bond issue (dollars per issue).
    $C_o =$ Fixed cost associated with floating a bond issue (dollars per issue).
    $C_h =$ Annual opportunity (carrying) cost associated with having cash on hand (dollars per dollar per year).
    $D =$ Annual cash needs (dollars per year).

It is important to note that C_h is expressed as a proportion or percentage of a dollar. For example, if $C_h = 0.06$, then the opportunity cost is \$0.06 on the dollar per year, or 6 percent annually.

    Assume that cash needs are uniform during the year, that funds can be obtained in a deterministic period of time, and that interest rates on bonds are constant and unaffected by the size of the bond issue.

a. Write a general expression for the total annual cost associated with borrowing and holding cash.

b. If $D = \$10$ million, $C_o = \$5,000$, and $C_h = \$0.06$ per dollar per year, determine the optimal size of each bond issue. How many times a year should bond issues be floated?

c. What is the annual cost of floating bonds? The annual opportunity cost associated with holding cash?

d. At what level of cash should a bond issue be initiated if it takes five days to float the issue? Assume 255 "trading" days in a year (that is, days when the bond market and the firm actively engage in their affairs).

52. In Exercise 51, the opportunity cost associated with holding cash was estimated at 6 percent per year. Because of the dynamics of the money market, analysts concede that this percentage may fluctuate between 4.5 and 7.75 percent. By conducting sensitivity analyses, determine the effects on your answers to parts (b), (c), and (d) in Exercise 51 if C_h assumes these extreme values.

53. Suppose that cash withdrawals for the firm in Exercise 51 are probabilistic according to the distribution indicated here. As before, assume a 5-day

Cash Withdrawals over Five Successive Trading Days ($1,000)	Probability
170	0.05
180	0.10
190	0.30
200	0.40
210	0.05
220	0.10

fixed lead time and 255 trading days in a year.

a. Confirm that the mean demand during the lead time translates into an expected annual demand which is approximately consistent with the annual demand used in Exercise 51.

b. Assume a shortage cost of $0.05 per dollar which is independent of time. Determine Q^*, R^*, and optimal buffer stock based on Model 1 in Section 11.5. Would you say that the shortage cost for this application should include a time factor? Explain.

**c. Determine the optimal policy by using Model 2 of Section 11.5. Use $C_p = 0.05$. Based on Equation (11.21), compare the expected annual cost of this policy to the expected annual costs of the policies in Exercise 51 and part (b) of this exercise.

**54. Derive expressions for Q^* and $C(Q^*)$ for a reorder point inventory model having the same assumptions as the classical model except that

$$C_o = a + b \cdot Q,$$

where a and b are fixed cost and variable cost parameters, respectively. Comment on differences between this model and the classic EOQ model.

**55. *Multi-item Constrained EOQ Model* Mathematical programming repre-
sents one approach to solving inventory models characterized by more
than one item subject to constraints on capital, storage area, storage volume, or other resource. Consider a simplified inventory situation whereby
inventory is to be carried for each of two liquid items. Assume that conditions for the classic EOQ model are approximated, except that the
maximum storage volume of both items combined must not exceed 400,-
000 gallons. Relevant weekly data are given below.

	Item 1	Item 2
D	1 million gallons per week	2 million gallons per week
C_h	$0.02 per gallon per week	$0.01 per gallon per week
C_o	$200 per order	$300 per order
t_L	1 week	2 weeks

a. Determine the unconstrained EOQ solution for each item and show
that the volume constraint is violated.

b. Formulate this model in terms of a mathematical programming
format; that is, minimize $z = (?)$ subject to $(?)$.

c. Solve the model in part (b) by the Lagrange multiplier method (see
Section 3.4, page 83). (Hint: Develop an expression for Q_i^* in terms
of λ^* and systematically assume trial values for λ^* until the constraint is approximately satisfied. Does Table 3–3 on page 87 predict the correct sign on λ^*?

12

Queuing Models

A "QUEUE" is a waiting line of "customers" (units) requiring service from one or more "servers" (service facility). Not without exaggeration, the comment has been made that "life is one big queue." Reflect for a moment about the waiting lines in which you have been a "unit": registration for the school term, red light at a traffic signal, ticket booth at a movie theater, checkout counter at a supermarket, busy signal when making a phone call, teller window at a bank, line or table at a dining hall or restaurant, and so on.[1]

Both the concept of "unit" and the concept of "service facility" can be applied very broadly. Although one first thinks of examples such as automobiles at toll booths, queuing models also are applicable to the arrival of rainfall to dams via rivers, arrivals of fire calls to fire departments, and money into and out of bank accounts.

Essentially, a queue forms whenever existing demand exceeds the existing capacity of the service facility, that is, whenever arriving customers cannot receive immediate service due to busy servers. This state of affairs is almost guaranteed to occur at some time in any system which has probabilistic arrival and servicing patterns. Tradeoffs between the cost of increasing service capacity and the cost of waiting customers prevent an easy resolution of the problem. In other words, if the cost of the service facility were no object, then theoretically enough servers could be marshalled to immediately service all incoming customers. It follows that a reduction in the capacity of the service facility results in a concurrent

---

[1] Philosophically, life itself can be conceptualized as a queuing system beginning with an arrival (birth) and ending with the inevitable departure (death).

increase in the costs associated with waiting units. Consider the $250,000 to $500,000 annual cost of acquiring and operating 24 hours per day an additional fire truck. Compare this with the hard-to-measure cost of having people (fires) wait for the arrival of fire-fighting equipment. The basic objective in most queuing models is to achieve a balance in this cost tradeoff.

The application of formal waiting line models began with the study of telephone congestion problems some seven decades ago. As with many models in MS/OR, the potential for application is almost unlimited; the theoretical "state of the art" continues to advance; and problems associated with implementation, while difficult, are being overcome slowly.

In this chapter, we begin by discussing the fundamentals of queuing systems, follow with an exposition of the most popular models (including models in an optimization framework), and end with an assessment of the field in general. The presentation is geared to your achieving an understanding of the assumptions and limitations for each model as well as to your acquiring a working knowledge of applied relationships for each model. The minor emphasis on proofs is relegated to Appendix 12A.

12.1 QUEUING SYSTEMS: AN OVERVIEW

Rather than immediately leaping into techniques of solution, we believe it is useful to first provide a foundation of concepts and a framework to help you establish your bearings. We start with a brief discussion on criteria and the managerial decision alternatives related to queuing models and thereafter provide a general representation of a queuing process. With this background, we can then examine in some detail the five basic features or characteristics of queuing systems, see how a taxonomy of queuing models can be structured by these features, and describe the analytical approaches which have been developed. At that point, the presentation of particular solution procedures can be accomplished in a more meaningful context.

Criteria and Decisions

Maximization of profit and minimization of cost represent two relatively global criteria for many queuing models. The optimum value is achieved when the costs of waiting are properly traded off with costs of providing service. A supermarket, for example, might wish to determine the number and type of servers which maximize the expected contribution to overhead and profit determined by expected revenue less costs of goods less server operating costs less implicit costs associated with customer waiting (or refusing to wait). The managerial decisions are what levels of service to provide and the operating conditions which allow for the achievement of these service levels. For the supermarket example, long-term decisions include the number and type of checkout counters (conveyor belts, computers, and so forth). Medium-term decisions include the size and composition of the labor force (number of checkers and baggers) as well as work schedules. Short-term decisions include when to operate express lines, when to open and close checkout counters, and when and how to shift personnel from stocking shelves to bagging groceries.

If the decisions appear to be difficult to pin down exactly, the cost criteria are even more slippery. Properly ascertaining incremental costs for service, difficult as they may be, are trivial compared to estimating waiting costs. What is the cost of waiting in supermarket lines? In having customers choose not to enter a queue? For students waiting to register for classes? For patients waiting in a hospital emergency room?

Appealing as the optimum waiting-service cost tradeoff may be, empirical problems often have to work with surrogate criteria related to **operating or behavioral characteristics** of queuing systems. Examples of operating characteristics include the average or expected waiting time and the probability that the server will be idle. Note that these two operating characteristics are respectively proportional to waiting and facility (idle) costs.

Thus, the decision maker will want to examine various service level policies (decision rules) in terms of various operating characteristics. Interest may be focused on both long-run expectations and specific levels for relevant operating characteristics. For example, although it may be of interest to know that the average waiting time at a checkout counter is four minutes, a decision maker might also be interested in the maximum waiting time, demand during periods preceding holidays, and the influences of starting with an empty store every morning.

Before we turn to the five basic features of queuing systems, it is useful for you to explicitly understand the role played by variability in queuing systems. In fact, waiting occurs primarily because of randomness or variability in the arrival pattern of units and because of variability in the times required to service those units. You will not be surprised to find that waiting times and other operating characteristics can be improved by reducing variability in either of these areas. Examples in reducing arrival time variability include appointments (for example, doctor's offices, beauty parlors, automobile service centers, and so forth) and smoothing via promotional efforts (for example, family discounts and double trading stamps on specific days). Reduction in service time variability can be equally advantageous, which suggests that alternative service facilities need to be evaluated in terms of both means and variances in their servicing times.

General Representation

Figure 12–1 is a general model of a **queuing process.** Units arrive from some defined **calling source** or **population** to require service from a **service facility** which can consist of none (self-service), one, or multiple servers. If the service facility can be entered immediately, the unit is served and then departs; otherwise, the unit joins a **queue or waiting line** (if it can or wants to) to await service. The term **queue configuration** refers to the number of available queues and their arrangement. Note that the **queuing system** itself only includes one or more queues (made up of units)

FIGURE 12–1

Schematic of Queuing Process

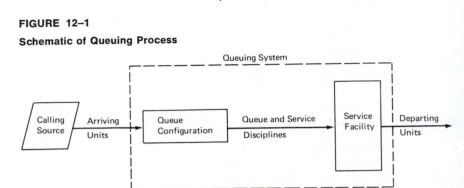

and the service facility (which can include one or more servers). **Queue and service disciplines** refer to the behavior and processing of units in the system. These will be discussed shortly.

Table 12–1 identifies selected real-world queuing systems which have been analyzed. The examples clearly indicate the scope and flexibility of what we term a queuing system. Notice that (1) customers and servers can be animate or inanimate, (2) queues can exist conceptually or physically in one or many locations, and (3) customers can go to servers or vice versa. The last section of the table includes criteria which might be of interest in making decisions.

12.2 FEATURES OF QUEUING PROCESS

Variations in the treatment of queuing systems can be described in terms of five important features: arrival process, queue configuration, queue discipline, service discipline, and service facility.

Arrival Process

The arrival process characterizes the arrival of units into the queuing system. We will consider eight possible states or arrival conditions. These are not necessarily mutually exclusive.

1. The calling source can consist of *single or multiple populations*. For instance, a queuing system for operating rooms can be analyzed in terms of a specific type of surgery (for example, brain or open heart) or in terms of several or all types of surgery combined.
2. The calling source can consist of a *finite or infinite number of units*. Water to replenish a reservoir originates from an infinite population, whereas malfunctioning machines in a particular machine shop are members of a finite population. For many applications, the populations, while not infinite, are large enough that models assuming infinite populations serve as adequate approximations.
3. *Single or bulk arrivals* can occur. At a restaurant, families may arrive singly to make reservations but in bulk to eat their meals.

TABLE 12–1

Queuing Examples

	Units	Servers	Queues	Possible Criteria
1.	Automobiles	Toll booths	Automobiles waiting to pay	Driver waiting, toll booth cost
2.	Machine breakdowns	Mechanics	Machines waiting to be fixed	Idleness of mechanics, cost of breakdown
3.	Patients	Surgeons	Patients waiting for surgery	Surgeon income, patient health
4.	Airplanes	Runways	Departing and arriving airplanes	Fuel costs, customer service
5.	Computer jobs	Computer	Jobs not yet begun	Machine utilization, turnaround time
6.	Boats	River locks	Waiting boats in both directions	River traffic, freight cost
7.	Vacationers	Rooms at resort hotel	Waiting list	Room utilization, "happy" travelers
8.	Callers	Reservations clerks	Calls on hold	Number of clerks, lost reservations
9.	Mechanics	Tool crib attendants	Waiting mechanics	Mechanic cost, attendant cost
10.	Freighters	Unloading docks	Freighters waiting to be unloaded	Stevedore cost; freighter leasing cost
11.	Documents	Typists	Documents to be typed	Size of typing pool, turnaround time
12.	Telephone calls	Switching equipment	Busy signals	Equipment needs, customer complaints
13.	River water	Dam locks	Quantity of water in reservoir	Flood control, irrigation benefits
14.	Orders	Sales personnel	Backorders	Lost backorders, payroll
15.	Criminal defendants	Trials	Defendants in jail or on bail	Justice, court costs, retention costs

4. Total, partial, or no *control of arrivals* can be exercised by the queuing system. The arrival of a component to be assembled in an automated assembly line is totally controlled; airplane arrivals at an airport are partially controlled; and automobiles arriving at toll booths are not controlled at all. Appointment schedules exercise a degree of arrival control.

5. Units can emanate from a *deterministic or probabilistic generating process*. If total control is exercised, then the arrival process is deterministic; if the time between arrivals is a random variable, then the generating process is probabilistic. Needless to say, most queuing problems are represented by the latter process.

6. A probabilistic arrival process can be described by either an *empirical or a theoretical probability distribution*. The Poisson model, for example, is one of several theoretical distributions which are widely used to describe arrival processes.

7. The arrival process can be characterized by *independent or conditional (dependent) arrivals*. If the state of the system or the sequence of preceding arrivals does not affect subsequent arrivals, then arrivals are said to be independent; otherwise, arrivals are conditional. Arrivals can be conditional by virtue of *correlation* or *state-dependence*. For example, the number of succeeding arrivals per time interval can be correlated due to *seasonal factors,* as when traffic intensity increases or decreases along a highway according to the time of day and the day of the week. Arrivals also can be affected by the number of units in (state of) the system. For example, if a finite calling source consists of ten operating machines, then the probability of four machine breakdowns in a one-hour period depends on how many machines are presently in the queue (broken down). *Behavioral factors* also account for state-dependence in the arrival rates. For instance the rate at which customers queue for a particular amusement at Disney World may be affected by the length of the waiting line.

8. A *stationary arrival process* may or may not exist. If the process is stationary, then the parameters (for example, mean and standard deviation) and form of the probability distribution which describes the arrival process remain constant over time. The usual assumption is a stationary process, as the mathematics become intractable otherwise. Nonstationary processes can be treated by monitoring changes in the process and/or by the use of forecasting models, in which cases stationary models can be reapplied.

Queue Configuration

Queue configuration refers to the number of queues in the queuing system, their relationship to the servers, and spatial considerations. A single queue can feed into a single server or multiple servers. Multiple queues typically align with an equal number of multiple servers (one queue in front of each server), although exceptions may exist as when several lanes of a highway converge into a smaller number of exit lanes. Queues may exist (1) physically in one place, (2) physically in disparate locations, as when telephone callers "hold the line" or machines wait to be repaired, (3) conceptually, as in a waiting list for hotel or airline reservations, or (4) not at all, as when calls to a busy number are rejected. Additionally, a queuing system may impose a restriction on the maximum number of units allowed in the queue (or system).

Queue Discipline

As used here, queue discipline refers to the behavior of arriving units both in the selection (or rejection) of a waiting line and in the act of waiting. We note six items which must be specified for any given queuing system.

1. If the system is filled to capacity, then the arriving unit is **rejected.** Examples include a busy signal when making a telephone call and a parking lot which is filled to capacity. Note that holding calls, such as is done by airlines, and waiting on the street for a parking space in the lot bring us back to queues. However, these queues also have a finite limit; at that point arriving units are rejected. In some instances a customer may be rejected by the primary system but accepted by a secondary system. A car which cannot enter a parking lot may "queue-up" in an informal waiting line of cars which are driving around the block waiting for entrance into the parking lot.

2. If the arriving customer's estimate of the waiting time is intolerably large (for example, as in a long queue which is moving slowly), then the customer might **balk,** or not join the queue. Note that this phenomenon is related to *state-dependence* in the arrival process.

3. If the customer does join the waiting line and subsequently decides that additional waiting is not worth it, then the customer **reneges,** or leaves the queue.

4. Customers exhibit **collusion** when the explicit processing of one unit represents the implicit processing of more than one unit, as when customers collude to buy movie tickets.

5. In multiple-queue systems, the possibility may or may not exist for customers to **jockey** between queues. (How many times have you had your grocery cart "revved-up" as you continuously scan the cashier lines for the purpose of changing queues?)

6. *Selection of a queue from among multiple queues* may be done by a variety of decision rules, including random selection, and shortest expected waiting time selection.

Customers who do not balk, renege, collude, jockey, and nonrandomly select from among multiple queues are said to be **patient.**

Service Discipline

Service discipline refers to the policy established for the service facility in selecting customers for processing. We note five types of service disciplines, with the last accommodating many varieties. It is useful to note that the selection of a service discipline represents a decision which can affect cost criteria.

1. *First-come first-served* **(FCFS)** or *first-in first-out* **(Fifo)** is often dictated by "fairness," as in the ticket numbering system of bakeries or butcher shops.
2. *Last-come first-served* **(LCFS)** or *last-in first-out* **(Lifo)** can be illustrated by an elevator queuing system whereby the last customers to enter are the first to exit on any given floor, or by coal to be removed from a coal pile.
3. *Service in Random Order* **(SIRO)** refers to some probabilistic process in selecting customers for service, as in a nail-packaging operation which packs nails randomly as they fall from a rotating drum, or in the selection of Bingo numbers. Service in random order does not require that anyone keep track of when units arrive at the queue.
4. **Round-robin service** is a sequential method of partially servicing units in the queuing system, as in the processing of jobs by a time-shared computer. Note that every unit in the queuing system is getting some service.
5. **Priority service** is a method of selection which biases the selection process according to predefined attributes. In general, units are serviced in order of decreasing priority. Examples include a time-sharing system which allocates CPU time on the basis of accumulated run time, favoring short-run jobs. Another is called "shortest operation next," which always processes that unit with smallest expected service time. The result is fewer units in the queue but longer expected waiting times for units with high service needs. A **preemptive** *priority discipline* specifies that a unit presently in service must be interrupted to service a newly arrived unit with higher priority; if the lower-priority unit presently in service is allowed to continue without interruption, then a **nonpreemptive** *priority discipline* has been specified. Emergency rooms in hospitals use priorities which are a function of the seriousness of the needs of the arriving customer and that of the customer being serviced.

Service Facility

In this section we describe characteristics associated with service facilities. These include both design attributes and operating characteristics.

1. The service facility can have *none, one, or multiple servers* **(channels).** Queuing systems in supermarkets, for instance, include both self-service (no server) for grocery items and multiple servers for checkouts.
2. Multiple servers can be **parallel,** in **series (tandem),** or *both*. Figure 12–2 illustrates various queue-server configurations. Interestingly, assuming patient customers, the case in part (*b*) can be analyzed as *c* separate cases of the type in part (*a*). The combined parallel-tandem case in part (*e*) is but one of many possible configurations. This case could be representative of a laundromat where the first type of service represents washing and the second represents drying. Channels in parallel can be **cooperative** (idle servers help busy servers) or **uncooperative.** By policy, parallel channels also can be **variable,** as when an additional teller's window is opened at a bank when the

FIGURE 12–2

Queue-Server Configurations

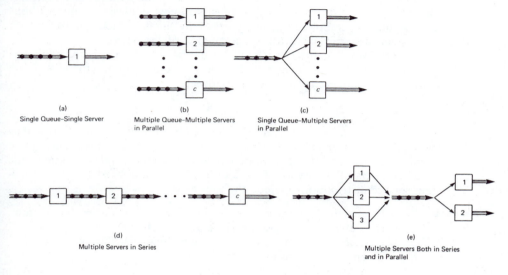

(a)
Single Queue–Single Server

(b)
Multiple Queue–Multiple Servers
in Parallel

(c)
Single Queue–Multiple Servers
in Parallel

(d)
Multiple Servers in Series

(e)
Multiple Servers Both in Series
and in Parallel

length of the queue exceeds a specified number. Job shop scheduling and network flow problems (see Chapter 16) characterize the case of channels in tandem.

3. As in the arrival process, service times can be deterministic or probabilistic. The time to process a car in an automated car wash is essentially deterministic. Most service-time distributions, however, are represented by random variables according to some specified empirical or theoretical probability distribution. For example, the exponential density function is commonly used to describe service times. As in the arrival process, *stationariness* is typically assumed.

4. *State-dependent service parameters* refer to cases where the mean, standard deviation, or other parameters of a service-time distribution are affected or changed by the **state** of (number of units in) the system. For example, cases where the service rate is affected by the length of a queue have been analyzed. Would you expect that the average service time increases or decreases as the length of the queue increases? Why? Can you think of examples?

5. *Breakdowns* among servers also can be considered. Such occurrences are possible not only among mechanical servers but also among human servers (as when someone takes ill).

12.3 CLASSIFICATIONS OF MODELS AND SOLUTIONS

In this section we first present an established scheme for classifying queuing models and then discuss general approaches for solving the models. The section ends with the very important consideration of time-dependency in the solutions.

Taxonomy of Queuing Models

Based on the various possibilities for each of the five queuing features, the number of distinct queuing models is almost endless. It goes without saying that the complete specification of any queuing model must include an explicit assumption with respect to each of the above variations. Still, it appears useful to broadly classify queuing models. D. G. Kendall has proposed a system of notation which has become popular for classifying parallel-server queuing models, as follows:

$$X/Y/Z$$

where position X contains a descriptive symbol for the particular distribution of time between arrivals (interarrival times), Y contains a descriptive symbol for the specific distribution of service times, and Z contains the number of parallel servers. The descriptive symbols used for the arrival and service distributions include the following:

$M \equiv$ Exponential interarrival or service time distribution (equivalent, respectively, to Poisson arrivals or departures).[2]
$D \equiv$ Deterministic interarrival or service-time distribution.
$E_k \equiv$ Erlangian distribution of order k.[3]
$GI \equiv$ General (any) distribution of interarrival times (or arrivals) which are independent.
$G \equiv$ General distribution of service times (or departures).

Thus, $M/M/1$ represents a Poisson arrival–exponential service time–single-server model; $D/M/c$ is a model with deterministic arrivals, exponential service times, and c parallel servers (but only one queue); and $GI/G/1$ indicates a single-server model with any probabilistic arrival process (as long as it is independent) and any probabilistic distribution of service times. Extensions by Lee and Taha have augmented the system of notation to include the type of service discipline, the maximum number of units allowed in the system, and the type of calling source (whether finite or infinite).[4] In this chapter, we will use Kendall's notation strictly and specify assumptions on the other characteristics in the description of the model.

Methods of Solution

Two methods of solution are available for queuing models: analytic and simulation. The analytical approach seeks to derive mathematical expressions for operating characteristics and (perhaps) optimal values for decision variables using probability theory and mathematical manipulations (for example, algebra and calculus), as illustrated in Appendix 12A and Section 12.7. The simulation approach seeks to artificially reproduce

---

[2] See Section A.3 in Appendix A under the negative exponential distribution.

[3] If $k = 1$, then the Erlangian and exponential distributions are identical.

[4] A. M. Lee, *Applied Queuing Theory* (New York: St. Marten's Press, 1966) and H. A. Taha, *Operations Research: An Introduction* (New York: The Macmillan Company, 1971).

the queuing process itself. We demonstrate this approach in the next chapter.

Often the characteristics of certain real-world queuing problems can be "adequately" approximated by analytical models. The "adequacy" of the approximations can be judged by statistical tests on historical or experimental data, as illustrated in Example A.3 on page 721. If the assumptions of available analytical queuing models are invalid for a particular application, then two courses of action are open: Derive a unique analytical solution or simulate. Since the mathematics associated with queuing solutions are difficult to understand for *all* but a select few (and limiting in general), the usual recourse is simulation. Simulation is appealing to most practitioners because it is conceptually uncomplicated. Great care (and expense), however, must be exercised in design, validation, and estimation. (See Section 13.6.)

Transient v. Steady-State Solutions

A final distinction is important at this time: the difference between transient-state and steady-state solutions. A solution in the **transient state** is one that is time-dependent (that is, the values of the operating characteristics depend on time), whereas a solution in the **steady state** is in statistical equilibrium (that is, time-independent). Typically, operating characteristics are transient during the early stages of operation because of their dependence on initial conditions, as illustrated by Figure 12–3. For example, the opening of a department store during a "normal" day or during a "big sale" day represent radically different initial conditions (small or nonexistent initial queue v. long initial queue which will affect the operating characteristics during the early part of the operating period). However, as time goes on, the system, given enough time, will effectively

FIGURE 12–3

Transient v. Steady-State Behavior

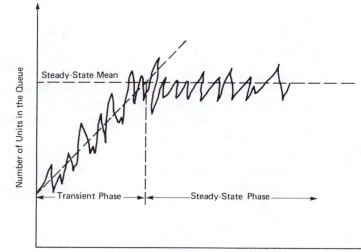

settle down to its long-run or steady-state tendencies. Mathematically, this is equivalent to letting the time variable approach infinity, a device which considerably simplifies the necessary mathematical tools.

Unfortunately, many queuing systems may never achieve an effective steady state, as in the following two cases: (1) the average rate of arrivals exceeds the average servicing capacity of the system, and (2) the time span of operation for the system is too short (as in an eight-hour day). Bhat has illustrated the latter case for an $M/D/1$ system.[5] Given mean arrivals of six customers per hour and service requiring seven minutes per customer, it takes more than half of an eight-hour day to achieve equilibrium. For both of these cases either simulation or complex mathematical formulas which include time as a variable (when available) must be used to estimate operating characteristics such as time spent in the queue or average number of units in the queue.

12.4 $M/M/1$ MODELS

This section presents the best-known set of queuing models. For each case, we state the relevant assumptions and follow with analytically derived formulas for estimating operating characteristics.

Standard $M/M/1$ Model

Every queuing model requires specific assumptions with respect to the five features in Section 12.2. The application of any queuing model, therefore, should include validation with respect to these assumptions.

The derivation of the standard $M/M/1$ model requires the following set of assumptions about the queuing process:

1. Arrival process—Single population with infinite number of units; single arrivals with no control exercised by queuing system; arrivals are independent and behave according to Poisson probability mass function; and stationary arrival process exists.[6]
2. Queue configuration—Single waiting line with no restriction on maximum length.
3. Queue discipline—No rejections; patient customers, (that is, no balking, reneging, or collusion). (Note that behavior associated with jockeying or queue selection need not be specified for a single queue.)
4. Service discipline—FCFS.
5. Service facility—One server (no parallel or series considerations); service times distributed according to exponential probability density function; service parameter and distribution are state-independent and stationary; no breakdowns.

There are several reasons for the popularity of this model, even though the above assumptions may seem unduly restrictive. First, transient and

---

[5] U. N. Bhat, "Sixty Years of Queuing Theory," *Management Science,* vol. 15 (1969), p. B-290.

[6] The Poisson function given by (A.24) implies independence between arrivals: Conversely, as already indicated, *interarrival times* are distributed according to the exponential density function given by (A.31). (See pages 714 and 716.)

TABLE 12–2

Steady-State Operating Characteristics for Standard $M/M/1$ Model

Operating Characteristics	Formula	Formula Number
Probability of zero units in system (probability of idle system)	$P_o = 1 - \rho$	(12.1)
Probability of busy period or busy system (probability of waiting or of delaying a unit)	$P(n > 0) = \rho$	(12.2)
Probability of n units in system (geometric distribution)	$P_n = P_o \rho^n$	(12.3)
Probability density function for time in system (exponential distribution)	$f(w) = (\mu - \lambda)e^{-(\mu-\lambda)w}, w \geq 0$	(12.4)
Expected number of units in system	$L_s = \dfrac{\lambda}{\mu - \lambda}$	(12.5)
Variance of number of units in system	$V_{ls} = \dfrac{\lambda\mu}{(\mu - \lambda)^2}$	(12.6)
Expected number of units in queue	$L_q = \dfrac{\rho\lambda}{\mu - \lambda}$	(12.7)
Expected number of units in queue for busy system	$L_b = \dfrac{\lambda}{\mu - \lambda}$	(12.8)
Expected time in system	$W_s = \dfrac{1}{\mu - \lambda}$	(12.9)
Variance of time in system	$V_{ws} = \dfrac{1}{(\mu - \lambda)^2}$	(12.10)
Expected time in queue	$W_q = \dfrac{\rho}{\mu - \lambda}$	(12.11)
Expected time in queue for busy system	$W_b = \dfrac{1}{\mu - \lambda}$	(12.12)

$\lambda \equiv$ Mean arrival rate (units per time period).
$\mu \equiv$ Mean service rate (units per time period).
$\rho \equiv$ Traffic intensity (λ/μ).
$w \equiv$ Random variate for time in system.
$n \equiv$ Number of units in system.
Note: System refers to queue plus service facility; formulas are valid only if $\rho < 1$.

steady-state derivations of operating characteristics are possible and easily applied; second, the assumptions have proved reasonable (especially Poisson-distributed arrivals) in some (but not many) applied problems; and, finally, the model can be used for planning purposes and insight. For example, results based on this model may lead to suggestions for subsequent approaches.[7]

In Table 12–2 we provide formulas, without proof, for the *steady-state* operating characteristics of this model. For those of you who are interested, the derivations for this model are presented in Appendix 12A.

Given the assumptions, you should understand that λ and μ are the parameters of the Poisson and exponential probability distributions, respectively. The restriction on **traffic intensity** $[\rho \equiv (\lambda/\mu) < 1]$ should make sense to you. If it were not restricted to a value less than one, then

---

[7] For an excellent example of what we mean by "insightful uses," see W. J. Erikson, "Management Science and the Gas Shortage," *Interfaces* (August 1974), pp. 47–51.

the steady state never would be achieved as an arrival rate greater than the service rate would result in an infinitely large queue as time approaches infinity. Also note that Equations (12.5), (12.7), (12.9), and (12.11), which are in Table 12–2, include customers who do not have to wait before moving into the service facility. Their inclusion results in lower expected values for these operating characteristics; Equations (12.8) and (12.12) provide operating characteristics which are more representative for those customers who must wait. For example, Equation (12.8) represents the steady-state mean number of customers in the queue when the single server is busy. Alternatively, (12.7) is the steady-state mean number of customers in the queue, including the queues of zero length whenever the server is idle. The steady-state mean in Figure 12–3 is, in fact, L_q.

Finally, note that the number of customers in the system (n) is a random variable with an associated probability distribution given by Equation (12.3). In other words, the actual number of customers in the system (n) will fluctuate about the mean number of customers in the system (L_s) according to the specified probability distribution (12.3) with variance given by (12.6).

Follow-up Exercises

1. Show that Equation (12.2) is obtained easily from (12.1).

2. Interpret the meanings, with respect to **system utilization,** of low and high values for Equations (12.1) and (12.2).

3. Using Equations (12.1) and (12.2), show that the **expected number in service** is $(1 - P_o)$ or ρ. (Note that a unit is either in service or not in service.)

4. Show that the expected number of units in the system equals the expected number in service plus the expected number in the queue.

5. If $1/\mu$ is the expected time in service (right?), show that the expected time in the system equals the expected time in the queue plus the expected time in service.

6. Show that the expected time in the queue can be determined as the expected number of units in the queue divided by the arrival rate. Does this make sense? Is this equivalent to $L = \lambda W$ for the system, queue, and busy-system queue?

7. Show that L_b can be determined as L_q divided by the probability of delaying a unit. Can you show why this is valid? (Hint: See Equation (13) in Appendix 12A.)

8. Show that W_b can be determined as W_q divided by the probability of waiting. Can you show why this is valid?

9. A measure of effectiveness for a queuing system is given by the **customer loss ratio,** (R), or the ratio of average time in waiting for service to the average time in service. Show that $R = \lambda/(\mu - \lambda)$ for the M/M/1 model. From the standpoint of the customer, are low or high values desired for R?

Example 12.1   Emergency Room Queuing System

In an emergency room queuing system, patients requiring treatment can be considered the units and the mechanism for treating them (for example, beds, physicians, and so forth) the servers. Suppose patients are treated by a single "server" on a FCFS basis, the arrival and service processes are as described in Examples A.1 and A.3 on pages 707 and 721, and other assumptions of the $M/M/1$ model are met.[8] (Note that the population is assumed infinite, which effectively means that it is of sufficient size to ensure that the assumption of infinity only minutely affects probabilities.)

Carefully note that the collection of data (step four in the paradigm) is a rather crucial step in the application of the correct queuing model. The chi-square test in Example A.3 indicates that the service distribution depicted in Table A–3 is exponential with mean 0.4 hour per patient. Thus, $\mu = 2.5$ customers per hour (that is, $1/\mu = 0.4$). In actual practice, μ is best estimated by fixing the number of units served and dividing by the total elapsed busy (service) time.

If you carried out a chi-square test in Exercise 19 of Appendix A on page 722, then you should have verified that the arrival process is Poisson with $\lambda = 2.1$ patients per hour. In general, λ can be estimated by fixing the number of arrivals and dividing by the total elapsed time or vice versa.[9]

The traffic intensity for this example is $\rho = 0.84$ (that is, 2.1/2.5), which implies that the server is busy (the system is utilized) 84 percent of the time. In other words, according to Equation (12.2), the probability of a busy period, or a busy system, or of waiting, or of delaying a unit is 0.84. Conversely, according to Equation (12.1), the probability of an idle server is 0.16.

The expected (mean) number of patients in the system, queue, and busy-system queue are, respectively, 5.25, 4.41, and 5.25 according to Equations (12.5), (12.7), and (12.8). A customer loss ratio (see Exercise 9) of 5.25 indicates that, on the average, customers spend more time in the queue than in service by a factor of 5.25 (or 525 percent). We see that the variance and standard deviation for the number of patients in the system, using Equation (12.6), are 32.8 and 5.73, respectively. From Equation (12.9), the mean time to process a patient from arrival to departure is 2.5 hours; from (12.11), the mean time that customers spend in a queue is 2.1 hours; from (12.12), the average time of waiting *for those who wait* (84 percent of the cases) is 2.5 hours; and from (12.10), the variance and standard deviation for time through the system are 6.25 hours^2 and 2.5 hours, respectively.

Now consider a sensitivity analysis based on the parameter μ. In Table 12–3 it can be seen that operating characteristics are highly sensitive to values of μ in the neighborhood of λ (that is, when ρ is close to 1); hence, especially precise estimations are needed in this neighborhood of high traffic intensities. Further note that a high traffic intensity promotes a large

---

[8] In actual practice, as previously mentioned, emergency room queuing systems must be analyzed using a priority service discipline based on, say, two priorities (for example, major and minor emergencies).

[9] These procedures for estimating λ and μ provide unbiased estimates of the population parameters; that is, the expected value of the sample statistic equals the population parameter. For Poisson and exponential distributions, respectively, they also provide maximum likelihood estimates; that is, they represent values for the parameters that maximize the probability of obtaining the observed sample outcome.

expected value for number of units and waiting time, which in turn results in a longer period of time for the system to achieve steady state. Moreover if the system got "out of whack" (for example, a five-car accident), then it would take a long time to get back into steady state.

The sensitivity table clearly is an important aid to decision making. If the hospital administrator finds that an average time above two hours for entirely processing a patient is intolerable, yet wishes to maintain a utilization (ρ) above 80 percent, then the service rate which must be achieved is 2.6 patients per hour, as indicated in the table. What controllable variables

TABLE 12–3

Sensitivity Analysis Based on μ for Example 12.1

μ	P_o	ρ	L_s, L_b	L_q	W_s, W_b	W_q
2.2.............	0.05	0.95	21.00	20.05	10.00	9.50
2.3.............	0.09	0.91	10.50	9.55	5.00	4.55
2.4.............	0.12	0.88	7.00	6.16	3.33	2.64
2.5.............	0.16	0.84	5.25	4.41	2.50	2.10
2.6.............	0.19	0.81	4.20	3.40	2.00	1.62
2.7.............	0.22	0.78	3.50	2.73	1.67	1.30
2.8.............	0.25	0.75	3.00	2.25	1.43	1.07

influence μ? In what ways can the hospital administrator increase the value of μ?

Follow-up Exercises

10. What service rate must be achieved to attain an average waiting time in the system (queue and service) which is one hour or less? What values result for the other operating characteristics?

11. Find the probabilities of 0, 1, 2, . . . , 7 patients in the system using Equation (12.3); find the cumulative probabilities of 0, 1, 2, . . . , 7 and less patients in the system.

12. Find the probabilities of 0, 1, . . . , 6 patients in the queue using the results of the preceding exercise; determine the associated cumulative probabilities.

13. What values for μ yield a customer loss ratio below 4 and system utilization above 75 percent? Interpret the meaning of the 4 and the 75 percent.

14. What value of μ satisfies the requirement that the probability of exactly no patients in the queue is 0.50.?

15. What values of μ satisfy the condition that the probability of one or more patients waiting at any given time must be less than 0.05?

16. Noting that $(\mu - \lambda)$ represents the parameter for the exponential density function in Equation (12.4), use (A.32) to determine the probability that a unit will take less than one hour to process. Between one and two hours? Between two and three hours?

Example 12.2 Bank Queuing System

Suppose that arrivals of customers to drive-in windows of a commercial bank are Poisson-distributed with rate $\lambda = 0.9$ car per minute. Goodness-of-fit tests indicate that the service time distribution for each of three tellers is exponential with rate $\mu = 0.4$ car per minute.

Notice that the example illustrates a multiple-server system; however, if we assume a queue in front of each teller, random selection of queues, and patient customers, then three separate single-server independent subsystems can be used to approximate the real system, as illustrated in Figure 12–4. If we adjust the arrival rate to 0.3 car per minute (that is, 0.9/3) for each

FIGURE 12–4

Independent Subsystems for Bank

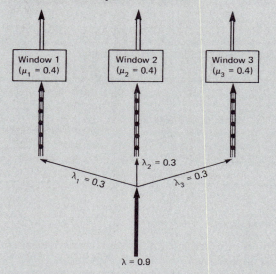

subsystem, then $P_o = 0.25$, $P(n > 0) = 0.75$, $L_s = L_b = 3$ cars, $L_q = 2.25$ cars, $V_{ls} = 12$ cars^2, $W_s = W_b = 10$ minutes per car, $W_q = 7.5$ minutes per car, and $V_{ws} = 100$ minutes^2. For the system as a whole, tellers are idle 25 percent of the time, 75 percent of the customers must wait an average of 10 minutes, on the average the waiting time in the queue is 300 percent greater than the waiting time in service (that is, $R = 3$), the expected number of cars in the system is nine (that is, 3 tellers $\times$ 3 cars per teller), and the associated variance is 36 cars^2 for the system (that is, $12 + 12 + 12$).

The use of $M/M/1$ formulas for approximating a multiple-queue $M/M/c$ system illustrates the flexibility of this simple model. In general, however, the realities of nonrandom queue selection, impatient customers, and utilization of indoor tellers due to rejection and balking suggest that the actual average time and average number of cars in the system will be less than 10 minutes and nine cars, respectively. At the very least, this model provides useful bounds for operating characteristics and serves as a benchmark for the application of more complex analytical or simulation models.

Follow-up Exercises

17. Draw a conclusion if only two drive-in windows are available.

18. Conduct a sensitivity analysis as in Table 12–3 for Example 12.2 based on $\mu = 0.3$, 0.35, 0.5. Conclusions?

19. What range of μ satisfies a customer loss ratio below two and system utilization above 60 percent? (Use data in Example 12.2.)

20. Determine operating characteristics if four drive-in windows are available each with $\mu = 0.4$ car per minute, and compare to the results in the example.

21. How many drive-in windows, each with $\mu = 0.4$ car per minute, would be needed to reduce the average time for those who wait to less than five minutes? What percentage of the time is each window busy? What is the probability a customer has to wait? What is the average number of customers in the system? In which direction are these figures biased and why?

22. Determine operating characteristics if four drive-in windows are available each with $\mu = 0.3$. Compare these results with the results in the example. (Note that the product $c \cdot \mu$, the average capacity of the entire system, equals 1.2 cars per minute for both cases.) Conclusions?

**23. Given three drive-in windows, each with $\mu = 0.4$ car per minute service and $\lambda = 0.3$ car per minute input, verify that the probability of exactly two cars in the *entire* system is given by $6(1 - \rho)^3 \rho^2 = 0.053$. (Hint: Derive this expression by applying Equations (A.6) and (A.3) to (12.3) for the six possible combinations which give two cars in the system.)

Other Service Disciplines

Except for a priority service discipline, the derivation of P_n for the standard $M/M/1$ model (as illustrated in Appendix 12A) is independent of whether FCFS, LCFS, or SIRO is used; in fact, the only difference among these three service disciplines is in the form and shape (but not the mean) of the waiting time distribution for the system. Thus, all equations in Table 12–2 are valid for these cases except for Equations (12.4) and (12.10). As noted before, however, service disciplines can affect operating characteristics in ways that are consistent with system design criteria.

Restriction on Maximum Number in System

We now consider a modification to the standard $M/M/1$ model by introducing a restriction on the allowable number of customers in the system. Suppose N represents the maximum number of customers allowed in the system, or for a single-server model, $N - 1$ indicates the maximum number of units in the queue. Thus, if a customer arrives at a point in time when N units are in the system, then that customer is rejected (that is, leaves the system without entering). Examples of this type of **finite-**

queue (or **truncated-queue**) **model** include telephone reservation systems with a finite number of calls which can be "held," a drive-in window with a driveway coming in from a busy street where one cannot stop, and so forth.

Except for rejection, all assumptions of the standard $M/M/1$ model are identical for this case.

Formulas for selected operating characteristics are given by (12.13) through (12.21) in Appendix 12B.

Since the waiting time distribution has not been considered explicitly, these formulas also hold for LCFS and SIRO service disciplines. *Note that a traffic intensity of unity ($\rho = 1$) or above is allowed for this model.* Can you explain why? Also, W_s and W_q relate to customers who join the system; otherwise, times of zero for those who are rejected would bias these characteristics downward. Furthermore, you should realize that P_N represents the **probability of rejection** and λP_N is the **expected number of customers rejected per unit time.** Finally, as you might have verified in Exercises 4 and 5, Equation (12.17) indicates that the expected number in the queue equals the expected number in the system less the expected number in service and (12.20) suggests that the expected time in the queue equals the expected time in the system minus the expected time in service.

Example 12.3   Bank Queuing System

Suppose $N = 2$ for each teller in the bank queuing system of Example 12.2. Then, with $\rho = 0.75$, you should verify that for each teller $P_o = 0.43$, $P(n > 0) = 0.57$, $L_s = 0.81$ customer, $L_q = 0.24$ customer, $L_b = 0.43$ customer, $W_s = 3.6$ minutes, $W_q = 1.1$ minute, and $W_b = 1.9$ minutes. As expected, dramatic decreases over the previous case are experienced in system utilization, line lengths, and waiting times. Of course, these are achieved at the expense of a high rejection rate (see Exercise 24).

Follow-up Exercises

24. Use Equation (12.15) to verify that the probability of rejection, P_2, is approximately 0.24. On the average, how many customers will be rejected per minute? Per hour? (Distinguish between each teller and the system.)
25. Calculate the customer loss ratio (R) for this example. Interpret its meaning.
26. Using data for this example, show that $P_o + P_1 + \cdots + P_N = 1$.
27. What value for N would guarantee a rejection rate of less than 10 percent? What effect does this have on P_o, L_s, L_q, L_b, W_s, W_q, and W_b when compared to results in Example 12.3 above?

Finite Population

In many queuing systems, the calling source is finite. This means, in turn, that the number of units presently in the system alters the probabilities of future arrivals (note that infinite populations are not so affected). The most commonly analyzed problem of this type is that where m machines are to be repaired by one or more service representatives. In this case, machine breakdowns represent "arrivals" and the number of machines to be repaired represents the queue. Obviously, the number of machines presently in the queuing system (that is, in the queue plus being serviced), affects the arrival rate and the probabilities of subsequent breakdowns. Conversely, any arrival or departure affects this probability. Other examples of finite populations as calling sources for queuing systems include those concerned with machine utilization by a limited number of personnel. Secretaries using a copying machine and analysts using computer terminals represent two common examples.

We might note that a subtle distinction exists between this model and other models with respect to the definition of the arrival rate. In the present case, λ is the arrival rate for *each* unit in a population of m units. This means that the *effective arrival rate* into the queuing system is given by the product of λ and the expected number of units outside the queuing system, that is, by $\lambda \cdot (m - L_s)$. Right? For example if each of 10 machines breaks down at the rate of 2 machines per day and the expected number of machines in the queuing system is 3, then the effective arrival rate is $2 \cdot (10 - 3)$, or 14 machines per day.

Except for the assumptions of a finite calling source and the manner in which λ is defined, all other assumptions of this model are identical to those in the standard $M/M/1$ model. As for the standard model, *LCFS* and *SIRO* also apply to this model. Finite populations which are "sufficiently" large can be treated as infinite populations with little or no error, as illustrated in the hospital emergency room and drive-in bank tellers problems. Rules-of-thumb for assessing the term "sufficiently" are not as clear-cut as in the case of sampling. Populations above 30 units may suffice if traffic intensity is low (say, below 75 percent). As ρ increases however, the number of units in the system must increase accordingly. Under these circumstances, the infinite population model will serve as a reasonable approximation to the finite population model if the size of the population is well above 30.

> Formulas for selected operating characteristics are given by Equations (12.22) through (12.30) in Appendix 12B.

In Formulas (12.22) through (12.30) m represents the number of units in the population and other symbols are as previously defined. Since hand-solution of these formulas for a particular problem can be tedious, tables have been published which greatly simplify the effort.[10] Repeated applications of queuing formulas, however, may warrant the development of an appropriate computer program.

---

[10] See, for instance, L. G. Peck and R. N. Hazelwood, *Finite Queuing Tables* (New York: John Wiley & Sons, Inc., 1958).

Example 12.4 Computer Terminal Service

The accounting office of a company is considering the installation of a single computer terminal for a staff of four members which is engaged in financial analysis. Trial runs have indicated that the time to complete a job is exponential with a mean of 40 minutes and the demand on the terminal by *each analyst* is Poisson with a mean of 1/20 of a demand per minute. Thus, $m = 4$, $\mu = 1/40$, and $\lambda = 1/20$, so that $\rho = 2$.[11] For the probability of zero in the system, we get:

$$P_o = \cfrac{1}{\frac{4!}{4!}(2)^0 + \frac{4!}{3!}(2)^1 + \frac{4!}{2!}(2)^2 + \frac{4!}{1!}(2)^3 + \frac{4!}{0!}(2)^4}$$

$$= \cfrac{1}{\frac{24}{24}(1) + \frac{24}{6}(2) + \frac{24}{2}(4) + \frac{24}{1}(8) + \frac{24}{1}(16)}$$

$$= \frac{1}{633}$$

$$\doteq 0.0016.$$

The following operating characteristics are expected: Essentially, the terminal will be fully utilized (that is, idle 0.16 percent of the time); on the average, 3.5 analysts will be in the queuing system (L_s); both the overall average number of waiting analysts (L_q) and the average number of waiting analysts when the system is busy (L_b) will be approximately 2.5; the average time for waiting and using the terminal (W_s) will be 140 minutes; the average time lost in waiting (W_q) will be 100 minutes; and the average time of waiting for those analysts who wait (W_b) will be just over 100 minutes. Needless to say, a single terminal would appear overburdened (which increases the probability of a breakdown), and analysts would waste a great deal of time waiting (unless they have alternative uses for their time).

The expected cost per day for this queuing system can be estimated by summing the expected costs per day of the service facility and the analysts' lost time due to waiting. The cost of service is based on costs associated with subscription to a time-sharing service and costs relating to the terminal itself: cost per unit of connect time, cost per resource unit (ru), cost of magnetic disk storage, maintenance cost, and capital (depreciation) cost.[12] This being the accounting office, we can have great confidence in the following estimates: $10 per hour for connect time; $1 per resource unit; $5 per day for required disk space; $0.50 per day for a maintenance contract; and $3 per day for capital cost. For an eight-hour day, the expected connect time is $8(1 - P_o)$, or approximately eight hours in this case. If each job averages 40 minutes, then the mean number of jobs per day will be given by the expected connect time per day (480 minutes) divided by the expected job time (40 minutes), or 12. If on the average 5 resource units are used per job, then on the average 60 resource units will be used per day. Thus, the total cost of service per day is illustrated in the accompanying table.

---

[11] Unlike the standard model, it is permissible for ρ to exceed unity in this case because an infinite queue buildup in the steady state is not possible. Right?

[12] A resource unit is based on the utilization of the Central Processing Unit (CPU), which primarily consists of CPU time and use of magnetic core.

Connect [(hours/day) · $P(n > 0)$ · ($/hour) = (8) · (0.9984) · (10)]....... $ 79.87
Resource [(jobs/day) · (ru's/job) · ($/ru) = (12) · (5) · (1)]............. 60.00
Disk space... 5.00
Maintenance.. 0.50
Capital cost (depreciation)....................................... 3.00

   Cost per day of service facility............................... $148.37

If the idle time of an analyst is costed at $15 per hour and the lost time per day is given as the product of L_s (Why not L_q?) and the number of hours in a day, then the cost per day associated with waiting is ($15 per analyst-hour) · (2.5 analysts) · (8 hours per day), or $300 per day; hence, the expected total cost for this queuing configuration is $448.37 per day.[13] Needless to say (but we'll say it anyway), this cost per day should be compared to the cost per day of alternative configurations, including the alternative of continuing under the present arrangement.

Follow-up Exercises

28.   Calculate P_1, P_2, . . . , P_4. What is the probability of two or less analysts in the system? More than three analysts? Does $P_0 + P_1 + \cdots + P_4 = 1$?

29.   Besides the customer loss ratio (R = mean time in queue divided by mean service time), other effectiveness measures for finite population models include E_1 = average number in system (L_s) divided by number in population (m) and E_2 = average number of facilities idle divided by number of facilities (c). Calculate R, E_1, and E_2 for this example.

30.   Determine the operating characteristics and costs associated with two computer terminals. Treat this system in the manner of Example 12.2, that is, as two separate and independent single line-single server subsystems. (Hint: Maintenance and depreciation costs will double; however, connect and resource costs will *not* increase proportionally. Also, m must be adjusted but not λ. Can you reason why?)

---

[13] The cost of idle time is most easily estimated as the hourly rate of pay, although more precisely it should be the hourly "worth" of the employee, which includes the return to the company less some adjustment if the employee is not entirely idle while waiting.

12.5   *M/M/c* MODELS

In this section we generalize single queue-single server models with Poisson arrivals and exponential service times to *single* queue-multiple server models.

Standard *M/M/c* Model

The assumptions for this model are identical to the assumptions for the standard $M/M/1$ model except for the additional restrictions that servers are uncooperative and service rates across channels are independent and identical (that is, $\mu_1 = \mu_2 = \ldots = \mu_c$). Additionally, the given operating characteristics apply to FCFS, LCFS, and SIRO service disciplines.

The standard $M/M/c$ model equations, Equations (12.31) through (12.39), appear in Appendix 12B.

The steady-state operating characteristics [given by Equations (12.31) through (12.39) in Appendix 12B] have the same interpretation as before, although the expressions are more complex. As before, $\rho = \lambda/\mu$. Note, however, that now $\rho < c$, or $(\lambda/\mu c) < 1$, is a necessary condition for steady state to be achieved. In other words, the mean overall service rate (μc) for the system must be greater than the mean arrival rate (λ). Further note that the probability of a busy period or of waiting is $P(n \geq c)$ and not $P(n > 0)$; that is, an arriving unit has to wait if the number of customers in the system is at least equal to the number of servers.

Interestingly, the distribution of *departures from the queuing system* for this model is Poisson. For a queuing system characterized by subsystems in tandem of the $M/M/c$ type, the above formulas can be used to analyze each subsystem separately.[14]

We now illustrate computations for this model. As you might imagine, the computations are *very* tedious. In actual practice, tables, graphs, or computer routines are used.

Example 12.5   Bank Queuing System Continued

In the bank queuing system (Example 12.2), a queue formed in front of each of the three drive-in tellers. Suppose the system is redesigned such that one queue feeds into the service facility. In this case, we have an $M/M/c$ system with $c = 3$, $\lambda = 0.9$ car per minute, $\mu = 0.4$ car per minute, and $\rho = 2.25 < 3$. This gives

$$P_o = \frac{1}{\frac{(2.25)^0}{0!} + \frac{(2.25)^1}{1!} + \frac{(2.25)^2}{2!} + \frac{(2.25)^3}{3!(1 - 2.25/3)}}$$
$$= 0.0748.$$

You should verify that appropriate substitutions in Equations (12.33) through (12.39) give the results in column (1) of Table 12–4. The second column in this table allows a direct comparison to the results in Example 12.2. In comparing methods (1) and (2) it appears that substantial improvements in performance measures are realized in switching from three queues to a single queue.[15] Have you noticed in recent years how banks have forced single queues for the indoor system of tellers? Not only has performance improved but also equity in the processing of customers and privacy of transactions

---

[14] We treat such a system in Example 12.7 and Exercises 45 and 46.

[15] As pointed out previously, the results for the $M/M/1$ treatment are upward biased. Do you remember why? Still, the differences are so substantial that a single queue appears warranted.

TABLE 12–4

$M/M/3$ v. Three Subsystems of $M/M/1$

Operating Characteristics	$M/M/3$ Model (1)	$M/M/1$ Model* (2)
P(wait)......................	0.57	0.75
L_s..........................	3.95 cars	9.00 cars (overall system)
L_q..........................	1.70 cars	2.25 cars (each of 3 queues)
L_b..........................	2.98 cars	9.00 cars (overall system)
W_s..........................	4.39 min. per car	10.00 min. per car
W_q..........................	1.89 min. per car	7.50 min. per car
W_b..........................	3.31 min. per car	10.00 min. per car

*Treated as three separate $M/M/1$ subsystems (as in Example 12.2).

have been gained. As is true for many real-world problems, however, perception can be a significant behavioral factor which must be taken into account. For example, McDonalds tried a single queue, but gave it up because "balky" customers perceived long waits when confronted with one long line.

Follow-up Exercises

31. Verify that the formulas for the $M/M/1$ model are special cases of the $M/M/c$ model for $c = 1$.

32. Confirm the calculations in column (1) of Table 12–4.

33. Repeatedly using Equation (12.32), find $P(n < 3)$ for Example 12.5. How is this result related to $P(n \geq 3)$, as given by (12.33)?

34. In general, the number of idle servers is a random variable given by $c - n$ when $n < c$ and by zero when $n \geq c$; hence, the **mean number of idle servers** is given by $cP_o + (c - 1)P_1 + (c - 2)P_2 + \cdots + 1P_{c-1} + 0P_{n \geq c}$. Right? Find the mean number of idle servers for Example 12.5.

35. Perform a sensitivity analysis for $\lambda = 0.8$ and $\lambda = 1.0$ in Example 12.5. Conclusions?

36. To what degree does performance improve in the emergency room problem (Example 12.1) if $c = 2$? $c = 3$?

Restriction on Maximum Length of Queue

As in the $M/M/1$ model, if $N \geq c$ is the maximum number of customers allowed in the system, then an arriving customer is rejected if $n = N$, or if the length of the queue is $N - c$. Other assumptions for this model are identical to the assumptions for the standard $M/M/c$ model.

Formulas for selected operating characteristics are given by Equations (12.40) through (12.48) in Appendix 12B.

As before, $(\rho/c) = (\lambda/\mu c)$ need not be less than one; W_s, W_q, and W_b reflect customers who join the system; P_N represents the probability that a customer will be rejected; and λP_N yields the expected number of rejections per unit time.

No Queue

In some cases the number of customers in the system is limited to the number of service facilities; that is, $n \leq c$. This situation, termed **absolute truncation,** is equivalent to stating that facilities are unavailable for the existence of a queue. Clearly, this represents a finite queue system with $N = c$; hence, the operating characteristics are given by Equations (12.40) through (12.48).

that $\lambda \cdot T \cdot P_N$ is the number of rejected cars and $\lambda \cdot T \cdot P_N$ $(1/\mu)$ is the associated number of lost hours over T due to rejection. Agree? Determine z if $c = 5$, $T = 10$ hours, and $p = \$0.50$ per car per hour.

**42. Write a computer program to solve for the operating characteristics of a parking garage with $c = 15$.

Finite Population

If the calling source is limited to m units and m is small, then finite population models must be used.[16]

Operating characteristics for an $M/M/c$ model with a finite population are given by Equations (12.49) through (12.57) in Appendix 12B.

As in the single-server model, $\rho/c \equiv \lambda/(\mu c)$ is not restricted to values less than unity for steady state to be achieved.[17]

Follow-up Exercises

43. Determine operating characteristics for the computer terminal problem (Example 12.4) if a single queue feeds into two terminals.
   a. Compare performance and costs to the results in Example 12.4.
   b. Compare L_s, L_q, W_s, and W_q to the results in Exercise 30. Comment?

44. For the preceding exercise, calculate R, E_1, and E_2 and compare to Exercise 29. In calculating E_2, the average number of idle facilities is given by $2P_0 + 1P_1$. Can you state a general expression given c service facilities? (See Exercise 34 for the answer.)

Self-Service

Given the assumptions of the standard $M/M/c$ model and unlimited self-service facilities (for practical purposes), the self-service model is simply the standard $M/M/c$ model as c approaches infinity.

Operating characteristics are given by Equations (12.58) through (12.60) in Appendix 12B.

In this case, $\rho \equiv \lambda/\mu$ can take on any value (less than infinity). Note that P_n is Poisson with mean ρ and that $L_q = W_q = 0$.

---

[16] See the discussion under "Finite Population" in Section 12.4 for an interpretation of "small."

[17] Peck and Hazelwood, *Finite Queuing Tables,* also include computational tables for this model.

Example 12.7   Supermarket Tandem System

The queuing systems at supermarkets are essentially tandem systems consisting of two subsystems or sets of servers. The first subsystem includes arrivals at the store who self-serve groceries; the second subsystem entails arrivals at the checkout queues for servicing by clerks. Poisson arrivals at the store and exponential self-service result in Poisson departures from the first subsystem and, consequently, Poisson arrivals for the second subsystem. In fact, Saaty has proved that **Poisson systems in series** (where each system is either standard $M/M/1$ or standard $M/M/c$) can be analyzed independently, each having the same steady-state input rate given by λ.[18]

Follow-up Exercises

45. Suppose customer arrivals at a supermarket are Poisson with rate 30 customers per hour and times to complete the "shopping list" are exponential with mean ½ hour per customer. What is the expected number of customers who are shopping? Find a cumulative Poisson table in some statistics text and determine the following: $P(n \leq 15)$, $P(n > 15)$, $P(n = 0)$, $P(n > 50)$, and $P(n > 75)$.

46. For the supermarket in the preceding exercise determine the expected number of customers and time spent in the checkout subsystem if management is experimenting with, (a) a queue in front of each of four checkout counters and (b) one queue feeding into four checkout counters. Checkout times are exponential with a mean of four minutes. Conclusions?

[18] T. L. Saaty, *Elements of Queuing Theory with Applications* (New York: McGraw-Hill Book Co., Inc., 1961).

12.6 OTHER QUEUING MODELS

Up to this point, the presentation has been limited to models of the Poisson type with varying assumptions regarding characteristics. Variations on the characteristics present an opportunity for an endless variety of models. As a result, the literature in this field is voluminous. For example, many models have been derived which treat Poisson-related distributions, non-Poisson distributions, priorities for service, bulk arrivals, impatient customers, facilities in series, and state-dependent arrival and service rates, to name a few. (See the references at the end of the chapter for some detailed treatments.)

In this section we begin by presenting some results which are rather general across models and end with the treatment of the $(M/G/1)$ model.

General Relationships

As you should have verified in Exercises 4 and 5, the following relationships hold generally by definition, where the symbol *"E"* denotes expected value or mean:

$$E[\text{number in system}] = E[\text{number in queue}] + E[\text{number in service}]$$

or

$$L_s = L_q + L_{se} \tag{12.61}[19]$$

and

$$E[\text{time in system}] = E[\text{time in queue}] + E[\text{time in service}]$$

or

$$W_s = W_q + E[t] \tag{12.62}$$

Additionally, Little has shown that the following relationships are relatively general providing the queuing process is stationary and steady state:[20]

$$L_s = \lambda W_s \tag{12.63}$$

and

$$L_q = \lambda W_q. \tag{12.64}$$

Did you verify these in Exercise 6 for the standard $M/M/1$ model? Can you give logical meaning to these?

If you were to check back over the various models we have presented, you would realize that Equations (12.61) through (12.64) either were directly used or can be proved in all cases. Their importance is evident if you realize that a knowledge of any three of the seven variables (either through sampling or analytical derivation) provides the solution to the remaining four variables. In some cases, however, care must be exercised in defining λ. For instance, in models with finite populations or finite queues, an *effective* λ must be used.[21]

Finally note that, although the relations hold for either single-server or multiple-server models with single queue, conditions for steady state must be met. This means that $\rho/c < 1$ must be satisfied where applicable and the period of sampling for statistical estimates must be sufficiently long to ensure an effective steady state.

Follow-up Exercises

47. Numerically confirm Equations (12.62) through (12.64) for the
     a. Standard $M/M/c$ model calculations in Table 12–4, column (1).
     b. Finite queue $M/M/1$ model of Example 12.3. (Hint: Effective λ is given by $\lambda \cdot (1 - P_N)$. Right?)

---

[19] Note that Equations (12.13) through (12.60) are in Appendix 12B.

[20] J. D. C. Little, "A Proof of the Queuing Formula: $L = \lambda W$," *Operations Research*, vol. 9 (1961), pp. 383–87. Also see W. S. Jewell, "A Simple Proof of $L = \lambda W$," *Operations Research*, vol. 15 (1967), pp. 1109–16; and S. Stidham, Jr., "A Last Word on $L = \lambda W$," *Operations Research*, vol. 22 (1974), pp. 417–21.

[21] Effective λ was illustrated under "Finite Population" in Section 12.4. Remember?

> c. Finite population $M/M/1$ model of Example 12.4. (Hint: Effective λ is given by $\lambda \cdot (m - L_s)$. Right?)
>
> 48. Consider a queuing system where $\lambda = 10$ units per day, $\mu = 5$ units per day, and $W_s = 0.5$ day per unit. Determine L_s, L_q, L_{se}, and W_q. Note that, for constant μ, $E[t] = 1/\mu$. Are your results valid for $c \leq 2$? What are the implications if λ, μ, and W_s were estimated by taking a "small" sample?

Pollaczek-Khintchine (P-K) Formula[22]

The P-K formula applies to an $M/G/1$ model having the same assumptions as the standard $M/M/1$ model except for the following: FCFS, LCFS, or SIRO service discipline; general (any) service time distribution with mean $E[t]$ and variance $V[t]$. Note that the condition $\rho < 1$ must still apply for the steady-state where $\rho = \lambda \cdot E[t]$.[23] Given these assumptions, we can prove that

$$L_s = \rho + \frac{\rho^2 + \lambda^2 V[t]}{2(1 - \rho)}. \tag{12.65}$$

Thus, knowing λ, $E[t]$, and $V[t]$, L_s can be determined from Equation (12.65) and L_q, W_s, and W_q follow from (12.62) through (12.64).

This result is significant because of the generality of the service time distribution. In other words, given a specific distribution such as exponential, normal, or deterministic, Equations (12.62) through (12.65) can be used to determine relevant operating characteristics.

Also, note the following very important observation: The appearance of a variance term in (12.65) proves the fallacy of deriving expected values without the explicit consideration of probabilistic behavior (as exhibited through variance); only if $V[t] = 0$ does variance not affect $E[$number in system$]$. Thus, we have shown explicitly what we said earlier in the chapter: Queues build up both because of traffic intensity (ρ) and because of variability in arrival and service times; improvements in operating characteristics can be effected from changes in either means or variances.

Example 12.8   Car Wash

Consider a planned car wash operation with four independent channels and a Poisson arrival pattern with rate 72 cars per hour for the entire sys-

---

[22] Correct pronunciation and spelling should be worth some sort of bonus for your course. Ask your instructor!

[23] If the average service rate (customers per unit time) is represented by μ, then $E[t] = 1/\mu$ so that $\rho = \lambda/\mu = \lambda \cdot E[t]$.

tem. Time-and-motion studies for similar service facilities indicate that $E[t] = 0.05$ hour per car and $V[t] = 0.01$ (hour per car)^2 for each server. For each channel it follows that $\lambda = 72/4 = 18$ and $\rho = \lambda \cdot E[t] = (18) \cdot (0.05) = 0.9$. According to (12.65),

$$L_s = 0.9 + \frac{(0.9)^2 + (18)^2(0.01)}{2(1-0.9)}$$
$$= 21.15 \text{ cars}$$

for each channel, or approximately 85 cars for the entire system. From (12.63),

$$W_s = L_s/\lambda$$
$$= 21.15/18$$
$$= 1.175 \text{ hours}$$

as the expected time in the system for each car. Rearranging (12.62) gives

$$W_q = W_s - E[t]$$
$$= 1.175 - 0.05$$
$$= 1.125 \text{ hours}$$

as the expected time in the queues. Finally, from (12.64),

$$L_q = (18)(1.125)$$
$$= 20.25 \text{ cars}$$

is the expected length of each queue.

Needless to say, the performance of this planned queuing system would be dismal. Costs aside, the number of servers definitely should be increased to avoid mass balking and reneging (if not rioting).

Follow-up Exercises

49. Noting that $\lambda = 24/c$ (cars per hour) for c independent single channel-single queue subsystems, determine operating characteristics for five car wash facilities. Is there much improvement?

50. At least how many car wash facilities would be needed to force the mean number of cars in each subsystem below three cars?

51. Suppose that total automation of each car wash facility effectively reduces variance to zero ($M/D/1$ model). Determine the resulting operating characteristics using the data in Example 12.8 and reflect on the results. Is the variance effect significant?

52. Using Equations (12.62) through (12.65), derive a set of formulas for the model $M/D/1$, noting that $E[t] = 1/\mu$ and $V[t] = 0$.

53. Do you remember the expression for the variance of an exponential distribution with parameter μ? (If not, see Appendix A) Prove that (12.62) through (12.65) provide the identical results for their equivalents in the standard $M/M/1$ model.

12.7 QUEUING OPTIMIZATION MODELS

Up to this point, primarily we have stressed the behavior (operating characteristics) of a queuing system. This section explicitly considers queuing models which optimize some objective function, a topic which is receiving increasing (and long-overdue) emphasis in recent years.

General Considerations

Figure 12–5 illustrates the economic tradeoff in a queuing system. Generally, increasing the degree of service results in lower waiting costs for customers at the expense of higher service costs for the facility. If the criterion to be optimized is stated in terms of minimizing these combined costs, then the decision is in terms of the best level of service to provide. An alternative objective which is relevant in retail establishments is the maximization of implicit contribution to overhead and profits, that is, revenue minus cost of service minus cost of waiting.

FIGURE 12–5

Economic Tradeoff in Queuing System

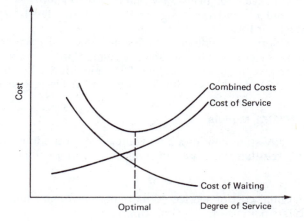

Typically, costs are stated on the basis of per unit time. The cost of service is based on *all* costs associated with the provision of that service. For instance, as in Example 12.4, the cost of a server (terminal) was comprised of connect, resource, task, maintenance, and capital costs on a per day basis. For the most part, service costs are readily attainable.

The estimated cost of waiting is another matter. If the waiting units are *internal* to the organization (for example, office personnel waiting to use equipment or mechanics waiting for supplies from a tool crib), then the cost of waiting usually can be estimated adequately. For units *external* to the organization, however, the cost of waiting is subtle. Examples include lost sales due to ill will, balking, or reneging; annoyances and "lost opportunities" due to waiting in long registration lines for the school term (usually costed at zero by universities); the "cost" (to the individual and society) associated with aggravated injuries or death in the queuing system of a hospital; and the "cost" of waiting for the response by fire or police departments. Because of the difficulty in estimating external waiting costs, many analyses focus on minimizing service costs subject to a constraint on a variable which is related to the cost of waiting (for example, W_q or L_q). Alternatively, **aspiration level models** seek to determine a level (or range) of service which satisfies two or more conflicting operating characteristics (for example, number of servers which would simultaneously not exceed predetermined levels for percent idle time and expected waiting time).[24] In either case, costs are treated *implicitly*. In short, there is no way of avoiding cost considerations. As in the past, we can ease our anxiety for risky parameter estimates by sensitivity analysis.

The degree of service is loosely defined, as it can take many forms. To wit: service rate (μ) setting, as in machines which are adjustable or servers which may have different configurations (for example, checkout clerk and bagger) or varying degrees of ability or experience; number of servers (c); traffic intensity (ρ); arrival rate (λ), as in scheduling patients for a clinic or setting the speed of conveyor belts in an automated assembly line; and allowable number of units in the system (N). More complicated cases include joint levels for decision variables (for example, μ and ρ, or μ and N, or λ and c) and the assignment of priority levels. (Can you think of examples for these?)

Methods of solution include marginal analysis for discrete variables, classical calculus for continuous variables, dynamic programming (Chapter 9), nonlinear programming (Chapter 10), and Markov decision processes (Chapter 15). In this section, we illustrate the first two methods.

Optimal μ for M/M/1 Models

Assuming steady-state conditions and linear cost functions for service and waiting, we see that the expected *total cost per unit time* is given by

$$z = c_s \cdot \mu + c_w \cdot L_s \qquad (12.66)$$

where c_s = marginal cost of service (dollars per customer) and c_w = cost of waiting (dollars per customer − unit time).

The expression for z in (12.66) is perfectly general for any single server model, excepting those that cost customers who renege or balk and those that truncate queues when N is a decision variable and rejected customers are costed. Substituting (12.5) for L_s gives the objective function for the standard $M/M/1$ model:

$$z = c_s\mu + c_w\left(\frac{\lambda}{\mu - \lambda}\right).$$

Setting the first derivative of z with respect to μ to zero and solving for optimal μ gives

$$\mu^* = \lambda + \left(\frac{c_w}{c_s} \cdot \lambda\right)^{1/2}. \qquad (12.67)$$

Note that (12.67) ensures $\lambda < \mu$ or $\rho < 1$. Furthermore, the process of taking the derivative assumes that z (and hence μ) is continuous.

---

[24] This idea was illustrated using Table 12–3 in determining μ for an $M/M/1$ model. Exercises 13 and 19 also illustrate the aspiration-level approach.

Follow-up Exercises

54. Suppose a particular electronic component is assembled by a machine with an adjustable service rate. Parts for assembly exhibit random (Poisson) arrivals with a mean of 40 parts per hour. Processing times are exponential. Determine the optimal machine assembly rate given that delayed components are costed at $5 per hour each and that the marginal cost of assembling a component is $2. How sensitive is μ^* to variations in the cost ratio? To variations in λ?

**55. Verify Equation (12.67) and test the second-order condition for a minimum.

**56. Express z for a finite queue single-server model where both μ and N are decision variables. Let $C_c \equiv$ cost per unit time of expanding the capacity of the facility to allow one more unit in the queue and $C_r \equiv$ cost of a rejected unit. Why is it inappropriate to differentiate this expression? How might you solve for μ^* and N^*?

**57. If the cost of waiting is defined in terms of waiting in the queue, then L_q or L_b must be used in place of L_s in (12.66). Determine z using L_q for the standard $M/M/1$ model. Show that the expression for μ^* (that is, $dz/d\mu = 0$) is a polynomial of degree 4. Can you solve for μ^* given values for the parameters as in Exercise 54?

**58. For the finite population $M/M/1$ model, L_s is given by (12.25). Determine the expression which must be solved for μ^*.

Optimal c for M/M/c Models

Assuming steady-state conditions, linearity in the cost functions, and the number of servers as the only relevant decision variable, the expected total cost per unit time is given by

$$z = c_s' \cdot c + c_w \cdot L \tag{12.68}$$

where c_s' is the cost per server per unit time, L is the expected number of customers in the system (L_s), or the expected number in the queue (L_q), or the expected number of customers in a busy-system queue (L_b), and c and c_w are as previously defined.

Since z is discontinuous (that is, c is an integer), we use marginal analysis to determine optimal c. Defining $z(c^*)$ as the minimum value of z when c is optimal, then the necessary conditions for minimum costs are

$$z(c^*) \leq z(c^* - 1)$$

and

$$z(c^*) \leq z(c^* + 1). \tag{12.69}$$

Try verbalizing these conditions. Substituting (12.68) into a combined inequality based on (12.69) gives

$$z(c^* - 1) \geq \quad z(c^*) \quad \leq z(c^* + 1)$$

$$c_s' \cdot (c^* - 1) + c_w \cdot L(c^* - 1) \geq c_s' \cdot c^* + c_w \cdot L(c^*)$$
$$\leq c_s' \cdot (c^* + 1) + c_w \cdot L(c^* + 1) \quad (12.70)$$

where $L(c^*)$ represents the value of L when using c^* servers. By algebraically manipulating (12.70), it can be shown that the necessary condition for an optimum number of servers is given by

$$L(c^*) - L(c^* + 1) \leq c_s'/c_w \leq L(c^* - 1) - L(c^*). \quad (12.71)$$

Example 12.9   Optimum Number of Tool-Crib Attendants

The tool crib in a production shop of a large industrial corporation services a large number of mechanics who are paid an average hourly wage of $6 (excluding fringe benefits). Two attendants in the service facility dispense tools on a FCFS basis according to a numbering system. Recently, the vice president of production has been receiving complaints of excessively long waiting lines. Upon first hearing of this, the assistant to the vice president (a recent M.B.A. graduate) immediately diagnosed this as a queuing problem. A subsequent study indicated that $\lambda = 48$ mechanics per hour, $\mu = 25$ mechanics per hour, and that the conditions of Poisson arrivals and servicing were satisfied adequately. Assuming a very large population of mechanics, the standard $M/M/c$ model should serve as a reasonable approximation to this queuing system. If tool-crib attendants are paid wages of $4 per hour (including fringe benefits), how many should be hired to service the facility?

In this case, $\rho = 1.92$, $c_s' = \$4$ per attendant-hour, and $c_w = \$6$ per mechanic-hour. If we assume that the time spent in the queue and in service is unproductive, then L_s, as given by (12.34), is appropriate for the criterion given by (12.68).

Table 12–5 indicates that $c^* = 3$ and $z^* = \$27.87$ per hour. Note that the cost ration ($c_s'/c_w = 0.667$) falls within the range (0.582–21.845) specified by Equation (12.71) for c^*.

TABLE 12–5

Results for Optimum Number of Tool-Crib Attendants

Number of Attendants c	Mean No. of Mechanics in System $L_s(c)$	Total Cost in Dollars per Hour* $z(c)$	$I_1 - I_2$†
1......................	∞	∞	—
2......................	24.490	$154.94	21.845–∞
3......................	2.645	27.87	0.582–21.845
4......................	2.063	28.38	0.111– 0.582
5......................	1.952	31.71	

* From equation (12.68).
† I_1 and I_2 represent, respectively, the left-hand–side and right-hand–side inequalities in (12.71).

Follow-up Exercises

59. Verify the calculations in Table 12–5.

60. Suppose the plant is operating at full capacity so that any time lost by mechanics must be made up with overtime at time and a half. Determine the new cost ratio and find optimal c.

61. Should the cost of waiting be expressed in terms of foregone marginal revenues or profits? Discuss pros and cons.

62. Why is Equation (12.71) an inappropriate rule for determining the optimal number of computer terminals as presented in Example 12.4?

**63. Verify Equation (12.71) starting with (12.70).

12.8 ASSESSMENT OF QUEUING THEORY

In recent years, theoretical developments in queuing models have proliferated at a rapid rate. Not only are theoretical models based on more realistic assumptions (for example, state-dependent parameters, dependent arrivals, general arrival and service distributions, priority service disciplines, and so on), but also powerful and sophisticated mathematical procedures have been developed to treat complex problems and transient solutions.

As in most fields characterized by rapid technological or theoretical developments, the application or practice of queuing theory has lagged behind the theoretical "state of the art." In part, this is due to a communications gap (or chasm) between mathematical theoreticians and applied researchers—a state of affairs for which both groups can share credit. For example, many of the theoretical results on, say, operating characteristics for complex models are in a form (called "transforms") which are either inconvenient or unuseable for numerical calculations. Progress has been made, however, in developing results which are computationally manageable, including approximation techniques. The alternative of simulation is available also, as demonstrated in the next chapter.

Other criticisms regarding the practice of queuing theory include the absence of statistical procedures and the indiscriminate uses of $M/M/c$ models and steady-state results. All too often, a disconcerting absence of proper sampling, estimation, and hypothesis testing procedures is noted. All assumptions inherent in a model (for example, types of distributions, parameters, state-independence, independent arrivals, and so forth) must be tested by such procedures, if possible, in order to select the correct model. While $M/M/c$ models are widely available and useful, their assumptions must be reasonably substantiated in any particular application. (Interestingly, Poisson input processes tend to be more common in real phenomena than exponential service times.) The limitations of and interpretations for steady-state solutions also must be assessed, as many queuing systems do not operate a sufficiently long period of time to achieve steady state.[25] This is not to say that decisions based on steady-state solutions are unjustified, but rather that their interpretations are based on an idealized concept.

In short, progress on all fronts is evident and, like Dr. Pangloss, we remain eternally optimistic (about tending our own garden).[26]

SELECTED REFERENCES

Cooper, R. B. *Introduction to Queuing Theory*. New York: The Macmillan Co., 1972.

Gross, D., and Harris, C. M. *Fundamentals of Queuing Theory*. New York: Wiley-Interscience, 1974.

Hillier, F. S., and Lieberman, G. J. *Introduction to Operations Research*, 2d ed. San Francisco: Holden-Day, Inc., 1974.

Jaiswal, N. K. *Priority Queues*. New York: Academic Press, 1968.

Lee, A. M. *Applied Queuing Theory*. New York: St. Martin's Press, 1966.

Panico, J. A. *Queuing Theory*. Englewood Cliffs, N.J.: Prentice-Hall, Inc., 1969.

Saaty, T. L. *Elements of Queuing Theory with Applications*. New York: McGraw-Hill Book Co., Inc., 1961.

Taha, H. A. *Operations Research: An Introduction*. New York: The Macmillan Company, 1971.

ADDITIONAL EXERCISES

64. *Gasoline Panic* Consider a one-pump gas station which satisfies the assumptions for the $M/M/1$ model. It is estimated that on the average, customers arrive to buy gas when the tank is $\frac{1}{8}$ full. The mean time to service a customer is four minutes and the arrival rate is six customers per hour.

    a. Determine the expected length of the queue and the expected number of minutes in the system.

    b. Suppose that customers perceive a gas shortage (when there is none) and respond by changing the fill-up criterion to more than $\frac{1}{8}$ full on the average. Assuming that changes in λ are proportional to changes in the fill-up criterion, compare results to part (a) when the fill-up criterion is $\frac{1}{4}$ full.

    c. Same as part (b) if the fill-up criterion is $\frac{1}{2}$ full. Do we have the makings of a behaviorally induced gasoline panic? (Remember the winter of 1974?)

    d. It is reasonable to assume that the time to service a customer will decrease as the fill-up criterion increases. Under "normal" conditions it takes an average of two minutes to pump gasoline and an average of two minutes to take the order, collect the money, and so forth. Rework parts (b) and (c) if the time to pump gasoline changes proportionally to changes in the amount of gasoline which must be pumped.

65. The $P–K$ model gives the same results as the $M/M/1$ model when service times are exponential. Show this for part (a) of the preceding exercise.

---

[25] Witness Examples 12.2 and 12.3.

[26] In Voltaire's *Candide*.

(Hint: The variance of the exponential distribution is given in Appendix A).

66. What is the optimum number of terminals for the problem described in Example 12.4? Assume a single queue and non proportional increases in the cost of providing service.

67. *Maintenance Service* Consider a company which holds maintenance contracts for repairing computer terminals whenever they break down. On the average each terminal breaks down every five days, where the time between breakdowns is exponential. The time to service a terminal, which includes travel time and repair time, is exponential with mean ¼ day. What is the maximum number of terminals that should be assigned to each service representative such that the probability of waiting to be serviced is less than 0.3?

68. *Typing Pool Model* Suppose that documents to be typed at an office arrive (Poisson) at the rate 100 per day and secretaries can type (Poisson) at the rate 50 documents per secretary per day. Each secretary earns $40 per day and the cost of holding documents in the system is estimated at $4 per document per day.

   a. Using the criterion total cost per day, find the optimal number of secretaries if each works with his/her own queue.

   b. Suppose that secretaries are to be combined into a typing pool with one queue. Determine the optimum number of secretaries and the associated cost by enumeration, that is, by evaluating (12.68) for 1, 2, 3, . . . secretaries. Is Equation (12.71) satisfied? Decision for pool or no pool? Any reservations about the validity of the analysis?

69. Consider the schematic below.

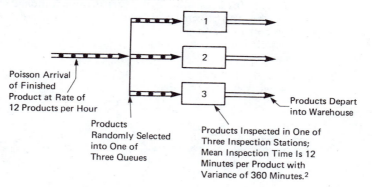

a. Determine the expected waiting time for a product, the expected length of each queue, and the expected number of products in the *overall* system.

b. Same as part (*a*) except for a variance of 36 min.²

c. Same as part (*a*) for $M/D/1$ model. Does the variance effect appear significant?

70. Given the schematic in the preceding exercise, determine the optimal number of inspection stations if each station costs $10 per hour to operate and the cost of holding each product in the system is $2 per hour.

71. *Pollution Control Model* A manufacturing company continuously operates five independent treatment facilities for cleaning out effluents which are discharged into a major river. The operation of each facility, however, is not completely reliable due to breakdowns. The time between breakdowns of each facility is exponential with mean 14 days. On the average, it takes a repair crew one day to repair a facility. As you might have guessed, repair times are exponential. Each repair crew costs the company $1,000 per day. The EPA does not allow the company to discharge untreated waste material; hence, whenever a facility is "down" the plant operates at less than planned capacity. This downtime is costed at $50,000 per day per facility. Determine the optimal number of repair crews to hire by enumerating total cost per day for 1, 2, 3, 4, and 5 repair crews. Is Equation (12.71) satisfied?

72. *Airline Reservation System* An airline reservation system has four telephone lines. For a particular shift, incoming phone calls are Poisson with rate ten calls per hour. The time to service a caller is exponential with a mean time of five minutes. If a call comes in and all reservationists are busy, then the call is placed on hold, providing a line is available; otherwise, the call is lost; that is, a busy signal rejects the caller. Callers encountering a busy signal are assumed to place reservations elsewhere. It is further assumed that calls on hold never renege.

    a. Determine the minimum number of reservationists needed to ensure a probability of rejection which is below 10 percent.

    b. Assuming that one reservationist is to be used, determine the minimum number of phone lines needed to ensure a probability of rejection below 10 percent.

    c. Discuss the tradeoffs between the two types of decisions indicated in parts (*a*) and (*b*). Specifically, determine the total cost per hour for each of the decisions above if $5 per hour is the cost of a reservationist, $0.25 per hour is the cost of an additional phone line, $2 is the cost of a rejected call, and $1 per hour per call in the system is the cost of waiting.

    d. Describe how you would determine the optimal joint decision for *c* and *N*.

73. Consider the following tandem queuing system for a product which requires two steps to assemble.

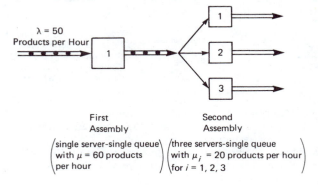

First
Assembly

Second
Assembly

$$\left(\begin{array}{l}\text{single server-single queue}\\ \text{with }\mu = 60\text{ products}\\ \text{per hour}\end{array}\right) \left(\begin{array}{l}\text{three servers-single queue}\\ \text{with }\mu_i = 20\text{ products per hour}\\ \text{for }i = 1, 2, 3\end{array}\right)$$

Given that the assumptions for the standard $M/M/c$ model are satisfied, determine the mean length of each queue and the expected time a product spends on the assembly line. (Hint: See Example 12.7.)

74. *State Unemployment Compensation* The agency of a particular state which handles compensation for those who are unemployed is considering two options for processing applications of potential recipients.

Option 1: Four clerks process applications in parallel from a single queue. Each clerk fills out the form for the application in the presence of the applicant based on information which is verbally related to the clerk. Processing time is exponential with mean 45 minutes.

Option 2: Each applicant first fills out the application without the help of a clerk. The time to accomplish this is exponential with mean 65 minutes. When the applicant finishes filling out the form, he/she joins a single queue to await a review by one of the four clerks. The time to review a form is exponential (what else?) with mean 5 minutes.

Given that the arrival of applicants is Poisson with rate 4.8 applicants per hour, compare the two options with respect to expected number of applicants in the system and expected time in the system.

APPENDIX 12A   DERIVATION OF STANDARD $M/M/1$ MODEL

In this appendix, we incompletely derive the operating characteristics given by Equations (12.1) through (12.10). Familiarity with the symbols and assumptions of the standard $M/M/1$ model is assumed.

Arrivals which are Poisson are said to occur randomly. This means that the probability of an arrival in some small interval of time (Δt) depends strictly on the length of Δt and not its starting point or the previous history of arrivals (*memoryless property*). Furthermore, it can be shown that Poisson arrivals with rate λ are equivalent to exponential interarrival times with parameter λ; hence, the probability of an interarrival time which is less that Δt, assuming *stationarity*, is given by (A.32) on page 716, the CDF for the exponential distribution:

$$F(\Delta t) = 1 - e^{-\lambda \Delta t}. \tag{1}$$

This is equivalent to stating that $F(\Delta t)$ is the probability of an arrival in the interval Δt. Agree? It follows, then that the probability of no arrival in the interval Δt is given by the complement of (1):

$$P(\text{no arrival in } \Delta t) = e^{-\lambda \Delta t}. \tag{2}$$

The expression in (2) can be estimated by its Taylor series expansion:[1]

$$e^{-\lambda \Delta t} = 1 - \lambda \Delta t + \frac{(-\lambda \Delta t)^2}{2!} + \frac{(-\lambda \Delta t)^3}{3!} + \cdots$$

For sufficiently small Δt, this can be approximated by

$$P(\text{no arrival in } \Delta t) = 1 - \lambda \Delta t, \tag{3}$$

since higher order terms tend to vanish. Now, (1) can be reexpressed as

$$P(\text{arrival in } \Delta t) = \lambda \Delta t. \tag{4}$$

---

[1] $f(x) = f(10) + \dfrac{f'(0)}{1!}x + \dfrac{f''(0)}{2!}x^2 + \cdots + \dfrac{f^n(0)x^n}{n!} + \text{Remainder}$

Similarly, assuming exponential service times with rate μ and that a customer is being serviced, we see that the corresponding probabilities are

$$P(\text{service not completed in } \Delta t) = 1 - \mu \Delta t \qquad (5)$$

and

$$P(\text{service completed in } \Delta t) = \mu \Delta t. \qquad (6)$$

Given (3) through (6), the basic derivation of operating characteristics hinges on the determination of $P_n(t)$, the probability that the *state* of the system is n at time t (that is, that n units are in the system at time t). If Δt is sufficiently small, then no more than one arrival or departure (or both) can occur during Δt. Three cases can be identified for the occurrence of n units in the system at time $t + \Delta t$: First, n units at t combined with no arrival and no departure during Δt; second, $n + 1$ units at t combined with no arrival and one departure during Δt; three, $n - 1$ units at t combined with one arrival and no departure during Δt. Assuming independence among an arrival, a departure, and the state of the system, we find that the probabilities for the preceding cases are determined by applying the multiplication rule given by (A.6): First, $P_n(t) \cdot (1 - \lambda \Delta t) \cdot (1 - \mu \Delta t)$; second, $P_{n+1}(t) \cdot (1 - \lambda \Delta t) \cdot \mu \Delta t$; third, $P_{n-1}(t) \cdot \lambda \Delta t \cdot (1 - \mu \Delta t)$. Since the system can have n units at time t in any of these three mutually exclusively ways, it follows that $P_n(t + \Delta t)$ is given by the sum of the three separate probabilities:[2]

$$P_n(t + \Delta t) = P_n(t) \cdot (1 - \lambda \Delta t) \cdot (1 - \mu \Delta t) + P_{n+1}(t) \cdot (1 - \lambda \Delta t) \cdot \mu \Delta t$$
$$+ P_{n-1}(t) \cdot \lambda \Delta t \cdot (1 - \mu \Delta t). \qquad (7)$$

Transposing $P_n(t)$ to the left-hand side of (7), dividing by Δt, and letting $\Delta t \to 0$, we get[3]

$$P_n'(t) = \begin{cases} \mu P_{n+1}(t) - \lambda P_n(t) & \text{for } n = 0 \\ \mu P_{n+1}(t) + \lambda P_{n-1}(t) - (\lambda + \mu)P_n(t) & \text{for } n > 0. \end{cases} \qquad (8)$$

The solution to this system of *linear differential equations* provides the *transient probabilities.*

In the steady state, probabilities are independent of time; hence, rates of change in the probabilities with respect to time (that is, $P_n'(t)$ for $n = 0, 1, \ldots$) equal zero. This gives, from (8), the *steady-state difference equations for the system:*

$$\mu P_1 - \lambda P_o = 0 \qquad (9)$$
$$\mu P_{n+1} + \lambda P_{n-1} - (\lambda + \mu)P_n = 0. \qquad (10)$$

The solution for P_n is obtained recursively. Starting with (9) we have

$$P_1 = \left(\frac{\lambda}{\mu}\right)P_o$$
$$= \rho P_o$$

---

[2] Rule of Addition according to (A.3).

[3] Note that the first derivative, according to Equation (2.9), is defined in this case as

$$P_n'(t) = \lim_{\Delta t \to 0} \frac{P_n(t + \Delta t) - P_n(t)}{\Delta t}.$$

Proceeding to (10) with $n = 1$ gives

$$\mu P_2 + \lambda P_o - (\lambda + \mu)P_1 = 0.$$

Substituting ρP_o for P_1 and solving for P_2 gives

$$P_2 = -\frac{\lambda}{\mu} P_o + \frac{(\lambda + \mu)}{\mu} (\rho P_o)$$
$$= -\rho P_o + \rho^2 P_o + \rho P_o$$
$$= \rho^2 P_o.$$

Continuing in the same manner, we can verify easily that

$$P_n = \rho^n P_o, \tag{12.3}$$

which is a geometric probability mass function. By definition for a pmf,

$$\sum_{n=0}^{\infty} P_n = 1.$$

Substituting Equation (12.3) provides

$$P_o \sum_{n=0}^{\infty} \rho^n = 1$$

or

$$P_o(1 + \rho + \rho^2 + \ldots) = 1.$$

You should recognize the parenthetic expression as an infinite geometric progression with common ratio ρ. If $\rho \equiv (\lambda/\mu) < 1$, then the series converges to the well-known sum $1/(1 - \rho)$. Note that if $\rho \geq 1$, then the series does not converge; that is, it sums to infinity. We have then

$$P_o \left(\frac{1}{1 - \rho} \right) = 1$$

or

$$P_o = 1 - \rho. \tag{12.1}$$

By the definition of expected value, L_s is determined from

$$L_s = \sum_{n=0}^{\infty} n P_n$$

$$= P_o \sum_{n=0}^{\infty} n \, \rho^n$$

$$= (1 - \rho) \cdot (0 + \rho + 2\rho^2 + 3\rho^3 + \cdots)$$
$$= (\rho + 2\rho^2 + 3\rho^3 + \cdots) - (\rho^2 + 2\rho^3 + 3\rho^4 + \cdots)$$
$$= \rho + \rho^2 + \rho^3 + \cdots$$
$$= \rho(1 + \rho + \rho^2 + \cdots)$$

$$= \frac{\rho}{1 - \rho}$$

or, since $\rho \equiv \lambda/\mu$,

$$L_s = \frac{\lambda}{\mu - \lambda}. \tag{12.5}$$

The expression for the variance, as given by Equation (12.6), can be obtained in a similar manner, although the procedure is tedious (there are better ways).

By definition, the expected number in the queue, L_q, is the expected number in the system, L_s, minus the expected number in service, L_{se}, or

$$L_q = L_s - L_{se}. \tag{11}$$

With only one server, 0 and 1 are the only two possible values for the random variable "number in service." Since their respective probabilities are P_o and $1 - P_o$, then by the definition of expected value,

$$\begin{aligned} L_{se} &= 0 \cdot P_o + 1 \cdot (1 - P_o) \\ &= 1 - P_o. \\ &= \rho. \end{aligned} \tag{12}$$

By substituting Equation (12.15) and (12) into (11) and simplifying we have

$$L_q = \frac{\rho^2}{1 - \rho}$$

or

$$\mathbf{L_q} = \frac{\rho\lambda}{\mu - \lambda}. \tag{12.7}$$

The expressions (12.9) and (12.11) for W_s and W_q can be obtained by respectively substituting (12.5) and (12.7) into (12.63) and (12.64). The expression for V_{ws}, Equation (12.10), is simply the variance of the exponential distribution for waiting times given by (12.4).

An alternative expression for L_q is

$$L_q = L_b \cdot (1 - P_o) + 0 \cdot P_o \tag{13}$$

where L_b is the expected number in the queue when the system is busy and $(1 - P_o)$ is the probability of a busy system. Solving for L_b gives

$$L_b = \frac{L_q}{1 - P_o}, \tag{14}$$

which can be verified easily as the equivalent of (12.8). Note that L_b simply removes the bias of an idle system; that is, it represents the mean queue length when the system is busy. Similarly,

$$W_b = \frac{W_q}{1 - P_o}, \tag{15}$$

which confirms (12.12).

With minor variations, the derivation of the standard $M/M/c$ model is identical (but messier).

APPENDIX 12B   FORMULAS FOR SELECTED $M/M/1$ AND $M/M/c$ MODELS

Definition of Symbols

$n =$ Number of units in system.
$\lambda =$ Mean arrival rate (units per time period).
$\mu =$ Mean service rate (units per time period).
$\rho =$ Traffic intensity (λ/μ).
$N =$ Maximum number allowed in system.
$m =$ Number of units in finite population.
$c =$ Number of servers.
$P_n =$ Probability of n units in system.
$L_s =$ Steady-state mean number of units in system.
$L_q =$ Steady-state mean number of units in queue.
$L_b =$ Steady-state mean number of units in queue for busy system.
$W_s =$ Steady-state mean time in system.
$W_q =$ Steady-state mean time in queue.
$W_b =$ Steady-state mean time in queue for busy system.

Finite Queue $M/M/1$ Model[1]

$$P_0 = \begin{cases} \dfrac{1-\rho}{1-\rho^{N+1}} & \text{for } \lambda \neq \mu \\[2ex] \dfrac{1}{N+1} & \text{for } \lambda = \mu \end{cases} \tag{12.13}$$

$$P(n > 0) = 1 - P_o \tag{12.14}$$

$$P_n = P_o\rho^n \quad \text{for } n \leq N \tag{12.15}$$

$$L_s = \begin{cases} \dfrac{\rho}{1-\rho} - \dfrac{(N+1)\rho^{N+1}}{1-\rho^{N+1}} & \text{for } \lambda \neq \mu \\[2ex] \dfrac{N}{2} & \text{for } \lambda = \mu \end{cases} \tag{12.16}$$

$$L_q = L_s - (1 - P_o) \tag{12.17}$$

$$L_b = \dfrac{L_q}{1 - P_o} \tag{12.18}$$

$$W_s = \dfrac{L_q}{\lambda(1 - P_N)} + \dfrac{1}{\mu} \tag{12.19}$$

$$W_q = W_s - \dfrac{1}{\mu} \tag{12.20}$$

$$W_b = \dfrac{W_q}{1 - P_o.} \tag{12.21}$$

---

[1] Note: $0 < \rho < \infty$.

Finite Population $M/M/1$ Model[2]

$$P_o = \frac{1}{\sum_{i=0}^{m}\left[\dfrac{m!}{(m-i)!}\cdot\rho^i\right]} \tag{12.22}$$

$$P(n > 0) = 1 - P_o \tag{12.23}$$

$$P_n = \frac{m!}{(m-n)!}\,\rho^n P_o, \qquad n \le m \tag{12.24}$$

$$L_s = m - \frac{1}{\rho}(1 - P_o) \tag{12.25}$$

$$L_q = m - \frac{(\lambda + \mu)(1 - P_o)}{\lambda} \tag{12.26}$$

$$L_b = \frac{L_q}{1 - P_o} \tag{12.27}$$

$$W_s = \frac{m}{\mu(1 - P_o)} - \frac{1}{\lambda} \tag{12.28}$$

$$W_q = \frac{1}{\mu}\left(\frac{m}{1 - P_o} - \frac{\lambda + \mu}{\lambda}\right) \tag{12.29}$$

$$W_b = \frac{W_q}{1 - P_o}\cdot \tag{12.30}$$

Standard $M/M/c$ Model[3]

$$P_o = \frac{1}{\left(\displaystyle\sum_{i=0}^{c-1}\frac{\rho^i}{i!}\right) + \dfrac{\rho^c}{c!\left(1 - \dfrac{\rho}{c}\right)}} \tag{12.31}$$

$$P_n = \begin{cases} \dfrac{\rho^n}{n!}\cdot P_o & \text{for } 0 \le n \le c \\[2ex] \left(\dfrac{\rho^n}{c!\,c^{n-c}}\right)\cdot P_o & \text{for } n \ge c \end{cases} \tag{12.32}$$

$$P(n \ge c) = \frac{\rho^c \mu c}{c!(\mu c - \lambda)}\cdot P_o \tag{12.33}$$

$$L_s = \frac{\rho^{c+1}}{(c-1)!\,(c-\rho)^2}\cdot P_o + \rho \tag{12.34}$$

$$L_q = L_s - \rho \tag{12.35}$$

---

[2] Note: $0 < \rho < \infty$.
[3] Note: $0 < \rho < c$.

$$L_b = \frac{L_q}{P(n \geq c)} \tag{12.36}$$

$$W_s = \frac{L_q}{\lambda} + \frac{1}{\mu} \tag{12.37}$$

$$W_q = \frac{L_q}{\lambda} \tag{12.38}$$

$$W_b = \frac{W_q}{P(n \geq c)} \tag{12.39}$$

Finite Queue $M/M/c$ Model[4]

$$P_o = \frac{1}{\left(\displaystyle\sum_{i=0}^{c} \frac{\rho^i}{i!} \right) + \left(\dfrac{1}{c!} \right) \cdot \left(\displaystyle\sum_{i=c+1}^{N} \frac{\rho^i}{c^{i-c}} \right)} \tag{12.40}$$

$$P_n = \begin{cases} \dfrac{\rho^n}{n!} \cdot P_o & \text{for } 0 \leq n \leq c \\[2ex] \dfrac{\rho^n}{c! \, c^{n-c}} \cdot P_o & \text{for } c \leq n \leq N \end{cases} \tag{12.41}$$

$$P(n \geq c) = 1 - P_o \sum_{i=0}^{c-1} \frac{\rho^i}{i!} \tag{12.42}$$

$$L_s = \frac{P_o \rho^{c+1}}{(c-1)!(c-\rho)^2} \left[1 - \left(\frac{\rho}{c} \right)^{N-c} - (N-c)\left(\frac{\rho}{c} \right)^{N-c} \cdot \left(1 - \frac{\rho}{c} \right) \right]$$
$$+ \rho(1 - P_N) \tag{12.43}$$

$$L_q = L_s - \rho(1 - P_N) \tag{12.44}$$

$$L_b = \frac{L_q}{P(n \geq c)} \tag{12.45}$$

$$W_s = \frac{L_q}{\lambda(1 - P_N)} + \frac{1}{\mu} \tag{12.46}$$

$$W_q = W_s - \frac{1}{\mu} \tag{12.47}$$

$$W_b = \frac{W_q}{P(n \geq c)} \tag{12.48}$$

---

[4] Note: $0 < \rho < \infty$.

Finite Population $M/M/c$ Model[5]

$$P_o = \cfrac{1}{\left(\sum_{i=0}^{c} \frac{m!}{(m-i)!i!} \cdot \rho^i\right) + \left(\sum_{i=c+1}^{m} \frac{m!}{(m-i)!c!c^{i-c}} \cdot \rho^i\right)} \qquad (12.49)$$

$$P_n = \begin{cases} \dfrac{m!P_o\rho^n}{(m-n)!\,n!} & \text{for } 0 \leq n \leq c \\[3mm] \dfrac{m!P_o\rho^n}{(m-n)!c!c^{n-c}} & \text{for } c \leq n \leq m \end{cases} \qquad (12.50)$$

$$P(n \geq c) = 1 - P_o \sum_{i=0}^{c-1} \frac{m!}{(m-i)!i!} \cdot \rho^i \qquad (12.51)$$

$$L_s = \frac{L_q + m\rho}{1 + \rho} \qquad (12.52)$$

$$L_q = \sum_{n=c+1}^{m} (n - c)P_n \qquad (12.53)$$

$$L_b = \frac{L_q}{P(n \geq c)} \qquad (12.54)$$

$$W_s = \frac{L_s}{\lambda(m - L_s)} \qquad (12.55)$$

$$W_q = \frac{L_q}{\lambda(m - L_s)} \qquad (12.56)$$

$$\bar{W_b} = \frac{W_q}{P(n \geq c)} \qquad (12.57)$$

Self-Service Model[6]

$$P_n = \frac{e^{-\rho}}{n!} \cdot \rho^n \qquad \text{for } n \geq 0 \qquad (12.58)$$

$$L_s = \rho \qquad (12.59)$$

$$W_s = \frac{1}{\mu} \qquad (12.60)$$

---

[5] Note: $0 < \rho < \infty$.
[6] Note: $0 < \rho < \infty$.

13

Simulation

OF ALL the "tools" in OR/MS, simulation leads the way in flexibility, comprehension, and (most probably) frequency of use. Its flexibility is apparent when one begins to list areas of application: production, inventory, and distribution systems; urban, industrial, and world systems; queuing and traffic flow systems; operating and information systems for airports, hospitals, and industrial organizations; environments involving conflict, such as military strategies and competitive market strategies; and many, many more. Its ability to be more comprehensive is evident in its treatment of large-scale and complex systems in a manner which requires less restrictive assumptions than its analytic counterparts. For example, operating characteristics for complex queuing systems can be estimated by simulation methods but not by the analytic methods illustrated in the preceding chapter.

In this chapter we (1) define and classify simulation, (2) relate it to the paradigm of Chapter 1, (3) discuss and illustrate its advantages, disadvantages, and complexities, and (4) present examples of its use in diverse and meaningful areas of application.

13.1 NATURE OF SIMULATION

Before presenting specific illustrations of simulation, we will first take the time to provide you with a meaningful frame of reference as to the nature of simulation.

Simulation Defined

In a broad sense, simulation is a methodology for conducting experiments using a model of the real system. OR/MS is primarily concerned with **digital** simulations, which involve the numerical manipulation of mathematical models. Other forms of simulation include **physical** simulations (for example, wind-tunnel and water-tank models of space flight) and **analog** simulations (that is, when one physical system is used to represent another, as when an electrical system is used to represent a mechanical system).

Given that the simulation is based on a mathematical model, further distinctions can be cited: deterministic versus stochastic, and static versus dynamic. **Deterministic** simulations involve variables and parameters which are fixed and known with certainty, whereas **stochastic** simulations assign probability distributions to some or all variables and parameters. In actual practice, both types are important, although many analysts are inclined to narrow their definition of simulation to those experiments based only on stochastic processes. We will take a broader perspective.

A **static** simulation is one where experiments are performed on a model having variables and parameters which are time-independent. A **dynamic** simulation, then, includes processes which change over time. Most simulations of economic and administrative interest are dynamic.

It is important for you to understand that digital simulation is to the OR/MS analyst as the laboratory is to the scientist or engineer. Simulation represents an experimental tool for operations research—a means to derive sample data and statistical estimates from a model. As such it is distinguishable from the analytic procedures which seek to optimize some criterion (such as linear programming and inventory models) or seek to predict the behavior of a system by formulas which are analytically derived (as do queuing models).

Simulation, Systems, and the Paradigm

Simulation is primarily concerned with experimentally predicting the behavior of a real system for the purpose of designing the system or modifying behavior. In essence, it replaces the need for either direct experimentation on the real system or analytic solutions of system behavior.

Because of the recurrent use of the word "system," simulation is often cast in the context of **systems analysis.** A **system** can be defined as a set of **components** or **entities** (for example, machines, resources, people) having **attributes** (for example, output rates, capacities, costs, skills) which *interact.* A **mathematical model** is a representation of the system of interest by sets of mathematical equations and logical relationships, and simulation is an *experiment* of (process of observing) the model.

The *process* of simulation involves all eight steps of the paradigm in Chapter 1. Simulation itself, however, is primarily concerned with model solution (Step 5), although in many cases simulation is strictly used for either data collection (Step 4) or validation (Step 6) of an analytic model.[1]

---

[1] Interestingly, the process of simulation itself might suggest (and therefore validate) appropriate analytic models. See, for instance, Edward J. Ignall et al., "Improving the Deployment of New York City Fire Departments," *Interfaces* (February 1975), pp. 48–61; P. Kolesar, "A Model for Predicting Average Fire Engine Travel Times," *Operations Research,* vol. 23, no. 4 (July–August 1975), pp. 603–13.

Motivations for Simulation

Many reasons can be advanced in support of simulation. In this section we indicate the more obvious.

1. Simulation can provide solutions when analytic models fail to do so. For example, transient (time-dependent) solutions for complex queuing models are not possible by analytic methods but are readily obtained by simulation methods.
2. Models to be simulated can represent a real-world process more realistically because fewer restrictive assumptions are required. Examples include the following: Lead times in an inventory model need not be deterministic (Section 13.5); arrivals or service times in a queuing process need not be Poisson-related; and parameters in a multiperiod production scheduling and inventory control problem need not be deterministic.
3. Changes in configuration or structure can be easily implemented to answer "What happens if . . . ?" questions. For example, various decision rules can be tested for altering the number of customers in a queuing system.
4. In most cases, simulation is less costly than actual experimentation; in other cases, it may be the only reasonable initial approach, as when the system does not yet exist, yet theoretical relationships are well-known. For example, solar energy thermal collection systems for homes have been tested by simulation, prior to being built, in order to help solve particular applications problems or to indicate problems in design not known to exist.
5. Simulation can be used for pedagogical (teaching) purposes either to illustrate a model, as in Table 13–12, or to better comprehend a process, as in management games.[2]
6. For many dynamic processes, simulation provides the only means for direct and detailed observation within specified time periods. The approach also allows **time compression,** whereby a simulation accomplishes in minutes what might require years of actual experimentation. These advantages are illustrated in Sections 13.4 and 13.5.

With these advantages and others (can you think of more?) one might ask "Why not approach all modeling through simulation?" First, simulation is time-consuming and costly compared to many analytic approaches. For example, a simulation to estimate optimal reorder levels and quantities for an inventory problem requires an extensive search for optimal values of controllable variables (as we illustrate in Section 13.5), whereas an analytic solution would not. Second, certain issues associated with design, validation, and estimation are complex at best and unresolved at worst. We take this up in some detail at the end of the chapter.

---

[2] J. G. H. Carlson and M. J. Misshauk, *Introduction to Gaming: Management Decision Simulations* (New York: John Wiley & Sons, Inc., 1972), and J. R. Frazer, *Business Decision Simulation: A Time Sharing Approach* (Reston, Va.: Reston Publishing Co., Inc., 1975).

Computers and Simulation Languages

Digital computers and programming languages have been important facilitators in increasing the frequency and ease of simulations. Without such technology the cost of implementing "meaningful" simulations would be prohibitive.

Once the construction of a simulation model (in mathematical or flow-chart form) is accomplished, the model must be programmed for runs (simulated experiments) on the computer. For this purpose, any of the available general-purpose languages can be used, for example, FORTRAN, PL/I, and so forth. These languages have the advantage of providing the most flexibility in tailoring the program both to the model and to the needs of the user; however, they also require great amounts of programming effort, which translates into more time and expense, especially in the process of debugging errors.

In recent years, specially designed simulation languages and programs have been developed to overcome the expense-error aspects of using general-purpose languages. In general, these languages simplify the process of transforming a model to a set of computer instructions and altering the model to answer "What happens if . . . ?" questions. Essentially, they accomplish these by providing a generalized structure which is easily manipulated and statistical reports which are useful for analysis. In this chapter we will illustrate two of these so-called simulation languages: DYNAMO (Section 13.2) and GPSS (Section 13.4).

13.2 DETERMINISTIC SIMULATION: SYSTEM DYNAMICS

This section describes an approach to the simulation of complex, dynamic systems as developed by Jay W. Forrester and his colleagues. As originally conceived, the approach was designed for industrial and economic systems and labeled **Industrial Dynamics.** Later the same methodology was applied to urban systems **(Urban Dynamics)** and global systems **(World Dynamics).** We use the term **System Dynamics** to represent the general approach.

Our objective here is to give you a descriptive sampling of the philosophy, methodology, and specific applications of a simulation approach which has become prominent. We make no attempt to be comprehensive.[3]

Overview of System Dynamics

System dynamics is an approach to analyzing, under dynamic conditions, a system having interacting components. Figure 13–1 illustrates the general structure of a simple dynamic system. As conceptualized by Forrester, the system has four hierarchies of structure: (1) closed boundary, (2) feedback loops, (3) level variables and rate variables, and (4) components of a rate variable.[4]

---

[3] If your appetite is "whetted," see J. W. Forrester, *Industrial Dynamics* (Cambridge, Mass.: M.I.T. Press, 1961); J. W. Forrester, *Urban Dynamics* (Cambridge, Mass.: M.I.T. Press, 1969); J. W. Forrester, *World Dynamics* (Cambridge, Mass.: M.I.T. Press, 1971); D. H. Meadows et al., 2d ed., *The Limits to Growth* (New York: Universe Books, 1972); and M. Mesarovic and E. Pestel, *Mankind at the Turning Point* (New York: E. P. Dutton & Co., Inc./Reader's Digest Press, 1974).

[4] Forrester, *Urban Dynamics.*

FIGURE 13–1

Structure of Simple Dynamic System

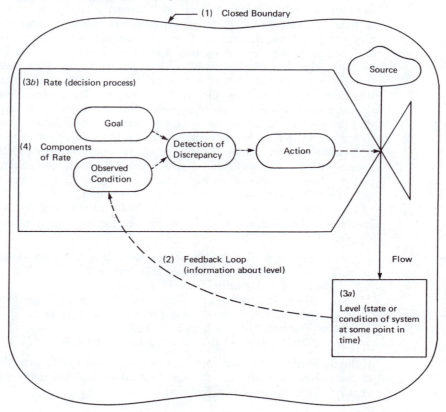

The **closed boundary** defines the limitations imposed on the system. It is chosen to include the interacting components which are necessary to adequately depict the behavior of interest. This is not to say that the system is unaffected by outside factors; rather outside factors affect conditions in the system but do not, in themselves, affect the manner in which the system behaves. For instance, suppose the dynamic system in Figure 13–1 represents the market for electronic calculators. If we let the **source** represent "demand per week for electronic calculators" and components of demand are of no interest to the system under study, then the closed boundary serves to exclude factors affecting demand for electronic calculators.

Feedback loops represent the conduits within which the dynamic behavior of a system is generated. **Levels** are accumulations (of objects, natural resources, population, capital, and so forth) within feedback loops; they are represented by **state variables.** **Rate variables** are a necessary second aspect of feedback loops; they represent the activity (that is, *flow* of objects, natural resources, population, capital, and so forth) within feedback loops. The rate of flow in Figure 13–1 is regulated by a "valve" which represents a **decision point.** In our electronic calculators example, we might represent level by "number of calculators in inventory at time t" and rate by "number of calculators to be produced during a given week." Note that rates of flow (decisions) cause changes in levels, and rate variables depend on **information** feedback about the levels. For example, the rate of production of calculators in the 10th week affects the inventory of calculators at the end of the 10th week; the level of inventory at the end of the 10th week provides information for the decision concerning the rate of production in the 11th week. Further note that the source, "demand per week for electronic calculators," also affects the rate decision; hence, it connects to the valve in Figure 13–1.[5]

Decisions come about because a *discrepancy* has been detected between the *observed condition* and the desired condition (*goal*), as illustrated by **components of a rate variable** in Figure 13–1. Decisions are in turn translated into *action,* which alters rates within the system.

Rate decisions are modeled by algebraic rate equations. Values for levels also are determined algebraically. In the electronic calculators example, let

$D_{jk} \equiv$ Demand rate (units per week) for calculators during period beginning at time j and ending at time k.
$L_j \equiv$ Level of inventory (units) at time j.
$R_{jk} \equiv$ Rate of production (units per week) of calculators during period beginning at time j and ending at time k.
$\Delta_{jk} \equiv$ Fraction of week between j and k.
$DL_k \equiv$ Desired level of inventory (units) at time k.

If the desired level of inventory is to be 20 percent higher than the demand in the *current* period, then the **level equations** for actual and desired inventory can be expressed as follows:

$$L_k = L_j + \Delta_{jk}(R_{jk} - D_{jk}) \tag{13.1}$$

and

$$DL_k = 1.2D_{jk}. \tag{13.2}$$

Note that j and k represent, respectively, the beginning and ending points of the current period. Since R and D are expressed on a per week basis, Δ_{jk} serves to correctly adjust for the period of time represented by the interval jk (assuming uniform production and demand over the time interval). For example, if each period is a week, then $\Delta_{jk} = 1$; if each period is one half of a week (that is, two periods per week), then $\Delta_{jk} = 0.5$. (Try verbalizing the level equation for L_k to convince yourself that it simply represents the usual accounting truism of ending inventory equals beginning inventory plus production minus sales.)

If the decision rule states that the production rate for the *next* period is to equal the previous period's demand plus 80 percent of the difference between desired and actual inventory levels at the end of the previous period, then the **rate equation** is

---

[5] Decisions which affect factors outside our system of interest can be represented by flows leading into **sinks.**

$$R_{kl} = D_{jk} + 0.8(DL_k - L_k) \tag{13.3}$$

where kl represents the time interval encompassing the next period. (Is the decision rule logical?)

To simplify the computer coding and associated input/output for system dynamic simulations, a computer simulation language (and compiler) has been developed called DYNAMO. Equation (13.1), written in DYNAMO, would appear as

$$L.K = L.J + (DT)(R.JK - D.JK) \tag{13.4}$$

where DT represents Δ_{jk}. Note that time subscripts are separated from variable names by the use of periods.

The system represented in Figure 13–1 is the simplest possible: one component (electronic calculators) and one feedback loop made up of one rate and one level. Complex systems exhibit many components and dynamic feedback loops which interact. Realities associated with *time delays, discrepancies* between perceived and actual conditions, and *perturbations (impulses)* of variables over time serve to further complicate the prediction of system behavior. Because of the complexities, dynamic interactions, delays, discrepancies, and impulses associated with real systems, results are often counterintuitive. Therein lies the danger of intuitive decision making and the value of system dynamics.

In the next three sections we briefly describe broad areas associated with the application of system dynamics. Our intent is to provide you with an appreciation of the power and flexibility of this methodology for modeling complex systems.

Follow-up Exercises

1. For our electronic calculators example, suppose that demand per week is constant at 100 calculators, each week consists of two time periods, inventory at the beginning of period 1 is 200 calculators, and production in the first period is at the rate of 50 calculators per week. Simulate this process for six weeks (12 periods) by completing the accompanying table (first confirm the calculations we have provided):

Week (t)	Period (jk)	D_{jk} (units/week)	L_j (units)	R_{jk}^* (units/week)	L_k^* (units)	DL_k (units)
1.........	1	100	200	50	175	120
	2	100	175	56	153	120
2.........	3	100		74		
	4	100				
.	.	.	.			
.	.	.	.			
.	.	.	.			

* Round off calculations to nearest whole number.

On a graph represent time periods on the horizontal axis and plot
curves for the behaviors of D_{jk}, R_{jk}, L_k, and DL_k. Conclusions?

2. Indicate the effects on the dynamic behavior of R_{jk} and L_k of (a) lower-
    ing by 50 percent and (b) increasing by 50 percent the 0.8 coefficient in
    the rate equation. Compute a table as in Exercise 1 and draw graphs.

3. Generate tables and graphs as in Exercise 2 for the case where a one-
    period impulse of +50 units occurs in the demand of period 5. Conclu-
    sions? (Note the amplifications.)

4. Complete a table and draw a graph as in Exercise 1 by replacing D_{jk}
    with $\bar{D}_{kl}$ in Equation (13.3), where $\bar{D}_{kl}$ represents forecasted demand in
    period kl based on a single exponential smoothing model with a coeffi-
    cient of 0.2. (See Section A.7 on page 733.) Assume actual demands for
    six weeks are 100, 110, 105, 112, 110, and 115.

**5. Write a general computer program (in BASIC, FORTRAN, or PL/1) to
    simulate the electronic calculators system. Strictly by changing input
    data, solve Exercises 1, 2, and 4. How might you handle the condition
    introduced in Exercise 3?

World Dynamics

The application of system dynamics to a global system has been termed
World Dynamics, as presented by Forrester, and implemented in the
classic study *The Limits to Growth,* which reports on the Club of Rome's
project on "The Predicament of Mankind."[6] With certain modifications,
the world model can be used to represent a nation. In *The Limits to
Growth* five global components which interact dynamically through more
than a hundred feedback loops are identified: population, agricultural
production, industrial production, natural resources, and pollution.

Simplified feedback loops and interactions for four of these components
are illustrated in Figure 13–2 (arrows indicate causal relationships which
may be immediate or delayed):

> Each year the population is increased by the total number of births
> and decreased by the total number of deaths that have taken place dur-
> ing that year. The absolute number of births per year is a function of
> the average fertility of the population and of the size of the population.
> The number of deaths is related to the average mortality and the total
> population size. As long as births exceed deaths, the population grows.
> Similarly, a given amount of industrial capital, operating at constant
> efficiency, will be able to produce a certain amount of output each year.
> Some of that output will be more factories, machines, and so forth, which
> are investments to increase the stock of capital goods. At the same time
> some capital equipment will depreciate or be discarded each year. To
> keep industrial capital growing, the investment rate must exceed the

---

[6] The Club of Rome is a loosely knit organization of international scientists,
industrialists, educators, economists, humanists, and others with the purpose of
fostering an understanding of and promoting policy initiatives and action in the
world's interdependent economic, political, natural, and social components. See also
Forrester, *World Dynamics,* and Meadows et al., *The Limits to Growth.*

FIGURE 13–2

Feedback Loops of Population, Capital, Agriculture, and Pollution

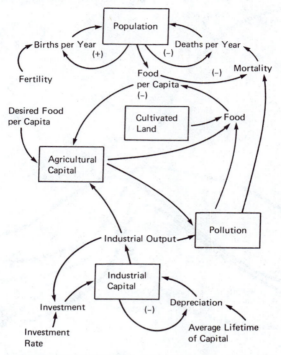

Source: D. H. Meadows et al., 2d ed; *The Limits to Growth* (New York: Universe Books, 1972), p. 97.

depreciation rate. . . . Some of the output of industrial capital is agricultural capital—tractors, irrigation ditches, and fertilizers, for example. The amount of agricultural capital and land area under cultivation strongly influences the amount of food produced. The food per capita (food produced divided by the population) influences the mortality of the population. Both industrial and agricultural activity can cause pollution. . . . Pollution may affect the mortality of the population directly and also indirectly by decreasing agricultural output. . . .

If everything else in the system remained the same, a population *increase* would decrease food per capita, and thus increase mortality, increase the number of deaths, and eventually lead to a population decrease. . . . If the food per capita *decreases* to a value lower than that desired by the population, there will be a tendency to increase agricultural capital, so that future food production and food per capita can *increase*.[7]

Figure 13–3 illustrates actual output from the world model. The form of the output is typical of the output generated by the DYNAMO compiler. It is worth noting that the focus is on the *mode of behavior* rather

[7] Meadows et al., *The Limits to Growth*, pp. 96–99.

FIGURE 13–3

Sample Runs of World Model

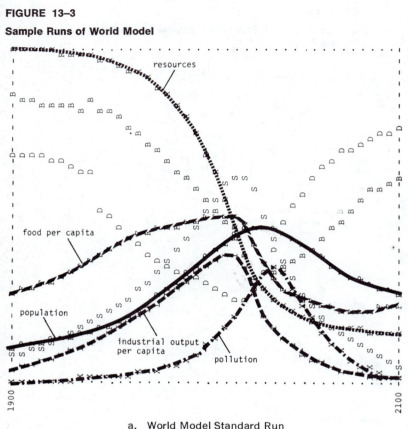

a. World Model Standard Run

The "standard" world model run assumes no major change in the physical, economic, or social relationships that have historically governed the development of the
world system. All variables plotted here follow historical values from 1900 to 1970.
Food, industrial output, and population grow exponentially until the rapidly diminishing resource base forces a slowdown in industrial growth. Because of natural delays
in the system, both population and pollution continue to increase for some time after
the peak of industrialization. Population growth is finally halted by a rise in the death
rate due to decreased food and medical services.

Source: D. H. Meadows et al., 2d ed.; *The Limits to Growth* (New York: Universe Books,
1972), pp. 124, 160, 162, 165, 168, 169.

FIGURE 13–3 (*continued*)

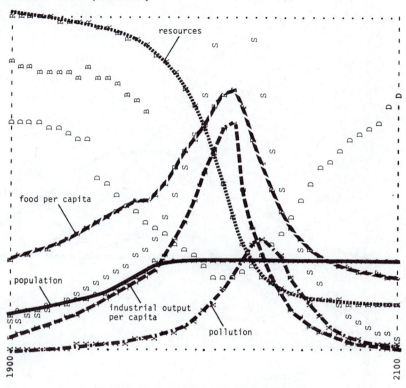

b. World Model with Stabilized Population

In this computer run, conditions in the model system are identical to those in the standard run . . . except that population is held constant after 1975 by equating the birth rate with the death rate. The remaining unrestricted positive feedback loop in the system, involving industrial capital, continues to generate exponential growth of industrial output, food, and services per capita. Eventual depletion of nonrenewable resources brings a sudden collapse of the industrial system.

FIGURE 13-3   *(continued)*

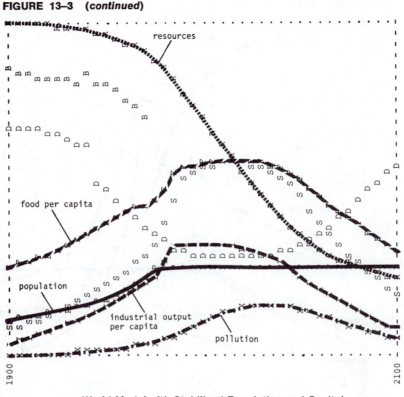

c.   World Model with Stabilized Population and Capital

Restriction of capital growth, by requiring that capital investment equal deprecia-tion, is added to the population stabilization policy. Now that exponential growth is halted, a temporary stable state is attained. Levels of population and capital in this state are sufficiently high to deplete resources rapidly, however, since no resource-conserving technologies have been assumed. As the resource base declines, indus-trial output decreases. Although the capital base is maintained at the same level, efficiency of capital goes down since more capital must be devoted to obtaining re-sources than to producing usable output.

FIGURE 13–3 (*continued*)

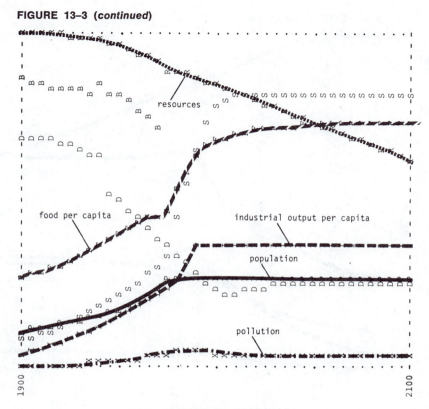

d. Stabilized World Model I

Technological policies are added to the growth-regulating policies of the previous run to produce an equilibrium state sustainable far into the future. Technological policies include resource recycling, pollution control devices, increased lifetime of all forms of capital, and methods to restore eroded and infertile soil. Value changes include increased emphasis on food and services rather than on industrial production.

Births are set equal to deaths and industrial capital investment equal to capital depreciation. Equilibrium value of industrial output per capita is three times the 1970 world average.

FIGURE 13–3 (continued)

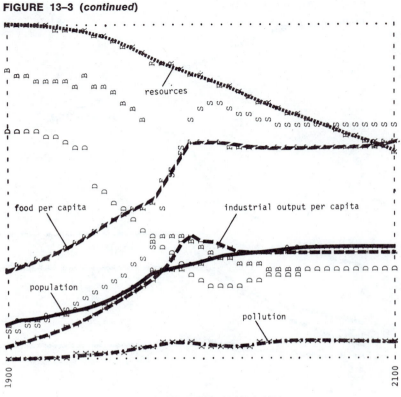

e. Stabilized World Model II

*If the strict restrictions on growth of the previous run are removed, and popula-
tion and capital are regulated within the natural delays of the system, the equilibrium
level of population is higher and the level of industrial output per capita is lower. Here
it is assumed that perfectly effective birth control and an average desired family size
of two children are achieved by 1975. The birth rate only slowly approaches the death
rate because of delays inherent in the age structure of the population.*

FIGURE 13–3 (concluded)

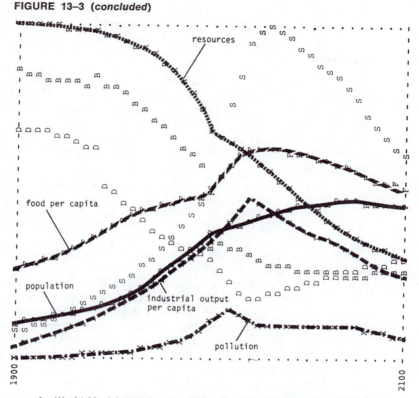

resources

food per capita

population

industrial output
per capita

pollution

1900

2100

f. World Model with Stabilizing Policies Introduced in the Year 2000

If all the policies instituted in 1975 in the previous figure are delayed until the year 2000, the equilibrium state is no longer sustainable. Population and industrial capital reach levels high enough to create food and resource shortages before the year 2100.

than on numerical predictions which require more exact data and relationships. In general, numerical changes in input data affect oscillation periods (times between peaks and troughs on a curve), growth rates, or collapse times (sudden drops of the curves), but they do not affect the fact that the basic mode is oscillation, growth, or collapse. Thus, the basic intent of the model is to answer "what happens if . . . ?" questions about modes of behavior.

We might mention that this brief treatment does not do justice to this type of modeling. Furthermore, the basic model appears to have its shortcomings.[8] Most critics and supporters, however, would agree on one point: The world model represents a long-overdue attempt to establish a scientific basis for solving critical and complex problems of world concern. As

---

[8] For an excellent critique of the world model see Richard H. Day and Evan F. Koenig, "On Some Models of World Cataclysm," *Land Economics* (February 1975), pp. 1–20.

such, it serves to focus on the issues and to provide a starting point from which subsequent models can be developed.[9]

Urban Dynamics

Forrester has applied system dynamics to an urban system, as described in the book *Urban Dynamics*. As in the world model, the urban model conceptualizes an urban system in terms of dynamic and interacting feedback loops.

The general model represents the life cycle of an urban area which traditionally shows growth followed by maturity followed by stagnation. The urban area

> . . . is a complex, self-regulating system that creates internal pressures to modify economic activity and shift the uses of land, structures, and people. The changes are dominated by the construction, aging, and demolition of industry and housing combined with concurrent population movements.[10]

Major components of the model include labor force, underemployed, managerial-professional, worker housing, underemployed housing, premium housing, declining industry, mature business, and new enterprise.

Forrester uses the model to show the factors and policies which lead to urban growth, aging, and revival. Common urban-management programs are examined to show that specific programs may actually worsen the conditions they are meant to improve. The model indicates that programs focusing on underlying causes rather than manifested symptoms suggest different approaches.

The underlying structures of both the world and urban models are theoretical and subject to scrutiny. As with all new approaches, confirmation of their value as methods of analyses for complex problems requires the test of time.

Industrial Dynamics

The methodology described in the book *Industrial Dynamics* for analyzing the aggregate behavior of large-scale industrial systems served as the forerunner to world and urban dynamics. As defined by Forrester:

> Industrial dynamics is the study of the information-feedback characteristics of industrial activity to show how organizational structure, amplification (in policies), and time delays (in decisions and actions) interact to influence the success of the enterprise. It treats the interactions between the flows of information, money, orders, materials, personnel, and capital equipment in a company, an industry, or a national economy. [It] provides a single framework for integrating the functional areas of management—marketing, production, accounting, research and development, and capital investment.[11]

---

[9] For later developments which have been reported in the news media, see "Club of Rome Revisited," *Time* (April 26, 1976), p. 56. For a more comprehensive world model, see Mesarovic and Pestel, *Mankind at the Turning Point*.

[10] Forrester, *Urban Dynamics*, p. 3.

[11] Forrester, *Industrial Dynamics*, p. 13.

As in the world and urban models, the aim is to explore the effects of alternative policies on the aggregate behavior of the system, rather than to make specific predictions.

Compared to the urban and world models, industrial dynamics (ID) models have been more widely examined. This is so for several reasons: First, ID models preceded the others by a decade; second, the "state of the art" of defining industrial structure is more advanced than urban and world counterparts; finally, there are orders of magnitude more industrial firms and applicable industrial problems. The best-known applications involve the study of steady-state systems for the purpose of stabilizing fluctuations in certain activities (for example, number of backorders, inventory levels, manpower, and so forth). Production-distribution systems are typical subjects. Growth systems such as product and industry life cycles and research and development projects also have been analyzed by this methodology. Additional applications include models of organizational policy relating to implementing change and analyzing power structure.[12]

Follow-up Exercises

6. Find copies of *The Limits to Growth*, and *Mankind at the Turning Point*; summarize their major conclusions.[13]
7. Do a literature search to find articles or books which either support or criticize (or both) world models.
8. Do a literature search and report on your findings relating to actual applications of (*a*) urban dynamics or (*b*) industrial dynamics.

13.3 FUNDAMENTALS OF MONTE CARLO SIMULATION

For the remainder of the chapter we focus on stochastic (probabilistic) simulation. As used here, "Monte Carlo" refers to an approach for reconstructing probability distributions based on the selection or generation of random numbers. Before proceeding we strongly urge you to review Sections A.1 through A.3 in Appendix A at the end of the book, as we rely heavily on the concepts presented therein.

Inverse Transformation Method for Generating Random Variates

The inverse transformation method (ITM) is a popular technique for generating random variates for either discrete or continuous random vari-

---

[12] For more detail and additional references, see H. Maisel and G. Gnugnoli, *Simulation of Discrete Stochastic Systems* (Chicago: S.R.A., Inc., 1972).

[13] Meadows et al., 2d ed., *The Limits to Growth,* and Mesarovic and Pestel, *Mankind at the Turning Point.*

ables.[14] To illustrate, consider the discrete random variable (X) "number of emergency room arrivals per hour" and the data in Table 13–1 (as originally presented in Table A–1).[15]

According to the relative frequency definition of probability, the probability of zero arrivals, or $P(X = 0)$, is 0.10, $P(X = 1) = 0.28$, . . . , and $P(X = 6) = 0.01$. Now, if it were possible to generate another random variable (U) which is *uniformly distributed* in the range $(0,1)$, then by definition $P(0.00 < U \le 0.10) = 0.10$, $P(0.10 < U \le 0.38) = 0.28$, . . . , and $P(0.99 < U \le 1.00) = 0.01$.[16] Since the probabilities for the given ranges of U are respectively identical to the probabilities for the given values of X, it follows that occurrences of U can be used to simulate or "artificially reconstruct" occurrences of X. If you study Table 13–1 and Figure 13–4 you should realize that random variates of U

TABLE 13–1

Distribution of Emergency Room Arrivals

Number of Arrivals per Hour (x)	Frequency of Occurrence	pmf f(x)	CDF F(x)	Range Along 0–1 Scale
0	10	0.10	0.10	0.00–0.10
1	28	0.28	0.38	0.10–0.38
2	29	0.29	0.67	0.38–0.67
3	16	0.16	0.83	0.67–0.83
4	10	0.10	0.93	0.83–0.93
5	6	0.06	0.99	0.93–0.99
6	1	0.01	1.00	0.99–1.00
	100	1.00		

within the specified intervals are equivalent to corresponding random variates of X. In other words, U can be used to artificially generate X precisely because the probabilities associated with the specified ranges of U are exactly equivalent to the probabilities associated with the corresponding values of X.

As you can see from Table 13–1, the Cumulative Distribution Function (CDF), $F(x)$, is equivalent to specified values of U. ITM gets its name from the fact that we are transforming from the U-scale to the X-scale. Note that this procedure is backward (inverse) from the usual procedure. Typically we map from specific X into specific U through $F(x)$, that is,

$$F(x) = u \qquad (13.5)$$

---

[14] Other methods exist. See T. H. Naylor et al., *Computer Simulation Techniques* (New York: John Wiley & Sons, Inc., 1966) for details.

[15] As in Appendix A, a random variate (specific value) of a random variable is represented by a lower case letter and the random variable itself is denoted by an upper case letter.

[16] See (1) under "Continuous Probability Distributions" in Section A.3 on page 713.

FIGURE 13-4

U-X Equivalents Based on Table 13-1

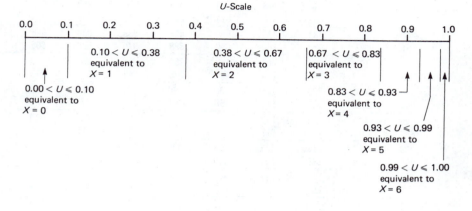

where u represents a specific cumulative probability. By the approach of the ITM, this procedure is reversed since given u we need to specify x, that is,

$$x = F^{-1}(u). \tag{13.6}$$

Table 13–2 illustrates a "hand" simulation for six one-hour periods based on the data in Table 13–1. The simulated number of arrivals for each time period first requires the generation of a random variate (u) from the distribution of U. To accomplish this we provide Table 13–3, which illustrates 500 random variates (or values for u) in the interval 0–1. Arbitrarily selecting column 5, we find the first number is 246, which represents $U = 0.246$. This corresponds to one simulated arrival $(X = 1)$ between 10 A.M. and 11 A.M., since 0.246 falls between 0.10 and 0.38 on the scale given in Table 13–1. Continuing down column 5 of Table 13–3, we find that $U = 0.514$ falls in the interval 0.38–0.67, which corresponds to $X = 2$ (two arrivals between 11 A.M. and noon). To check your understanding, you should confirm the remaining entries in Table 13–2. Approaches to generating values of U as in Table 13–3 are discussed in the next section.

TABLE 13-2

Sample Simulation of Emergency Room Arrivals between 10 A.M. and 4 P.M.

Time Period (24-hour clock)	0–1 Random Variate (u)	Number of Arrivals During Specified Time Period (x)
10–11	0.246	1
11–12	0.514	2
12–13	0.898	4
13–14	0.030	0
14–15	0.152	1
15–16	0.573	2

TABLE 13–3

Random Numbers

1	2	3	4	5	6	7	8	9	10
104	900	150	296	246	812	725	250	612	999
223	321	465	925	514	096	842	039	484	009
241	211	483	475	898	413	838	038	048	990
421	021	930	830	030	888	376	520	605	800
375	198	399	287	152	759	267	655	583	487
779	383	888	774	573	075	261	972	773	478
995	107	799	123	480	690	491	527	054	227
963	799	322	849	558	393	962	577	853	190
895	439	236	772	462	343	230	943	313	439
854	262	309	917	245	025	484	755	200	302
289	587	611	433	468	448	075	731	684	794
635	169	349	564	940	430	604	670	663	707
094	678	743	242	427	094	470	918	992	637
103	917	253	078	717	075	238	653	078	597
071	440	442	098	906	713	553	631	061	456
510	346	695	575	110	366	849	844	142	450
023	310	082	654	181	893	783	159	413	754
010	744	527	853	275	446	275	405	898	612
521	333	491	242	215	145	288	938	056	434
070	718	975	011	651	639	963	142	757	609
556	002	893	868	375	903	336	194	942	098
204	847	436	188	037	688	067	922	719	665
203	553	943	111	623	193	682	154	167	244
112	939	806	291	830	790	429	813	430	358
465	345	285	278	323	203	999	122	085	091
549	128	563	635	478	095	035	649	916	657
411	809	098	428	335	267	750	228	388	257
640	617	605	822	012	317	042	295	784	912
070	116	499	272	334	593	085	899	415	796
074	895	985	934	815	937	884	193	213	938
588	728	220	698	448	028	299	731	279	221
355	271	284	471	392	866	365	625	770	327
517	811	435	424	201	968	746	097	653	966
328	959	772	300	832	040	560	521	744	709
007	887	982	497	661	947	733	715	362	861
514	627	829	667	669	353	949	652	358	324
869	374	186	522	729	249	527	540	852	607
316	010	840	919	397	917	497	147	203	845
523	672	564	745	906	544	688	936	103	214
979	152	263	443	097	753	202	916	249	420
370	575	698	784	535	441	926	296	914	009
448	670	395	433	625	508	576	989	126	523
391	837	633	447	092	139	875	729	189	018
098	191	066	267	834	849	113	429	226	086
568	545	478	310	911	811	572	054	054	106
800	868	301	727	743	917	344	617	251	660
524	199	592	107	240	441	050	092	209	516
122	493	915	730	755	553	582	872	865	196
681	200	279	565	790	841	626	671	901	136
327	734	849	367	161	713	219	965	382	512

FIGURE 13–5

Graphical Illustration of $2 = F^{-1}(0.514)$ for Discrete Random Variable in Table 13–1

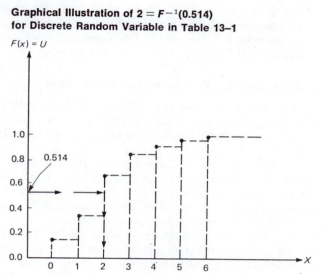

The transformation of u to x for our present example is shown graphically in Figure 13–5. In general, the simulation of a *discrete* random variable can be represented by the graph of its CDF. Conceptually, the simulation of a *continuous* random variable is treated in the same manner, as indicated in Figure 13–6.

Actual simulations of *empirical* probability distributions can be effected in the manner of Tables 13–1 and 13–2. For *theoretical* distributions (for example, Poisson, exponential, and so forth), however, random variates of X are generated through the use of algorithms or formulas for $F^{-1}(u)$.

FIGURE 13–6

Graphical Illustration of $x = F^{-1}(u)$ for Continuous Random Variable

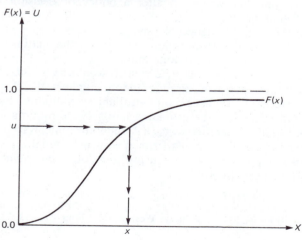

The Appendix at the end of this chapter illustrates methods of generating exponential and Poisson variates.[17] Given an empirical probability distribution, some analysts prefer to generate the simulation from a theoretical probability distribution for which the empirical distribution "fits" based on a goodness-of-fit test, as in Section A.4 on page 719.

Generation of 0–1 Uniformly Distributed Random Variates

As you now know, the simulation of a stochastic process (for example, arrivals at the emergency room of a hospital) requires the generation of a sequence of random numbers (variates of U) uniformly distributed over the interval 0 to 1.

The process which generates U *must* satisfy the conditions of (1) a *uniform distribution* in the parent population and (2) *independence* (absence of correlation) in the sampled observations (variates) from that population. Additionally, it is desirable that the process be (3) *fast (or cheap)*, and (4) have a *long period* should it repeat itself.

Processes for generating U include (*a*) the use of random number tables which are available either in published form or on computer tapes, (*b*) special machines or physical phenomena (for example, fluctuations in some electronic process), and (*c*) the application of a numerical process. Of these, numerical processes based on so-called *congruential methods* most nearly satisfy the four criteria outlined above. In fact, Table 13–3 was generated by a congruential method on an IBM/370–155 computer. Suffice it to say that all manufacturers of general-purpose digital computers make available computational procedures (usually in the form of subroutines) for generating random numbers. Therefore, a simulation model programmed for a digital computer need only incorporate the appropriate subroutine for generating U.

Random numbers for U based on numerical methods are called **pseudorandom numbers,** as opposed to *true* random numbers which are generated by some physical process. Believe it or not, pseudorandom numbers are preferable because the exact same sequence of random numbers is capable of being repeated at will by the experimenter. This has control value when the experimenter wishes to alter a policy or decision variable in answering "What happens if . . . ?" questions. Without the capability of repeating the same sequence of random variates, experimental results would differ because of both conscious changes by the analyst and random changes due to a different random number sequence. The latter effect would represent a confounding factor which would have to be isolated by replications of the experiment. Pseudorandom numbers, therefore, uniquely isolate the effects of changes in controllable conditions. Furthermore, purely random effects can be estimated easily by re-running experiments with changed **random number seeds.** (A random number seed is an arbitrary number provided by the experimenter which initializes the random number subroutine.) The value of using pseudorandom numbers will be illustrated in the next two sections.

---

[17] Computer packages for generating binomial, Poisson, normal, exponential, . . . processes are widely available. For example, see T. E. Vollmann, *Operations Management* (Reading, Mass.: Addison-Wesley Publishing Co., 1973), pp. 303–4.

Follow-up Exercises

9. Besides the methods indicated above for generating U, more pedestrian methods (for example, manual) can be described. If you were given 100 poker chips and a "magic marker" pen, describe how you could manually simulate the arrival process in Table 13-1. Comment on the degree to which the four criteria for generating U are satisfied.

10. Theoretically, why need we not worry about $U = 0.10$, $U = 0.38$, and so on in using the ITM for the process in Table 13-1? Need we be concerned from a practical standpoint?

11. Determine $f(u)$, $F(u)$, $E(U)$, $V(U)$, $P(U \leq 0.1)$, $P(0.10 \leq U \leq 0.38)$, and $P(0.38 \leq U \leq 0.67)$ when U is uniform over the interval $(0, 1)$. (Hint: Go back to Appendix A.) Are your probabilities consistent with corresponding values of $f(x)$ in Table 13-1?

Applications of Monte Carlo Simulation

Two primary factors account for the widespread application of Monte Carlo simulation: The real world is probabilistic, and simulation is a flexible approach to modeling rather than a specific technique. In this section we overview the widespread use of Monte Carlo approaches with no attempt to be comprehensive.

Complex queuing systems have been significant subjects of Monte Carlo simulation, especially since the development of the GPSS simulation language. In Section 13.4 we treat the simulation of queuing systems in some detail. Other primary areas of application include inventory systems characterized by complexities which cannot be modeled analytically (Section 13.5); involved production and job shop scheduling systems with probabilistic demands and processing times (Chapter 16); and project scheduling with probabilistic completion times (Chapter 14).

Military and business games represent another important area of application. For example, a common business game simulates an oligopolistic industry of three to six firms, where each firm is represented by a team of students or business executives. The game is played over a specified number of time periods (usually quarters). Teams must input decisions for each time period regarding prices, production rates, advertising expenditures, acquisitions, and expansions. Outputs for each period include balance sheets and income statements for each firm.

Other areas of probabilistic simulation include econometric models of a firm, industry, or economy; behavioral models of learning and human behavior; urban applications such as traffic flow patterns and the positioning and allocation of emergency response units; financial simulations of stock market portfolios and cash flows of a firm; military models concerned with logistics and effectiveness of weapons systems; hospital applications such as the scheduling of out-patient clinics, utilization of in-patient facilities, management of blood banking, and ambulatory care in emergency and out-patient departments; and airport models of airplane arrival and departure patterns, maintenance support, and baggage handling.

13.4 SIMULATION OF QUEUING SYSTEM

In this section we illustrate a "hand" simulation for a $GI/G/1$ system and present the results of a simulation for an $M/M/c$ system with state-dependent service rates. The latter simulation is implemented using GPSS, the output of which we will illustrate. First, however, we motivate the use of simulation for queuing systems.

Motivation for Simulating Queuing Systems

As with inventory systems, the primary motivation for simulating queuing systems is the inability to generate meaningful analytic solutions for complex queuing structures. Typical system complexities include:

1. Arrival processes having empirical distributions with no theoretical counterparts, or characterized by certain theoretical distributions (for example, normal), or exhibiting nonstationarity, seasonal patterns (for example, rush hours), or serial correlation.
2. Service facilities with certain empirical or theoretical service time distributions, or specific forms of state dependence in the service rate (as illustrated later in this section), or tandem and parallel servers (as in job shop systems which process simultaneous orders and assembly line production systems), or breakdown and fatigue failures, or nonstationary service distributions.
3. Queuing processes for which transient solutions are required (that is, the system never operates long enough to achieve steady state) but are unavailable (which is the case for most non-$M/M/c$ systems).

GI/G/1 System

To give you a better "feel" for the process of Monte Carlo simulation, we now illustrate a procedure for simulating any single-channel queuing system. For simplicity we adopt the assumptions of the standard $M/M/1$ model (page 440), except for the relaxation of interarrival times and service times to the general case.

Consider the interarrival-time (that is, time between successive arrivals) distribution and service-time distribution given in Table 13–4. Two ran-

TABLE 13–4

Empirical Probability Distributions for Queuing Simulation

Range of Interarrival Times (minutes)	Probability	Range of Service Times (minutes)	Probability
0 but under 4	0.4	0 but under 2	0.4
4 but under 8	0.3	2 but under 4	0.4
8 but under 12	0.2	4 but under 6	0.2
12 but under 16	0.1		

TABLE 13–5

Simulation Structure for B

Random Variates for Interarrival Times b	Probability f(b)	Cumulative Probability F(b)	Ranges of 0–1 Uniformly Distributed Random Number u_1
2............................	0.4	0.4	0.0–0.4
6............................	0.3	0.7	0.4–0.7
10...........................	0.2	0.9	0.7–0.9
14...........................	0.1	1.0	0.9–1.0

dom variables are to be directly simulated: interarrival time (B) and service time (T). Tables 13–5 and 13–6 provide the structure for simulating these random variables. Note that the random variates are determined as the midpoints of the ranges in Table 13–4. Further note the cumulative probabilities identify the upper point of each range for the random numbers on the U-scales.

TABLE 13–6

Simulation Structure for T

Random Variates for Service Times t	Probability f(t)	Cumulative Probability F(t)	Ranges of 0–1 Uniformly Distributed Random Number u_2
1............................	0.4	0.4	0.0–0.4
3............................	0.4	0.8	0.4–0.8
5............................	0.2	1.0	0.8–1.0

Table 13–7 illustrates a simulation for a period of time encompassing ten arrivals. The items below should help to clarify the logic.

1. The 0–1 random variates (u_1 and u_2) are taken from columns 2 and 9 in Table 13–3. The simulated random variates (b and t) are determined from Tables 13–5 and 13–6 once u_1 and u_2 are given.
2. The first arriving unit initializes CLOCK1. By the definition of b, the column labeled CLOCK1 now can be filled. An empty initial system is assumed; hence, Unit 1 enters service immediately (CLOCK2 = 0) and departs at the end of 3 minutes. Other entries in this first row should be self-explanatory.
3. Unit 2 enters the system 14 minutes into the simulation (CLOCK1 = 14). Since Unit 1 departed the system at time 3, it follows that Unit 2 enters service immediately (CLOCK2 = 14). Given that it takes 3 minutes to service Unit 2, this unit departs at time 17 (CLOCK3 = 17). Note that the server is idle for 11 minutes (that is, the difference between CLOCK3 = 3 for Unit 1 and CLOCK2 = 14 for Unit 2).
4. Unit 3 enters at CLOCK1 = 16. Since Unit 2 does not leave service until time 17, it follows Unit 3 must wait 1 minute in the queue before entering service. Unit 3 enters at time 17 and departs at time

Douglas Salter
748-8666

TABLE 13-7

GI/G/1 Simulation

Arriving Unit	u_1	b	Enter System at Time (CLOCK1)	Length of Queue at Entry	Time Spent in Queue	Enter Service at Time (CLOCK2)	u_2	t	Leave Service at Time (CLOCK3)	Server Idle Time
1.........	—	—	0	0	0	0	0.612	3	3	—
2.........	0.900	14	14	0	0	14	0.484	3	17	11
3.........	0.321	2	16	0	1	17	0.048	1	18	0
4.........	0.211	2	18	0	0	18	0.605	3	21	0
5.........	0.021	2	20	0	1	21	0.583	3	24	0
6.........	0.198	2	22	0	2	24	0.773	3	27	0
7.........	0.383	2	24	0	3	27	0.054	1	28	0
8.........	0.107	2	26	1	2	28	0.853	5	33	0
9.........	0.799	10	36	0	0	36	0.313	1	37	3
10.........	0.439	6	42	0	0	42	0.200	1	43	5

18. No idle time is experienced by the server between Units 2 and 3.

5. The simulation continues in the same manner until the desired number of arriving units have been generated, after which relevant operating characteristics can be estimated. The question of "How many units to simulate?" depends on factors relating to costs of implementing the simulation and variability in estimating operating characteristics such as mean length of the queue. This tradeoff will be considered in detail in Section 13.6.

6. Note that the length of the queue when a unit enters the system will be zero whenever CLOCK1 for the entering unit is *greater than* or *equal to* CLOCK2 for the immediately preceding unit; however, if CLOCK1 for the entering unit is *less than* CLOCK2 for the immediately preceding unit, then a queue which is at least 1 unit long must exist (as "viewed" by the entering unit). The exact length of the queue will equal the number of preceding CLOCK2's that are *greater than* the CLOCK1 for the entering unit. Right?

Time Flow Mechanisms

The simulation just described is classified as a **variable time increment** simulation because the clock which times the simulation is not changing by equal intervals of time. This simulation also can be labeled as a **next event** simulation because the simulation moves forward by the occurrence of "events." In this case events are based on the arrivals and departures of units, and the clock is updated by the amount of time necessary for the next event to occur. Alternatively, **fixed time increment** simulations proceed by equal increments of the clock. At each interval of time the system is scanned in order to record the occurrence or nonoccurrence of events. The DYNAMO simulation language which we described in the preceding section uses fixed time increments.

The choice of a **time flow mechanism** (fixed or variable) will affect the efficiency and cost of a particular simulation; hence, this represents a design issue which is nontrivial.[18]

Follow-up Exercises

12. Calculate the following operating characteristics for the queuing system of Table 13–7.

   a. Mean time in queue.
   b. Mean time in busy-system queue.
   c. Mean length of queue at entry.
   d. Mean length of queue weighted by the proportion of time the queue is at a given length. (Note: This is equivalent to L_q of Chapter 12 in the steady state.)
   e. Same as part d for busy-system queue.
   f. Mean time in system.
   g. Probability of an idle system. (Hint: Total clock time for the simulation is given by CLOCK3 of the last unit.)

13. Extend the simulation of Table 13–7 to 25 units and calculate the operating characteristics of the preceding exercise. (Note: Continue down columns 2 and 9 of Table 13–3.) Explain why these are more reliable estimates than those in the preceding exercise.

Multiserver Queuing System with State-Dependent Service Rates and Implicit Profits

We now describe the development of a general single queue-multiserver queuing model with two distinguishing characteristics: implicit (as opposed to accounting) profit as a criterion and service rates which can be modified behaviorally as a function of queue length. The stated criterion provides a desirable economic framework for retail establishments which incorporate both facility costs and waiting time (*implicit* or *opportunity*) costs, the latter by formulating an opportunity cost function in terms of customer waiting time. Additionally, functionally relating service times to queue lengths may have its behavioral justifications, especially for retail establishments having human beings as servers. For instance, longer queues may decrease the mean time of service, perhaps because of an increased level of dissonance or anxiety in the server which is induced by irate customers, superiors, or the realization that long queues encourage lost sales (there have been empirical studies which bear out these allegations).

For known revenue and opportunity cost distributions, the implicit revenue contribution of the ith customer can be expressed as

---

[18] See the references for greater detail on the cost implications of time flow mechanisms.

$$r_i = q_i - w_i \qquad (13.7)$$

where q is a variate of the random variable customer contribution to operating and overhead expenses (Q) or, alternatively, revenue from a sale less the cost of goods sold, and w is a variate of the random variable W, the opportunity cost ($W > 0$) or gain ($W < 0$).

A policy which creates ill will is said to represent an opportunity cost. Conversely, the creation of good will represents an opportunity profit (negative opportunity cost) to the firm. Ignoring variables such as courtesy, quality of service and merchandise and price differentials, we can see that the reality of impatient or pleased customers can be incorporated by expressing opportunity cost (W) as a function of the random variable waiting time in the queue.

For a specified time horizon, H, the total implicit revenue for K customers is

$$R_H = \sum_{i=1}^{K} r_i \qquad (13.8)$$

and the implicit profit, exclusive of overhead, is

$$P_H = R_H - \sum_{j=1}^{c} O_j \qquad (13.9)$$

where c is the number of servers in operation during H and O_j is the operating expense for the jth service station over H.

The objective is to determine a value for the decision variable c such that P_H is maximized. Since revenue contribution and marginal operating expenses are not treated as decision variables, the formulation implicitly assumes that product prices and factor costs are market-determined parameters.

The term **state-dependent service rate** refers to a service rate (customers per unit time) which is a function of the number of customers in the system (n). We incorporate this concept behaviorally as follows. Under "normal" operating conditions, a mean service time (time units per customer) for the jth service station, $E[t_j]$, is to be determined or assumed. Service time is to be a function of queue length (L) as defined by the following conditions:

1. The service time for the ith customer is to be modified by a *service time multiplier* (m) such that the resulting service time will be a variate from a distribution with mean

$$E[t_{ij}] = m_i E[t_j]; \qquad (13.10)$$

2. The range of m will be specified by an upper limit (v) and a lower limit (k) which represent, respectively, the maximum increase and decrease in mean service time multiples, $k \leq m \leq v$.
3. The "normal" service time $E[t_j]$ has been observed when L_N customers have been in the queue; that is, $m = 1$ when $L = L_N$.

The last two assumptions suggest the curve in Figure 13–7 for the

FIGURE 13-7

Service-Time Multiplier Function

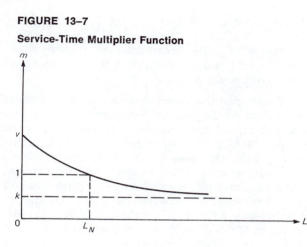

service-time multiplier function, which may be described as a modified exponential.[19]

Simulation Using GPSS

General Purpose System Simulation (GPSS) is a special purpose simulation language which is uniquely designed for implementing complex queuing simulations. Our intent is not to describe the simulation language itself, but rather to illustrate its convenient output.[20] The queuing system to be simulated is based on the model just described, according to the following conditions:

1. A multiserver retail establishment characterized by stationary exponential interarrival and service times $(M/M/c)$, where mean interarrival time is 6 minutes and mean service time is 20 minutes.
2. Around-the-clock operation of the firm.
3. First-come, first-served service discipline from a single queue.
4. Service times which are independent from customer expenditures.
5. Absence of balking and reneging.
6. Normally distributed revenue contributions with mean of $100 per customer and standard deviation of $20 per customer.
7. Operating cost per hour per service station of $100.
8. A positive opportunity cost which increases at a decreasing rate to a maximum of $100 as waiting time increases above 10 minutes and a negative opportunity cost which decreases (becomes more negative)

---

[19] Its mathematical function is given by $m = k + ab^L$, where a and b can be determined given v,k, and $(L_N,1)$.

[20] For details of the simulation language itself, see P. A. Bobillier, B. C. Kahan, and A. R. Probst, *Simulation with GPSS and GPSS V* (Englewood Cliffs, N.J.: Prentice-Hall, Inc., 1976), and G. Gordon, *The Application of GPSS V to Discrete System Simulation* (Englewood Cliffs, N.J.: Prentice-Hall, Inc., 1975).

at a decreasing rate to a minimum of $-\$50$ as waiting time decreases below 10 minutes.[21]

9. Maximum changes of ± 20 percent in mean service time (that is, $k = 0.8$ and $v = 1.2$) and normal service times at a queue length of five customers (that is, $L_N = 5$).

We might emphasize that the model described in the preceding section is in no way dependent on the specific conditions (1) through (6). Any specified service and arrival time distributions, empirical or theoretical, can be utilized. An $M/M/c$ queuing system was chosen for referencing (benchmarking). Should the assumption of 24-hour operation prove untenable, it would be an easy matter to reprogram the simulation. Such a procedure, while more realistic, necessitates replication runs and obviates a direct comparison with analytic steady-state solutions. Other conditions, such as multiple queues with specific selection heuristics, also can be programmed easily in GPSS. Should service times and customer expenditures exhibit covariation, a conditional probability distribution of service time given customer revenue contribution must be specified. Explicit balking and reneging can be programmed once the distributions are specified. If a space constraint is active, the likelihood of balking is certain (for example, parking lot filled). Finally, should expected interarrival times exhibit seasonal variations across time periods (that is, hourly, daily, and so on), it might be of benefit to so vary the arrival distribution. One possible way of accommodating this condition is not unlike the multiplier used in changing the service-time distribution. Given each seasonal arrival time multiplier (index), it would be a simple matter to modify the mean and/or variance of the distribution.

Figure 13–8 illustrates the type of output provided by a GPSS simulation. This particular run generated 25,000 arrivals into a five-server queuing system as previously described. The first part of the exhibit summarizes statistics for each server (facility). For example, the third server was busy 78.4 percent of the time, served 5,115 customers, and averaged 21.262 minutes to service each customer.[22] The second part provides summary statistics for the queue. The third part is a frequency distribution for "waiting time in the queue." This distribution is one of many which can be specified by the programmer. For example, the same computer run also provided frequency distributions for revenue contribution (Q), opportunity cost (W), total implicit revenue (R_H), service-time multiplier (m), service times, and total implicit profit (P_H).

Table 13–8 provides simulated statistics for 1,500 arrivals. The results indicate that the "optimal" number of servers is six, with an associated maximum total implicit profit of $126,000 over the time horizon.[23]

Table 13–9 summarizes some comparisons to theoretical steady-state predictions given by the analytic formulas of the standard $M/M/c$ model.

---

[21] To avoid unnecessary detail in the formulation, the specific functions for W have been omitted.

[22] In GPSS parlance, "entry" or "transaction" is synonymous with "customer" or "unit."

[23] The resulting GPSS "clock count" was 8,620, which gives an elapsed time horizon of 8,620 minutes, or approximately six days.

FIGURE 13-8

Partial GPSS Output*

FACILITY	AVERAGE UTILIZATION	NUMBER ENTRIES	AVERAGE TIME/TRAN
1	.872	5589	21.631
2	.838	5379	21.613
3	.784	5115	21.262
4	.723	4673	21.476
5	.666	4244	21.774

QUEUE	MAXIMUM CONTENTS	AVERAGE CONTENTS	TOTAL ENTRIES	ZERO ENTRIES	PERCENT ZEROS	AVERAGE TIME/TRANS	$AVERAGE TIME/TRANS
1	17	1.444	25000	12190	48.7	8.011	15.636

$AVERAGE TIME/TRANS = AVERAGE TIME/TRANS EXCLUDING ZERO ENTRIES

TABLE 2						
ENTRIES IN TABLE 25000		MEAN ARGUMENT 8.011		STANDARD DEVIATION 11.867		SUM OF ARGUMENTS 200299.000

UPPER LIMIT	OBSERVED FREQUENCY	PERCENT OF TOTAL	CUMULATIVE PERCENTAGE	CUMULATIVE REMAINDER	MULTIPLE OF MEAN	NON-WEIGHTED DEVIATION FROM MEAN
0	12190	48.75	48.7	51.2	-.000	-.675
5	3017	12.06	60.8	39.1	.624	-.253
10	2552	10.20	71.0	28.9	1.248	.167
15	1974	7.89	78.9	21.0	1.872	.588
20	1564	6.25	85.1	14.8	2.496	1.010
25	1235	4.93	90.1	9.8	3.120	1.431
30	814	3.25	93.3	6.6	3.744	1.852
35	569	2.27	95.6	4.3	4.368	2.274
40	429	1.71	97.3	2.6	4.992	2.695
45	286	1.14	98.5	1.4	5.616	3.116
50	147	.58	99.1	.8	6.240	3.538
55	123	.49	99.5	.4	6.864	3.959
60	51	.20	99.8	.1	7.488	4.380
65	26	.10	99.9	.0	8.112	4.802
70	19	.07	99.9	.0	8.736	5.223
75	2	.00	99.9	.0	9.361	5.644
80	1	.00	99.9	.0	9.985	6.066
85	1	.00	100.0	.0	10.609	6.487

REMAINING FREQUENCIES ARE ALL ZERO

* Source: Authors' computer run using GPSS/360/OS version 1, Program number 360A-CS-17X(VIMi).

TABLE 13-8

Results of GPSS Simulation

Number of Servers (c)	Mean Waiting Time for Those Who Waited (minutes)	Mean Service Time Multiplier ($\bar{m}$)	Total Implicit Revenue in $1,000 ($R_H$)	Total Implicit Profit in $1,000 ($P_H$)
3	84.1	0.88	43	-1
4	26.6	1.06	156	99
5	14.0	1.14	195	124
6*	9.5	1.17	212	126*
7	7.4	1.18	219	119
8	5.2	1.19	222	108
9	3.6	1.19	224	96
10	3.0	1.19	224	82

* Optimal solution.

TABLE 13–9

Comparisons of Theoretical Steady State and Simulations*

Number of Servers (c)	Waiting Time for Those Who Waited (minutes)			Average System Utilization		
	Theoretical Steady State	Value of m Fixed at Unity	Variable m	Theoretical Steady State	Value of m Fixed at Unity	Variable m
5.............	12.0	11.9	14.0	0.67	0.70	0.78
6.............	7.5	8.4	9.5	0.56	0.58	0.67
7.............	5.5	5.4	7.4	0.48	0.50	0.57

* Based on 1,500 arrivals.

When m is restricted to values of unity, the simulated model is identical to the standard $M/M/c$ model of Section 12.5. The "closeness" of the results is an indication of the validity of the simulation model (or of the analytic formulas, depending on your perspective).[24] Note the predictable effect on mean waiting time and mean system ultilization when average m is greater than one (that is, from Table 13–8, $\overline{m} = 1.14$, 1.17, and 1.18, respectively, when $c = 5,6,7$)—increased service times increase both utilization and waiting times.

Follow-up Exercises

14. Sketch the service rate multiplier function for the data in condition 9. Is the function conceptually reasonable? How might you go about designing a sampling plan for obtaining this function for, say, a state unemployment benefits agency with a numbering system for servicing potential recipients?

15. The literature on queuing theory defines two main approaches to handling the behavior of arrivals as a function of "number of customers presently in the system" (n): Modify the arrival rate as a function of n or specify balking and reneging probability distributions.

    a. Discuss how each might be incorporated in a simulation.
    b. Discuss the pros and cons of these approaches v. our opportunity cost approach.

16. With respect to Figure 13–8.

    a. Determine overall average utilization for the queuing system. Compare to Table 13–9. (Note the difference in number of generated customers.)

---

[24] Ignoring the existence of serial correlation in observed waiting times (as discussed in the next section), we see that analytic steady-state values were within 99-percent confidence limits about the sampled mean.

b. Identify consistencies in the generated statistics between the second and third parts of the output.

c. Estimate the following probabilities: of more than 17 customers in the queue; of spending 10 minutes or less in the queue; of spending more than 30 minutes in the queue; of going into service without having to wait in the queue; of waiting in the queue.

17. With respect to Table 13–8.

a. Describe the behavior of mean waiting time for those who waited as a function of number of servers. Is the function logical?
b. Describe the behavior of $\bar{m}$ as a function of c. Is the function logical? What maximum value for $\bar{m}$ is approached as $c \to \infty$?
c. Describe the behavior of R_H. Is the function logical?
d. Describe the behavior of P_H. Is the function logical?
e. Given an elapsed time horizon of 8,620 minutes and a cost of $100 per server per hour, confirm $P_H = \$126,000$ given $R_H = \$212,000$.

18. With respect to Table 13–9, confirm (for $c = 5$) the mean steady-state waiting time for those who waited using Equation (12.39) on page 473.

13.5 SIMULATION OF INVENTORY SYSTEM

Our next illustration of a stochastic simulation is that of a reorder point inventory system with probabilistic demands and lead times. Although the model is conceptually simple, analytic solutions are restrictive and not generally available.

Motivation for Simulating Inventory Systems

Inventory systems are simulated when analytic solutions are not possible. System conditions under which it is necessary to simulate include:

1. Stochastic demands *and* lead times characterized by specific probability distributions which may be theoretical or empirical.
2. Nonstationarities as when demands exhibit pattern or trend over time.
3. Nonlinearities and/or discontinuities in the cost functions which negate analytic solutions.
4. Elaborate or comprehensive systems (for example, constraints, multi-products, multiechelons, queuing considerations as in production-inventory systems, and so forth).

Extension of Reorder Point Inventory Model

As you may recall from Chapter 11, the reorder point model is concerned with estimating the reorder point (R) and reorder quantity (Q) which minimize the sum of average holding, ordering, and shortage costs per unit time. In this section we simulate a reorder point inventory model which incorporates both stochastic demands and stochastic lead times.

Tables 13–10 and 13–11 illustrate sample data for empirical probability distributions of demand per day (D), and days of lead time (T_L), respectively. As before, the assignments of random number ranges are based on the cumulative probabilities (CDF). Note that the random variates for D and T_L are approximated as class midpoints. Also, we assume that the given probability distributions typify the random behaviors of D and T_L, and are stationary.

Figure 13–9 and Table 13–12 describe the procedure for this type of inventory simulation. Carefully study these figures and relate them to one another. Note the following:

1. Holding cost for a given day (H) is based on the ending inventory (I) for that day as long as $I > 0$; that is, $H = C_h \cdot I$. If $I \leq 0$, then $H = 0$. Depending on the application, C_h could also be based on the beginning inventory or average inventory for the day.

2. Shortage cost for a given day (S) is strictly based on the *lost sales* for that day; that is, $S = C_s \cdot |I|$, when $I < 0$. If ending inventory for a given day is negative $(I < 0)$, then the beginning inventory for the next day is set to zero. (See Days 8, 11, and 16.) Thus, *backordering* is not allowed. Other models could base this cost on the number of outstanding backorders per day, in which case the unit of measurement on C_s is dollars per unit per day. Still other models could use a mixture of lost sales and backorders, if appropriate.

3. If the ending inventory for a given day is less than the reorder point (that is, if $I < R$), then an order for Q units is placed and an ordering cost (C_o) is incurred. At this point a random number for the lead time variate is generated to determine when the order is to be received. (See Days 3, 6, 9, 12, and 18.) For example, the order placed in Day 3 can be used in Day 5, since the lead time is two days. Note that only one order can be outstanding at any one time. Quantity discounts can be incorporated easily by making C_o a function of Q.

4. Beginning inventory is augmented by Q on the day an order is received. (See Days 5, 9, 12, and 17.)

5. If a random number exactly equals a class boundary, then the event corresponding to the lower class limit is assigned (See Day 20.) This occurrence is rare in actual practice (when using, say seven digits). For practical purposes, this slight bias may be ignored.

Note that Table 13–12 represents an illustration of a *20-day* simulation $(n = 20)$ for *specific* values of the decision variables $(R = 300, Q = 400)$. In an actual simulation, a greater number of days (sample size) would be needed to more accurately estimate the criterion mean total cost per day, $\overline{C} = \overline{H} + \overline{O} + \overline{S} = \$181 + \$5 + \$50 = \$236$. (Can you draw an analogy in assessing the balance of a coin in 10 flips v. 1000 flips?) Also, you should realize that the beginning inventory for Day 1 will affect cost calculations; however, this effect diminishes as n becomes larger. We discuss the tradeoff between sampling error and cost of implementation (sample size) in Section 13.6.

FIGURE 13–9

Logic for Inventory Simulation

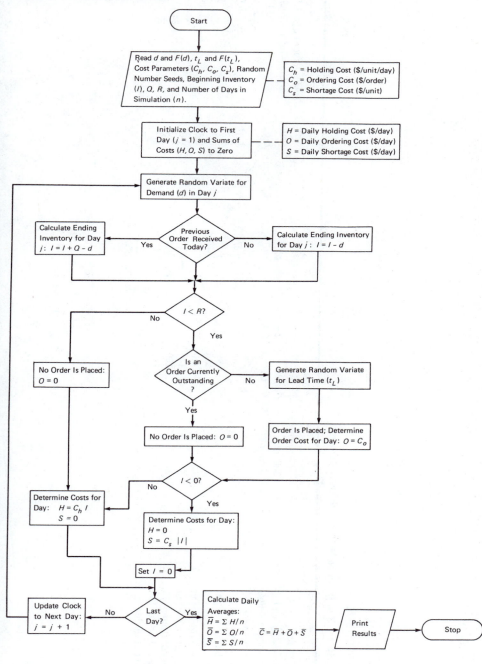

TABLE 13–10

Assignment of Random Numbers to Daily Demand

Number of Units Demanded Daily	Number of Days in Which Specified Demand Occurred	Random Variate for Demand (d)	pmf f(d)	CDF F(d)	Ranges of 0-1 Uniformly Distributed Random Number (u_i)
0 but under 50........	0	—	—	—	—
50 but under 70.......	24	60	0.07	0.07	0.00–0.07
70 but under 90.......	50	80	0.14	0.21	0.07–0.21
90 but under 110......	65	100	0.18	0.39	0.21–0.39
110 but under 130.....	103	120	0.29	0.68	0.39–0.68
130 but under 150.....	59	140	0.16	0.84	0.68–0.84
150 but under 170.....	41	160	0.11	0.95	0.84–0.95
170 but under 190.....	18	180	0.05	1.00	0.95–1.00
190 but under ∞	0	—	—	—	—
	360		1.00		

TABLE 13–11

Assignment of Random Numbers to Days of Lead Time

Number of Days between Placement and Receipt of Order	Number of Orders for Which Specified Lead Time Occurred	Random Variate for Lead Time (t_L)	pmf $f(t_L)$	CDF $F(t_L)$	Ranges of 0–1 Uniformly Distributed Random Number (u_2)
0............	0	—	—	—	—
1............	3	1	0.06	0.06	0.00–0.06
2............	10	2	0.20	0.26	0.06–0.26
3............	20	3	0.40	0.66	0.26–0.66
4............	10	4	0.20	0.86	0.66–0.86
5............	7	5	0.14	1.00	0.86–1.00
≥6...........	0	—	—	—	—
	50		1.00		

TABLE 13–12

Sample Inventory Simulation*

Day	Units of Beginning Inventory	Units Received (Q)	u for Demand (u₁)	Units of Demand (d)	Units of Ending Inventory	u for Lead Time (u₂)	Days of Lead Time (tₗ)	Holding Cost in $ (H)	Order Cost in $ (O)	Shortage Cost in $ (S)	Total Cost in $ (C)
1	500	0	0.104	80	420	—	—	420	0	0	420
2	420	0	0.223	100	320	—	—	320	0	0	320
3	320	0	0.241	100	220	0.150	2	220	20	0	240
4	220	0	0.421	120	100	—	—	100	0	0	100
5	100	400	0.375	100	400	—	—	400	0	0	400
6	400	0	0.779	140	260	0.465	3	260	20	0	280
7	260	0	0.995	180	80	—	—	80	0	0	80
8	80	0	0.963	180	0	—	—	0	0	500	500
9	0	400	0.895	160	240	0.483	3	240	20	0	260
10	240	0	0.854	160	80	—	—	80	0	0	80
11	80	0	0.289	100	0	—	—	0	0	100	100
12	0	400	0.635	120	280	0.930	5	280	20	0	300
13	280	0	0.094	80	200	—	—	200	0	0	200
14	200	0	0.103	80	120	—	—	120	0	0	120
15	120	0	0.071	80	40	—	—	40	0	0	40
16	40	0	0.510	120	0	—	—	0	0	400	400
17	0	400	0.023	60	340	—	—	340	0	0	340
18	340	0	0.010	60	280	0.399	3	280	20	0	300
19	280	0	0.521	120	160	—	—	160	0	0	160
20	160	0	0.070	80	80	—	—	80	0	0	80
Totals.........	4,040		—	2220	3620	—	—	3,620	100	1,000	4,720
Average.........	202		—	111	181	—	—	181	5	50	236

*For $R = 300$ units, $Q = 400$ units, $C_h = \$1$ per unit per day, $C_o = \$20$ per order, $C_s = \$5$ per unit, and initial inventory of 500 units; u_1 and u_2 taken from columns 1 and 3 of Table 13–3.

Interactive Computer Model

An actual simulation of the inventory model would be characterized both by an adequately large sample size and by the search for an "optimal" $R - Q$ combination; hence, it would be desirable to implement the simulation using a computer package which automatically allows the systematic evaluation of mean total cost $(\overline{C})$ based on specified $R - Q$ ranges. Figure 13–10 illustrates the I/0 for a time-shared version of the inventory model presented in this section. A chronological explanation of the I/0 follows.

The purpose of the random number seed has been explained previously, and the issue of "how many days of simulation" will be taken up subsequently. Inputs for the demand and lead time distributions are consistent with Tables 13–10 and 13–11. The costs ($C_s = \$5$ per unit, $C_h = \$1$ per unit per day, and $C_o = \$20$ per order) and the beginning inventory (500 units) are identical to those used in the "hand" simulation of Table 13–12.

Next, the user must specify appropriate ranges for R and Q. In effect, this means that ranges for R and Q must be indicated *within* which the (hopefully) *universal optimal* $R - Q$ will be found. "Quick-and-dirty" starting points are provided by the basic EOQ formula for Q,

$$Q^* = \left[\frac{2C_oE(D)}{C_h}\right]^{1/2}, \tag{13.11}$$

and by the *expected* demand between placement and receipt of an order for R,

$$R = E(D) \cdot E(T_L) \tag{13.12}$$

where $E(D) \equiv$ mean demand per unit time and $E(T_L) \equiv$ mean time between placement and receipt of an order. Note that Equation (13.11) will tend to be too low, as shortage costs are ignored. The estimate given by (13.12) should make sense in that the computation provides the expected demand between the placement and receipt of an order; hence, on the average, inventory will be at zero level when an order arrives.

From Tables 13–10 and 13–11, using the formula given by (A.12) on page 710, we get $E(D) = 117.2$ units per day and $E(T_L) = 3.2$ days. This gives $Q^* = 68$ units and $R \doteq 370$ units with Equations (13.11) and (13.12). Therefore, ranges of 0–700 for R and 100–700 for Q should be reasonable first approximations within which we might expect to find optimal $R - Q$, as shown in Figure 13–10.

Based on the first output matrix for $\overline{C}$, optimal R and Q are 400 and 300 units, respectively. This policy would cost a total of $233.20 per day, on the average. At this point, we can be reasonably certain that the "universal" minimum $\overline{C}$ has been "bracketed," rather than some "local" optimum. This is because 233.20 is "well-imbedded" in the matrix. That is, if you were to conceptualize the first cost matrix as a topographical map with "ridges" outlining a "valley," you can see that 233.20 is on the valley floor with high ridges all around the perimeter of the matrix. Right? Convince yourself that if we had specified ranges of 0–200 for R and

FIGURE 13-10

Computerized Inventory Simulation

Enter random number seed (any number)? 2001
How many simulations ?1000

What is the possible number of demands? 7

Enter the demand and associated cumulative probability, one pair
per line.

?60, .07
?80, .21
?100, .39
?120, .68
?140, .84
?160, .95
?180, 1.0

How many lead times are possible? 5

Enter the lead time and associated cumulative probability, one pair
per line

?1, .06
?2, .26
?3, .66
?4, .86
?5, 1.0

What is the shortage cost, holding cost, order cost, beginning
inventory?5, 1, 20, 500

What is the first reorder point, last one, and the step? 0, 700, 100

What is the first order quantity, last one, and the step? 100, 700, 100

Do you want a printout for the first few days (ans. yes or no)? no

Reorder			Quantities Ordered (Q)				
Points (R)	100	200	300	400	500	600	700
0	449.10	376.94	346.30	333.38	354.70	357.82	386.78
100	435.78	329.84	303.70	302.58	315.40	342.06	365.34
200	425.00	307.68	260.66	267.64	289.18	322.32	360.52
300	433.30	293.88	240.08	257.24	289.88	327.80	368.28
400	433.06	301.46	233.20	275.44	325.28	371.10	421.12
500	433.32	310.34	234.28	327.06	402.26	453.00	524.64
600	430.92	303.18	239.12	370.44	488.06	561.74	583.46
700	432.48	300.42	256.16	415.90	579.46	626.06	703.92

The lowest average total cost is $233.20 when R = 400, Q = 300.

FIGURE 13–10 (cont.)

Do you want to make any input changes (ans. yes or no)? yes

How many changes? 3

Choose the change (one at a time) and type in the corresponding number.

1 =#simulation, 2=#demands, 3=demand vs. cum.prob., 4=#lead times
5 = lead times vs. cum. prob., 6=costs and begin. inven., 7=reorder
points, 8=order quantities, 9=R.N. seed

?7

What is the first reorder point, last one, and the step? 250,550,50

?8

What is the first order quantity, last one, and the step? 250,350,50

?1

How many simulations? 5000

Any more changes (ans. yes or no)? no

Do you want a printout for the first few days (ans. yes or no)? no

Reorder	Quantities Ordered (Q)		
Points (R)	250	300	350
250	262.60	240.29	246.95
300	261.59	235.99	240.91
350	258.60	236.48	240.80
400	257.52	235.35	249.64
450	258.16	239.96	255.04
500	258.85	238.35	266.05
550	258.79	240.89	279.38

The lowest average total cost is $235.35 when R=400 and Q = 300.

Do you want to make any value changes (ans. yes or no)? no

Stop.

100–300 for Q, the minimum given by 260.66 would represent a local minimum, as suggested by its "hillside" location.

Now that we have located the approximate floor of the valley, we "zoom in" to get a better fix on optimal R and Q. The computer run continues by narrowing the ranges for R (250–550) and Q (250–350) and lowering the increments (steps) to 50 units instead of 100 units. Also note that the number of days in the simulation (n) has been increased from 1,000 to 5,000 in order to further reduce sampling error.

The results given by the second cost matrix indicate that the valley floor is fairly flat between 300 and 400 for R and 300 for Q. Thus, an optimal policy is suggested by $Q = 300$ paired with $R = 300$ to 400.

Follow-up Exercises

19. Modify the logic of Figure 13–8 and the data in Table 13–12 if

    a. C_s is based strictly on backorders which are subsequently filled, where $C_s = \$5$ per unit per day.

    b. Forty percent of shortages represent lost sales and 60-percent backorders, where C_s for lost sales is $5 per unit and C_s for backorders is $2 per unit per day;

    c. The mix of lost sales and backorders when units are short is probabilistic as shown:

Percent of Shortages Going to		
Lost Sales	Backorders	Probability
30%	70%	0.6
40	60	0.3
50	50	0.1

    Assume costs as in part (b). (Hint: You need a third random number generator. Use column 10 of Table 13–3. Note: When backorders are outstanding, the receipt of a shipment first satisfies backorders; hence, track must be kept of outstanding backorders.)

20. Find $\overline{C}$ for the simulation in Table 13–12 if

    a. $C_s = \$10$ per unit (C_h and C_o as in the example).

    b. $C_o = \$100$ per order (C_s and C_h as in the example).

    c. $C_h = \$1.50$ per unit per day (C_s and C_o as in the example).

    d. Beginning inventory for Day 1 is 1,500 units.

    How sensitive is $\overline{C}$ to each of these changes? Compare each to the optimal values of $\overline{C}$ in Table 13–13. Words of wisdom?

21. Continue the use of columns 1 and 3 in Table 13–3 to extend the simulation of Table 13–12 to 40 days. Do you have more confidence in $\overline{C}$? (Check your result against the result in Figure 13–10.)

22. Appropriately modify Table 13–12 for

    a. $R = 300$ and $Q = 700$.

    b. $R = 600$ and $Q = 400$.

    Check each result against the corresponding cell in the matrix of Figure 13–10. Comment on the differences in $\overline{C}$ estimates.

**Sensitivity Analysis Using Multiple Regression

Table 13–13 gives the behavior of *optimal* values of $\overline{C}$, R, and Q when cost parameters are varied as indicated. For each of the 12 cases the

TABLE 13–13

Sensitivity Data for Inventory Simulation

Run	Optimal $\overline{C}$ (1)	Optimal R (2)	Optimal Q (3)	Cost Parameters		
				C_s (4)	C_h (5)	C_o (6)
1........................	89.80	300	200	1	1	20
2........................	233.20	400	300	5	1	20
3........................	312.24	400	400	10	1	20
4........................	93.68	200	100	1	1.5	20
5........................	291.01	400	300	5	1.5	20
6........................	400.60	500	300	10	1.5	20
7........................	114.86	0	200	1	1	100
8........................	258.32	400	300	5	1	100
9........................	334.24	400	400	10	1	100
10........................	119.92	200	100	1	1.5	100
11........................	316.13	400	300	5	1.5	100
12........................	425.96	500	300	10	1.5	100

same random number seed (2,001) was used. Do you remember why? All other data were fixed as in Figure 13–10. Note that Run 2 corresponds to the result given in Figure 13–10.

Table 13–14 provides selected results of three separate multiple regression runs of the functional forms given by

$$\overline{C} = b_o + b_1 C_s + b_2 C_h + b_3 C_o \qquad \text{(Function 1, for data in columns 1, 4, 5, 6 of Table 13–13).}$$

$$R = b_o + b_1 C_s + b_2 C_h + b_3 C_o \qquad \text{(Function 2, for data in columns 2, 4, 5, 6 of Table 13–13).}$$

$$Q = b_o + b_1 C_s + b_2 C_h + b_3 C_o \qquad \text{(Function 3, for data in columns 3, 4, 5, 6 of Table 13–13).}$$

where b_o represents the intercept and b_1, b_2, and b_3 represent regression coefficients (slopes).[25]

The usefulness of multiple regression in assessing the results of sensitivity analysis is well illustrated here. For instance, the linear fit of Function 1 is highly "significant" (for example, multiple correlation = 0.95 and critical $F = 8.85$ for 3 degrees of freedom in the numerator and 8 in the denominator); however, looking at the t-values for each regression coefficient (noting that with 8 degrees of freedom and a 5-percent level of significance, the critical value of t is 2.31) shows that the *marginal* effect of C_s on optimal $\overline{C}$ is highly significant ($t = 9.85$), that of C_h on optimal $\overline{C}$ is marginally significant ($t = 2.35$), and that of C_o on optimal $\overline{C}$ is quite insignificant ($t = 1.15$). Furthermore, a \$1 change in C_s gives an average change of \$28.87 in optimal $\overline{C}$ (that is, $b_1 = 28.87$);

---

[25] At this time you might find it helpful to review Section A.6, page 726.

TABLE 13–14

Selected Regression Results for Inventory Simulation

	Independent Variables			Adjusted Multiple Coefficient of Correlation	F
	C_s	C_h	C_o		
Function 1 (optimal $\overline{C}$ as dependent variable)					
Regression coefficients........	28.87	101.55	0.31		
Standard errors...............	2.93	43.15	0.27	0.95	34.6
t-values.....................	9.85	2.35	1.15		
Function 2 (optimal R as dependent variable)					
Regression coefficients........	29.71	100.00	−0.62		
Standard errors...............	7.36	108.44	0.67	0.76	6.0
t-values.....................	4.04	0.92	−0.92		
Function 3 (optimal Q as dependent variable)					
Regression coefficients........	21.72	−133.33	0.00		
Standard errors...............	3.57	52.57	0.00	0.89	14.5
t-values.....................	6.08	−2.54	—		

a \$1 change in C_h results in a mean change of \$101.55 in optimal $\overline{C}$; and \$1 change in C_o yields an average change of \$0.31 in optimal $\overline{C}$.[26]

We leave the interpretations associated with the inventory decision (optimal $R - Q$ values) to a follow-up exercise. Note, however, that the shortage cost (C_s) has very strong influences on optimal values of $\overline{C}$, R, and Q. This implies that its estimation and use must be very carefully considered.

Follow-up Exercises

23. Fully interpret the regression results for optimal R and Q in Table 13–14. Note that, strictly speaking, the decision is bivariate (optimal R and Q) so that the separate treatment of each is an (gross?) over-simplification. More appropriate analyses for bivariate and multivariate criteria include response surface techniques and canonical correlation analysis.

24. If you're not familiar with **canonical correlation analysis, look up an introductory description of the philosophy, its use, and interpretation.[27]

---

[26] We might caution that all interpretations of marginal effects and "significance" are predicated on the assumption of linearity in the functional form of the regression equation; in many analyses, nonlinear forms may be warranted. Also, interpretations are limited to the space defined by the chosen ranges for C_s, C_h, and C_o.

[27] See, for example, P. E. Green and D. S. Tull, *Research for Marketing Decisions* (Englewood Cliffs, N.J.: Prentice-Hall, Inc., 1966), pp. 357–62.

Now find a computer package and apply canonical correlation to the data in Table 13–13. Let columns 2 and 3 (R and Q) represent the criterion variables and columns 4 through 6 ($C_s, C_h,$ and C_o) the predictor variables. Assess the overall "fit" and the importance of each predictor. Compare conclusions to those in Exercise 23.

13.6 **VALIDATION AND ESTIMATION

In this section we briefly discuss some "thorny" problems concerned with the validation of simulation experiments and the estimation of criteria and controllable variables. Our purpose here is simply to create an awareness of the pitfalls associated with simulation, particularly with respect to estimation. Familiarity (if not mastery) with the contents of Sections A.4 and A.5 (page 719) is assumed.

Validation

The process of validation seeks to answer the question "Does the simulation experiment accurately represent the problem environment?" Two aspects of this process can be identified: (1) *internal validation* with respect to logical and programming errors and (2) *external validation* with respect to the degree to which the experiment replicates the phenomenom in question.

Various means can be used to internally validate what we assume to be a computer program of the simulation model. For example, hand calculations can be compared to generated output under various conditions. Another popular procedure is to compare simulated results to analytic results which may be available. For instance, the service rate was held constant in the queuing simulation of Section 13.4 so as to compare simulated output with analytic predictions (Table 13–9). For the inventory problem of Section 13.5, demand and/or lead times can be held constant for comparisons to the analytic formulas in Chapter 11. (See Exercise 33.)

External validation creates both philosophical and practical problems. The former relates to the issue of "What is truth?" which may well be irreconcilable.[28] In contrast, the practical approach seeks to apply statistical tests to simulated data v. either historical data or future data (when it becomes available). For instance, a chi-square test (Section A.4) or other statistical tests can be performed to test the null hypothesis that simulated and actual data are from the same underlying distribution. Another approach for, say, time series data is to regress (Section A.6) generated data on actual data to test the null hypothesis that the population intercept equals 0 and the population slope equals 1. (See Exercise 34c.)

---

[28] See Naylor, *Computer Simulation Techniques,* for a brief discussion of various philosophical positions.

Sample Sizes and Simulated Probability Distributions

Monte Carlo simulations seek to artificially reproduce underlying probability distributions by the methods described earlier. A design issue immediately becomes evident: What size sample (n) should be taken to ensure a given degree of accuracy between simulated and theoretical observations? Prior to the experiment, the answer to this question usually takes the form of determining sample sizes (number of simulated observations) which provide sample statistics for estimating population parameters within specified maximum errors and confidence levels according to the Central Limit Theorem.

Table 13–15 illustrates calculations for means of the demand and lead time distributions of the inventory simulation in Section 13.5. Note the exponential increases in n as error decreases, which clearly illustrates the price you pay (in increased computer time) for greater accuracy in esti-

TABLE 13–15

Required Sample Size for 95-Percent Confidence and Specified Percentage Error in Estimating Means of Demand and Lead Time Distributions

	Demand (D)	Lead Time (T_L)
Estimated theoretical mean......................	117.2	3.2
Estimated theoretical standard deviation.........	31.0	1.1
Sample size (n) for 1% error......................	2,688	4,540
Sample size (n) for 5% error......................	108	182
Sample size (n) for 10% error.....................	27	46

Note: $E(D) = 117.2$ units and $E(T_L) = 3.2$ days were calculated using (A.12) on Tables 13–10 and 13–11, respectively; $\sigma_D = 31.0$ units and $\sigma_{T_L} = 1.1$ days were determined using the square root of (A.14) on the same tables; n was calculated using (A.45), although theoretically the standard deviation of the population should be known rather than estimated (a minor hindrance, when n is, say, above 50).

mating population parameters with sample statistics. In the initial set of simulations, sample sizes of 1,000 days were used, which provided approximately 2-percent maximum errors with 95-percent confidence in reproducing the assumed population means for demand and lead time.

Other approaches include the calculation of required n for maximum error and confidence in estimating the population standard deviation and the application of goodness-of-fit tests between the assumed theoretical probability distribution and the generated empirical probability distribution.

Estimation of Criteria

The estimation of criteria is beset with pitfalls for the statistically unwary. To illustrate what we mean, consider the results in Table 13–16 for estimating the criterion "mean total cost per day" in the inventory model of Section 13.5. Note that three sets of simulations (**replications**) have been run for each level of n by simply changing the random number seed and restarting the simulation under otherwise identical conditions. For example, three separate runs for 1,000 days of simulation gave values for

TABLE 13-16

Mean Total Cost per Day ($\overline{C}$) as a Function of Sample Size (n)

n	Three Replications of $\overline{C}$			Average $\overline{C}$ ($\overline{\overline{C}}$)	Unbiased Estimated Standard Error of $\overline{C}$ ($\hat{\sigma}_{\overline{C}}$)
25	228.80	256.80	218.40	234.67	19.80
100	257.00	250.20	217.60	241.60	21.06
500	250.16	243.84	246.84	246.95	2.74
1,000	230.82	242.04	239.52	237.46	5.89
2,000	242.09	242.45	241.55	242.03	0.45
5,000	241.84	242.36	235.35	239.85	3.90
10,000	242.31	242.47	242.19	242.32	0.14

Note: Results based on the computer model of Section 13.5 with $R = 400$, $Q = 300$, $C_s = 5$, $C_h = 1$, and $C_o = 20$.

$\overline{C}$ of 230.82, 242.04, and 239.52; the average of these three means gives a grand mean ($\overline{\overline{C}}$) of 237.46; and the unbiased estimated standard error of $\overline{C}$ is 5.89.[29]

The principle of **stochastic convergence** is well-illustrated by the column labeled $\overline{\overline{C}}$ and the plot of the first replication of $\overline{C}$ in Figure 13-11; that is, as the sample size increases the sample statistic ($\overline{C}$) converges about the *steady-state value* (which apparently is in the neighborhood of $242 per day). Furthermore, as predicted by (A.40) and verified by $\hat{\sigma}_{\overline{C}}$ in Table 13-16, variation about the expected value decreases as n increases. (The somewhat erratic behavior of $\hat{\sigma}_{\overline{C}}$ is a consequence of its being estimated by only three observations.) Also note that $\hat{\sigma}_{\overline{C}}$ could have been (and usually is) determined by directly calculating $\hat{\sigma}_C$ based on (A.42) for any one of the replications and then applying (A.40).

If a steady-state estimate of the criterion is desired, then care must be exercised so that **transient effects** do not confound the calculations. For instance, size of the initial inventory affects the calculation of $\overline{C}$ in the inventory model, and the starting length of a queue affects the estimation of the steady-state waiting time in a queuing simulation. By definition, in the steady state, succeeding observations of the criterion are time-independent; hence, the observations used to estimate the steady-state criterion should not exhibit correlation over time (termed **serial correlation**). One approach (of many) to this problem is to calculate a serial correlation coefficient for a block of the first k observations and test for significance. If significant, assume the first k observations are part of the transient phase and repeat the procedure on the *next* k observations by continuing the simulation at the point where it previously ended. This procedure is continued until the first block of k observations is found which accepts the null hypothesis of no correlaton. At this point, the k observations in that block can be used to estimate the steady-state criterion.

---

[29] Note that $\hat{\sigma}_{\overline{C}}$, the unbiased estimated standard error of the sampling distribution of $\overline{C}$, is directly estimated by applying Formula (A.42) to the three values and taking the square root.

FIGURE 13–11

Stochastic Convergence for the Inventory Problem

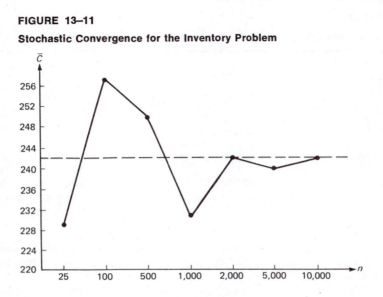

A more straightforward (but no less costly) approach is "reasonably" initializing values for the necessary parameters and variables and simulating until stochastic convergence is exhibited. The usual problem with this approach is that one may not know what "reasonable" (that is, near steady state) values to use. For the inventory problem, this approach works well because we can derive "ball park" figures based on simple analytic formulas; that is, $Q = 68$ and $R = 370$ based on Equations (13.11) and (13.12) suggested that a beginning inventory of 400 or 500 units would not be unreasonable. Therefore, we could rely on a long simulation to "wash out" transient effects. A glance at Table 13–16 or Figure 13–11 should confirm that stochastic convergence is in the neighborhood of 2,000 days of simulation, with an associated criterion of approximately $242 per day.

Because stochastic convergence is slow, its realization is costly in terms of computer time. For this reason, much research has centered on **variance reduction techniques,** which provide lower standard errors than the conventional approach for a given n. At present, however, there is no definitive answer to the problem of estimating steady-state criteria, although recent research shows promise.[30]

Assuming that the mean steady-state value of the criterion has been estimated in a manner which is free of transient effects, it is possible to establish a **confidence interval** based on (A.44). For the inventory simulation, with $n = 5,000$ and the first replication, we get

$$241.84 \pm (1.96)(3.90)$$
$$241.84 \pm 7.64,$$

---

[30] See F. S. Hillier and G. S. Lieberman, *Introduction to Operations Research* (San Francisco: Holden Day, Inc., 1974), pp. 641–48, for an illustration of estimation by the cycle method.

or 234.20 to 249.48 as the 95-percent confidence interval for the true mean total cost per day.[31]

Optimization

If a single criterion is being used and its optimization is desired, then the problem becomes one of finding optimal values for the decision variables. The output of a simulation (as measured by the criterion) is affected not only by (1) the controllable variables but also by (2) initial conditions, (3) randomness in the uncontrollable variables, and (4) values of parameters (for example, number of simulations, cost of carrying inventory, and so forth). Care, therefore, must be exercised in accounting for and isolating the effects of the last three factors.

The effects of initial conditions and parameters can be assessed by sensitivity analysis (as in Section 13.5) or by experimental design techniques such as analysis of variance; transient and steady-state phases can be approximated by varying the length of the simulation; and sampling error can be estimated and controlled by properly manipulating the random number seed. In the latter case, replications under the same conditions, except for the setting of the random number seed, allow for an estimation of sampling error, as demonstrated in Table 13–16. Alternatively, by fixing the random number seed and varying some other factor, the random effect can be controlled or eliminated. For example, differences in the cost criterion for each cell in Figure 13–10 are due strictly to changes in R and Q since the random number seed was initialized to the same value for each $R - Q$ combination.

In an experimental framework, the use of a **search procedure** (Chapter 10) is typical for finding optimal values of the decision variables. For a single controllable variable with a reasonable number of finite alternatives, you can simply **enumerate** for the optimal solution, as shown in Table 13–8. If the simulation includes two controllable variables, then a **visual grid or lattice** can be used, as illustrated by Figure 13–10. For more than two controllable variables, **response surface** techniques are appropriate. These techniques sequentially (iteratively) search for the optimum by applying sets of mathematical decision rules, whereby each iteration determines the manner in which the decision variables must change to move in the "direction" of the optimum.[32]

We conclude with two words of caution once you think you have found an optimal solution. First, the optimal point may be "local" and not "global." For the queuing and inventory examples, the criteria appear to be "well-behaved," which suggests a global extremum for each. Second,

---

[31] If transient effects are considered relevant to estimation, then the standard error is affected by serial correlation, in which case a formula other than (A.40) must be used. See H. M. Wagner, *Principles of Operations Research* (Englewood Cliffs, N.J.: Prentice-Hall, Inc., 1975), p. 923.

[32] See R. C. Meier, W. T. Newell, and H. L. Pazer, *Simulation in Business and Economics* (Englewood Cliffs, N.J.: Prentice-Hall, Inc., 1969), and J. W. Schmidt and R. E. Taylor, *Simulation and Analysis of Industrial Systems* (Homewood, Ill.: Richard D. Irwin, Inc., 1970), for straightforward illustrations of selected search techniques.

the estimated criterion represents a point estimate for the true criterion; hence, sampling error should be accounted for by either constructing confidence intervals or testing for significant differences among points in the vicinity of the derived optimum (as in Exercise 32).

Follow-up Exercises

25. Calculate the mean, $E(D)$, and variance, $V(D)$, for demand from Table 13–10 and compare to your calculations of the sampled mean $(\bar{d})$ and unbiased variance $(\hat{\sigma}_D^2)$ in Table 13–12. Is $E(D)$ within a 95-percent confidence interval constructed from $\bar{d}$ and $\hat{\sigma}_D^2$ and based on the t-distribution?

26. Same as Exercise 25 for the random variable lead time (T_L).

27. Confirm the sample size calculations in Table 13–15 for (a) demand and (b) lead time. Note that E in (A.45) is absolute error, not percent error; that is, $E =$ (percent error $\div$ 100) $\cdot$ (assumed theoretical mean).

28. Confirm the results for $\bar{\bar{C}}$ and $\hat{\sigma}_{\bar{C}}$ in Table 13–16 for $n = 1,000$.

29. Calculate the 95-percent confidence interval for the true mean total cost when $n = 10,000$ (Table 13–16). Does it make sense that this interval is narrower than the interval we calculated for $n = 5,000$? Why? Why do you think it's a narrower interval for $n = 2,000$ than for $n = 5,000$?

30. Determine the 95-percent confidence interval for true $\bar{C}$ based on the simulation in Table 13–12. In words explain the meaning of this interval. Is the mean cost in Figure 13–10 for $R = 300$ and $Q = 400$ within this interval?

31. Same as Exercise 30 for the simulation in Exercise 21. Is this interval more narrow than the one in Exercise 30? Explain.

32. With respect to the second grid in Figure 13–10 (for $n = 5,000$):

   **a. Treat each cell mean as a single observation and perform a two-way analysis of variance to assess the effects of Q and R on the criterion. Conclusions?

   b. Suppose the unbiased sample standard deviation for C (that is, $\hat{\sigma}_c$) associated with each cell has been calculated as $200 per day (in actual practice it would differ from cell to cell). Construct the 95-percent confidence interval for true $\bar{C}$ predicted by each cell mean. Conclusion relating to the $R - Q$ combination(s) associated with optimal $\bar{C}$?

   **c. Test the null hypothesis of no difference between the means of cells (4, 2) and (3, 2); cells (4, 2) and (1, 2); cells (4, 2) and (4, 1); cells (4, 2) and (5, 3). Use a 0.05 level of significance and assume that $\hat{\sigma}_c = 200$ for each cell.

   Conclusion relating to the $R - Q$ combination(s) associated with optimal $\bar{C}$?

33. Validate the inventory simulation using appropriate analytic formulas from Chapter 11 given the following simulated results based on 5,000 simulations when demand is fixed at 120 per day, lead time is fixed

at one day, the cost of ordering is $500, and the holding cost is $0.48 per unit per day:

Total Cost

R \ Q	450	500	550
120	247.20	242.62	248.51
140	258.03	250.13	255.33
160	258.03	252.61	255.33

**34. Test the null hypothesis that a simulated criterion is consistent with the actual criterion given the data below.

	Time Period									
	1	2	3	4	5	6	7	8	9	10
Actual....................	10	12	15	20	18	17	24	28	30	25
Simulated...............	8	14	12	17	20	19	23	30	32	27

Use a 0.05 level of significance and the following statistical tests:

a. *Matched t*-test.
b. Wilcoxon (rank-sum) test.
c. Regression of simulated criterion (dependent variable) on actual criterion (independent variable). (Test the null hypotheses of zero population intercept using $t = a/\hat{\sigma}_a$ and of unit population slope using $t = (b - 1)/\hat{\sigma}_b$; look up formulas for the estimated standard errors $\hat{\sigma}_a$ and $\hat{\sigma}_b$.) Comment on the results.

SELECTED REFERENCES

Bobillier, P. A.; Kahan, B. C.; and Probst, A. R. *Simulation with GPSS and GPSS V*. Englewood Cliffs, N.J.: Prentice-Hall, Inc., 1976.

Carlson, J. G. H., and Misshauk, M. J. *Introduction to Gaming: Management Decision Simulations*. New York: John Wiley & Sons, Inc., 1972.

Dutton, J. M., and Starbuck, W. H. *Computer Simulation of Human Behavior*. New York: John Wiley & Sons, Inc., 1971.

Emshoff, J. R., and Sisson, R. L. *Design and Use of Computer Simulation Models*. London: The Macmillan Co., 1970.

Forrester, J. W. *Industrial Dynamics*. Cambridge, Mass.: M.I.T. Press, 1961.

————. *Urban Dynamics*. Cambridge, Mass.: M.I.T. Press, 1969.

————. *World Dynamics*. Cambridge, Mass.: M.I.T. Press, 1971.

Frazer, J. R. *Business Decision Simulation: A Time Sharing Approach*. Reston, Va.: Reston Publishing Co., Inc., 1975.

Gordon, G. *System Simulation*. Englewood Cliffs, N.J.: Prentice-Hall, Inc., 1969.

————. *The Application of GPSS V to Discrete System Simulation*. Englewood Cliffs, N.J.: Prentice-Hall, Inc., 1975.

Hillier, F. S., and Lieberman, G. J. *Introduction to Operations Research.* San Francisco: Holden Day, Inc., 1974.

Maisel, H., and Gnugnoli, G. *Simulation of Discrete Stochastic Systems.* Chicago: S.R.A., Inc., 1972.

McMillan, C., and Gonzalez, R. F. *Systems Analysis.* Homewood, Ill.: Richard D. Irwin, Inc., 1973.

Meadows, D. H. et al. 2d ed. *The Limits to Growth.* New York: Universe Books, 1972.

Meier, R. C.; Newell, W. T.; and Pazer, H. L. *Simulation in Business and Economics.* Englewood Cliffs, N.J.: Prentice-Hall, Inc., 1969.

Mesarovic, M., and Pestel, E. *Mankind at the Turning Point.* New York: E. P. Dutton & Co., Inc./Reader's Digest Press, 1974.

Mize, J. H., and Cox, J. G. *Essentials of Simulation.* Englewood Cliffs, N.J.: Prentice-Hall, Inc., 1968.

Naylor, T. H. et al. *Computer Simulation Techniques.* New York: John Wiley & Sons, Inc., 1966.

Schmidt, J. W., and Taylor, R. E. *Simulation and Analysis of Industrial Systems.* Homewood, Ill.: Richard D. Irwin, Inc., 1970.

Vollmann, T. E. *Operations Management.* Reading, Mass.: Addison-Wesley Publishing Co., 1973.

Wagner, H. M. *Principles of Operations Research.* Englewood Cliffs, N.J.: Prentice-Hall, Inc., 1975.

Wheelwright, S. C., and Makridakis, S. G. *Computer Aided Modeling for Managers.* Reading, Mass.: Addison-Wesley Publishing Co., 1972.

ADDITIONAL EXERCISES

35. *Simulation of Dependent Variables* For the inventory model of Section 13.5, consider the case where the random variable D, "number of units demanded per day," is determined by the random variable Y, "unit price in dollars," where Y fluctuates daily based on factors beyond the control of our firm. Thus, we have a compound experiment with two statistically dependent events: First, a random variate of Y is generated for the day; next, based on the value of Y, a random variate from the appropriate distribution of D is generated.

   a. Run a 20-day simulation as in Table 13–12 given the probability distributions below:

		If Y = 5		If Y = 6		If Y = 7	
y	f(y)	d	f(d|Y = 5)	d	f(d|Y = 6)	d	f(d|Y = 7)
5	0.5	120	0.20	60	0.07	40	0.05
6	0.3	140	0.35	80	0.14	50	0.20
7	0.2	160	0.25	100	0.18	60	0.40
		180	0.10	120	0.29	70	0.25
		200	0.07	140	0.16	80	0.10
		220	0.03	160	0.11		
				180	0.05		

Note: In Table 13–3 use columns 7, 8, and 9 to generate Y, D, and T_L, respectively.

b. Can you think of an alternative procedure for generating D without first having to generate Y? (Hint: Determine the *marginal* distribution of D utilizing the Rules of Multiplication and Addition.) Is this approach theoretically equivalent to the approach in part (a)?

36. *Patterned Behavior* As you might recall from Appendix A, the relative definition of probability requires that trials in the random experiment be as uniform as possible. This means, for example, that the probability distribution of demands exhibited in Table 13–10 must be free of identifiable irregularities and patterned behavior over time. By patterned behavior we mean the existence of trend, seasonal, and cyclical effects, or factors which can cause serial correlation.

a. Suppose demand for the inventory problem exhibits stationary seasonal patterns by day of the week, with Monday through Friday seasonal indices of 0.8, 1.1, 0.9, 1.2, and 1.0, respectively (assuming a five-day week). Since the data in Table 13–10 have been deseasonalized, it is necessary to appropriately adjust (that is, seasonalize) the random variate once it has been generated. For example, assuming Day 1 in Table 13–12 represents Monday, we note that the demand of 80 is deseasonalized; hence, it must be seasonalized by its appropriate seasonal index to $(0.8) \cdot (80)$, or 64. Rework the simulation in Table 13–12 by seasonalizing each demand. Do you expect that steady-state $\overline{C}$ will be affected? Do you expect that the timing of orders will be affected?

b. Suppose that, in addition to being seasonal, demand exhibits a simple linear trend of +5 units per day. In other words, the data in Table 13–10 have been detrended to the present by the time series model

$$\hat{y}_t = 117.2 + 5t,$$

where t represents the number of days from time zero. (Note that the intercept of 117.2 turns out to be the mean of the probability distribution for D. Right?) This means, for example, that Monday's ($t = 1$) generated demand of 80 must be adjusted for trend to 85 and then seasonalized to $(0.8) \cdot (85)$, or 68; Tuesday's ($t = 2$) demand becomes $(1.1) \cdot [100 + (5) \cdot (2)]$, or 121; Wednesday's ($t = 3$) demand becomes $(0.9) \cdot [100 + (5) \cdot (3)]$, or 104; and so forth. Rerun the simulation in Table 13–12 by incorporating both trend and seasonal factors. What effect does trend have with respect to the interpretation of mean total cost ($\overline{C}$)? (Hint: Is steady state achievable?)

37. *Port Facility Management* Consider a port with a single dock that can unload a specialized type of cargo off of a freighter. Frequency distributions based on 100 freighters are given in the accompanying table, as determined empirically by a "hotshot" OR consultant.

Times between Arrivals of Successive Freighters (hours)	Frequency	Times to Unload Freighter (hours)	Frequency
5 but under 15	30	0 but under 12	40
15 but under 25	25	12 but under 24	25
25 but under 35	20	24 but under 36	16
35 but under 45	15	36 but under 48	9
45 but under 55	10	48 but under 60	6
		60 but under 72	4

Freighters are unloaded on a first-come first-served basis. Moreover, the port operates around the clock.

a. Initialize the number of units in the system to zero and simulate this port facility for 20 arrivals. Use columns 1 and 2 in Table 13–3, respectively, for the two probability distributions. Calculate the operating characteristics described in Exercise 12.

b. Assuming that the assumptions for the standard $M/M/1$ queuing model are valid for this port facility, calculate the steady-state operating characteristics determined in part (a) by using appropriate analytic formulas from Chapter 12. Are the two sets of calculations consistent? Comment on reasons for any divergences. (Hint: First you must calculate mean interarrival and mean service times using Formula [A.12]. Then, you must determine λ and μ using Formula [A.33].)

c. Initialize the simulation in part (a) to six freighters in the port facility (five waiting to be unloaded and one just starting to unload). Simulate 20 arrivals and calculate operating characteristics. Are these closer to the theoretical operating characteristics determined in part (b)? Comment. (Note: The first six service times must be assigned to the initial freighters in the port.)

**d. Use appropriate statistical tests to test the null hypothesis that the probability distributions are exponential. (Hint: See Appendix A.) What other assumptions need to be realized for the $M/M/1$ model to hold? Of these, what assumptions are necessary for the simulation to be a valid representation of reality?

38. Construct a flow chart of the type given in Figure 13–8 for the $GI/G/1$ simulation in Section 13.4. Make sure that a variable name is assigned to each column of Table 13–7.

39. *Coin Flip Game*—Sharpie, a long-time resident of Las Vegas, has proposed a game to Orsa, the "budding" collegian who is the offspring of a prominent OR analyst (unknown to Sharpie, of course).

Sharpie: I have a game you can't refuse.

Orsa: O yeah?

Sharpie: Yeah. You flip a coin until the difference between the number of heads and the number of tails reaches three.

Orsa: What kind of bread are we talking about?

Sharpie: Well, you pay me $1 for each flip. When the game ends I pay you $8. O.K.?

Orsa: (Skeptical) Well, I'll tell you what. Give me a few minutes to interact with my computer terminal and then I'll get back to you.

Sharpie: (Doubtful) Well, O.K.

How sharp is Sharpie? (Hint: Define a criterion in terms of an appropriate random variable which must be estimated and, using random numbers, simulate ten games. You wouldn't be so crass as to use a real coin, would you?) Identify some statistical issues in estimating the criterion.

40. *Emergency Room* Design a simulation for the emergency room of Gotham City Hospital as described in Exercise 3 of Chapter 1 (page 14). Use five-minute *fixed time increments*. Assume one queue and the ability of the emergency room to treat ten patients at one time. Use

column 6 of Table 13–3 to simulate arrivals and column 7 to simulate treatment times. Assume an empty emergency room at the beginning of the simulation and simulate for one hour (12 time periods). For simplicity, assume that treatment for any patient arriving during a time interval starts at the beginning of the time interval, which is the same as saying that patients arrive at the beginning of an interval. In your simulation table keep track of "number in system," "number in queue," and "number of idle servers," all defined at the *end* of a time interval.

Theoretically, what do you expect will happen in this system as time approaches infinity? How many "servers" would be needed to avert this theoretical happening? What factors in reality prevent this theoretical happening? In your simulation, indicate how you would handle 15 "servers." Will this increase in the number of servers improve operating characteristics? Explain.

41. *Solar Energy Collection System* A solar energy collection system consists of four basic components: solar collection panels, thermal energy storage tank, thermal distribution system, and control system. The ability to provide the energy needs for a particular building or house is determined by the design configuration of the system (that is, area and efficiency of collectors, quality of control system, size and efficiency of storage tank, design and efficiency of distribution system) and by uncontrollable variables such as ambient temperatures and amount of sunlight. Meteorological data for the month of January in a particular geographical region are given here.

Percent Amount of Sunlight per Day	Probability	Average Ambient Temperature per Day (°F)	Probability
0	0.25	0	0.10
20	0.20	10	0.30
40	0.25	20	0.40
60	0.10	30	0.15
80	0.05	40	0.05
100	0.15		

A contractor for a large housing development is considering the installation of thermal collection systems in houses which are essentially similar with respect to construction and living area. Two designs are under consideration, each differing with respect to amortized cost per day of the system and cost per day of providing supplementary energy needs. This latter cost is a reality because solar energy systems may not be capable of providing 100 percent of the energy needs every day, in which case an auxiliary conventional heating system supplements the solar system. Relevant cost data are given in the accompanying table. Can

Design	Amortized Cost per Day ($)	Supplementary Heating Cost per Day* ($)
1	1.00	$\dfrac{30}{T_i + 0.5\,T_{i-1}} + \dfrac{20}{10 + S_i + 0.4\,S_{i-1}}$
2	1.50	$\dfrac{30}{T_i + 0.8\,T_{i-1}} + \dfrac{20}{20 + S_i + 0.7\,S_{i-1}}$

* S_i = Percent sunlight in day i; T_i = average °F in day i.

you reason out why weather factors in the preceding day have an effect on the current day's supplementary heating cost? How are the efficiencies of each design accounted for in the costs?

a. Estimate the average total cost per day in January for each design given that on December 31 the average temperature is 20° F and the average percent sunlight is 50 percent. (Use columns 1 and 2 of Table 13–3 for variates of S and T, respectively.) Recommendation?

**b. Determine a 95 percent confidence interval for the average total cost of each design. (Ignore serial correlation in supplementary heating costs.) Conclusion?

42. *Stock Market Investment Strategy* Adam Smith, Jr., is an up-and-coming investor. (It runs in the family.) For many trading days he has observed the closing price (per share) behavior of a particular stock that

Price Change Any Given Day to Nearest $1	Price Change the Following Day			
	Down $1	Same	Up $1	Up $2
Down $1	0.4	0.3	0.2	0.1
Same	0.3	0.3	0.3	0.1
Up $1	0.2	0.4	0.2	0.2
Up $2	0.3	0.4	0.2	0.1

he has taken a fancy to, as depicted above. Adam's parents have just given him 100 shares of this very same stock, which currently closed up $1 at $20 a share. This gift, however, is not without a very specific condition: Adam must cash in his shares at the end of 30 days, as the cost realized from this sale will become his expense money for his first year in college. Needless to say, Adam is concerned with having a good (extracurricular) time his first year in college, so he has devised an investment strategy which "can't lose," as follows:

1. Sell all shares owned at the end of a trading day whenever the price of the stock increases.
2. Buy as many shares as cash allows whenever the price of the stock has declined at the end of a trading day.
3. Do nothing if price remains the same.

a. Simulate Adam's cash position at the end of 30 days given that 1 percent of the price of each share goes to the broker as commission whenever shares are bought or sold. Use column 6 of Table 13–3.

b. Would Adam have been better off at the end of 30 days if he had just let the shares "ride," while spending his time at the beach?

c. Can you think of other investment strategies?

**d. Discuss the statistical implications associated with estimating cash position.

43. *Accounting Simulation*[33] A firm wishes to predict the status of certain items in its financial structure one year from now. Specifically, it would like to know what its acid test ratio (the sum of cash plus accounts receivable divided by accounts payable), cash balance, accounts receivable, and accounts payable will be if current sales and credit patterns prevail and if current inventory and financial policies are maintained.

Merchandise is sold both for cash and on credit. Cash and credit sales

---

[33] Adapted from the seminar "Monte Carlo Simulation for Financial Analysis," Executive Development Program, University of Cincinnati, 1970.

vary from month to month, but these variations are not attributable to seasonal or cyclical factors. Rather, they reflect the influence of essentially chance or random forces. Analysts know that the basic factors underlying these chance variations have remained stable over the past several years and believe that they will not change significantly over the coming year. The accompanying table shows these variations.

Cash Sales (millions of dollars per month)	Probability	Credit Sales (millions of dollars per month)	Probability
3	0.5	6	0.1
4	0.3	7	0.2
5	0.1	8	0.4
6	0.1	9	0.2
		10	0.1

Each month, a certain percentage of the preceding month's accounts receivable (resulting entirely from credit sales) is collected. The next table shows the firm's credit payment experience over the past several years.

Percentage of Preceding Month's Accounts Receivable Collected in Current Month	Probability
0.1	0.1
0.2	0.2
0.3	0.4
0.4	0.2
0.5	0.1

As part of its inventory policy, the firm finds it desirable to begin each month with an inventory level equal to a retail valuation of $16 million. Since inventory is obtained from outside vendors, and since the *markup* on each item is 20 percent of the selling price, the firm makes *purchases* at the end of each month which amount to 80 percent of that month's total dollar sales. These purchases are paid in full at the end of the next month. If the cash balance is not adequate for this purpose, the deficit is carried over to the next month under accounts payable and paid off then, if cash funds are sufficient then. Carryovers to succeeding month's accounts payable continue as long as the cash balance remains inadequate. As a matter of policy, the firm pays cash dividends of $500,000 every third month.

At the beginning of the first month, the retail value of inventory is $16 million, the cash balance is $5 million, accounts receivable are $10 million, and accounts payable are $2 million.

a. Conduct a 12-month simulation by completing a table with the following headings: Month, Random Number for Cash Sales, Cash Sales, Random Number for Credit Sales, Credit Sales, Total Sales, Random Number for Percentage of Preceding Month's Accounts Receivable Collected, Percentage of Preceding Month's Accounts Receivable Collected, Preceding Month's Accounts Receivable Collected, Total Cash Inflow, Purchases, Dividends, Total Cash Outflow, Beginning Cash Balance, Ending Cash Balance, Accounts Receivable,

Accounts Payable, Acid Test Ratio. (Use columns 8, 9 and 10 of
Table 13–3, respectively, to generate the three random number sequences.)

b. What happens to the financial structure if the inventory policy is
changed to beginning inventories of $12 million? (Note: If total sales
for a month exceed beginning inventory, then assume that the difference is lost to credit sales.)

c. What happens to the financial structure if the markup is changed to
30 percent? (What else must you assume?)

d. Do you have statistical confidence in your estimates? Explain.

**44. Write a computer program for one of the following in order to facilitate
sensitivity analyses and larger sample sizes.

a. Exercise 37.
b. Exercise 39.
c. Exercise 40.
d. Exercise 41.
e. Exercise 42.
f. Exercise 43.

APPENDIX: PROCESS GENERATION OF EXPONENTIAL AND POISSON RANDOM VARIATES

In this appendix we illustrate methods of generating random variates
from exponential and Poisson processes. The general approach typifies
the treatment of process generation for many other theoretical probability
distributions. We repeat that computer subroutines are widely available
for process generation of standard probability distributions.

If X is an exponential random variable with parameter λ, then its pdf
is given by

$$f(x) = \lambda e^{-\lambda x}, x \geq 0. \tag{1}$$

Its CDF, therefore, is given by

$$\begin{aligned}
F(x) &= P(X \leq x) \\
&= \int_0^x f(x)dx \\
&= \int_0^x \lambda e^{-\lambda x}dx \\
&= -e^{-\lambda x}\big|_0^x \\
&= 1 - e^{-\lambda x}.
\end{aligned} \tag{2}$$

Letting $F(x) = u$, where u is a random variate in the interval $(0, 1)$,
and noting that we wish to express x as a function of u when using the
ITM, then from Equation (2):

$$\begin{aligned}
u &= 1 - e^{-\lambda x} \\
e^{-\lambda x} &= 1 - u \\
-\lambda x \ln e &= \ln(1 - u)
\end{aligned}$$

$$x = \frac{-\ln(1 - u)}{\lambda}. \tag{3}$$

Note that the right-hand–side expression in Equation (3) represents
$F^{-1}(u)$. Thus, given the ability to generate uniformly distributed random

variates in the interval 0 to 1 as represented by u, exponential random variates of X are easily determined using (3).

If X is Poisson with parameter λ, then it can be proved that the continuum (for example, time) between any two Poisson occurrences is exponential with the same parameter λ. For example, if the number of arrivals per unit time (X) in a queuing process is Poisson with mean λ, then the time between successive arrivals (S) is exponential with mean $1/\lambda$ (or parameter λ). Now, if x Poisson arrivals occur over some arbitrary number of unit time intervals (t), then the sum of times between the x arrivals *must be* less than t. If s_i represents the time between arrivals $(i-1)$ and i, then the following must be true:

$$\sum_{i=1}^{x} s_i \le t < \sum_{i=1}^{x+1} s_i. \tag{4}$$

Thus, Poisson random variates (x) with parameter λ can be generated by summing exponential random variates (s_i) until (4) is satisfied. Note that s_i is based on (3); that is,

$$s_i = \frac{-\ell n(1 - u_i)}{\lambda}$$

where u_i is the ith 0–1 uniform random variate.

Follow-up Exercises

45. Is

$$F^{-1}(u) = \frac{-\ell n\ u}{\lambda}$$

as valid as (3) for generating exponential random variates? Why or why not?

46. Using the u's in Table 13–2, determine x for the 10–11 period if X is Poisson with $\lambda = 2.1$ patients per hour (as in Table A–1 or Example 12.1) and $t = 1$. What if $t = 2$?

47. Suppose that the random variable X represents the time to service an emergency room patient, as in Examples A.3 and 12.1. Given that X is exponential with parameter $\lambda = 2.5$ patients per hour, simulate the times required to treat five patients using the first five random numbers in column 3 of Table 13–3.

48. Carry out the simulation in part (a) of Exercise 37 by assuming that interarrival times and service times are exponential with parameters $\lambda = 0.04$ and $\mu = 0.0468$, respectively. How is this procedure advantageous over the procedure in Exercise 37?

49. Determine $F^{-1}(u)$ if X is uniform in the interval (a, b).

14

Project Management and Other Network Models

THE KEY to implementing change in many organizations is to clearly delineate projects; to determine the detailed activities necessary to complete a particular project, to estimate the resources and times required for each activity, to plan start and completion times for each activity, to prepare a schedule of resource needs (especially labor) over the life of the proposed project, to commit the resources (from within the organization and outside it) to specified time periods, and to monitor and control time and cost performance for the project.

In this chapter we present some models which are well-suited to the design and implementation of major projects. Variations of these models have been successfully applied in the construction of large buildings or public works, in military research and development programs, and in the development and introduction of new products, to name a few. We also deal with some important organizational issues for users of project management models, and we include an Appendix on the use of mathematical programming for solving these models.

Although the majority of this chapter deals with project management models, these are but a subset of a general class of models called network models. At the end of the chapter we overview the framework of network models and discuss three classic network problems.

14.1 PLANNING WITH THE BASIC MODEL

Two fundamental analytic techniques were proposed in the late 1950s for planning, scheduling, and controlling complex projects: **Performance**

Evaluation and Review Technique (PERT) and **Critical Path Method (CPM).** Although the techniques were developed concurrently and independently, they were surprisingly similar. Aside from minor differences in terminology, notation, and structure, only two major differences usefully distinguished the two methods. First, PERT acknowledged uncertainty in the times to complete activities, while CPM did not. Second, PERT restricted its attention to the time variable, whereas CPM included time-cost tradeoffs. For our purposes we will not differentiate between the two methods, as subsequent developments have blurred the distinctions between them.

Example 14.1 Choo-Chew Restaurants, Inc., or CCRI

The most straightforward way to understand project management models is by example. Let us consider the problems faced by a franchised restaurant operation, Choo-Chew Restaurants, Inc. CCRI grew from a highly successful first restaurant made from two turn-of-the-century railroad cars. Similar restaurants followed and the decor, menus, and operating procedures were standardized.

One critical aspect of the franchise arrangement is design and construction of the restaurant itself. CCRI has broken this job into the set of tasks or activities presented as Table 14–1.

TABLE 14–1

Restaurant Design and Construction Activities

Activity		Preceding Activities	Estimated Duration (days)
A	Purchase and renovate coaches..............	—	10
B	Purchase restaurant equipment..............	—	3
C	Hire personnel................................	—	1
D	Select and purchase site.....................	—	2
E	Obtain necessary permits and licenses.......	D	7
F	Site preparation............................	E	3
G	Move coaches onto site......................	A, F	5
H	Install utilities..............................	G	4
I	Install equipment...........................	B, H	4
J	Decorate....................................	B, H	3
K	Stock bar and kitchen.......................	I, J	6
L	Advertise and promote......................	G	3
M	Train personnel.............................	C, I	4
N	Undertake Pilot Operation...................	K, L	7

Precedence Requirements

As noted in Table 14–1, the project can begin with purchases of the coaches, the restaurant equipment, and the site. The purchases are divided into three activities because they involve different procedures and vendors. At the same time, we can undertake the hiring process for the required personnel. The other activities should be self-explanatory.

In the second column of the table, **precedence requirements** are presented. That is, it is necessary to accomplish activity D (select and purchase site) before starting activity E (obtain necessary permits and licenses). Similarly, we need to obtain the permits associated with activity E before activity F (site preparation) can be started. Activity G (move coaches onto site) requires the completion of both site preparation (F) and purchase-renovation of coaches (A). Note, however, that activities I (install equipment) and J (decorate) have the same sequential requirements; this means that these two activities can proceed simultaneously. Do the other precedence relationships make sense?

The third column of Table 14-1 contains an estimate for the time required to accomplish each activity. Methods for estimating durations include those discussed in Appendix A (Sections A.5 through A.7).

We might mention that the construction of a table such as Table 14-1 represents a rather formidable task for complex projects. First, the nature and number of activities must be specified, which relates to the *level of aggregation* problem discussed in Chapter 1; that is, what level of detail should define activities? For example, should we separate the renovation of coaches from the purchase of coaches? Is renovation itself complex enough to warrant separate activities? Ultimately, these and other answers must be based on experience, "art," and the usefulness of results. Second, great care must be exercised in establishing meaningful precedence relationships, as their nature can very much affect differences between predicted and actual results.

Network Representation

Before illustrating the so-called network representation of Table 14-1, we formalize the previous discussion with some key definitions.

Events are specific accomplishments which occur at recognizable points in time. For example, the *completion* of activity J (decorate) in Table 14-1 represents an event. Similarly, the *initiation* of activity N represents an event.

An **activity** is the work required to complete a specific event. Activities, unlike events, require time and utilize resources.

The **project** is the complete set of interrelated activities. By convention, the "start" of the project is indicated by an **originating event;** the "end" of the project is denoted by a **terminal event.**

The **network** for the project is a display of its activities and events, and their interrelationships. Figure 14-1 represents a network for the restaurant project defined in Table 14-1. Activities are represented by line segments with arrows, termed **directed arcs.** Events are represented by numbered circles, called **nodes.** Note that nodes 1 and 11 represent, respectively, the originating event **(source)** and terminal event **(sink).**

Two simple rules must be observed in the construction of such a network:

Rule 1— Each activity must be represented by one and only one directed arc.

Rule 2— No two activities may begin *and* end on the same two nodes.

Rule 1 is obvious because of the need to represent activities uniquely. Rule 2 is necessary to avoid notational problems when using solution methods. For example, activities *I* and *J* are concurrent activities which must precede activity *K*. Figure 14–2a shows an incorrect representation because *I* and *J* cannot be uniquely identified when using the "coordinate" convention of coding an activity by its beginning and ending event; that is, the coordinate (6, 9) would fail to distinguish between activities *I* and *J*. Part (*b*) of the figure (as does Figure 14–1) correctly identifies activity *I* as (6, 8) and activity *J* as (6, 9).

The implementation of Rule 2 in Figure 14–2b required the use of a **dummy activity** (D_1). Such activities do not require time or utilize resources, but are necessary either (1) to preserve Rule 2 or (2) to properly

FIGURE 14–1

Network for Restaurant Project in Table 14–1

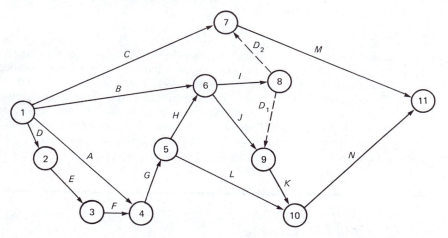

FIGURE 14–2

Use of Dummy Activity to Avoid Notational Problems

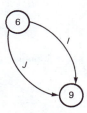

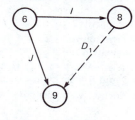

(a) Incorrect
(b) Correct

FIGURE 14–3

Use of Dummy Activities to Avoid Precedence Problems

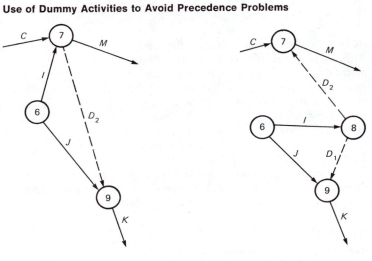

(a) Incorrect   (b) Correct

represent certain logical relationships. To illustrate the latter, consider Figure 14–3. Part (a) shows an incorrect precedence relationship for activity K. According to Table 14–1, I and J are to precede K, and C and I are to precede M. The dummy (D_2), therefore, is inserted to allow I to precede K. Doing so, however, implies that C *also* must precede K, which is incorrect. Part (b) of Figure 14–3 (as does Figure 14–1) shows the correct relationships. Note that dummies are represented by "broken" directed arcs.

Follow-up Exercises

1. Confirm that Figure 14–1 is correctly based on Table 14–1. Do so by answering the following questions for each activity in the network: (a) What activity or activities must be completed immediately before this activity can start? (b) What activity or activities must immediately follow this activity? (c) What activity or activities must occur concurrently with this activity?

2. Construct a new network for the restaurant project if activity J need not precede activity K but must precede activity N.

3. Construct a new network for the restaurant project if activities C and K (rather than C and I) must precede activity M.

4. Construct a new network which combines the conditions in Exercises 2 and 3.

Time Concepts

A primary objective in project management is the determination of a schedule which shows starting and finishing dates for each activity. Concepts helpful in the construction of such a schedule are discussed next.

Figure 14–4 shows the network for the restaurant project (Table 14–1) with estimated durations for each activity labeled on the arcs. Note that activities are now referenced using (i, j) notation. For example, activity C in Figure 14–1 is now activity $(1, 7)$ in Figure 14–4.

FIGURE 14–4

Restaurant Network with Estimated Durations and Critical Path (→)

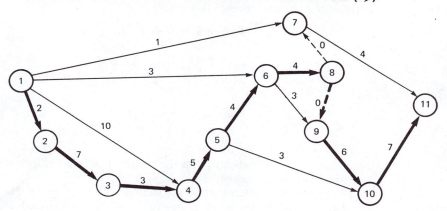

We begin with two important definitions associated with *each event:*

1. The **earliest starting time** (E_i) for all activities *leaving* event i is the earliest time at which the event can occur such that all precedence relationships relevant to the event are implemented.
2. The **latest finishing time** (L_i) for all activities *entering* event i is the latest time at which the event can occur without delaying the completion of the project.

E_i for each event is calculated during a *forward* pass of the network. Since node 1 is the initiating event, it follows that $E_1 = 0$. Now look at the network in Figure 14–4. The earliest time for event (node) 2 is identical to the earliest starting time for the activity which *leaves* node 2, or the end of the second day for activity $(2, 3)$. Thus, $E_2 = 2$; for event 3 we have $E_3 = 9$; and for event 4, $E_4 = 12$. Did you think, perhaps, that E_4 was 10 because of activity $(1, 4)$? E_4 cannot be 10 because it is supposed to represent the earliest starting time for activity $(4, 5)$; the earliest starting time for activity $(4, 5)$ must be the end of the 12th day because activity $(3, 4)$, which has a duration of 3 days coupled with an earliest starting time at the end of the ninth day $(E_3 = 9)$, precedes activity $(4, 5)$. Thus, the earliest time for an event is given by the path of *maximum* length into that event.

Consider event 8. Three paths are possible in arriving at node 8: 1–6–8, 1–4–5–6–8, and 1–2–3–4–5–6–8. The three paths have durations of 7 days, 23 days, and 25 days, respectively; hence, $E_8 = 25$ since the activities along those paths which precede event 8 must be completed before activities *leaving* event 8 can start.

Fortunately, we need not enumerate all the possible paths going into event j to determine E_j, as the following formula accomplishes the purpose:

$$E_j = \max_i \{E_i + d_{ij}\}, \tag{14.1}$$

for all relevant (i, j) activities which *enter* node j, where d_{ij} is the estimated duration of activity (i, j). Table 14–2 provides the earliest time calculations for each event. For example,

$$\begin{aligned} E_6 &= \max \{E_1 + d_{16}, E_5 + d_{56}\} \\ &= \max \{0 + 3, 17 + 4\} \\ &= \max \{3, 21\} \\ &= 21 \end{aligned}$$

and

$$\begin{aligned} E_8 &= \max \{E_6 + d_{68}\} \\ &= \max \{21 + 4\} \\ &= 25. \end{aligned}$$

Note that $E_{11} = 38$ indicates that the earliest possible (estimated) completion time for the project is 38 days.

To determine the latest time associated with each event (L_i), a *backward* pass must be undertaken beginning with the terminal event (node 11). The latest finishing time for activities which *enter* node 10—that is, activities $(9, 10)$ and $(5, 10)$—such that the completion of the project is not delayed *beyond 38 days* is $(38 - 7)$, or $L_{10} = 31$. In other words, if either activity $(9, 10)$ or activity $(5, 10)$ were to be completed beyond the 31st day, then the entire project would be delayed *beyond its earliest completion date* of 38 days because 7 days are required for the successor activity $(10, 11)$.

TABLE 14–2

E_i and L_i for Restaurant Project

Event i	E_i	L_i
1	0	0
2	2	2
3	9	9
4	12	12
5	17	17
6	21	21
7	25	34
8	25	25
9	25	25
10	31	31
11	38	38

Now consider event 8. Two paths lead out of event 8 to the terminal event. Path 8–7–11 requires 4 days and path 8–9–10–11 requires 13 days. As far as path 8–7–11 is concerned, activity (6, 8) can be completed as late as the end of the 34th day $(38 - 4)$ without delaying the project. The 13-day duration of path 8–9–10–11, however, requires that activity (6, 8) be completed by the end of the 25th day $(38 - 13)$; hence, $L_8 = 25$.

In general,

$$L_i = \min_i \{L_j - d_{ij}\}, \tag{14.2}$$

for all relevant (i, j) activities which *leave* node i. For example,

$$
\begin{aligned}
L_9 &= \min \{L_{10} - d_{9,10}\} \\
&= \min \{31 - 6\} \\
&= 25
\end{aligned}
$$

and

$$
\begin{aligned}
L_8 &= \min \{L_9 - d_{89}, L_7 - d_{87}\} \\
&= \min \{25 - 0, 34 - 0\} \\
&= \min \{25, 34\} \\
&= 25.
\end{aligned}
$$

The second column of Table 14–2 illustrates the complete set of calculations for L_i, $i = 1, \ldots, 11$. Note that, for a network with n nodes, the condition $L_n = E_n$ is always true when starting the backward pass procedure. (Can you reason why?)

Slacks

The **total slack** for activity (i, j), or TS_{ij}, is defined as the maximum time to perform the activity less the estimated duration of the activity. Since the maximum time to perform activity (i, j) is the difference between its earliest starting date and its latest completion date $(L_j - E_i)$, then

$$TS_{ij} = L_j - E_i - d_{ij}. \tag{14.3}$$

For example, the total slacks for activities (1, 6) and (3, 4) are, respectively,

$$
\begin{aligned}
TS_{16} &= L_6 - E_1 - d_{16} \\
&= 21 - 0 - 3 \\
&= 18 \text{ days}
\end{aligned}
$$

and

$$
\begin{aligned}
TS_{34} &= L_4 - E_3 - d_{34} \\
&= 12 - 9 - 3 \\
&= 0 \text{ day.}
\end{aligned}
$$

This means that we have 18 days of "play" or "float" within which we can choose to delay the *start* of activity (1, 6) *without delaying the 38-day completion time for the project*. No delay, however, is allowed in the start of activity (3, 4) if we wish to complete the project in 38 days.

Table 14–3 provides relevant time calculations for each activity. (Carefully note the use of i, j subscripting and the utilization of E_i and L_j values from Table 14–2.)

It must be noted that the total slack value associated with a particular activity is not strictly unique to that activity. For example, activity $(1, 7)$ has 33 days of total slack and its successor $(7, 11)$ has 9 days of total slack. Looking at Figure 14–4, we see that if the start of $(1, 7)$ were to be delayed for 33 days, then event 7 would be achieved at the end of day 34, and $(7, 11)$ would need to start immediately to achieve event 11 at the end of day 38. It can be seen then that total slack often occurs *in*

TABLE 14–3

Time Calculations for Restaurant Project

Activity	Code for Activity (i, j)	Duration in Days (d_{ij})	Ending Day of Earliest Starting Time (E_i)	Ending Day of Latest Finishing Time (L_j)	Days of Total Slack (TS_{ij})	Days of Free Slack (FS_{ij})
A	(1, 4)	10	0	12	2	2
B	(1, 6)	3	0	21	18	18
C	(1, 7)	1	0	34	33	24
D	(1, 2)	2	0	2	0	0
E	(2, 3)	7	2	9	0	0
F	(3, 4)	3	9	12	0	0
G	(4, 5)	5	12	17	0	0
H	(5, 6)	4	17	21	0	0
I	(6, 8)	4	21	25	0	0
J	(6, 9)	3	21	25	1	1
D_2	(8, 7)	0	25	34	9	0
D_1	(8, 9)	0	25	25	0	0
K	(9, 10)	6	25	31	0	0
L	(5, 10)	3	17	31	11	11
M	(7, 11)	4	25	38	9	9
N	(10, 11)	7	31	38	0	0

series, whereby the use of total slack by one activity negates its availability to one or more other activities.

The shortcoming of total slack with respect to uniqueness has led to the definition of **free slack**, which is unique to activities in series. If activities in series were to begin as *early* as possible, then free slack (FS_{ij}) for activity (i, j) can be defined as the difference between *available time* $(E_j - E_i)$ and duration (d_{ij}):

$$FS_{ij} = E_j - E_i - d_{ij}. \tag{14.4}$$

The free slack for each activity in the restaurant example is shown in Table 14–3. Thus, the total slack of 33 days for activity $(1, 7)$ is made up of 24 days of free slack and 9 days of slack shared with activity $(7, 11)$. This means that a delay in $(1, 7)$ between 0 and 24 days has no effect on the slack available to $(7, 11)$, but a delay beyond 24 days reduces the slack of $(7, 11)$ by the exact amount of the additional delay.

The Critical Path

The **critical path** for a project is a path which spans the network such that activities along the path (termed **critical activities**) have zero total slack. Thus, a delay in the start of any activity along the critical path delays the entire project. In effect, the critical path is the *longest path* in the network. Put another way, the sum of durations for critical activities represents the *shortest* possible time to complete the project.

The critical activities in Table 14–3 are those having zero total slack. Since they represent activities on the critical path, they must form a chain which spans the network, as indicated in Figure 14–4.

In the Appendix of this chapter, we present mathematical programming procedures for finding directly the critical path.

Follow-up Exercises

5. Confirm the calculations in Table 14–2 using the formulas given by Equations (14.1) and (14.2).
6. Confirm the calculations in Table 14–3.
7. Convince yourself that a critical path need not be unique by changing the duration of activity (5, 10) in Figure 14–4 from 3 days to 14 days.
8. Complete a table such as Table 14–3 for the network in Exercise 4. Identify the critical path for this network.

14.2 SCHEDULING

The network calculations provided by the basic model serve as the planning tool for actually scheduling the activities. In this section we illustrate the construction of a time chart for scheduling activities, and then touch on the important topic of allocating resources.

Time Chart

The **time chart** for the restaurant project is given in Figure 14–5. The first step is the scheduling of critical activities. From Table 14–3, critical activities are located as those having zero total slack. Then, they are plotted sequentially, the length of each line corresponding to the duration of the corresponding activity. Note that dummy activities need not be plotted, as they take up zero time. Next, each noncritical activity is plotted separately. The beginning and end of each line correspond, respectively, to the earliest starting time (E_i) and the latest finishing time (L_j) for the given activity. For example, activity J can begin as early as (the end of) day 21 and must be completed by (the end of) day 25. Since its duration is 3 days, its **latest starting time** is (the end of) day 22, which necessarily corresponds to a total slack of 1 day (that is, 22 minus 21). Latest starting times for noncritical activities are located by dots ($\bullet$) on the solid lines.

FIGURE 14–5

Time Chart for Restaurant Project

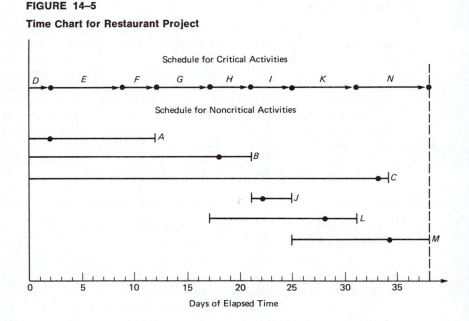

Days of Elapsed Time

The time chart readily identifies scheduling flexibilities because of the visual ease in identifying the total slack associated with each noncritical activity (as given by the distance between the beginning of each line and the dot, which is the difference between earliest and latest starting times). For example, the purchase of restaurant equipment (*B*) and the hiring of personnel (*C*) represent activities with very flexible starting dates. Scheduling the start of purchase-renovation of coaches (*A*) or decoration (*J*), however, is not very flexible.

Resource Allocation

Up to now we have assumed unlimited resources in scheduling activities. In actual practice, it is probable that the initial schedule will call for more labor, equipment, funds, or other resources than is available for a particular time period.

To illustrate our point, consider the labor requirements in Table 14–4. Figure 14–6 provides a schedule of labor requirements over time based on the scheduling of all noncritical activities according to the earliest starting time (part *a*) or the latest starting time (part *b*). For example, in part *b*,

TABLE 14–4

Labor Requirements for Restaurant Project

Activity	A	B	C	D	E	F	G	H	I	J	K	L	M	N
Number of Personnel	4	2	1	2	1	3	2	4	5	2	3	1	2	2

FIGURE 14-6

Labor Schedules for Restaurant Project

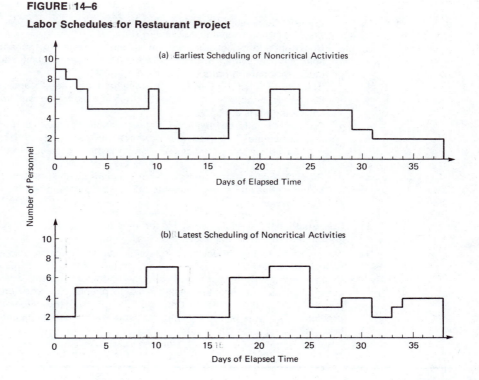

the number of personnel required for days 10, 11, and 12 (that is, for the end of day 9 to the end of day 12) is 7. If the maximum number of available personnel is 7, then it would not be desirable to schedule activities *A, B,* and *C* as early as possible, since 9 and 8 personnel would be required in days 1 and 2, respectively.

It should be evident that by shifting noncritical activities between earliest and latest *starting* times, either reduction in the maximum number of personnel or **resource (or load) leveling** can be achieved (assuming that units of the resource are perfect substitutes for one another). By load leveling we mean the smoothing of fluctuations in the requirements for a particular resource. At this time, computationally feasible models for optimizing the allocation of resources do not exist. Good heuristic (rule-of-thumb) approaches do exist, however, as discussed in Chapter 16.

Follow-up Exercises

9. Construct a time chart for the project in Exercise 8. Identify what appear to be scheduling flexibilities.

10. With respect to Figure 14-6:

a. Confirm the personnel needs in part (a).
b. Confirm the personnel needs in part (b).
c. Construct a labor schedule for the restaurant project by scheduling noncritical activities midway between earliest and latest starting dates. Compare to parts (a) and (b).
   (Hint: First label Figure 14–5 to include labor needs and duration of each activity; then use this revised figure to aid you in answering parts a, b, and c.)
d. For the 38 daily observations of the variable "number of personnel," calculate the mean and variance for part (a) and for part (b). Based on these measures, which schedule best levels the load?
e. By shifting the starting times of noncritical activities, is it possible to reduce maximum requirements below seven personnel? Illustrate your answer.

11. Construct labor schedules as in Figure 14–6 for the project of Exercise 9. Compare results to the needs in Figure 14–6.

12. Why must there be perfect substitutability across activities among resource units when leveling? Given the nature of the labor resource (people) and the variety of activities in the restaurant project, does this assumption appear tenable? (Assume some people can work on certain activities and not others.) Can you think of ways to overcome this problem? Can you think of resources which are more homogeneous than labor?

14.3 INCORPORATING PROBABILITIES

Up to now the duration of each activity has been treated as a deterministic variable. For example, the time required to purchase and renovate coaches in the restaurant project had been fixed at ten days, with no possibility of variation. In this section a model is presented which defines the time to complete each activity as a random variable.

Activity Durations as Random Variables

The original version of PERT requires three time estimates of the duration of activity (i, j) from people who are most intimately involved with accomplishing the activity, as follows:

1. An *optimistic* time (a_{ij}), such that the probability is "small" that the activity can be completed in less time.
2. A *most likely (modal)* time (m_{ij}), which should occur under "normal" operating conditions.
3. A *pessimistic* time (b_{ij}), such that the probability is "small" that the activity will take longer.

The time (d_{ij}) to complete activity (i, j) is assumed to be a random variate from a probability distribution with a specified mean and variance.

FIGURE 14–7

Beta Distributions for Durations of Activity (i, j).

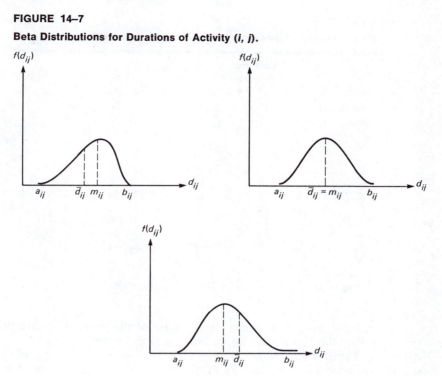

The *mean* ($\bar{d}_{ij}$) is estimated as a weighted average of the three time estimates, with the mode receiving four times the weight of either extreme:

$$\bar{d}_{ij} = \frac{a_{ij} + 4m_{ij} + b_{ij}}{6}. \tag{14.5}$$

The *variance* (v_{ij}) for the time to complete activity (i, j) is estimated by assuming that the range given by $(b_{ij} - a_{ij})$ encompasses six standard deviations of the distribution.[1] Thus,

$$6\sqrt{v_{ij}} = b_{ij} - a_{ij}$$

or

$$v_{ij} = \left(\frac{b_{ij} - a_{ij}}{6}\right)^2. \tag{14.6}$$

Under certain restrictive assumptions, it can be proved that $\bar{d}_{ij}$ and v_{ij} are the mean and variance of a Beta distribution (Section A.3). As illustrated in Figure 14–7, this continuous distribution has finite limits, is unimodal, and can assume flexible shapes. The main concern in our calcu-

---

[1] According to the Chebyshev Inequality, we can guarantee that *at least* 89 percent of the durations will fall within the range given by $(b_{ij} - a_{ij})$ regardless of the specific form of the probability distribution. If the probability distribution is normal, for example, then the probability is 0.9973 that d_{ij} falls within this range.

TABLE 14–5

Time Estimates, Means, and Variances for Restaurant Project*

Activity	Code for Activity (i, j)	a_{ij}	m_{ij}	b_{ij}	$\bar{d}_{ij}$	v_{ij}
A................	(1, 4)	5	7	27	10	13
B................	(1, 6)	0	3	6	3	1
C................	(1, 7)	1	1	1	1	0
D................	(1, 2)	0	1	8	2	2
E................	(2, 3)	3	6	15	7	4
F................	(3, 4)	1	3	5	3	0
G................	(4, 5)	0	6	6	5	1
H................	(5, 6)	1	2	15	4	5
I................	(6, 8)	2	4	6	4	0
J................	(6, 9)	2	3	4	3	0
K................	(9, 10)	3	5	13	6	3
L................	(5, 10)	3	3	3	3	0
M................	(7, 11)	2	3	10	4	2
N................	(10, 11)	1	8	9	7	2

* All estimates and calculations to the nearest day.

lations, however, is not the exact form of the probability distribution, but rather the "goodness" of $\bar{d}_{ij}$ and v_{ij} as estimates.

Table 14–5 provides time estimates and calculations of mean and variance for each activity of the restaurant project. Note that we have cleverly "fixed" the time estimates (a_{ij}, m_{ij}, and b_{ij}) to give us the same durations as before (that is, $\bar{d}_{ij}$ equals the previously used d_{ij} for all i and j).

Probabilistic Events

Given probabilistic durations of activities along specific paths in the network, it follows that elapsed times for achieving events along those paths are also probabilistic. We now present a procedure for assessing the probability that an event will be attained within its allotted time according to a given schedule.

Let e_i represent a random variate from the distribution of *"earliest*

FIGURE 14–8

$E(e_i^*)$ and $V(e_i)$ Estimates

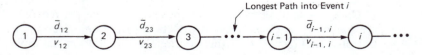

Mean of "earliest times for achieving event i":
$$E(e_i) = \bar{d}_{12} + \bar{d}_{23} + \cdots + \bar{d}_{i-1,i}.$$

Variance of "earliest times for achieving event i":
$$V(e_i) = v_{12} + v_{23} + \cdots + v_{i-1,i}.$$

Where, for each activity, $\bar{d}_{ij}$ represents mean duration and v_{ij} represents variance in durations.

times for achieving event i." If durations along the *longest* path into event i are statistically independent, then the mean, $E(e_i)$, and the variance, $V(e_i)$, of the distribution of earliest times for achieving event i can be estimated as the sums of the means ($\bar{d}_{ij}$'s) and variances (v_{ij}'s), respectively, of the durations for activities along the longest path.[2] (See Figure 14–8.) To illustrate, turn to Figure 14–4. For event 4,

$$E(e_4) = \bar{d}_{12} + \bar{d}_{23} + \bar{d}_{34}$$
$$= 2 + 7 + 3$$
$$= 12$$

and (from Table 14–5)

$$V(e_4) = v_{12} + v_{23} + v_{34}$$
$$= 2 + 4 + 0$$
$$= 6.$$

Note that 1–2–3–4 and not 1–4 is the *longest* path into event 4. Also note that $E(e_i)$ is equivalent to the earliest starting time (E_i), since the latter was determined by summing expected durations along the longest path into event i. In other words, $E(e_i) = E_i$ for all i, as calculated in Table 14–2. Finally, if two or more paths into event i are of equal length, then $V(e_i)$ is conservatively estimated from the path yielding the highest sum of variances.

Given that k independent activities precede event i (on the longest path into i) and that e_i is the sum of the k independent and identically distributed observations (that is, the k durations represent a random sample), then according to the **Central Limit Theorem** (Section A.5) e_i is approximately normally distributed with mean $E(e_i)$ and variance $V(e_i)$ for "large" k. This allows us to estimate the probability that the "earliest time for achieving event i" (e_i) is less than or equal to some "scheduled time for event i" (S_i). In other words, $P(e_i \leq S_i)$ is given by the shaded area of the normal curve shown in Figure 14–9, where the "standardized random variate" (z_i) is defined by

$$z_i = \frac{S_i - E(e_i)}{\sqrt{V(e_i)}}. \tag{14.7}$$

To illustrate the calculation of event probabilities, consider the probability that event 4 in the restaurant project occurs prior to the end of day 14. Previously we found that $E(e_4) = 12$ and $V(e_4) = 6$. Thus,

$$P(e_4 \leq S_4) = P\left(Z_4 \leq \frac{S_4 - E(e_4)}{\sqrt{V(e_4)}}\right)$$

$$P(e_4 \leq 14) = P\left(Z_4 \leq \frac{14 - 12}{\sqrt{6}}\right)$$

$$= P(Z_4 \leq 0.82)$$
$$= 0.79.$$

---

[2] The justification for this statement is based on theorems in statistics which state that: (1) the expected value of a sum of n variables equals the sum of the n expected values; (2) the variance of a sum of n variables equals the sum of the n variances, provided the n variables are statistically independent (uncorrelated).

If $S_4 = 9$, then

$$P(e_4 \leq 9) = P\left(Z_4 \leq \frac{9 - 12}{\sqrt{6}}\right)$$
$$= P(Z_4 \leq -1.22)$$
$$= 0.11$$

Thus, the probability is 79 percent that event 4 is achieved in 14 days or less and 11 percent that it is achieved in 9 days or less.[3]

Table 14–6 presents the calculations for determining the probability that each event in the restaurant project finishes by a time (S_i) according to some schedule. Note that determinations of $E(e_i)$ are based on E_i from Table 14–2; $V(e_i)$ calculations are based on the sum of v_{ij}'s (from Table 14–5) for the longest path into event i.

FIGURE 14–9

Normal Curve for e_i

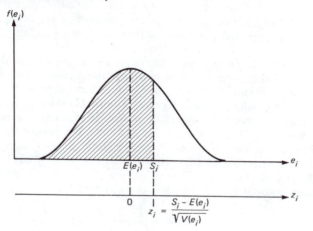

Probability tables of this type aid project planners in assessing whether or not schedules and resource commitments are reasonable. For example, the probability that the project is completed in 40 days or less is estimated as 0.69. If this is considered too low, then additional resources must be committed along the critical path to reduce estimated durations and/or variances (or, perhaps, the scheduled completion date needs to be increased).

The procedure provided by PERT for assessing uncertainties, while not rigorous in a probabilistic sense, has been workable in actual practice.

---

[3] You should confirm these probabilities by turning to the normal curve table in your "Stat" book and looking up the appropriate areas corresponding to $z = 0.82$ and $z = -1.22$. Note, however, that normality is hardly guaranteed when $k = 2$ (that is, e_i is based on only two observations).

TABLE 14–6

Event Probabilities for Restaurant Project

Event (i)	Longest Path into Event i	$E(e_i)$	$V(e_i)$	S_i	z_i	$P(e_i \leq S_i)$, or $P(Z_i \leq z_i)$
2...........	1–2	2	2	2	0.00	0.50
3...........	1–2–3	9	6	10	0.41	0.66
4...........	1–2–3–4	12	6	11	−0.41	0.34
5...........	1–2–3–4–5	17	7	20	1.13	0.87
6...........	1–2–3–4–5–6	21	12	24	0.87	0.81
7...........	1–2–3–4–5–6–8–7	25	12	34	2.60	1.00
8...........	1–2–3–4–5–6–8	25	12	27	0.58	0.72
9...........	1–2–3–4–5–6–8–9	25	12	28	0.87	0.81
10...........	1–2–3–4–5–6–8–9–10	31	15	32	0.26	0.60
11...........	1–2–3–4–5–6–8–9–10–11	38	17	40	0.49	0.69

We must caution, however, that a number of assumptions have been made in this section. To recap, we have assumed that:

1. Expected activity durations and variances are accurately estimated by Equations (14.5) and (14.6).
2. Activities are statistically independent for computing event variances.
3. Time observations for activity durations represent "large enough" random samples for the Central Limit Theorem to be operable.
4. The distribution of times for the longest path into an event represents a reasonable estimate of earliest times for that event, which means that it is not possible for alternative paths into i to have greater cumulative times. (This assumption considerably simplifies statistical manipulations.)

We ask you to think further about these assumptions in Exercise 20.

In closing we might mention that an alternative to probabilistic PERT has emerged in recent years called **GERT (Graphical Evaluation and Review Technique).** This appears to be a promising technique for directly analyzing probabilistic events in generalized activity networks. First used in industrial engineering applications, more recently it has been applied to new product planning simulations.[4]

Follow-up Exercises

13. Verify the calculations in Table 14–5.
14. For each activity in Table 14–5 identify whether its durations are symmetric, negatively skewed, or positively skewed (be careful with B).

---

[4] A. A. Pritsker and G. E. Whitehouse, "GERT, Graphical Evaluation and Review Technique," *The Journal of Industrial Engineering*, (pp. 1 and 2) nos. 5 and 6 (1966), pp. 267–74, 293–301; C. H. Bellas and A. C. Samli, "Improving New Product Planning with GERT Simulation," *California Management Review, vol.* 15, no. 4 (1973), pp. 14–21.

What can you say about activities *C* and *L*? Is it reasonable to state that activities having low variance are fairly standardized or routine?

15. Confirm the calculations in Table 14–6.

16. Determine the probability that the project is completed by its earliest expected completion date of 38 days.

17. In general, what can you say about the probability that an event along the critical path is completed by its latest date? In other words, $P(e_i \leq L_i) = ?$ when event *i* is critical.

18. Find the following probabilities for the restaurant project:

    a. That the project is completed in 45 or less days.
    b. That the project is completed in 35 or less days.
    c. That the project is completed between 35 and 45 days, inclusive.
    d. That event 7 has not been completed by the end of day 30.

19. Compute a probability table for the project of Exercises 4 and 8. Assume all scheduled times are 20-percent higher than latest event dates; that is, $S_i = 1.2 \ L_i$ for all *i*. Also, assume the time estimates in Table 14–5.

20. With respect to the four assumptions outlined at the end of the section:

    a. Do Equations (14.5) and (14.6) appear to be reasonable or logical? Why or why not? On what basis do they appear to be statistically justified?
    b. Activities are assumed to be statistically independent in order to avoid statistical problems associated with estimating covariances or correlations. Can you think of factors or circumstances in a real project which would cause dependence?
    c. For purposes of the Central Limit Theorem (CLT), a "large enough" sample is usually assumed to be 30 or more. Under what conditions is normality approximated for small samples? (Hint: It has to do with the shapes of the distributions of activity durations.) Would you say that size restrictions imposed on *k* (number of activities preceding event *i* along the longest path) by the CLT are a problem for real-world projects? (Hint: Real-world projects using PERT-CPM consist of hundreds and even thousands of activities.) Why do you feel more confident in probability estimates for events in the late part of the network than for events in the early part? (Hint: It has to do with the size of *k* and the CLT.) Since (1) variances associated with durations are estimated rather than known and (2) sample sizes (*k*) may be small, what probability distribution for event times is more appropriate than the normal curve?
    d. Would you say that the longest elapsed time into, say, event 4 of the restaurant project is *always* given by path 1–2–3–4? (See Figure 14–4.) The answer is "no" because, given probabilistic durations, it is quite possible that it will take longer to complete activity (1, 4) than to complete the sequence of activities given by (1, 2), (2, 3), and (3, 4). To convince yourself, assume that the elapsed time along path 1–4 is normal with mean 10 and variance 13 (from Table 14–5), and that elapsed time along path 1–2–3–4 is normal with mean 12 and variance 6 (from Table 14–6). Determine (1) the probability that elapsed time along 1–4 is *greater* than 12

days, (2) the probability that elapsed time along 1–2–3–4 is *less* than 12 days, and (3) the probability that the events in (1) and (2) occur simultaneously. Note that when elapsed time along 1–4 is greater than along 1–2–3–4, activity (1, 4) becomes critical and activities (1, 2), (2, 3), and (3, 4) becomes noncritical. Can you think of alternative definitions for the critical path?

21. Criticisms of Equations (14.5) and (14.6) for estimating the means and variances of activities have led to the development of alternative formulas:

$$\bar{d}_{ij} = \frac{a_{ij} + 0.95 m_{ij} + b_{ij}}{2.95} \tag{14.8}$$

and

$$v_{ij} = \left(\frac{b_{ij} - a_{ij}}{3.25}\right)^2, \tag{14.9}$$

where a_{ij} and b_{ij} are estimates for the 5 and 95 percentiles of the probability distribution and m_{ij} is the mode.[5] The authors claim that these formulas are more accurate than Equations (14.5) and (14.6) and are relatively distribution free (for example, their use is not predicated on the assumption of a specific distribution such as the Beta). Based on (14.8) and (14.9), generate alternative tables to Tables 14–5 and 14–6. Comment on the differences.

---

[5] C. Perry and I. D. Greig, "Estimating the Mean and Variance of Subjective Distributions in PERT and Decision Analysis," *Management Science,* vol. 21, no. 12 (1975), pp. 1477–80.

Simulation

If the distributions of activity times for all activities in a network are known (or can be approximated), then Monte Carlo simulation (Section 13.3) represents an ideal procedure for generating a probability distribution of elapsed times for each event.[6]

To illustrate, suppose each activity of the restaurant project has durations which are distributed according to the Beta distribution, with mean and variance as given in Table 14–5. A *single* simulation run would consist of the following steps:

1. Generate a random variate for the duration of *each* activity from the appropriate distribution.
2. Determine the critical path.
3. Determine earliest elapsed time for each event in the network.

Repeating this procedure an "adequate" number of times (in order to satisfy error criteria in estimation) would allow the construction of mean-

---

[6] We say that the procedure is ideal because assumptions 2 through 4 at the end of the previous section need not hold. Of course, complete knowledge of the distribution of activity times may be a "fairy tale" in actual practice.

TABLE 14–7

Simulated Frequency Distribution of Elapsed Time for Entire Project

Number of Days	Frequency	Relative Frequency
30 to 34....................	100	0.10
35 to 39....................	500	0.50
40 to 44....................	200	0.20
45 to 49....................	150	0.15
50 to 54....................	50	0.05
	1,000	1.00

ingful frequency distributions or histograms for the earliest times of any given event.

For example, if 1,000 simulations were conducted for the restaurant project, a frequency distribution for event 11 (completion of project) might appear as in Table 14–7. Thus, the probability that the project takes between 40 and 44 days is 0.20; that it takes less than 30 days is 0; and so forth. Note that $E(e_{11})$ and $V(e_{11})$ are estimated by the mean (39.7) and variance (30.2) of this frequency distribution.

Follow-up Exercise

**22. Consider the following network and distribution for each activity.

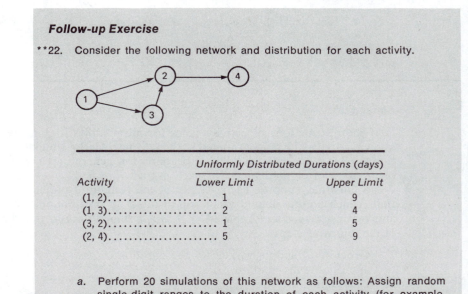

	Uniformly Distributed Durations (days)	
Activity	Lower Limit	Upper Limit
(1, 2)......................	1	9
(1, 3)......................	2	4
(3, 2)......................	1	5
(2, 4)......................	5	9

a. Perform 20 simulations of this network as follows: Assign random single-digit ranges to the duration of each activity (for example, 1 through 9 for the first activity and 2 through 4 for the second activity); locate the first digit of column (1) in Table 13–3 on page 494; sequentially assign durations to each activity by going down the column (skip digits outside specific ranges). For example, the first column includes the following digits: 1, 2, 2, 4, 3, 7, 9, · · · This would result in the following simulated durations: $d_{12} = 1$,

$d_{13} = 2$, $d_{32} = 2$, (skip 4 and 3 because not in 5–9 range), $d_{24} = 7$ (end of first simulation), $d_{12} = 9$, · · · · When you get to the end of column (1), go to the first digit in column (2), and so on. Construct a frequency distribution for e_4 and calculate $E(e_4)$ and $V(e_4)$ directly from the frequency distribution. Estimate $P(e_4 \leq 13)$ and $P(e_4 \leq 16)$.

b. Estimate $E(e_4)$, $V(e_4)$, $P(e_4 \leq 13)$, and $P(e_4 \leq 16)$ by the procedures of Section 14.3. Compare to the simulated results. In which set of results do you have more confidence? (Note: $\bar{d}_{ij}$ and v_{ij} are determined by Formulas (A.29) and (A.30), respectively.)

c. Extend part (a) to 50 simulations and compare to part (b). Comments?

14.4 INCORPORATING COSTS

Our presentation up to now has strictly focused on the time element of project management. In this section, we introduce the idea of time-cost tradeoffs in rescheduling activities and follow with a brief description of PERT/Cost.

Crashing

Three categories of cost can be identified for any given project: (1) *direct* costs associated with the commitment of resources (labor,

FIGURE 14–10

Costs for Hypothetical Project

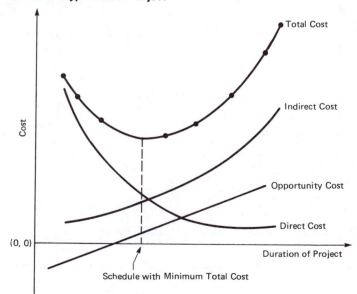

materials, equipment, and so forth) to activities; (2) *indirect* or *overhead* costs such as expenses associated with utilities, administration, and supervision; and (3) *opportunity* costs such as penalties for completing a project beyond a certain date or bonuses (benefits or negative costs) for completing a project prior to a specified date.

In general, the time to complete an activity can be shortened by committing additional resources to that activity; necessarily, the direct costs for that activity will increase. By decreasing the durations of critical activities, it follows that the project can be completed at an earlier date than previously scheduled, but at higher direct costs and lower indirect and opportunity costs. Figure 14–10 illustrates the identification of a schedule which resolves this tradeoff by minimizing the total cost (sum of direct, indirect, and opportunity costs) of a hypothetical project.

The original version of CPM approached this problem by first requiring the identification of normal and crash points for each activity. The **normal point** for activity (i, j) is identified as a coordinate on its **direct cost-time function,** which indicates the duration (DN_{ij}) and associated direct cost (CN_{ij}) for this activity under "normal" conditions. DN_{ij}, for example, can be represented by the most likely duration (m_{ij}) or the expected duration $(\bar{d}_{ij})$ defined in Section 14.3. The **crash point** for activity (i, j) is the coordinate on its direct cost-time function which indicates the duration (DC_{ij}) and associated direct cost (CC_{ij}) if direct cost were of no concern in expediting this activity. In other words, DC_{ij} is the limiting duration for activity (i, j) such that an additional commitment of resources cannot further expedite this activity. Figure 14–11 illustrates these concepts under the usual *linear* assumption for the direct cost-time function. Note that the crash point is necessarily "northwest" of the normal point, but that the function passing through the two points is not

FIGURE 14–11

Direct Cost-Time Function for Activity (i, j)

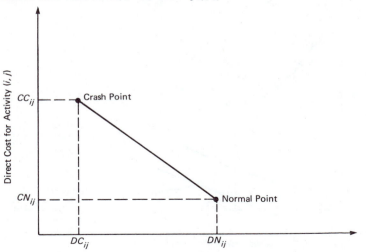

Duration of Activity (i, j)

necessarily linear. Further note that the slope (or first derivative) of this function gives the *cost of expediting this activity per unit of time.*

Given the determination of a critical path based on normal times, the act of **crashing** involves the sequential time compression of critical activities from normal durations to crash durations. The end result of this effort is a set of schedules yielding direct cost as a discrete function of project duration. When this function is combined with the indirect and opportunity cost functions, a discrete version of the total cost function in Figure 14–10 can be constructed. We now illustrate one of many approaches to crashing. In the appendix to this chapter, a more rigorous linear programming version is presented.

Example 14.2 "Crashing in One Easy Lesson"

Table 14–8 provides cost and time estimates for a seven-activity project. As indicated in part (a) of Figure 14–12, the earliest time to complete the project under "normal" conditions is 16 weeks, for a total direct cost of

TABLE 14–8

Cost-Time Estimates

Activity (i, j)	Time Estimates (weeks) Normal	Crash	Direct Cost Estimates ($1,000) Normal	Crash	Linear Slope (cost to expedite)
(1, 2)...........	2	1	10	15	5
(1, 3)...........	8	5	15	21	2
(2, 4)...........	4	3	20	24	4
(3, 4)...........	1	1	7	7	—
(3, 5)...........	2	1	8	15	7
(4, 6)...........	5	3	10	16	3
(5, 6)...........	6	2	12	36	6
			82	134	

$82,000. Part (b) illustrates the extreme (but unnecessary) act of crashing *all* activities. It serves the useful purpose of providing the least possible duration for the project (9 weeks). As you will see, however, this same duration can be achieved at a cost which is lower than $134,000.

The first step is to expedite an activity along the critical path of the normal network. Noncritical activities are ignored because further reductions in their durations do not lower the earliest completion date for the project. Of the three critical activities given by (1, 3), (3, 5), and (5, 6), activity (1, 3) is crashed because it has the *least* cost per unit time to expedite; that is, according to the last column of Table 14–8, it costs $2,000 per week to expedite activity (1, 3), whereas it costs $7,000 per week and $6,000 per week to expedite activities (3, 5) and (5, 6), respectively. Crashing activity (1, 3) from 8 weeks to 5 weeks reduces the time of project completion from 16 weeks to 13 weeks and increases direct cost from $82,000 to

FIGURE 14–12

Crashing a Project

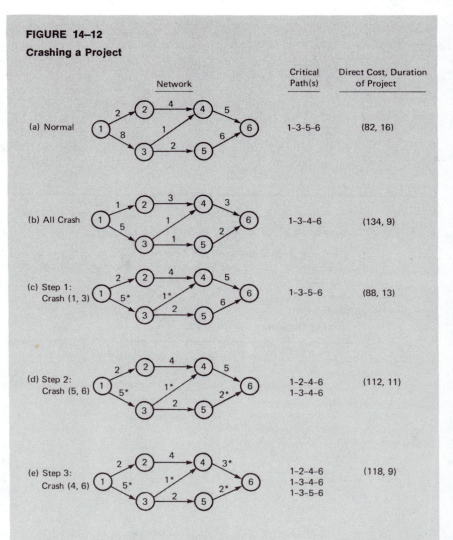

	Network	Critical Path(s)	Direct Cost, Duration of Project
(a) Normal		1-3-5-6	(82, 16)
(b) All Crash		1-3-4-6	(134, 9)
(c) Step 1: Crash (1, 3)		1-3-5-6	(88, 13)
(d) Step 2: Crash (5, 6)		1-2-4-6 1-3-4-6	(112, 11)
(e) Step 3: Crash (4, 6)		1-2-4-6 1-3-4-6 1-3-5-6	(118, 9)

$88,000. For convenience, a **crashed activity** (that is, an activity at its crash point) is identified by an asterisk (*) above its duration along the appropriate arc in the network. Note that activity (3, 4) is already at its crash point.

In general, at each step of the crashing procedure, our heuristic (rule-of-thumb) calls for crashing the *uncrashed critical activity* which yields the least linear direct cost per unit of time to expedite, or the minimum

$$S_{ij} = \frac{CC_{ij} - CN_{ij}}{DN_{ij} - DC_{ij}} \qquad (14.10)$$

for all (i, j) along the *current* critical path.

Given the current critical path 1–3–5–6 in part (c), it is evident that activities (3, 5) and (5, 6) are critical and uncrashed. Because $S_{56} = 6$ is less than $S_{35} = 7$, we crash activity (5, 6) in Step 2. Now the estimated duration of the project is 11 weeks at a direct cost of $112,000. Note that two paths are now critical. Activity (4, 6) is chosen next for crashing because it has the minimum S_{ij} (that is, $S_{46} = 3$) of all uncrashed activities along the two critical paths.

Step 3 yields a project duration of 9 weeks, a direct cost of $118,000, and three critical paths. According to the all-crash network in part (b), we cannot lower the project's completion below 9 weeks. Furthermore, all activities which were previously crashed are currently critical; hence, our procedure terminates at this point.

In general, crashing terminates when the "all-crash" time is reached *and* when current *noncritical* activities which have been crashed (or compressed), and have the *highest* S_{ij}, are *uncrashed* (or uncompressed) up to the point where they become critical.[7] To illustrate the second part of this

TABLE 14–9

Total Cost Calculations for Project of Example 14.2

Elapsed Time (weeks)	Direct Cost ($1,000)	Indirect Cost ($1,000)	Opportunity Cost ($1,000)	Total Cost ($1,000)
16	82	35	12	129
15	84	33	9	126
14	86	31	6	123
13	88	29	3	120
12	94	27	0	121
11	100	25	−3	122
10	109	23	−6	126
9	118	21	−9	130

stopping rule, suppose the network in part (d) satisfies the first part (that is, 11 represents the all-crash time). Activity (5, 6) is currently noncritical and has been crashed previously. By increasing its duration from 2 to 4 weeks, it follows that 1–3–5–6 also becomes critical, that the project's duration remains at 11 weeks, and that direct cost declines from $112,000 to $100,000.

Note, therefore, that the *least* direct cost is achieved *for each step* by uncrashing previously crashed (or uncompressing previously compressed) activities with *highest* S_{ij} along *uncritical* paths up to the point where they become critical. This gives a minimum direct cost of $100,000 for Step 2 after activity (5, 6) is uncrashed from 2 to 4 weeks.[8]

Now, suppose that indirect cost ($1,000's) is given by the function $3 + 2t$ and opportunity cost ($1,000's) is given by the function $-36 + 3t$, where t represents elapsed time in weeks. According to the calculations in Table 14–9, total cost for the project is minimized at $120,000 for the 13-week schedule suggested by the network in part (c) of Figure 14–12.

[7] Take care with our terminology. If an activity is at its crash point, then we say it is crashed; moving it off its crash point is called uncrashing. If an activity is between its crash and normal points, then we say it is compressed; increasing its time further is called uncompressing.

[8] That is, $112,000 - (4 \text{ weeks} - 2 \text{ weeks}) \cdot S_{56}$, or $112,000 - (2 \text{ weeks}) \cdot ($6,000 \text{ per week})$.

Follow-up Exercises

23. Confirm the S_{ij} calculations in the last column of Table 14–8.

24. What difficulties do you foresee in crashing if the function passing through the normal and crash points is nonlinear?

25. Confirm the calculations in Table 14–9. Determine direct costs by compressing critical activities with lowest S_{ij} one week at a time. That is, for direct costs, generate a figure such as Figure 14–12, but having seven steps. Note that when two or more paths are currently critical, as in part (d) of Figure 14–12, a reduction of one time period in the completion of the project requires the compression of the activity with lowest S_{ij} (and no asterisk) along each critical path. This method, compared to the method in the example, requires more calculations but provides more comprehensive schedules.

**26. Given the table below for the restaurant project (Example 14.1), determine the minimum total cost schedule using the crashing procedure described in (a) Example 14.2 and (b) Exercise 25. Assume that indirect cost ($1,000) is given by $2 + t$ and opportunity cost is given by $-15 + 0.5\,t$, where t is elapsed time in days.

Activity	Time Estimates (days)		Direct Cost Estimates ($1,000)	
(i, j)	Normal	Crash	Normal	Crash
(1, 4)	10	6	50	60
(1, 6)	3	1	35	36
(1, 7)	1	1	1	1
(1, 2)	2	1	25	27
(2, 3)	7	5	1	1
(3, 4)	3	2	8	11
(4, 5)	5	4	12	20
(5, 6)	4	2	3	8
(6, 8)	4	3	8	12
(6, 9)	3	2	5	8
(9,10)	6	4	12	15
(5,10)	3	3	2	2
(7,11)	4	2	3	8
(10,11)	7	4	5	6

PERT/Cost

PERT/Cost is a cost accounting technique for achieving realistic estimates of costs associated with activities and for providing an information system which allows excellent control of interim project costs. The federal government, which originally published the technique, uses it regularly for controlling cost overruns in governmental contracts.

The need for an accounting system which is conceptually consistent with project management becomes evident when one considers that traditional cost accounting systems group costs not by activities but by organizational areas, flows of materials, and time periods. PERT/Cost provides a means for structuring costs which is consistent with project management models.

With respect to planning and scheduling, PERT/Cost generates cumulative and average expenditures on a period-by-period basis for alternative schedules. This feature is useful in deciding when activities should be started between their earliest and latest starting dates.

Additionally, the information system for PERT/Cost provides reports which allow project managers to control costs and evaluate performance with respect to the schedule. For example, suppose *actual* cost for an activity is 80 percent of *budgeted* cost at some point in time. One might think that cost is under control; however, the activity may be only 50 percent complete. PERT/Cost provides this information routinely each period, for each activity, and for the project as a whole.

14.5   IMPLEMENTATION AND CONTROL

Our discussions of PERT/CPM models have focused on the planning and scheduling of projects. As noted in PERT/Cost, however, there is at least an equal need for monitoring and, perhaps, replanning as progress on the project takes place. The project management concept is a viable way to implement change; and in this section we will attempt to illustrate this viability with concrete examples.

Implementation at Ethan Allen

One of the authors served as a consultant to the Ethan Allen furniture company for several years. In 1972, a critical need for additional capacity led to major plant expansion projects in seven furniture factories (in addition to minor increases in the other factories). The typical expansion project consisted of a 100 percent or greater increase in volume, design and construction of large buildings, layout and purchase of new equipment, rearrangement of existing facilities, and the hiring and training of new employees.

Large capital expenditures were committed to these expansion projects, and there were substantial pressures to get the additional capacities on line as quickly as possible. The vice president of manufacturing was very concerned about cost and time performance. This was the largest set of expansion projects ever taken on by the company; if past time-cost experiences were to be repeated, the company would need to go back into the money markets and customer complaints would reach an all-time high.

Each major expansion project was planned as a PERT network with a bar chart constructed to show week by week expectations for each activity. As actual results were achieved, these were colored onto the charts to show progress. A weekly progress report was required from each expansion project manager.

A detailed description of this entire effort would take more space than can be allotted, but there are several interesting aspects that can be highlighted. At the outset of the use of PERT, most of the plant managers responsible for the major projects did not understand the models. They had all participated in expansion projects before, felt they knew how to do them, and that the PERT approach was largely a "pain in the neck."

Initial responsibility for preparing the PERT plan was often delegated to someone who did not understand the complexities of the project. As a result, original plans had great variability in quality. Eventually, the requirement of PERT planning and reporting forced managers to understand the technique as well as to explain early deviations in plans. The result was better control and attention to meeting detailed objectives. Furthermore, extensive replanning resulted in better matches of time and cost schedules to reality than would otherwise have been achieved.[9]

At one point, it was necessary to plan an education program for people actively engaged in major expansion projects. Included were the basics of project management models, the reporting and control procedures, and a case study. This session was intensive, lasted three days, and took place after the projects had been in the design stages for several months. At that point, each person had made major mistakes which could be shared, and the validity of project management models became obvious.

A critical reason for previous poor time-cost performance at Ethan Allen was a tendency to focus attention on the physical or "hard" aspects of a plant expansion. For example, the construction of buildings, placement of utilities, and ordering of equipment received a great deal of attention; but the design of a production scheduling system for the expanded volume or the training of 150 new employees did not receive the same degree of concerted effort.

This tendency to focus on hard activities to the detriment of "soft" activities was clearly shown in the planning models for Ethan Allen. Almost all of the projects included no provision for activities such as project scheduling, quality control procedures, plant maintenance and protection, shop floor control, production scheduling, personnel planning, capital budgeting, start up budgets and pro forma statements, standard cost calculations, product engineering, safety, hiring, training, or incentive wage determination.

When attention was clearly focused on the importance of considering soft activities as well as the hard activities, a very interesting learning experience took place. When each of these activities is included, it is necessary to identify the resources that will be used. That is, for example, *who* will design the new production scheduling system? The resources required for soft activities are almost always managerial people, and the analysis of the work loads placed on these individuals can be frightening. It is not hard to see why past failures were so prevalent.

Another Case History

To build on these ideas, let us now turn to another example of project management in the real world. One of the authors was called in as a consultant to a manufacturing company which mined and converted a raw

---

[9] As projects progress over time, new schedules need to be developed periodically because initially scheduled times deviate from actual times. New networks and time charts can be generated by assigning zero durations to completed activities and remaining durations to partially completed activities.

material into a consumer product. The company perceived an inadequate return from its manufacturing sector, but the exact definition of the consulting assignment was kept open-ended and broad in nature to avoid artificial roadblocks to fundamental understanding. An important part of the consulting relationship involved problem delineation, which steadily evolved during the consultation period.

The study focused initially on a manufacturing audit and the identification of potential cost reductions. Two major varieties of cost reduction seemed possible: across the board increases in worker productivity with the existing set of methods or technology, and significant changes in the methods themselves. The latter approach was taken by identifying projects which resulted in major cost reductions.

As these projects were identified, some broader issues became apparent. Perhaps the most fundamental observation was the perception of great potentiality for cost reduction within the company. In fact, many of the specific cost-saving proposals suggested by the consulting study had been previously identified by manufacturing personnel. The problem as seen by the middle managers in the manufacturing function was a lack of personnel to study and implement the cost-saving proposals. These middle managers also felt that there was insufficient direction from top management as to the priority of cost-reduction projects.

At this point, the focus of the consulting study shifted from the identification of potential cost reductions to the *process* of implementing improvements within the company, to causes of sluggishness, and to ways in which the implementation process might be improved.

One of the main reasons for failure to implement improvements was that the line organization could not carry out improvement projects while taking care of day-to-day activities. This situation seemed to require staff support for operations improvement projects in two major areas: in the technical or engineering area, and in managerial-project planning. Present improvement projects were accomplished largely by line managers whose technical talents were limited and who were clearly occupied with many other activities. Projects were undertaken without use of techniques such as PERT; few projects were finished on schedule, substantial cost overruns were frequent, and the number of projects which could be initiated was limited.

A project management concept was recommended for major capital appropriation items and for problems which crossed functional authority boundaries. One particular project was selected by manufacturing people from several which reasonably might be completed within 6 to 12 months. A project team was set up to plan, evaluate, and coordinate the project, and a project manager was appointed. The team included the plant manager, chief engineer, supervisor directly responsible for the area in which the improvement was planned, purchasing agent (during the early stages), and project manager. The total job was broken down into activities, and a network and schedule of required resources were thereafter prepared.

The project management concept had the approval and commitment of top management. This meant that resources needed for this project would have priority over alternative uses. This was most important in utilizing personnel resources, particularly engineering personnel. The project required one engineer's time for almost six months, which was crucial in completing the project within a reasonable time period.

When the detailed list of required technical activities was finalized, the project team seemed rather surprised. The improvement project called for purchase of a new piece of capital equipment, and at the outset it was felt that only a minimal amount of engineering talent would be required. As it turned out, however, installation of the equipment required design of concrete footings, changes in handling systems for very heavy materials, structural steel designs for some auxiliary equipment, major changes in the electric power system, and redesign of a system for pumping abrasive materials.

Improvement projects within this company prior to the establishment of project management concepts resulted in a strong commitment of financial resources but a weak commitment of personnel resources. As a result, many projects did not have *someone* clearly responsible for completion of specific tasks at specific times as well as *someone* clearly responsible for coordinating activities between different individuals and/or departments who might accomplish those tasks.

The project management concept resulted in the first project being completed within 10 percent of estimated cost, with cost savings that were greater than those stated at the outset, but with a slippage in the final time schedule of two months from the anticipated seven months. Although the two-month slippage was unfortunate and potentially avoidable in future projects, the company felt that the overall timing was extraordinarily good and that without the close control and integration of all activities which the project management concept provided for, the actual time would have been at least doubled and probably tripled.

14.6 ASSESSMENT OF PERT/CPM

Specific *technical* criticisms of PERT/CPM techniques abound: difficulty in accurately estimating durations, variances, and costs; validity of Beta distributions in representing durations; validity of statistical independence of activities; validity of applying the Central Limit Theorem for estimating event probabilities; the optimistic effect of assuming that the critical path is always the longest path (which ignores variances along near-critical paths); and the existence of nonlinear direct cost-time functions in CPM.

Additionally, *administrative* and *behavioral* problems arise, as discussed in the case histories of the previous section. Another problem which we have not mentioned is the "mountain" of computer printout produced for the project team's "ingestion." A delightful editorial by Andrew Vazsonyi suggests that the final resolution for large PERT systems (having hundreds and even thousands of activities) is a "Shredmaster Conveyor 400" that has the incredible ability to gobble up and shred into pulp 2,500 lb. of computer printout per hour.[10]

In the final analysis, judgment must rest with the answer to "Do we get

---

[10] Andrew Vazsonyi, "L'Histoire de Grandeur et de la Decadence de la Methode PERT," *Management Science*, vol. 16, no. 8 (April 1970), p. 455.

better results using project management models than alternative procedures?" If so, "Does the additional cost justify the benefits?" According
to various surveys, a number of real-world projects have answered both of
these questions in the affirmative, including the Polaris submarine, the
Braves stadium, and the Houston Astrodome.

14.7 OTHER NETWORK MODELS

Network analysis has considerably wider application than PERT and
CPM. It has been applied in areas involving physical systems such as oil
distribution systems, telecommunication systems, and computer networks,
and in less tangible areas such as airline scheduling and organizational
structures. Its flexibility is further illustrated by its applicability to the
transportation and assignment problems of Chapter 7 and to the traveling
sales representative problem of Chapter 8. In this section we will provide
additional terminology in network theory, and we will overview a few
classical network problems and approaches to their solution.

Network Terminology: A Review

Although we have introduced the terms *network, directed arc, node,
source,* and *sink* in Section 14.1 as they pertain to PERT, it will be useful
in this section to generalize these definitions, as well as others, for the
discussion which follows. Networks are typically represented by graphs.
The graphs consist of **nodes,** denoted by circles, which usually represent
locations. Some pairs of nodes may be connected by **arcs** or **branches**
which imply a relationship between the connected nodes. A typical arc
connecting two nodes may suggest that movement is allowed between the
nodes. Arcs may be further characterized by measures which express the
distance, cost, or time to travel between two nodes. **Directed arcs** are arcs
which have a specified direction. In Figure 14–13 the arc connecting
nodes 2 and 3 is a directed arc while that connecting nodes 2 and 4 is not.
The sequence of arcs connecting two nodes is called a **path** between the
nodes. The arcs connecting nodes 1–3–2 constitute a path between nodes
1 and 2. A **directed chain (directed path)** is a path made up of nodes and
directed arcs which actually allows for flow between two nodes. The path
1–3–2–5 is a directed chain between nodes 1 and 5. A path which begins
and ends at the same node is called a **loop.**

Often the arcs represent channels for the flow of some resource (cars,
information, fluids, and so forth). When all arcs associated with a node

FIGURE 14–13

A Network Diagram

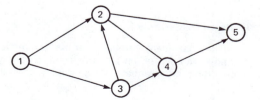

are oriented away from the node, it is referred to as a **source.** Node 1 is a source in Figure 14–13. When all arcs associated with a node are directed toward the node it is referred to as a **sink.** Node 5 is a sink in Figure 14–13. Finally, arcs may be characterized by a **flow capacity.** Flow capacities simply indicate a limit on the quantity of flow along an arc in a feasible direction.

Shortest-Route Problem

Network analysis can provide a useful framework for solving shortest-route problems. The classic shortest-route problem involves finding the shortest route from some origin node to a destination node. As mentioned above, however, the context of a shortest-route problem may require the minimization of costs to complete some project, where branches represent alternative activities required to complete the project; or, another problem might involve identifying the sequence of activities which will minimize the total time to complete a project.

Our purpose in mentioning this type of problem is to create awareness that it can be solved within the framework of network analysis. Because we discussed the dynamic programming solution to this problem in Chapter 9, we will not present other solution approaches in this chapter.

Minimal Spanning Tree Problem

Another classic network problem requires selection of the set of arcs for a network which provides a route between all pairs of nodes and minimizes the total distance (cost or time) to do so. Another way of viewing this problem is that it involves selecting the network which forms a *tree* that *spans* the nodes of interest. In network terminology, a **tree** is a network without loops which connects every pair of nodes.

This type of problem has wide applicability, especially to transportation and telecommunication networks. As an example, consider a "planned community" which is in the process of drawing up blueprints for sewer service in the community. It knows the locations of the users (nodes) and it wishes to provide sewer service to all users at a minimum cost of construction. In this instance, the minimum spanning tree problem requires identification of the network of sewers which reaches all users and minimizes the total amount of sewer pipe. Take a minute to think of other minimal spanning tree problems.

Although a number of algorithms exist for solving this type of problem, the following example illustrates a very simple procedure.

Example 14.3   Agricultural Irrigation

A corporate food producer has many farms under its "umbrella." One major farm for producing corn on each of ten fields is in the planning stage. A primary concern is providing an adequate water supply to the fields.

Supply of water itself is not the problem. The firm wishes, though, to minimize the cost of installing a water pipe network which reaches all fields. A well will be drilled at one of the fields from which all others will be supplied. Figure 14–14 is a graph where each node represents a field and each arc represents a potential water pipe link between respective fields. The numbers attached to each arc represent costs (in $1,000's) associated with installing the link. Costs primarily reflect the cost of pipe, labor, and equipment. Although usually a linear function of pipe length, some differentials exist according to difficulty in laying the pipe (for example, blasting rock formations or installing overhead pipes).

One way of identifying the minimum cost network is to apply the following **minimal spanning tree algorithm:**

1. Select *any* node and identify the least distant (cost or time) node. Connect the two. (Break any ties arbitrarily.)
2. Identify the *unconnected* node which is the least distant from any *connected* node and connect the two. (Break any ties arbitrarily.)
3. Repeat step (2) until all nodes have been connected.

To illustrate this algorithm, consider the farming problem in Figure 14–14. Arbitrarily, we begin with node 1. The shortest arc (costwise) emanating from node 1 is that leading to node 2. Thus, these two nodes are connected. Applying step (2), the next shortest arc leads from connected node 2 to unconnected node 5, and these two are connected. Comparing all unconnected nodes with nodes 1, 2, and 5, the next least costly arc results in node 5 being connected with node 6. Table 14–10 summarizes the steps which lead to the spanning tree with minimum cost. Figure 14–15 illustrates this network. Minimum total costs are $53,000.

FIGURE 14–14

Network for Farm Irrigation Example

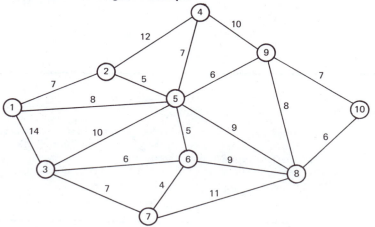

TABLE 14–10

Solution Summary for Example 14.3

Solution Step	Nodes Connected	Cost of Connection ($1,000's)	Cumulative Cost ($1,000's)
1..................	1–2	7	7
2..................	2–5	5	12
3..................	5–6	5	17
4..................	6–7	4	21
5..................	6–3	6	27
6..................	5–9	6	33
7..................	5–4	7	40
8..................	9–10	7	47
9..................	10–8	6	53

FIGURE 14–15

Minimal Spanning Tree for Farm Irrigation Problem

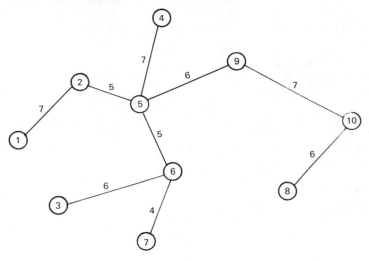

Follow-up Exercise

27. Verify that the algorithm presented above is valid regardless of the initial node selected by beginning (a) at node 10 and (b) at node 7. (Hint: To help yourself along, start with a "tree" having only nodes and no branches. Thereafter, connect the appropriate nodes at each step of the algorithm.)

The Maximal Flow Problem

The maximal flow problem is concerned with determining the maximum flow which can pass from one input node or *source* through a network and out one output node or *sink* during a specified time period. Examples include maximizing the flow of oil through pipelines, cars through highway systems, passengers through airports, and so forth. Flow capacities associated with arcs of the network set restrictions on the amount of flow between nodes. Pipe size, number of traffic lanes, and number of check-in counters and gates all affect flow capacities in the examples above.

The following example illustrates the nature of the maximal flow problem and presents a simple solution algorithm.

Example 14.4   Postal Routing

The post office at city 1 is preparing for the Christmas rush. A heavy volume of mail always moves from city 1 to city 3, and the post office wants to determine the maximum number of pieces it can deliver each day. Mail moves by either air, truck, or rail from city 1 through city 2 to city 3. Mail may move via the same mode of transportation for the complete trip or it may switch modes at city 2. Figure 14–16 indicates the delivery network. Arcs labeled *A, T,* and *R* represent air, truck, and rail links, respectively. Nodes 2′, 2″, and 2‴ all represent city 2 in the network. The flow capacities (in 10,000's of pieces per day) along an arc are indicated next to each node. Notice that these capacities may vary according to direction of flow and that each node indicates the flow capacities in a direction *away from* the node.

The following algorithm finds the solution to the maximal flow problem, where f_{ij} is the flow capacity from node i to node j.

1. Identify *any* path from the origin to the sink having *positive* flow capacities, f_{ij}, (in the direction of the path) along each arc of the path. If no such path exists, then the optimal solution has been found.
2. Determine the *minimum* positive flow capacity between any two nodes on the path, f_{ij}^*. Increase the flow along the path by f_{ij}^*.
3. Compensate for the flow assignment in (2) by *reducing* the flow capacities in the direction of the flow assignment by f_{ij}^* for all nodes on the path. *Increase* the respective capacities in the reverse direction along the path by the same quantity.
4. Repeat steps (1) through (3) until an optimal solution has been identified.

Referring to Figure 14–16, we first identify path 1–2′–3 (shipment by air from city 1 to city 3) as allowing positive flows through each arc on the path. The flow capacity for arc 1–2′ ($f_{12'} = 16$) is compared with that for arc 2′–3 ($f_{2'3} = 23$), which gives $f_{12'}^* = 16$. Thus, 16 (10,000's) pieces of mail are allocated along this path. Flow capacities for all nodes

FIGURE 14–16

Network for Example 14.4

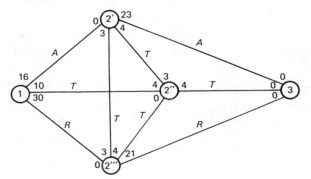

FIGURE 14–17

Intermediate Networks for Example 14.4

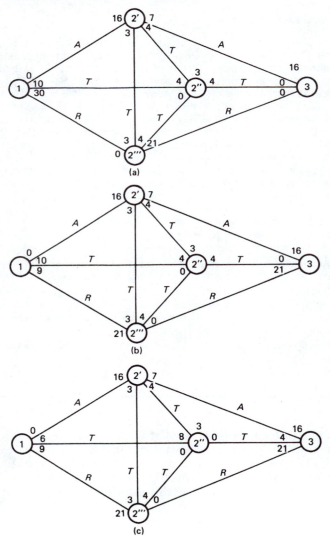

on the path are adjusted according to step (3), as indicated in Figure 14–17*a*.

Arbitrarily, we next identify flow potential along the path 1–2‴–3. Comparing $f_{12\cdots} = 30$ to $f_{2\cdots 3} = 21$, we see that 21 (10,000's) pieces of mail can be allocated to move by rail from city 1 to city 3. Flow capacities for all nodes on this path are adjusted as indicated in Figure 14–17*b*.

From Figure 14–17*b*, flow potential is identified for the path 1–2″–3. You should verify that 4 (10,000's) pieces of mail may be delivered by truck from city 1 to city 3. The resulting network is shown in Figure 14–17*c*.

At this stage, single mode delivery alternatives have been exhausted. There are, however, other possibilities for shipping mail from city 1 to city 3. For example, mail can go by rail to city 2, then by truck to the air terminal in city 2, then by air to city 3. How many paths are possible in this network?

You should verify that the maximal flow between cities 1 and 3 is 470,000 pieces of mail per day. Table 14–11 summarizes the allocations.

TABLE 14–11

Allocations for Example 14.4

Allocation	Path	Quantity
1	1–2′–3	16
2	1–2‴–3	21
3	1–2″–3	4
4	1–2″–2′–3	3
5	1–2‴–2′–3	3

Follow-up Exercises

28. Draw the intermediate networks associated with allocations 4 and 5 in Table 14–11. What specifically in the delivery network restricts the shipment of more mail? What alternatives are available to increase the flow? Are there other criteria the postal authorities should be considering in this problem?

29. Resolve Example 14.4 by making the initial allocation of 4 units along the path 1–2′–2″–3. Do you get the same solution? Draw the final network diagram for both this solution and the solution in Example 14.4. Compare the final flow capacities for the two diagrams. Are they same?

**30. In Exercise 29 there is an initial flow of 4 units along arc 2′–2″. At a later step in the solution process a flow of 7 units occurs in the reverse direction from 2″–2′. When a reverse flow occurs along an arc, one can think of this as canceling the previous equivalent flow along the arc. The net effects of the 7-unit allocation are:

1. The original flow of 4 units along path 1–2′–2″–3 is negated and these 4 units are "reallocated" to path 1–2′–3.

2. Four of the 7 units of flow from 1–2″ are allocated along the path 1–2″–3.
3. The remaining 3 of the 7 units are allocated along the path 1–2″–2′–3.

Verify a similar reversal of flow along arc 2‴–2′ if the *initial* allocation in Exercise 29 is a 3-unit flow along the path 1–2′–2‴–3. Verify that the solution in this instance is the same as that for Exercise 29.

SELECTED REFERENCES

Ford, L. R., Jr., and Fulkerson, D. R. *Flows in Networks.* Princeton, N.J.: Princeton University Press, 1962.

Frank, H., and Frisch, I. T. *Communication, Transmission, and Transportation Networks.* Reading, Mass.: Addison-Wesley Publishing Co., 1971.

Giffin, Walter C. *Introduction to Operations Engineering.* Homewood, Ill.: Richard D. Irwin, Inc., 1971.

Hillier, Frederick S., and Lieberman, Gerald J. *Introduction to Operations Research.* 2d ed. San Francisco: Holden Day, Inc., 1974.

Levin, R., and Kirkpatrick, C. A. *Planning and Control with PERT/CPM.* New York: McGraw-Hill Book Co., 1966.

Moder, Joseph J., and Phillips, Cecil R. *Project Management with CPM and PERT.* 2d ed. New York: Van Nostrand, 1970.

Wagner, Harvey M. *Principles of Operations Research.* 2d ed. Englewood Cliffs, N.J.: Prentice-Hall, Inc., 1975.

Wiest, J. D., and Levy, F. *A Management Guide to PERT/CPM.* Englewood Cliffs, N.J.: Prentice-Hall, Inc., 1969.

ADDITIONAL EXERCISES

31. *Product Development* Consider this simplified scenario for the development of a consumer product through the market test phase.

Activity	Symbol	Preceding Activities	Time Estimate (weeks)
Design promotion campaign	A	—	3
Initial pricing analysis	B	—	1
Product design	C	—	5
Promotional costs analysis	D	A	1
Manufacture prototype models	E	C	6
Product cost analysis	F	E	1
Final pricing analysis	G	B,D,F	2
Market test	H	G	8

a. Draw the network for this project.
b. Calculate total slacks and free slacks, and interpret their meaning.
c. Determine the critical path and interpret its meaning.
d. Construct a time chart and identify scheduling flexibilities.

32. For the product development project in the preceding exercise consider the detailed time estimates given below. Note that time estimates in the preceding exercise are equivalent to modal time estimates in this exercise.

	Time Estimates (weeks)		
Activity	Optimistic	Most Likely	Pessimistic
A.....................	1	3	4
B.....................	1	1	2
C.....................	4	5	9
D.....................	1	1	1
E.....................	4	6	12
F.....................	1	1	2
G.....................	1	2	3
H.....................	6	8	10

a. Relabel your network in the preceding exercise to include $\bar{d}_{ij}$ (in place of d_{ij}) and v_{ij}. Use Formulas (14.5) and (14.6).
b. Compare total slacks and free slacks to the preceding exercise.
c. Has the critical path changed?
d. Determine the following probabilities:

 1. That the project will be completed in 22 weeks or less.
 2. That the project will be completed by its earliest expected completion date.
 3. That the project takes more than 30 weeks to complete.

33. Use Equations (14.8) and (14.9) to calculate $\bar{d}_{ij}$ and v_{ij} and answer the same questions as in the preceding exercise. Compare results to the preceding exercise.

34. Consider the cost-time estimates for the product development project of Exercise 31 as given here.

	Time Estimates (weeks)		Direct Cost Estimates ($1,000's)	
Activity	Normal	Crash	Normal	Crash
A.....................	3	1.0	3.5	10.0
B.....................	1	0.5	1.2	2.0
C.....................	5	3.0	9.0	18.0
D.....................	1	0.7	1.0	2.0
E.....................	6	3.0	20.0	50.0
F.....................	1	0.5	2.2	3.0
G.....................	2	1.0	4.0	9.0
H.....................	8	6.0	100.0	150.0

Indirect cost is made up of two components: a fixed cost of $5,000 and a variable cost of $1,000 per week of elapsed time. Also, for each week the project exceeds 17 weeks, an opportunity cost of $2,000 per week is assessed.

a. Construct a time chart for the minimum total cost schedule.
b. Construct a two-part schedule of direct costs (of the type illustrated in Figure 14–6) based on the time schedule in part (a). Of the two, which schedule yields the lowest peak cost? Of the two, which schedule levels cost the most based on variance?

35. *Space Module Assembly* An aerospace company has received a contract from NASA for the final assembly of a space module for an upcoming mission. A team of engineers has determined the activities, precedence constraints, and time estimates given below.

Activity	Symbol	Preceding Activities	Time Estimate (days)
Construct shell of module................	A	—	30
Order life support system and scientific experimentation package from same supplier..................................	B	—	15
Order components of control and navigational system......................	C	—	25
Wire module............................	D	A	3
Assemble control and navigational system.	E	C	7
Preliminary test of life support system.....	F	B	1
Install life support system in module......	G	D,F	5
Install scientific experimentation package in module.......................	H	D,F	2
Preliminary test of control and navigational system...........................	I	E,F	4
Install control and navigational system in module...............................	J	H,I	10
Final testing and debugging.............	K	G,J	8

a. Draw the network for this project. (Hint: You should have ten events and two dummy activities.)
b. Calculate total slacks and free slacks, and interpret their meaning.
c. Determine the critical path and interpret its meaning.
d. Construct a time chart and identify scheduling flexibilities.

36. A more careful analysis of time estimates for the space module assembly of the preceding exercise is given here. Note that the "most likely estimates" are identical to the "time estimates" in the preceding exercise.

Activity	Time Estimates (days)		
	Optimistic	Most Likely	Pessimistic
A.....................	25	30	45
B.....................	10	15	20
C.....................	20	25	35
D.....................	3	3	5
E.....................	5	7	12
F.....................	1	1	1
G.....................	4	5	7.
H.....................	2	2	3
I.....................	4	4	6
J.....................	8	10	14
K.....................	6	8	15

a. Relabel your network in the preceding exercise to include $\bar{d}_{ij}$ (in place of d_{ij}) and v_{ij}. Use Equations (14.5) and (14.6).
b. Compare total slacks and free slacks to the preceding exercise.
c. Has the critical path changed?
d. Determine the following probabilities:

1. That the project will be completed in 54 days or less.
2. That the project will be completed by its earliest expected completion date.
3. That the project takes more than 70 days to complete.

37. Use Equations (14.8) and (14.9) to calculate $\bar{d}_{ij}$ and v_{ij} and answer the same questions as in the preceding exercise. Compare results to the preceding exercise.

38. A project has 11 activities that can be accomplished either by one person working alone, or by several people working together. The activities, precedence constraints, and time estimates are shown here.

Activities	Preceding Activities	Person-Days Required
A...............	—	10
B...............	A	8
C...............	A	5
D...............	B	6
E...............	D	8
F...............	C	7
G...............	E,F	4
H...............	F	2
I...............	F	3
J...............	H,I	3
K...............	J,G	2

Suppose that you have up to five people that can be assigned on any given day. A person must work full days on each activity, but the number of people working on an activity can vary from day to day.

a. Prepare a network diagram, calculate the critical path, total slacks, and free slacks assuming that one person (independently) is working on each task.
b. Prepare a time chart.
c. Prepare a daily assignment sheet for personnel so as to finish the project in minimum time.
d. Prepare a daily assignment sheet to "best" balance the workforce assigned to this project.
e. How many days could the project be compressed if unlimited personnel resources were available?

39. The Sour Grapes Winery has the following project defined for refurbishing one of their vats:

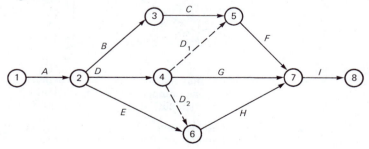

| | | | Crash Data | |
Task	$\bar{d}_{ij}$ (days)	$\sqrt{v_{ij}}$ (days)	Maximum Possible Compression (days)	Expediting Cost per Day ($)
A.	6	2	0	—
B.	2	0	1	50
C.	12	3	2	80
D.	8	1	2	175
E.	7	2	1	100
F.	16	4	0	—
G.	23	2	1	100
H.	25	5	3	300
I.	4	1	1	1000

a.   Find the critical path, total slacks, and free slacks.
b.   Find the probability of completion within 45 days.
c.   Find the minimum cost increase to reduce the expected project dura-
     tion by one day.
d.   Find the minimum cost increase to reduce the expected project dura-
     tion by two days.
e.   Find the minimum project duration and the expected cost increase.

40.   *Ski Resort Management*   A Colorado ski resort is planning for the com-
      ing season. Management wishes to determine the maximum number of
      skiers who can be transported to the top of the mountain with existing
      lift facilities. The figure indicates the network of lifts and flow capacities
      (in 100's of skiers per hour).

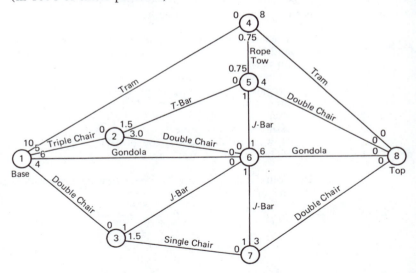

a.   Determine the maximal flow per hour to the top of the mountain.
b.   What are the constraining arcs for this network?
c.   How much flow should go through each lift facility?

41.   *Physical Plant Management*   A new community college is being estab-
      lished and the Director of Physical Plant is planning the sewer system

which will be used to service the ten buildings which will be constructed on the campus. The Director wants to minimize the amount of sewer pipe necessary to link all of the buildings.

In the figure, the nodes represent the building locations and the arcs represent the pairs of buildings which can be feasibly linked. The distances (in yards) between buildings are denoted on the arcs. Determine the minimum amount of sewer pipe needed to connect all buildings.

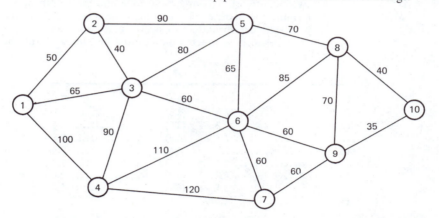

42. *Highway System Capacity* A European city has been named host for the upcoming summer Olympics. Municipal officials are concerned about the ability of the existing highway network to handle the volume of vehicles converging upon Olympic Village. All vehicular traffic must cross a river via one bridge and then choose different routes (as illustrated) to the village.

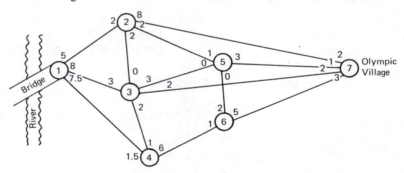

The network indicates flow capacities along each arc (in 1,000s of vehicles per hour). What would a capacity of zero indicate?

   a. Determine the maximum number of vehicles per hour which can reach the Olympic Village via the current network of highways.

   b. How much flow should go over each road to achieve this maximum?

   c. What highways are most restrictive to the flow of traffic?

43. *Highway Planning* Suppose that the network in the preceding exercise represents the layout for a proposed Olympic Village. Assume that no roads have been constructed and that each node represents a spectator interest area (for example, stadium, swimming complex, and so forth). The Board of Olympic Governors wants to establish a road network

which links each area. However, budget overruns on other construction activities require that the total length of roads be minimized. Given that d_{ij} equals the distance in miles between nodes i and j, the accompanying table enumerates distances for road links under consideration (links may not be included because of natural barriers such as rivers or because of distances which are obviously too long).

a. Draw the network, labeling each node and the length of each arc.
b. Determine the plan which minimizes the total length of roads necessary to span all spectator areas. If road construction costs \$10,000 per mile, then how much funds should be allocated for the highway plan?

(i, j)	$d_{i,j}$	(i, j)	$d_{i,j}$
(1,2)...................	2.5	(3,5)...................	2.2
(1,3)...................	2.2	(3,6)...................	2.4
(1,4)...................	2.7	(4,5)...................	2.8
(2,3)...................	1.9	(4,6)...................	2.5
(2,5)...................	2.4	(5,6)...................	1.0
(2,7)...................	4.2	(5,7)...................	2.6
(2,6)...................	3.1	(6,7)...................	2.4
(3,4)...................	1.8		

APPENDIX: MATHEMATICAL PROGRAMMING APPLIED TO PROJECT MANAGEMENT MODELS

In this appendix we illustrate the use of mathematical programming in determining (1) the earliest completion time for the project, (2) the critical path, and (3) the schedule which minimizes direct cost for the project.

Earliest Event Times and Critical Path

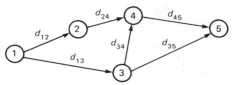

For the illustrative network given by the accompanying figure, we define E_j as the earliest time for event j and d_{ij} as the duration of activity (i, j). Our objective is to *minimize* the earliest time of completing the project (as given by E_5) such that constraints imposed by the definition of E_j are not violated. That is, our constraints must guarantee that E_j is at least equal to or greater than the sum of durations along *all* paths leading into event j. For example, with respect to event 4, the following two constraints guarantee that E_4 is no less than the *longest* path into event 4, as suggested by Equation (14.1):

$$E_4 \geq E_2 + d_{24}$$

and

$$E_4 \geq E_3 + d_{34}.$$

For the entire network, you should easily confirm the following LP formulation for determining earliest event times:

Minimize

$$z = E_5$$

subject to

$$
\begin{array}{llll}
E_2 & & \geq d_{12} & \text{(1)} \\
& E_3 & \geq d_{13} & \text{(2)} \\
-E_2 & \quad + E_4 & \geq d_{24} & \text{(3)} \\
& -E_3 + E_4 & \geq d_{34} & \text{(4)} \\
& -E_3 \quad + E_5 & \geq d_{35} & \text{(5)} \\
& -E_4 + E_5 & \geq d_{45} & \text{(6)}
\end{array}
$$

$$E_j \geq 0 \text{ for all } j.$$

Inspection of the right-hand–side constants in (1) through (6) should convince you that the number of constraints always equals the number of activities. Furthermore, it can be shown that the dual of this primal problem (after certain modifications) is equivalent to a formulation for finding the *longest* path in the network. The optimal values of dual variables (*shadow prices*) indicate whether an activity is critical (value of unity) or noncritical (value of zero); hence, the critical path can be determined by examining shadow prices in the optimal solution to the primal problem. Since for each constraint in the primal there is a corresponding dual variable, it follows that (in our example) the shadow price corresponding to constraint (1) indicates whether or not activity (1, 2) is critical, the shadow price corresponding to constraint (2) determines the nature of activity (1, 3), and so forth.

Follow-up Exercises

44. Formulate the LP model for the restaurant project.

45. Confirm our solution to the restaurant project by solving the LP model. Inspect shadow prices to determine the critical path. Interpret the meaning of surplus variables. (Hint: See Equation (14.4).)

46. Formulate and solve by linear programming the network given in part (a) of Figure 14–12. Confirm the critical path from shadow prices and interpret the meaning of surplus variables.

47. What recourse do you have if all E_j are restricted to integer values?

**48. Find the critical path for the network in part (a) of Figure 14–12 by dynamic programming. Treat each event as a stage. (Hint: See Exercises 43 and 44 of Chapter 9, page 349.)

Minimum Cost Schedules

In Section 14.4, we presented a cumbersome "hand" technique for generating direct cost curves based on the concept of crashing. Assuming a linear function between crash and normal points (see Figure 14–11) and an intercept on the cost axis given by A_{ij}, the direct cost contribution of activity (i, j) is given by

$$A_{ij} - S_{ij} \cdot x_{ij}, \tag{1}$$

where S_{ij} is the slope defined by (14.10) and x_{ij} is the *scheduled duration* for activity (i, j).[11] The objective function is determined by summing (1) over all defined (i, j) activities:

Minimize

$$z = \sum_{(i, j)} (A_{ij} - S_{ij} \cdot x_{ij}). \tag{2}$$

The first set of constraints ensures that all x_{ij} are assigned values between crash (DC_{ij}) and normal (DN_{ij}) durations:

$$
\begin{aligned}
x_{ij} &\le DN_{ij}, & \text{all defined } (i, j) \\
x_{ij} &\ge DC_{ij}, & \text{all defined } (i, j).
\end{aligned} \tag{3}
$$

The next set of constraints guarantees that all free slacks, as given by Equation (14.4), must be greater than or equal to zero:

$$E_j - E_i - x_{ij} \ge 0, \qquad \text{all defined } (i, j), \tag{4}$$

where E_j is the earliest time for event j. Note that (4) avoids the inconsistency of a duration being longer than its allotted time, as given by $(E_j - E_i)$. Also, in addition to all x_{ij}, all E_j are treated as decision variables. Finally, the duration of the project, as specified by t, must conform to the earliest time for the terminal event (n):

$$E_n = t. \tag{5}$$

The solution to this LP problem yields the schedule (E_j's and x_{ij}'s) which minimizes direct cost for a project of length t, which represents a point on the "Direct Cost" function of Figure 14–10. The entire function can be constructed by varying t in steps between its appropriate limits and solving (2) through (5) for each step. A far more efficient (and elegant) approach is the use of parametric linear programming (Chapter 10) for generating optimal z as a function of t.

---

[11] Certain nonlinear functions can be modeled by piecewise LP (Section 4.6) or by other methods, some of which are described in Chapter 10.

Follow-up Exercises

49. Explain why it would be valid to maximize

$$z' = \sum_{(i,j)} S_{ij} \cdot x_{ij}$$

in finding optimal values for x_{ij} and E_j. Is z' equivalent to direct cost?

50. In general, within what limits can t be varied?

51. How can you be sure that E_j represents the *earliest* time for event j?

52. Formulate the LP version for the project in Example 14.2.

53. Solve the preceding exercise (and compare to Table 14.9) for

    a. $t = 9$.
    b. $t = 10, \ldots, 16$.

54. Formulate the LP version for the restaurant project as given in Exercise 26.

**55. Solve the preceding exercise for $t = 25, \ldots, 38$.

15

Stochastic Processes

A STOCHASTIC PROCESS is a process of observation which can be repeated and which has two or more outcomes that are determined by chance factors. In this sense it is synonymous with the notion of a *random experiment,* as discussed in Section A.1 on page 702. Such a broad perspective, however, would include all of probability theory. The accepted perspective, which we adopt, takes a more narrow point of view by basing the definition of a stochastic process on a time parameter; that is, outcomes in the process are "indexed" or identified at specific points in time.

In this chapter, we begin by establishing the nature of stochastic processes, follow with the development of a specific type of stochastic process called a Markov process, and thereafter present analytical models of Markov processes which have been useful in actual applications. Our aim throughout this chapter is based on your achieving a sound conceptual understanding of these models and their uses.

15.1 NATURE OF STOCHASTIC PROCESSES[1]

As noted above, a stochastic process is a random experiment over time whereby some attribute of interest assumes numerical values according to chance factors (probability laws). This attribute, which may take on nominal (categorical) values, is termed a *random variable.*

A **stochastic process** is defined by the family or *set* of random variables $\{X_t\}$, where t is a time parameter (index) from a given *set* T. For example, if X_t is defined as the number of customers observed in a camera shop queuing system at the end of each hour (that is, at time t), then $\{X_1, X_2, X_3, X_4, X_5, X_6, X_7, X_8\}$ represents a stochastic process for

---

[1] Knowledge of the concepts in Sections A.1 and A.2 in Appendix A at the end of the book is assumed throughout this chapter.

an eight-hour working day, and {2, 5, 3, 6, 10, 4, 3, 5} represents the *realization* of this process (that is, two customers were observed at the end of the first hour, five at the end of the second hour, . . .). In this case, T represents the set of hours in an eight-hour working day, or $T = \{1, 2, 3, 4, 5, 6, 7, 8\}$.

As another example, suppose that X_t represents the number of pints of a particular type of blood demanded in day t from the blood bank inventory of a hospital. $\{X_t\}$, or $\{X_1, X_2, X_3, . . .\}$, is a general representation of the stochastic process for blood demand, where t takes on values from the countably infinite set $T = \{1, 2, 3, . . .\}$. If the recorded demands for the first four days are 200, 175, 195, and 215 pints, then the realization of this stochastic process is depicted by {200, 175, 195, 215, . . .}.

A specific value for the random variables is termed a **state.** Hence, in the terminology of stochastic processes, the random variable X_t is termed a **state variable.** The **state space** (S) is simply the sample space for all possible values of X_t. If S exclusively contains discrete values, then $\{X_t\}$ is termed **a discrete state stochastic process.** In other words, S contains the mutually exclusive and exhaustive states (outcomes) associated with the process (experiment). The camera shop queuing example represents such a process since $S = \{0, 1, 2, . . . , N\}$ is the possible number of customers in the shop. In this case, N represents the capacity of the camera shop. Likewise, demand for blood is a discrete state stochastic process, since $S = \{0, 1, 2, 3, . . .\}$. In general, discrete state spaces may be *countably finite* (that is, the number of outcomes in S is finite) or *countably infinite* (that is, the number of outcomes in S is infinitely large). S for the camera shop is countably finite, while S for the blood bank example is countably infinite. Right?

If S is defined in terms of real (continuous) values along the line from $-\infty$ to ∞, then $\{X_t\}$ is classified as a **real-valued stochastic process.** For example, if X_t represents the weight of inventory in kilograms at time t for a specific type of raw material, then $\{X_t\}$ is real-valued. When S is real-valued, it may also be defined in two or more dimensions. Suppose X_t represents the coordinates of a special ocean buoy for tracing the flow of pollutants. In this case, possible latitude and longitude coordinates represent the state space. In general, a stochastic process is a **k-vector process** if S is represented by a coordinate system in k-space.

In the same manner, the **index parameter** T can be discrete or continuous. If T is restricted to integer values; that is, $T = \{0, 1, 2, . . .\}$, then $\{X_t\}$ is a **discrete parameter stochastic process.** As described, the camera shop and blood bank examples represent discrete parameter stochastic processes. However, if X_t were defined as the number of customers in the camera shop at *any point* in time, then $\{X_t\}$ would be a **continuous parameter stochastic process.** Similarly, depending on how the time parameter is defined, the raw material inventory example and the ocean buoy can be treated as either discrete parameter or continuous parameter stochastic processes.

Table 15–1 summarizes the four possible categories for these examples. It follows that any stochastic process can be classified into one of these four categories. Why is the classification important? Because the manner

TABLE 15–1

Categories of Stochastic Processes

	Definition of T	
Definition of S	Discrete Parameter (DP)	Continuous Parameter (CP)
Discrete State (DS)......	1. X_t = Number of customers in camera shop at *end* of hour *t*. 2. X_t = Pints of blood demanded *during* day *t*.	1. X_t = Number of customers in camera shop at *any* point in time *t*.
Real-Valued (RV)........	3. X_t = Kilograms of raw material in inventory at *end* of week *t*. 4. X_t = Coordinate of ocean buoy at 4 P.M. on day *t*.	3. X_t = Kilograms of raw material in inventory at *any* instant in time *t*. 4. X_t = Coordinate of ocean buoy at *any* point in time *t*.

in which S and T are defined determines the type of analytic model which is used to describe the stochastic process. For example, *DS-DP* (discrete state-discrete parameter) stochastic processes can be described by manipulating discrete probability distributions using tools in finite mathematics, whereas *RV-CP* (real-valued–continuous parameter) stochastic processes require the more mathematically sophisticated continuous probability distributions with tools in the calculus. In this chapter we will focus on the analytic properties of *DS-DP* stochastic processes.

Once the category of a stochastic process is identified, the *dependency relationships* among the random variables in the set must be specified by identifying appropriate probability distributions. When this is done we say the process is *well-defined*. If a stochastic process is well-defined, then it can be modeled analytically, as we will subsequently demonstrate.

Example 15.1   Income Tax Audits

Consider a problem which is dear (not to mention frightening) to many of us: the possibility that the Internal Revenue Service (IRS) will audit our taxpayer's return. Suppose that records for a particular taxpayer are shown in the accompanying table.

Year (*t*)	1	2	3	4	5	6	7	8	9	10
Audit ?	No	No	No	Yes	No	No	Yes	Yes	Yes	No

In this case, the state variable is discrete and can take on one of two values. Let $X_t = 0$ if there is no audit in year *t* and $X_t = 1$ if there is an audit in year *t*. $\{X_t\}$ then is a discrete state and discrete parameter stochastic process where $S = \{0,1\}$ and $T = \{1,2, \ldots\}$. For a ten-year period, $\{X_t\} = \{X_1, X_2, \ldots, X_{10}\}$ is a general representation of this stochastic process and $\{0,0,0,1,0,0,1,1,1,0\}$ is its realization.

15.2 MARKOV PROCESSES

Markov processes represent one of the best-known and most useful classes of stochastic processes. In this section we present some of their fundamental properties.

Markovian Property

A stochastic process is a **Markov process** if it satisfies the following condition, which is called the **Markovian property:**

> Given that the present (or most recent) state is known, the *conditional* probability of the next state is independent of states prior to the present (or most recent) state.

More specifically, for a discrete state and discrete parameter stochastic process, the conditional probability of a specific *next* state (that is, of $X_{t+1} = x_{t+1}$) given the *present* state (that is, given $X_t = x_t$) and given all states prior to the present state (that is, given $X_0 = x_0$, $X_1 = x_1 \ldots$, $X_{t-1} = x_{t-1}$) is identical to the conditional probability of a specific next state given the present state:

$$P(X_{t+1} = x_{t+1} \mid X_0 = x_0, X_1 = x_1, \ldots, X_t = x_t)$$
$$= P(X_{t+1} = x_{t+1} \mid X_t = x_t) \qquad (15.1)$$

for $t = 0, 1, \ldots$ and all possible sequences for state values. Note that an upper-case letter represents the random variable and a lower-case letter represents a specific value of the random variable (termed a random variate).

Equation (15.1) is the proper statement of the Markovian property for discrete state and discrete parameter stochastic processes. In the case of, say, a real-valued and continuous parameter process, the mathematical statement is given by

$$P(a < X_{t_{k+1}} \le b \mid X_{t_0} = x_0, X_{t_1} = x_1, \ldots, X_{t_k} = x_k)$$
$$= P(a < X_{t_{k+1}} \le b \mid X_{t_k} = x_k) \qquad (15.2)$$

where the points-in-time are chronological; that is, $t_0 < t_1 < \cdots < t_k < t_{k+1}$. In this case, t_k is the point-in-time for the most recent occurrence of a state and t_{k+1} represents the point-in-time for the next occurrence. As in Appendix A, a and b define a specific range for the random variable.

Example 15.2

If the discrete state and discrete parameter stochastic process in Example 15.1 is known to be Markovian, then the conditional probability of an audit in the 11th year can be stated according to the Markovian property given by Equation (15.1):

$$P(X_{11} = 1 \mid X_1 = 0, X_2 = 0, \ldots, X_{10} = 0) = P(X_{11} = 1 \mid X_{10} = 0).$$

This implies that *how* we got to the present state is not a factor in affecting the probability of the next state. In other words, the probability of an audit in year 11 is only conditional (dependent) on the fact that no audit occurred in year 10.

Follow-up Exercises

1. For the IRS example, state the Markovian property given by Equation (15.1) for the state "no audit in year 11."
2. Mathematically state the Markovian property for a (a) discrete state and continuous parameter Markov process and (b) continuous state and discrete parameter Markov process.

Transition Probabilities

The conditional probabilities given by the right-hand sides of Equations (15.1) and (15.2) represent so-called **transition probabilities.** Thus, a transition probability is defined as the conditional probability that the process will be in a specific future state given its most recent state. These probabilities are also termed *one-step* transition probabilities, since they describe the system between t and $t + 1$ in the discrete case and between t_k and t_{k+1} in the continuous case. Similarly, we refer to an m-step transition probability as the conditional probability describing states in the system between t and $t + m$ in the discrete case and between t_k and t_{k+m} in the continuous case.

A convenient representation of one-step transition probabilities for the discrete state case is given by the following **transition matrix:**[2]

$$
\mathbf{P} = \begin{array}{c} \\ \\ 1 \\ 2 \\ . \\ . \\ . \\ n \end{array}
\begin{array}{cccc}
1 & 2 & \ldots & n \\
\begin{pmatrix} p_{11} & p_{12} & \ldots & p_{1n} \\ p_{21} & p_{22} & \ldots & p_{2n} \\ . & & & \\ . & & & \\ . & & & \\ p_{n1} & p_{n2} & \ldots & p_{nn} \end{pmatrix}
\end{array}
$$

$$
\begin{array}{c} \text{To} \\ \text{From} \qquad \text{State} \\ \text{State} \end{array}
$$

where n is the number of exhaustive and mutually exclusive states and p_{ij} is the transition probability of going from the present (ith) state to the next (jth) state. Thus, rows represent the possible present states and columns represent the possible future states for the next outcome. Carefully note that the specific values of i and j represent identification numbers for discrete states, not their values. For example, the identification

---

[2] The notion of a matrix is reviewed in Appendix B at the end of the book.

numbers for the possible states in Example 15.1 are 1 and 2; however, the value for state 1 is $X_t = 0$ and for state 2 is $X_t = 1$.

By definition, the elements in **P** must satisfy the following two properties:

1. $0 \leq p_{ij} \leq 1$ for all i, j.

2. $\sum_{j=1}^{n} p_{ij} = 1, \quad i = 1, 2, \ldots, n.$

The first property follows from the definition of a probability. The second property states that each row of the transition matrix must sum to one. This follows from the Rule of Addition for mutually exclusive events which are exhaustive; that is, given that the system is presently in the ith state, the probability of its being next in state 1 or state 2 or . . . or state n is one.

Example 15.3

Suppose that the stochastic process in Example 15.1 is Markovian and that the transition matrix between year 10 and year 11 is given by

$$\mathbf{P} = \begin{pmatrix} p_{11} & p_{12} \\ p_{21} & p_{22} \end{pmatrix}$$
$$= \begin{pmatrix} 0.6 & 0.4 \\ 0.5 & 0.5 \end{pmatrix}.$$

In this case, row 1 ($i = 1$) represents a state of no audit in year 10 (that is, $X_{10} = 0$) and row 2 ($i = 2$) represents an audit in year 10 (that is, $X_{10} = 1$); column 1 ($j = 1$) represents no audit in year 11 (that is, $X_{11} = 0$) and column 2 ($j = 2$) represents an audit in year 11 (that is, $X_{11} = 1$).

The transition probability p_{11} states that the probability of not having an audit in the 11th year ($j = 1$) given that no audit was performed in the tenth year ($i = 1$) is 0.6. Mathematically,

$$p_{11} = P(X_{11} = 0 \mid X_{10} = 0) = 0.6.$$

Similarly,

$$p_{12} = P(X_{11} = 1 \mid X_{10} = 0) = 0.4.$$

Note that both properties of **P** are satisfied by this matrix.

Markov Chains

A **Markov chain** is a stochastic process with the following properties:

1. Discrete state space.
2. Markovian property.

3. One-step transition probabilities which remain constant over time (termed *stationary* transition probabilities).

If additionally the discrete state space has a finite number of states, then a **finite-state Markov chain** has been defined.

Markov chains constitute a prominent class of Markov processes which have desirable computational properties for real-world implementation. As we show in Section 15.4, a Markov chain is completely determined once we specify (with certainty) the transition matrix and the set of unconditional probabilities for initial states. Knowledge of these two sets of probabilities allows the probabilistic prediction of specific states at future points in time. Prior to computational considerations, however, we take the time in the next section to present scenarios of applications which have proven useful in actual practice.

Example 15.4

In Example 15.3 we presented a transition matrix for the Markov process described in Example 15.1. If a finite-state Markov chain is to be assumed, then the property of stationary transition probabilities prescribes that

$$\mathbf{P} = \begin{pmatrix} 0.6 & 0.4 \\ 0.5 & 0.5 \end{pmatrix}$$

remains constant over time.

Typically, the theoretical or true transition matrix is unknown in actual practice. The usual procedure for specifying **P** first assumes that the observed (historical) stochastic process is a random sample from the true process. If this is the case, then there is theoretical justification for basing point estimates of transition probabilities on the empirical probabilities obtained from a contingency table. To illustrate, the historical stochastic process in Example 15.1 given by

$$\{X_t\} = \{0,0,0,1,0,0,1,1,1,0\}$$

can be described by this *contingency* table. For example, three times the

From a Specific State in a Given Year	To a Specific State in the Following Year		Row Sum
	No Audit	Audit	
No audit....................	3	2	5
Audit.......................	2	2	4

state of the system went from "no audit" to "no audit" in adjoining years (that is, from $X_1 = 0$ to $X_2 = 0$, from $X_2 = 0$ to $X_3 = 0$, and from $X_5 = 0$ to $X_6 = 0$); hence, a 3 is placed in cell (1,1) of the table. (Can you confirm the other entries?)

By definition, p_{11} is the probability of "no audit" in a succeeding year given that there was "no audit" in the current year. From the contingency table, out of 5 "no audit" current years (the sum of row 1), 3 "no audit" succeeding years followed; hence, $p_{11} = \frac{3}{5}$. Similarly, $p_{12} = \frac{2}{5}$, or 2 "audit" years followed "no audit" years out of a possible 5. For the entire matrix, we have

$$\mathbf{P} = \begin{pmatrix} p_{11} = \frac{3}{5} & p_{12} = \frac{2}{5} \\ p_{21} = \frac{2}{4} & p_{22} = \frac{2}{4} \end{pmatrix},$$

which is consistent with the matrix we used previously.

Follow-up Exercises

3. Verbalize the implication and plausibility of each of the three assumptions (properties) in treating Example 15.1 as a Markov chain.

4. In estimating **P** for the IRS problem, would you prefer more than ten observations? Explain.

5. Suppose that a year has passed in the IRS problem. If an audit was performed in year 11, how would you update **P**? Would you say that the history of the stochastic process is relevant when **P** is not known with certainty? Explain. If so, does this necessarily violate the Markovian property? Explain.

6. Let f_{ij} represent the number of observations in cell (i,j) of a contingency table for **P**. Write down a general expression for calculating all p_{ij}.

15.3 APPLICATIONS OF MARKOV CHAINS

Early uses of Markov models are found in the physical sciences. For example, this type of analysis has been used to study the behavior of gas particles in a container, to model the development of biological populations, and to forecast weather patterns in meteorology. More recently, managerial applications include analyses of inventory and queuing systems; replacement and maintenance policies for machines; brand loyalty in marketing; time series of economic data such as price movements of stocks; accounts receivable in accounting; hospital systems such as the movements of coronary and geriatric patients; management of resources such as water and wildlife; and expected payout of life insurance policies. In this section we describe scenarios for three of these applications. In every case, a Markov chain is assumed. In the exercises at the end of the chapter, other applications will be described for you to formulate and analyze.

Brand Switching Model

Markov chains of brand switching behavior in the marketplace have been used for over a decade as diagnostic tools for suggesting marketing strategies. To illustrate a specific formulation, consider the brandswitching behavior depicted in Table 15–2 for a panel of 500 consumers. According to the first row, of the 100 consumers enjoyed by Brand 1 in Week 26, 90

TABLE 15.2

**Number of Consumers Switching from Brand i
in Week 26 to Brand j in Week 27**

Brand (j) 1	2	3	Total
(i)			
1 90	7	3	100
2 5	205	40	250
3 30	18	102	150
Total 125	230	145	500

repurchased Brand 1 in Week 27, 7 switched to Brand 2, and 3 switched to Brand 3. Note, however, that 5 customers switched from Brand 2 to Brand 1 and 30 customers switched from Brand 3 to Brand 1 (according to the first column); hence, for Brand 1, the loss of 10 customers $(7 + 3)$ was more than compensated by the gain of 35 customers $(5 + 30)$, yielding a net gain of 25 customers from one week to the next (100 v. 125). The market share for Brand 1 increased from 0.2 of the sample market (100/500) to 0.25 of the sample market (125/500).

Contingency tables of this type are useful because they not only show the net changes and market shares but also show the sources of change. For example, Brand 1 showed a net loss of 2 customers $(5 - 7)$ to Brand 2 and a net gain of 27 customers $(30 - 3)$ from Brand 3.

Additionally, such tables directly yield the *current* one-step matrix of transition probabilities, as given in Table 15–3. Note that **P** in this case represents a sample estimate of the underlying or true transition matrix. (See Example 15.4.) Further note that p_{ii} is a reflection of the "holding power" of Brand i, since it represents the probability that a consumer purchases Brand i given that the preceding purchase was Brand i. Similarly, p_{ij} reflects the "attraction power" of Brand j, in that it is an estimate of the probability that Brand j is purchased next given that Brand i was the preceding purchase.

If we define the state variable X_t as the brand purchased in Week t, then $\{X_t\}$ represents a discrete state and discrete parameter stochastic process where $S = \{1, 2, 3\}$ and $T = \{0, 1, 2, \ldots\}$. If we can establish

TABLE 15.3

Empirical Transition Probabilities (p_{ij}'s)

Brand (j) 1	2	3
(i)		
1 $\frac{90}{100} = 0.90$	$\frac{7}{100} = 0.07$	$\frac{3}{100} = 0.03$
2 $\frac{5}{250} = 0.02$	$\frac{205}{250} = 0.82$	$\frac{40}{250} = 0.16$
3 $\frac{30}{150} = 0.20$	$\frac{18}{150} = 0.12$	$\frac{102}{150} = 0.68$

that $\{X_t\}$ exhibits the Markovian property given by Equation (15.1) and that $\mathbf{P}$ is stationary, then a Markov chain should be a reasonable representation of *aggregate* consumer brand switching behavior.[3]

Uses of Markov analyses of brand switching behavior include, but are not restricted to, the following:

1. Prediction of market shares at specific future points in time.
2. Assessment of rates of change in market shares over time.
3. Prediction of market share equilibriums (if they exist).
4. Assessment of the specific effects of marketing strategies in changing undesirable market shares.
5. Evaluation of the process for introducing new products.

In the next section, we will present computational methods for realizing these uses.[4]

Follow-up Exercises

7. With respect to Table 15–3:

    a. Interpret the meanings of $p_{11} = 0.90$, $p_{22} = 0.82$, and $p_{33} = 0.68$.
    b. To which brand is Brand 2 most likely to lose customers?
    c. Which brand has the most "loyal" customers?
    d. Which brand has the least "loyal" customers?

8. Add a fourth state to the state space which represents "no purchase of Brands 1, 2, or 3 in week *t*." Construct a new transition matrix given the contingency table below.

Brand (*j*)	1	2	3	4	Total
(*i*)					
1	90	5	3	2	100
2	5	200	40	5	250
3	25	15	80	10	130
4	5	10	5	0	20
Total	125	230	128	17	500

Is this table more comprehensive than the preceding table? Interpret the meaning of p_{44}. Identify two explanations for the occurrence of $X_t = 4$. (Hint: When $X_t = 4$ does it necessarily mean that the consumer did not purchase this product in week *t*?)

---

[3] Section 15.7 discusses the nature of statistical inference in Markov analysis as a means to assess the validity of dependence and stationarity.

[4] For more comprehensive treatments (and additional references) of brand switching Markov models see D. B. Montgomery and G. L. Urban, *Management Science in Marketing* (Englewood Cliffs, N.J.: Prentice-Hall, Inc., 1969).

9. Consider the three-brand market presented in the example. Define a state space which includes the possibilities of zero, one, or two purchases of the product in a given week.

10. *Homogeneity Assumption* You should realize that a contingency table such as Table 15–2 and the resulting matrix of transition probabilities represent the *aggregate* switching behavior in a *sample* of the defined *population*. They do not represent *individual* consumer behavior in the sense of predicting what a particular consumer will do. The purchasing pattern for a particular consumer represents a stochastic process which could be modeled by a Markov chain. To illustrate, you should construct **P** for the following nine-week purchasing pattern of a specific consumer: {2,2,2,1,1,3,1,1,1}. For practical reasons firms are interested in aggregate rather than individual behavior. The act of aggregating consumers, however, implicitly assumes that consumers are *homogeneous* with respect to their transition matrices. Put another way, the construction of empirical probabilities as point estimates for true probabilities requires that the experiments (that is, consumers in the sample) be performed under "identical" conditions (that is, homogeneous consumers). Can you think of procedures for designing the sample which more nearly guarantee homogeneity?

11. *Marketing Strategies* To illustrate how marketing strategy can affect consumer switching behavior in a Markov model, consider the following. Suppose that the relationship below is empirically valid:

$$p'_{ij} = p_{ij} + a(s_{it} - \bar{s}_{it})$$

where

p_{ij} = Current (stationary) transition probability.
p'_{ij} = New (stationary) *unadjusted* transition probability.
s_{it} = Selling price of Brand i in week t.
$\bar{s}_{it}$ = Mean selling price of all brands other than Brand i in week t.
a = Parameter ($a = 0.01$ when $i \neq j$ and $a = -0.05$ when $i = j$).

Thus, when $i \neq j$, a price for Brand i in week t which is above the market average of all other prices (that is, $s_{it} > \bar{s}_{it}$) will have the effect of increasing the attraction power of other brands (that is, p'_{ij} will be greater than p_{ij}). Given expected prices in week t, it follows that this prediction model can be used to construct a new transition matrix. Note, however, that row sums will not be unity; hence, the unadjusted p'_{ij} for each row must be adjusted to yield a sum of unity. For example, if unadjusted $p'_{11} = 0.9$, $p'_{12} = 0.5$, and $p'_{13} = 0.6$, then the adjusted values for the first row would be determined as follows (noting that unadjusted $p'_{11} + p'_{12} + p'_{13} = 2.0$): $p'_{11} = 0.9/2.0 = 0.45$; $p'_{12} = 0.5/2.0 = 0.25$; $p'_{13} = 0.6/2.0 = 0.3$. Note: If unadjusted $p'_{ij} < 0$, then set to zero before adjusting.

a. Reason out changes in p_{ij} when $s_{it} > \bar{s}_{it}$ and $i = j$; $s_{it} < \bar{s}_{it}$ and $i \neq j$; $s_{it} < \bar{s}_{it}$ and $i = j$; $s_{it} = \bar{s}_{it}$. Does the logic of this model reflect the phenomenom of "price-snobbery?"

b. Construct the new transition matrix for the main example (Table 15–3) given that expected market prices in week 28 are $1, $3, and $2 for Brands 1, 2, and 3, respectively. Reflect on the changes.

Hospital Administration Model

Decision problems in the field of health administration have proven to be fertile territory in recent years for OR/MS models. Here we illustrate a Markov model for analyzing the flow of patients in the geriatric ward of a state hospital.[5]

For the hospital in question, a resocialization program (RP) has been initiated in the geriatric ward to reduce the number of patients who become "institutionalized," or totally dependent upon the hospital for their needs. After five years of running RP, hospital administrators felt that it was a success but were unsure of means to measure its effectiveness in terms of both monetary cost to the state and the welfare of its patients. Fortunately, one of the administrators (a young, aspiring M.B.A. graduate) had recently taken a course in Management Science, and so suggested that the services of her professor (a young, aspiring Ph.D. graduate) be commissioned.

Following a fair amount of interaction with the administrators, much study, and tedious data collection, the consultant constructed Table 15–4.

TABLE 15.4

Transition Probabilities

State	1	2	3	4
1 RP...............	0.85	0.03	0.11	0.01
2 Ward.............	0.01	0.97	0.01	0.01
3 Home............	0.02	0.02	0.95	0.01
4 Dead.............	0.00	0.00	0.00	1.00

The problem has been conceptualized as a discrete state (four states) and discrete parameter (one month time unit) stochastic process. Thus, $S = \{1, 2, 3, 4\}$ and $T = \{0, 1, 2, \ldots\}$, where $T = 0$ represents an initial month.

Based on the information provided in the table, patients are classified in one of four states in any given month. Patients who are in RP live in a special ward of the hospital and participate in a four-step program which combines group activities and special training aimed at fostering independence. Patients who are not in RP but who live in the hospital are classified as "Ward" ($X_t = 2$). Patients classified in State 3 have been discharged to an approved boarding home outside the hospital grounds. Patients living in such homes are deemed resocialized because they are more active and independent than their peers living in the hospital. The other (very real) possibility for the geriatric patient is death.

Based on data analysis using statistical procedures, the consultant con-

[5] This model is based on Jack Meredith, "A Markovian Analysis of a Geriatric Ward," *Management Science,* vol. 19, no. 6 (February 1973), pp. 604–12. For other Markov models in hospital administration see Peter Kolesar, "A Markovian Model for Hospital Admission Scheduling," *Management Science,* vol. 16, no. 6 (February 1970), pp. 384–96; E. P. C. Kao, "Modeling the Movement of Coronary Patients within a Hospital by Semi-Markov Processes," *Operations Research,* vol. 22, no. 4 (July–August 1974), pp. 683–99.

cluded (1) that patients were essentially homogeneous (see Exercise 10), (2) that future states were basically dependent only on the present state (Markovian property), and (3) that the transition matrix was independent of time (stationary); hence, a Markov chain is a satisfactory representation of this flow of patients. It was noted, however, that a patient's aging affects the probability of death. This means that the Markov chain may be unreliable for long-run predictions. Furthermore, the probability of moving from one state to another was a function of not only the current state but also how long a patient had been in the current state. This effect, however, was weak.

The transition matrix for this problem is a good indication of RP's effectiveness. For example, we might conclude that for patients beginning their stay in the regular ward of the hospital ($X_0 = 2$), the probability of being discharged to a home in the next month is no better than the probability of dying [that is, $P(X_1 = 3 \mid X_0 = 2) = P(X_1 = 4 \mid X_0 = 2) = 0.01$]; however, for a patient beginning in RP ($X_0 = 1$), the odds of being discharged in the next month rather than dying are 11 to 1, that is, 11-percent probability v. a 1-percent probability, or $P(X_1 = 3 \mid X_0 = 1) = 0.11$ v. $P(X_1 = 4 \mid X_0 = 1) = 0.01$.

In the next two sections we develop computational procedures for further analyzing the expected effectiveness of the RP program.

Follow-up Exercises

12. State 4 in this example is termed an "absorbing" or "trapping" state in Markov analysis. Can you define an absorbing state?

13. If the amount of time in a given state affects the probabilities of subsequent states very much, do we still have a Markov chain? a Markov process? A stochastic process? Explain.

Stock Market Model

The fluctuation of stock prices over time is an example of a stochastic process of an economic time series. The field of finance known as "security analysis" is concerned with predicting the future behavior of prices of securities (stocks, bonds, treasury bills, and so forth) for the purpose of formulating investment strategy. A popular class of models for this type of decision making is mathematical programming applied to portfolio analysis (Example 10.10). In the present example, we describe a simplified Markovian scenario which is based on an actual application.[6]

Let $\{C_t\}$ and $\{D_t\}$ represent, respectively, the stochastic process of *closing daily prices* over time and the stochastic process over time of

---

[6] B. D. Fielitz and T. N. Bhargava, "The Behavior of Stock Price Relatives— A Markovian Analysis," *Operations Research,* vol. 21, no. 6 (November–December 1973), pp. 1183–99.

TABLE 15–5

States for Stock Market Model

X_t	Description	Realization if
1	Up	$c_t > c_{t-1}$ or $d_t > 0$
2	No change	$c_t = c_{t-1}$ or $d_t = 0$
3	Down	$c_t < c_{t-1}$ or $d_t < 0$

Note: c_t represents actual price at close of day t; d_t represents actual difference between two successive daily closing prices, or $d_t = c_t - c_{t-1}$.

differences in closing prices from one day to the next (that is, $D_t = C_t - C_{t-1}$). Based on these price movements, we can now define a discrete three-state and discrete parameter stochastic process $\{X_t\}$ with respect to actual changes in the price of a stock from one day to the next, as indicated in Table 15–5. For example, if the price of a stock at the end of a trading day (Day t) has increased from the preceding day, then State 1 $(X_t = 1)$ has occurred on this day. It follows that $\{X_t\}$ represents a discrete state and discrete parameter stochastic process with $S = \{1, 2, 3\}$ and $T = \{0, 1, 2, \ldots\}$, where T is indexed on days.

Table 15–6 shows the realization of $\{C_t\}$, $\{D_t\}$, and $\{X_t\}$ over a 20-day

TABLE 15–6

Realization of Stochastic Processes for Stock Market Model

Day T	Closing Price (dollars per share) $\{C_t\}$	Price Difference (dollars per share) $\{D_t\}$	Classification of Price Difference $\{X_t\}$
0	10¼	—	—
1	10⅞	⅝	1
2	11½	⅝	1
3	11	−½	3
4	13½	2½	1
5	13½	0	2
6	12¼	−1¼	3
7	15⅛	2⅞	1
8	18¾	3⅝	1
9	16	−2¾	3
10	15⅞	−⅛	3
11	14½	−1⅜	3
12	14	−½	3
13	16⅛	2⅛	1
14	20¾	4⅝	1
15	20	−¾	3
16	19¼	−¾	3
17	19½	¼	1
18	21	1½	1
19	21½	½	1
20	19⅞	−1⅝	3

.

.

.

period of time for a selected stock. The stochastic process given by $\{X_t\}$ is a Markov chain if the assumptions relating to dependence (Markovian property) and stationarity are satisfied. In the next two sections we develop computational procedures for you to further analyze this model.

Follow-up Exercises

14. In the context of this problem, what two conditions must be statistically validated if $\{X_t\}$ is to be considered a Markov chain? Comment on the logical reasonableness of these two conditions.

15. Based on $\{X_t\}$ in Table 15–6, construct a matrix of transition probabilities. In words, what is $P(X_t = 1 \mid X_{t-1} = 3)$?

16. It can be argued that Up, No Change, and Down states should be based not only on the direction of change, but also on the magnitude of change. Consider the following scheme for assigning states where $\bar{d}$ is the mean of price differences and $\hat{\sigma}_d$ is the unbiased estimate of the standard deviation of price differences: If $d_t > \bar{d} + 0.5\hat{\sigma}_d$, then $X_t = 1$; if $d_t < \bar{d} - 0.5\hat{\sigma}_d$, then $X_t = 3$; otherwise, $X_t = 2$.

   a. State in words the meaning of these "state rules."
   b. State an advantage of this scheme with respect to small changes in price.
   c. Generate $\{X_t\}$ for $\{D_t\}$ given in Table 15.6. (Note: $\bar{d} = 0.5$ and $\hat{\sigma}_d = 1.9$.)
   d. Construct a transition matrix and compare to Exercise 15. Comments?

15.4 COMPUTATIONAL PROPERTIES OF MARKOV CHAINS

Up to now we have presented the nature, uses, and sample formulations of stochastic processes in general and Markov chains in particular. In this section we illustrate computational techniques for the probability analysis of future states in a Markov chain.

Transient Solutions: Classical Approach

Consider the IRS problem previously presented (Example 15.1). Assuming the validity of a Markov chain (Example 15.4), we can predict the probability of any future state given any present state by simply applying the Rules of Addition and Multiplication given by formulas (A.3) and (A.6) on pages 704 and 705.

Figure 15–1 illustrates a **probability tree** which depicts the present state in year 10 ("no audit" or $X_{10} = 0$) and, possible future states in years 11, 12, and 13. Each node in the tree represents a specific state in year t which is either "no audit" ($X_t = 0$) or "audit" ($X_t = 1$). The branch between any two states represents a possible path of travel between those two states. For convenience, the conditional or branch probabilities are

FIGURE 15–1

Probability Tree for IRS Problem

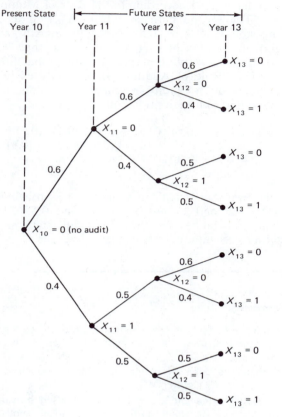

included in the figure just above each branch. Note that these branch probabilities are, in fact, the transition probabilities between any two successive states.

The probability of "no audit" in year 11 ($X_{11} = 0$) given "no audit" in year 10 ($X_{10} = 0$) is simply

$$P(X_{11} = 0 \mid X_{10} = 0) = p_{11}$$
$$= 0.6.$$

The probability of "no audit" in year 12 ($X_{12} = 0$) given "no audit" in year 10 ($X_{10} = 0$) is given by

$$P(X_{12} = 0 \mid X_{10} = 0) = P(X_{11} = 0 \mid X_{10} = 0) \cdot P(X_{12} = 0 \mid X_{11} = 0)$$
$$+ P(X_{11} = 1 \mid X_{10} = 0) \cdot P(X_{12} = 0 \mid X_{11} = 1)$$
$$= (0.6) \cdot (0.6) + (0.4) \cdot (0.5)$$
$$= 0.36 + 0.20$$
$$= 0.56.$$

Looking at the tree, we reason that it is possible to achieve $X_{12} = 0$ by one of two paths. The first takes us from $X_{10} = 0$ to $X_{11} = 0$ to $X_{12} = 0$ with probability $(0.6) \cdot (0.6)$ according to the Rule of Multiplication for dependent events. The second path runs from $X_{10} = 0$ to $X_{11} = 1$ to $X_{12} = 0$ with probability $(0.4) \cdot (0.5)$. Since these paths are mutually exclusive, the probability of achieving $X_{12} = 0$ given that we started at $X_{10} = 0$ is given by the sum of the separate path probabilities $(0.36 + 0.20)$ according to the Rule of Addition for mutually exclusive events. Finally, the probability of "no audit" in year 13 given "no audit" in year 10 is given by the sum of four path probabilities:

$$P(X_{13} = 0 \mid X_{10} = 0) = (0.6) \cdot (0.6) \cdot (0.6) + (0.6) \cdot (0.4) \cdot (0.5)$$
$$+ (0.4) \cdot (0.5) \cdot (0.6) + (0.4) \cdot (0.5) \cdot (0.5)$$
$$= 0.216 + 0.120 + 0.120 + 0.100$$
$$= 0.556.$$

To summarize, given "no audit" in year 10, the probabilities of "no audit" in years 11, 12, and 13 are 0.6, 0.56, and 0.556, respectively. These conditional probabilities for the "no audit" state are known as **transient probabilities** because they are changing over time.

Follow-up Exercises

17. Using Figure 15–1, determine the transient probabilities for audits in years 11, 12, and 13 given that "no audit" was performed in year 10.

18. Confirm that $P(X_{14} = 0 \mid X_{10} = 0) = 0.5556$. Do you notice anything interesting about the behavior of the transient probabilities over time given by $P(X_t = 0 \mid X_{10} = 0)$, $t = 11, \ldots, 14$?

19. Draw a probability tree and determine the following transient probabilities for a "typical" customer in the brand switching model of Table 15–3: Given that the current purchase is Brand 3 ($X_0 = 3$), determine the conditional probabilities that Brand 1 will be purchased next week ($X_1 = 1$), two weeks hence ($X_2 = 1$), and three weeks hence ($X_3 = 1$).

20. For the hospital administration model depicted in Table 15–4, draw probability trees and determine the following:

    a. The probabilities that a customer currently in RP will be in a home next month, two months from now, and three months from now.
    b. The probabilities that a customer currently in a ward will be in a home next month, two months from now, and three months from now. Compare these to part (a) and draw a conclusion as to the effectiveness of RP.

21. For the stock price model with transition matrix given in Exercise 15, find the probabilities that two days from now the price will increase, remain the same, and decrease given that the current state is "down." Why should these probabilities sum to unity?

Transient Solutions: Matrix Approach

The method of probability trees for calculating transient probabilities is instructive but cumbersome, as you should have realized by solving the preceding set of exercises. A more efficient (and elegant) procedure involves the application of matrix multiplication, as we now demonstrate.[7]

Example 15.5

For the IRS problem (Examples 15.1 through 15.4), with transition matrix given by

$$\mathbf{P} = \begin{pmatrix} 0.6 & 0.4 \\ 0.5 & 0.5 \end{pmatrix},$$

we know that the first row represents the conditional probabilities of possible states in the *next* period given that State 1 (no audit) is observed in the *current* period. Thus, given "no audit" in the current period, $p_{11} = 0.6$ and $p_{12} = 0.4$ are the probabilities of "no audit" and "audit," respectively, in the next period. Similarly, the second row represents all conditional probabilities in the next period given that State 2 (audit) is observed in the current period (that is, $p_{21} = 0.5$ and $p_{22} = 0.5$).

To determine all conditional probabilities two periods hence (that is, $p_{ij}^{(2)}$ for all i and j) we simply square $\mathbf{P}$ as follows:

$$\mathbf{P}^2 = \mathbf{P} \cdot \mathbf{P}$$

$$= \begin{pmatrix} 0.6 & 0.4 \\ 0.5 & 0.5 \end{pmatrix} \cdot \begin{pmatrix} 0.6 & 0.4 \\ 0.5 & 0.5 \end{pmatrix}$$

$$= \begin{pmatrix} 0.56 & 0.44 \\ 0.55 & 0.45 \end{pmatrix}.$$

This indicates, for example, that $p_{11}^{(2)} = 0.56$ is the probability of "no audit" 2 years hence given that in the current year there was "no audit," and $p_{22}^{(2)} = 0.45$ is the probability of an audit 2 years from now given that there was an audit in the current year. Can you interpret $p_{12}^{(2)}$ and $p_{21}^{(2)}$?

Three years from now, the conditional probabilities are given by

$$\mathbf{P}^3 = \mathbf{P}^2 \cdot \mathbf{P}$$

$$= \begin{pmatrix} 0.56 & 0.44 \\ 0.55 & 0.45 \end{pmatrix} \cdot \begin{pmatrix} 0.6 & 0.4 \\ 0.5 & 0.5 \end{pmatrix}$$

$$= \begin{pmatrix} 0.556 & 0.444 \\ 0.555 & 0.445 \end{pmatrix}.$$

Thus, $p_{12}^{(3)} = 0.444$ represents the probability that there is an audit three years from now given that there was no audit in the current year.

For the conditional probabilities four years into the future, we simply evaluate $\mathbf{P}^4$ by taking $\mathbf{P}^3 \cdot \mathbf{P}$ or $\mathbf{P}^2 \cdot \mathbf{P}^2$. In general, so-called *k-step transition probabilities* for k time periods into the future (which we label as $p_{ij}^{(k)}$) are determined by calculating $\mathbf{P}^k$.

---

[7] For a review of matrix multiplication see Appendix C at the end of the book.

Notice that the $p_{11}^{(2)} = 0.56$ and $p_{11}^{(3)} = 0.556$ transient probabilities which were determined in the previous section for years 12 and 13 (2 and 3 years beyond the current year given by year 10) are readily located in cell (1,1) of $\mathbf{P}^2$ and $\mathbf{P}^3$, respectively.

Follow-up Exercises

22. Why must *each row* of $\mathbf{P}^k$ sum to unity?

23. Confirm the probability for year 14 requested in Exercise 18 by calculating $\mathbf{P}^4$. Label this probability using $p_{ij}^{(k)}$ notation.

24. Use matrix multiplication to answer (a) Exercise 19, (b) Exercise 20, and (c) Exercise 21.
    Does the matrix approach readily provide more information than the classical approach? Illustrate for any one of the problems in parts *a, b,* or *c.*

Unconditional v. Conditional Probabilities

In the preceding section, $p_{ij}^{(k)}$ was defined as the k-step transition probability between States i and j. Just as in the case of the one-step transition probability (p_{ij}), this probability is a *conditional* probability because the probability of State j after the Markov chain goes through k transitions is statistically dependent on the initial State i. If the *unconditional* or *absolute* probability of State j after k transitions $(u_j^{(k)})$ is desired, then the following product must be determined:

$$\mathbf{u}^{(k)} = \mathbf{u}^{(o)} \cdot \mathbf{P}^k \tag{15.3}$$

where $\mathbf{u}^{(k)} = [u_1^{(k)} \ u_2^{(k)} \ \ldots \ u_n^{(k)}]$ is the row vector of unconditional probabilities for all n states after k transitions, $\mathbf{u}^{(o)}$ is the row vector of *initial* unconditional probabilities, and $\mathbf{P}$ is the one-step transition matrix.

Example 15.6

In the brand switching model, the column totals in Table 15–2 represent market shares for the current week (week 27). Alternatively, we can say that the absolute probability is 125/500 (or 0.25) that a consumer selected at random (from among the 500 in the sample) has purchased Brand 1 in the current week. Similarly, the unconditional probabilities that Brands 2 and 3 were purchased in the current week are 0.46 and 0.29, respectively. These probabilities represent the initial unconditional probabilities, so

$$\mathbf{u}^{(o)} = (0.25 \quad 0.46 \quad 0.29).$$

To predict market shares for, say, week 29 (that is, 2 weeks into the future), we simply apply Equation (15.3) with $k = 2$, $\mathbf{u}^{(o)}$ as above, and $\mathbf{P}$ as given by Table 15–3:

$$\mathbf{u}^{(2)} = (0.25 \quad 0.46 \quad 0.29) \cdot \begin{pmatrix} 0.90 & 0.07 & 0.03 \\ 0.02 & 0.82 & 0.16 \\ 0.20 & 0.12 & 0.68 \end{pmatrix}^{2}$$

$$= (0.25 \quad 0.46 \quad 0.29) \cdot \begin{pmatrix} 0.8174 & 0.1240 & 0.0586 \\ 0.0664 & 0.6930 & 0.2406 \\ 0.3184 & 0.1940 & 0.4876 \end{pmatrix}$$

$$= (0.32723 \quad 0.40604 \quad 0.26673).$$

Thus, the expected market shares two weeks hence are 32.723 percent for Brand 1, 40.604 percent for Brand 2, and 26.673 percent for Brand 3.

Follow-up Exercises

25. Calculate expected market shares three weeks into the future by

    a. Utilizing $\mathbf{u}^{(o)}$ and the fact that $\mathbf{P}^3 = \mathbf{P}^2 \cdot \mathbf{P}$, where $\mathbf{P}^2$ has already been determined.
    b. Taking the product of $\mathbf{u}^{(2)}$ and $\mathbf{P}$. Which approach is easier?

26. Show that, in general,

$$\mathbf{u}^{(k)} = \mathbf{u}^{(k-1)} \cdot \mathbf{P} \tag{15.4}$$

27. Suppose that the transition matrix in the IRS problem was based on a sample of homogeneous taxpayers. Calculate the proportion of taxpayers that will be audited (a) next year, (b) two years from now, and (c) four years from now, if we have knowledge that the number of taxpayers audited in the current year was 10 percent.

28. For the hospital administration problem, determine $\mathbf{u}^{(2)}$ given that $\mathbf{u}^{(o)} = (0.3\ 0.4\ 0.2\ 0.1)$. Interpret $\mathbf{u}^{(2)}$ and compare to $\mathbf{u}^{(o)}$.

Steady-State Solutions

To illustrate the nature of steady-state (time-independent) probabilities in Markov chains, consider the calculations in Table 15–7 for the IRS problem. First of all, focus on any $p_{ij}^{(k)}$ as k increases. For example, the series given by $p_{11} = 0.6$, $p_{11}^{(2)} = 0.56$, $p_{11}^{(3)} = 0.556$, $p_{11}^{(4)} = 0.5556$, and $p_{11}^{(5)} = 0.55556$ indicates that these transient probabilities change by smaller and smaller increments for each step. This implies that $p_{ij}^{(k)}$ is asymptotically approaching a steady-state value as k increases.

Now, focus on the rows of $\mathbf{P}^k$ as k increases. As you can see, the rows are becoming identical. For example, the rows of $\mathbf{P}^5$ are identical to four significant digits. This illustrates the interesting fact that *the probability of any future state is becoming independent from its initial state* as we go further and further into the future. Furthermore, from our previous observation, this probability is converging to its steady-state value (u_i^*) either

TABLE 15–7

***k*-Step Transition Matrices for IRS Problem**

k	$\mathbf{P}^k$
1........................	$\begin{pmatrix} 0.6 & 0.4 \\ 0.5 & 0.5 \end{pmatrix}$
2........................	$\begin{pmatrix} 0.56 & 0.44 \\ 0.55 & 0.45 \end{pmatrix}$
3........................	$\begin{pmatrix} 0.556 & 0.444 \\ 0.555 & 0.445 \end{pmatrix}$
4........................	$\begin{pmatrix} 0.5556 & 0.4444 \\ 0.5555 & 0.4445 \end{pmatrix}$
5........................	$\begin{pmatrix} 0.55556 & 0.44444 \\ 0.55555 & 0.44445 \end{pmatrix}$

from above (if $p_{ij} > u_j^*$) or from below (if $p_{ij} < u_j^*$), as indicated in Figure 15–2.

Carefully note that the steady-state probability for State j indicates that the probability of finding the stochastic process in State j after a "large" number of transitions tends toward the value given by u_j^*. Since this tendency manifests itself regardless of initial states or initial probability distributions, it follows that u_j^* is an *unconditional* probability for State j.

From the preceding observation, we can conclude that absolute probabilities do not change once steady state is reached; hence, based on Equation (15.4), the following must be true:

$$\mathbf{u}^* = \mathbf{u}^* \cdot \mathbf{P} \tag{15.5}$$

FIGURE 15–2

Transient Probability Asymptotically Approaches Steady-State Probability

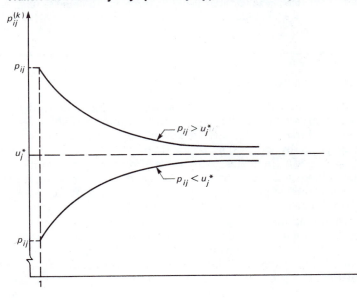

where $\mathbf{u}^*$ is the row vector of n steady-state probabilities. This condition, together with the fact that the elements in $\mathbf{u}^*$ must sum to one, that is,

$$\sum_{j=1}^{n} u^*_j = 1, \tag{15.6}$$

allows us to readily calculate steady-state probabilities, as we now illustrate.

Example 15.7

Applying Equation (15.5) to the brand switching model, we get

$$(u^*_1 \quad u^*_2 \quad u^*_3) = (u^*_1 \quad u^*_2 \quad u^*_3) \cdot \begin{pmatrix} 0.90 & 0.07 & 0.03 \\ 0.02 & 0.82 & 0.16 \\ 0.20 & 0.12 & 0.68 \end{pmatrix},$$

which translates into 3 equations in 3 unknowns after multiplication:[8]

$$u^*_1 = 0.90u^*_1 + 0.02u^*_2 + 0.20u^*_3 \tag{1}$$
$$u^*_2 = 0.07u^*_1 + 0.82u^*_2 + 0.12u^*_3 \tag{2}$$
$$u^*_3 = 0.03u^*_1 + 0.16u^*_2 + 0.68u^*_3. \tag{3}$$

Furthermore, from Equation (15.6), the following must be true:

$$u^*_1 + u^*_2 + u^*_3 = 1. \tag{4}$$

This gives a total of 4 equations in 3 unknowns. Since $\mathbf{u}^* = (0 \quad 0 \quad 0)$ represents a trivial solution to (1) through (3) which is invalidated by (4), it follows that there is one redundant equation among the first three. Arbitrarily discarding (3) and solving (1), (2), and (4) simultaneously, we get (to three significant digits) $u^*_1 = 0.474$, $u^*_2 = 0.321$, and $u^*_3 = 0.205$.

These results indicate that, over time, the market share of Brand 1 will increase from its present value of 0.25 (see Example 15.6) to its long-run stable value of 0.474. The market shares of Brands 2 and 3 will erode, respectively, from 0.46 to 0.321 and from 0.29 to 0.205. Therefore, if present conditions continue, we can expect market share gains for Brand 1 at the expense of losses for the other two brands. Note, however, that under steady-state conditions customers will continue to switch according to the stationary transition matrix. It is the absolute probabilities (market shares) that will change over time and finally stabilize.

---

[8] Note that the product given by $\mathbf{u}^* \cdot \mathbf{P}$ results in a (1×3) matrix which is then equated to $\mathbf{u}^*$ according to (15.5). Equating term by term gives the first three simultaneous equations. In general, this procedure provides n simultaneous equations in n unknowns.

Two points are in order at this time. First, steady-state predictions are never achieved in actual practice because of a combination of (1) error in estimating $\mathbf{P}$, (2) changes in $\mathbf{P}$ over time, and (3) changes in the nature of dependence relationships among states. As in queuing theory, however, the use of steady-state values is an important diagnostic tool for the decision maker.

Second, not all transition matrices lend themselves to the analysis of steady-state properties as presented here. In fact, steady-state probabilities may not exist for certain types of Markov chains. If a Markov chain is **ergodic,** then u_j^* as the limit of $p_{ij}^{(k)}$ will exist; that is,

$$u_j^* = \lim_{k \to \infty} p_{ij}^{(k)}$$

is guaranteed. Basically, a Markov chain is ergodic if the process allows the achievement of any future state from any initial state after one or more transitions.[9] For example, consider the following two matrices:

$$\mathbf{P}_1 = \begin{pmatrix} 0.4 & 0 & 0.6 \\ 0.3 & 0.3 & 0.4 \\ 0 & 0.5 & 0.5 \end{pmatrix}$$

and

$$\mathbf{P}_2 = \begin{pmatrix} 0.7 & 0 & 0 & 0.3 \\ 0.2 & 0.2 & 0.4 & 0.2 \\ 0.6 & 0.1 & 0.1 & 0.2 \\ 0.2 & 0 & 0 & 0.8 \end{pmatrix}$$

$\mathbf{P}_1$ is checked as follows. If State 1 is the initial state, then State 3 can be reached after one transition but not State 2; however, State 2 can be reached once State 3 is reached. Therefore, any state can be achieved from an initial state given by State 1. If the initial state is State 2, then any state can be achieved after one transition. Finally, if State 3 is the initial state, then State 2 can be achieved after one transition, but not State 1. Once State 2 is achieved, however, State 1 can be achieved. Thus, the chain described by $\mathbf{P}_1$ is ergodic, since it is possible for the process to go from any one state to any other state. Using the same reasoning, show why the chain described by $\mathbf{P}_2$ is *not* ergodic.

Follow-up Exercises

29. Confirm the calculations for **u*** in Example 15.7.

30. Calculate steady-state probabilities for the IRS example. Interpret their meaning.

31. The nearly identical rows of $\mathbf{P}^5$ in Table 15.7 indicates the irrelevancy of initial states with respect to the probabilities of states far enough into the future. For the IRS example, demonstrate the long-run irrelevancy of initial absolute probability distributions by comparing $\mathbf{u}^5$ using $\mathbf{u}^{(0)} = (0.9\ 0.1)$ in Equation (15.3) against $\mathbf{u}^{(5)}$ using $\mathbf{u}^{(0)} = (0.1\ 0.9)$ in Equation (15.3). Compare $\mathbf{u}^{(5)}$ to $\mathbf{u}^*$. Conclusions?

---

[9] For a technical definition of ergodic Markov chains, see H. A. Taha, *Operations Research,* (New York: The Macmillan Company, 1971), or S. Karlin, *A First Course in Stochastic Processes* (New York: Academic Press, 1966).

32. a. The Markov chain described in the hospital administration model is not ergodic. Can you answer why? This type of chain is termed *absorbing* (see Exercise 12). Certain long-run properties (for example, expected number of time periods before absorption) for this type of chain can be analyzed by other procedures. Show that $\mathbf{u}^* = (0 \quad 0 \quad 0 \quad 1)$ for this problem. Interpret this result.

   b. Show what happens when you try to calculate $\mathbf{u}^*$ for the nonergodic chain described by the transition matrix $\mathbf{P}_2$ above.

   c. If a transition matrix $\mathbf{P}$ has all nonzero entries, then does it necessarily describe an ergodic chain?

15.5 MARKOVIAN DECISION MODELS

This section explicitly incorporates decision making in a Markovian framework. We begin by introducing concepts which relate criteria, decisions, and policies; thereafter, we illustrate solutions by enumeration and discuss more advanced optimization procedures.

Decision-Making Framework

Assume that a specific *discrete decision* (D_m) is made for period t which, when coupled with the *realized state* (X_t), results in a value for some *criterion, $Z(D_m, X_t)$*. In other words, a criterion which is of interest to the decision maker (for example, cost, profit) is affected both by the state of a Markov process and by a decision which has been (or is to be) made. A **policy** (Q) is a statement or *decision rule* which specifies a *specific* decision for *each* possible state. For example, if $(D_1, D_2, \ldots, D_M)$ represents the set of decisions of interest, then a policy would assign a specific decision $(D_1$ or D_2 or $\cdots$ or $D_M)$ to each possible value of the state variable.

Given a state which has just been observed (X_{t-1}) and a set of defined policies $(Q_1, Q_2, \ldots, Q_L)$, the problem is to determine the policy which optimizes the criterion.

In general, the Markov process given by $\{X_t\}$ now develops over time as a result of both probability laws (Markovian property) and decisions. Observed states, however, need not be affected by decisions. Furthermore, transition probabilities may or may not be affected by actions of the decision maker. Finally, the number of decision alternatives (M) may or may not be affected by the state of the system.

Example 15.8   IRS Problem

For our IRS problem, let $X_{t-1} = 0$ if no audit has been undertaken in the year just passed and $X_{t-1} = 1$ if an audit has been undertaken in the year just

TABLE 15–8

$Z(D_m, X_t)$ for IRS Problem

	State	
Decision	$X_t = 0$	$X_t = 1$
D_1	250	300
D_2	0	500

passed. Consider two decisions of interest: Hire (D_1) or do not hire (D_2) a "top-flight" certified public accountant (CPA) to prepare your return for the current year.

Suppose it costs $250 to hire a CPA. It is widely held that the IRS usually collects 'back taxes" whenever it audits a return. According to past records, if the return has been prepared by a CPA, then the average collection of back taxes is $50 when the return is audited; however, if the audited return has not been prepared by a CPA, then the taxpayer has had to pay average back taxes of $500. Table 15.8 illustrates possible values for the cost criterion (Z) based on the conditions just stated. For example, if a CPA is hired (D_1) and the return is audited ($X_t = 1$), then $Z(D_1, 1) = 300$, or it costs the taxpayer $300 (that is, $250 to the CPA and $50 to the IRS). Can you interpret $Z(D_2, 1) = 500$?

Table 15–9 indicates the four possible policies ($L = 4$) for this problem. Thus, Q_1 specifies that a CPA is not to be hired in year t (that is, decision D_2) if no audit was performed in year $t - 1$ (that is, if $X_{t-1} = 0$); a CPA is to be hired in year t if an audit was performed in year $t - 1$. Can you verbalize Q_2, Q_3, and Q_4?

TABLE 15–9

Policies for IRS Problem

	State from Preceding Year	
Policy	$X_{t-1} = 0$	$X_{t-1} = 1$
Q_1	D_2	D_1
Q_2	D_1	D_2
Q_3	D_1	D_1
Q_4	D_2	D_2

In this problem we assume that decisions in any one year affect neither states nor transient probabilities. In the next section, we illustrate the determination of an optimal policy for this problem.

Example 15.9   Brand Switching Problem

According to Table 15–2, Brand 2 has a 50 percent market share in week 26; however, if present conditions were to continue, as represented by the transition matrix

$$P = \begin{pmatrix} 0.90 & 0.07 & 0.03 \\ 0.02 & 0.82 & 0.16 \\ 0.20 & 0.12 & 0.68 \end{pmatrix},$$

then its long-run market share will slip to 32.1 percent according to the calculation for u_2^* in Example 15.7. Suppose that two promotion campaigns (*A* and *B*) are under consideration for reversing this trend:

Campaign *A*. Aims to achieve 90 percent retention of its customers (holding power) by reducing the attractive power that Brand 3 has on Brand 2 customers (that is, aims to increase p_{22} from 0.82 to 0.90 and simultaneously decrease p_{23} from 0.16 to 0.08).

Campaign *B*. Aims to increase by half the attractive power of Brand 2 for Brand 3 customers at the expense of Brand 1 (that is, aims to increase p_{32} from 0.12 to 0.18 and decrease p_{31} from 0.20 to 0.14).

A marketing research study shows that **P** is representative of a potential market of 50 million customers. Exclusive of additional promotion, each customer represents a potential profit of $0.50 per week. What decision should be made by the company if the cost of *A* is $500,000 per week and the cost of *B* is $400,000 per week?

Since states (X_t) for this process are based on individual consumer behavior and **P** is based on aggregate behavior, it should be evident that X_{t-1} is not a factor for defining policies. In this case, therefore, policies and decisions are essentially synonymous. Let

$Q_1 \equiv D_1 \equiv$ No additional promotion campaign.
$Q_2 \equiv D_2 \equiv$ Undertake Campaign *A*.
$Q_3 \equiv D_3 \equiv$ Undertake Campaign *B*.
$Z(D_m) \equiv$ Long-run profit per week when decision D_m is made.

This problem, then, illustrates a situation where the most recent state (X_{t-1}) has no bearing on a policy, yet decisions affect transition probabilities and, consequently, affect the evolution of the stochastic process over time. We solve this problem in the next section.

Follow-up Exercises

33. Suppose that, in addition to the costs depicted in Table 15–8, a benefit of $100 is realized when a CPA prepares a return. In other words, with the CPA's expert knowledge you pay $100 less than what you would have paid if you had prepared the return yourself. Appropriately modify Table 15–8.

34. For the brand switching problem:

    a. State **P** and determine **u*** for Q_2.
    b. State **P** and determine **u*** for Q_3.

    Compare effects on long-run market shares relative to Q_1.

35. Let Q_4 represent a policy to undertake both promotion campaigns. If the effects of these campaigns are independent of each other, state **P** and determine **u***. Compare to the preceding exercise.

36. Consider the pricing strategy described in Exercise 11 on page 592. Brand 2 currently sells for $1.50 per unit. In addition to the current price, management is considering alternative prices of $1.25, $2.00, and $3.00. Marginal profit is given by price less variable cost of $1 per unit. The potential market is 50 million customers. Define policy and decision variables. Define the criterion. Determine **P** for each decision if Brands 1 and 3 are expected to hold prices at $1 and $2 per unit, respectively.

37. For the stock market model, consider two decisions: Sell a share at the beginning of the trading day or buy a share at the beginning of the trading day. Now consider two policies: (1) Sell if the closing price from the preceding day increased or remained the same from its opening price on that day; buy if it declined; (2) buy if the closing price from the preceding day increased or remained the same from its opening price on that day; sell if it declined.

    a. Construct a Q_t v. X_{t-1} table.
    b. From Table 15–6, determine the average price increase per day for the days when the stock closed up. Determine the average price decrease per day for the days when the stock closed down. Define your criterion in terms of gains or losses per share per day due to price changes. Construct a table for $Z(D_m, X_t)$.
    c. Can you define additional policies? Can decisions affect **P** or X_t?

Solution by Complete Enumeration

When the number of policies is small, a practical solution procedure involves the evaluation of expected values for the criterion for each possible policy. In this case, we find that the "optimal" policy is that policy (from among those enumerated) which yields the most favorable expected value for the criterion *per unit time,* assuming the existence of steady-state probabilities. If criteria are based on cash flows (for example, costs, profits, revenues), then a popular alternative is to optimize the discounted total flow.

Example 15.10   Solution of IRS Problem

In Exercise 30 you should have confirmed that $u_1^* = 5/9$ and $u_2^* = 4/9$. This means that in the long-run 5/9 of the time there will *not* be an audit and 4/9 of the time there will be an audit. Now consider policy Q_1 according to Table 15–9. Based on the long-run probabilities, it follows that 5/9 of the time decision D_2 (do not hire CPA) is made and 4/9 of the time decision D_1 (hire CPA) is made. From the transition matrix,

$$\mathbf{P} = \begin{pmatrix} 0.6 & 0.4 \\ 0.5 & 0.5 \end{pmatrix},$$

TABLE 15–10

Expected Cost per Year for Policy Q_1

Verbal Joint Event	Symbolic Joint Event	Joint Probability	Cost	Expected Cost
Do not hire CPA and no audit in year t ..	D_2 and $X_t = 0$	$(5/9) \cdot (0.6) = 3/9$	0	$(3/9) \cdot (0)$
Do not hire CPA and audit in year t......	D_2 and $X_t = 1$	$(5/9) \cdot (0.4) = 2/9$	500	$(2/9) \cdot (500)$
Hire CPA and no audit in year t......	D_1 and $X_t = 0$	$(4/9) \cdot (0.5) = 2/9$	250	$(2/9) \cdot (250)$
Hire CPA and audit in year t......	D_1 and $X_t = 1$	$(4/9) \cdot (0.5) = 2/9$	300	$(2/9) \cdot (300)$
Total..........		$9/9$		$2100/9 = \$233.33$ per year

we know that given no audit in the preceding year (which for policy Q_1 is the same as saying "given decision D_2") the probability of no audit in year t is 0.6; hence, the long-run probability of no audit in the preceding year $(X_{t-1} = 0)$ *and* no audit in the subsequent year $(X_t = 0)$ is $(5/9) \cdot (0.6)$, or $3/9$. Since under these circumstances decision D_2 will have been made and no audit will have occurred, it follows that a cost of zero dollars will have resulted according to $Z(D_2, 0) = 0$ in Table 15–8. A cost of \$500 will be incurred with probability $(5/9) \cdot (0.4)$, or $2/9$, if D_2 is coupled with an audit in year t.

Table 15–10 summarizes for policy Q_1 the four possible joint events, their probabilities, and their costs. If policy Q_1 were to be adopted, then the expected (long-run) cost per year would be \$233.33. (Why must the sum of the joint probabilities always equal unity?)

Table 15–11 summarizes the calculations for policies Q_2, Q_3, and Q_4. (Can

TABLE 15–11

Expected Costs per Year for Policies Q_2, Q_3, and Q_4

Policy	Joint Event	Joint Probability	Cost	Expected Cost
Q_2..............	D_1 and $X_t = 0$	$(5/9) \cdot (0.6) = 3/9$	250	$750/9$
	D_1 and $X_t = 1$	$(5/9) \cdot (0.4) = 2/9$	300	$600/9$
	D_2 and $X_t = 0$	$(4/9) \cdot (0.5) = 2/9$	0	$0/9$
	D_2 and $X_t = 1$	$(4/9) \cdot (0.5) = 2/9$	500	$1000/9$
Total.......		$9/9$		$2350/9 = \$261.11$ per year
Q_3..............	D_1 and $X_t = 0$	$(1) \cdot (5/9) = 5/9$	250	$1250/9$
	D_1 and $X_t = 1$	$(1) \cdot (4/9) = 4/9$	300	$1200/9$
Total.......		$9/9$		$2450/9 = \$272.22$ per year
Q_4..............	D_2 and $X_t = 0$	$(1) \cdot (5/9) = 5/9$	0	$0/9$
	D_2 and $X_t = 1$	$(1) \cdot (4/9) = 4/9$	500	$2000/9$
Total.......		$9/9$		$2000/9 = \$222.22$ per year

you verbalize the joint events and confirm their probabilities and costs by referencing Tables 15–8 and 15–9?) Based on this long-run criterion (expected cost per year), the best policy is Q_4 (never hire a CPA).

Example 15.11   Solution of Brand Switching Problem

In Example 15.9, three policies were enumerated. Table 15–12 shows the transition matrix and corresponding steady-state market shares for each policy. (Did you confirm u^* for Q_2 and Q_3 in Exercise 34?) If we assume that (1) the effect of a promotion campaign on **P** is immediate, but weekly promotion expenditures must be continued to maintain the new **P;** and (2) prices, costs, size of potential market, and transition probabilities are all static and known with certainty, then the expected steady-state value of the criterion (profit per week) for policy Q_i is given by $Z(Q_i) =$ Expected market share for Brand 2) $\times$ (Size of potential market) $\times$ (Marginal profit per week) less (Promotional expenditures per week).

TABLE 15–12

P and u* for Stated Policies

Policy	P			u*		
Q_1	0.90	0.07	0.03	(0.474	0.321	0.205)
	0.02	0.82	0.16			
	0.20	0.12	0.68			
Q_2	0.90	0.07	0.03	(0.393	0.456	0.151)
	0.02	0.90	0.08			
	0.20	0.12	0.68			
Q_3	0.90	0.07	0.03	(0.393	0.380	0.227)
	0.02	0.82	0.16			
	0.14	0.18	0.68			

Table 15–13 summarizes the calculations. Accordingly, policy Q_2 should be undertaken, which is to say that promotion campaign A yields the highest expected profit per week.

TABLE 15–13

Expected Values of Criterion for Stated Policies

Policy	Long-Run Profit per Week, $\bar{Z}(Q_i)$
Q_1	$(0.321) \cdot (50,000,000) \cdot (0.5) - \quad 0 = \$\ 8,025,000$ per week
Q_2	$(0.456) \cdot (50,000,000) \cdot (0.5) - 500,000 = \$10,900,000$ per week
Q_3	$(0.380) \cdot (50,000,000) \cdot (0.5) - 400,000 = \$\ 9,100,000$ per week

Follow-up Exercises

38.   Determine the optimal policy for Exercise 33.

39.   Determine $\bar{Z}(Q_4)$ based on your results in Exercise 35. Compare to the policies in Table 15–13. Conclusion?

40. Determine the best price of those considered in Exercise 36. Does this price necessarily yield a universal optimum (that is, might there be some other price which was not considered but which gives a higher value for the criterion)? What "heroic" assumptions need to be realized for this decision model to be accurate?

41. Determine the optimal policy in Exercise 37 based on **P** in (a) Exercise 15 and (b) Exercise 16.

Optimization Algorithms

When the number of states is large or countably infinite, complete enumeration is far too costly a procedure for finding the optimal policy. Not surprisingly, therefore, actual large-scale Markov decision processes have been solved by some of the optimization procedures with which you are already familiar: *linear programming* and *dynamic programming*. Particularly noteworthy is the **policy improvement algorithm** developed by Howard, which applies dynamic programming to a discounted cost criterion.[10]

The usual computational and storage problems associated with large-scale mathematical programming, however, have necessitated the development of alternative computational approaches for large real-world processes. One popular algorithm for discounted cost problems is the **method of successive approximations.** Unfortunately, its rate of convergence to a solution can be slow; hence, the speed with which these algorithms converge on optimal or near-optimal solutions has been a topic of great research interest.[11]

15.6 OTHER STOCHASTIC PROCESSES

In this chapter we have focused on Markov chains as a specific stochastic process with important applicability. So as to not leave you with the impression that a Markov chain is the only stochastic process of interest, we now briefly identify other stochastic processes which are prominent.

Markovian processes with continuous state spaces (termed **diffusion processes**) and continuous time parameters are widely discussed in the literature. **Birth and death processes** represent a special case of continuous time Markov chains with general applicability to queuing, genetic, and biological growth-decay problems.

Markov processes when the time between states is itself a random

---

[10] R. Howard, *Dynamic Programming and Markov Processes* (Cambridge, Mass.: M.I.T. Press, 1960).

[11] See F. S. Hillier and G. L. Lieberman, *Introduction to Operations Research,* 2d ed. (San Francisco: Holden Day, Inc., 1974), for the LP formulation and the policy improvement algorithm. For an empirical comparison of convergence properties for selected algorithms, see M. Zaldivar and T. J. Hodgson, "Rapid Convergence Techniques for Markov Decision Processes," *Decision Sciences,* vol. 6, no. 1 (January 1975), pp. 14–24.

variable have also been analyzed. Such processes are termed *variable time* rather than *fixed time*. When variable times are applied to a Markov chain, we have what is called an **imbedded Markov chain.** Conceptually and analytically, imbedded Markov chains have been very useful in analyzing queuing problems.

Counting processes represent another important class of stochastic processes. A counting process is a continuous time stochastic process, $\{N_t, t \geq 0\}$, where N_t is the total number of events which have occurred up to time t. A **Poisson process** is a special type of counting process if certain conditions for N_t are met—most notably that the number of events in a time interval is Poisson-distributed. A counting process where the times between events are independently and identically distributed with an arbitrary probability distribution is termed a **renewal process.** Poisson and renewal processes have been widely applied to the solution of queuing and reliability (failure-replacement) problems.

Other classes of stochastic processes and numerous variations within classes also have been analyzed in the literature. For the most part, their presentation requires mathematical sophistication and their relevance tends to be limited to applications in the physical sciences.

15.7 ASSESSMENT

The simple fact that models of stochastic processes directly address an uncertain environment lends value and credibility to such approaches. For this reason alone, applications in economics and the social and physical sciences have been widespread.

As with all OR/MS modeling, however, problems arise in the divergence between the theoretical model and the real process itself. Since all models necessarily rely on assumptions for their derivations, it follows that analysts must assess the degree of this divergence by appropriate tests in inferential statistics. Specifically, for Markov chains, the goodness of the model should be assessed by appropriate tests for (1) stationarity, (2) the Markovian property, and (3) homogeneity (where applicable).[12] All too often these assumptions are not tested.

Other problems which arise in implementation include the need for substantial data estimation and the cost of convergence for large-scale decision processes. As discussed in Section 15.5, current research is alleviating the latter problem. Unfortunately, for many applications, the collection of adequate data is either too costly or impossible. In part, data collection is facilitated for consumer behavior applications (for example, brand switching) by the existence of established consumer panels. In other cases, the existence of large data banks reduces the cost of data collection. In financial applications, for example, COMPUSTAT tapes provide a wealth of time-series data for corporations and industries.

A final issue relates to the relevancy of long-run assumptions for decision problems. For example, in reality stationarity and equilibrium are never really achieved for brand switching models. We all know that such markets are dynamic as a result of changing competitive strategies and

---

[12] See Fielitz and Bhargava, "Stock Price Relatives," for some appropriate testing procedures.

changing consumer preferences. Even under these conditions, however, the use of equilibrium criteria is widespread. This leads us to conclude that equilibrium approaches represent valid diagnostic tools for making decisions.

SELECTED REFERENCES

Hillier, F. S., and Lieberman, G. J. *Introduction to Operations Research.* 2d ed. San Francisco: Holden Day, Inc., 1974.

Howard, R. *Dynamic Programming and Markov Processes.* Cambridge, Mass.: M.I.T. Press, 1960.

Karlin, S. *A First Course in Stochastic Processes.* New York: Academic Press, 1966.

Montgomery, D. B., and Urban, G. L. *Management Science in Marketing.* Englewood Cliffs, N.J.: Prentice-Hall, Inc., 1969, chap. 2.

Parzen, E. *Stochastic Processes.* San Francisco: Holden Day, Inc., 1962.

Ross, S. M. *Applied Probability Models with Optimization Applications.* San Francisco: Holden Day, Inc., 1970.

Shamblin, J. E., and Stevens, G. T. *Operations Research: A Fundamental Approach.* New York: McGraw-Hill Book Company, 1974.

Taha, H. A. *Operations Research: An Introduction.* New York: The Macmillan Company, 1971.

ADDITIONAL EXERCISES

42. *Credit (Accounts Receivable) Control* In recent years a number of consumer credit applications have appeared in the literature regarding control of accounts receivable. To illustrate a simplified approach, consider the accompanying table based on the accounts (in millions) of Muster Charge, a nationally prominent credit card company.[13] For example, of

Days Past Due On July 1	Days Past Due on August 1			
	0–29	30–59	60+	Total
0–29	3.0	2.0	0.0	5.0
30–59	0.5	1.8	0.7	3.0
60+	0.6	0.8	0.6	2.0
Total	4.1	4.6	1.3	10.0

10 million total accounts, 5 million were 0–29 days past due on July 1. Of these 5 million, 3 million remained in the 0–29 status and 2 million lapsed into the 30–59 category. Note that it is not possible in one month to go from 0–29 days past due to 60 or more days past due. Accounts remaining in the 0–29 category means that customers paid on time (that is, within 30 days). In actual practice, more past-due categories would exist.

   a. Define the state variable, state space, and index parameter for this problem. Categorize this stochastic process.

---

[13] For a more realistic, but complicated, model see L. H. Liebman, "A Markov Decision Model for Selecting Optimal Credit Control Policies," *Management Science,* vol. 18, no. 10 (1972), pp. B-519–25.

    b. Predict the proportion of accounts in each category for September 1, October 1, and November 1. Show why this chain is ergodic. Predict the steady-state proportions and interpret their meaning. (Note: Express the entries in **P** to two decimal places.)

    c. What assumptions need to be realized for your predictions in part (*b*) to be valid?

    d. A monthly total cost given by the sum of administrative cost, receivable carrying cost (including opportunity cost), and bad debt cost is associated with each account in each state. The estimated total costs (dollars per account per month) for the states 0–29, 30–59, and 60+ are, respectively, 2, 5, and 20. Predict monthly costs for the months ending on September 1, October 1, and November 1. Predict steady-state monthly costs. (Assume 10 million accounts throughout.)

  ***e.* Suppose that the company makes one of two decisions each month for customers in each state: "Do nothing other than the usual late notice" or "phone the customer." (Can you think of other alternatives in actual practice?) If the company selects the first decision, then the *row* in the transition matrix *for that state* remains unaffected, and the expected cost per customer per month is the same as in part (*d*); however, if the company phones the customer, then the added expense of $.50 per customer per month is incurred *and* that particular *row* of the transition matrix is altered as follows: Increase the 0–29 transition probability by 6 percentage points (that is, by 0.06) and decrease all other nonzero entries uniformly. For example, row 2 of **P** would change from (0.17 0.60 0.23) to (0.23 0.57 0.20). Do you see the logic? Construct a Z-table and policy table for this problem and determine the policy which yields minimum expected (long-run) cost per month. (Hint: You must consider eight policies.)

43. *Maintenance Model* Markov processes have been applied to a wide variety of maintenance scenarios. To illustrate one approach, consider the following problem. Turbines in a power generating plant are inspected daily. At the end of each day, a turbine is classified into one of the following states: $X_{t-1} = 1$ if operating efficiently; $X_{t-1} = 2$ if operating inefficiently; and $X_{t-1} = 3$ if inoperable. The operating costs in Day *t* for these states are estimated as $100 per day, $200 per day, and $1,000 per day, respectively. The increased cost for State 3 reflects the higher operating cost of securing supplementary power from a regional combine of utility companies.

    Current maintenance policy calls for "no repair" (D_1) in Day *t* whenever State 1 or State 2 is observed the previous night (that is, decision D_1 whenever $X_{t-1} = 1$ or $X_{t-1} = 2$) and "undertaking a major repair" (D_2) in Day *t* whenever State 3 is observed the previous night (that is, decision D_2 whenever $X_{t-1} = 3$). Assume that the major repair always takes one full day, is always successful in the sense of returning the turbine to State 1, and costs $500. Note that when a turbine is being repaired, the daily cost for that turbine is $1,500, or $1,000 for auxiliary power and $500 for the parts and labor associated with the repair.

    The matrix for transitions between X_{t-1} and X_t is given by

$$\mathbf{P} = \begin{pmatrix} 0.8 & 0.2 & 0 \\ 0 & 0.9 & 0.1 \\ 1 & 0 & 0 \end{pmatrix}.$$

Note that **P** is dependent upon the policy. For example, Row 3 indicates that if the machine is inoperable at the end of Day $t-1$, then it is over-hauled and will be operating efficiently by the end of Day t; that is, if $X_{t-1} = 3$, then $X_t = 1$ with certainty.

a. Define the state space and index parameter for this stochastic process. What assumptions need to be realized in reality for this problem to be modeled as a Markov chain? Is this chain ergodic? Explain.

b. In the long run, how many turbines will need repair per day on the average if the facility has 16 turbines?

c. Determine the expected cost per day for the current policy.

d. Determine the optimal policy by assessing all other possible policies. (Hint: For two decisions and three states there are eight possible policies; also note that **P changes according to the policy.)

e. Can you think of other possible states and other possible decisions for this model?

44. *Scheduling Hospital Admissions*[14]   Consider the following definitions of variables for a model which schedules the admission of patients into a specific ward of a hospital:

$X_t =$ Number of occupied beds at *end* (midnight) of day t.
$N_t =$ Nonscheduled arrivals during Day t.
$A_t =$ Scheduled arrivals during Day t.
$D_t =$ Discharges, transfers, and deaths during Day t.

For this stochastic process, X_t represents the state variable; N_t is a random variable over time which is independent and identically distributed; D_t is a random variable over time which is dependent (conditional) on the occupancy of the ward in Day $t-1$; and A_t represents the deterministic decision variable.

By policy of the hospital, all scheduled arrivals for Day t are admitted, but nonscheduled arrivals are admitted into this ward only if beds are available; hence, N_t is not synonymous with admissions. Also, patients who are admitted on Day t are never discharged on the same day. To keep the problem manageable for you, we limit the number of beds in this ward to three.

Empirical probability distributions have been determined for N_t and for D_t given X_{t-1}, as shown in the accompanying table. For example, the

N_t	$P(N_t)$	X_{t-1}	D_t	$P(D_t|X_{t-1})$
0	0.2	0	0	1.0
1	0.1	1	0	0.8
2	0.4		1	0.2
3	0.2	2	0	0.6
4	0.1		1	0.3
			2	0.1
		3	0	0.3
			1	0.4
			2	0.2
			3	0.1

---

[14] Based in part on P. Kolesar, "Markovian Model for Hospital Admission Scheduling," pp. 384–96.

probability of three nonscheduled arrivals on any given day is 20 percent. Note that discharges, transfers, and deaths on any given day cannot exceed the number of occupied beds at the *beginning* of the day; that is, $D_t \leq X_{t-1}$. Also, the value of D_t is probabilistically dependent on the value of X_{t-1}. For example, if two beds are occupied at the beginning of any one day, then the probability that one patient is discharged, is transferred, or dies is 30 percent.

a. Specify the state space and the index parameter for this stochastic process.

b. Finish constructing the following one-step transition matrix for this model if the hospital follows a policy of always scheduling one admission (that is, $A_t = 1$ for all t):

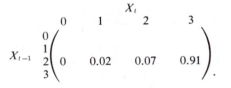

To help you along, we will describe the given calculations for the third row of the transition matrix. In general, the number of beds which are occupied at the end of Day t will be either three (the capacity of the ward) or $(X_{t-1} + N_t + A_t - D_t)$, whichever is smaller. Can you verbalize the algebraic expression? Thus, for $A_t = 1$, it follows that

$$X_t = \min [3, (X_{t-1} + N_t - D_t + 1)].$$

O.K. so far? Now, to determine the third row of **P**, it is necessary to evaluate the conditional probabilities $(P(X_t \,|\, X_{t-1} = 2)$ for all possible values of X_t. To help you conceptualize this, consider the probability tree given in Figure 15–3. A node ($\bullet$) with a number on top represents a realized value for that random variable. The probability of achieving that node is labeled parenthetically on the branch leading into that node. To illustrate, consider the path with the starred (*) ending node. In this case, two beds were occupied at the beginning of the day $(X_{t-1} = 2)$, two nonscheduled arrivals $(N_t = 2)$ and one departure $(D_t = 1)$ occurred, and one scheduled arrival was admitted $(+1)$. Thus, there was a demand for four beds $(2 + 2 - 1 + 1)$. Since only three beds are available, it follows that the number of beds occupied at the end of the day must be three $(X_t = 3)$. Since $N_t = 2$ *and* $D_t = 1$ must occur for this path, it should be evident that achieving $X_t = 3$ via this path is given by the *joint* probability

$$P(X_t = 3 | X_{t-1} = 2) = P(N_t = 2) \cdot P(D_t = 1 | X_{t-1} = 2) =$$
$$(0.4) \cdot (0.3) = 0.12.$$

Noting that the paths through the tree are all mutually exclusive, you should readily confirm the entries in row 3 of **P** by the Rule of Addition in probability (page 704 in Appendix A).

c. Explain why the described stochastic process is a finite state Markov chain. Do you have quarrel with any of the assumptions? Is this chain ergodic? Explain.

FIGURE 15–3

Probability Tree for Hospital Admission Model

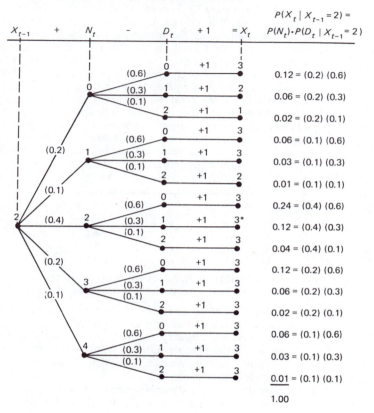

$$P(X_t \mid X_{t-1}=2) =$$

X_{t-1}	+	N_t	−	D_t	+ 1	= X_t	$P(N_t) \cdot P(D_t \mid X_{t-1}=2)$
			(0.6)	0	+1	3	$0.12 = (0.2)(0.6)$
		0	(0.3)	1	+1	2	$0.06 = (0.2)(0.3)$
			(0.1)	2	+1	1	$0.02 = (0.2)(0.1)$
	(0.2)		(0.6)	0	+1	3	$0.06 = (0.1)(0.6)$
		1	(0.3)	1	+1	3	$0.03 = (0.1)(0.3)$
	(0.1)		(0.1)	2	+1	2	$0.01 = (0.1)(0.1)$
2	(0.4)	2	(0.6)	0	+1	3	$0.24 = (0.4)(0.6)$
			(0.3)	1	+1	3*	$0.12 = (0.4)(0.3)$
			(0.1)	2	+1	3	$0.04 = (0.4)(0.1)$
	(0.2)		(0.6)	0	+1	3	$0.12 = (0.2)(0.6)$
		3	(0.3)	1	+1	3	$0.06 = (0.2)(0.3)$
	(0.1)		(0.1)	2	+1	3	$0.02 = (0.2)(0.1)$
			(0.6)	0	+1	3	$0.06 = (0.1)(0.6)$
		4	(0.3)	1	+1	3	$0.03 = (0.1)(0.3)$
			(0.1)	2	+1	3	$0.01 = (0.1)(0.1)$

1.00

d. Calculate the steady-state probability distribution for number of occupied beds and the expected number of occupied beds.

e. In the preceding parts, the decision variable A_t was specified as 1
for all t. In actual practice, this analysis would be undertaken for
the purpose of determining the policy which provides optimal control
of the process. In this case, the possible number of policies $(Q_1, Q_2,$
. . . , $Q_L)$ is determined by the possible assignments of decisions to
each possible value of the state variable X_{t-1}. In other words,
given the number of occupied beds at the end of Day $t-1$, a decision
is made for the number of admissions to schedule the next day (A_t).
Criteria to be optimized include maximization of expected occupancy
subject to a constraint for an upper limit on the probability that an
arriving patient is rejected from the ward; or, conversely, minimizing
this "overflow" probability subject to a constraint on average bed
utilization. You might be surprised to learn that this model can be
solved by linear programming. Determine the possible number of
policies for the three-bed ward if more than 3 patients are never
scheduled into the ward. How many policies are possible for a 20-bed
ward if more than 20 patients are never scheduled for admission?

Might there be a cost problem in solving the 20-bed model by enumeration?

45. *Periodic Review* (s,S) *Inventory Model* The Seers Co., a prominent merchandising firm with more than 1,000 retail stores across the country, is currently analyzing the inventory policies it recommends to its retail stores. The current focus is on the *very* expensive Zony Model 2001 television set. The *periodic review* (s,S) *policy* under study is the following: At the *end* of a week, order enough sets to bring inventory *up to* two sets (that is, $S = 2$) whenever the ending inventory for the week is *less than* one set (that is, $s = 1$); if the ending inventory is one or more sets, then no order is placed. The distribution system of Seers is so efficient that once an order is placed at the end of the week, the new sets are guaranteed to arrive for business at the beginning of the next week (that is, zero lead time). Weekly demands for this particular type of television set are independent and distributed according to the stationary probability distribution given here. Assume that sales are lost if demand

Demand in Week t D_t	Probability $P(D_t)$
0	0.3
1	0.5
2	0.2

exceeds inventory on hand. (Customers go to the Monty Ward Company, which always keeps many units in inventory.)

a. Specify the state space and the index parameter if the state variable, X_t, is defined as ending inventory in Week t.

b. Construct the one-step transition matrix for this model, where rows represent the possible states in Week $t - 1$ and columns represent the possible states in Week t. Note that X_t depends on the (s,S) policy and on both X_{t-1} and D_t.

c. Explain why the described problem is a finite state Markov chain. What assumption is most likely not satisfied in reality? Is the chain ergodic? Explain.

d. Given that the ending inventory for the current week is 2 sets, determine the probabilities of 0, 1, and 2 sets at the end of next week and the following week.

e. Determine the expected (long-run) carrying (holding) cost per week if ending inventory is costed at $3 per set per week.

**f. Besides carrying costs, two other types of costs are incurred: ordering costs and shortage costs (lost profits). Suppose that the shortage cost is $150 per set and the ordering cost is estimated by a fixed cost component ($20 per order) and a variable cost component ($5 per television set which is ordered). Determine the expected total cost per week for the (s,S) inventory policy given by (1,2). (Hint: For each possible state, determine total cost in Week t as the carrying cost at the end of Week $t - 1$ plus the ordering cost at the end of Week $t - 1$ plus the *expected* shortage cost during Week t.) Note that the expected shortage cost first requires you to determine the expected number of units short during Week t. The actual shortage during Week t, of course, is dependent upon the particular (s,S) policy and the values of X_{t-1} and D_t.

**g. Calculate expected total cost per week for all other possible (s,S) policies. Assume that inventory never exceeds 2; that is, maximum

S is 2. (Do you see why a greater upper limit for S would be non-optimal?) (Hint: You must consider two more (s,S) policies. Don't forget that the (s,S) policy affects **P**.) What is the optimal periodic review policy for this inventory system?

46. *Probabilistic Dynamic Programming* In Chapter 9 we treated the topic of dynamic programming in detail. In all cases, the models which were solved were of the deterministic type. In this exercise, we extend dynamic programming to include stochastic states. Since dynamic programming is a sequential approach to optimization, its use in a Markovian framework is often referred to as **Markovian sequential decision process.**[15]

To illustrate a Markovian sequential decision process, we return to the maintenance model of Exercise 43. The equivalent dynamic programming structure is as follows.

1. A **stage** is equivalent to a day. Therefore, the number of stages (n) will equal the number of days in the planning horizon.
2. The **decision variables** for stage i are defined as $x_i = 1$ for no repair in stage i and $x_i = 2$ for major repair in stage i.
3. The **state** *following* or *leaving* stage i is labeled s_i. It will take on one of three values:
   $s_i = 1$ if the turbine is operating efficiently.
   $s_i = 2$ if the turbine is not operating efficiently.
   $s_i = 3$ if the turbine is inoperable.
4. The general **transformation function** can be depicted as in Chapter 9: $s_{i-1} = T(s_i, x_i)$. This means that, given s_i and x_i, it is possible to determine s_{i-1}. Note, however, that the state variable is now stochastic. Its next value is determined by a chance process based on the current state and decision. In other words, the current state and decision do not determine the next state (as in the deterministic case); they determine the *probability distribution* for the next state. In a Markovian framework, this probability distribution is based on a *row* of an enlarged transition matrix. The appropriate row is determined by both the current state s_i and the current decision x_i, as indicated by the transformation function. Since we have three states and two decisions, it is necessary to specify six distinct rows:

		Next State (s_{i-1})		
		1	2	3
Current	1,1	0.8	0.2	0
State-Decision	1,2	1	0	0
(s_i, x_i)	2,1	0	0.9	0.1
	2,2	1	0	0
	3,1	0	0	1
	3,2	1	0	0

For example, if the current state is "operating efficiently" $(s_i = 1)$, then a decision "no repair" $(x_i = 1)$ would yield transition probabilities of (0.8 0.2 0) for the next state (as in Exercise 43); however, again if $s_i = 1$, then a decision "major repair" $(x_i = 2)$ would result in transition probabilities (1 0 0); that is, the next state is guaranteed to be "operating efficiently." Can you interpret the remaining four rows?

---

[15] For applications in airline and hotel reservation systems, see M. Rothstein, "Hotel Overbooking as a Markovian Sequential Decision Process," *Decision Sciences*, vol. 5, no. 3 (1974), pp. 389–404.

5. The **return** for Stage i, r_i, depends on the state and decision associated with Stage i. As in Exercise 43, it represents (operating cost + repair cost) for Stage i.
6. The **optimal recursive equation** is given by

$$f_i^* = \min_{\text{all } x_i} [r_i + E(f_{i-1}^*)],$$

where f_i^* is the cumulative optimal cost per turbine over the first i stages and $E(f_{i-1}^*)$ is the *expected* cumulative optimal cost through Stage i-1. The expected value for f_{i-1}^* is found by weighting each possible f_{i-1}^* by the probability of its associated state s_{i-1}. These probabilities are given by the appropriate row in the enlarged transition matrix.

Now, suppose that a turbine is currently in State 2 and we wish to determine an optimal policy (sequence of optimal decisions) for the next four days. Because of this given state, we formulate this as a **backward recursion** according to the diagram. Carefully note that

$$s_4 = 2 \quad \boxed{\begin{array}{c}\text{Stage 4}\\(\text{Day 1})\end{array}} \quad s_3 \quad \boxed{\begin{array}{c}\text{Stage 3}\\(\text{Day 2})\end{array}} \quad s_2 \quad \boxed{\begin{array}{c}\text{Stage 2}\\(\text{Day 3})\end{array}} \quad s_1 \quad \boxed{\begin{array}{c}\text{Stage 1}\\(\text{Day 4})\end{array}} \quad s_0$$

the state following stage i (s_i) is equivalent to the *beginning* state for the day associated with stage i. For example, $s_2 = 1$ would mean that the turbine is operating efficiently at the beginning of Day 3. This, of course, also represents the ending state for Day 2.

Now that you're thoroughly (partially?) confused, we will "straighten" you out by providing the first two tableaus. Carefully confirm the logic of all calculations based on the above explanations.

Stage 1 (Day 4): $f_1 = r_1 + E(f_0^*)$

s_1 \ x_1	1	2	x_1^*	f_1^*
1	$100 + 0 = 100$	$1{,}500 + 0 = 1{,}500$	1	100
2	$200 + 0 = 200$	$1{,}500 + 0 = 1{,}500$	1	200
3	$1{,}000 + 0 = 1{,}000$	$1{,}500 + 0 = 1{,}500$	1	1,000

Note: $s_1 \equiv$ Beginning state for Day 4.

Stage 2 (Day 3): $f_2 = r_2 + E(f_1^*)$

s_2 \ x_2	1	2	x_2^*	f_2^*
1	$100 + [(0.8)(100) + (0.2)(200) + (0)(1{,}000)] = 220$	$1{,}500 + [(1)(100) + (0)(200) + (0)(1{,}000)] = 1{,}600$	1	220
2	$200 + [(0)(100) + (0.9)(200) + (0.1)(1{,}000)] = 480$	$1{,}500 + [(1)(100) + (0)(200) + (0)(1{,}000)] = 1{,}600$	1	480
3	$1{,}000 + [(0)(100) + (0)(200) + (1)(1{,}000)] = 2{,}000$	$1{,}500 + [(1)(100) + (0)(200) + (0)(1{,}000)] = 1{,}600$	2	2,000

Note: $s_2 \equiv$ Beginning state for Day 3.

a. Determine the optimal policy for Days 1, 2, 3, and 4 and the associated optimal cost when the turbine is in State 2 at the beginning of Day 1.

b. Same as part (a) for initial states of 1 and 3. Do the results make sense? Explain.

c. Answer part (a) for a five-day planning horizon. Assess differences in policy and optimal cost between the four-day and five-day problems. Why might a longer horizon be desirable?

d. Answer part (a) for the case where an additional decision is possible: $x_t = 3$ represents "minor repairs." A minor repair costs $150 per day per turbine and guarantees the return of a previously efficient or inefficient turbine to an efficient state; however, a minor repair cannot restore an inoperable turbine to an operable state. Assume that auxiliary power for a minor repair is costed at $300 per day. Compare optimal cost to part (a).

Heuristic Programs

THIS CHAPTER continues our broadening orientation toward decision making by examining larger systems—including multiple criteria—and decreasing the interest in "pure optima." With your present understanding of how optimum-producing algorithms work, we can now go on to some important problems that either cannot be solved optimally, or the cost of obtaining the optimal solution makes optimal solutions impractical. After a brief introduction to the nature of heuristics, one particular problem (the assignment of facilities to locations) will be treated in detail. Thereafter, some classic OR applications of heuristics will be overviewed, followed by an overview of marketing heuristics and some less traditional applications.

16.1 THE NATURE OF HEURISTICS

Without actually labeling them as such, several heuristic procedures have been treated in previous chapters. In Chapter 7, three heuristics were presented for obtaining initial solutions to transportation problems. The Northwest Corner Method is a heuristic technique which has the objective of finding a starting solution with little time or effort. The Least Cost and Vogel's Approximation methods seek initial solutions which are as near optimal as possible. As you will recall, these methods often achieve very good starting solutions; sometimes they are even optimal. As noted in Chapter 7, however, transportation solutions can be tested to determine if they are optimal. If the test for optimality did not exist, or one did not choose to make the test, then these techniques would be in exactly the same category as the models we will consider in this chapter.

Heuristic Defined

The term "heuristic" is somewhat difficult to define. Webster's New Collegiate Dictionary defines heuristic as "to discover." The word heuristic also ". . . is related to the word 'eureka' (I have found it, from the Greek *heuriskein,* which means to discover, find)."[1] For many OR analysts it refers to styles of reasoning, computer programming, problem investigation, or intelligence. Meier, Newell, and Pazer define heuristic methods as being composed of three subsets of techniques, not necessarily mutually exclusive. The first of these subsets is **heuristic problem solving,** which is problem-oriented and strives to reduce search efforts in achieving a satisfactory solution to a problem. The second subset is **artificial intelligence,** which uses computer-oriented heuristics in problems requiring searches over a solution space, pattern recognition, or organizational planning. The subset can even be extended to focus upon learning behavior (program modification resulting from experience) and inductive inference. "The orientation is toward efficient use of the computer to obtain apparently intelligent behavior rather than to attempt to reproduce the step-by-step thought process of a human decision maker."[2] The last subset is **simulation of human thought,** which is concerned with computer replication of thought processes of a human decision maker.

Our concern in this chapter will be primarily with the first of the three subsets, heuristic problem solving. For the moment, we simply define a **heuristic** as "a rule-of-thumb for solving some aspect of a problem." A collection of such rules-of-thumb for solving some overall problem is termed a **heuristic program.**

Simon believes that the primary differences between the traditional operations research approach and a heuristic approach are that in the heuristic approach:

1. Explicit consideration is given to a number of factors (for example, computer storage capacity and solution time) in addition to the quality of the solution produced.
2. The evaluation of heuristic approaches is usually done by inductive rather than deductive procedures. That is, specific heuristics are justified not because they attain an analytically derived solution (for example, an optimum) but rather because experimentation has proven that they are useful in practice.[3]

We all use heuristics, most often in combination with other heuristics or with more formal analyses of particular situations. In chess, for example, rules-of-thumb include having control over the center of the board, defending the king, not bringing the queen into play too early, clearing the way for a castle, and trading undeveloped pieces for developed pieces.

---

[1] James R. Slagle, *Artificial Intelligence: The Heuristic Programming Approach* (New York: McGraw-Hill Book Co., 1971), p. 3.

[2] Robert C. Meier, William T. Newell, and Harold L. Pazer, *Simulation in Business and Economics* (Englewood Cliffs, N.J.: Prentice-Hall, Inc., 1969), p. 150.

[3] H. A. Simon, "Modeling Human Processes," *Proceedings of the 1961 Western Joint Computer Conference,* p. 11.

These rules can be in harmony or conflict in specific circumstances and are obviously overridden by particular strategies. Similar kinds of heuristics exist for everyday living such as in driving a car in traffic (for example, stay in the fast lane unless cars begin to pass on the right). In baseball, a heuristic might be to counter the entrance of a right-handed relief pitcher with a left-handed pinch hitter.

Heuristics may also be distinguished as being **special-purpose** or **general-purpose.** Many of the chess heuristics would be considered as special-purpose since they are suitable only for the game of chess. The rule of first-come-first-served (or first-in-first-out) is a general-purpose heuristic which has applicability in a wide variety of circumstances, including inventory valuation and queuing theory. The heuristic of "working backward" is widely used as a general approach to solving a problem. Students often apply this approach in solving homework problems when the answer is given.

A heuristic program is typically implemented through a computer program. This dependence on the computer has resulted in substantive research contributions by computer scientists in applying heuristic programming to artificial intelligence. Their efforts to get machines to exhibit intelligent behavior have resulted in heuristic programs in which the computer plays games of chance, solves mathematical problems, proves mathematical theorems, composes music, and programs itself.

Problem Features

Heuristics can be used for many kinds of problems. Perhaps the most typical application in operations research is for solving large combinatorial problems for which the determination of an optimal solution by enumeration or mathematical (integer) programming would be prohibitively expensive (as we demonstrate in Section 16.2). The usual approach is to break down a problem into steps, or smaller problems, each of which can be solved efficiently. The analyst then hopes that the overall solution so derived (while not optimal) is satisfactory.

Heuristics are also usefully employed in problems that are vague or not definitively stated. For example, for most high-level problems in management, it is hard to state definitive criteria. If one embraces the systems viewpoint embodied in Industrial Dynamics, the emphasis shifts to overall results, the interdependencies and feedbacks among specific solutions are recognized, and the necessity (if not elegance) of the "quick and dirty" becomes obvious.

Tonge characterizes the applicable problem features in another way. "Heuristics techniques are most often used when the goal is to solve a problem whose solution can be described in terms of acceptability characteristics rather than by optimizing rules."[4] This is particularly true of problems with multiple, conflicting objectives, in which a "satisficing" solution is acceptable.

---

[4] F. M. Tonge, "The Use of Heuristic Programming in Management Science," *Management Science*, vol. 7 (April 1961), pp. 231–37.

Model Construction

Heuristic construction usually is driven by surrogate criteria, which may or may not be optimized; in many instances, the validity of the surrogate relationship is questionable. For example, a grocery shopper might compute the cost per ounce for all brands of items on the shopping list and use the following heuristic: Buy that package with the lowest cost per ounce. That rule might, however, result in the purchase of 50-gallon containers of milk or 20-pound jars of mustard. Inclusion of constraining decision rules might rectify gross mistakes, but the rules would still tend to produce a large pantry stock. Explicitly trading-off pantry inventory investment with quantity discounts can be achieved, but quality of foodstuffs and other use criteria have been omitted in the criteria set. For example, as one well-known bleach manufacturer claims: "It is the number of washings per dollar that counts, not the number of ounces per dollar."

It is this noncongruency between overall criteria and surrogate criteria, as well as the overwhelming size and complexity of many problems, that often results in heuristic procedures providing only one input to the final decision process. For example, the heuristic program which assigns facilities to locations (Section 16.2) is a model of only one aspect of plant or office layout. Minimization of materials flow has to be integrated with aesthetic features, personal feelings, and many other attributes of the decision environment. The right modeling interaction will encourage the decision maker to evaluate qualitative considerations in terms of quantitative ramifications.

There are two basic approaches to heuristic design. The first is to replicate the actions taken by a human decision maker; the ultimate test of the heuristic is whether the solutions obtained from the model are identical to those designed by the decision maker. This approach is called **cognitive simulation.**

The second approach to heuristic design, *artificial intelligence,* does not attempt to duplicate the analytic process used by some decision maker. Although the same kinds of reasoning *may* be used, this is not usually the case. The goal is to produce solutions that are superior to those obtained by human decision makers.

Follow-up Exercises

1. State any "rules-of-thumb" which you use in helping to make decisions about your personal life.

2. For those of you familiar with the card game of blackjack, state a heuristic for determining whether or not to "take a hit." What factors influence this heuristic? Would the factors differ if you were the dealer?

3. Would you conclude that selection of the origin as an initial basis in the simplex method is a heuristic? Explain.

> 4. In what area of project management models (Chapter 14) would you say heuristic programming is most applicable? Can you think of a reasonable heuristic in this area?

16.2 THE ASSIGNMENT OF FACILITIES TO LOCATIONS

The preceding general remarks will become more operational by working through a detailed example. The assignment of facilities to locations is a combinatorial problem in which considerable interest has been shown by operations researchers. The most widely addressed real-world problem has been the plant or office layout problem, that is, the relative placement of people or departments in physical locations.

The Problem

Although many empirical problems involve facilities of different size, the most straightforward formulation of the problem is to assign n equally-sized facilities to n homogeneous fixed locations within a prescribed area boundary based on the "cost" (c_{ikjl}) of placing facility i in location k and facility j in location l:

$$c_{ikjl} = f_{ij} \cdot d_{kl} \tag{16.1}$$

where

f_{ij} = The flow of "materials" over some defined time period *between* the ith *facility* and the jth *facility* ($f_{ij} = 0$ for $i = j$)

d_{kl} = The distance between locations k and l ($d_{kl} = 0$ for $k = l$).

Notice that the direction of material flow between two facilities is of no interest. The objective is to minimize a measure of the volume of material flow weighted by the distance that volume travels.

The "classic" 12-department problem considered in the literature is shown in Figure 16–1. The top half of the figure indicates the possible locations for positioning the 12 departments within the prescribed boundary. The problem can be thought of as being similar to having an egg carton wherein departments (eggs) are to be placed. The lower half of the figure is a 12×12 matrix split into two sections. The section above the diagonal (upper right) contains the "city block" distances between locations (for example, $d_{16} = 2$).[5] The section below the diagonal (lower left) indicates a measure of the flows (units, volume, pounds, and so forth) of materials between departments (for example, $f_{83} = 5$).

The assignment of facilities problem can be viewed as a mathematical

---

[5] Note that each distance in the matrix is determined from the locations in the top half of the figure. For example, two units of distance (as measured by city block or perpendicular movements) separate the midpoints of locations 1 and 6; three units separate locations 1 and 7, and so on.

FIGURE 16–1

Data for a Classic 12-Department Layout Problem

Locations within Prescribed Boundary

1	2	3	4
5	6	7	8
9	10	11	12

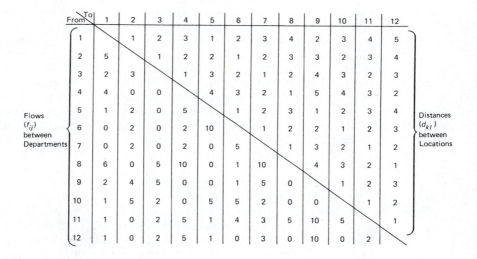

Flows (f_{ij}) between Departments (lower-left) — Distances (d_{kl}) between Locations (upper-right)

From\To	1	2	3	4	5	6	7	8	9	10	11	12
1		1	2	3	1	2	3	4	2	3	4	5
2	5		1	2	2	1	2	3	3	2	3	4
3	2	3		1	3	2	1	2	4	3	2	3
4	4	0	0		4	3	2	1	5	4	3	2
5	1	2	0	5		1	2	3	1	2	3	4
6	0	2	0	2	10		1	2	2	1	2	3
7	0	2	0	2	0	5		1	3	2	1	2
8	6	0	5	10	0	1	10		4	3	2	1
9	2	4	5	0	0	1	5	0		1	2	3
10	1	5	2	0	5	5	2	0	0		1	2
11	1	0	2	5	1	4	3	5	10	5		1
12	1	0	2	5	1	0	3	0	10	0	2	

program with a quadratic objective function (Chapter 10), linear constraints, and zero–one decision variables (Chapter 8):

Minimize

$$z = \tfrac{1}{2} \sum_{i=1}^{n} \sum_{k=1}^{n} \sum_{j=1}^{n} \sum_{l=1}^{n} c_{ikjl}\, x_{ik}\, x_{jl} \qquad (16.2)$$

subject to

$$\sum_{i=1}^{n} x_{ik} = 1, \quad k = 1, \ldots, n$$

$$\sum_{k=1}^{n} x_{ik} = 1, \quad i = 1, \ldots, n \qquad (16.3)$$

$$x_{ik} = 0 \text{ or } 1, \text{ for all } i, k$$

where

c_{ikjl} = The "cost" for some time period of placing facility i in location k, and facility j in location l.

x_{ik} = One if facility i is located in location k; zero if facility i is not located in location k.

x_{jl} = One if facility j is located in location l; zero if facility j is not located in location l.

When formulated as a quadratic assignment problem, it can be seen that $n!$ feasible solutions exist. Determining the optimal solution by complete enumeration is infeasible for problems of interesting size; for example, it would take a large computer approximately one year to enumerate the 479,001,600 solutions in a 12-department problem. The use of branch-and-bound procedures (Chapter 8) can substantially reduce the solution space to be evaluated. Nevertheless, the enormity of the computational burden in combinatorial problems is simply staggering; a semi-enumerative procedure (such as branch-and-bound) that "prunes" 95 percent of the final "leaves" off the total enumeration tree would still require 23,950,080 layouts to be evaluated in the 12-department case.

There are two basic approaches to solving this layout problem. One is to start with an "empty egg carton" and *construct* a solution by assigning each department a specific location based on a heuristic program or an optimization procedure. The other approach is to start with some initial departmental placement and *improve* the solution by exchanging departments.

An efficient branch-and-bound algorithm has been written for solving the layout problem by the first approach.[6] Achieving an optimum solution to the classic 12-department problem required approximately 2 hours of computer CPU time (GE-Honeywell 635). Solving 1/15 of the analogous 15-department problem (an *easy* 1/15) required approximately 55 hours.

The heuristic procedure that is described below obtained solutions for the 12-department and 15-department problems in approximately 7 and 16 seconds, respectively. For the 12-department problem, a comparison of the heuristic solution with the known optimal solution indicated the former to be within 3 percent of the optimum. Clearly the cost of generating a solution must be considered in addition to the quality of the solution when evaluating a heuristic program.

Best Pairwise Exchange Heuristic

Best pairwise exchange is an improvement (as opposed to construction) heuristic which starts with some initial layout. The starting solution may be the existing layout, one which has been randomly generated, or some other proposed solution. The procedure computes the value of the objective function according to Equations (16.1) and (16.2) for the

---

[6] Richard Mojena, Thomas E. Vollmann, and Yoshihiro Okamoto, "On Predicting Computational Time of a Branch and Bound Algorithm for the Assignment of Facilities," *Decision Sciences,* vol. 7, no. 4, (1976), pp. 856–867.

initial solution, finds the potential improvements in the objective function gained by exchanging all pairs of departments $[n(n-1)/2$ evaluations], makes the change resulting in the largest improvement, and repeats the procedure until no pairwise exchange will reduce the value of the objective function.

As noted above, this heuristic produces solutions within a few percent of optima (for those cases where optima are known) and it does so at a relatively small cost compared with that required to achieve the optimal solution.[7] The computation time does grow rapidly, however, as the number of departments is increased. For this reason, other heuristics have been proposed which produce results of comparable quality at substantially less computational cost.

Greatest to Least Heuristic

The best pairwise exchange heuristic is essentially a "brute force" procedure that does not make efficient use of problem information. The technique creates a ranked table of all pairwise exchanges which would reduce the objective function and then only utilizes the first entry in the table. For the next iteration, the entire table is recomputed even though many of the values in the former table have a high probability of being unchanged in the subsequent table.

The **greatest to least heuristic** maintains the ranked exchange table and examines in rank order a specified percentage of the best entries in the table (20 percent has been found in some studies to be about right). Each time an exchange in the ranked table is considered, its cost reduction has to be recalculated (but only *its* cost reduction—not all pairwise possibilities) since the conditions on which the reduction was based are no longer true after the first exchange. When the specified percentage of pairs from the original exchange table has been examined, a new ranked table of all pairwise exchanges is constructed. The process is repeated until no pairwise exchange will reduce costs (an empty table).

The greatest to least procedure, by effectively utilizing problem information, obtains results that are not statistically different from the "best pairwise method"; however, they are derived at a computational cost which is approximately 20 percent of that for the best pairwise method.

Any Improvement Heuristic

An alternative strategy to either best pairwise or greatest to least is the elimination of ranked lists of improvements; the **any improvement heuristic** simply makes any exchange that will reduce the objective function whenever it is found. "Any improvement" will make many more exchanges than a heuristic which searches out the most important exchanges first, but the speed of making each exchange is greatly increased. Results are achieved that are similar in quality to those obtained by greatest to

---

[7] Best pairwise exchange does not produce a guaranteed optimum because only pairs of departments are considered for improvement; three-way, four-way, and so forth, exchanges are not evaluated.

least; the computational cost is roughly 15 percent of that for the best pairwise method.

Other Heuristics

A variety of other heuristics have been proposed for this problem. An alternative to best pairwise exchange considers *three-way exchanges* as well. This allows the selection of the best two- or three-way exchange at each iteration. The **Hillier-Conners heuristic** determines desirability of moves by computing cost reductions resulting from singular movements of a department or facility to an adjacent location to the left, right, up, or down.[8] The **ranked product** procedure combines attributes of the previously mentioned heuristics to produce quality solutions with small computational effort. It was originally designed to cope with an empirical problem involving the placement of 121 departments, and its results were impressive compared with other techniques.[9]

There have been some *construction* (that is, start with an empty "egg crate") heuristics proposed in the literature, but all have been shown to produce results inferior to improvement heuristics. The usual approach is to sum the flows for each facility, place high flow facilities in the middle, and attempt to place departments adjacent to those with high interaction. The inferiority of construction procedures is probably due to their inability to trade-off all flows at the same time; placement of any one facility precludes another in that location.

Finally, a procedure called **biased sampling** can be applied to any heuristic procedure. For best pairwise exchange, it assigns weighted probabilities to cost reductions for pairwise moves in any particular exchange table, generates a random number to decide which exchange to make, and repeats the procedure for a specified number of simulations in order to construct a probability distribution of final solutions. As it turns out, the minimum of this distribution is almost always better than the minimum found by deterministic means.

The Surrogate Criterion Relationship

When Equation (16.1) is used in (16.2) the objective function represents the volume of material flow weighted by the distance that volume travels, which is a surrogate for "materials handling" cost. Materials are assumed to be loads transported between departments in a job shop or people walking for face-to-face communication in offices. There are some heroic assumptions involved in using this one criterion for evaluation of layout "goodness." Multiple criteria affect layout decisions; the basis for grouping individuals or pieces of equipment into "departments" tends to

[8] F. S. Hillier and M. M. Connors, "Quadratic Assignment Problem Algorithms and the Location of Indivisible Facilities," *Management Science,* vol. 13 (September 1966).

[9] T. E. Vollmann, C. E. Nugent, and R. L. Zartler, "A Computerized Model for Office Layout," *The Journal of Industrial Engineering,* vol. 17 (July 1968), pp. 321–27.

be somewhat arbitrary; the incremental nature of materials handling cost is open to question in many layout investigations; the data used are typically historical rather than forecasted; and the interaction of the layout problem with other organizational issues tends to be ignored (for example, a good production scheduling system creates better tolerance of poor layout—also, scheduling *creates* the materials flows).

Additional considerations include constraints on relative or absolute placements, such as separating flammable materials from welding shops, or satisfying the chief executive's desire for the corner office. In addition, the flows of materials are typically gathered from operation sheets which show the sequential nature of each part or product conversion. The assumption that future product routings will be the same may be tenuous. Moreover, the sequence data are based upon routing conventions that often are easily changed, and the source of these data tend to be from a low-level clerical operation.

All of these real-world considerations do not, however, negate the use of layout models. If anything, they focus attention appropriately on the illusory nature of "optima" and on the need to create a modeling environment where tradeoffs between subjective and objective criteria are more explicitly considered.

Follow-up Exercises

5. Verbalize the meaning of the constraints given by Equation (16.3).

6. Four departments are to be located in four locations as indicated. The distances between locations are presented in the upper right-hand side

Locations

1	2
3	4

of the accompanying table, and the daily flows between departments are presented in the lower left-hand portion of the table.

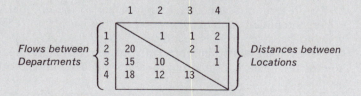

		1	2	3	4	
	1		1	1	2	
Flows between	2	20		2	1	Distances between
Departments	3	15	10		1	Locations
	4	18	12	13		

   a. Confirm each distance in the matrix.
   b. Find the optimal solution by enumerating all 24 feasible solutions.

7. Starting with an initial solution that has department *i* in location *k* where $i = k$, solve this problem using the "best pairwise exchange"

heuristic. (Verify that the value of the objective function in the initial solution is 116 flow-distance units.) Compare quality of solution v. computational effort to Exercise 6.

16.3 CLASSIC HEURISTIC APPLICATIONS IN OPERATIONS RESEARCH

In this section we describe some early applications of heuristic programming in operations research. You should find many similarities to the assignment of facilities example: in problem structure, heuristic construction, and surrogate criteria selection.

Assembly Line Balancing

Assembly line balancing is one of the first applications of heuristic models in operations research. The problem is how to divide the work required for the assembly of a complex product such as an automobile. For many of these problems, there are hundreds or even thousands of individual tasks of varying length which must be combined into work stations in a manner which efficiently utilizes the people at the stations. Sequential considerations further complicate the combining of tasks; for example, the suspension system for an automobile must be installed before the body. The objective is to minimize labor costs by employing the smallest possible number of workers which achieve the desired output rate. This objective can be accomplished when the individual tasks are combined so that the **cycle time** (time to complete the required tasks) for each work station is the same (that is, the line is balanced). When this has been achieved, there is no idle time at any station, and the cycle time matches the desired output rate.

The line balancing problem is a combinatorial problem. Approaches to solving these problems include integer programming and network models, but as was true for the assignment of facilities, computational cost grows exponentially as the size of the problem increases; thus, heuristic approaches are needed for most real-world problems.

To illustrate a few heuristic approaches to the line balancing problem, a *very* simplified problem is presented in Figure 16–2. The hypothetical item to be assembled is made up of 20 tasks ($A - T$), with the times and sequential constraints presented at the top of the figure. At the bottom of the figure is a precedence chart which is similar to the PERT networks in Chapter 14.

We begin by assuming that the desired production rate for this item is one every 3 minutes. That would indicate three stations with not more than 3 minutes of work in each (that is, 8.6 minutes total time divided by 3 minutes desired cycle time per station gives approximately 2.9, which is three stations, to the next highest integer). A quick solution is A, B, C, D, E for Station 1 (3.0 minutes); F, G, H, I, J, K, L, M, N for Station 2

FIGURE 16–2

Simplified Line Balancing Problem

Task	Time (minutes)	Preceding Task(s)
A....................	0.4	—
B....................	0.5	A
C....................	0.2	A
D....................	1.0	A
E....................	0.9	B
F....................	0.6	B
G....................	0.3	B
H....................	0.1	C
I....................	0.5	D
J....................	0.6	E
K....................	0.1	F, G
L....................	0.2	H, I
M....................	0.5	J
N....................	0.1	K
O....................	0.2	K
P....................	0.1	L
Q....................	0.1	M, N
R....................	0.5	O
S....................	1.6	P
T....................	0.1	Q, R, S
Total............	8.6	

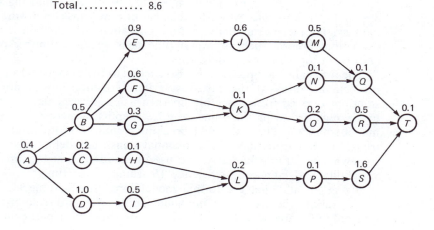

(3.0 minutes); and O, P, Q, R, S, T for Station 3 (2.6 minutes). Note that Station 3 has an idle time of 0.4 minute per item produced.

If, however, the desired output rate is one every 2.9 minutes, then the problem becomes more complex. One possible solution is the groupings of tasks given by (A, B, C, D, H, I, L), (E, F, G, J, K, N, O, P), and (M, Q, R, S, T). Stating a heuristic which will accomplish this result for large problems can be extremely difficult.

Our heuristic adds tasks to a particular station until the maximum time is reached, always adding the task with the largest time next (from those which satisfy sequential constraints). Ties between tasks may be broken in alphabetical order. This **largest time next rule** will leave small tasks unassigned to "fill in the holes." Applying this heuristic to the immediately preceding problem results in (A, D, B, E), (F, J, I, M, G, C, H, K), and (L, O, R, N, P, S, Q, T).

A conclusion that largest time next is a good heuristic would be erroneous for most empirical problems. It works well here because there are many tasks of small magnitude relative to the cycle time and because the sequencing constraints are not very limiting.

Another heuristic suggested by Kilbridge and Wester assigns tasks which have the smallest number of predecessor tasks first, with ties broken by largest time next.[10] Still another heuristic assigns that task next whose followers have the largest total time.[11] Both of these heuristics attempt to avoid limitations near the end caused by sequential constraints.

Other rules allow for backtracking when trouble occurs, perhaps taking the next most desirable candidate at the previous step. A particularly intriguing approach is suggested by Tonge.[12] This method combines several heuristics which initially are selected at random. As the heuristics are applied, those which produce better results have their selection probabilities increased.

Finally, a heuristic approach that is somewhat similar to Tonge's has been developed by Arcus.[13] The Arcus procedure applies **biased sampling** in a manner similar to its use in the assignment of facilities. A fast computer sampling scheme examines large numbers of line balancing solutions and picks the best one. At each inclusion of a new task to a work station, the tasks are picked randomly, but the probability of selection is weighted by various criteria such as largest time next, greatest number of predecessors, or total time of predecessors.

The line balancing problem is also similar to the assignment of facilities problem in terms of the surrogate criteria relationships. Although the solutions derived from assembly line heuristics are very useful, they have to be regarded with the same healthy skepticism necessary for layout model solutions. The process of breaking a total job into subtasks is not trivial; both partitioning and sequential constraint definitions are often somewhat arbitrary. Similarly, the use of standard times ignores worker variability and increasing efficiency (learning) over time.

We might add that the formal models are usually subjected to other considerations before being implemented; a standard rule-of-thumb is that only 90 percent of the cycle time is assigned to a particular station.

---

[10] M. D. Kilbridge and L. Wester, "A Heuristic Model of Assembly Line Balancing," *The Journal of Industrial Engineering*, vol. 12 (July–August 1961). pp. 292–98.

[11] W. B. Helgeson and D. P. Birnie, "Assembly Line Balancing Using the Ranked Positional Weight Technique," *The Journal of Industrial Engineering*, vol. 12 (November–December 1961), pp. 394–98.

[12] F. M. Tonge, *A Heuristic Program for Assembly Line Balancing* (Englewood Cliffs, N.J.; Prentice-Hall, Inc., 1961).

[13] A. L. Arcus, "COMSOAL: A Computer Method of Sequencing Operations for Assembly Lines," in *Readings in Production and Operations Management*, ed. E. Buffa (New York: John Wiley & Sons, Inc., 1966), pp. 336–60.

Furthermore, interactions with users are encouraged. For example, industrial engineers can usually improve a solution by redefining tasks, relaxing sequential constraints, and selectively placing superior workers.

Follow-up Exercises

8. Verify that the idle times for Stations 1, 2, and 3 are 0, 0, and 0.1 minute, respectively, for the example which yields a desired output rate of 2.9 minutes.

9. Verify the results given by the "largest time next" heuristic by completing the following computational table:

Station	Step	(1) Available Choices from Those Whose Sequential Constraints Have Been Satisfied	(2) Selection from Column (1) with Maximum Task Time (if within 2.9 minute allowable total time for stations)	(3) Task Time (minutes)	(4) Cumulative Task Time for Station (2.9 minute maximum)
1........	1	A	A	0.4	0.4
	2	B, C, D	D	1.0	1.4
	3	B, C, I	B	0.5	1.9
	4	C, I, E, F, G	E	0.9	2.8
2........	5	C, I, F, G, J	F	0.6	0.6
	6	C, I, G, J	J	0.6	1.2
	7	C, I, G, M	I	0.5	1.7
	.				
	.				
	.				

Note that B, C, and D are not available choices until A has been chosen; I is not available until D has been chosen; and so on. Also note that the available choices in Step 5 all have times greater than 0.1 minute, which precludes any for consideration in Station 1; otherwise, the maximum total time of 2.9 minutes would be exceeded by Station 1. It follows that Step 5 represents the first choice for Station 2. Further note that B is selected over I in Step 3 (both are tied at 0.5 minute) by applying the tie-breaking rule. Finally, note that K will not be available until both F and G have been chosen.

10. Use the largest time next heuristic to balance the line for four stations of 2.2 minutes each.

Job Shop Scheduling

Another problem which has received considerable attention is job shop scheduling. For an enterprise with several work centers and jobs which

require varying amounts of work at some or all work centers, how should
the jobs be scheduled? In what order should the jobs waiting at each work
center be selected for processing?

Real-world examples obviously include the traditional job shop, exemplified by the metal-working machine shop. Another example is automobiles requiring different services at a garage with various work centers,
such as wheel alignment and engine tuneup. Still another is a hospital with
service capacities such as operating room, x-ray, and laboratories for
taking care of a set of particular patient needs. Job shop problems can
be formulated and optimally solved by integer programs. Beyond two or
three work centers, however, the cost of optimal solutions becomes prohibitive. Subsequently, problems of interesting size are solved by heuristic
programs.

A distinction has been drawn between the **static job shop** and the
dynamic job shop. The former is concerned with processing a fixed set of
jobs which are all available at the outset, whereas the dynamic job shop
is concerned with jobs continuously arriving. The static case typically
begins with all facilities empty and idle.

In the static case, the most frequent criterion is to minimize the total
elapsed time from start to completion of a specified set of jobs. There
are analogs for selected sets of jobs in the dynamic case, but other criteria
are usually considered as well. Surrogate criteria include the number of
orders processed in some time period, measures of machine center utilization, percentage of orders completed after due date, total number of
days late, variability in lateness, work-in-process inventory levels, and
labor force utilization.

The heuristics are essentially "dispatching" rules for which job to
process next at any given work center. The best known rules are (1)
process that job next with the shortest expected completion time, (2)
first-come, first-served, (3) last-come, first-served, (4) process that job
next with the largest number of remaining operations, (5) process that
job next with the earliest due date, and (6) various slack rules based on
due dates and remaining processing times.

The most commonly used dispatching rules are those in the general
category of (6). The tendency for rule (1) to perform poorly on long-
running jobs rules it out in most real-world applications. Rules that consider potential lateness and minimize variability in lateness tend to produce
results more in line with higher order criteria, such as the good will of the
customer. Of course, the critical nature of dispatching rules is directly
related to the match between capacity and need. With substantial excess
capacity almost any dispatching rules will work, and no rule can make
up for a lack of sufficient capacity. As capacity gets "tight," however,
some rules will utilize capacity much better than others.

Resource Leveling and Allocation in Project Management

A problem that is somewhat related to job shop scheduling is to smooth
out the resource needs generated from a planning schedule provided by
project management models (Section 14.2). The basic issue involves

scheduling noncritical path activities at times which minimize fluctuations in expected needs for the resource. In this way, the resource is more effectively utilized. Basic models assume unlimited resource availability, which is clearly unrealistic for many environments. Activities on parallel paths in a network may compete for the same resources. Consequently, limited resources may force sequential scheduling of activities which are not related by precedence relationships.

Linear programming models have been applied, but they are only appropriate for small projects having substantially less than 100 activities.[14] As before, the alternative is to turn to heuristic methods.

There are two basic approaches to scheduling with limited resources: resource leveling and resource allocation. In **resource leveling,** peak resource requirements are smoothed to reduce maximum capacity needs—consistent with meeting the scheduled completion date. In **resource allocation** the duration of the project is minimized (usually beyond the scheduled completion date provided by the basic model) subject to appropriate resource and sequential constraints.

The resources that are to be leveled or allocated will be of different types (for example, money, labor, machinery, and so forth). Furthermore, capacities in various work centers (each resource is a work center) may or may not be transferable to other work centers or activities. For example, a particular type of skilled labor may be appropriate only for certain activities.

The heuristic approach used by Levy, Thompson, and Weist for resource leveling of labor first generates a schedule of tasks based upon earliest start dates. This schedule is then used to prepare a labor schedule **(loading chart)** with day-to-day labor requirements for each work center. Maximum capacities are then set in each work center at one labor-unit below the peak capacity requirement. Jobs not on the critical path which contribute to the "overloads" in each work center are rescheduled into the future, one at a time, until all capacity maxima are satisfied. At that point the maxima are reduced by another labor-unit and the process is repeated.

Some work center capacities can be reduced much more than others, and it should be clear that there is some ability to trade-off capacities. Also, the *costs* of additional capacities may vary substantially. The Levy, Thompson, and Weist program allows the user to specify cost criteria (average hourly pay). By reducing capacities sequentially in descending order of cost, total cost may be reduced (perhaps with greater capacity in low-cost work centers).

An interesting feature of this heuristic is random selection of the noncritical job to be rescheduled. By running the program several times, alternative schedules are generated. The approach is very similar to biased sampling as applied to layout and line balancing.

Heuristic approaches which allocate resources attempt to reduce completion time for the project subject to work center capacities. Various heuristics have been proposed for determining which activity to process

---

[14] J. D. Weist and F. K. Levy, *A Management Guide to PERT/CPM* (Englewood Cliffs, N.J.: Prentice-Hall, Inc., 1969), p. 101.

next. The usual approach uses remaining slack time as a priority rule. That is, the activity which is closest to being critical is processed next, providing resources are available.

16.4 HEURISTICS IN MARKETING

In the past decade, heuristic programming has been applied rather extensively in marketing. In this section we will overview several of the areas in which applications have been reported in the literature.

Media Selection

Media selection is obviously a problem of major concern if one considers the enormous sums of money invested on advertising each year. A number of heuristic approaches have been proposed for overcoming the shortcomings associated with the mathematical programming versions presented in Chapters 4 and 10. Taylor devised a graphical heuristic procedure which attempts to determine the point where the marginal return from the last advertisement equals the marginal cost of the advertisement.[15] The heuristic relies upon a preliminary determination of the optimal size for an advertisement in each medium, and it then determines for each medium the number of advertisements to place.

Other heuristics also employ the "marginal approach." One interesting procedure deals with the dynamic period-to-period allocation of a budget such that exposure targets are met for each period. In any period, the first advertisement selected is that which results in the lowest cost per consumer reached. Prior to the selection of the next ad, "reach" estimates are adjusted to account for duplication, and costs are revised to reflect quantity discounts offered by the media. Media insertions continue until the exposure target for each period has been attained. This procedure is repeated in each period with the objective of satisfying the exposure targets at the lowest possible cost.

MEDIAC is an on-line media selection system which allows users to plan, evaluate, and alter advertising programs for multiple time periods.[16] Segments of this model include heuristic methods which are designed to search for good, and it is hoped optimal, solutions. As with the above heuristics, those in this model operate using a marginal approach. One heuristic option is the **maximum-seeking heuristic.** The approach is ". . . simply that of adding to a schedule those insertions that produce a high increment of response per dollar and deleting those that produce a low decrement of response per dollar."[17] For those of you familiar with advanced regression analysis, the procedure is analogous to that used in

---

[15] Usual criteria for media selection models include *frequency* (expected number of advertisements seen by a consumer in the target audience) and *reach* (total number of target-market consumers exposed to at least one advertisement). C. J. Taylor, "Some Developments in the Theory and Application of Media Scheduling Methods," *Operational Research Quarterly,* vol. 14 (September 1963), pp. 291–305.

[16] John D. C. Little and Leonard M. Lodish, "A Media Planning Calculus," *Operations Research,* vol. 17 (January–February 1969), pp. 1–35.

[17] Ibid., p. 24.

stepwise regression. The model also incorporates a second heuristic which can be applied when media discounts are available.

Follow-up Exercise

11. Refer to the LP formulation of Example 4.8 (Media Mix Model) on page 118. Utilize a heuristic which allocates the advertising budget in $100,000 increments to the various media. This "greedy" heuristic will allocate among the media beginning with the one having the greatest number of exposures per dollar, followed by the other media in decreasing order. With each marginal allocation, make sure that no constraints are violated. If an allocation results in the violation of a constraint, move to the next highest rated medium. Does this heuristic generate a feasible solution? Is it as good as the LP solution?

Physical Distribution

The physical distribution of goods and services is an extremely important part of our economy. Enormous amounts of money are expended in this complex network of activities. The area is also one in which OR efforts have been successfully implemented. One component of distribution systems consists of warehouses which serve as intermediate storage locations for goods. One critical decision relates to the location of such warehouses. Heuristic approaches have been proposed and used in the selection of sites.

An example of such a heuristic approach is that proposed by Kuehn and Hamburger.[18] Capable of evaluating problems involving several hundred potential sites and several thousand shipping destinations, the heuristic program consists of a main program and a "bump-and-shift" routine. The main program locates warehouses one at a time until no additional warehouses can be added without increasing costs. This portion of the program uses three main heuristics:

1. Most geographical locations are not promising sites for a regional warehouse; locations with promise will be at or near concentrations of demand.
2. Near-optimum warehousing systems can be developed by locating warehouses one at a time, adding at each stage of the analysis that warehouse which produces the greatest cost savings for the entire system.
3. Only a small subset of all possible warehouse locations need be evaluated in detail at each stage of the analysis to determine the next warehouse site to be added.[19]

---

[18] Alfred A. Kuehn and Michael J. Hamburger, "A Heuristic Program for Locating Warehouses," *Management Science,* vol. 9 (July 1963), pp. 643–66.

[19] Ibid., pp. 645–46.

In the second stage, the bump-and-shift portion, warehouses are eliminated which have become uneconomical due to subsequent assignments. In addition, the remaining warehouses are examined to determine if locations can be shifted in an economical manner.

Heuristics have also been applied in other areas of warehouse analysis. Examples of simple heuristic rules used to reduce materials handling costs in merchandise layout include the **popularity method** (locate high turn-over items nearest to the shipping docks), the **volume method** (locate items according to their size or volume), and the **cube-per-order-index** (which combines the two previous techniques to guarantee movement of the largest stock volume over the shortest possible distance).

Sales Force Allocation

Expenditures on personal selling are often the largest single item in marketing budgets. Given that a firm has established a budget for sales effort, decisions must be made which allocate sales effort to customers, sales territories, and time. OR has provided useful inputs for these types of decisions. An example of the application of a heuristic procedure to this type of problem is a model developed by Cloonan.[20] In a modification of the *traveling sales representative problem* (Example 8.8), the approach begins with the solution which minimizes the travel time to visit each account and return home. The effects of deviating from this route in order to increase the effectiveness of the sales effort are then examined (the presumptions, here, are that the effectiveness of a visit depends upon the time between visits to a particular customer and that customers could be visited more than once during a tour). A heuristic compares the opportunity cost of deviating from the minimum time (cost) route to the expected increases in sales resulting from the change in schedule. The result is a schedule of calls which considers both the time and cost of the sales effort as well as the expected sales volume.

Another model developed by Montgomery, Silk, and Zaragoza was concerned with which items in a product line should be promoted by personal sales calls.[21] There are three major aspects of this model that should be noted. First, the approach uses judgmental data from users about the sales effects of pushing or not pushing particular products. Second, the judgmental data become a critical input to a fairly simple "improvement" heuristic that allocates sales efforts to company products over time. Third, and perhaps most importantly, the entire approach integrates the analysis into the style of decision making and reasoning used by the particular managers in the company. Interactive conversational computer programs are used, which allows immediate feedback on the effect of changing an assumption.

---

[20] J. B. Cloonan, "An Analysis of Sales Tours," in *Applications of Management Science in Marketing,* ed. D. B. Montgomery and G. L. Urban (Englewood Cliffs, N.J.; Prentice-Hall, Inc., 1969).

[21] D. B. Montgomery, A. J. Silk, and C. E. Zaragoza, "A Multiple Product Sales Force Allocation Model," *Management Science,* vol. 18, no. 4, pt. 2 (December 1971), pp. 2–24.

Dynamic Pricing

Another heuristic model worthy of mention was developed by Morgenroth for how a firm might react to competitive price moves.[22] The model was developed for a company in an industry where prices can be very dynamic, such as lumber, meatpacking, or retail gasoline. The approach used in model validation is interesting because it is fundamentally different from that used for the other heuristics we have considered. Morgenroth attempted to duplicate the pricing decision process used by company executives (cognitive simulation) rather than building a model which produced results at least as good as those attained by the executives (artificial intelligence). The model is essentially descriptive; that is, it attempts to understand an existing situation. Although there is always a strong interest in normative models (what decision *should* be made), the descriptive model can be a very important factor in affirmatively answering "Do decision makers *use* the model?"

16.5 LESS TRADITIONAL HEURISTIC APPLICATIONS

In this section, a few additional heuristic applications will be overviewed briefly. No attempt will be made to be exhaustive, nor will explanations include much detail; the intent is merely to broaden your appreciation of the general applicability of heuristic techniques and to show how these models can be an integral part of the decision-making environment.

Political Districting

An interesting application of heuristics is in political districting. The problem is how to partition an area, such as a state, into districts for the assignment of representatives. This is a problem of current interest because of court rulings regarding gerrymandering and the issue of what constitutes disproportionate populations in districts. Other criteria include contiguity, compactness, and minimal crossing of county or other subdivision lines. The problem has been solved optimally by integer programming using an algorithm designed by Garfinkle and Nemhauser.[23] As is true for other combinatorial models, the computational burden increases dramatically as the number of districts exceeds 40. Consequently, several heuristic programs have been proposed by Garfinkel and Nemhauser.

Desegregation

A somewhat related problem concerned a plan to schedule classes in a large city so as to achieve desegregation while specializing at particular schools in topical areas such as foreign languages. Students would have

---

[22] W. M. Morgenroth, "A Method for Understanding Price Determinants," *Journal of Marketing Research* (August 1964), pp. 17–26.

[23] R. S. Garfinkel and G. L. Nemhauser, "Optimal Political Districting by Implicit Enumeration Techniques," *Management Science,* vol. 16, no. 8 (April 1970), pp. B495–508.

the same "home" school but would travel to other schools as their program of required classes dictated. The surrogate objective was minimization of total weekly student travel time. The problem was formulated as a zero-one quadratic programming problem, but the computational burden was too great.[24] A proposed heuristic approach proved particularly valuable because the model was time-shared and capable of being overridden by the administrators for reasons such as scheduling activity blocks for varsity athletics. Although the single surrogate criterion did not adequately reflect all important issues in class scheduling for a large city, the model provided a critical focal point; subjective considerations could be evaluated, and an overall structure was provided for a complex and potentially explosive problem.

A related issue is the **school bus scheduling problem.** The structure of this problem is similar to the traveling sales representative problem; however, the sheer size of the required model prohibits an efficient solution by mathematical programming methods. Angel, Caudle, and Whinston have developed and implemented a heuristic model which attempts to minimize total mileage traveled, avoid overloading buses, and keep route time below some maximum specified by school administrators.[25]

Urban Systems

Throughout the book, we have discussed different applications indicative of the activity of OR analysts in the area of urban systems. The operational problems of police departments, fire departments, emergency ambulance services, waste disposal systems, and urban transportation systems have all been subjected to systematic analyses by operations researchers. In the area of emergency response systems, the allocation of resources usually includes decisions regarding (a) the number of units to have on duty, (b) design of response areas or patrol areas, (c) location of units, and (d) relocation of units.

Heuristics have been applied in analyzing each of these areas. In some instances the heuristics have been established by departmental policy. An example deals with the repositioning of police patrol cars whenever one unit becomes unavailable. Sample heuristics under these circumstances might include (1) no repositioning of available cars, (2) a free unit patrols both sectors uniformly, (3) the free unit is located at a fixed point between the two sectors. In many situations, heuristics have been developed to search for acceptable solutions to problems which otherwise cannot be solved by analytic means. Kolesar and Walker have proposed a heuristic related to the fire equipment positioning problem.[26] This model was discussed in Chapter 8 (Example 8.7) in the context of having fire

---

[24] R. R. Lutz, M. D. Devine, H. J. Kumin, and W. C. Smith, "An Application of Operations Research to School Desegregation," *Management Science,* vol. 19, no. 4 (December 1972), pp. 17–26.

[25] R. D. Angel, R. N. Caudle, and A. Whinston, "Computer-Assisted School Bus Scheduling," *Management Science,* vol. 18, no. 6 (1972), pp. B279–88.

[26] P. Kolesar and W. E. Walker, "An Algorithm for the Dynamic Relocation of Fire Companies," *Operations Research,* vol. 22, no. 2 (March–April 1974), pp. 249–74.

districts "covered." This meant that at least one engine company can respond to each district within some specified maximum time. If one or more districts are to be uncovered for an undesirable period of time, Kolesar and Walker proposed a heuristic which first determines which vacant houses to fill and then which available units to relocate to these houses. Developed and tested in New York City, the method allows for "good" decisions in short periods of time.

Simulation of Human Thought

As mentioned at the beginning of this chapter, heuristic programs are often developed to replicate the thought processes of human decision makers. The objective is to simulate as exactly as possible these processes, with little concern for the efficiency of solutions. In most of these efforts, the **protocol method** is used whereby the decision maker verbalizes thought processes while actually making decisions. An analysis of these protocols results in their translation into the simulator. A classic example of this procedure includes Clarkson's simulation of the decision-making processes of trust investment officers.[27] This model simulates three stages of the decision process: selection of the current list of stocks, choice of the appropriate investment policy, and selection of the portfolio.

In a similar manner, Dickson has modeled the process of vendor selection by purchasing agents.[28] Other areas of application include a simulation of processing procedures for overdrafts by bank officers, screening procedures used by credit officers in issuing credit, and screening procedures used by admissions officers to admit students to college.

16.6 CONCLUDING REMARKS

In this chapter, attention has been focused largely on heuristic models developed for managerial problems. Necessarily, a thorough presentation of heuristics and heuristic problem solving must remain outside our present scope. Philosophical topics have been purposely omitted. For example, we have not attempted to raise (or answer) questions about either the intrinsic nature of problems that can be analyzed by formal algorithms, or those problems which are suited to computerized heuristics v. those which can be implemented only by persons. (Can computers *think?*)

On a less philosophical plane, we emphasize two major observations. First, there is a striking similarity in the approaches embodied by heuristic models which analyze seemingly different problems. The use of fast computers permits a large degree of searching or testing of alternatives— relative to what a person can accomplish. In comparison to the totality of possible alternatives, however, the search is restricted to a very small subset. Typically, the heuristics define the subset, usually a step at a time. Furthermore, in all cases, the user must be aware of alternative heuristics

[27] G. P. E. Clarkson, *Portfolio Selection: A Simulation of Trust Investment* (Englewood Cliffs, N.J.: Prentice-Hall, Inc., 1962).

[28] G. W. Dickson, "An Analysis of Vendor Selection Systems and Decisions," *Journal of Purchasing*, vol. 2, no. 1 (February 1966).

or optimization procedures which trade-off between the cost of solution and the quality of solution.

Second, heuristics promote interaction between the model and the decision maker, and are especially valuable for multiple-criteria problem situations. Proper attention to this man-machine interface can provide decision alternatives that are superior, with reduced costs of obtaining those solutions. You should expect to see heuristic models increasingly applied to ill-defined problems, in concert with the decision makers who can best articulate and trade-off the multiple objectives that affect these decisions.

SELECTED REFERENCES

Belmore, M., and Nemhauser, G. L. "The Traveling Salesman Problem: A Survey." *Operations Research*. Vol. 16, No. 3 (May–June 1968), pp. 538–58.

Clarkson, Geoffrey, P. E. *Portfolio Selection: A Simulation of Trust Investment*. Englewood Cliffs, N.J.: Prentice-Hall, Inc., 1962.

Conway, R. W.; Maxwell, W. L.; and Miller, L. W. *Theory of Scheduling*. Reading, Mass.: Addison-Wesley Publications Co., 1967.

Feigenbaum, E. A., and Feldman, J. *Computers and Thought*. New York: McGraw-Hill Book Co., 1963.

Ignall, E. J. "A Review of Assembly-Line Balancing." *Journal of Industrial Engineering*. Vol. 16, No. 4 (July–August 1965), pp. 244–54.

Meier, Robert C.; Newell, William T.; and Pazer, Harold L. *Simulation in Business and Economics*. Englewood Cliffs, N.J.: Prentice-Hall, Inc., 1969.

Montgomery, David B., and Urban, Glen L. *Management Science in Marketing*. Englewood Cliffs, N.J.: Prentice-Hall, Inc., 1969.

Nugent, C. E.; Vollmann, T. E.; and Ruml, J. "An Experimental Comparison of Techniques for the Assignment of Facilities to Locations." *Operations Research*. Vol. 16, No. 1 (January–February 1968), pp. 150–73.

Simon, H. A. *The New Science of Management Decision*. New York: Harper & Bros., 1960.

Simon, H. A., and Newell, A. "Heuristic Problem Solving: The Next Advance in Operations Research." *Operations Research*. Vol. 6 (January–February 1958), pp. 1–10.

Thoreson, I., and Littschwager, J. "Legislative Districting by Computer Simulation." *Behavioral Science*. Vol. 12 (1967), pp. 237–47.

Weist, J. D. "A Heuristic Model for Scheduling Large Projects with Limited Resources." *Management Science*. Vol. 13, No. 6 (February 1967), pp. B359–77.

ADDITIONAL EXERCISES

12. In the Stepping Stone Method of Chapter 7, the incoming variable at each iteration is selected by computing the improvement indices, I_{ij}, for all nonbasic cells and choosing the one which results in the largest *marginal* improvement in the objective function. An alternative selection heuristic is to sequentially compute nonbasic variable improvement indices. The entering variable is the first which leads to an improved solution.

    a.   Comment on the expected benefits and disbenefits of using each of these entrance heuristics. Specifically, consider relative effort and rate of convergence.

    b.   Apply the latter heuristic to the solution of Example 7.8 on page 244. Compare your results with those obtained by the Stepping Stone heuristic.

13.   The following is an alternative to the selection heuristics discussed in the preceding exercise: Select the entering variable as the one leading to the greatest *total improvement* in the objective function. This determination requires identification not only of each variable with a favorable improvement index, but also the largest quantity of each which may be entered. Combining this information, one can compare *total improvement* for all candidate variables.

    a.   Comment on the expected benefits and disbenefits of this heuristic versus the other two heuristics.

    b.   Apply this heuristic to Example 7.8 and compare your results with those in the preceding exercise.

    c.   Can these two alternative heuristics be applied in the simplex method?

14.   A consulting firm is doing a relayout of a small bank made up of the following six departmental areas: (1) Estates, (2) Filing, (3) Trusts, (4) Accounting, (5) Data Processing, and (6) Board Room.

The office space configuration is illustrated here (with department 1 in location 1, department 2 in location 2, and so forth):

1	2	3
4	5	6

The flow and distance matrices are:

From \ To	1	2	3	4	5	6
1		1	2	1	2	3
2	1		1	2	1	2
3	10	0		3	2	1
4	1	2	5		1	2
5	1	1	2	1		1
6	5	10	0	0	1	

    a.   Calculate the total flow-distance cost for the existing layout.

    b.   Use the best pairwise exchange heuristic to make the first two iterations.

15.   For the preceding exercise:

    a.   Use the greatest to least heuristic to make the first two iterations.

    b.   Use the any improvement heuristic to make the first two iterations.

    c.   Compare the results of applying the three heuristics. Given the relative progress of the three, comment on each as regard benefit v. effort.

16.   The following assembly problem is to be performed on a four-person line. Assign the tasks "by eyeball" so that the line is balanced with the

smallest cycle time you can manage (note that the theoretical minimum is $12.8/4 = 3.2$ minutes).

Task	Time (minutes)	Preceding Tasks
A...	1.2	—
B...	0.5	A
C...	0.7	A
D...	1.6	B
E...	0.9	B
F...	3.2	C
G...	1.8	C
H...	1.0	E, G
I...	0.6	D, F
J...	1.3	I, H

17. Solve Exercise 16 with the "largest time next" heuristic, and compare your efforts.

18. Solve Exercise 16 for a three-person line using the "largest time next" heuristic.

19. For Exercise 16:

   a. Verify the following table.

Task	Number of Predecessors
A...	0
B...	1
C...	1
D...	2
E...	2
F...	2
G...	2
H...	5
I...	5
J...	9

   b. Solve Exercise 16 with the Kilbridge and Wester heuristic.

20. For Exercise 16:

   a. Verify the following table.

Task	Time of Following Tasks
A...	11.6
B...	5.4
C...	7.9
D...	1.9
E...	2.3
F...	1.9
G...	2.3
H...	1.3
I...	1.3
J...	0

   b. Solve Exercise 16 with the Helgeson and Birnie heuristic.

21. Draw conclusions from Exercises 17, 19, and 20 with respect to difficulty of solution and degree of performance.

22. *Investment Strategy*   Read Exercise 42 in Chapter 13 on page 530.

a. Carry out the simulations and compare the performances and required efforts for the two heuristic strategies identified in parts (*a*) and (*b*) of that exercise.

b. Invent at least one other investment heuristic and compare its performance to the two already specified.

23. *Relocation of Patrol Cars*   Consider a simplified emergency response system whereby each sector of a city is patrolled by one patrol car. To further simplify the scenario, consider the two adjacent sectors diagrammed, where each lattice (+) represents the location of a potential emergency call. The street layout is such that movements of the patrol

North

Sector 1

```
 3 ┤   +    +    +

 2 ┤   +    +    +

 1 ┤   +    +    +

 0 ┼───┬────┬────┬──────────────▶ East
       1    2    3

-1 ┤   +    +    +

-2 ┤   +    +    +
```

Sector 2

vehicles must be in North–South or East–West directions. The "city block" distance between each lattice is approximately 0.1 mile.

In any 30-minute time interval, the probability of one emergency call is 0.5 in Sector 1 and 0.3 in Sector 2. Within this 30-minute time increment, the probability of two or more calls in either sector is negligible. Within each of the sectors, the probability that the emergency call originates at any one lattice is the same as the probability for any other lattice. Moreover, the two sectors are statistically independent.

Now, suppose that the patrol vehicle for Sector 2 is absent; for example, it is disabled or it is needed outside the sector. This means that the patrol vehicle for Sector 1 now must cover both sectors, with preference given to Sector 1 whenever calls originate within the same time interval in both sectors. Two heuristics are under consideration for repositioning the vehicle for Sector 1:

1. Stay in current location until next call.
2. Return to location (2,0) after servicing each call, where it is assumed that calls can always be serviced by the end of any 30-minute time interval.

a. Conduct five Monte Carlo simulations of movements of the patrol vehicle, where each simulation lasts ten time periods. Compare the two heuristics based on "average mileage traveled in response to a call." Assume that at the beginning of each simulation, the vehicle is located at coordinate (2,0). (Note: For each sector and each time interval, you must generate a random number to determine whether or not a call originates. If a call does originate in any one sector, then a random number must be generated for its location. Use columns 5 and 6 in Table 13–3 on page 494 to generate your random numbers.)

b. Suggest some other heuristic and evaluate it.

17

Decision Analysis

THROUGHOUT THIS TEXTBOOK we have presented models for decision making under conditions of certainty and uncertainty in the environment. The optimization models of Chapters 2 through 10 all assumed that parameters and uncontrollable variables were known with certainty, although this extreme assumption was relaxed through the use of sensitivity analysis. Most of the models illustrated in Chapters 11 through 16 directly incorporated uncertainty by specifying the probability distributions of random variables. In this chapter we introduce an area of specialization which provides a formal analytic framework for decisions under conditions of uncertainty and conflict.

17.1 FUNDAMENTALS

Decision analysis, which is often called **decision theory,** is a popular field of study which provides an insightful framework for statistically analyzing decisions characterized by uncertain environments. Before illustrating the basic structure of decision models, we first present a motivating example.

Example 17.1 Portfolio Model

In financial analysis, "portfolio" refers to the number and types of investments which are undertaken by an individual or institution. The usual investment alternatives are represented by stocks and bonds, which allows for wide latitude in the number and types of investments in the portfolio.

Consider a decision whereby an institutional investor plans to invest $10 million, in one of two or both investment alternatives. Such a situation might arise in deciding how much to invest in each of two alternatives for a retirement fund.[1] To simplify matters, only three decisions are under consideration:

$D_1 \equiv$ all $10 million invested in Alternative A.
$D_2 \equiv$ $5 million invested in Alternative A and $5 million invested in Alternative B.
$D_3 \equiv$ all $10 million invested in Alternative B.

To further simplify (or complicate, depending on your point of view) the illustration, suppose that the annual rate of return for Alternative A will be either −0.05 or 0.10 and that for Alternative B will be either −0.10 or 0.20; however, which return will be associated with each investment alternative is not known with certainty.[2] Furthermore, the rates of return between the two investment alternatives are statistically dependent. The interactions are shown in Table 17–1. Thus, θ_1 represents a year in which Alternative A

TABLE 17–1

Rates of Return Relationships

		Rates of Return for Alternative B	
		−0.10	0.20
Rates of Return for Alternative A	−0.05	θ_1	θ_2
	0.10	θ_3	θ_4

had a −0.05 rate of return and Alternative B had a −0.10 rate of return; θ_2 represents the outcome −0.05 for A and 0.20 for B; and so forth.

---

[1] College professors might recognize this as being similar to the TIAA-CREF portfolio decision.

[2] Annual rate of return = (Value at end of year plus dividends or interest, minus value at beginning of year) ÷ (Value at beginning of year).
For example, if a share of stock is bought for $10, provides $0.20 interest, and sells for $11 one year later, then the rate of return is $(11 + 0.2 − 10)/10$, or 0.12.

Basic Structure of Decision Tables

Table 17–2 illustrates a type of decision table called a **payoff table.** Rows represent the **decision alternatives** to be considered and columns represent the possible **states of nature.**
In a decision theory context, states of nature represent conditions outside the control of the decision maker which influence the outcomes associated with decisions. States of nature may be indicated by values for

TABLE 17–2

Payoff Table for Example 17.1 (millions of dollars)

	θ_1	θ_2	θ_3	θ_4
D_1.............	9.50	9.50	11.00	11.00
D_2.............	9.25	10.75	10.00	11.50
D_3.............	9.00	12.00	9.00	12.00

continuous random variables such as the rate of inflation during a particular period of time, or they may be reflected by discrete or categorical random variables such as weather conditions (rain, snow, sunny, and so forth). In the portfolio example, states of nature are specified by a *joint* random variable, since the simultaneous behavior of the two investments depicted in Table 17–1 is of interest.

The interaction of a decision D_i and a state of nature θ_j results in a **consequence.** In this case, consequences are represented by monetary "payoffs," as indicated by the cell values in Table 17–2. For example, if all $10 million are invested in Alternative A (that is, decision D_1) and both investments have positive rates of return over the following year as indicated in Table 17–1 (that is, state of nature θ_4), then the investor will end up with $11 million at the end of the year.[3] This payoff, then, is entered in cell (D_1, θ_4) of the payoff table.

If consequences are represented by a measure which reflects "cost," then the decision table is called a **loss table** rather than a payoff table; otherwise its structure is identical to that of a payoff table.

Measures of subjective preferences, called **utilities,** are still another way of reflecting consequences. Utilities represent individualized desirability measures for risky consequences. In essence, these measures reflect the extent of need satisfaction as perceived by the decision maker. A simple way of relating to utility is to think of the satisfaction that $50 would bring to a pauper v. the satisfaction that $50 would bring to a millionaire. Most likely the utility measure of that identical payoff would be quite different between these two individuals. When utilities replace payoffs, the payoff table is labeled a **utility table.** When utilities replace losses, however, the loss table is called a **disutility table** as the consequences reflect measures of dispreferences. In Section 17.6, we will discuss procedures for "quantifying" utilities.

As an alternative to payoff, loss, and utility tables, for some applications it is desirable to specify an **opportunity loss** or **regret table** as given by Table 17–3. The **opportunity loss** for a given decision–state of nature combination is the numerical difference between the realized consequence (payoff, loss, or utility) and the consequence associated with the optimal decision for the given state of nature. For example, suppose decision D_3 is made and θ_3 occurs, resulting in a $9 million payoff according to Table 17–2. In retrospect, if we had known that θ_3 would occur, then the best decision would have been D_1 with a payoff of $11 million. The difference

---

[3] $10 million original investment plus $1 million increase in value due to the 0.10 rate of return for investment Alternative A. Can you confirm the other entries in Table 17–2?

TABLE 17–3

Regret or Opportunity Loss Table for Example 17.1 (millions of dollars)

	θ_1	θ_2	θ_3	θ_4
D_1..................	0.00	2.50	0.00	1.00
D_2..................	0.25	1.25	1.00	0.50
D_3..................	0.50	0.00	2.00	0.00

of \$2 million between the optimal decision and the nonoptimal decision for state of nature θ_3 represents a loss we would not have incurred if we had made the best decision; hence, it is termed an opportunity loss or regret for cell (D_3, θ_3). Can you confirm the other entries in Table 17–3?

Components of Decision Problems

In general four components must be specified for the analysis of all decision problems:

1. $\{D\}$, the *set* of decision or action variables (alternatives).
2. $\{\theta\}$, the *set* of uncontrollable variables or states of nature.
3. $f(\theta)$, the probability distribution for the states of nature.
4. the payoff function, $R(D, \theta)$, the loss function, $L(D, \theta)$, or the utility function, $U(D, \theta)$.

Decision variables can be *discrete* or *continuous*. As described, the portfolio problem identified three discrete alternatives: $\{D\} = \{D_1\,D_2\,D_3\}$. If the decision, however, had been stated in terms of the proportion of funds to be invested in each alternative, then the decision variable would have been continuous.

Another issue relating to decision variables is the number and timing of decisions. **Single stage decision problems** are those which require a single decision followed by some chance event. The portfolio example is of this type. **Multistage or sequential decision problems** are characterized by a sequence of decisions. Following each decision a chance event occurs, which in turn influences the next decision. This topic is discussed more fully in Section 17.7.

States of nature can also be discrete or continuous. In the portfolio problem, each investment alternative was characterized by only two possible rates of return, which gave four permutations when the investments were considered jointly. The permutations represent four discrete states of nature, $\{\theta\} = \{\theta_1\,\theta_2\,\theta_3\,\theta_4\}$, as depicted in Table 17–1. Typical portfolio problems, however, exhibit rate of return behavior which is best represented by continuous random variables. When both decision variables and states of nature are continuous, the usual approach for solving portfolio problems is mathematical programming, as illustrated in Example 10.10 on page 376. Note that the use of payoff, loss, or utility tables is restricted to discrete $\{D\}$ and $\{\theta\}$. Why?

The solution of a decision problem also requires the specification of a probability distribution $f(\theta)$ for states of nature. If states of nature are discrete, then a probability mass function must be specified; continuous states of nature require the identification of a probability density function. As discussed in Appendix A, these probability distributions can be empirical, subjective, or theoretical. In the theoretical case, empirical evidence should substantiate the use of a specific theoretical distribution. In this chapter, we will focus on the solution of decision problems having discrete decisions and discrete states of nature.

Finally, a payoff function, a loss function, or a utility function must be specified. Each of these functions provides a measure for the specific consequences resulting from the interaction of decisions and states of nature. For this reason we attach the argument (D, θ) to the symbols which represent payoffs, losses, and utilities, that is, $R(D,\theta), L(D,\theta)$, and $U(D, \theta)$. In effect, these functions embody the criterion set with which the decision maker evaluates actions. **Payoffs** are generally represented by gains, profits, revenues, net worth, or any other measure which reflects something which is desirable. **Losses** are usually taken to mean opportunity losses or some other measure which reflects something to be avoided (for example, costs, error). The literature on decision theory exhibits a distinct preference for reflecting consequences in terms of losses, primarily because they are easier to determine and can give useful theoretical insights, as demonstrated in Section 17.3. **Utilities** represent preference measures for consequences. Conceptually, they are superior to payoffs or losses in that they take into account a decision makers' subjective attitude toward risk. Section 17.6 develops this concept in more detail.

Once the four elements of a decision problem have been specified, it is necessary to solve the problem. This is accomplished by determining the optimal act or decision with respect to some criterion. Methods of solution are presented in Sections 17.2 through 17.5.

Follow-up Exercises

1. Construct a payoff table for the portfolio problem which also includes the following decisions:

    $D_4 \equiv$ \$2.5 million in A and \$7.5 million in B.
    $D_5 \equiv$ \$7.5 million in A and \$2.5 million in B.

2. Construct the regret table for Exercise 1.
3. Construct a payoff table for the portfolio problem which includes a 0.0 rate of return for investment Alternative A.
4. Construct the regret table for Exercise 3.

17.2 PRIOR ANALYSIS

Prior analysis refers to methods of solving decision problems which utilize the originally specified probability distribution $f(\theta)$ for states of nature. This probability distribution is termed the **prior probability distribution** because it is specified *prior* to the act of seeking additional information about states of nature. Procedures which revise prior probabilities based on additional experimentation or sampling will be discussed in Section 17.3.

Assessment of Prior Probabilities

If past data are available, then the *relative frequency* or *empirical* definition of probability (Section A.1) may be used to define the probability distribution for states of nature. This procedure is quite acceptable if the future environment is not expected to differ appreciably from the historical environment which provided the data; however, if the decision maker feels that historical data will not be representative of future data, then empirical probabilities can be altered subjectively to accommodate this belief.

Subjective probabilities represent the likelihood of occurrences for the specific states of nature based on the personal feelings and experiences of the decision maker. They are not "wild" guesses, but rather represent degrees of belief based on informed judgment. In some cases, these subjective probabilities may reflect or utilize available empirical data, as mentioned previously. In other cases, however, historical data may be unavailable, in which case subjective likelihoods represent the only alternative for specifying prior probabilities. Interestingly, the willingness of decision theorists to use subjective probabilities is a clear break with the classical school of statistics.

Alternatively, $f(\theta)$ can be based on a theoretical distribution such as binomial, Poisson, or normal. The use of theoretical distributions, however, should be justified by logic or by empirical evaluation, as demonstrated by Example A.3 on page 721.

Example 17.2 Highway Patrol Model

Two primary functions of the highway patrol relate to reducing the number of accidents by preventive patrol and to servicing accidents when they do occur. Consider a 200-mile turnpike which is under the jurisdiction of a captain. Each day, for the shift between 9 A.M. and 5 P.M., a decision must be made regarding the type of patrol which is to be conducted. Two choices are available. Decision D_1 refers to normal patrols whereby patrol cars combine roadside parking (waiting in "ambush") with some highway driving. Decision D_2 involves the use of police escorts, which means that patrol cars spend most of their time driving the turnpike at or near the speed limit. The average operating costs per shift are $800 for normal patrols and $1,100 for patrol escorts.

Records and judgment indicate that accidents appear to be random with respect to time of day within the 9–5 shift, with no differences in daily patterns between Monday and Friday or from June through August; hence, our model is applicable to weekday shifts between 9 A.M. and 5 P.M. during June, July, and August.

Based on records and the judgment of the highway patrol captain, accidents along the entire turnpike will average one, five, or ten per shift when normal patrols are used and one or five when escorts are used. Furthermore, after some probing by an OR analyst, the captain estimates that for normal patrols the chances of averaging one or five accidents are approximately the same and twice as likely as averaging ten accidents. For escorts, the captain estimates that an average of ten is not possible, but that an average of one accident per shift is four times more likely than an average of five accidents per shift.[4] The estimated mean cost of servicing an accident is $50.

Table 17–4 is the loss table for this example. D_1 refers to the use of

TABLE 17–4

Loss Table for Highway Patrol Model

	$\theta_1:1$	$\theta_2:5$	$\theta_3:10$
D_1.............	850	1,050	1,300
D_2.............	1,150	1,350	1,600

normal patrols and D_2 to the use of escorts. The states of nature represent the three possible mean number of accidents per shift. Based on the likelihoods given, it follows that $f(\theta_1) = 0.4$, $f(\theta_2) = 0.4$, and $f(\theta_3) = 0.2$ when D_1 applies; that is, θ_1 and θ_2 are equally likely to occur and both are twice as likely as θ_3. Note that the sum of these probabilities must be unity since $\{\theta_1\ \theta_2\ \theta_3\}$ represents the specified set of mutually exclusive and collectively exhaustive outcomes. Similarly, $f(\theta_1) = 0.8$, $f(\theta_2) = 0.2$, and $f(\theta_3) = 0.0$ for the case given by D_2. Further note that the prior probabilities $f(\theta)$ *are dependent on the decision* in this example.

Losses in this case are defined as the expected total cost per shift to the highway patrol. For example, $L(D_1, \theta_1) = \$850$, or $800 for the expected operating expense of normal patrols plus $50 for the one expected accident; and $L(D_2, \theta_2) = \$1,350$, or $1,100 for escorts plus $250 for the expected five accidents.

---

[4] Detailed procedures for estimating subjective probabilities are presented in T. R. Dyckman, S. Smidt, and A. K. McAdams, *Management Decision Making under Uncertainty* (London: The Macmillan Company, 1969), chap. 10; R. L. Winkler, *Introduction to Bayesian Inference and Decisions* (New York: Holt, Rinehart and Winston, 1972), chaps. 2 and 3; and R. V. Brown, A. S. Kahr, and C. Peterson, *Decision Analysis for the Manager* (New York: Holt, Rinehart and Winston, 1974), pp. 160–71.

Decision Rules

Many rules are available on which to base a decision. In most instances the rules reflect an attitude toward risk which should be consistent with the situation and the decision maker. We will discuss the following four:

1.   Min-max (for losses) or max-min (for payoffs).
2.   Min-min (for losses) or max-max (for payoffs).
3.   Min-max regret.
4.   Minimize expected loss or maximize expected payoff.

Min-max and **max-min** rules reflect a pessimistic decision maker. This decision maker assumes that, given any decision which is made, the worst possible outcome will occur. Consequently, the decision maker identifies the worst outcome associated with each decision alternative and selects the alternative having the *best* of these outcomes (a "best of the worst" strategy). Table 17–4 indicates that the worst possible loss for each decision is $1,300 for D_1 and $1,600 for D_2. These figures represent the maximum values for each row in the table. The min-max rule states that one should select the decision which *min*imizes these *max*imum losses. Thus, a pessimistic highway patrol captain would use normal patrols (D_1) since a $1,300 expenditure is less than one of $1,600. If consequences are expressed in terms of payoffs, then a pessimistic decision maker would *max*imize the *min*imum returns. If we apply the max-min rule to the portfolio problem, we can see in Table 17–2 that the minimum return for each decision is 9.50 for D_1, 9.25 for D_2, and 9.00 for D_3. The maximum of these is 9.50; hence, the investor should invest all funds in Alternative A (that is, select D_1).

Min-min and **max-max** rules accommodate the eternal optimist. This decision maker expects that "fate" will deal the best possible outcome for whatever decision is selected. From Table 17–4, $850 for D_1 and $1,150 for D_2 represent the minimum costs for each row. The *min*imum of these *min*ima yields $850. Thus, based on min-min, the captain would select D_1. Of course, the captain *could* incur a $1,300 loss by selecting D_1 (if θ_3 occurs), but then we did say the captain is being optimistic. From Table 17–2, max-max would select D_3 since 12.00 is greater than 11.50 (for D_2) and 11.00 (for D_1).

Min-max regret selects the decision which *min*imizes the *max*imum regret for each decision. A regret table is first developed and the maximum regret is identified for each decision alternative. The decision maker then selects the alternative having the smallest of these maximum regret values. From Table 17–3, the maximum regrets are 2.50 for D_1, 1.25 for D_2, and 2.00 for D_3. In this case the proper decision would be D_2.

In some circumstances, one of the first three decision rules may be desirable. For example, max-min may be appropriate for the portfolio problem if the investor *must* have at least $9.5 million by the end of the year. In general, however, the first three decision rules suffer from an inability to use the specified prior probabilities, which presumably are relevant to the problem. To illustrate this point, note that $L(D_2, \theta_3) = 1,600$ was entered in Table 17–4; yet, based on prior probability assessments, we know that $f(\theta_3) = 0$ for D_2.

Additionally, it can be demonstrated that the first three rules implicitly utilize a subjective probability distribution coupled with an expected value criterion.[5] It can be argued, therefore, that subjective prior probabilities

---

[5] See Exercises 9 through 11.

can always be assigned for use by the expected value rule. In other words, one cannot support the position that the first three rules are relevant when prior probabilities are unknown.

The **expected value** rule specifies the selection of the decision $D*$ which maximizes the expected return given by

$$E(R) = \sum_\theta R(D, \theta) \cdot f(\theta) \qquad (17.1)$$

or minimizes the expected loss given by

$$E(L) = \sum_\theta L(D, \theta) \cdot f(\theta), \qquad (17.2)$$

where the decision set $\{D\}$ and the states of nature set $\{\theta\}$ are both discrete.[6] $D*$ is termed the **optimal prior decision,** where "optimality" is based on the expected value rule.

Table 17–5 indicates that decision D_1 (normal patrols) is the optimal

TABLE 17–5

Expected Losses for Highway Patrol Model

Decision	Loss $L(D,\theta)$	Prior Probability $f(\theta)$	Expected Loss $L(D,\theta) \cdot f(\theta)$
D_1....................	850	0.4	340.
	1,050	0.4	420.
	1,300	0.2	260.
Total..............		1.0	$E(L) = 1,020.$
D_2....................	1,150	0.8	920.
	1,350	0.2	270.
	1,600	0.0	0.
Total..............		1.0	$E(L) = 1,190.$

prior decision for the highway patrol model (that is, $D* = D_1$), with an expected optimal cost of $E(L*) = \$1,020$ per shift.

Follow-up Exercises

5. Determine the min-max regret strategy for the highway patrol model.
6. Revise Table 17–4 to reflect an expected damage and injury loss of $300 per accident.

[6] If $\{\theta\}$ is continuous, then expected values are found by integration rather than by summation. If $\{D\}$ is continuous, then the optimal values must be found by optimization procedures, for example, differentiation or mathematical programming. If either $R(D,)$ or $L(D,)$ is a random variable, which is the case in the highway patrol model, then its probability distribution can be replaced by its mean. For this proof, see G. Hadley, *Introduction to Probability and Statistical Decision Theory* (San Francisco: Holden Day, Inc., 1967), pp. 445–50.

a. Determine the best decision according to each of the four decision rules. Compare results to what was obtained previously. Comments?

b. Explain how injuries might be costed. Would you feel uneasy about the estimates? Explore the implications of considering fatalities.

7. For the portfolio problem in Table 17–2, suppose $f(\theta_1) = 0.1$, $f(\theta_2) = 0.5$, $f(\theta_3) = 0.3$, and $f(\theta_4) = 0.1$. Determine the optimal prior decision using the expected value decision rule. Interpret the meaning of $E(R^*)$.

8. Determine the best decision for each of the four decision rules using the payoff table of Exercise 1 and $f(\theta)$ as given in the preceding exercise. Would you conclude that diversification (investing in more than one investment alternative) is undesirable when expected monetary value is the only criterion? In general, why is diversification desirable?

9. Show that the min-max rule for Table 17–4 is nothing more than an expected value rule where $f(\theta_1) = 0$, $f(\theta_2) = 0$, and $f(\theta_3) = 1$ for both D_1 and D_2. Do these probability assignments make sense for the pessimist?

10. Show that the max-min rule for Table 17–2 is in reality an expected value rule where $f(\theta_1$ or $\theta_2) = 1.0$, $f(\theta_3) = 0$, and $f(\theta_4) = 0$ for D_1; $f(\theta_1) = 1.0$, $f(\theta_2) = 0$, $f(\theta_3) = 0$, and $f(\theta_4) = 0$ for D_2; and $f(\theta_1$ or $\theta_3) = 1.0$, $f(\theta_2) = 0$, and $f(\theta_4) = 0$ for D_3. Do these probability assignments make sense for the pessimist?

11. For Table 17–2, assign implicit subjective probabilities $f(\theta)$ according to the max-max rule. Find the decision which maximizes the expected value. Is this identical to the max-max rule?

17.3 POSTERIOR ANALYSIS

Up to now we have not considered the possibility of seeking additional information about the states of nature. For example, an investor might achieve a better return on a portfolio by subscribing to a service which forecasts stock prices; likewise, the highway patrol captain might make better decisions if the number of accidents tomorrow were related to the number of accidents today (for example, early morning fog on both mornings). In this section we present methods which incorporate the availability of additional information.

Example 17.3 New Product Model

A product manager is to make a decision regarding whether or not a new product is to be developed and introduced to the market. Based on judgment and past experience with similar products, the payoff table for this venture is represented by Table 17–6. In this case, states of nature are defined by degrees of market penetration. For example, θ_1 indicates that the product will capture 5 percent ($p = 0.05$) of the market. Payoffs represent the present value of estimated profits in millions of dollars. Note that all payoffs for act

TABLE 17-6

Payoffs ($1 million) for New Product Model

	$\theta_1: p = 0.05$	$\theta_2: p = 0.10$	$\theta_3: p = 0.15$
D_1: Introduce...............	−2	1	5
D_2: Do not introduce.........	0	0	0

D_2 are zero, as revenues are not generated and costs relating to development, manufacturing, and distribution are not incurred.

In actual practice, penetration would be a continuous random variable; however, the manager believes that the three specified penetrations adequately represent the states of nature. Table 17-7 suggests the reasoning behind this assertion. The product is expected to achieve no less than 2.5 percent and no' more than 17.5 percent of the market. Penetrations within each of the first two class intervals are judged to occur with twice the likelihood of penetrations within the last class; hence, classes are represented by class midpoints and prior probabilities for states of nature are defined by the given $f(\theta)$.

You should confirm that prior analysis yields $E(R) = 0.6$ for D_1 and $E(R) = 0$ for D_2. Thus, without additional information on which to base a decision, the optimal prior act is to develop and introduce the product, which is expected to yield $600,000 of profit in present value terms.

TABLE 17-7

Potential Market Penetrations

State of Nature θ	Range of Potential Penetration	Midpoint (p)	Probability $f(\theta)$
θ_1...............	0.025 but less than 0.075	0.05	0.4
θ_2...............	0.075 but less than 0.125	0.10	0.4
θ_3...............	0.125 but less than 0.175	0.15	0.2

Value of Perfect Information

In general, applications of decision theory include the option of seeking additional information about the states of nature. An interesting hypothetical question is the expected upper limit for the value of this information. In other words, what would be the value of information which is so perfect that the true state of nature can be predicted with certainty.

Consider the new product example. If θ_1 were predicted with certainty, then D_2 should be chosen with payoff $0; if θ_2 were predicted with certainty, then D_1 is the best with payoff $1 million; finally, if θ_3 were predicted with certainty, then D_1 would yield $5 million. The expected value of this combination of best decisions and certain states of nature is determined by weighting these payoffs by their respective probabilities of occurrence, as defined by $f(\theta)$. Thus, the **expected value under certainty (EVUC)** is $(0) \cdot (0.4) + (1) \cdot (0.4) + (5) \cdot (0.2)$, or $1.4 (million).

Given that $600,000 is the expected value of the optimal act *prior* to any additional information about states of nature, it follows that $800,000 is the most that the product manager should be willing to pay for perfect information.

In general,

$$\text{EVUC} = \sum_{\theta} R(D^*, \theta) \cdot f(\theta) \tag{17.3}$$

when consequences are expressed as payoffs and

$$\text{EVUC} = \sum_{\theta} L(D^*, \theta) \cdot f(\theta) \tag{17.4}$$

when consequences are in terms of losses, where D^* identifies the best act for a certain θ. Note that the calculation of EVUC requires that $f(\theta)$ *not be affected by decisions*. Consequently, EVUC is not defined for the highway patrol model of Example 17.2.

The upper bound of $800,000 is called the **expected value of perfect information (EVPI);** that is, it is the difference between the expected return or loss under certainty ($1,400,000) and the expected return or loss of the optimal act given by prior analysis ($600,000). In general,

$$\text{EVPI} = \text{EVUC} - E(R^*) \tag{17.5}$$

for payoffs and

$$\text{EVPI} = E(L^*) - \text{EVUC} \tag{17.6}$$

for losses, where $E(R^*)$ and $E(L^*)$ represent the appropriate expected values of the optimal act for prior analysis.

Revision of Prior Probabilities[7]

Posterior analysis provides a means for revising prior probabilities based on new information which has become available. The vehicle for revising probabilities is **Bayes' Rule,** which is given by

$$f(\theta|x) = \frac{f(\theta) \cdot f(x|\theta)}{f(x)} \tag{17.7}$$

for *discrete* θ and X where

θ = State of nature.
X = Random variable representing additional information based on a sample survey or an experiment.
x = Specific value of X.
$f(\theta|x)$ = Revised or conditional probability of θ given x (termed the **posterior probability**).
$f(\theta)$ = Prior probability.
$f(x|\theta)$ = Conditional probability of x given θ.
$f(x)$ = Marginal probability of x.[8]

---

[7] This section assumes knowledge of the concepts in Section A.1.

[8] For posterior analyses based on continuous θ and/or X see Hadley, *Introduction to Probability;* L. Weiss, *Statistical Decision Theory* (New York: McGraw-Hill, Inc., 1961); and Winkler, *Bayesian Inference.*

To continue the new product model, suppose that a market survey based on a consumer panel of 100 customers yields the additional information that only 3 customers would buy this product. In this case, we assume that the binomial distribution, as given by Equation (A.20) on page 714, is an adequate representation of the experimental process where $n = 100$, $X = 3$, and p is given by the appropriate θ in Table 17–6. The calculation of posterior probabilities is summarized in Table 17–8.

TABLE 17–8

Calculation of Posterior Probabilities

θ	$f(\theta)$	$f(3\|\theta)$	$f(\theta) \cdot f(3\|\theta)$	$f(\theta\|3)$
$\theta_1 : p = 0.05$	0.4	0.1396	0.05584	0.95912
$\theta_2 : p = 0.10$	0.4	0.0059	0.00236	0.04054
$\theta_3 : p = 0.15$	0.2	0.0001	0.00002	0.00034
	1.0		$f(3) = 0.05822$	1.00000

Note that $f(x|\theta)$ is, in fact, the binomial probability mass function. For example, 0.1396 is the probability of 3 "successes" $(X = 3)$ in 100 trials $(n = 100)$ of a binomial experiment when the probability of success in any one trial is $p = 0.05$.

The joint probability of θ and x is given by

$$f(\theta \text{ and } x) = f(\theta) \cdot f(x|\theta) \qquad (17.8)$$

according to Formula (A.6) on page 705. For example, from Table 17–8, the joint probability of $X = 3$ and θ_1 is 0.05584. Since x can be achieved any number of mutually exclusive ways depending on the value of θ, it follows that Formula (A.3) can be applied to the joint event $(\theta \text{ and } x)$ across all possible values of θ:

$$f(x) = \sum_{\theta} f(\theta) \cdot f(x|\theta). \qquad (17.9)$$

Having determined that $f(3) = 0.05822$ according to Equation (17.9), we now apply (17.7) to revise the prior probabilities for the states of nature. This provides the last column in Table 17–8. Thus, based on the experimental result, we revise the probability of θ_1 (that is, that the market penetration will be 0.05) from 0.4 to 0.95912, of θ_2 from 0.4 to 0.04054, and of θ_3 from 0.2 to 0.00034. This means that our current best likelihoods for achieving 0.05, 0.10, and 0.15 market penetrations are approximately 96, 4, and 0 percent, respectively. Note that the application of (17.7) insures that these revised probabilities sum to unity. Further note that the experimental result (3 customers out of 100) is much more consistent with θ_1 than with θ_2 and θ_3; hence, the revised probabilities reflect the changes in likelihoods that one would logically expect.

To determine the optimal posterior decision $\mathbf{D}_B^*$, termed the **Bayes' decision**, the expected value rule given by Equation (17.1) or (17.2) is applied after replacing the prior probability distribution $f(\theta)$ by the posterior probability distribution $f(\theta|x)$:

$$E'(R) = \sum_{\theta} R(D, \theta) \cdot f(\theta|x) \qquad (17.10)$$

or

$$E'(L) = \sum_{\theta} L(D, \theta) \cdot f(\theta|x) \qquad (17.11)$$

were E' denotes the posterior expected value.

Table 17–9 illustrates calculations for the new product example. Since the expected return associated with introducing the new product (D_1) is now a loss of $1,876,000, it follows that the Bayes' decision subsequent to the consumer panel results is not to introduce this product (that is, $D_B^* = D_2$) with an optimal expected return of $E'(R^*) = 0$.

TABLE 17–9

Expected Posterior Payoffs for New Product Model

Decision	Payoff $R(D,\theta)$	Posterior Probability $f(\theta|x)$	Expected Payoff $R(D,\theta) \cdot f(\theta|x)$
D_1	-2	0.95912	-1.91824
	1	0.04054	0.04054
	5	0.00034	0.00170
		1.00000	$E'(R) = -1.87600$
D_2	0	0.95912	0.0
	0	0.04054	0.0
	0	0.00034	0.0
		1.00000	$E'(R) = \quad 0.0$

Follow-up Exercises

12. With respect to the portfolio problem:
    a. Up to how much should you be willing to pay for an investment service which guarantees you perfect forecasts for Table 17–2?
    b. It can be proved that EVPI *is equivalent to the minimum expected regret.* Show this for the portfolio problem of Tables 17–2 and 17–3. Is the decision associated with minimum expected regret the same as the decision associated with maximum expected payoff?

13. Determine D_B^* if 3 consumers out of a panel of 20 indicate their preference for the new product.

14. Suppose that an investment service for the portfolio model of Table 17–2 accurately forecasts the correct θ with twice the likelihood of the other θ's. This means, for example, that $f(x_1 | \theta_2) = 0.2$, $f(x_2 | \theta_2) = 0.4$, $f(x_3 | \theta_2) = 0.2$, and $f(x_4 | \theta_2) = 0.2$, where x_j is the forecast for θ_j. Thus, if the actual state of nature turns out to be θ_2, then $f(x_1 | \theta_2) = 0.2$ indicates that 20 percent of the time θ_1 was forecasted erroneously, $f(x_2 | \theta_2) = 0.4$ says that θ_2 was forecasted accurately 40 percent of the

time, and so on. Note that these conditional probabilities must sum to one. Further note that the above conditional probabilities are only 4 of the 16 which must be specified for this problem. Can you verbalize the following complete set of conditional probabilities?

Conditional Probabilities, $f(x \mid \theta)$

State of Nature	Forecast				
	x_1	x_2	x_3	x_4	Total
θ_1.....................	0.4	0.2	0.2	0.2	1.0
θ_2.....................	0.2	0.4	0.2	0.2	1.0
θ_3.....................	0.2	0.2	0.4	0.2	1.0
θ_4.....................	0.2	0.2	0.2	0.4	1.0

In Exercise 7 on page 658, you should have confirmed that D_3 is the optimal decision by prior analysis with $E(R^*) = \$10.8$ million. Using the prior probabilities given in Exercise 7, determine the posterior probabilities, the expected values, and the Bayes' decision by posterior analysis if the forecast for next year is (a) x_1 and (b) x_3.

When you compare the posterior probabilities in this exercise to the prior probabilities in Exercise 7, are the directions of change logical? Based on the magnitudes of these changes, would you conclude that the forecasting service is effective?

15. In Exercise 14, change the elements in the main diagonal of the $f(x \mid \theta)$ table from 0.4 to 0.7, and change all other elements to 0.1. Rework the problem and draw a conclusion with respect to the "information content" of main-diagonal elements.

16. For the highway patrol model of Example 17.2, suppose that normal patrols are specified for the first hour of each 9–5 shift. During this first hour, all accidents which occur are reported to headquarters. At the end of this first hour, a decision is made regarding the continuation of normal patrols v. a switch to escorts. In this case, we treat the number of accidents in the first hour as a random variable X from a *Poisson* process with parameter $\lambda = 1$ (for θ_1), $\lambda = 5$ (for θ_2), or $\lambda = 10$ (for θ_3) with $t = \frac{1}{8}$ (the first hour represents $\frac{1}{8}$ of the shift). In this case, Formula (A.24) on page 714 represents the conditional probabilities $f(x|\theta)$. For example, given θ_2, the probability of zero accidents in the first hour $(X = 0)$ is

$$f\,(0|\theta_2) = \frac{[(5)(\frac{1}{8})]^0 \cdot e^{-(5)(1/8)}}{0!}$$

$$= 0.535.$$

Assuming that the costs in Table 17–4 appropriately reflect the new conditions, determine the Bayes' decision if the number of accidents in the first hour is (a) zero and (b) two. (Note that the prior probabilities associated with D_2 do not get revised.)

17. Show that Bayes' Rule is nothing more than the applications of Equations (A.5) and (A.6) to the conditional probability $f(\theta|x)$.

17.4 PREPOSTERIOR ANALYSIS

As you already know, prior analysis does not consider the act of obtaining new information about the states of nature, whereas posterior analysis provides a means to incorporate new information *after* it becomes available. Up to now, however, we have not considered the issue of whether additional information *should* be acquired in the first place. In other words, since the acquisition of information incurs a cost, it is of interest to assess *beforehand* whether the potential benefit of this information is worth the cost. **Preposterior analysis** addresses itself to this issue at a point in time which precedes the actual acquisition of new information. It is instructive to point out that preposterior analysis can evaluate not only whether new information should or should not be acquired, but also the manner (that is, alternative sample designs) by which this information is to be acquired.

Example 17.4   Nuclear Power Plant Model

Consider a $1 billion nuclear power plant which, after seven years, is nearing completion. It is being built by Ocean Gas & Electric (OG & E) in a certain western state which shall remain unnamed (to protect the innocent). OG & E has applied for an operating license to the Nuclear Regulatory Commission (NRC). Unfortunately, the power needs of this most progressive state required that the plant be located in an area near a most famous geological fault. Should a severe earthquake rupture the plant, radioactive particles would be released into the atmosphere in the form of a colorless, odorless cloud that not only would contaminate everything in its path but also would cause untold death and human misery primarily in the form of cancers and genetic defects.

The NRC is well aware of this potential catastrophe. As a result, it requires that all atomic power plants which are located in earthquake zones must be constructed to withstand the most severe shaking ever recorded in that location. To comply with this ruling, OG & E engineers designed a plant with a reinforced concrete foundation which is 15 feet thick and a reinforced concrete dome over each reactor which is 4 feet thick. It is estimated that this design would withstand a jolt of 7.0 on the Richter scale.

An analysis by the OR staff of NRC yields the information provided by Table 17–10, where

$\theta_1 \equiv$ Reading of $R \leq 7$ on the Richter scale over the life of the plant.
$\theta_2 \equiv$ Reading of $7 < R \leq 8$.
$\theta_3 \equiv$ Reading of $R > 8$.
$D_1 \equiv$ Award operating license unconditionally.
$D_2 \equiv$ Award operating license conditional on additional concrete reinforcement which is to withstand 8.0 on the Richter scale.
$D_3 \equiv$ Do not award operating license.

The loss function $L(D,\theta)$ represents the present value of expected cost to the consumer in billions of dollars over the life of the plant. D_2 represents higher costs than D_1 because expensive construction rework must be under-

TABLE 17–10

Loss Table for Nuclear Power Plant Model (billions of dollars)

	θ_1	θ_2	θ_3
D_1...............	70.0	8,000.0	8,000.0
D_2...............	70.1	70.1	8,000.1
D_3...............	100.0	100.0	100.0

taken, the cost of which eventually gets passed on to the consumer in the form of higher rates. This amounts to $0.1 billion (that is, the difference between 70 and 70.1 when no rupture occurs for D_1 and D_2). D_3 implies that the power plant is to be abandoned as a nuclear generating facility, resulting in higher rates for alternative sources of power and/or for reduced levels of commercial activity due to a lack of generating power. It follows that costs for D_3 are independent of θ. The consequence of a ruptured nuclear plant is costed at $7,930 billion, which is reflected by the difference between 8,000.0 and 70.0 in the D_1-row or between 8,000.1 and 70.1 in the D_2-row.[9]

Now suppose that the prior probabilities for states of nature are estimated as $f(\theta_1) = 0.999990$, $f(\theta_2) = 0.000009$, and $f(\theta_3) = 0.000001$. You should confirm that prior analysis yields $E(L) = 70.0793$ for D_1, $E(L) = 70.10793$ for D_2, and $E(L) = 100.0$ for D_3; hence, the license should be granted unconditionally based on prior analysis.

---

[9] As in the highway patrol model, any attempt to cost human death or suffering in terms of dollars is impossible to justify, yet costing is always implicit. For example, the "cost" of waiting in the emergency room of a hospital effectively can be reduced to zero by providing extremely costly facilities. Since such facilities are never provided, it follows that death and suffering caused by waiting are implicitly costed by our institutions; that is, a cost trade-off is acknowledged. The expression of losses in terms of disutilities (Section 17.6) perhaps provides a more meaningful approach to this dilemma.

Bayes' Decision Rules

Prior to making one of the decisions D_1, D_2, or D_3, the NRC has the option of seeking additional information about the states of nature θ. Past geological surveys in other regions often have discovered new faults, causing revisions in the projected magnitudes of tremors. A special geological survey over an area encompassing a 50-mile radius centered on the plant can provide forecasts for θ, but at a cost of $1 million to the consumers (courtesy of the NRC). Should the NRC require the survey? If so, what decision is best for each possible forecast?

Before answering these questions, it is of interest to determine EVUC and EVPI. Thus, based on Equations (17.4) and (17.6),

$$\text{EVUC} = (70.0) \cdot (0.999990) + (70.1) \cdot (0.000009) + (100.0) \cdot (0.000001)$$
$$= 70.0000309$$

and

$$EVPI = 70.0793000 - 70.0000309$$
$$= 0.0792691.$$

This indicates that \$79.2691 million (exclusive of fee) is the most that can be gained by a perfect survey. Since the cost of an imperfect survey is \$1 million, it follows that a wide margin exists for the realization of cost gains. We have yet to answer, however, whether the benefit from an imperfect survey outweighs its cost.

The geological survey under consideration is capable of providing a forecast on the maximum magnitude of tremors for a particular region. Let the random variable X represent forecasted maximum reading on the Richter scale so that

$x_1 =$ Forecast of $R \leq 7$.
$x_2 =$ Forecast of $7 < R \leq 8$.
$x_3 =$ Forecast of $R > 8$.

Needless to say, forecasts are not perfectly reliable. Past experience combined with expert judgment provide the conditional probabilities in Table 17–11.

TABLE 17–11

Conditional Probabilities $f(x|\theta)$

| | Experimental Result (Forecast) | | |
State of Nature	x_1	x_2	x_3
θ_1........................	0.7	0.2	0.1
θ_2........................	0.3	0.5	0.2
θ_3........................	0.0	0.1	0.9

For example, the first row of probabilities can be interpreted as follows:

$f(x_1|\theta_1) = 0.7$ means that in regions with maximum $R \leq 7$, the correct forecast is 70 percent reliable.
$f(x_2|\theta_1) = 0.2$ means that in regions with maximum $R \leq 7$, the erroneous forecast $7 < R \leq 8$ is given with 20-percent probability.
$f(x_3|\theta_1) = 0.1$ means that in regions with maximum $R \leq 7$, the erroneous forecast $R > 8$ is given with 10-percent probability.

Can you interpret the other rows? Why do row probabilities sum to unity?

From Section 17.3 we know that a specific forecast is going to cause a revision in the prior probability for each state of nature according to Bayes' Rule. Table 17–12 provides results which facilitate the calculation

TABLE 17–12

Joint and Marginal Probabilities

	x_1	x_2	x_3	Marginal, $f(\theta)$
θ_1........................	0.6999930	0.1999980	0.0999990	0.999990
θ_2........................	0.0000027	0.0000045	0.0000018	0.000009
θ_3........................	0.0000000	0.0000001	0.0000009	0.000001
Marginal, $f(x)$............	0.6999957	0.2000026	0.1000017	1.000000

of these posterior probabilities. The nine cell entries in the main body of the table represent joint probabilities according to Formula (17.8). For example, the joint probability of θ_3 and x_3 is

$$
\begin{aligned}
f(\theta_3 \text{ and } x_3) &= f(\theta_3) \cdot f(x_3|\theta_3) \\
&= (0.000001) \cdot (0.9) \\
&= 0.0000009,
\end{aligned}
$$

where $f(\theta_3)$ is the prior probability given in Example 17.4 and $f(x_3|\theta_3)$ is the conditional probability given in Table 17–11. Note that the sum of the joint probabilities in a given row gives the prior probability $f(\theta)$ for that row, as expressed in the column of marginal probabilities. Similarly, the sum of any column gives the marginal probability $f(x)$. For example. $f(x_3) = 0.1000017$ is the probability of the forecast $R > 8$.

TABLE 17–13

Posterior Probabilities, $f(\theta|x)$

	x_1	x_2	x_3
θ_1	0.9999961	0.9999770	0.9999730
θ_2	0.0000039	0.0000225	0.0000180
θ_3	0.0000000	0.0000005	0.0000090
Total	1.0000000	1.0000000	1.0000000

The results in Table 17–12 are now used to generate the nine posterior probabilities in Table 17–13. For example, if the forecast is $X = x_3$, then the posterior probability of θ_3 is given by Equation (17.7):

$$
\begin{aligned}
f(\theta_3|x_3) &= \frac{f(\theta_3) \cdot f(x_3|\theta_3)}{f(x_3)} \\
&= \frac{f(\theta_3 \text{ and } x_3)}{f(x_3)} \\
&= \frac{0.0000009}{0.1000017} \\
&= 0.0000090
\end{aligned}
$$

where the numerator and denominator are taken from Table 17–12. Note the meaning of this result. Prior to a geological survey, the probability that a jolt registers above 8 on the Richter scale is $f(\theta_3) = 0.0000010$; however, if a geological survey forecasts that the given area will receive a jolt above 8, this prior probability is revised upward by a factor of nine to 0.0000090.

We are now in a position to calculate the Bayes' decision for each possible forecast. Consider the forecast $X = x_3$. From Table 17–13, the revised probabilities for each state of nature are $f(\theta_1|x_3) = 0.9999730$, $f(\theta_2|x_3) = 0.0000180$, and $f(\theta_3|x_3) = 0.0000090$. Substituting these posterior probabilities and the losses in Table 17–10 into Formula (17.11), we get

$$E'(L) = (70.0) \cdot (0.9999730) + (8{,}000.0) \cdot (0.0000180)$$
$$+ (8{,}000.0) \cdot (0.0000090)$$
$$= 70.21411 \text{ for } D_1,$$

$$E'(L) = (70.1) \cdot (0.9999730) + (70.1) \cdot (0.0000180) + (8{,}000.1) \cdot (0.0000090)$$
$$= 70.17137 \text{ for } D_2,$$

and

$$E'(L) = (100.0) \cdot (0.9999730) + (100.0) \cdot (0.0000180) + (100.0) \cdot (0.0000090)$$
$$= 100.0 \text{ for } D_3.$$

This result indicates that D_2 (award licence conditional on more reinforcement) is the Bayes' decision should the results of the survey yield $X = x_3$ (a forecast for a tremor above 8 on the Richter scale). The optimal posterior expected loss is $E'(L^*) = 70.17137$ for this decision.

Table 17–14 summarizes the Bayes' decision for each possible experi-

TABLE 17–14

Summary of Preposterior Analysis

Forecast	Bayes' Decision	Optimal Posterior Expected Loss	Marginal Probability
X	D_B^*	$E'(L^*)$	$f(x)$
x_1..................	D_1	70.030927	0.6999957
x_2..................	D_2	70.103965	0.2000026
x_3..................	D_2	70.171370	0.1000017
Total..............			1.0000000

mental result. The first two columns of this table define the **Bayes' strategy, Bayes' policy,** or **Bayes' decision rule** for this model. A Bayes' decision rule Q is a function which specifies the Bayes' decision to be taken for each possible experimental result (value of X); that is

$$D_B^* = Q(x). \tag{17.12}$$

Thus, if the geological survey yields $X = x_1$, then the NRC should select D_1; if $X = x_2$, then D_2 is the best decision; and if $X = x_3$, then D_2 is prescribed.[10]

Expected Value of Experimentation

Although we have prescribed an optimal (Bayes') decision for each possible experimental result, we have yet to consider the issue of whether or not the geological survey should be commissioned. The third column in Table 17–14 gives the optimal posterior expected loss for each Bayes' de-

---

[10] Note that this concept of policy is also utilized by the Markovian decision models of Section 15.5. In that case, however, the optimal policy was sought from among those which were enumerated. In this section, the optimal policy is defined as that which yields Bayes' decisions.

cision. Since the probability of each Bayes' decision is exactly equivalent to the probability of the experimental outcome (value of X) which corresponds to each Bayes' decision, it follows that the probability of each $E'(L^*)$ is defined by $f(x)$, as indicated in the fourth column of Table 17–14 (which is taken from the last row in Table 17–12).

If you're still with us, then you should realize that the **expected loss with experimentation (ELE)** is the expected value of $E'(L^*)$ plus the cost of experimentation, C, or

$$\text{ELE} = \sum_x E'(L^*) \cdot f(x) + C. \tag{17.13}$$

For the atomic power plant example,

$$\begin{aligned}
\text{ELE} &= (70.030927) \cdot (0.6999957) + (70.103965) \cdot (0.2000026) + (70.171370) \\
&\qquad\qquad\qquad\qquad\qquad\qquad\qquad\qquad\qquad \cdot (0.1000017) + 0.001 \\
&= 70.06057933.
\end{aligned}$$

This means that the expected loss is \$70,060,579,330 if the geological survey is to be undertaken. By the prior analysis in Example 17.4, the optimal decision with no experimentation was determined as D_1, yielding $E(L^*) = 70.0793$, or an **expected loss without experimentation** of \$70,079,300,000. The difference between the expected loss without experimentation and the expected loss with experimentation is termed the **expected value of experimentation (EVE)**:

$$\text{EVE} = E(L^*) - \text{ELE}. \tag{17.14}$$

For the example,

$$\begin{aligned}
\text{EVE} &= 70.07930000 - 70.06057933 \\
&= 0.01872067,
\end{aligned}$$

which indicates that the decision to require a geological survey results in an expected net savings of approximately \$18.7 million over the decision not to direct the survey.

To summarize, the NRC first should require a geological survey. Based on the result of this survey, it should then make a decision according to the decision rule specified in Table 17–14.

If consequences are expressed as payoffs, then the **expected payoff with experimentation (EPE)** is given by

$$\text{EPE} = \sum_x E'(R^*) \cdot f(x) - C \tag{17.15}$$

and

$$\text{EVE} = \text{EPE} - E(R^*). \tag{17.16}$$

When alternative experimental plans are available, let EVE_k represent the expected value of experimentation for plan k. If $\text{EVE}_k < 0$ for all k, then experimentation should not be undertaken; otherwise, select the plan which yields maximum EVE_k.

Follow-up Exercises

18. Confirm the results for x_1 and x_2 in Table 17–14.

19. Suppose that the NRC has the option of a more elaborate and reliable geological survey costing $5 million. Determine

    a. $D_B^* = Q(x)$
    b. EVE,

    if the conditional probabilities $f(x|\theta)$ are given by the table below.

	x_1	x_2	x_3
θ_1	0.9	0.1	0.0
θ_2	0.1	0.8	0.1
θ_3	0.0	0.0	1.0

    Should the NRC select this survey over the other survey?
    c. Judging from the conditional probabilities, why do we say this survey is more "reliable" than the other? Would you say that good estimates for prior probabilities become less important as more reliable experiments are used? Explain.
    d. Based on joint probabilities, show that the probability of a correct forecast for this survey is greater than for the other survey. Is this a good measure of reliability?

20. For the portfolio problem in Exercise 15:

    a. Generate the table of joint and marginal probabilities.
    b. Generate the table of posterior probabilities.
    c. Determine $D_B^* = Q(x)$.
    d. Calculate EVE if the investment service costs $50,000. Do you recommend subscribing to the investment service? What is the maximum the investor should be willing to pay the investment service?

21. For the new product model described in Example 17.3, consider a consumer panel of 4 members (instead of 100 members). Also, assume that you are at a point in time prior to a market survey.

    a. Theoretically, what is the most the company should be willing to pay for a market survey?
    b. Generate the table of conditional probabilities.
    c. Generate the table of joint and marginal probabilities.
    d. Generate the table of posterior probabilities.
    e. Determine $D_B^* = Q(x)$.
    f. Calculate EVE if the market survey costs $100,000. Do you recommend a market survey? What maximum cost should the company tolerate for a market survey? Should a larger consumer panel be considered? Explain.

**22. *Optimal sample size* An interesting issue for binomial sampling plans of the type in the preceding exercise is the determination of the optimal sample size. As the size of the sample n becomes larger, the expected value of the optimal posterior expected loss $E'(L^*)$ becomes smaller [or the expected value of the optimal posterior expected return $E'(R^*)$ gets larger]. Can you reason why? As n becomes larger, however, the cost of the experiment C increases. Right? This tradeoff is reflected by ELE or EPE, so that the optimal sample size n^* is that which minimizes ELE or maximizes EPE. The solution for n^* is straightforward once C is specified as a function of n. In fact, EVE is well-behaved (that is, exhibits a single maximum which is global) so that by incremental analysis the following must be true: $EVE_{n^*} > EVE_{n^*-1}$ and $EVE_{n^*} > EVE_{n^*+1}$. Right? Thus, the computational procedure "only" needs to determine EVE_n for $n = 1, 2, \ldots, n^* + 1$.

a. Determine n^* for Example 17.3 if $C = 400{,}000 + 50{,}000n$.
b. In general, would you say that the computer is recommended for solving optimal binomial sampling plans? Explain by example.

17.5 DECISION TREES

Decision trees represent a useful means by which to structure decision problems. Figure 17–1 illustrates the complete decision tree for the nuclear power plant model of the previous section. (At this point we recommend that you close your eyes and breathe deeply if you're in a state of panic from an overabundance of visual stimuli.) It is not as bad as it looks. In fact, we would be willing to bet that decision trees will become your preferred tool for analyzing decision problems.

First, study the legend so as to reorient yourself to this model. Note that the decisions to not undertake or to undertake the geological survey are identified by the new decision variables D_4 and D_5, respectively. Next, follow each of the following steps in sequence.

Basic Tree Structure

The first step is preliminary: Determine all relevant states of nature θ, decisions D, and experimental outcomes X. Next, structure the relationships among these variables in the form of a tree having "forks" and "branches." Branches identify specific values of θ, D, and X. A fork identifies the type of branches that emanate from the fork. The branches following **decision forks** identify specific decisions D. The branches following **chance forks** identify either specific states of nature θ or specific experimental outcomes X.

The tree "flows" from left to right in chronological order. For example, the Nuclear Regulatory Commission first must decide D_4 or D_5; hence, D_4 and D_5 are the first set of branches. Since these are decision branches, they must emanate from a decision fork (labeled $\boxed{1}$). If D_4 is selected, then the NRC must next decide on D_1, D_2, or D_3, which gives $\boxed{2}$ and its three branches. For each of these three branches, any one of three possible states of nature will follow; thus, θ_1, θ_2, and θ_3 depart from the

FIGURE 17–1

Decision Tree for Nuclear Power Plant Model

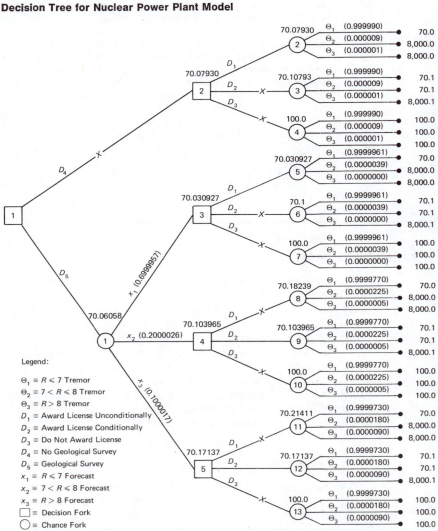

Legend:

$\Theta_1 \equiv R \leqslant 7$ Tremor
$\Theta_2 \equiv 7 < R \leqslant 8$ Tremor
$\Theta_3 \equiv R > 8$ Tremor
$D_1 \equiv$ Award License Unconditionally
$D_2 \equiv$ Award License Conditionally
$D_3 \equiv$ Do Not Award License
$D_4 \equiv$ No Geological Survey
$D_5 \equiv$ Geological Survey
$x_1 \equiv R \leqslant 7$ Forecast
$x_2 \equiv 7 < R \leqslant 8$ Forecast
$x_3 \equiv R > 8$ Forecast
$\square \equiv$ Decision Fork
$\bigcirc \equiv$ Chance Fork

chance forks given by ②, ③, and ④. If the NRC selects D_5, then the experimental results of the geological survey will follow. This gives the chance fork ① and its three possible branches (x_1, x_2, and x_3). Following the experimental result, the NRC must decide D_1, D_2, or D_3. Since three experimental results are possible, this gives ③, ④, and ⑤, with their sets of decision branches. These decision branches, in turn, must lead into the chance forks ⑤ through ⑬, each of which provides a fork for the states of nature θ. Right? (Don't let the numbers bother you at this point; just focus on the relationships indicated by the flows.)

Incorporating Probabilities

Now we are ready to include probabilities in the decision tree. First of all, note that probabilities parenthetically follow chance outcomes only (that is, θ_1, θ_2, θ_3, x_1, x_2, and x_3). The probabilities for θ_1, θ_2, and θ_3 following ②, ③, and ④ are the *prior probabilities* specified in Example 17.4: $f(\theta_1) = 0.999990$, $f(\theta_2) = 0.000009$, and $f(\theta_3) = 0.000001$. This must be so because no experimental outcomes precede these chance forks.

Now consider the probabilities for θ_1, θ_2, and θ_3 following ⑤, ⑥, and ⑦. For each of these chance forks, the experimental outcome x_1 is a precedent; hence, these probabilities must be the *posterior probabilities* $f(\theta|x_1)$. Similarly, the posterior probabilities $f(\theta|x_2)$ follow ⑧, ⑨, and ⑩; and $f(\theta|x_3)$ follow ⑪, ⑫, and ⑬. These posterior probabilities are given, respectively, by the columns in Table 17–13.

Finally, the probability for each experimental outcome must be the *marginal probability* $f(x)$. They cannot be the conditional probabilities $f(x|\theta)$ because θ does not precede X in the tree. Thus, $f(x_1) = 0.6999957$, $f(x_2) = 0.2000026$, and $f(x_3) = 0.1000017$, according to Table 17–12.

Backward Induction

The optimal set of decisions is found by the method variously called **backward induction, roll-back principle,** or **averaging out and folding back.**

First, place the appropriate loss $L(D, \theta)$ or payoff $R(D, \theta)$ at each terminal point of the tree. For example, the losses in the first row of Table 17–10 are placed following the appropriate end points of branches emanating from ②, ⑤, ⑧, and ⑪. The second and third rows of Table 17–10 are placed similarly.

Second, move backward or "roll-back" on the tree to the chance forks labeled ② through ⑬. Immediately above each chance fork place the expected loss for the outcomes following this fork. You should recognize the entries above ②, ③, and ④ as the expected losses $E(L)$ for prior analysis. Thus, for D_1 we place

$$E(L) = (70.0) \cdot (0.999990) + (8,000.0) \cdot (0.000009) + (8,000.0) \cdot (0.000001)$$
$$= 70.07930$$

above fork ②. The procedure is identical for forks ⑤ through ⑬, which you should recognize as the expected posterior losses $E'(L)$ based on Formula (17.11).

Next, we roll back to the decision forks ② through ⑤. Above each of these decision forks we place the loss of the optimal decision following that fork. For example, above ③ we place 70.030927 since D_1 yields the lowest expected loss following ③. At the same time we "prune" the nonoptimal branches by indicating the symbol (×). You should recognize that the branches which are *not* pruned following ③ through ⑤ represent the Bayes' decisions in Table 17–14. The decision D_1 following ② represents the optimal prior decision.

Finally, we roll back to ① and calculate the expected loss plus the cost of experimentation at this point in the tree:

$$(70.030927) \cdot (0.6999957) + (70.103965) \cdot (0.2000026)$$
$$+ (70.17137) \cdot (0.1000017) + 0.001 = 70.06058.$$

This, of course, is identical to the expected loss of experimentation (ELE) according to Equation (17.13). Since the expected loss for D_5 is less than the expected loss for D_4, the latter is pruned.

The optimal set of decisions can be summarized now: Select D_5; if x_1 is the experimental outcome, then select D_1; if x_2 or x_3, then D_2.

Follow-up Exercises

23. Solve Exercise 19 by using a decision tree.
24. Solve Exercise 20 by using a decision tree.
25. Solve Exercise 21 by using a decision tree.

17.6 UTILITY THEORY

In Section 17.1 we noted that consequences can be expressed in terms of a preference measure $U(D, \theta)$ called a utility function. In this section we justify and illustrate the use of utility functions.

Rationale

Consider the following hypothetical scenario. A benefactor offers you two alternative decisions:

$D_1 \equiv$ Flip a coin once, wherein either you win $1 million if a head comes up or you win nothing if a tail comes up.
$D_2 \equiv$ Accept a gift of $300,000.

What would *you* decide? Experience shows that most people would accept the *certain* payoff of $300,000 for D_2 than the *expected* payoff of $500,000 for D_1. Why? Because the consequences associated with D_1 are risky, and most decision makers are risk avoiders. In this case we would say that the expected preference for D_2 is greater than the expected preference for D_1.

The above scenario suggests that the selection of an act based on the decision rule of optimal expected value may not be appropriate when "great" risk is involved. Consider another scenario. A Las Vegas casino offers you a coin-flip game. If head comes up, then you win $2; otherwise, you lose $1. The expected monetary value of this game to you is $(2) \cdot (0.5) + (-1) \cdot (0.5)$, or $0.50. Most likely you would play against this foolish casino. Suppose, however, that the payoffs were $2,000 and $-1,000 instead of $2 and $-1, respectively. Your expected payoff is now $500. Would you still play? How about if the payoffs were $200,000 and $-100,000?

The lesson should be evident by now. A decision involving less expected payoff and less risk is often selected over a decision involving greater expected payoff and greater risk. Evidence of this type of risk-avoiding behavior is common, particularly in life and casualty insurance applications. For example, almost all homeowners carry homeowners' insurance; yet the expected values of such policies to homeowners must be negative, as the insurance companies presumably set rates to yield expected profits. What is needed, then, is a preference measure which incorporates the subjective risk associated with uncertain monetary payoffs.

In other situations, a preference measure is desirable when the use of monetary payoffs or losses may be inappropriate. For example, monetary cost is not the most desirable measure to use when reflecting human casualties due to the rupture of a nuclear power plant.

Besides the ability to incorporate subjective risk and nonmonetary payoffs, utility concepts can be used in *multiple criteria environments*. For example, utility functions have been applied to the solution of mathematical programming problems characterized by multiple concave objective functions.[11]

Construction of Utility Functions

We define a **utility index** $U = U(D, \theta)$ as a real number which represents the preference measure for some consequence. In this section we illustrate one procedure for constructing the utility function $U(D, \theta)$ when it is based on monetary payoffs. In other words, rather than expressing U functionally in terms of the consequences (D, θ), we express U functionally in terms of the monetary payoffs:[12]

$$U = U[R(D, \theta)]$$
$$= U(R).$$

Consider once again the portfolio model of Example 17.1. The payoff table is reproduced here as Table 17–15. Our present purpose is to replace

TABLE 17–15

Monetary Payoffs (millions of dollars)

	θ_1	θ_2	θ_3	θ_4
D_1...........	9.50	9.50	11.00	11.00
D_2...........	9.25	10.75	10.00	11.50
D_3...........	9.00	12.00	9.00	12.00

these monetary payoffs with utility indices, based on the following procedure.

1. Determine the lowest $(R_{\min} = 9)$ and the highest $(R_{\max} = 12)$ monetary payoffs and assign corresponding utility indices of $U_{\min} = 0$

---

[11] S. Zionts and J. Wallenius, "An Interactive Programming Method for Solving the Multiple Criteria Problem," *Management Science*, vol. 22, no. 6 (1976), pp. 652–63.

[12] For other procedures see the references at the end of the chapter.

and $U_{max} = 1$. The selection of end points on the utility scale is arbitrary (as long as $U_{max} > U_{min}$); however, the selection of 0 and 1 as end points makes for an attractive interpretation of utility indices as probabilities (see Exercise 31). We have now established coordinates 1 and 2 on the utility function, or **preference curve,** for the investor, as illustrated in Figure 17–2.

FIGURE 17–2

Preference Curve for Portfolio Model

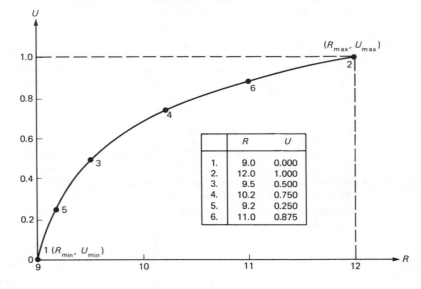

	R	U
1.	9.0	0.000
2.	12.0	1.000
3.	9.5	0.500
4.	10.2	0.750
5.	9.2	0.250
6.	11.0	0.875

2.   Next, the **certainty equivalent (CE)** is established. The CE represents a payoff for which the decision maker is indifferent between (a) the option of receiving the uncertain payoffs R_1 and R_2, each with probability 0.5, and (b) the option of receiving the CE with certainty. For example, suppose that it were possible to offer the investor the following options: (a) an asset position of \$9 million ($R_1 = 9$) with probability $\frac{1}{2}$ or an asset position of \$12 million ($R_2 = 12$) with probability $\frac{1}{2}$; (b) an asset position of \$9.2 million with certainty. If the investor answers option (a), we then increase option (b) to, say, \$10 million. If now the investor prefers option (b), then we revise the certain figure downward and ask the same question. Suppose that after a number of such questions the investor decides that a certain asset position of \$9.5 million is no more or less desirable than uncertain asset positions of \$9 million or \$12 million, each with probability $\frac{1}{2}$. In this instance, we conclude that the $CE = 9.5$ when $R_1 = 9$ and $R_2 = 12$. Note that the expected value of option (a) is \$10.5 million, yet the investor is willing to accept option (b) if just over \$9.5 million can be guaranteed with certainty. This means that our investor is exhibiting risk-averse (avoidance) behavior; that is,

the 50-percent probability of ending up with $9 million is considered so risky that the investor is willing to accept a riskless $9.5 million over a risky expected payoff of $10.5 million. The difference of $1 million between $10.5 million and $9.5 million is called a **risk premium;** that is, in effect the investor is willing to "sacrifice" an expected value of $1 million to avoid this risk.

3. Given the CE from the preceding step, it is now possible to establish another coordinate on the preference curve. Since the investor is indifferent between the riskless $9.5 million of option ($b$) and the equally likely $R_1 = 9$ and $R_2 = 12$ of option (a), it follows that the utility associated with the $CE = 9.5$ must be equal to the *expected* utility associated with $R_1 = 9$ and $R_2 = 12$; hence,

$$U(9.5) = \tfrac{1}{2} \cdot U(9) + \tfrac{1}{2} \cdot U(12)$$
$$= (\tfrac{1}{2}) \cdot (0) + (\tfrac{1}{2}) \cdot (1)$$
$$= 0.5.$$

This gives (9.5, 0.5) as the third coordinate on the preference curve of Figure 17–2. In general,

$$U(CE) = \tfrac{1}{2} \cdot U(R_1) + \tfrac{1}{2} \cdot U(R_2). \tag{17.17}$$

4. Steps 2 and 3 are repeated a number of times until a reasonably smooth preference curve is obtained. Note that you are free to select values of R_1 and R_2 so long as the values selected have known utility indices. Thus, R_{min} and R_{max} must always be used for R_1 and R_2 to establish the third coordinate. Once the third coordinate is established, R_1 and R_2 for the fourth coordinate are based on either R_1 or R_2 from the third coordinate paired with the CE from the third coordinate. In general, R_1 and R_2 for the next coordinate can be based on any previous R_1, R_2, or CE. Table 17–16 provides the

TABLE 17–16

Certainty Equivalents and Corresponding Utilities

R_1	R_2	CE	$U(R_1)$	$U(R_2)$	$U(CE)$
9.0	12.0	9.5	0.000	1.000	0.500
9.5	12.0	10.2	0.500	1.000	0.750
9.0	9.5	9.2	0.000	0.500	0.250
10.2	12.0	11.0	0.750	1.000	0.875

$R_1 - R_2 - CE$ triads and the corresponding utilities which were used to establish the preference curve of Figure 17–2. For example, given $R_1 = 10.2$, $R_2 = 12.0$, and $CE = 11.0$, it follows from Equation (17.17) that

$$U(11.0) = \tfrac{1}{2} \cdot U(10.2) + \tfrac{1}{2} \cdot U(12.0)$$
$$= (\tfrac{1}{2}) \cdot (0.750) + (\tfrac{1}{2}) \cdot (1.000)$$
$$= 0.875.$$

Can you confirm $U(10.2) = 0.750$ and $U(9.2) = 0.250$? Note that the CE and $U(CE)$ columns in Table 17–16 represent, respectively, the R and U coordinates in Figure 17–2.

Based on the sketched preference curve it is now possible to replace the payoffs in Table 17–15 by utility indices.[13] For example, consider $R(D_2, \theta_3) = 10$ for the portfolio model in Table 17–15. From Figure 17–2, $R = 10$ approximately corresponds to $U = 0.7$; hence, in Table 17–17 we let $U(D_2, \theta_3) = U(10) = 0.7$. Can you confirm the remaining entries in Table 17–17?

TABLE 17–17

Utility Table for Portfolio Model

	θ_1	θ_2	θ_3	θ_4
D_1	0.50	0.50	0.88	0.88
D_2	0.31	0.85	0.70	0.95
D_3	0.00	1.00	0.00	1.00

Incorporating Utility Functions

Once $U(D, \theta)$ is specified as in Table 17–17, prior, posterior, and preposterior analyses are undertaken as before. The primary differences are notational: $U(D, \theta)$ is used in place of $R(D, \theta)$ or $L(D, \theta)$; $E(U)$ in place of $E(R)$ or $E(L)$; and $E'(U)$ in place of $E'(R)$ or $E'(L)$.

We might note that $U(D, \theta)$ is interpreted as a **disutility function** when it replaces the loss function $L(D, \theta)$. In other words, rather than minimizing expected loss we minimize expected dispreference.[14]

Additionally, when undertaking preposterior analysis, the cost of experimentation (C) must be added to $L(D, \theta)$ or subtracted from $R(D, \theta)$ *before* $U(D, \theta)$ is determined. For example, the losses at the end points of forks ⑤ through ⑬ in Figure 17–1 must be increased by 0.001 before losses are converted to disutilities. This is the same as saying that $R(D, \theta)$ and $L(D, \theta)$ must include the cost of experimentation.

To illustrate the use of $U(D, \theta)$, consider the prior analysis for the portfolio problem. Given $f(\theta_1) = 0.1$, $f(\theta_2) = 0.5$, $f(\theta_3) = 0.3$, and $f(\theta_4) = 0.1$ and the payoffs in Table 17–15, we get $E(R^*) = \$10.8$ million and $D^* = D_3$. This says that an investment of $10 million in Alternative B is optimal according to the $E(R)$ decision rule, yielding an expected worth of $10.8 million one year hence.

---

[13] The estimation of an analytic utility function is an alternative to curve-fitting by hand. See Exercise 32.

[14] Based on a set of axioms, it can be proved that maximization of expected utility or minimization of expected disutility is consistent with the optimizing behavior of a "rational" decision maker. See Dyckman, Smidt, and McAdams, *Management Decision Making;* Hadley, *Introduction to Probability;* H. Raiffa, *Decision Analysis* (Reading, Mass.: Addison-Wesley Publishing Co., 1968); or Winkler, *Bayesian Inference.*

According to the utilities in Table 17–17, however, we get $E(U) = 0.652$ for D_1, $E(U) = 0.761$ for D_2, and $E(U) = 0.600$ for D_3. Thus, $E(U^*) = 0.761$ and $D^* = D_2$. This means that the investor should diversify (that is, invest \$5 million in A and \$5 million in B) when risk is taken into consideration.

The selection of D_2 as optimal in the utility sense yields an $E(R)$ of \$10.45 million; hence, the investor pays a "price" of \$350,000 (that is, $10.80 - 10.45$) by selecting the alternative with lower risk. In effect, the investor is willing to trade-off a higher expected return for a lower expected risk. Those of you who are financial wizards recognize this as the key argument for diversification in portfolios.[15]

Behavioral Implications

As mentioned earlier, utility theory provides an attractive means by which to describe the subjective preferences of decision makers in en-

FIGURE 17–3

Behavioral Prototypes

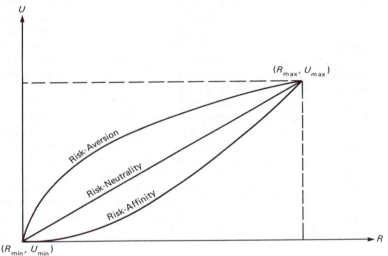

vironments characterized by risk. Figure 17–3 illustrates three prototype configurations to describe risk behavior. You are already familiar with the conservative individual who exhibits **risk-aversion.** This decision

---

[15] We know that the investor is risk-averse because of the concave utility function of Figure 17–2. By deduction, therefore, we might conclude that if D_2 yields a lower expected return, then it must also yield a lower expected variance (the traditional measure of risk). Using (A.14) on Table 17–15 and $f(\theta)$ from above gives $V(R) = 0.54$ for D_1, $V(R) = 0.36$ for D_2, and $V(R) = 2.16$ for D_3, which is consistent with our reasoning. This result also is consistent with the thrust of mathematical programming applications of portfolio theory (see Example 10.10).

maker is willing to pay a risk premium for averting risk, resulting in a preference curve which is concave.

If the preference curve for a decision maker is linear, then the decision maker professes **risk-neutrality.** That is, this individual is indifferent toward risk. Note that a linear preference curve equates the CE to the expected value of R_1 and R_2. Thus, the linear function always yields the expected value of R_1 and R_2.

More importantly, it can be proved that *maximization of* $E(U)$ *and maximization of* $E(R)$—*or minimization of* $E(U)$ *and minimization of* $E(L)$—*yield identical results for linear preference curves.* This result is significant in justifying the simpler approach of utilizing payoffs or losses for situations characterized by either low risk or small disparities in monetary values.

A decision maker with a convex utility function exhibits **risk-affinity.** This individual can be characterized as a gambler, as there is a willingness (up to a point) to favor risk situations having a lower expected payoff than no-risk situations. This is evident by the fact that the CE is greater than the expected value of the $R_1 - R_2$ gamble for any given utility (that is, for any U, the R-value for the curve with risk-affinity is greater than the R-value for the linear function).

Interestingly, a study which constructed preference curves for a sample of corporate executives indicated predominant risk-aversion.[16] In fact, many of the curves were S-shaped, showing slight convexity when $R < 0$ and pronounced concavity when $R > 0$. This conservative behavior suggests that "managers are surely not the takers of risk so often alluded to in the classical defense of the capitalistic system."[17]

It appeared that lower-echelon executives tended to make decisions based on personal preference curves which perhaps were at variance with the preference curves deemed desirable by top management. The rationale for this is not unlike that of portfolio diversification. The diversification of decisions and projects which characterizes a corporate environment yields a total risk which is smaller than the sum of individual risks. This means that the corporation can afford risk taking for individual decisions. Top management, therefore, should take steps to correct such risk-averse behavior in lower management, perhaps by altering its system of rewards and punishments for managers.

Follow-up Exercises

26. Conduct a prior analysis for the portfolio model of Exercise 1. Use the $f(\theta)$ and $U(R)$ given in this section.

27. Construct $U(R)$ for the portfolio model in this section given the following triads:

---

[16] Ralph O. Swalm, "Utility Theory—Insights into Risk Taking," *Harvard Business Review* (November–December 1966).

[17] Ibid., pp. 135–36.

R_1	R_2	CE
9.0............	12.0	10.0
10.0............	12.0	10.5
9.0............	10.5	9.9
9.0............	9.9	9.7
9.0............	9.7	9.5

What type of behavior is exhibited by $U(R)$? Determine $U(D, \theta)$ and conduct a prior analysis using $f(\theta_1) = 0.1$, $f(\theta_2) = 0.5$, $f(\theta_3) = 0.3$, and $f(\theta_4) = 0.1$.

28. Modify the decision tree in Exercise 24 such that all consequences are expressed in terms of utility indices. Use Figure 17–2 as the utility function. (Don't forget the $50,000 cost of experimentation.) Determine $D_B^* = Q(x)$. Is the investment service desirable? Compare to Exercise 20.

29. Construct $U(R)$ and $U(D, \theta)$ for the new product model of Example 17.3 if the triads below are relevant.

R_1	R_2	CE
−2.0.............	5.0	0.5
−2.0.............	0.5	−0.5
0.5.............	5.0	2.5
2.5.............	5.0	3.7
−2.0.............	−0.5	−1.0

Assess the behavioral implications of this preference curve. Modify the decision tree in Exercise 25 accordingly. Don't forget the $100,000 cost of the market survey. Compare prior and preposterior results to what was obtained previously.

30. Construct $U(L)$ and $U(D, \theta)$ for the nuclear power plant model of Example 17.4 if the triads below are relevant. Note that L replaces R in the notation.

L_1	L_2	CE
70.0..............	8,000.1	2,000.0
70.0..............	2,000.0	700.0
70.0..............	700.0	200.0
2,000.0..............	8,000.1	3,000.0
3,000.0..............	8,000.1	4,000.0

Assess the behavioral implications of this dispreference curve. Modify the decision tree in Figure 17–1 accordingly. Compare prior and preposterior results to what was obtained in Section 17.4.

31. The choice of $U_{min} = 0$ and $U_{max} = 1$ for end points on the utility scale makes for the following interpretation of utility: The utility $U(R)$ for a certain payoff R is equivalent to an **indifference probability** (p) for the option of receiving R_{max} with probability p and R_{min} with probability $(1 - p)$. Show this algebraically.

**32. Determine an appropriate *analytic* utility function for the preference curve of Figure 17–2. Try regression analysis for

a. The quadratic, $U = b_0 + b_1R + b_2R^2$.
b. The third degree polynomial, $U = b_0 + b_1R + b_2R^2 + b_3R^3$.
c. The modified exponential, $U = 1 - e^{-bR}$.

Compare estimated values of U based on the analytic function to the values of U in Table 17–17. Which approach do you prefer, analytic utility functions or hand-sketched utility functions? Explain.

17.7 OTHER DECISION STRUCTURES

In this chapter we have focused strictly on discrete and finite decisions and states of nature. This allowed the construction of a payoff, loss, or utility table and the mathematically straightforward development of prior, posterior, and preposterior analyses. In the current section we overview other decision structures of interest.

Continuous States of Nature and Decisions

Textbooks which specialize in decision theory usually include a relatively extensive treatment of various cases where $\{\theta\}$ is continuous and $\{D\}$ is discrete. Various situations arise depending on the probability density function (pdf) specified for θ and the functional form of $R(D, \theta)$ or $L(D, \theta)$. A common case is a *normal* pdf for $f(\theta)$ combined with a *linear* payoff or loss function. In general, the mathematical requirements for these cases include integral calculus and other concepts from mathematical statistics.

The treatment of D as a continuous decision variable introduces another level of mathematical complexity. In this case optimization requires the application of differential calculus or other mathematical programming procedures.

Sequential Decision Processes

In recent years a great deal of effort has been expended in defining and solving sequential (multistage) decision problems. For such processes a time variable is relevant; that is, decisions are made chronologically. The observed process is termed sequential because a decision is followed by a chance event, followed by another decision, followed by another chance event, and so on. Often the occurrences of chance events can be described as Markovian, in which case the decision framework of Section 15.5 can be adapted for what is called a **Markovian sequential decision process.** This is illustrated in Exercise 46 of Chapter 15 on page 619, wherein dynamic programming is used to solve the model.

Without your realizing it, you have already dealt with a special case of sequential decision processes. The type of preposterior analysis exhibited in Figure 17–1 requires the consideration of two sequential decisions (D_5 and D_1, D_2, or D_3) separated in time by the occurence of a chance event (x_1, x_2, or x_3). It follows that the roll-back procedure represents one approach for solving sequential problems.

A second, widely used approach for solving sequential decision problems is **probabilistic dynamic programming.** If you were assigned Chapter 9, then you might have realized (being the whiz that you are) that the backward induction procedure of Section 17.5 is conceptually the same as a backward recursion in dynamic programming. In this case, the stage is indexed on a time variable and the state is a random variable. (See Exercise 45 at the end of this chapter.)

Many real problems are so large that enumerative decision tree procedures and semienumerative dynamic programming procedures are computationally infeasible. For this reason, research interest continues to be expressed in developing efficient algorithms for solving large-scale sequential decision processes.

Game Theory

Game theory represents an analytic approach to decision making involving conflict and cooperation among two or more decision makers.

> It recognizes that conflict arises naturally when various participants have different preferences and that such problems can be studied quantitatively rather than as a mere illness or abnormality which should be cured or rectified. Game theory attempts to abstract those elements which are common and essential to many different competitive situations and to study them by means of the scientific method. It is concerned with finding optimal solutions or stable outcomes when various decision makers have conflicting objectives in mind. In brief, a game consists of players who must choose from a list of alternatives which will then bring about expected outcomes over which the participants may have different preferences. The game model describes in detail the potential payoffs which one expects to occur, and it points out how one should act in order to arrive at the best possible outcome in light of the options open to one's opponents. Game theory attempts to provide a normative guide to rational behavior for a group whose members aim for different goals.[18]

The placement of game theory in this textbook implies that it is a special case of decision theory, whereby a decision maker "plays" against other decision makers rather than against an indifferent state of nature. A strong advocate of game theory, however, would counter that decision theory is a special case of game theory, whereby the set of opposing players is represented by Mother Nature. We suspect that the truth is somewhere in between. Without question, however, game theory is an important area of specialization in OR/MS which is quite distinct from decision theory.

Most introductory textbooks of OR/MS treat the topic of game theory in its simplest form: **two-person, zero-sum games** with no cooperation. Zero-sum refers to a strictly competitive situation whereby what one player loses the other player gains. Real-world interest in game theory, however, is concerned with more than two players, nonzero sum games,

---

[18] William F. Lucas, "An Overview of the Mathematical Theory of Games," *Management Science,* vol. 18, no. 5, pt. 2 (1972), p. 3.

cooperation as a way of life, and sequential (over time) games. Unfortunately, the mathematics for such games are esoteric for the nonspecialist. For these reasons, we have chosen to entirely omit detailed game theory models.

Game theory scenarios have been formulated in diverse fields including economics, management theory, political science, military science, and psychology. For the most part, these models have been *normative* (what ought to be done) rather than *descriptive* (what is done). This in itself is not bad, however, as normative models can serve as an instrument for effecting change. To date, unlike other OR/MS models, game theory models have had a negligible impact with respect to operating decisions; however, their usefulness as a conceptual and insightful framework for structuring certain types of real-world phenomena is generally acknowledged.

17.8 ASSESSMENT

Evidence of the increasing use of decision analysis by major corporations has been accumulating since the early 1960s.[19] For several reasons, the trend is expected to continue:

1. Decision analysis has great potential for effectively structuring decision problems characterized by uncertainty.
2. The pool of managers conversant with decision analysis continues to grow due to M.B.A. and Executive Development Programs.
3. The growing use of the computer by managers (particularly time-sharing) facilitates the computational implementation of decision analysis.

For the most part, problems associated with the effective implementation of decision analysis, as with most OR/MS, are due to organizational, behavioral, and educational issues (see Sections 1.1 and 18.2). Implementation problems are not due to the technological state of the art of decision analysis, as the available tools of analysis appear to outpace the capacity of current management to use them.

Finally, as with all quantitative decision making, the effective use of models requires "good" estimates for parameters and uncontrollable variables (states of nature). If subjective estimates and preferences are to be used at all, however, then it is best to bring them "out of the closet" and into the scrutiny of a structured framework. Therein lies the strength of decision analysis.

SELECTED REFERENCES

Brown, R. V.; Kahr, A. S.; and Peterson, C. *Decision Analysis for the Manager*. New York: Holt, Rinehart and Winston, 1974.

Dyckman, T. R.; Smidt, S.; and McAdams, A. K. *Management Decision Making under Uncertainty*. London: The Macmillan Company, 1969.

[19] See Brown, Kahr, and Peterson, *Decision Analysis,* pp. 61–73 and Rex V. Brown, "Do Managers Find Decision Theory Useful?" *Harvard Business Review* (May–June 1970), pp. 78–89.

De Groot, M. H. *Optimal Statistical Decisions*. New York: McGraw-Hill, Inc., 1970.

Hadley, G. *Introduction to Probability and Statistical Decision Theory*. San Francisco: Holden Day, Inc., 1967.

Halter, A. N., and Dean, G. W. *Decisions under Uncertainty*. Cincinnati: South-Western Publishing Co., 1971.

Newman, J. W. *Management Applications of Decision Theory*. New York: Harper and Row, Inc., 1971.

Raiffa, H. *Decision Analysis*. Reading, Mass.: Addison-Wesley Publishing Co., 1968.

Schlaifer, R. *Analysis of Decisions under Uncertainty*. New York: McGraw-Hill, Inc., 1969.

Weiss, L. *Statistical Decision Theory*. New York: McGraw-Hill, Inc., 1961.

Winkler, R. L. *Introduction to Bayesian Inference and Decisions*. New York: Holt, Rinehart and Winston, 1972.

ADDITIONAL EXERCISES

33. Compare similarities and differences between Markovian decision models (Section 15.5) and models in decision analysis. Use the four components of decision analysis models as a basis for comparison.

34. *Single-Period Inventory Model* Consider an inventory situation whereby an item is to be stocked at the *beginning* of some time period for the purpose of meeting stochastic demand *during* that time period. It is not possible to restock during the period; hence, if demand is greater than the amount stocked, then sales are lost. If more units are stocked than are demanded, however, then items are left over which *must* be disposed of at some salvage value. We are dealing, then, with a perishable product which must be totally renewed at the beginning of the next time period, which implies that decisions can be made in isolated time periods without regard to other time periods, providing that lost sales do not affect subsequent demand distributions. Note that this model is particularly suitable to perishable products. The scenario is a "classic" in inventory theory and is often referred to as the "newsboy" (newsgirl? newsperson?) problem.

   Suppose that a large supermarket chain is in the process of reassessing its inventory policy for ½-gallon containers of milk. The current policy of stocking 2,500 containers at the beginning of the week has caused some concern because of a recent federal ruling that milk is to be taken off display after one week. Each container sells for $0.90 and costs the store $0.60. Unsold containers left over at the end of the week can be sold to a food salvage company for $0.20 per container. The penalty cost for shortages has been assessed at $0.35 per container, which includes lost profit and ill will. A recent analysis of demands for a "pilot" store indicates the probability distribution below.

Weekly Demand	Probability
1,000	0.1
1,500	0.3
2,000	0.4
2,500	0.2

a. Denote unit selling price by p, cost by c, salvage value by s (where $s < c$), and penalty cost by C_p (where $C_p > p\text{-}c$). Define D and θ, and state a general expression for $R(D, \theta)$ in terms of p, c, s, C_p, D, and θ, where R represents weekly "contribution to profit and overhead" in dollars. (Hint: $R(D, \theta)$ requires two expressions, depending on whether $\theta \leq D$ or $\theta > D$.)

b. Construct a payoff table for the stocking alternatives 1,000; 1,500; 2,000; and 2,500 containers. How many containers should be stocked at the beginning of the week? What is the expected savings in contribution to profit and overhead of this optimal policy v. the current policy?

35. Rework the preceding exercise if a carrying cost (C_h) of $0.05 per container per week is assessed on *average* inventory for the week.

36. A time-sharing company has offered its services to the supermarket chain described in Exercise 34. For an estimated $50 per week, each supermarket can access a forecasting program for predicting demand in the coming week. Past experience with this forecasting package shows that, given any realized demand, the probability of a correct forecast is 70 percent; the probabilities of erroneous forecasts, given any realized demand, are approximately evenly distributed among the remaining 30 percent. Does the time-sharing service appear worthwhile for the pilot supermarket? If so, how many containers of milk should be stocked for each possible forecast?

37. In actual practice, it is not necessary to construct the payoff table for the single-period inventory model described in Exercise 34, as it can be proved that D^* is the *smallest* number of units stocked (d) for which the following expression holds:[20]

$$F(d) \geq \frac{p + C_p - c}{p + C_p - s}.$$

The symbols p, C_p, c, and s have been defined in Exercise 34; $F(d)$ represents the cumulative distribution function for demand, that is, the probability that demand is less than or equal to some specific value (d). Confirm that the described decision rule yields the same D^* as in Exercise 34.

38. The decision rule described in the preceding exercise is particularly useful for considering stocking alternatives in increments of one unit when demand is represented by some theoretical probability distribution. Consider a single-period inventory situation whereby a certain type of spare part for a highly technological aircraft is to be stocked for one year. The price is $500, the cost is $400, the salvage value is $1, and the penalty cost is $150.

a. Determine the optimal number of parts to stock if demand is Poisson with mean 5 parts per year.

b. Determine the range in penalty cost outside of which the optimal decision in part (a) changes. Would you say that the optimal decision is sensitive to this parameter?

39. *Forest Management Model* A pulp and paper firm wishes to determine the percentage of timber for the next fiscal year which it will supply itself from company-owned timberlands. Three possible alternatives are under

---

[20] See Hadley, *Introduction to Probability*, p. 170.

consideration: 25-percent internal supply and 75-percent external supply; 50-percent internal and 50-percent external; 75-percent internal and 25-percent external. It is estimated that demand for timber (in thousands of cords) will be 600, 700, or 800 for the year, with respective probabilities 0.3, 0.5, and 0.2. The cost per cord for externally supplied wood has been guaranteed by the supplier at $30 per cord, regardless of the amount purchased. The internal cost to the firm of supplying its own wood is estimated as a convex function of the amount of harvested wood, as indicated below.

	Thousands of Cords Harvested Internally								
	150	175	200	300	350	400	450	525	600
Cost (dollars per cord)......	36	34	32	30	29	29	29	35	40

a. Construct a loss table for this problem in terms of annual cost of supplying wood in millions of dollars. How should the firm supply its wood and what is the expected annual cost?

b. Suppose that the external supplier guarantees prices of $30 or $34 with probabilities 0.6 and 0.4, respectively. What is the optimal decision and associated annual cost for the firm? (Hint: You must redefine θ.)

40. *Environmental Protection Model* The following scenario is based, in part, on a description in *Time,* June 28, 1976, p. 53. Among other duties, a regional office of the Environmental Protection Agency (EPA) is charged with investigating complaints regarding industrial pollution, when "warranted." A complaint is investigated by sending a panel of three experts, collectively called the "proboscis patrol," to the site of the alleged offender. By concensus, the proboscis patrol then renders one of three opinions: low level, medium level, or high level of pollution. (We might note that the human nose has yet to find an electronic "equal" in detecting offending odors.) Following an opinion, the regional director of the EPA then has the option of issuing or not issuing a citation to the offender. Alternatively, the EPA may choose not to investigate the complaint and then make a decision regarding issuance or nonissuance of a citation.

A joint team of economists, ecologists, and management scientists has determined the economic impact to the region of various consequences. If a citation is issued, then the present values of "net pollution costs" are $3 million, $5 million, and $10 million, respectively, should low, medium, or high levels of pollution come to be realized. The equivalent costs for not issuing a citation are 0, 8, and 25 (in millions of dollars). By "net pollution costs" we mean the direct costs associated with pollution (for example, medical illness, purifying water, cleaning buildings, and so forth) plus the costs of altered economic activity as a result of enforcing pollution standards (for example, potential reduction in tax revenues, higher prices for consumer goods, and so forth). For present value purposes, a 20-year planning horizon and an 8 percent per year discount rate have been assumed. It is estimated that the cost of maintaining the proboscis patrol is $50,000 per year, which in present value terms over a 20-year horizon at 8 percent translates into approximately $490,000.

Past experience and judgment indicate that alleged offenders achieve low, medium, and high actual levels of pollution with probabilities 0.5, 0.4, and 0.1, respectively. Also, for any given actual level of pollution, the proboscis patrol has been accurate in predicting the correct level 80 percent of the time and equally wrong in predicting each of the other two levels the remaining 20 percent of the time.

Completely analyze this problem in order to advise the director of the EPA as to (1) whether or not to investigate complaints and (2) whether or not to issue citations depending on the circumstances.

41. Completely analyze the preceding exercise based on the following disutility function: $U(L) = 0.065L - 0.001L^2$.

42. *Single-Stage Capital Investment Model*   An industrial plant is faced with two capital investment alternatives for a planning horizon encompassing the next five years: Modernize the existing plant at a capital cost of $10 million or do not modernize the existing plant. The effect of the capital investment decision is realized through the capacity of the company to operate efficiently and to meet sales demand over the next five years. For example, if market demand over the next five years is high, then a modernized plant can meet projected demand and operate more efficiently. The projected present values of net cash flows (revenues less operating costs) in millions of dollars for the six possible consequences are given here. Probabilities for low, medium, and high demands are estimated as

Demand	Modernize	Do Not Modernize
Low	8	10
Medium	38	30
High	75	50

0.2, 0.5, and 0.3, respectively. Construct an appropriate payoff table and apply the four decision rules with which you are familiar. Relate these decision rules to behavioral prototypes.

43. *Two-Stage Capital Investment Model*   Suppose that the analysis of the capital investment model of the preceding exercise is extended to a second stage (the years 6 through 10). At the beginning of the sixth year, a decision on modernization or no modernization is to be made once again. If the plant was modernized at the beginning of the first year, then the alternative at the beginning of the sixth year is no modernization; however, if modernization was not carried out in the first year, then both options are open once again in the sixth year. Treating this problem as a sequential decision is attractive because one of the chance (experimental) events has occurred by the sixth year. In other words, the company is in a better position to assess subsequent demands. The accompanying table reflects these relationships by indicating the conditional probabilities of demand in Stage 2 given demand in Stage 1.

Demand During First Stage	Demand During Second Stage		
	Low	Medium	High
Low	0.8	0.2	0
Medium	0.1	0.7	0.2
High	0.1	0.3	0.6

The present value of the capital investment for modernizing in the sixth year is estimated as $12 million. The present values of net cash flows in the second stage are projected as indicated.

	Decision in Stage 2	
	---	---
Demand in		Do Not
Stage 2	Modernize	Modernize
Low..........................	9	10
Medium.....................	40	30
High........................	80	50

Using the expected value decision rule, determine the optimal decision for the first year. Specify the decision to be made in the sixth year for each possible demand level during the first five years. (Hint: Draw a decision tree.)

44. *Pipeline Construction Model* The following exercise is a variation of the classical "machine set-up" problem. The installation of an oil pipeline which runs from an oil field to a refinery requires the welding of 1,000 seams. Two alternatives have been specified for conducting the weldings: strictly use a team of ordinary and apprentice welders (B-Team) or use a team of master welders (A-Team) who check and rework (as necessary) the welds of the B-Team. If the B-Team is strictly used, then it is estimated from past experience that 5 percent of the seams will be defective with probability 0.30, or 10 percent will be defective with probability 0.50, or 20 percent will be defective with probability 0.20. However, if the B-Team is followed by the A-Team, then a defective rate of 1 percent is almost certain.

   Material and labor costs are estimated at $400,000 when the B-Team is used strictly, whereas these costs rise to $530,000 when the A-Team is also brought in. Defective seams result in leaks which must be reworked at a cost of $1,200 per seam, which includes the cost of labor and spilled oil but ignores the cost of environmental damage.

   a. Determine the optimal decision and its expected cost. How might environmental damage be taken into account?

   b. A worker on the pipeline with a Bayesian inclination (from long years of wagering on sporting events) has proposed that management consider x-ray inspections of five randomly selected seams *following* the work of the B-Team. Such an inspection would identify defective seams, which would provide management with more information for the decision on whether or not to bring in the A-Team. It costs $5,000 to inspect the five seams. Financially, is it worthwhile to carry out the inspection? If so, then what decision should be made for each possible result of the inspection?

**45. *Probabilistic Dynamic Programming for Sequential Decision Problems* In Section 17.7 we mentioned that probabilistic dynamic programming can be used to solve sequential decision problems. In fact, you might have already done just that by having solved the Markovian sequential decision model in Exercise 46 of Chapter 15 (page 619). The same table structure as was used in Chapter 9 can be applied to the solution of probabilistic dynamic programs with discrete decisions and discrete states. Conceptually, there are only two differences between the deterministic case and the probabilistic case. In the latter, the states are random variables from defined probability distributions; additionally, the recursive equation is given by

$$f_i = r_i + E[f^*_{i-1}],$$

where, as before, r_i is the return in Stage i and f_i is the cumulative return through stage i. Now, however, the optimal cumulative return through the preceding stage, f_{i-1}^*, is an *expected value* and denoted by $E[f_{i-1}^*]$. Its value is based on the probability distribution associated with states in stage i-1. Thus,

$$E[f_{i-1}^*] = \sum_{\text{all } s_{i-1}} f_{i-1}^* \cdot g(s_{i-1}),$$

where $g(s_{i-1})$ represents the discrete probability distribution for states in stage i-1.

Solve the two-stage problem of Figure 17–1 by dynamic programming. (Hint: Use a backward recursion based on the diagram.)

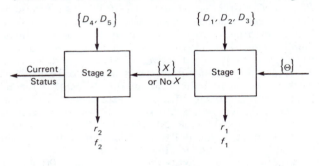

18

Decisions, Implementation, and Control

FOR MANY OF YOU, coming to the last chapter is a distinct pleasure, to be exceeded only by completing the chapter and your course in operations research. We will try to move you quickly toward that pleasure. Our primary purpose here is to briefly review the decision-making paradigm and to focus upon the very important issues of decision making and preparing for change, implementation, and control.

18.1 MAKING THE DECISION

The Decision-Making Paradigm Revisited

In Chapter 1 we presented an eight-step paradigm for decision making that we believe provides a very useful perspective for your course in operations research. Rather than repeating substantial portions of this description, our emphasis here will be on synthesis and reinforcement.

Take 30 minutes (by the clock) to review the paradigm as presented in Chapter 1. Start with the brief statement of the eight steps on page 3, and make sure you review Figures 1–2, 1–3, and 1–4. Key words that you should understand include criteria, surrogates, congruence, user-designer concept, evolution, variables, parameters, constraints, objective function, model building process, level of aggregation, system of measurements and scales, management information system, model validation, solution validation, satisficing, suboptimization, and decision rules.

We have contended from the outset that quantitative analysis can be of considerable assistance in making better decisions. The decision-making paradigm provides a logical framework for integrating quantitative methods into the decision-making process. We have commented frequently on the evolutionary nature of model construction and the fact that in an actual application there may be considerable cycling through the steps of the paradigm before a satisfactory solution is identified. At each step in the process, and with each iteration through the stages of the paradigm, there is continual reference back to the overall goals or criteria against which the final solution will be evaluated. We have also stressed the *user-designer concept* as an approach which will offer greater assurances of implementing better solutions.

One Input to the Decision Process

A decision maker often has access to a great deal of information at the time the final decision is made. This information constitutes a set of *inputs* for consideration. The nature of these inputs ranges from those which are purely subjective (such as one's "gut feelings"), to those which are derived through quantitative analysis, to those which relate to other issues (such as political, ethical, or behavioral considerations). Implicitly, the decision maker assigns a subjective weight to each input which expresses its significance. Alternatively, one may think of these inputs as criteria which must be weighted in making a final decision.

It should be clear that the recommendation based on an OR study constitutes *one* input to the decision process. In some cases it may be the primary input; in others it may be one of many. In some cases it may be a highly significant input; in others, it may be of little value. In some cases its monetary benefit exceeds its cost of implementation; in other cases it does not. Thus, decision makers who are receiving quantitatively derived inputs must be capable of assessing their significance.

Several factors can facilitate one's ability to assess the "significance" of quantitatively derived inputs. A person with a technical educational background is more likely to understand the key aspects of quantitative solution procedures and scientific methodology. In addition, this person is in a better position to bridge the communications gap which often exists between technical specialists and nontechnical decision makers. At this point, *you* should find yourself in a position to be a more effective user of quantitative inputs. *You* should be able to ask the "right" questions of OR analysts, to critique assumptions which have been made in the analysis, and to be generally familiar with the types of quantitative tools which were employed.

Participating "in the evolutionary process" is another way of improving one's ability to assess inputs. This is the user-designer concept.

Use of Management Science/Operations Research

By now we should have convinced you that MS/OR modeling can be effective in "capturing the essence" of reality, clarifying complex relationships, and providing a "laboratory" for exploring policy implications and answering "What if. . . ?" types of questions. The primary justification for the use of MS/OR, however, is *cost effectiveness;* that is, the difference between the benefits of using MS/OR and the costs of developing and implementing MS/OR solutions can exceed that of any other approach. This is particularly true for one-time major projects (for example, construction of the Superdome, selection of major capital investments, and so forth) and on-going projects (for example, production and inventory control systems).

Conversely, MS/OR should not be used when it is not cost effective. (For example, the cost of collecting data for the model may exceed any potential monetary benefits from using the model, or an alternative approach may be more cost effective, or decisions need to be made within a time span which is too short for a legitimate MS/OR analysis.) To illustrate, consider the franchised outlets for a national food chain. The development of a computerized inventory control system exclusively for one outlet would probably result in adverse cost effectiveness because of high developmental costs; however, the development of this system by the national organization for use by all outlets may result in substantial net benefits for the entire organization.

18.2 IMPLEMENTATION

Operations research survived the "honeymoon" period during the 50s and 60s in which a number of our OR forefathers were preoccupied with the glories of the newly developed quantitative techniques. Exquisite mathematical models were painstakingly constructed at huge expense to organizations, and top management patiently waited for the "word" to come down which would lead their firms to the "promised land." Unfortunately, many firms never reached the promised land and management's opinion of their "prophets" began to sour. The fault must be shared by both OR specialists and management. In some instances, the OR analysts developed solutions which were either inappropriate or incapable of being implemented. In other cases, technically valid solutions were developed, but management as well as OR personnel failed to properly prepare the organization for the change which was associated with implementation of the solution.

Both parties have learned some useful lessons, and they should realize now that implementation of change within organizations not only is a critical aspect in the process but also represents a delicate and sensitive stage in which our colleagues in the behavioral sciences can be of considerable assistance.

Preparing the Organization for Change

A major implication of decision making is change in the operating environment for at least one level of an organization. Major policy decisions can have far-reaching implications. A decision as simple as changing the frequency with which raw materials are purchased has ramifications which may affect the purchasing, receiving, production, and accounting functions within the buyer's organization and the sales, shipping, purchasing, warehousing, and accounting functions of the seller's organization.

The complexity of behavioral change is very often underestimated by decision makers and analysts. In implementing a solution, there is a clear need to go beyond convincing key decision makers that results from a model are useful: Ultimate users of the proposed system or procedures are of critical importance to successful implementation. Without active user support, potentially excellent systems may fail. Alienation of workers, as exemplified in the extreme by the General Motors Lordstown crises of the early 70s, is the kind of implementation environment that can occur. Clearly implementation of *any* change in this type of environment is difficult if not impossible.

It has been our experience (as well as that of many others) that organizational climates change over time; what may be possible to implement at one point in time may not have been possible at an earlier date. To some extent, the climate is a function of perceived necessity or urgency, but there is even more to it; one needs to crawl before walking and walk before running. Thus, logical transition states need to be explicitly considered in implementation of organizational change.

A closely related issue concerns the *commitment* to a problem made by all levels in the organization. Commitment means more than a pat on the back and stated support from management. It even means substantially more than a financial commitment. Too many organizations (including governments) have erroneously concluded that once funds have been allocated to a particular project, the project will succeed. For many problems, the solution involves changes in the way decisions are to be made and in who is to make them. Since decisions are implemented by people, it follows that those people whose decision making will be changed will best understand the reasons for change through the process of involvement. Moreover, the key players in implementing change usually need to be provided *released time* in order to actively participate in the project. Simply adding the project on to an existing set of job activities can seriously thwart implementation goals.

This involvement of key players becomes more important as the scope of the problem crosses organizational boundaries. The solution can easily imply change in the relative delegation of authority; decisions formerly made by individuals in isolation may now require consultation or compromise. The decisions may in fact at some point be "made by the system" through sets of decision rules.

Education

Perhaps you will think we are showing our bias in stressing the critical need for education if implementation involves more than a trivial change in the organization; however, many consultants involved in implementing complex systems have emphasized the importance of educating users about system design. The educational job is almost always underestimated, and the need for redundancy and repetition is amazing to those not familiar with education, retention, and the difference between understanding in a detached way v. integrating that knowledge into present decision-making practice.

Dedication to a thorough program of education recognizes explicitly the "here to there" problem. It is simply too easy to expect an environment to change because management wishes it to change. Even if operating personnel agree with the proposed changes, they have to see how these changes are to be implemented and exactly what changes are required in their own decision making.

A very good way for this to be accomplished is to recognize a fundamental "law" of organization: All managers can see clearly the need for educating those *below* them organizationally; some can see the need for educating those *above* them; very few can see the need for educating themselves. By involving themselves intimately in the education of their subordinates, managers enhance their own education.

Plunkett Hospital Equipment Company[1]

The Plunkett Hospital Equipment Company is a midwestern company manufacturing hospital furniture. Sales in 1976 were approximately $50 million, and growing at about 15 percent per year. The company is well-managed, having good basic product design, methods, materials control systems, quality control, and so on. The growth in sales, however, indicated that major expansion would be required; materials flow control would become increasingly difficult in the future and the present manual systems would become overloaded. Moreover, new product lines were becoming more technically complex, incorporating expanded options of electronic monitoring equipment and other patient-care innovations.

The Vice President of Manufacturing became convinced that a new system of materials flow control was necessary, and that MRP (Chapter 11) was the way to go. The president and several key officers attended an intensive three-day education session on MRP. Thereafter, a consultant was brought into the company to help implement MRP.

The climate for change was carefully assessed as a first step. The consultant found that prior work in data base design was supportive, that reporting systems for shop floor conditions were in place, that accurate data were being transmitted, and that a program of security was underway. More importantly, it was found that the personnel were ready for change, there were no illusions about the task ahead, the resources were ready to be committed, and whatever time was considered necessary would be forthcoming.

An operating group of 15 people was formed, chaired by the Vice President of Manufacturing. Included were individuals from sales, customer service, marketing research, purchasing, finance, systems, manufacturing, engineering, and production control. The group devoted one day per week to meetings (primarily education) and significant portions of the rest of their time to data collection and analyses for the weekly meetings.

Progress toward the objective of a fully operational MRP system was swift and sure, with the desired results being achieved. The point here, however, is not MRP; it is the change environment, and how that en-

---

[1] Disguised name.

vironment was carefully prepared and monitored. This particular company can be contrasted with others who were equally desirous of the end results, as aware of the benefits, and who even spent the money. Without the right environment, however, the changes simply did not occur.

Planning for Change

Implementation is the phase during which the right people must stand up and be counted. It follows that it is crucial to identify these "right people and *plan* how and by what means they *will* stand up to be counted. All of the prior stages in the decision-making paradigm are of no consequence if successful implementation does not occur, and one must remember that the value of a solution cannot be tested unless implementation is achieved.

To a considerable degree, improving the implementation "batting average" involves planning based upon understanding of the *behavioral sciences*. Individual and group decision-making processes, cognitive styles, reactions to uncertainties, educational requirements and individual as well as organizational ability to change authority relationships are representative issues.

The user-designer concept attempts to deal with these issues by involving the key players deeply in the model-building and implementation process. These users will be more likely to produce decision alternatives that are capable of being implemented, and timing can be planned on a basis which is consistent with organizational realities.

In developing an implementation plan the goal is to have all individuals who will be affected by the new solution (either directly or indirectly) engaged in the process. Their participation induces a favorable environment, enables the cultivation of cooperative attitudes and relationships, and reduces the likelihood of misunderstanding, anxiety, and efforts to sabotage the new system. All plans for implementation must have timetables that are consistent with achieving these characteristics.

As implied earlier in this chapter, it is essential that OR personnel follow through on projects and be involved in the implementation stages. For most projects, there is a good likelihood that at least minor adjustments in the solution will need to be made at the time of implementation. Since OR personnel possess the greatest understanding of the technical aspects of the solution, they are the logical persons to be making judgments regarding technical modifications.

Whenever possible, the implementation plan should allow for pretesting the solution. This is especially important when the solution involves widespread changes in an organization. Pretesting the solution on a small scale allows one to work out the "bugs" prior to a complete program of implementation. Marketing researchers utilize this approach regularly by selecting test markets in which to experiment with new products or promotion strategies.

The implementation plan also should provide the capability of "manual override"; that is, the user should be able to make a decision without the use of the MS/OR system. This is particularly helpful in the initial stages of implementation if the user is not fully "comfortable" with the new system. Experience indicates that the frequency of manual overrides declines over time.[2]

Manual overrides and pretesting not only facilitate implementation procedures, but also provide feedback regarding the performance of the new solution. Actual benefits can be compared with expected benefits to determine the relative success of the new program. If actual benefits are not as great as expected, then reasons must be sought which provide an explanation. This brings us to the issue of control.

18.3   CONTROL

The final concept that we want to emphasize is that of control, or system monitoring, after an on-going solution has been implemented. In this section we discuss why control systems are necessary, the nature of a feedback control system, and the importance of management information systems in this stage.

It's a Dynamic Environment!

The most significant reasons for control systems are to make sure that the implemented system is living up to expectations and that the solution maintains continuing validity over time. Once the new system is in place and is performing satisfactorily, the need for control arises because the future cannot be predicted with certainty, because of unexpected combinations of factors (such as high inventories simultaneously with stockouts), and because the conditions leading to the need for the original decision change *because* of the decision. Changes which can occur in a system or model may be classified as changes in:

1.   The importance of criteria.
2.   The degree of control over decision variables.
3.   The values of parameters and uncontrollable variables.
4.   The constraints on the system.
5.   The structure of the system.

The first classification of change simply recognizes that the measures of performance which are used in developing the new solution may not always retain the same level of importance. Lower-level criteria may, over time, replace those originally deemed most important, or new criteria may be identified which supplant those in the original criterion set. During the gasoline shortage of 1974, the normal criteria used by firms or individuals in selecting and purchasing gasoline (minimize cost, maximize quality of gasoline, maximize level of customer service, and so forth) were supplanted in most instances by a criterion which sought to maximize the availability of gasoline. This was true for both customers and suppliers.

The second category of change simply suggests that internal and external factors may indeed change over time. A firm which operates within

---

[2] See J. L. Bishop, Jr., "Experience with a Successful System for Forecasting and Inventory Control," *Operations Research,* vol. 22, no. 6 (1974), pp. 1224–31, and R.E.D. Woolsey, "On Doing Good Things and Dumb Things in Production and Inventory Control," *Interfaces,* vol. 5, no. 3 (1975), pp. 65–67.

a regulated industry, such as the airline industry, may find that its ability to make certain types of decisions changes as the degree of industry regulation changes. An example of this is the price that a firm charges for its goods or services. Collective bargaining may dramatically change the discretion which management has in making decisions about its employees. Similarly, the general state of the economy can have a widespread influence over what is controllable. For example, the ability to float a bond issue (think of New York City in 1975) and the expected yield from the financial program are subject, in part, to economic conditions.

Third, the values of parameters and uncontrollable variables are very likely to change, even over the short run. A good example of this is the effect of a changing technology. The technology in manufacturing electronic calculators underwent a rapid change in which unit-cost parameters, and consequently price decision variables, decreased significantly over a short period of time. The costs of a firm's factors of production may change, causing modifications in objective function and/or constraint relationships.

Fourth, the constraints on a system are likely to change over time. That which was constraining in the original problem may not be so in the future. As an example, the discovery of new and cheaper energy sources might eliminate an energy constraint, or at least reduce the extent to which energy is a constraint. On the other hand, conditions which were not constraining originally may later become significant. Recent legislation regarding pollution standards has created constraints for companies which previously had none. Companies are required to alter their operating policies so as to meet both federal and state requirements on solid waste disposal and air pollutant emissions.

Finally, the structure of the system itself may change. A merger with another firm—say, a major supplier—may generate significant changes in both the structure and operation of the two component firms. A federal mandate for socialized medicine would cause significant changes in the health care delivery system.

Feedback Control Systems

The existence of a dynamic environment raises the need for an effective control system; otherwise, the implemented solution will degrade over time. In effect, a control system will detect the previously discussed changes and make appropriate adjustments in the solution. Notice that the act of making decisions in itself *causes* conditions to change. For example, if inventories are too high, it would not be uncommon to put pressure on the sales force, who in turn may increase sales efforts, which could increase sales, which could decrease inventories.

What we have just described is **feedback control.** In a general sense, an on-going view of the decision-making process can be diagrammed as in Figure 18–1. At the left-hand side is the decision-making process, as described by the eight-step paradigm. This process yields a decision or set of decision outputs, which in turn leads to results. Information channels are used to gain knowledge of the results which are transformed

FIGURE 18–1

Decision Making as a Feedback Control Process

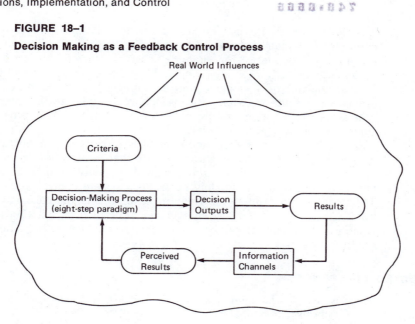

into a set of perceptions about the actual results, which act as an input to further decision making. Notice that this process interacts continuously with the real world; the real-world influences affect each and every aspect of the process.

In order to have an effective feedback control system, certain elements are essential. There is a need for both a system and a method of measurement. There is also a need for a method of comparison between planned and actual results. In addition, there must exist an activating mechanism which responds to comparisons which fall outside of predetermined performance tolerances. This mechanism signals to the decision-making authority that the process is out of control and that there is need for corrective action. Analytic methods for implementing feedback control include **systems dynamics models** (Chapter 13) and **optimal dynamic control models.**[3] We now turn our attention to the information channels which collect and transmit system information.

Management Information Systems

For many management problems, decisions must be based upon aggregations of large data bases. Implied are computers and computerized information systems.

A computerized **Management Information System (MIS)** can be viewed as a set of computer software and hardware for converting raw data into information which is useable for management. For instance, disaggregated data (for example, costs of raw materials or sales of single products for

---

[3] See, for example, Gene K. Groff and John F. Muth, *Operations Management Analysis for Decisions* (Homewood, Ill.: Richard D. Irwin, 1972), chap. 9.

specific time periods) can be stored on disk files for access by remote computer terminals through computer programs which allow desired aggregation of the data (for example, cost parameters for an LP model or demands for a forecasting model). The MIS also may contain programs for the analysis of aggregated and disaggregated data. Some of the programs are unique or special-purpose (how to compute the payroll) and others are part of a general-purpose "model bank" (linear programming, statistical routines, and so forth).

The effectiveness of feedback control is directly dependent upon MIS design. In fact, we can categorically state that information is the *medium of control;* the timely flow and imaginative analysis of well-chosen information aggregates ultimately determines system control and evolution. The provision of "timely information flows," "imaginative analysis," and "well-chosen aggregates" is what makes MIS such an exciting and challenging field today. However, all of this is another course and another book!

SELECTED REFERENCES

Anthony, R. N. *Planning and Control Systems, A Framework for Analysis.* Cambridge, Mass.: Harvard University Press, 1965.

Beer, Stafford. *Decision and Control.* New York: John Wiley & Sons, Inc., 1966.

Huysmans, J. *The Implementation of Operations Research.* New York: John Wiley & Sons, Inc., 1970.

McCarthy, D. S.; Minichiello, R. J.; and Curran, J. R. *Business Policy and Strategy: Concepts and Readings.* Homewood, Ill.: Richard D. Irwin, Inc., 1975, chaps. 7–9.

McFarlan, F. W.; Nolan, R. L.; and Norton, D. P. *Information Systems Administration.* New York: Holt, Rhinehart and Winston, Inc., 1973.

Mockler, Robert J. *The Management Control Process.* New York: Appleton-Century Crofts, 1971.

Newman, W. H. *Constructive Control Design and Use of Control Systems.* Englewood Cliffs, N.J.: Prentice-Hall, Inc., 1975.

Tannenbaum, A. S. *Control in Organizations.* New York: McGraw-Hill Book Co., 1968.

Thierauf, R. J. *Systems Analysis and Design of Real-Time Management Information.* Englewood Cliffs, N.J.: Prentice-Hall, 1975.

Appendix A   Review of Probability, Estimation, and Forecasting

ALTHOUGH PROBABILITY and statistics are not usually considered fields of specialization in operations research, their concepts are utilized so extensively both by theoreticians and practitioners that it is worthwhile to review some highlights. We stress "review" and "highlights."

This Appendix reviews basic probability, probability distributions, statistical inference, and forecasting. The review obviously cannot replace a two-semester statistics course; our objectives are to emphasize the use of these concepts in decision making through operations research and to lay a foundation for the chapters which directly utilize probability.

Essentially, OR's use for probability and statistics falls into two categories. First, the theory of probability plays a significant role in the derivation of all stochastic or probabilistic models. For example, probability distribution theory plays an integral part in the derivation of stochastic inventory models (Chapter 11), queuing models (Chapter 12), Markov processes (Chapter 15), and decision theory (Chapter 17).

Second, the utilization of OR requires the estimation of parameters and uncontrollable variables—both for the deterministic models and for the stochastic models. Procedures for effecting this step of data collection (Step 4 of the paradigm in Chapter 1) include **sample survey methods, estimation** (including **regression analysis**) in inferential statistics, and statistical **forecasting.**

We cannot overemphasize the OR analyst's need for data collection tools. By and large the collection of viable data has not received proper emphasis from both practitioners and (especially) teachers of OR. We hope this Appendix will rectify this deficiency. Why the importance? Because the most elegant OR model is only as useful as the data that drive it. (At this time, you might find it informative to reread Section 1.5.)

A.1 BASIC CONCEPTS IN PROBABILITY

Experiments and Events

A **random experiment** is a process of observation which can be repeated and which has two or more results (**outcomes** or **sample points**) that are affected by chance factors. A **sample space** (S) is the set of all possible outcomes in the experiment, an **event** (E_i) is a defined subset of S, and the **complement** of an event (E_i') consists of all outcomes not in E_i. Figure A–1 illustrates these concepts for an M.B.A. class of 100 students (sample points). In this case the experiment consists of selecting a student's file and observing (classifying) the attributes "entrance examination score" and "academic performance." The set E_1 consists of students whose scores on the GMAT examination were greater than 550 (60 out of 100 students). The set E_2 represents those students whose undergraduate academic grade point average is greater than 3.25 (65 out of 100 students). Note that E_1' has 40 outcomes and E_2' has 35 outcomes.

Another experiment might be defined as rolling a die and observing the

FIGURE A–1

Sample Space for M.B.A. Class

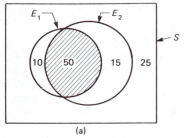

(a)

Venn Diagram

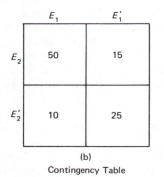

(b)

Contingency Table

E_1 = Student with GMAT score > 550.
E_2 = Student with grade point average > 3.25.

face that comes up; the sample space has six outcomes, or $S = (1, 2, 3, 4, 5, 6)$. Two possible events are "the maximum value," $E_1 = (6)$, and "three or less," $E_2 = (1, 2, 3)$, as indicated in Figure A–2.

Two events are said to be **mutually exclusive** if they cannot occur simultaneously in the same experiment. E_1 and E_2 are mutually exclusive in the die experiment but not in the M.B.A. experiment. A set of events is said to be **collectively exhaustive** if the outcomes represented by the set include all possible points in the sample space. E_1 and E_2 are not collectively exhaustive events in the die experiment because of their failure to account for the outcomes 4 and 5.

The **alternative event** $(E_1 \text{ or } E_2)$ is the event consisting of outcomes in either E_1 or E_2 or both. In set theory, the alternative event $(E_1 \text{ or } E_2)$ is represented by the *union* of E_1 and E_2. Thus $(E_1 \text{ or } E_2)$ can be repre-

FIGURE A–2

Sample Space for Die Experiment

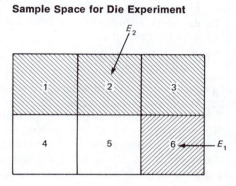

sènted by 75 outcomes in the M.B.A. experiment and by the outcomes $(1, 2, 3, 6)$ in the die experiment.

The **joint event** $(E_1 \text{ and } E_2)$, represented by the *intersection* between two events, consists of outcomes common to both events. Thus the joint event $(E_1 \text{ and } E_2)$ consists of 50 outcomes in the M.B.A. experiment (shaded region in Figure A–1a) and $(E_1 \text{ and } E_2) = \phi$, the *null set,* in the die experiment.

A **compound random experiment** is two or more random experiments performed in succession and its resulting event is termed a **compound event.** For example, three successive rolls of the die is a compound experiment which could result in the compound event E_1 and E_2 and E_2. Can you think of a compound experiment and event for the M.B.A. example?

Assignment of Probabilities to Single Events

The probability of an event is simply the likelihood of the occurrence of that event. When you conclude that the probability of flipping a balanced coin and obtaining the event "head" is 0.5, you really mean that on the average, over many flips of the coin, 50 percent of the flips will result in heads. Probabilities can assume values between 0 and 1, where a value of 0 implies certainty of nonoccurrence of an event and a value of 1 implies certainty of occurrence of the event.

Single events can be assigned probabilities in one of three ways: **a priori** (sometimes termed classical, predetermined, logical, or axiomatic), **empirical** (or relative frequency), and **subjective.** If the possible outcomes in E_i are known beforehand and if the outcomes in S are collectively exhaustive, mutually exclusive, and equally likely, then the probability that an event (E_i) occurs can be determined a priori as

$$P(E_i) = \frac{\text{Number of outcomes in } E_i}{\text{Number of outcomes in } S}. \qquad (A.1)$$

For example, $P(E_2) = \frac{3}{6}$ in the die experiment and $P(E_1) = \frac{60}{100}$ if a file is selected at random from among the 100 files in the M.B.A. experiment.

If outcomes are not equally likely and/or if it is not practical or possible to draw up a collectively exhaustive list of outcomes, then an experiment can be performed n times *under identical conditions.* In this case the empirical probability of an event is defined as

$$P(E_i) = \lim_{n \to N} (f/n) \qquad (A.2)$$

where f is the frequency of occurrence of E_i and where the sample size n approaches some maximum value N (which could be infinity). The probability of rolling a "1" with an unbalanced die, the probability that an American male of age 45 will live to be 55, the probability that an M.B.A. student taking the GMAT examination in 1976 scored above 600, and the probability that more than 50 units of a product will be demanded in one week are all examples of probabilities which could be estimated using the relative frequency definition. In actual practice, the critical issues are in satisfying conditions of "identical experiments" and of sufficient sample size. We will see that the sample size issue can be resolved by estimating the standard error of the sampling distribution.

The third approach to the assignment of probabilities is to use subjective opinion. Although this approach might not appear as elegant as a priori or relative frequency, for many kinds of problems it is very appropriate. This procedure allows for the translation of the experience and feelings of the decision maker into an estimate of the likelihood of occurrence of an event. This form of "educated guessing" can be effective in actual practice, for example, determining odds for sporting events ("Jimmy the Greek"?) and the estimation of success levels for new products by brand managers.

The probabilities for mutually exclusive alternative events can be determined by the **Rule of Addition:**

$$P(E_1 \text{ or } E_2 \text{ or } \ldots \text{ or } E_k) = \sum_{i=1}^{k} P(E_i). \qquad (A.3)$$

If the events are not mutually exclusive, then the probability for two alternative events is

$$P(E_1 \text{ or } E_2) = P(E_1) + P(E_2) - P(E_1 \text{ and } E_2). \qquad (A.4)$$

For the M.B.A. experiment, $P(E_1 \text{ or } E_2) = 0.60 + 0.65 - 0.50 = 0.75$, and, for the die experiment, $P(E_1 \text{ or } E_2) = \frac{1}{6} + \frac{3}{6} = \frac{2}{3}$ and $P(E_1' \text{ or } E_2) = \frac{5}{6} + \frac{3}{6} - \frac{3}{6} = \frac{5}{6}$. Can you verify these results using a *Venn diagram* approach? (See Figure A–1a.)

The **marginal probability** of an event is simply the probability of the event. In the M.B.A. example, the probability of selecting a student having an undergraduate grade point average above 3.25, or $P(E_2)$, is 0.65. Note that this probability can be expressed opposite E_2 in the right-hand "margin" of the *contingency table* of Figure A–1b.

The **conditional probability** of E_i relative to E_j (that is, the probability of E_i given the occurrence of E_j) is defined as

$$P(E_i|E_j) = \frac{P(E_j \text{ and } E_i)}{P(E_j)} . \tag{A.5}$$

For the M.B.A. example, given that a student has scored above 550 on the GMAT Examination, what is the probability that the student had an undergraduate grade point average above 3.25? In other words, given E_1 what is the probability of E_2? According to (A.5),

$$\begin{aligned}
P(E_2|E_1) &= \frac{P(E_1 \text{ and } E_2)}{P(E_1)} \\
&= 0.50/0.60 \\
&= \tfrac{5}{6} \\
&= 0.83.
\end{aligned}$$

Carefully note that knowledge of E_1 has altered the probability of E_2; that is, the conditional probability is different from the marginal probability for this example.

The probability of a **joint event** for a single experiment is simply the probability that both E_1 and E_2 occur simultaneously in the same experiment; for example, $P(E_1 \text{ and } E_2) = 0.5$ in the M.B.A. example.

Assignment of Probabilities to Compound Events

Events can be classified as being either statistically **independent** or statistically **dependent.** When events are independent, the occurrence (or nonoccurrence) of any one event in no way affects the probabilities of the others. Examples of states of statistical independence include successive flips of a coin, rolls of dice, and sampling with replacement (such as drawing a card from a deck). Under statistical dependence, the probability of an event is related to or affected by the occurrence or nonoccurrence of other events. With certain types of illnesses, the probability of survival often depends upon the number of days survived since contracting the disease. The likelihood of having your birthdate selected *next* in the former military draft lottery was dependent upon the number of birthdates selected previously.

For a compound experiment, the probability of a joint or compound event is given by solving for the numerator in the right-hand side of (A.5); that is,

$$P(E_j \text{ and } E_i) = P(E_j) \cdot P(E_i|E_j). \tag{A.6}$$

The presence of a conditional term in (A.6) implies that the events E_i and E_j are dependent, or the occurrence of one event affects or alters the probability of the other event. The usual example of this dependence is sampling "without" replacement. Thus, in the M.B.A. example, removal of the file for a student having a GPA over 3.25 alters the probability that the random draw of the next file is for a student with a GPA over 3.25, unless the first file is returned before the second is drawn. If two files are removed without replacement and the first file indicates the occurrence of E_2, then the probability that the second file also yields E_2 is not $P(E_2)$ but $P(E_2$ in the second experiment $\mid E_2$ in the first experiment), so according to (A.6)

$$P(E_2 \text{ and } E_2) = (65/100) \cdot (64/99).$$

If the events are not dependent, then (A.6) can be generalized by the **Multiplication Rule:**

$$P(E_1 \text{ and } E_2 \text{ and } \ldots \text{ and } E_k) = P(E_1) \cdot P(E_2) \cdot (\ldots) \cdot P(E_k)$$

$$= \prod_{i=1}^{k} P(E_i). \tag{A.7}$$

For example, the events in our compound die experiment of three rolls are independent so

$$P(E_1 \text{ and } E_2 \text{ and } E_2) = (1/6) \cdot (3/6) \cdot (3/6).$$

Follow-up Exercises

1. For the M.B.A. example, determine $P(E_1')$, $P(E_2)$, $P(E_2')$, $P(E_1' \text{ and } E_2')$, and $P(E_1' \text{ or } E_2')$ in a single experiment; for a compound experiment of drawing three files at random, determine the probability that all three are of students having scored below 550 on the GMAT.

2. For the die example, find the probability of (a) rolling four successive aces; (b) $P(E_1' \text{ or } E_2')$ in a single roll; and (c) $P(E_1 \mid E_2')$ in a single roll.

A.2 RANDOM VARIABLES AND PROBABILITY DISTRIBUTIONS

For most random experiments, interest is centered not on the individual sample points of the sample space but on some value associated with the attribute being measured. For instance, a market researcher might be interested in the probability that, out of n customers who purchase a particular type of product, p purchase brand $Y;$ analysis of an inventory system would consider the demand per time period (d) over the next n periods and the variability in that demand; and a study of emergency room operations in a hospital might center around the distribution of arrivals per unit time (a) and the distribution of times to serve patients (s). Attributes which assume numerical values based on the outcome of a random experiment, as in the examples above, are termed **random** or **stochastic variables.** In these instances, we need to be able to estimate probabilities that specific values will occur, such as the probability of selling 20 units next period. Also we are concerned with ranges such as the probability that sales next period will be between 15 and 25. We do this with probability distributions which, given some value for the random variable (x), permit the assignment of probabilities by the function $f(x)$.

Discrete Random Variables and Probabilty Mass Functions

If the sample space contains a countably infinite or finite number of sample points, then it is termed a **discrete sample space.** Variables defined on discrete sample spaces are identified as **discrete random variables,** that is, random variables which assume integer or discrete values. Conversely, a **continuous sample space** consists of elements which are uncountably infinite, and variables defined on them are termed **continuous random variables.** That is, for some kinds of experiments outcomes are restricted to certain values, such as 4 or 5 in rolling a die but not 4.3. For other experiments, the values, the time to run 100 yards or the diameter of a shaft, are only restricted by measurement equipment. In the illustrations above, p is discrete, d can be either discrete or continuous (for example, units or pounds), a is discrete, and s is continuous.

Example A.1   Emergency Room Arrivals

A study has been undertaken to improve the emergency room operation of a hospital. In Chapter 12 this project is treated as a waiting line or queuing model. For now, consider the collection of data pertaining to arrivals during "off-peak" hours. Assume that adjustments have been made for seasonal variations and other identifiable "noise," such as a natural disaster, a train derailment, and so forth.[1] (Can you guess why this must be done?)

Let the discrete random variable X represent the number of arrivals per hour, x a particular value of X, $f(x)$ the probability of x arrivals per hour, and $F(x)$ the probability of x or less arrivals each hour. Table A–1 illustrates sample arrival data for 100 time periods of one hour each. For the 100 time periods under observation, seven or more arrivals per hour never occurred (although theoretically the sample space contains a finite number of points given by the population of the world). Carefully note that the process of data "deseasonalizing" and other "smoothing" is undertaken in order to ensure that trials in the experiment (time periods) are as uniform as possible

---

[1] Raw data can be "deseasonalized" by dividing the value for each observation by its corresponding seasonal index. Methods for constructing seasonal indices are explained in textbooks on managerial, business, or economic statistics. Adjusting data for identifiable random movements can be accomplished by various ad hoc procedures; for example, if on a given day excessive arrivals at an emergency room can be traced to a local airplane disaster, then the number of victims involved in the disaster can be subtracted from the total number of arrivals on that day.

TABLE A–1

Distribution of Emergency Room Arrivals

x	Number of One-Hour Time Periods	$f(x)$	$F(x)$
0..	10	0.10	0.10
1..	28	0.28	0.38
2..	29	0.29	0.67
3..	16	0.16	0.83
4..	10	0.10	0.93
5..	6	0.06	0.99
6..	1	0.01	1.00
Total.......................	100	1.00	—

so that the relative frequency definition of probability is valid. The question of whether or not $n = 100$, is large enough will be taken up subsequently.

The ordered pairs given by x, $f(x)$ in Table A–1 represent a **discrete probability distribution.** Thus, for example, the probability that the random variable X takes on a value of 3; that is, $P(X = 3)$, is given by $f(3) = 0.16$. For a discrete random variable, $f(x)$ is termed a **probability mass function (pmf),** a designation which becomes clear if the plotted points for the probability functions in Figure A–3 are perceived as "masses."

Notice that we use the convention of an upper-case symbol for the random variable itself (X) and a lower-case symbol for specific values that the random variable can take on (termed **random variates**).

In general, the pmf is defined as

$$f(x) = P(X = x) \tag{A.8}$$

such that the following two conditions are met:

$$0 \leq f(x_i) \leq 1, \quad i = 1, \ldots, k \tag{A.9}$$

and

$$\sum_{i=1}^{k} f(x_i) = 1 \tag{A.10}$$

where k represents the possible number of values for the random variable. The condition given by Equation (A.9) defines the acceptable probability range, and (A.10) ensures that the defined events are collectively exhaustive and mutually exclusive. Note that (A.10) is simply the application of (A.3).

The **cumulative distribution function (CDF)** for a discrete random variable is defined as

$$F(x_i) = P(X \leq x_i)$$

$$= \sum_{j=1}^{i} f(x_j). \tag{A.11}$$

For Example A.1, the CDF is calculated in Table A–1 and plotted in Figure A–3b.

FIGURE A–3

Plots for Example A.1

(a) Probability Mass Function

(b) Cumulative Distribution Function

The **expected value** or **mean** for a discrete random variable is given by

$$E(X) = \sum_{i=1}^{k} x_i \cdot f(x_i) \qquad \text{(A.12)}$$

and the extent of the dispersion about this mean, as measured by the **variance,** can be estimated from either

$$V(X) = \sum_{i=1}^{k} [x_i - E(X)]^2 \cdot f(x_i) \qquad \text{(A.13)}$$

or

$$V(X) = \sum_{i=1}^{k} x_i^2 \cdot f(x_i) - [E(X)]^2. \qquad \text{(A.14)}$$

The **standard deviation** (σ_X) is simply the square root of the variance. For example A.1, $E(X) = 2.1$, $V(X) = 1.93$, and $\sigma_X = 1.39$. The expected value indicates that during "off-peak" hours there are an average of 2.1 arrivals per hour.

Follow-up Exercises

3. Does the pmf in Example A.1 satisfy Equations (A.9) and (A.10)?
4. Verify the calculations for $E(X)$, $V(X)$, and σ_x in Example A.1.

Continuous Random Variables and Probability Density Functions

If X is a continuous random variable, then its probability function, $f(x)$, termed a **probability density function (pdf),** must satisfy the following two conditions:

$$f(x) \geq 0 \qquad \text{(A.15)}$$

and

$$\text{Area under the function} = 1.0. \qquad \text{(A.16)}$$

The first condition ensures nonnegative probabilities, and the second condition guarantees the property of a collectively exhaustive and mutually exclusive sample space. Note that (A.15) and (A.16) are analogs of (A.9) and (A.10).

The probability that the random variable assumes a real value in the interval (a, b) where $a < b$, is given by

$$P(a \leq X \leq b) = \text{Area (density) under } f(x) \text{ between } a \text{ and } b, \quad \text{(A.17)}$$

as depicted in Figure A–4a.[2] It follows that $P(X = x) = 0$ when X is a continuous random variable. (Can you reason this out logically if, say,

---

[2] As you probably know, such areas are typically determined by evaluating definite integrals.

FIGURE A–4

Probability Functions for Continuous Random Variables

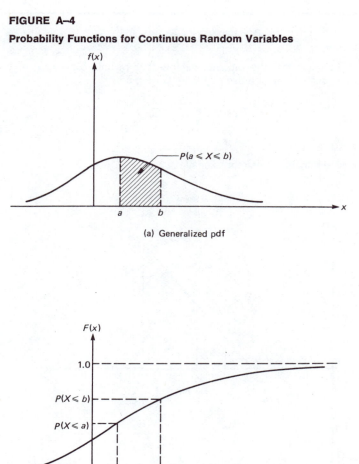

(a) Generalized pdf

(b) Generalized Continuous CDF

X represents the weight of baby girls living in New York City on their second birthday?)

The CDF for a continuous random variable is given by

$$F(x) = P(X \leq x) \tag{A.18}$$

as illustrated in Figure A–4b. From (A.18) it follows that (A.17) can be expressed as

$$P(a \leq X \leq b) = F(b) - F(a). \tag{A.19}$$

The expected value $E(X)$ and the variance $V(X)$ of a continuous random variable are defined in a manner similar to (A.12) and (A.13) by replacing the summation symbol by the integral symbol. Their values for a specific function can be determined by the methods of integral calculus.

Example A.2

Suppose that the random variable "air pollution index, x, in New York City" can be characterized by the following pdf:

$$f(x) = \begin{cases} \dfrac{-3}{80} + \dfrac{x}{800}, & 30 \leq x \leq 70 \\[2mm] 0, & \text{otherwise.} \end{cases}$$

FIGURE A–5

Probability Functions for Example A.2

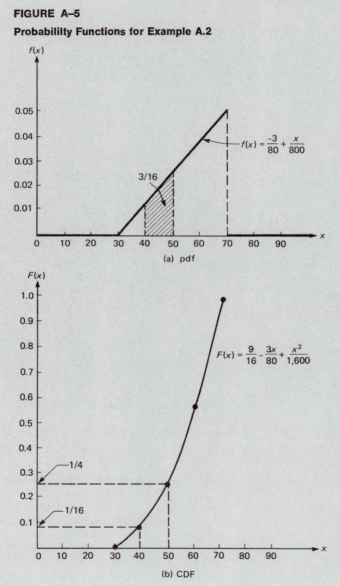

(a) pdf

(b) CDF

The probability of an air pollution index between 40 and 50 units can be determined either by evaluating the area indicated in Figure A–5a or by integrating the definite integral of $f(x)$ using limits of 40 and 50. In either case, $P(40 \leq X \leq 50) = 3/16$. Alternatively, given the CDF in Figure A–5b and utilizing (A.19), we see that $P(40 \leq X \leq 50) = F(50) - F(40) = 1/4 - 1/6 = 3/16$. The expected value and variance can be determined as 170/3 and 800/9, respectively.

Follow-up Exercises[3]

5. Does the pdf in this example satisfy Equations (A.15) and (A.16)? Can you state the distinctions between a pdf and a pmf?

6. Find $P(2 \leq X \leq 4)$ and $P(X \leq 3)$ by sketching $f(x)$ and $F(x)$ given that

$$f(x) = \begin{cases} 1/4, & 1 \leq x \leq 5 \\ 0, & \text{otherwise.} \end{cases}$$

   Verify that this is a pdf.

** 7. Integrate $f(x)$ for Example A.2 to verify that

$$F(x) = \frac{9}{16} - \frac{3x}{80} + \frac{x^2}{1600}.$$

** 8. Verify that

$$f(x) = \begin{cases} \dfrac{1}{b-a}, & a \leq x \leq b \\ 0, & \text{otherwise} \end{cases}$$

   is a pdf. Derive expressions for $F(x)$, $E(x)$, and $V(X)$. Let $a = 1$ and $b = 5$ and verify your results in this exercise using your results in Exercise 6.

** 9. Determine $F(x)$, $P(X \leq 10)$, $P(4 \leq X \leq 8)$, $P(X > 12)$, $E(X)$, and $V(X)$ given that

$$f(x) = 0.1e^{-0.1x}, \qquad x \geq 0.$$

   Sketch $f(x)$ and $F(x)$. (e is the base of natural logarithms.)

**10. Verify that

$$f(x) = \lambda e^{-\lambda x}, \qquad x \geq 0$$

   is a pdf where e is the base of natural logarithms. Derive expressions for $F(x)$, $E(X)$, and $V(X)$. Do your results agree with Exercise 9?

---

[3] Exercises preceded by two asterisks are for those who are "up" on integral calculus.

A.3 SELECTED THEORETICAL PROBABILITY DISTRIBUTIONS

Both discrete and continuous probability distributions can be represented by theoretical functions of specific mathematical form. Theoretical pmf's and pdf's are useful for several reasons. First, they simplify the calculation of probabilities; second, they provide specific mathematical functions with which to "fit" empirical data; finally, they play a central role in the derivation of many stochastic models in operations research, for example, queuing, inventory, and decision theory models, among others. This section presents a review of distributions which have been especially useful.

Discrete Probability Distributions

First, a random variable X has a **binomial distribution** if its pmf is given by

$$f(x) = (_nC_x) \cdot (p^x) \cdot (1 - p)^{n-x}, \qquad x = 0, 1, \ldots, n \qquad \text{(A.20)}$$

where n is the number of *Bernoulli* trials (distinct random experiments with only two possible outcomes, "success" or "failure," per trial) which are performed under identical conditions; p is the constant probability of success per trial; x is the total number of successes; and

$$_nC_x = \frac{n!}{(n - x)!x!} \qquad \text{(A.21)}$$

is the number of combinations of n items taken x at a time. Note that only two parameters, n and p, completely describe this distribution.

The mean and variance for the binomial distribution are

$$E(X) = n \cdot p \qquad \text{(A.22)}$$

and

$$V(X) = n \cdot p \cdot (1 - p). \qquad \text{(A.23)}$$

To illustrate, suppose ten market survey questionnaires have been sent out to a "homogeneous" market segment, and past experience indicates that the probability of getting any one back is 0.2. The probability that four will be returned is

$$\begin{aligned} f(4) &= (_{10}C_4) \cdot (0.2)^4 (0.8)^6 \\ &= 0.0881, \end{aligned}$$

the probability that four or more will be returned is 0.1209 (Can you verify this using a table in any statistics text?), the expected number which will be returned is 2, and the variance in the number returned is 1.6.

In OR, the binomial distribution has been useful in certain queuing models, in marketing research simulations, in the sample design related to survey data collection, and in some Bayesian decision theory models. We illustrate its usefulness in Chapter 17.

Second, a random variable X has a **Poisson distribution** if its pmf is given by

$$f(x) = \frac{(\lambda t)^x \cdot e^{-\lambda t}}{x!} \qquad x = 0, 1, 2, \ldots \qquad \text{(A.24)}$$

where λ is the expected number of "successes" per unit of continuum (for example, time, distance, area, and so forth); t is the number of continuum units; x is the number of successes over t continuum units; and e is the irrational number 2.71818 . . . (the base of natural logarithms).

Interestingly, the mean and variance are identical and given by

$$E(X) = \lambda \cdot t \tag{A.25}$$

and

$$V(X) = \lambda \cdot t. \tag{A.26}$$

Since both x and t must be specified in any given problem, λ is the only parameter in this distribution. This feature of the Poisson pmf makes it especially amenable to analytical use.

As an illustration, suppose that the hospital emergency room arrival data (Table A–1) are considered to be adequately represented by a Poisson distribution with mean (λ) of two arrivals per hour. The probability of five arrivals in any three-hour off-peak period (noting that $\lambda = 2$ and $t = 3$) is

$$f(5) = \frac{(6)^5 \cdot e^{-6}}{5!}$$
$$= 0.1606.$$

Underlying assumptions for this model include a constant λ over the continuum and irrelevancy of the beginning point of the continuum (that is, any three-hour off-peak period in the above example). As with the binomial distribution, tables for the Poisson distribution are readily available so that typically Equation (A.24) does not have to be solved.

The Poisson distribution is extensively applied in waiting line systems (Chapter 12), has been used in estimating the demands for certain products, and can serve as an approximation to the binomial distribution if n is large (say, 100) and p is small (say, 0.1).

Continuous Probability Distributions

First, a random variable X has a **rectangular** or **uniform distribution** if

$$f(x) = \begin{cases} \dfrac{1}{b - a}, & a \le x \le b \\ 0, & \text{otherwise} \end{cases} \tag{A.27}$$

where a and b are specified parameters (Figure A–6a). Its CDF is given by

$$F(x) = \frac{x - a}{b - a}, \qquad a \le x \le b \tag{A.28}$$

and its mean and variance by

$$E(X) = \frac{b + a}{2} \tag{A.29}$$

and

$$V(X) = \frac{(b - a)^2}{12}. \tag{A.30}$$

(Is this what you got in Exercise 8?)

The primary use for the uniform distribution is in the generation of uniformly distributed random numbers in the interval (0, 1) for simulation, as you will see in Chapter 13.

FIGURE A–6

Selected pdf's

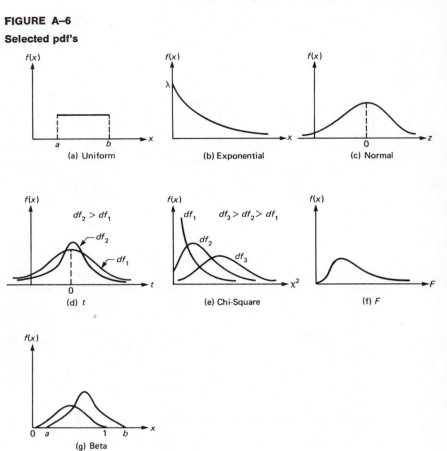

(a) Uniform

(b) Exponential

(c) Normal

(d) t

(e) Chi-Square

(f) F

(g) Beta

Second, a random variable X has a **negative exponential distribution** if

$$f(x) = \lambda e^{-\lambda x}, \qquad x \geq 0 \tag{A.31}$$

where λ is a specified parameter (Figure A–6b). Its CDF, mean, and variance are determined from

$$F(x) = 1 - e^{-\lambda x}, \qquad x \geq 0 \tag{A.32}$$

$$E(X) = 1/\lambda \tag{A.33}$$

and

$$V(X) = 1/\lambda^2. \tag{A.34}$$

(Do these agree with your results in Exercise 10?)

Interestingly, there is a unique relationship between the Poisson and exponential distributions. To illustrate, if X is the number of arrivals in a queuing system over a period of time t and it is Poisson-distributed with λ

representing the average arrival rate per unit of time, then the random variable "time between successive arrivals" is distributed according to the exponential distribution with the same parameter λ. For example, if $\lambda = 2$ customers per hour, then according to (A.32) the probability of an inter-arrival time of less than 0.5 hour is

$$F(0.5) = 1 - e^{-2(0.5)}$$

$$= 1 - \frac{1}{2.718 \ldots}$$

$$= 0.6321.$$

Further note that the mean of the exponential distribution is the inverse of the mean of the Poisson distribution, as it should be.

The exponential distribution has been exceedingly useful in queuing systems and in describing certain phenomena such as the "life" of both telephone conversations and electronic components.

A **standardized** random variable

$$Z = \frac{X - E(X)}{\sigma_X} \qquad (A.35)$$

has a **unit normal** or **Gaussian distribution** (Figure A–6c) if

$$f(z) = \frac{e^{-(1/2)z^2}}{\sqrt{2\pi}} \qquad (A.36)$$

where e is as before and $\pi = 3.14 \ldots$, the ratio of the circumference to the diameter of a circle. Recall that this distribution is perfectly symmetrical about its mean and that its tails approach the z-axis asymptotically.

Notice that X is also normally distributed with mean $E(X)$ and standard deviation σ_X. The standardized variable Z has a mean of zero and a standard deviation of unity. In effect, this scale change allows the application of a single normal CDF table to all normal curve problems.[4]

For those of you who are "rusty," find a normal curve table and confirm that if $x = 20$, $E(X) = 14$, and $\sigma_X = 4$, then $z = 1.5$ and

$$P(X \leq 20) = F(Z = 1.5)$$
$$= 0.9332.$$

The normal curve commands a central role in sampling, can be used to approximate either the binomial distribution for large n or p close to 0.5 or the Poisson distribution for large λ (say, greater than 15), has described a variety of real-world phenomena, and has been incorporated in queuing, inventory, and decision theory models.

For modeling and applications in OR, a familiarity with four other probability distributions would round out your repertoire. In the interest of avoiding "shell shock," we omit the pdf's. For greater detail, consult your statistics text. (You do have one, don't you?)

The **t distribution** is similar to the unit normal distribution in its symmetry about a mean of zero, its bell shape, and its asymptotic tails to the abscissa (Figure A–6d). Furthermore, the random variate t is cal-

---

[4] The CDF is tabulated because (A.36) cannot be integrated.

culated in the identical manner as z, that is, by Equation (A.35). This distribution is central to inference which is based strictly on sample data (see Section A.5). Its shape is a function of a parameter termed **degrees of freedom (df),** which is determined by the sample size less the number of parameters (including the parameter n or total frequency in a sample) used to calculate the statistic under investigation; that is, df is the number of independent random observations in the sample. As with the normal curve, its tabular CDF is commonplace. Find a t-table and verify that for $P(T \leq t) = 0.95$ and $df = 30$, the value of t is 1.697. Also note that for any probability in a t-table, as df approaches infinity, the t-value approaches the corresponding z-value in the normal curve table. Do you remember why?

The **chi-square** (χ^2) **distribution** (Figure A–6e) is useful primarily for testing statistical hypotheses relating to equality of variances, goodness-of-fit, frequencies, and statistical independence. As with the t distribution, its shape is strictly dependent on the degrees of freedom. In Section A.4, we illustrate its applied use for testing the fit of empirical data to theoretical probability distributions. Find a table for the chi-square distribution and verify that for $df = 3$, $P(\chi^2 \leq 7.81) = 0.95$.

The **F distribution** (Figure A–6f), as with chi-square and t, serves primarily to test statistical hypotheses. Its most common application is the analysis of variance (ANOVA). We will illustrate its use in testing the "goodness" of a regression model (Section A.6). Theoretically, the F distribution is the ratio of two chi-square distributions; hence, a degree of freedom is associated with the numerator (df_1) and another with the denominator (df_2). Interestingly, in the particular case of testing the fit of simple linear regression (that is, the hypothesis that the population slope is zero), it turns out that $F = t^2$. Now that you are adept at finding tables, verify that $P(F \leq 4.17) = 0.95$ for $df_1 = 1$ and $df_2 = 30$.

The **Beta distribution** (Figure A–6g) is another two-parameter family of distributions which has been useful in project scheduling models (Chapter 14) and Bayesian decision theory (Chapter 17). By specific assignments of values to its parameters, it can be used to generate random numbers either uniformly or nonuniformly distributed between 0 and 1; by scale changes, other limits (a, b) can be chosen, as illustrated in the figure. Furthermore, wide latitude in the degree of symmetry or asymmetry is possible. Its cumulative distribution for $0 < x < 1$ is extensively tabulated in specialized texts as the **incomplete Beta distribution.**

Follow-up Exercises

11. If X is binomial with $n = 20$ and $p = 0.5$, find $P(X \leq 10)$, $P(X = 10)$, $E(X)$, and $V(X)$. Try it again for $n = 100$ and $p = 0.1$ and compare.

12. If X is Poisson with $\lambda = 5$ and $t = 2$, find $P(X \leq 10)$, $P(X = 10)$, $E(X)$, and $V(X)$. Compare your results to Exercise 11. Any conclusions? Recompute for $\lambda = 10$ and $t = 1$. Any conclusions?

13. What are the forms of $f(x)$, $F(X)$, $E(X)$, and $V(X)$ for the uniform distribution over the unit interval $(0, 1)$?

14. If X is exponential with $\lambda = 10$, find $P(X \leq 0)$, $P(X \leq 0.1)$, $P(X \leq 0.2)$, $P(X \leq 0.5)$, and $P(X \leq 1)$. Also find $E(X)$ and $V(X)$. What can you conclude about skewness?

15. If Z is normal, find z for $F(z) = 0.95$, $F(z) = 0.98$, $F(z) = 0.99$, $P(-z < Z < z) = 0.95$, $P(-z \leq Z \leq z) = 0.98$, and $P(-z \leq Z \leq z) = 0.99$. Distinguish between one-tail and two-tail probabilities.

16. If X is t-distributed, $E(X) = 14$, $\sigma_x = 4$, and $df = 10$, estimate $P(X \leq 20)$. Estimate again for $df = \infty$. Compare the latter to the sample normal calculation given in the third part of this section. Any conclusions? Compare the last row of the t-table ($df = \infty$) to its equivalent in a normal curve table. Would you conclude that $T \rightarrow$ normal Z as $df \rightarrow \infty$?

A.4 STATISTICAL INFERENCE: ESTIMATING PROBABILITY DISTRIBUTIONS

In this and the following two sections, we present some fundamental concepts regarding sampling, sample design, and statistical inference with respect to the nature of underlying probability distributions and the estimations of means. An understanding of these concepts is very important to the successful conduct of OR studies which require real data.

Sampling and Sample Design

For any study which requires data, there is a target set of objects about which information regarding some attribute is desired. This set of objects is termed the **universe** or **population.** Illustrative attributes and populations include the following: the probability distribution for "interarrival times" (attribute) for "all possible arrivals at the emergency room of a hospital" (population); the average "response velocity for a particular type of emergency vehicle" (attribute) among "all the possible responses in a given section of a city" (population); the expected "total cost of producing any given number of items over some planning horizon" (attribute) from among the "set of items of the same type which will be, could be, or would have been produced" (population).

If every item of the population is to be examined, a **census** is to be undertaken; if some subset of the population is to be examined, then a **sample** will be undertaken. **Inferential statistics** is the area of study which is concerned with the making of generalizations or inferences about some population characteristic based on the results of a sample.

The motivation for sampling is strong. In many cases, a census either is not feasible (for example, an infinite population) or is insane (for example, determination of the attribute requires the destruction of the object). In most cases, sampling is considerably less costly with little or no sacrifice in estimation error.

The method of selecting a sample is a field of study in itself **(sample survey methods)** requiring substantial expertise. Essentially, samples can be selected in one of two ways: **judgment samples** and **probability samples.**

In the first approach, an individual (or set of individuals) selects items which are "known" to be typical with respect to the desired attribute(s); in the latter approach, the selection of items is based on a plan which requires a knowledge of the probability that any given item will be selected. Only for the latter can we estimate the degree of **sampling error,** which is a measure of the variability in estimating a statistic such as the mean. Of the various methods for selecting probability samples (for example, simple random, systematic, cluster, stratified random, and variants or combinations thereof), we will exclusively deal with **simple random sampling,** that is, where each element of the population has an equal probability of being selected.

Goodness-of-Fit Test

In this section, we illustrate the use of the chi-square distribution to test the hypothesis that an empirical distribution based on some random variable represents a sample from some theoretical distribution.

Given an empirical probability distribution with observed frequencies (o_i) and a theoretical probability distribution with expected frequencies (e_i), both with k categories as illustrated in Table A–2,

TABLE A–2

Setup for Chi-Square Test

Range of Random Variable $a_i \leq X \leq b_i$ (Category i)	Empirically Observed Frequency (o_i)	Theoretically Expected Frequency (e_i)
1	o_1	e_1
2	o_2	e_2
.	.	.
.	.	.
.	.	.
k	o_k	e_k

the statistic

$$s = \sum_{i=1}^{k} \frac{(o_i - e_i)^2}{e_i} \qquad (A.37)$$

approaches a chi-square (χ^2) distribution with $df = k - m$ degrees of freedom as the sample size n approaches infinity (m stands for the number of parameters or restrictions which apply in the calculations). As a rule, $n \geq 50$ gives satisfactory results as long as all expected frequencies are greater than five; otherwise, additional refinements must be incorporated in the test. Note that small values for s imply "good" fits between the empirical and theoretical distributions; for example, if $o_i = e_i$ for all i, then the fit would be perfect (giving $s = 0$).

The idea then is to evaluate (A.37) utilizing the expected frequencies for some assumed theoretical distribution. The **null hypothesis** would state that the empirical distribution represents a sample of observations from the assumed theoretical distribution. If this were true, then differences between observed and expected frequencies would be due only to sampling error and values for s would be small; on the other hand, a "surprisingly" high value for s would raise the suspicion that the empirical data are inconsistent with the assumed underlying distribution, which implies a rejection of the null hypothesis.

Example A.3   Emergency Room Service

Consider the emergency room problem first introduced in Example A.1. A simple random sample of 100 cases has been selected from among a large number of case records and the attribute "time to treat a patient" was recorded as in Table A–3. As before, data have been smoothed to en-

TABLE A–3

Data and Computations for Exponential Service Distribution

Service Time per Patient in Hours ($a_i \leq X < b_i$)	Observed Frequency (o_i)	$P(X \leq a_i)$ $F(a_i)$	For Exponential pdf with $\lambda = 2.5$ $P(X \leq b_i)$ $F(b_i)$	$P(a_i \leq X \leq b_i)$ $F(b_i) - F(a_i)$	Expected Frequency (e_i)	$\dfrac{(o_i - e_i)^2}{e_i}$
0.0 0.2	38	0.0000	0.3935	0.3935	39.35	0.05
0.2 0.4	25	0.3935	0.6321	0.2386	23.86	0.06
0.4 0.6	17	0.6321	0.7769	0.1448	14.48	0.44
0.6 0.8	9	0.7769	0.8647	0.0878	8.78	0.01
0.8 1.0	6	0.8647	0.9179	0.0532	5.32	0.09
1.0 1.2	5	0.9179	0.9507	0.0328	3.28 ⎱ 1.26
Over 1.2	0	0.9507	1.0000	0.0493	4.93 ⎰
Total...	100					1.91

sure the elimination of identifiable "noise." Furthermore, a previous statistical study showed no appreciable differences in the distribution of treatment times for various physicians.

Using (A.12), we calculate the sample mean as 0.4 hour. Suppose we formulate the null hypothesis that the observed distribution is a sample from an exponential distribution with $E(X) = 0.4$. Furthermore, suppose we specify a probability of no more than 0.01 for the wrong decision of rejecting a true hypothesis (this establishes a 0.01 **level of significance** or right-tail area and a corresponding value for the **critical value** of χ^2 as in Figure A–7).

According to (A.33), $\lambda = 1/0.40 = 2.5$. Based on (A.32), it follows that the assumed distribution has a CDF given by

$$F(x) = 1 - e^{-2.5x}.$$

We can now determine the probability of a theoretical observation within any specified category or class (a_i, b_i) in the table. For example, in the third class ($a_3 = 0.4$, $b_3 = 0.6$), we have

$$P(0.4 \leq X \leq 0.6) = [1 - e^{-2.5(0.6)}] - [1 - e^{-2.5(0.4)}]$$
$$= 0.7769 - 0.6321$$
$$= 0.1448.$$

Expected frequencies for each class are now determined as the product of the total number of observations ($n = 100$) and the probability of an observation in that class. For the third class, $e_3 = 100(0.1448) = 14.48$. Calculations for each class are shown in Table A–3. Note that the last two classes in the table have been combined in order to avoid an expected frequency of less than five in any class. This changes the number of categories to $k = 6$.

The last column illustrates the calculation of $s = 1.91$ according to (A.37). For $df = 6 - 2 = 4$ (two parameters, n and λ, were needed, or $m = 2$), the critical value of χ^2 which gives a 0.01 level of significance is 13.28. (See Figure A–7.) Since $s < 13.28$, we conclude that the exponential distribution with $\lambda = 2.5$ is a reasonable theoretical distribution to represent this process.

FIGURE A–7

Chi-Square Distribution for Hypothesis Test

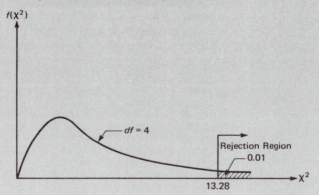

Follow-up Exercises

17. Plot the empirical and theoretical CDFs for this example and compare.

18. Test the null hypothesis that the empirical distribution in Table A–3 is a sample from an underlying normal distribution with $E(X) = 0.4$ and $V(X) = 0.16$. Use 1-percent and 5-percent levels of significance.

19. Test the null hypothesis that the empirical distribution in Table A–1 is a sample from an underlying Poisson distribution. Use a 5-percent level of significance. Calculate $E(X)$ according to (A.12) to determine λ based on (A.25).

A.5   STATISTICAL INFERENCE: ESTIMATING MEANS

In this section we review the concepts of a sampling distribution and point and interval estimations.

Sampling Distributions and Estimation of Population Parameters

Given the motivation to estimate the parameter of some population (for example, mean or variance), the usual procedure is to design a probability sample which would provide a **sample statistic** for estimating the parameter of interest. For example, we might estimate the parameter true average cost (population mean, μ) with the statistic average cost (sample mean, $\bar{x}$) based on a sample; or we might estimate the proportion of taxpayers who cheated on their 1975 income tax returns (population proportion, π) by using the proportion based on a sample (sample proportion, p). When a single estimate based on a sample is used to estimate the population parameter ($\bar{x}$ for μ or p for π), it is termed a **point estimate.** While such estimates are indispensable data for models(think back to all of our "estimates" in the LP examples), you can appreciate that they provide no judgment as to the extent of random sampling error. **Interval estimates** allow us to specify the maximum expected error and associated probability that a point estimate would diverge from the population parameter.

By realizing that the sample statistic that is calculated is only one of many possible that could be calculated, it is not difficult to conceptualize the existence of a distribution of possible sample statistics, termed the **sampling distribution of a statistic.**[5] Now for the crux of sampling theory. If the shape or form of the sampling distribution can be specified, then it would be possible to base errors on probability judgments. For example, if p is used to estimate π, then the sampling distribution of p turns out to be binomial (which can be approximated by the normal curve if n is sufficiently large), assuming the conditions underlying the binomial process are met; if $\bar{x}$ is used to estimate μ, then the sampling distribution of $\bar{x}$ turns out to be approximately normally or t-distributed. Given a specified shape for the sampling distribution, interval estimates are made easily, as illustrated next.

Sampling Distribution of the Mean

If $x_1, x_2, \ldots, x_n$ represent independent and identically distributed random variates (that is, variates from a random sample of size n), then the sample mean (point estimate for the population mean, μ) can be calculated from:[6]

$$\bar{x} = \frac{\sum_{i=1}^{n} x_i}{n}. \tag{A.38}$$

---

[5] If N is the size of the population and n is the size of the simple random sample, then the number of possible samples (and therefore the number of $\bar{x}$'s if the population mean is being estimated) is given by combinations of N taken n at-a-time, as determined by (A.21).

[6] Note that for a simple random sample, $P(X = x_i) = f(x_i) = 1/n$, so that (A.38) is a special case of (A.12). Also, we make no effort to explain methods of calculating point estimates (for example, moments, maximum likelihood, Bayesian),

If n is sufficiently large (say, above 30) and the population standard deviation is known, then we have the result guaranteed by the **Central Limit Theorem (CLT):**

If $x_1, x_2, \ldots, x_n$ represents a random sample from a population with $E(X) = \mu_x$ and $V(X) = \sigma_x^2$, then the distribution of $\bar{x}$ approaches a *normal distribution* with

$$E(\bar{X}) = \mu_X \tag{A.39}$$

and

$$V(\bar{X}) = \sigma_{\bar{X}}^2 = \sigma_X^2/n. \tag{A.40}$$

as n approaches infinity.

In short, this allows us to establish probability ranges of $\bar{x}$ about μ_X. Carefully note that the CLT is operative if and only if (1) the variates are independently and identically distributed, (2) n is sufficiently large, and (3) σ_X is known. Condition (1) and the derivation of (A.40) require that sampling is from an infinite population or from a finite population with replacement; otherwise, a so-called **finite population correction** factor must be applied to (A.40):

$$\sigma_{\bar{X}}^2 = \frac{\sigma_X^2}{n} \cdot \left(\frac{N-n}{N-1}\right). \tag{A.41}$$

If n is small or σ_X is unknown, then the sampling distribution of $\bar{X}$ will be distributed according to the t distribution, providing the population for X is normally distributed. Note that the normality of $\bar{X}$ as specified by the CLT makes absolutely no assumptions about the form of the X distribution. The application of the t distribution, however, requires that X itself be normally distributed. If σ_X^2 is unknown (the usual case), it is estimated by the **unbiased sample variance:**

$$\hat{\sigma}_X^2 = \frac{\sum_{i=1}^{n}(x_i - \bar{x})^2}{n-1} \tag{A.42}$$

If n is large or small, σ_X is unknown, and X is *not* normally distributed, then the appropriate statistical procedure is "punt." For practical purposes, however, a large n (above 50) under these conditions will give satisfactory results.

Once $\bar{x}$ and the **standard error of the mean,** $\sigma_{\bar{X}}$, are determined, the maximum error and **confidence interval** in estimating μ_X are given by

$$\mu_X = \bar{x} \pm z \cdot \sigma_{\bar{X}} \tag{A.43}$$

or

---

although the Least Squares Method will be reviewed in the next section. Finally, a discussion on criteria for evaluating methods of point estimation (that is, consistency, efficiency, sufficiency, and unbiasedness) is omitted.

$$\mu_X = \bar{x} \pm t \cdot \hat{\sigma}_{\bar{X}} \qquad (A.44)$$

as the case may be, where $\hat{\sigma}_{\bar{x}}$ is the estimated standard error when (A.42) is used in place of σ_x^2 in (A.40) or (A.41).

Example A.4 Police Patrol Sector

In Example 4.1, 10 mph is used as the velocity of travel for a police patrol vehicle in an east-west direction along a particular sector. Suppose this figure represents a point estimate (that is, $\bar{x} = 10$) for the mean of the population of all possible response velocities based on a simple random sample of 61 observations (that is, $n = 61$). The population variance (σ_x^2) is unknown, but has been estimated as $\hat{\sigma}_x^2 = 2$ using (A.42). Seasonal factors based on shift, day of week, and month of year have been controlled to ensure as much as possible that random variates are independent and identically distributed.[7] The assumption of a random sample was further buttressed by a previous study which showed that response velocities do not vary significantly with individual drivers. Finally, a chi-square test on the null hypothesis that the random sample of 61 observed velocities came from a normal distribution was accepted. This cleared the way for using the t distribution as representative of the $\bar{X}$ distribution.

Since the population is infinite, we substitute $\hat{\sigma}_x^2$ for σ_x^2 in (A.40), which gives $\hat{\sigma}_{\bar{x}}^2 = \frac{2}{61}$, or $\hat{\sigma}_{\bar{x}} = 0.18$ mph. For $df = n - 1 = 60$ and a 0.95 **level of confidence** (that is, 0.025 of the area lies in each tail), the value of t is 2.0; hence, according to (A.44),

$$\mu_X = 10 \pm (2.0)(0.18)$$
$$= 10 \pm 0.36.$$

This means that the probability is 95 percent that the estimate of 10 mph is *within* 0.36 mph of the population (true) average velocity. Alternatively, the 95-percent confidence interval for μ is 9.64 to 10.36 mph. These **confidence limits** can be used as extreme values of this parameter for performing sensitivity analysis.

Follow-up Exercises

20. Determine the confidence limits if $n = 21$, all other things equal. Conclusion?

21. Estimate maximum error for μ if $\bar{x} = 50$, $n = 30$, and $\sigma_x = 10$. Use 95-percent and 99-percent confidence intervals.

22. If σ_x is known, then the maximum error for a given level of confidence is given by $E = z \cdot \sigma_{\bar{x}}$ or $E = z \cdot \sigma_x / \sqrt{n}$ when (A.40) applies. It follows that

---

[7] This can be accomplished by selecting the sample either from a particular shift-day-month combination or from a group of such combinations that appear to be statistically similar with respect to response velocities. A less likely alternative includes deseasonalizing velocities using seasonal indices.

$$n = \left(\frac{z \cdot \sigma_x}{E}\right)^2 \qquad \text{(A.45)}$$

provides the required sample size which satisfies a given maximum error and confidence level. For the police sector problem, determine the required sample size if $\sigma_x = 1.41$ and an error of no more than 0.5 mph with 99-percent confidence is desired. What sample size must be taken if $E = 0.1$? Conclusion as to behavior of n as E changes?

A.6 STATISTICAL INFERENCE: REGRESSION ANALYSIS

The **Least Squares Method** in regression analysis is an alternative method for point and interval estimates of population parameters. The gist of the technique is to discover linear association or covariation between the variable to be estimated (called the **dependent** or **criterion variable**) and some other set of variables (called the **independent** or **predictor variables**) having values accessible to or under the control of the decision maker.[8] If the set of predictor variables consists of a single variable, then the form of the analysis is called **simple** or **bivariate regression;** otherwise, **multiple regression** applies. Throughout this section it should be understood that we are dealing only with **linear regression** (which *can* include nonlinear functions) and not **nonlinear regression.** The term "linear" refers to linearity in the parameters of the model and not to linearity in the variables themselves.

Estimating the Simple Regression Function

In bivariate regression, the objective is to find the functional (mathematical) relationship between the criterion variable (y) and the predictor variable (x), that is, to explicitly determine

$$y = f(x). \qquad \text{(A.46)}$$

The simplest and most widely used form of (A.46) is the linear function:

$$y_c = a + bx \qquad \text{(A.47)}$$

where a is the y-intercept, b is the slope or **regression coefficient,** and y_c is the calculated or estimated value for y. Other forms of (A.46) include nonlinear functions which by some transformation can be converted to linear form. For example, the popular *exponential*

$$y = a \cdot b^x \qquad \text{(A.48)}$$

---

[8] In some cases the purpose of regression analysis is not to predict or estimate some variable but rather to discover associations for explanatory purposes (for example, as a means to structurally substantiate some theory such as "lip velocity in the combustion of a jet engine is related to the fuel/air ratio").

is converted easily to the form in (A.47) by taking the logarithm of both sides.

Given a set of n paired observations for the criterion and predictor variables, $[(y_1, x_1), (y_2, x_2), \ldots, (y_n, x_n)]$, based on a random sample, the method of least squares "fits" a linear function to these observations such that the sum of squared deviations from the line is minimized. (See Figure A–8.) In other words, we wish to find the values for a and b which minimize the **residual sum of squares** or **unexplained variation (UV):**

$$UV = \sum_{i=1}^{n} [y_i - (a + bx_i)]^2. \tag{A.49}$$

The procedure, as illustrated in Example 3.6, involves taking the partial derivatives of UV with respect to a and b, setting the two simultaneous equations to zero, and solving for a and b. You can find computational equations for a and b in any textbook on statistics.

FIGURE A–8

Linear Function Fit to n Data Points

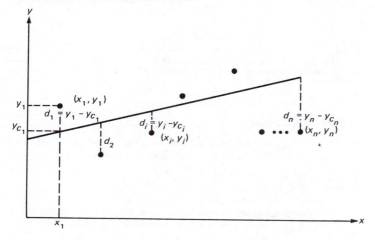

Example A.5

Table A–4 illustrates regression information provided by a time-shared computer package (STATPACK) for the demand data in the MBTA example of Chapter 3. (Note that in our present example we have reversed the criterion and predictor variables.) The results indicate a regression equation of the form

$$y_c = 22.5 - 0.5x.$$

Estimated y_i values (y_{c_i}) are determined by plugging corresponding x_i values in the regression equation. Note that the sum of the residuals will always equal zero (except for rounding errors).

TABLE A–4

Sample Statistics from Computer Output*

Volume y_i	Price x_i	Estimated Volume y_{c_i}	Residual $d_i = y_i - y_{c_i}$	Intercept (a) = 22.500 Regression coefficient (b) = −0.500
10.0	25	10.0	0.0	Coefficient of determination (r^2) = 1.000
12.6	20	12.5	0.1	Coefficient of correlation (r) = −1.000
14.9	15	15.0	−0.1	Estimated standard error of regression coefficient ($\hat{\sigma}_b$) = 0.007
17.4	10	17.5	−0.1	t-test on regression coefficient = −68.445
20.1	5	20.0	0.1	Estimated standard error of estimate ($\hat{\sigma}_e$) = 0.116
$\bar{y} = 15$	$\bar{x} = 15$		0.0	

*Above results are standard output for most commercial computer packages. Computational formulas for these statistics are readily found in textbooks on managerial statistics.

Follow-up Exercises

23. Construct a **scatter diagram** for this example by plotting (x_i, y_i) and the regression line. Confirm the y_{c_i} and d_i columns in Table A–4.

24. Confirm the results given in Example 3.6 either by hand calculation (for shame!) or by an available computer package.

25. Suppose that a firm wishes to establish the relationship between the total cost of placing orders and the number of orders placed for an item it carries in inventory. A "random" sample of eight observations (one observation for each of eight quarters) provides the following paired (cost, order) data where costs have been deflated by the consumer price index: ($560,2), (640,5), (780,9), (620,4), (700,6), (580,3), (640,4), and (700,7). Fit a least squares line to these data and construct a scatter diagram. Try to accomplish this by using an available computer program. On the average, what is the change in cost per unit change in orders?

Judging Goodness-of-Fit

The precision of a regression fit can be judged by the relationships exhibited in Table A–5.

TABLE A–5

Analysis of Variance (ANOVA) Table for Bivariate Regression

Source of Variation	Sum of Squares	Degrees of Freedom	Mean Square	F Statistic
Regression............	EV	1	$MEV = EV/1$	
Residual..............	UV	$n - 2$	$MUV = UV/(n - 2)$	$F = \dfrac{MEV}{MUV}$
Total............	TV	$n - 1$	—	

Total variation *for the criterion variable* is given by the numerator of the variance term, or

$$TV = \sum_{i=1}^{n} (y_i - \bar{y})^2. \qquad (A.50)$$

The variation due to or explained by the regression fit (EV) represents the portion of TV which we have been able to account for by the regression model. Ideally, we would like $EV = TV$, or a "perfect" fit. The variation which remains unexplained (UV) represents the extent to which the observations fall off the line. In fact, this was the objective of our minimization as given by (A.49).

The mean squares are the sums of squares adjusted for (divided by) the degrees of freedom. The F-statistic allows the analyst to test the null hypothesis that the *population* regression coefficient (β) is zero (note that b represents the *sample* regression coefficient). If the null hypothesis were true, then there is no linear relationship between y and x. (Why?) If $\beta = 0$, then it can be proved that the expected value of F is unity. Note that if it were true that $\beta = 0$, it would still be possible for the sample statistics (F or b) to diverge from their expected values due to random sampling error. Note also that the greater the value of F, the better (or more significant) is the regression fit.

The **coefficient of determination (r^2)** also provides a measure of goodness in that it represents the proportion of variation explained by the model; that is,

$$r^2 = EV/TV. \qquad (A.51)$$

The **coefficient of correlation (r)** is simply the square root of the coefficient of determination. If $r = 0$, the worst possible fit has occurred (a horizontal line); if $r = 1$, perfect positive correlation exists; if $r = -1$, perfect negative correlation exists. (Note that the sign on r is consistent with the sign on b.)

Because b is an observation from the **sampling distribution of b** with expected value β and the estimated **standard error of the regression coefficient** ($\hat{\sigma}_b$) is analogous to $\hat{\sigma}_{\bar{x}}$, the t-statistic given by

$$t = \frac{b - \beta}{\hat{\sigma}_b}$$
$$= b/\hat{\sigma}_b \qquad (A.52)$$

allows for the test of the null hypothesis that $\beta = 0$. As mentioned in Section A.3, $F = t^2$ for simple linear regression.[9]

Example A.6

Continuing our previous example, we see that Table A–6 illustrates the computer output for the ANOVA table. As can be seen, out of a total variation of 62.54 in the criterion variable (volume), all but 0.04 remains unex-

TABLE A–6

ANOVA Table for Example A.5

Source	SS	df	MS	F
Regression...............	62.50	1	62.500	
Residual.................	0.04	3	0.013	4684.7
Total...............	62.54	4	—	—

plained. The F statistic of 4684.7 is extremely high, as the critical F value is only 34.1 for $df_1 = 1$ and $df_2 = 3$ at a significance level of 0.01.

To three significant digits, the coefficient of determination (from Table A–4) indicates that approximately 100 percent of the variance in volume was explained (actually it is 62.5/62.54). The coefficient of correlation correspondingly suggests a perfect negative correlation between price and volume. Finally, the t value of -68.445 concurs with a highly significant regression fit; that is, the null hypothesis of a zero population slope is soundly rejected. (Do you get the feeling we contrived the data?) In actual practice, regression fits never quite measure up to the standard we have just set. In fact, such a small number of observations rarely gives meaningful results in the sense of achieving reject signals from F and t.

Follow-up Exercises

26. Determine relevant goodness-of-fit statistics for the problem in Example 3.6. Compare these results with our results in Example A.6. Conclusions? Does $F = t^2$?

27. Determine goodness-of-fit statistics for the inventory problem in Exercise 25. Make a judgment as to the precision of the regression model.

Point and Interval Estimates

The calculated value, y_{c_i}, represents a point estimate for the mean (expected or average) value of y_i conditional on (or given) x_i.

---

[9] All inferences in regression analysis are predicated on the assumption that the residuals are independent, have zero mean, a constant variance, and are normally distributed. A rigorous analysis would test these assumptions.

The confidence interval for the *expected* value of y_i given x_i is determined from

$$\text{Expected } y_i = y_{c_i} \pm t \cdot \hat{\sigma}_m \qquad \text{(A.53)}$$

where $\hat{\sigma}_m$ is the **estimated standard error of expected (mean)** y_i, a statistic which is also analogous to the standard error of the mean (that is, it represents the estimate for the standard deviation of the sampling distribution of mean y_i). For bivariate regression analysis, $df = n - 2$ and

$$\hat{\sigma}_m = \hat{\sigma}_e \sqrt{\frac{1}{n} + \frac{(x_i - \bar{x})^2}{\Sigma (x - \bar{x})^2}} \qquad \text{(A.54)}$$

where $\hat{\sigma}_e$ is the **estimated standard error of estimate** (as given in Table A–4). We might note that $\hat{\sigma}_e$ is an unbiased estimate of the standard deviation of residuals about the population regression line:

$$\hat{\sigma}_e = \sqrt{\frac{UV}{n - 2}}. \qquad \text{(A.55)}$$

Similarly, the confidence interval for an *individual* y value given x_i is determined from

$$\text{Individual } y_i = y_{c_i} \pm t \cdot \hat{\sigma}_f \qquad \text{(A.56)}$$

where $\hat{\sigma}_f$ is the **estimated standard error of the forecast:**

$$\hat{\sigma}_f = \hat{\sigma}_e \sqrt{1 + \frac{1}{n} + \frac{(x_i - \bar{x})^2}{\Sigma (x - \bar{x})^2}}. \qquad \text{(A.57)}$$

Again $df = n - 2$. Note that individual y_i values are distributed about the expected y_i value.

Example A.7

Continuing our volume-price example, for $df = 3$ and 99-percent confidence, the critical value of t is 5.841, so that for, say, $x_i = 12$

$$\text{Expected } y_i = [22.5 - 0.5(12)] \pm (5.841)\left\{(0.116) \cdot \left[\frac{1}{5} + \frac{(12 - 15)^2}{250}\right]^{1/2}\right\}$$

$$= 16.50 \pm (5.841)(0.056)$$

$$= 16.50 \pm 0.33$$

and

$$\text{Individual } y_i = 16.50 \pm (5.841)\left\{(0.116) \cdot \left[1 + \frac{1}{5} + \frac{(12 - 15)^2}{250}\right]^{1/2}\right\}$$

$$= 16.50 \pm (5.841)(0.129)$$

$$= 16.50 \pm 0.75.$$

In other words, for a fare of $0.12, the expected number of passengers is 16.5 thousand. Alternatively, we can state that the probability is 99 percent that the mean number of passengers will fall between 16.17 thousand and 16.83 thousand when a fare of $0.12 is charged. Furthermore, the probability is 99 percent that a single observation falls in the interval 15.75 thousand to 17.25 thousand for a fare of $0.12. Note that the unexpected width of the intervals is due to the small df and its correspondingly high t.

Follow-up Exercises

28. For Exercise 26, establish a 95-percent confidence interval for the average price given a volume of 15; for the same volume establish a 95-percent confidence interval for an individual price. Interpret these intervals.

29. For the inventory problem in Exercise 27, construct a 99-percent confidence interval for average and individual cost given the placement of six orders. Interpret these intervals.

Multiple Regression

Functionally, conceptually, and computationally the multiple linear regression model given by

$$y_c = b_0 + b_1x_1 + b_2x_2 + \cdots + b_nx_n \tag{A.58}$$

is a straightforward extension of (A.47).[10] Statistics of interest (as in Tables A–4 and A–5) and their interpretations remain almost the same.[11] The model given by (A.58) is useful from several perspectives: first, most real-world phenomena tend to be multivariate (for example, incidence of coronaries is related to factors such as age, weight, blood pressure, extent of cigarette smoking, and so forth); second, if the analyst is having difficulty establishing what predictor variable(s) to use in the analysis, it saves time to overspecify the number of variables for the purpose of "cranking" through a multiple regression (preferably stepwise) analysis which effectively does some "fishing"; third, it is useful in assessing the results of sensitivity analysis, as we illustrate in Section 13.5; finally, (A.58) can handle a nonlinear function such as

$$y_c = b_0 + b_1x_1 + b_2x_1^2 + b_3 \cdot (\log x_1) \tag{A.59}$$

by simply letting x_2 represent x_1^2 and x_3 represent $\log x_1$ in the data matrix. Equation (9.9) on page 327 could have been determined in just such a way.

---

[10] Using matrix algebra.

[11] A common oversight for this type of analysis is the problem of **multicollinearity** (correlation among the predictor variables), as its existence affects the precision and interpretation of individual regression coefficients. To some extent, **stepwise regression procedures** overcome this problem by sequentially including or excluding variables.

A.7   FORECASTING

The term forecasting, as used here, refers to the estimation of some random variable *over time*. All of our previous estimating procedures implicitly assumed estimation for a given point in time (or that the estimate would not vary over time). Yet many models in OR require the specification of some variable or parameter which could vary over time (for example, inventory models, production planning models, and so forth). In this section we have the modest objective of simply making you aware of this particular specialization by very briefly describing a typology of forecasting procedures and illustrating one methodology in particular called exponential smoothing.

Typology of Forecasting Procedures

The first (and perhaps most often used) approach is **subjective forecasts** primarily based on the intuition and expertise of the analyst regarding the variable or process being forecasted. If rapid responses are needed and/or if the cost of forecast error is small relative to the cost of implementing a more sophisticated forecasting system, then subjective forecasts can be justified; otherwise, mathematical and statistical procedures may be warranted.

Classical time series models express the criterion variable as a mathematical function of time (t) so as to provide forecasts ($\hat{y}_t$) by simple extrapolation:

$$\hat{y}_t = f(t). \tag{A.60}$$

For instance, a polynomial model of degree 3 would appear as

$$\hat{y}_t = b_0 + b_1 t + b_2 t^2 + b_3 t^3 \tag{A.61}$$

and an exponential model as

$$\hat{y}_t = a \cdot b^t \tag{A.62}$$

or

$$\hat{y}_t = a \cdot e^{bt} \tag{A.63}$$

where b is the growth rate and e is the natural number. Models of this type are most often fit by the use of linear regression procedures. More sophisticated versions first **decompose** the historical time series into trend, seasonal, cyclical, and noise components, analyze each component separately, and finally recompose for the forecast. Such models have fared well for long-term predictions of relatively stable processes (for example, GNP and world population growth) but are far too unresponsive to short-term movements.

Hybrid time-series models express the criterion either as a function of both independent variables (x_i's) and time (t) or as a function of variables which lead-lag the criterion. The former has been illustrated by Equation (9.9) and the latter can be illustrated by

$$\hat{y}_{t+6} = b_0 + b_1 x_t \tag{A.64}$$

where the variable x_t (say, housing starts in period t) leads the variable y (say, demand for mortgage money) by six periods. The effectiveness of both types of models is limited only by the availability of values for the predictors and by structural stability in the process over time.

Naïve models include a plethora of models with ad hoc forecasting formulas; for example, the forecast in period $t + 1$ equals the value of the variable in the present period ($\hat{y}_{t+1} = y_t$); and include others founded on the important classes of **simple moving averages** and **exponentially weighted moving averages** based on past observations. For example, a moving average of n periods provides the following forecast one period ahead (period $t + 1$):

$$\hat{y}_{t+1} = \frac{1}{n}(y_t + y_{t-1} + \cdots + y_{t-n+1}). \tag{A.65}$$

For the most part, naïve models have fared well, both from the standpoint of good forecast accuracy and ease of implementation. Among the most popular is the exponentially weighted moving average or **exponential smoothing.**

Econometric models specify structural relations among variables using mathematical and statistical methods. For instance, in a capital investment application (for example, see page 116), the estimation of present value is dependent, among other things, on future prices which in turn are dependent on supply-and-demand functions which in turn. . . . If correctly specified, these models can be quite effective; however, the required expenditure of time and the need for personnel with specialized knowledge in econometrics discourage their widespread use other than in large organizations.

Stochastic time-series models include a host of mathematically sophisticated procedures which treat the time series (sequence of observations) as a set of jointly distributed random variables. From a theoretical perspective, these models are the most appealing and appear to be the most effective for certain **autoregressive** (future observations correlated to past observations) and nonstationary processes.

Often the distinction between a **forecast** and a **prediction** is useful. Any of the above procedures results in a forecast. There may be causal factors at work, however, that will not be exhibited in the data. For example, forecasted sales for some product can be strongly influenced by the introduction of a competitive product or by the onset of a recession. Inclusion of such anticipated events results in a prediction based on a subjective revision of the forecast. In such instances, the **Delphi method** of prediction has proved useful.[12]

---

[12] Prediction by the Delphi method is based on a revised group consensus arrived at by a process which collates, summarizes, and "feeds" back to the group individual predictions of experts. For an overview, see J. Pill, "The Delphi Method: Substance, Context, a Critique and Annotated Bibliography," *Socio-Economic Planning Sciences,* vol. 5, no. 1 (1969).

Exponential Smoothing

The simplicity, low cost of implementation, and relative effectiveness of exponential smoothing models have been prominent factors in their widespread use. Here we illustrate the simplest of these, sometimes termed *single* exponential smoothing.

The smoothed value for the variable in the tth period $(\hat{y}_t)$ is defined as a *weighted average* of the current and n past observations $(n \rightarrow \infty)$;

$$\hat{y}_t = Ay_t + A(1 - A)y_{t-1} + A(1 - A)^2 y_{t-2} + \cdots + A(1 - A)^n y_{t-n} \quad (A.66)$$

where A is termed the **smoothing coefficient** $(0 < A < 1)$. The smoothed value $\hat{y}_t$ approaches a true weighted average as n approaches infinity because the sum of the weights approaches unity (they form a geometric progression with a ratio less than unity). Factoring $(1 - A)$ beginning with the second term in (A.66) gives the basic computational formula for single exponential smoothing as

$$\hat{y}_t = Ay_t + (1 - A)\hat{y}_{t-1}. \quad (A.67)$$

Thus, the smoothed value in period t is simply a weighted average of the current observation and the smoothed value in the previous period.

Note that (1) past observations are progressively less important, a feature which is intuitively appealing;[13] (2) n should be large (say, above 30) to justify theoretically the concept of a weighted average and to ensure lower sampling error; (3) higher values for A place more emphasis on the current observation (y_t) than on the composite of all past observations $(\hat{y}_{t-1})$; and (4) we need only keep track of four calculations at one time and not the entire past history (compare this feature to regression analysis).

The choice of a value for A poses an interesting dilemma for the analyst: High values for A (close to 1) make for a model which is highly responsive (but unstable) to changes in the time series; low values for the smoothing coefficient (close to 0) make for a model which is stable (but unresponsive) to changes in the time series. If the series is undergoing real changes, as when it is trending, then high values for A are called for. However, if much of the variability of the series is caused by random factors (noise), then low values for A are best. This tradeoff in stability and responsiveness often can be resolved by an analysis which evaluates forecast errors over a range of values for A.

Assuming that the y_t's represent deseasonalized values and that no trend is present, we can forecast k periods into the future by

$$\hat{y}_{t+k} = \hat{y}_t \quad (A.68)$$

and the forecast error by

$$d_{k,t} = y_{t+k} - \hat{y}_{t+k}. \quad (A.69)$$

Needless to say, more meaningful exponential smoothing models exist, including those that incorporate and smooth seasonal indices and trends.

---

[13] By contrast, all past observations are equally important (weighted) in *classical* regression analysis Alternatively, *Bayesian* regression analysis allows the revision of regression coefficients based on new observations.

Example A.8

To illustrate the model given by (A.67), consider the calculations in Table A-7 for the first five observations of a series using two values for A.

TABLE A-7
Calculations for Single Exponential Smoothing

		Smoothed Values A		One Period Forecast Error A	
		0.1	0.8	0.1	0.8
t	y_t	$\hat{y}_t$	$\hat{y}_t$	$d_{1,t}$	$d_{1,t}$
1	5	5.0	5.0	—	—
2	7	5.2	6.6	2.0	2.0
3	8	5.5	7.7	2.8	1.4
4	10	5.9	9.5	4.5	2.3
5	10	6.3	9.9	4.1	0.5
.					
.					
.					

In both cases, $\hat{y}_1$ was initialized by setting it to y_1.[14] Notice that a higher smoothing coefficient $(A = 0.8)$ gives better results than a smaller coefficient $(A = 0.1)$ for a series which exhibits trend as evidenced by closer fits of $\hat{y}_t$ to y_t and lower one period forecast errors given by $d_{1,t} = y_t - \hat{y}_{t-1}$. (Can you explain why this is so?)

Follow-up Exercises

30. Given the time series (10, 15, 18, 22, 26, 32, 37, 44, 48, 55) construct a table such as Table A-7 and compare average $d_{1,t}$ and $d_{2,t}$ for $A = 0.1$ and 0.8. Conclusions?

31. Do as in Exercise 30 for the time series (50, 60, 42, 55, 47, 45, 55, 40). Conclusions?

32. Use the first five observations of the series in Exercise 30 to fit the regression model $\hat{y}_t = a + bt$. Forecast the last five periods using this

---

[14] Better procedures exist. Can you think of any?

model and calculate average error. Compare this result to the one-period forecasts when $A = 0.8$ in Exercise 30 (for the last five periods).

33. Apply the model $\hat{y}_{t+1} = y_t$ to the series in Exercises 30 and 31. Compare errors.

34. What would be your forecast for the tenth observation of the series in Exercise 30 if you were to fit the regression model $\hat{y}_{t+1} = a + by_t$ to the first nine observations? Why is this model costly to implement?

SELECTED REFERENCES

Boot, J. C. G., and Cox, E. B. *Statistical Analysis for Managerial Decisions.* 2d ed. New York: McGraw-Hill Book Co., 1974.

Chou, Ya-lun. *Statistical Analysis.* 2d ed. New York: Holt, Rinehart and Winston, Inc., 1975.

Hays, W. L., and Winkler, R. L. *Statistics: Probability, Inference, and Decision.* New York: Holt, Rinehart and Winston, Inc., 1970.

Hughes, A., and Grawoig, D. *Statistics: A Foundation for Analysis.* Reading, Mass.: Addison-Wesley Publishing Co., 1971.

Nelson, C. R. *Applied Time Series Analysis for Managerial Forecasting.* San Francisco: Holden Day, Inc., 1973.

Neter, John; Wasserman, W.; and Whitmore, G. A. *Fundamental Statistics for Business and Economics.* 4th ed. Boston: Allyn and Bacon, Inc., 1973.
———. *Applied Linear Statistical Models.* Homewood, Ill.: Richard D. Irwin, Inc., 1974.

Summers, G.; Peters, W.; and Armstrong, C. *Basic Statistics in Business and Economics.* 2d ed. Belmont, Calif.: Wadsworth Publishing Co., 1977.

Wonnacott, R. J., and Wonnacott, T. H. *Econometrics.* New York: John Wiley & Sons, Inc., 1970.

Appendix B   Solving Systems of Equations

A VARIETY OF PROCEDURES can be used to solve systems of simultaneous equations. (Chapter 5 discusses one method which is fundamental to the Simplex solution technique for linear programming problems.) To serve as a review, this appendix presents one procedure for solving systems of linear and nonlinear equations having the same number of equations as unknown variables. By "solving" a system of simultaneous equations, you are attempting to determine whether there are any values of the variables which will "satisfy" all of the equations at the same time.

B.1   LINEAR EQUATIONS

You may remember that linear equations involving two variables and having the form

$$a_1x_1 + a_2x_2 = b$$

are geometrically represented by straight lines in two dimensions. In solving a system of linear equations involving two independent variables, we are looking for any points which are common to *all* of the straight lines. Linear equations involving three variables and having the form

$$a_1x_1 + a_2x_2 + a_3x_3 = b$$

are geometrically represented by *planes* in three dimensions. Similarly, linear equations involving n variables $(n > 3)$ and having the form

$$a_1x_1 + a_2x_2 + a_3x_3 + \cdots + a_nx_n = b$$

738

are geometrically conceived as *hyperplanes* in n dimensions, although it is impossible to graph in greater than three dimensions.

In general, when solving a system of linear equations there will be a *unique* solution (a single point common to all equations), an *infinite number* of solutions, or *no* solution. You should attempt to describe or illustrate the circumstances which would lead to each type of solution in two and three dimensions.

Probably the most popular solution procedure by hand is the **elimination-substitution technique.** This approach begins with the original $n \times n$ system and forms $n - 1$ linear combinations of pairs of equations, each linear combination eliminating the same variable. Care must be taken to assure that each of the n equations is used at least once in forming the linear combinations. The result of this process is the reduction of the $n \times n$ system to one which has $n - 1$ equations and $n - 1$ variables. The elimination procedure is repeated using each successive system until there is one equation and one variable. If this result occurs, a *unique* solution exists and the values of the other $n - 1$ variables can be found by substitution backward through the intermediate subsystems of equations. If during the elimination procedure a contradiction occurs (for example, $0 = 4$), there is no solution to the original system of equations; if an identity condition results (for example, $0 = 0$), there are an infinite number of solutions to the original system.

The following examples illustrate the elimination-substitution procedure for 2×2 and 3×3 systems of equations.

Example B.1

$$3x_1 + 2x_2 = 16 \qquad \text{(B.1)}$$
$$x_1 + 5x_2 = 27 \qquad \text{(B.2)}$$

Multiplying Equation (B.2) by (-3) and adding to Equation (B.1) to eliminate x_1, we get

$$
\begin{array}{ll}
3x_1 + 2x_2 = 16 & \text{(B.1)} \\
-3x_1 - 15x_2 = -81 & -3\text{(B.2)} \\
\hline
-13x_2 = -65 & \text{(B.3)} = \text{(B.1)} - 3\text{(B.2)} \\
x_2 = 5. &
\end{array}
$$

Substituting back into Equation (B.1), we get

$$3x_1 + 2(5) = 16$$
$$3x_1 = 6$$
$$x_1 = 2.$$

For this system, there is a unique solution when $x_1 = 2$ and $x_2 = 5$.

Example B.2

$$3x_1 + 2x_2 = 20 \qquad \text{(B.4)}$$
$$-6x_1 - 4x_2 = -20 \qquad \text{(B.5)}$$

Multiplying Equation (B.4) by 2 and adding to Equation (B.5), we get

$$
\begin{aligned}
6x_1 + 4x_2 &= 40 & 2(\text{B.4}) \\
-6x_1 - 4x_2 &= -20 & (\text{B.5}) \\
\hline
0 &\neq 20. & (\text{B.6}) \neq 2(\text{B.4}) + (\text{B.5})
\end{aligned}
$$

This is a contradiction, implying there is no solution to the original system of equations.

Example B.3

$$
\begin{aligned}
x_1 + x_2 + x_3 &= 3 & (\text{B.7}) \\
5x_1 - x_2 + 2x_3 &= 3 & (\text{B.8}) \\
2x_1 - 3x_2 + x_3 &= -4 & (\text{B.9})
\end{aligned}
$$

x_2 can be eliminated from Equations (B.7) and (B.8) by adding the two equations, or

$$6x_1 + 3x_3 = 6. \qquad (\text{B.10}) = (\text{B.7}) + (\text{B.8})$$

x_2 can be eliminated from Equations (B.7) and (B.9) by multiplying Equation (B.7) by 3 and adding to Equation (B.9), or

$$5x_1 + 4x_3 = 5. \qquad (\text{B.11}) = 3(\text{B.7}) + (\text{B.9})$$

The resulting 2×2 system of equations is

$$
\begin{aligned}
6x_1 + 3x_3 &= 6 & (\text{B.10}) \\
5x_1 + 4x_3 &= 5. & (\text{B.11})
\end{aligned}
$$

x_1 can be eliminated by multiplying Equation (B.10) by -5, multiplying Equation (B.11) by 6, and adding the resulting equations, or

$$
\begin{aligned}
-30x_1 - 15x_3 &= -30 & -5(\text{B.10}) \\
30x_1 + 24x_3 &= 30 & 6(\text{B.11}) \\
\hline
9x_3 &= 0 & (\text{B.12}) = -5(\text{B.10}) + 6(\text{B.11}) \\
x_3 &= 0.
\end{aligned}
$$

Substituting $x_3 = 0$ into Equation (B.10), we get

$$6x_1 + 3(0) = 6$$

or

$$x_1 = 1.$$

And finally substituting the values for x_1 and x_3 into Equation (B.7), we get

$$
\begin{aligned}
1 + x_2 + 0 &= 3 \\
x_2 &= 2.
\end{aligned}
$$

Thus, there is a unique solution to the original system when $x_1 = 1$, $x_2 = 2$, and $x_3 = 0$.

B.2 NONLINEAR EQUATIONS

Procedures of solution for systems of nonlinear equations represent a topic in **numerical analysis** which is far too advanced for this textbook.

Rather than completely skirting the issue, however, we will present a simple example which illustrates once more the elimination-substitution method.

Example B.4

$$x_1^2 - 3x_1 + x_2 = 2 \qquad\qquad (B.13)$$
$$4x_1 + 5x_2 = 6 \qquad\qquad (B.14)$$

Multiplying Equation (B.13) by -5 and adding to Equation (B.14), we get

$$
\begin{aligned}
-5x_1^2 + 15x_1 - 5x_2 &= -10 \qquad &-5(B.13)\\
4x_1 + 5x_2 &= 6 \qquad &(B.14)\\
\hline
-5x_1^2 + 19x_1 &= -4 \qquad &(B.15) = -5(B.13) + (B.14)\\
(5x_1 + 1)\cdot(-x_1 + 4) &= 0 \\
x_1 &= 4, -1/5.
\end{aligned}
$$

Substituting each of these results into Equation (B.14) and solving for x_2, we get the pair of solutions: $x_1 = 4$ and $x_2 = -2$; $x_1 = -\tfrac{1}{5}$ and $x_2 = 1.36$.

Appendix C   Matrix Concepts

A MATRIX is a rectangular array of numbers. It is described as being of dimensions $(m \times n)$ if it has m rows and n columns. In the generalized matrix below, the elements are denoted by a_{ij} where i is the row and j is the column in which the element is located.

$$A = \begin{pmatrix} a_{11} & a_{12} & a_{13} & \ldots & a_{1n} \\ a_{21} & a_{22} & a_{23} & \ldots & a_{2n} \\ \cdot & \cdot & \cdot\cdot & & \cdot \\ \cdot & \cdot & \cdot & \cdot\cdot & \cdot \\ \cdot & \cdot & \cdot & & \cdot \\ a_{m1} & a_{m2} & a_{m3} & \ldots & a_{mn} \end{pmatrix}$$

Matrices provide a powerful, practical, and efficient vehicle for both representing and manipulating data. They are compact in their representation and lend themselves well to computer applications. In fact, the manipulation of matrices for an important class of linear models in mathematics and statistics has become so central that the field of **linear (or matrix) algebra** has evolved.

C.1   THE DETERMINANT

Any **square matrix** (that is, a matrix with $m = n$) has an associated scalar value called the **determinant** of the matrix. If a matrix is denoted by the symbol **A**, then the determinant of the matrix is represented as $|\, A \,|$. Although the determinant can be defined rigorously in terms of permutations of the elements in the matrix and its importance in mathematics can

742

be illustrated, we will devote our present efforts to calculating the value of the determinant. An appreciation of its usefulness will be deferred to other sections of the textbook.

If a matrix is (1×1) in dimension, then the determinant is equal to the element in the matrix. For example, if

$$A = (-6)$$

then

$$|A| = -6.$$

If a matrix is of dimensions (2×2) and has the general form

$$A = \begin{pmatrix} a & b \\ c & d \end{pmatrix},$$

then

$$|A| = a \cdot d - c \cdot b.$$

For example, if

$$A = \begin{pmatrix} 2 & -5 \\ 6 & 3 \end{pmatrix},$$

then

$$|A| = (2)(3) - (6)(-5)$$
$$= 36.$$

The most generalized approach for finding a determinant is the **method of cofactors**. For this method, the determinant can be found by expanding along *any* row or column. The expansion is performed by selecting any row or column, multiplying each element in the row or column by its cofactor, and algebraically summing. For any row, i, of an $(m \times m)$ matrix,

$$|A| = \sum_{j=1}^{m} a_{ij} \cdot c_{ij} = a_{i1} \cdot c_{i1} + a_{i2} \cdot c_{i2} + \cdots + a_{im} \cdot c_{im}$$

where c_{ij} = the cofactor associated with matrix element a_{ij}. For any column, j, of an $(m \times m)$ matrix,

$$|A| = \sum_{i=1}^{m} a_{ij} \cdot c_{ij} = a_{1j} \cdot c_{1j} + a_{2j} \cdot c_{2j} + \cdots + a_{mj} \cdot c_{mj}.$$

A cofactor can be defined for each element of a square matrix. If a_{ij} represents the element contained in row i and column j of the original matrix, c_{ij} is used to represent the cofactor associated with a_{ij}. To find the cofactor, c_{ij}:

1. Eliminate row i and column j of the original matrix.
2. Calculate the **minor,** which is the determinant of the remaining sub-matrix.

3. Find the cofactor by multiplying the minor by either plus or minus one, depending upon the position of the original element in the matrix. Specifically,

$$c_{ij} = (-1)^{i+j} \cdot |S_{ij}|$$

where $|S_{ij}|$ is the minor associated with element a_{ij}, that is, the determinant of the submatrix S_{ij}.

Example C.1

Find the cofactor for the element a_{11} in the 3 × 3 matrix

$$A = \begin{pmatrix} 5 & 2 & 4 \\ 1 & 0 & 6 \\ 2 & 3 & 2 \end{pmatrix}$$

Crossing off row 1 and column 1 leaves the (2 × 2) submatrix

$$S_{11} = \begin{pmatrix} 0 & 6 \\ 3 & 2 \end{pmatrix}$$

The determinant of the submatrix equals −18 and is the minor. The cofactor, c_{11}, is found as

$$c_{11} = (-1)^{1+1}(-18)$$
$$= -18.$$

You should verify that the matrix below contains the cofactors for all elements in the original matrix.

$$C = \begin{pmatrix} -18 & 10 & 3 \\ 8 & 2 & -11 \\ 12 & -26 & -2 \end{pmatrix}.$$

You should also verify that by expanding along any row or column, the determinant is found to have a value of −58. For example, expanding down column 3,

$$|A| = a_{13} \cdot c_{13} + a_{23} \cdot c_{23} + a_{33} \cdot c_{33}$$
$$= 4(3) + 6(-11) + 2(-2)$$
$$= -58.$$

Do you see any advantages to expanding along either row 2 or down column 2? Computational efficiencies are introduced if you expand along any row or column containing zeros in the original matrix. For such elements, it is unnecessary to compute the cofactor.

The method of cofactors is valid for matrices larger than (3 × 3). In a (4 × 4) matrix, the computation of cofactors requires finding the determinant of (3 × 3) submatrices. For (5 × 5) matrices, it is necessary to find the determinants of (4 × 4) matrices, and so forth. Obviously, the process of finding determinants for matrices larger than (3 × 3) becomes tedious by hand calculations. Those of us regularly requiring determinants need not despair, however; computer packages for evaluating determinants are common.

C.2 MATRIX MULTIPLICATION

Matrix algebra facilitates the manipulation of data which is stored in matrix form. In this section we present a brief discussion of matrix multiplication, an understanding of which is useful in Chapter 15.

Let us define a matrix, $\mathbf{A}$, as having dimensions (rows and columns) of m_1 by n_1, or $(m_1 \times n_1)$. Another matrix, $\mathbf{B}$, has dimensions of $(m_2 \times n_2)$. Two matrices may be multiplied if and only if the number of columns in the first matrix equals the number of rows in the second matrix. As an example, the multiplication of matrix $\mathbf{A}$ times matrix $\mathbf{B}$, defined by $\mathbf{AB}$, is possible if and only if $n_1 = m_2$. Similarly, the product $\mathbf{BA}$ is possible if and only if $n_2 = m_1$.

If it is determined that matrix multiplication is possible, then the resulting matrix will have dimensions of $(m \times n)$ where m equals the number of rows contained in the first matrix and n equals the number of columns in the second matrix. Referring to the matrices $\mathbf{A}$ and $\mathbf{B}$, we see that if $\mathbf{AB}$ is possible and

$$\mathbf{AB} = \mathbf{C},$$

then the product matrix, $\mathbf{C}$, will have dimensions equal to $(m_1 \times n_2)$. Similarly, if $\mathbf{BA}$ is possible and

$$\mathbf{BA} = \mathbf{D},$$

then $\mathbf{D}$ will have dimensions of $(m_2 \times n_1)$.

To actually compute the product matrix, consider the product

$$\mathbf{AB} = \mathbf{C}.$$

Let c_{ij} be a generalized element which is located in row i and column j of the product matrix. To compute any c_{ij}, the elements in row i of matrix $\mathbf{A}$ are multiplied times the respective elements in column j of matrix $\mathbf{B}$ and are algebraically summed. This operation is often called a **vector product.** This rule will be illustrated by the following examples.

Example C.2

If

$$\mathbf{A} = \begin{pmatrix} 1 & 4 \\ 5 & -3 \end{pmatrix}$$

and

$$\mathbf{B} = \begin{pmatrix} 1 \\ 4 \end{pmatrix}$$

then **A** is a (2×2) matrix and **B** is a (2×1) matrix. If we desire to find the product **AB**, then we must first examine the dimensions of the matrices. The product **AB** involves multiplying matrices with dimensions

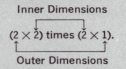

This product is defined because the "inner" dimensions are equal; that is, the number of columns of **A** equals the number of rows of **B**. The product matrix **C** will have dimensions equal to the "outer" dimensions indicated above, that is, (2×1). Thus, the product will be of the form

$$AB = C$$

or

$$\begin{pmatrix} 1 & 4 \\ 5 & -3 \end{pmatrix} \begin{pmatrix} 1 \\ 4 \end{pmatrix} = \begin{pmatrix} c_{11} \\ c_{21} \end{pmatrix}.$$

To compute the elements of **C**,

$$c_{11} = \begin{pmatrix} 1 & 4 \end{pmatrix} \begin{pmatrix} 1 \\ 4 \end{pmatrix} = (1)(1) + (4)(4)$$
$$= 17$$

and

$$c_{21} = \begin{pmatrix} 5 & -3 \end{pmatrix} \begin{pmatrix} 1 \\ 4 \end{pmatrix} = (5)(1) + (-3)(4)$$
$$= -7,$$

or

$$C = \begin{pmatrix} 17 \\ -7 \end{pmatrix}.$$

The product, **BA**, is not defined because the inner dimensions do not match; that is, it involves multiplying a (2×1) matrix times a (2×2) matrix and the number of columns of **B** *does not equal* the number of rows of **A** $(1 \neq 2)$.

Example C.3

If

$$A = \begin{pmatrix} 1 & 0 & 6 \\ 2 & -3 & 1 \end{pmatrix}$$

and

$$B = \begin{pmatrix} 1 & 0 & 0 \\ 0 & 1 & 0 \\ 0 & 0 & 1 \end{pmatrix},$$

then **AB** is defined because inner dimensions match. In this case **C** will have dimensions (2×3):

$$AB = C$$

or

$$\begin{pmatrix} 1 & 0 & 6 \\ 2 & -3 & 1 \end{pmatrix} \begin{pmatrix} 1 & 0 & 0 \\ 0 & 1 & 0 \\ 0 & 0 & 1 \end{pmatrix} = \begin{pmatrix} c_{11} & c_{12} & c_{13} \\ c_{21} & c_{22} & c_{23} \end{pmatrix}.$$

The elements of C are computed as follows:

$$c_{11} = (1 \quad 0 \quad 6) \begin{pmatrix} 1 \\ 0 \\ 0 \end{pmatrix} = (1)(1) + (0)(0) + (6)(0)$$
$$= 1,$$

$$c_{12} = (1 \quad 0 \quad 6) \begin{pmatrix} 0 \\ 1 \\ 0 \end{pmatrix} = (1)(0) + (0)(1) + (6)(0)$$
$$= 0,$$

$$c_{13} = (1 \quad 0 \quad 6) \begin{pmatrix} 0 \\ 0 \\ 1 \end{pmatrix} = (1)(0) + (0)(0) + (6)(1)$$
$$= 6,$$

$$c_{21} = (2 \quad -3 \quad 1) \begin{pmatrix} 1 \\ 0 \\ 0 \end{pmatrix} = (2)(1) + (-3)(0) + (1)(0)$$
$$= 2,$$

$$c_{22} = (2 \quad -3 \quad 1) \begin{pmatrix} 0 \\ 1 \\ 0 \end{pmatrix} = (2)(0) + (-3)(1) + (1)(0)$$
$$= -3,$$

and

$$c_{23} = (2 \quad -3 \quad 1) \begin{pmatrix} 0 \\ 0 \\ 1 \end{pmatrix} = (2)(0) + (-3)(0) + (1)(1)$$
$$= 1,$$

or

$$C = \begin{pmatrix} 1 & 0 & 6 \\ 2 & -3 & 1 \end{pmatrix}.$$

Notice anything peculiar about the preceding example? Matrix **B** is called a (3×3) **identity matrix.** By definition, an identity matrix is a square matrix with 1's along the main diagonal and 0's elsewhere. If the product of an identity matrix, **I**, and another matrix, **A**, is defined, then the resultant product matrix will simply equal matrix **A**, or

$$\textbf{AI} = \textbf{A}$$

In effect, **I** is to matrix multiplication what the number 1 is to scalar multiplication. For this reason, $\textbf{A} \equiv \textbf{C}$ in Example C.3. Note, however, that the product **BA** or **IA** is not defined in Example C.3. Why?

Index

This book has been set in 10 and 9 point Times Roman, leaded one point. Chapter numbers are 72 point Vanguard Light and chapter titles are 24 point Helvetica. The overall size of the type page is 27 picas by 47½ picas.